8.95

D1483928

PLAYS FOR THE THEATRE

An Anthology of World Drama

PLAYS FOR THE THEATRE

An Anthology of World Drama

THEATRE

Second Edition

Edited by

OSCAR G. BROCKETT
INDIANA UNIVERSITY

and

LENYTH BROCKETT

HOLT, RINEHART AND WINSTON, INC.
New York, Chicago, San Francisco, Atlanta,
Dallas, Montreal, Toronto

Copyright © 1967, 1974 by Holt, Rinehart and Winston, Inc.
All rights reserved
Library of Congress Cataloging in Publication Data
Brockett, Oscar Gross, comp.
  Plays for the Theatre
  1. Drama—Collections   I. Brockett, Lenyth, joint comp.   II. Title.
PN6112.B74   1974   808.82   74-842
ISBN: 0-03-089444-1

Printed in the United States of America
  6789   090   987654

The editors of *Plays for the Theatre: An Anthology of World Drama* are grateful to the following publishers, playwrights, and translators for permission to reprint the plays in this volume:

Oedipus Rex of Sophocles: An English version by Dudley Fitts and Robert Fitzgerald, copyright, 1949, by Harcourt, Brace & World, Inc., and reprinted with their permission. Inquiries on all rights should be addressed to Harcourt, Brace & World, Inc., 757 Third Avenue, New York, N.Y. 10017.

The Menaechmi by Plautus: Translated by Richard W. Hyde and Edward C. Weist; reprinted with the permission of the President and Fellows of Harvard College.

The Second Shepherds' Play: Reprinted from *An Anthology of English Drama Before Shakespeare* by permission of the editor, Robert B. Heilman.

Tartuffe by Molière: Translated by John Wood, from *Misanthrope and Other Plays*; reprinted by permission of Penguin Books Ltd.

The Wild Duck by Henrik Ibsen is reprinted with minor adaptation, with the permission of Charles Scribner's Sons from Volume VIII, *The Collected Works of Henrik Ibsen*, translated by William Archer. Copyright 1907 Charles Scribner's Sons; renewal copyright 1935 Frank Archer.

From Morn to Midnight by Georg Kaiser: Translation and copyright 1964 under title *From Morn till Midnight* by Ulrich Weisstein; reprinted with his permission and with the permission of the publishers Kiepenheuer & Witsch, Cologne-Berlin and the Georg Kaiser-Archives, Berlin.

The Good Woman of Setzuan by Bertolt Brecht: Translated by Eric Bentley. Copyright © 1947, 1948, 1956, 1961 by Eric Bentley; Epilogue copyright © 1965 by Eric Bentley. Originally published in the volume *Parables for the Theatre: Two Plays by Bertolt Brecht* by the University of Minnesota Press. Reprinted by permission.

Death of a Salesman by Arthur Miller. Copyright 1949 by Arthur Miller. Reprinted by permission of the Viking Press, Inc. This play in its printed form is designed for the reading public only. All dramatic rights in it are fully protected by copyright, and no public or private performance—professional or amateur—may be given without the written permission of the author and the payment of royalty. As the courts have also ruled that the public reading of a play constitutes a public performance, no such reading may be given except under the conditions stated above. Communication should be addressed to the author's representative, International Famous Agency, Inc., 1301 Avenue of the Americas, New York, N.Y. 10019.

The New Tenant by Eugene Ionesco, translated by Donald Watson. Reprinted by permission of Grove Press, Inc. Copyright © 1958 by John Calder Publishers, Ltd.

Sticks and Bones by David Rabe. Copyright © 1969, 1972, 1973 by David Rabe. Reprinted by permission of The Viking Press, Inc. Caution: Professionals and amateurs are hereby warned that *Sticks and Bones*, being fully protected under the Copyright Laws of the United States of America, and the British Commonwealth, including the Dominion of Canada, and all other countries of the International Copyright Union and the Universal Copyright Convention, is subject to royalty. All rights, including professional, amateur, motion picture, recitation, lecturing, public reading, radio and television broadcasting, and the rights of translation into foreign languages, are strictly reserved. Particular emphasis is laid on the question of readings, permission for which must be secured from the author's agent in writing. The stock and amateur acting rights of *Sticks and Bones* are controlled exclusively by Samuel French, Inc., 25 West 45th Street, New York, New York, 10036, without whose permission in writing no performance of it may be made. Inquiries concerning all other rights should be addressed to Bohan-Neuwald Agency, Inc., 905 West End Avenue, New York City, New York, 10025.

CAUTION:

All the plays listed above are fully protected under the copyright laws of the United States of America, the British Empire including the Dominion of Canada, and all other countries, members of the Copyright Union. All rights including professional, amateur, motion picture, recitation, lecture, public reading, radio broadcasting, televised performance, and the rights of translation into foreign languages are strictly reserved in their present form. These plays are for the reading public only. All inquiries for such rights must be addressed to the copyright owners. Also see special cautions under acknowledgments.

FOR
CHESSIE

Contents

Introduction

Selecting the plays for an anthology of world drama is a task accompanied by both anguish and risk—anguish at the realization of how many excellent plays must be left out, and risk because it is always uncertain whether plays traditionally regarded as masterpieces will still speak to the contemporary reader. Any selection is arbitrary to a degree, but we have chosen plays that have stood the test of long performance in the theatre or, in the case of recent dramas, those that seem to have the likelihood of doing so. We have also selected plays that are representative of various periods, cultures, and genres. Obviously, the impression of world drama gained by knowing only some of its masterpieces is incomplete. Nevertheless, a useful if limited view of past drama can be obtained by reading some outstanding examples, much as one might get acquainted with a new terrain by noting its highest mountain peaks. This collection, then, offers a rough map of Western drama as revealed by significant plays ranging from the classic to the contemporary.

Oedipus Rex [c. 430 B.C.]   The world's oldest surviving dramas are the tragedies that were presented during the fifth century B.C. at the religious and civic festivals held in Athens to honor the god Dionysus.

Oedipus Rex is usually considered to be the greatest of these works and in modern times has probably been the most frequently produced of all Greek plays. Aristotle, in his celebrated discussion of tragedy (written in the fourth century B.C.) refers to it often as an ideal example of the tragic form.

The most striking feature of Greek tragedy is the alternation of dramatic episodes (or scenes) with choral passages. Little is known for certain about the Greek tragic chorus, but in Sophocles' day it probably included fifteen performers who sang (or recited) and danced the choral passages to flute accompaniment. The chorus (in *Oedipus Rex* composed of Elders from the city of Thebes) acts as a group, gives advice to the leading characters, expresses the community's point of view (and sometimes the playwright's), and functions as an "ideal spectator." Other typical features of Greek tragedy are the small number of individualized characters, the restriction of the action to a single place, the tightly unified plot, the serious and philosophic tone, and the poetic language.

The action of *Oedipus Rex* is extremely concentrated, for a complete reversal of the hero's position takes place in a relatively short time. The story follows Oedipus, King of Thebes, as he attempts to discover the murderer of Laius, the former king, after an oracle has declared that the plague now destroying the people will not be lifted until the guilty one is cast out. Oedipus' search gradually uncovers terrible truths about the past and his own origins. The initial suspicion that Oedipus himself may be the slayer of Laius is a moment of high dramatic tension; it is followed by other electrifying moments (such as Jocasta's recognition that she is both Oedipus' wife and his mother) and the ultimate outcome: blindness, exile, and anguish for the once mighty king.

Sophocles is particularly admired for his skillful management of extensive plot materials: he accomplishes the gradual unveiling of mystery after mystery and a steady increase in dramatic tension with the utmost economy of means. Although, as with many great plays, *Oedipus Rex* is open to many interpretations, most critics have agreed that its central concern is the uncertainty of fate and man's helplessness in the face of destiny.

The Menaechmi [c. 184 B.C.]   Of the few Roman plays that survive, the majority are comedies. Indeed, rollicking farces (exemplified by Plautus' *The Menaechmi*) designed solely for entertainment are a peculiarly Roman contribution to the development of drama. The subject matter of surviving Roman comedies is drawn from everyday domestic life and features intrigues that turn on mistaken identity, misunderstood motives, and deliberate deception. The characters are familiar, if sometimes exaggerated types: the old man obsessed with his money or children, the young man who rebels against parental authority, the clever slave, the parasite who lives by flattery and trickery, the courtesan or mistress, the shrewish wife, the unscrupulous slave dealer, and the cowardly soldier. Latin comedy has no chorus, but the action is sometimes interrupted by songs. Thus, it often resembles modern musical comedy.

Plautus opens *The Menaechmi* with a prologue designed to put the audience at ease and to set forth humorously all the information needed to understand what is to come. The opening scenes introduce the characters and situation, the comical possibilities of which are then fully exploited as the twins are in turn mistaken for each other. Plautus' inventiveness is everywhere evident, but especially in the reunion, for its potential sentimentality is subverted by good-natured cynicism when Menaechmus I offers all his property for sale—including his wife.

Although wholly different in tone, Latin comedy shares with Greek tragedy many structural conventions: a story is taken up near the climactic moment; action and time are restricted in scope; and there is no intermingling of serious and comic elements. In the Renaissance, when dramatists turned to antiquity for guidance, it was the Latin writers, above all, from whom they learned. Thus Roman comedy is important not only in its own right but also for its influence on later practices.

The Second Shepherds' Play [1425–1450 A.D.]   After Rome was overrun by invaders in the sixth century A.D., public performances financed by the state ceased, and thereafter for approximately four hundred years theatrical activity in Western Europe was at best sporadic. Then drama was revived by the Catholic Church, although in a form radically different from that seen in Greece or Rome. Beginning in the tenth century, short playlets dramatizing Biblical events were performed in Latin in connection with church services. Around 1200, plays began to be presented out of doors, and eventually they were elaborated into lengthy series, or cycles, of plays dramatizing events ranging from the Creation to the Last Judgment. Productions of cycles were usually financed by trade guilds or religious societies; written in the vernacular language, they often required several days to perform in their entirety. *The Second Shepherds' Play* is the thirteenth segment (out of a total of thirty-two) from the cycle performed at Wakefield (in England). Thus it is only one part of a much larger whole.

The Second Shepherds' Play is an elaboration of a single sentence in the New Testament (Luke 2:8): "And there were in the same country shepherds abiding in the field, keeping watch over their flock by night." This hint has been transformed into a short play rich in contemporary medieval detail and farcical humor. The anonymous author opens his story with a scene in which each of three shepherds complains of his hardships; thus, characters and situation are introduced in a leisurely fashion. Forward movement of the action does not begin until Mak appears, but thereafter it progresses swiftly as Mak steals a sheep, takes it home, and attempts to pass it off as a newborn baby when the suspicious shepherds arrive looking for the missing animal; the ruse is discovered and Mak is punished. Then, in a manner not unusual in medieval literature, the tone of the play alters suddenly, an angel appears to announce the birth of Christ, and the shepherds go to Bethlehem to worship him. The Biblical text, thus, is the basis for a short, entertaining farce that has been linked to a wholly serious and devotional playlet celebrating the birth of Christ. The mingling of such diverse elements and the rapid shift in tone and locale, typical of medieval practice, clearly distinguishes the drama of this age from that of the classical era.

King Lear [c. 1605]   For many reasons, but primarily because of divisive religious controversies, the production of medieval cycles was forbidden or abandoned in the sixteenth century. This separation of drama from the church stimulated the development of a wholly secular theatre. The first country to produce a drama of lasting excellence was England during the years between 1580 and 1640. Indeed, the plays of William Shakespeare, which date from this period, are often said to be the finest ever written.

The plays of the early English Renaissance were still sufficiently close to their medieval predecessors to retain many practices from the earlier era: a sprawling, often episodic plot; scenes set in many times and places; and intermingled comic and serious elements. Before the end of the sixteenth century, however, renewed interest in classical drama had modified and refined medieval practices considerably to create more complex conceptions of dramatic form and characterization. A synthesis of medieval and classical inheritances can be noted in Shakespeare's works, which are both numerous and of varied dramatic types. Shakespeare's genius is probably seen at its best, however, in the tragedies, of which *King Lear* is an outstanding example.

Like *Oedipus Rex*, *King Lear* depicts the struggle of a man first to control and then to comprehend his destiny. But Shakespeare uses a much broader canvas than does Sophocles and includes within his drama more facets of the story, more characters, and a wider range of times and places. Shakespeare's structural skill is shown especially in his ability to interweave the two plots and make each illuminate the other. *King Lear* develops several themes. One concerns the relationship of parents and children; this is found both in the main plot, about Lear and his daughters, and in the subplot, about Gloucester and his sons. A second motif is appearance versus truth. Both Lear and Gloucester are deceived on very little evidence by an appearance of guilt in children who are actually true and loyal. A contrast is drawn between physical sight and spiritual blindness, dramatized by real blindness in Gloucester's case and symbolized by madness in Lear's. A third theme is the degree to which man is subject to fate; Shakespeare seems to suggest that man is an intelligent being who must choose his own path and accept the responsibility for his actions. Shakespeare's dramatic poetry is generally conceded to be the finest in the English language. The basic medium is blank verse, which allows the flexibility of ordinary speech while elevating it through imagery and rhythm.

Because of its universal themes, compelling story, powerful characters, and great poetry, *King Lear* is one of the world's finest achievements in drama. Although it embodies many ideas typical of its time, it transcends the limitations of a particular era. It continues to move spectators in the theatre as it has since its first presentation in the early seventeenth century.

Tartuffe [1669]   While English drama retained many medieval traditions, continental dramatists were more inclined to follow Greek and Roman practices. This conscious imitation of the classics led to a set of literary standards summed up in the term *neoclassicism*; these included the unities of time, place and action; strict distinction between tragedy and comedy, with no intermingling of serious and comic elements; the use of universalized character types; and the demand that drama teach moral lessons. Most of the plays written in compliance with these rules now seem lifeless, but the tragedies of Racine and the comedies of Molière, written in France during the seventeenth century, reached a peak of artistry in the neoclassical mode. Molière is one of the most skillful and inventive of comic dramatists of all times, and *Tartuffe* is one of his best plays. Here, within the restricted frame of one room, one day, and one main story, using a limited number of characters and little physical action, Molière has created an excellent comedy of character in the neoclassic style.

The plot of *Tartuffe* can be divided into five stages: the demonstration of Tartuffe's complete hold over Orgon; the unmasking of Tartuffe; Tartuffe's attempted revenge; the foiling of Tartuffe's plan; and the happy resolution. Each scene of the play, with the possible exception of the young lovers' quarrel, contributes to the main action and hence to the play's unity. The scene in which Orgon hides under the table while Tartuffe attempts to seduce Elmire, Orgon's wife, is one of the most amusing in all comic drama. Molière has been criticized for delaying Tartuffe's appearance until the third act, but he makes skillful use of this delay by having other characters discuss Tartuffe at length, thereby establishing clearly his hypocrisy and Orgon's gullibility in trusting him. The final resolution, in which Tartuffe is suddenly discovered to be a notorious criminal, has also been criticized as overly contrived, but it is emotionally satisfying since it punishes Tartuffe and reestablishes the norm. *Tartuffe* was first presented in its five-act form in 1669 and has since remained in the repertory almost continuously. It is still performed more often than any other play by Molière.

The School for Scandal [1777]   In England the neoclassic rules (which dominated French drama to the end of the eighteenth century) were recognized but not followed slavishly. In Sheridan's *School for Scandal* the unity of time prescribed by neoclassic theory is retained, but unity of place is broadly interpreted to include four different though neighboring houses, and the single plot is replaced by several related intrigues. Thus the play may be called an English response to continental critical precepts. It is also related to other important developments, particularly the comedies of manners written by English dramatists of the late seventeenth century. Like these earlier playwrights, Sheridan satirizes upper-class social foibles with wit and urbanity.

The main action is set against the background of a "school for scandal" in which a circle of malicious men and women, over their teacups, destroy reputations and the impressionable young Lady Teazle tries to ape their sophisticated manners. The shallowness of this group allows hypocrites to flourish, since the group cannot distinguish between fashionable behavior and true character. Sheridan places much of the blame for this state of affairs on the then-current vogue for sentimentalism, epitomized by the comic villain, Joseph Surface, who is admired because he sprinkles his conversation with moral maxims. On the other hand, Charles, his brother, is widely condemned merely because his speech and behavior are natural for a young man of his age and situation. Sheridan is thus concerned with the distinction between true virtue and pious words, but he treats this contrast comically. But if Sheridan satirizes sentimentality, he has not succeeded in freeing his own play from it. His admirable characters are themselves inclined to moralize or fall into "sentiments," and the play as a whole illustrates the lesson typical of sentimental comedy: true virtue will be rewarded—and with a sizable fortune. Sheridan is free of the worst excesses of sentimentality, however, and his moralizing is lightened by amusing dialogue and an air of high spirits.

Sheridan's skill in play construction is especially evident in the way he integrates the subplot and the main plot. At the beginning of the play, the Sir Peter-Lady Teazle story has little connection with the Joseph-Maria-Charles story. As the play progresses, however, the two stories move closer and closer together, and in the "screen scene" (one of the most skillfully contrived in the history of drama) the revelation of Joseph's relationship to Lady Teazle leads to the resolution of both the subplot and the main plot.

The School for Scandal has been called the greatest comedy of manners written in the English language. Its story, its urbane and polished dialogue, and its comic inventiveness have made it popular with each succeeding generation.

The Wild Duck [1884]   During the nineteenth century a revolt against the ideals of romanticism and sentimentality gave rise to a new literary mode, realism. Many influences contributed to the realistic outlook, among them deepening interest in the emerging sciences of sociology and psychology and emphasis on environment as a determinant of human behavior. The result was a drama based on contemporary events closely observed and carefully rendered through lifelike dialogue and detailed settings. Henrik Ibsen's plays epitomize the new trend so well that he is often called the founder of modern realism. *The Wild Duck* illustrates many of the techniques Ibsen used; it reproduces the speech and actions of ordinary people of the middle and lower classes in a fully detailed environment that plays an essential part in the story. In his dialogue Ibsen abandoned the older devices of the aside and soliloquy; instead, his characters reveal themselves as they would in real life, through indirection rather than explicit statement.

In *The Wild Duck*, the idealistic Gregers Werle returns home after an absence of fifteen years, decides that the lives of all his acquaintances are based on lies, and determines to make them face the truth. His efforts lead to catastrophe: in forcing some unwelcome truths on his former schoolmate, Hjalmar Ekdal, he sets in train a series of events that end with a child's suicide. Opposed to Gregers in this tug of war between truth and illusion is Dr. Relling, who believes that people need a "saving lie" in order to endure life. Hjalmar illustrates this principle, for he enjoys a lazy, happy and self-centered life under the illusion that he will some day discover a great invention. Because of Ibsen's ironic treatment of Hjalmar the play has many passages of genuine humor that relieve the generally sombre tone.

Ibsen's themes are related to the central motif of the wild duck which seems to symbolize various stages in human experience: the unfettered freedom of youth, the wounds of experience, the effort to escape, and the necessity of going on living, though wounded and in an environment composed of illusions (symbolized by the Ekdals' attic). An engrossing play because of its tightly woven story, believable characters, and skillful balance of the serious and the satiric, *The Wild Duck* is significant from a historical viewpoint both as one of the works that helped to establish a new realistic drama and as a forerunner of Symbolist drama which was to become important in the next decade.

From Morn till Midnight [1916]   Of the several revolts against realism in the late nineteenth and early twentieth centuries, the earliest was symbolism. Rejecting the realists' belief that truth is discovered by close observation of the environment, the Symbolists held that external appearances were merely the mask of inner spiritual realities that could only be communicated through the use of symbols. Although the appeal of this drama was limited, it foreshadowed other antirealistic movements, including expressionism, which emerged in Germany around 1912. The Expressionists proclaimed the supreme importance of the human spirit, which they believed was being crushed or distorted by materialism and industrialization; like the Symbolists, they regarded appearance as the mask of significant inner truths. Thus to comprehend Expressionist drama the reader must be prepared to accept and interpret its deliberate distortions.

From Morn till Midnight has been compared to those medieval dramas that portray the "stations" of martyrdom; thus, the Teller is said to be a modern Everyman and the time of the action, from morning to midnight, to represent the span of human life. The unity of the play derives from a central theme (man's frustrating search for spiritual identity in a hostile environment) and its central character (the Teller, who is present throughout). In the first two scenes the Teller is depicted as robotlike, rapping for attention, taking in and paying out money, and entering sums in a book. This routine is broken by the exotic Lady from Italy, whose sensuous appeal awakens the Teller from his machinelike state and motivates his theft of the money. In succeeding scenes the Teller, confident that money will buy happiness, is shown in a frantic search for fulfillment as he tries and rejects domestic life (his home), the political and social world (symbolized in the race track), sensual pleasure (the dance-hall scene) and finally religion, where, in the Salvation Army hall he receives the most telling demonstration of humanity's grasping materialism. The Teller dies with arms outstretched as on a cross, thus reinforcing the theme of modern man's martyrdom on the cross of materialism.

From Morn till Midnight is representative of both the outlook and techniques of expressionism. The episodic structure, telegraphic speech and distorted visual elements are typical of the movement, as is Kaiser's blend of mysticism and savage irony.

The Good Woman of Setzuan [1940]   The Expressionists' idealistic dream of transforming mankind foundered in disillusionment after World War I. Some writers came to believe that society could be improved only by adopting a program of concrete political action, and in the theatre they sought to focus attention on the grave difference between human needs and existing conditions. Attempts to use the theatre as a weapon of social action took several forms, but the most significant and fruitful from an esthetic viewpoint was Epic Theatre, exemplified in the plays of Bertolt Brecht. Brecht used many of the devices of Expressionist drama, such as episodic structure, unity derived from theme or thesis, and nonillustionistic visual elements. But Brecht, unlike the Expressionists, did not suggest that external appearance is untruthful or insignificant; rather, he wished to focus attention on the immediate world and its injustices, and believed he could do so most effectively if his audience remained fully conscious that it was in a theatre. Rejecting the theatre of illusion on the basis that it merely lulls the spectator's critical faculties, Brecht devised several techniques (such as inserted songs, and speeches addressed directly to the audience) to reduce the empathic response and intensify the spectator's awareness of social, economic, and political conditions and their shortcomings. It was his hope that the spectator would be sufficiently moved by what he saw to work for change outside the theatre.

The Good Woman of Setzuan is a parable about the difficulties of remaining good under existing social and economic conditions. The "good woman," Shen Te, is generous and well-intentioned but she soon finds herself exploited and betrayed. Her solution is to disguise herself as her cousin Shui Ta—that is, to let the evil side of her character determine her actions. As time passes, she finds herself more and more frequently forced into taking on the role of the ruthless "cousin." Brecht uses this device to suggest the progressive deterioration of morality. The play ends in a stalemate, for the Gods leave Shen Te with the same simplistic message they delivered in the prologue—"Be good"—and she is no nearer to knowing how to accomplish this.

The play alternates short and long scenes. The short scenes serve the purposes of breaking up and commenting on the action. They contribute to Brecht's aim of forcing the audience to think by giving it clues about the significance of what it has seen and time in which to reflect upon it. The long scenes are broken up by the insertion of songs and speeches delivered directly to the audience. While not all the songs are closely related to the plot, they do serve to underscore Brecht's main ideas about society. Throughout the play Brecht skillfully and persistently reminds the audience that Shen Te's predicament is a universal human situation—and one that might be solved by taking the right social and political action.

Death of a Salesman [1949]   Symbolism, expressionism, Epic Theatre, and other antirealistic styles have by no means replaced realism in the modern theatre, but they have unquestionably altered it as a style. Contemporary realistic plays, therefore, are radically different in tone and technique from the works of Ibsen and earlier realists. In general outlook, they differ from earlier drama principally by portraying human personality as more complex, and by being less optimistic about the likelihood of improving society. At the same time, the dramatic techniques used in contemporary realistic plays have been altered because many devices have been taken over from nonrealistic drama.

Many of these results are seen to good effect in Miller's *Death of a*

Salesman. The play's structure, with its fluid handling of time and place which follow the shifting thoughts of the protagonist, is so unlike the drama of Ibsen that on first acquaintance it may seem an entirely different style. Yet, like Ibsen, Miller evokes a specific social milieu, carefully observed and rendered, and creates a highly individualized protagonist, the vivid and memorable Willy Loman.

Death of a Salesman develops a primary conflict in the American consciousness: its tendency to measure success in wholly material terms even though it upholds love and family cohesiveness as major values. As a result, the play suggests, Americans often unconsciously mingle these goals in such a way that love and approval are withheld from those who have not succeeded materially. Miller has embodied this conflict in Willy Loman's obsessive desire to succeed and his confusion of success with the right to be loved. Miller has used two characters to represent the poles between which Willy is pulled. Uncle Ben, Willy's brother, epitomizes material success, while Linda, Willy's wife, represents love given without question or conditions.

It is interesting to compare Miller's play with works from earlier periods. Both *Death of a Salesman* and *Oedipus Rex* involve a search into the past to find the roots of present evils. The scenes in *Oedipus Rex*, however, all take place in the present, and the past is revealed only through narration. *Death of a Salesman*, on the other hand, uses "flashbacks" to transport the audience backward in time to witness various scenes. The play shares with *From Morn till Midnight* and *The Good Woman of Setzuan* a concern for the destructiveness of materialistic values.

In *Death of a Salesman* Miller has combined believable characters and a plausible environment with technical devices taken over from non-realistic styles. When first produced, the play seemed startlingly novel because of this mixture of elements, but subsequent developments have served to define it more clearly as modified realism. After twenty-five years, it is still considered to be one of the most effective and moving of all American plays.

The New Tenant [1953]   In the 1950s a new style, now usually called absurdism, became evident. (*Absurdism* is a term coined by the English critic Martin Esslin to describe the work of Eugène Ionesco, Samuel Beckett, Jean Gênet, and several other European dramatists.) To the Absurdists, ultimate truth consists of the chaos, formlessness, and inanities that make up everyday existence, for though each person may construct a set of values by which to live, his values can never be verified. According to Ionesco, however, all men share certain preoccupations and anxieties, "mysterious nostalgias," "nameless regrets," and a "true community of fear" about the "void at the center of things" of which the final expression is death. Even a hint that the world is absurd terrifies the average person, who tries to insulate himself against the void by surrounding himself with material objects, with comforting clichés, and with rigid ideologies.

The New Tenant develops several themes typical of Absurdist drama. Its action is very simple: a Gentleman arrives to claim his apartment, has a brief discussion with the Caretaker, and supervises two movers who gradually fill the room with furniture and then leave him alone in it. This simple story is used to embody two principal themes. First, it shows how language has been reduced to empty clichés: the Caretaker talks volubly, spouting commonplaces, uncaring that she contradicts herself, for to her language serves not as communication but as reassurance. The Gentleman cares only about his material possessions and wishes to insulate himself from the rest of humanity; he directs the movers to block the room's only window and allows them to place a radio by his chair only when he has been assured that it does not work. When finally he has been so walled in by his possessions that he can no longer move, he directs them to turn out the light.

The repercussions of this dehumanizing process extend far beyond the Gentleman's room, however, for the movers report that furniture now clogs the streets, subways, and even the river. Thus, Ionesco seems to suggest that what has happened in this room is also happening in the world at large as people seek to deny the threat of a spiritual void by filling physical space to overflowing. In *The New Tenant*, the stage spectacle is perhaps the most important element, for the play as a whole represents the visualization of a perception—how material objects fill space that should be occupied by people—and, symbolically, how preoccupation with materialism dwarfs the spirit and crowds out any concern for truly human values.

Sticks and Bones [1971]   Since 1960 every area of human endeavor has been subjected to intense questioning. Thus, it is not surprising that plays have been used to raise issues about many institutions and values previously taken for granted. *Sticks and Bones* is a play about the American family, but the play suggests much about society in general. On one level, the play tells a relatively realistic story about how a family's life is disrupted by the return of a son from Vietnam and how, after failing to adjust to him, they persuade him to commit suicide. But the suicide itself, and many other elements as well, are so grotesque as to make us look behind the realistic surface and beyond the living room in which the action occurs.

Rabe has made an ironic commentary on the story by giving the family of *Sticks and Bones* names taken from a well-known television series of the 1950s and 1960s (Ozzie, Harriet, David, and Rick). Thus his subject is the popular "glossy" ideal of the perfect American family, contrasted with the realities that lie behind that picture. Harriet, the sweet conventional wife and mother, is shown to harbor ugly prejudices. Ozzie, whose psychological equilibrium is threatened by David, is discontented and anxiety-ridden. The cheerful, fudge-gobbling Ricky is blandly amoral. These three present a united front against David, whom they regard as a "defector" from the family circle, partly because he is blind, angry, and resentful, and also because he has violated the clan's taboo by loving a Vietnamese girl. David tries to force his family to acknowledge his anguish and face unpleasant truths, but he is unable to reach them, and at the end of the play he acquiesces in his own death, calmly watched by his family, who are relieved to return to the ordinary tenor of their life.

The structure of *Sticks and Bones* is relatively simple, with incidents arranged in strict chronological order. The principal emphasis is on character relationships and ideas rather than on story, and perhaps for that reason the incidents are only loosely related causally. Nevertheless, there is a strong sense of growing tension leading to crisis and resolution. Thus, the play follows traditional structural patterns. What is new and compelling is the play's almost surrealistic tone, its powerful dialogue, and its successful integration of elements of fantasy, comedy, and horror. *Sticks and Bones* won the 1972 Tony Award for the best play on Broadway. Rabe's is indeed a promising new voice in the theatre.

Detailed analyses of the plays in this volume, accompanied by a description of contemporary theatrical conditions and pertinent historical information will be found in Oscar G. Brockett's *The Theatre: an Introduction* (Holt, Rinehart and Winston, Inc., 1974).

PLAYS FOR THE THEATRE

Oedipus the King directed by Tyrone Guthrie, 1955. Center: Douglas Campbell as Oedipus. Rear: Robert Goodier as Creon. Production photograph by Donald McKague, courtesy of the Stratford Shakespearean Festival Foundation of Canada.

Production photograph of Plautus' *The Menaechmi*. Directed by Harrold Shiffler; scenery by Richard Baschky.

A production photograph of a scene from *The Second Shepherds' Play* at the Mermaid Theatre, London. Courtesy of the Mermaid Theatre.

The opening scene of *King Lear* at the Oregon Shakespeare Festival, 1958. Courtesy Oregon Shakespearean Festival Association. Photograph—Dwaine Smith.

Tartuffe's first meeting with Dorine in the production presented at Stratford in 1968. William Hutt as Tartuffe; Pat Galloway as Dorine. Courtesy Stratford Shakespearean Festival Foundation of Canada.

The screen scene from the original production of *The School for Scandal*, 1777. Note the forestage, proscenium doors, stage boxes, clearly defined wings, and the similarity of the actors' costumes to those worn by the spectators. Courtesy Yale University Library.

Setting used for *The Wild Duck* by André Antoine. Courtesy Bibliothèque de l'Arsenal, Paris.

From Morn till Midnight. Scene 5, the first gallery, as staged by the Theatre Guild. Photograph—Bruguière. Collection of the Library and Museum of the Performing Arts at Lincoln Center.

Scene from Brecht's *The Good Woman of Setzuan,* as presented at the University of Texas. Directed by Francis Hodge; setting by John Rothgeb; costumes by Paul Reinhardt.

Scene from the first production of *Death of a Salesman.* Directed by Elia Kazan. Setting by Jo Mielziner. Courtesy Graphic House, Inc.

Scene from the first production given in Paris of Ionesco's *The New Tenant*. Directed by Jean-Marie Serreau; setting by Sine. Photograph—Bernand.

A scene from the New York production of *Sticks and Bones* by David Rabe. David, Drew Snyder; Rick, Cliff DeYoung; Ozzie, Tom Aldridge; Harriet, Elizabeth Wilson. Photograph —Friedman-Abeles.

SOPHOCLES

OEDIPUS REX

English Version by
Dudley Fitts
and Robert Fitzgerald

PERSONS REPRESENTED

OEDIPUS
A PRIEST
CREON
TEIRESIAS
IOCASTE [JOCASTA]
MESSENGER
SHEPHERD OF LAÏOS
SECOND MESSENGER
CHORUS OF THEBAN ELDERS

THE SCENE——*Before the palace of* OEDIPUS, *King of Thebes. A central door and two lateral doors open onto a platform which runs the length of the façade. On the platform, right and left, are altars; and three steps lead down into the "orchestra," or chorus-ground. At the beginning of the action these steps are crowded by suppliants who have brought branches and chaplets of olive leaves and who lie in various attitudes of despair.* OEDIPUS *enters.*

PROLOGUE

OEDIPUS: My children, generations of the living
    In the line of Kadmos, nursed at his ancient hearth:
    Why have you strewn yourselves before these altars
    In supplication, with your boughs and garlands?
    The breath of incense rises from the city
    With a sound of prayer and lamentation.
                                    Children,
    I would not have you speak through messengers,
    And therefore I have come myself to hear you—
    I, Oedipus, who bear the famous name.
        [*To a* PRIEST.]
    You, there, since you are eldest in the company,
    Speak for them all, tell me what preys upon you,

7

Whether you come in dread, or crave some blessing:
Tell me, and never doubt that I will help you
In every way I can; I should be heartless
Were I not moved to find you suppliant here.
PRIEST: Great Oedipus, O powerful King of Thebes!
You see how all the ages of our people
Cling to your altar steps: here are boys
Who can barely stand alone, and here are priests
By weight of age, as I am a priest of God,
And young men chosen from those yet unmarried;
As for the others, all that multitude,
They wait with olive chaplets in the squares,
At the two shrines of Pallas, and where Apollo
Speaks in the glowing embers.
                                    Your own eyes
Must tell you: Thebes is tossed on a murdering sea
And can not lift her head from the death surge.
A rust consumes the buds and fruits of the earth;
The herds are sick; children die unborn,
And labor is vain. The god of plague and pyre
Raids like detestable lightning through the city,
And all the house of Kadmos is laid waste,
All emptied, and all darkened; Death alone
Battens upon the misery of Thebes.

You are not one of the immortal gods, we know;
Yet we have come to you to make our prayer
As to the man surest in mortal ways
And wisest in the ways of God. You saved us
From the Sphinx, that flinty singer, and the tribute
We paid to her so long; yet you were never
Better informed than we, nor could we teach you:
It was some god breathed in you to set us free.

Therefore, O mighty King, we turn to you:
Find us our safety, find us a remedy,
Whether by counsel of the gods or men.
A king of wisdom tested in the past
Can act in a time of troubles, and act well.
Noblest of men, restore
Life to your city! Think how all men call you
Liberator for your triumph long ago;
Ah, when your years of kingship are remembered,
Let them not say *We rose, but later fell*—
Keep the State from going down in the storm!
Once, years ago, with happy augury,

You brought us fortune; be the same again!
No man questions your power to rule the land:
But rule over men, not over a dead city!
Ships are only hulls, citadels are nothing,
When no life moves in the empty passageways.

OEDIPUS: Poor children! You may be sure I know
All that you longed for in your coming here.
I know that you are deathly sick; and yet,
Sick as you are, not one is as sick as I.
Each of you suffers in himself alone
His anguish, not another's; but my spirit
Groans for the city, for myself, for you.

I was not sleeping, you are not waking me.
No, I have been in tears for a long while
And in my restless thought walked many ways.
In all my search, I found one helpful course,
And that I have taken: I have sent Creon,
Son of Menoikeus, brother of the Queen,
To Delphi, Apollo's place of revelation,
To learn there, if he can,
What act or pledge of mine may save the city.
I have counted the days, and now, this very day,
I am troubled, for he has overstayed his time.
What is he doing? He has been gone too long.
Yet whenever he comes back, I should do ill
To scant whatever duty God reveals.

PRIEST: It is a timely promise. At this instant
They tell me Creon is here.

OEDIPUS: O Lord Apollo!
May his news be fair as his face is radiant!

PRIEST: It could not be otherwise: he is crowned with bay,
The chaplet is thick with berries.

OEDIPUS: We shall soon know;
He is near enough to hear us now.
          [*Enter* CREON.]
                              O Prince:
Brother: son of Menoikeus:
What answer do you bring us from the god?

CREON: A strong one. I can tell you, great afflictions
Will turn out well, if they are taken well.

OEDIPUS: What was the oracle? These vague words
Leave me still hanging between hope and fear.

CREON: Is it your pleasure to hear me with all these
Gathered around us? I am prepared to speak,
But should we not go in?

OEDIPUS: Let them all hear it.
It is for them I suffer, more than for myself.
CREON: Then I will tell you what I heard at Delphi.

In plain words
The god commands us to expel from the land of Thebes
An old defilement we are sheltering.
It is a deathly thing, beyond cure;
We must not let it feed upon us longer.
OEDIPUS: What defilement? How shall we rid ourselves of it?
CREON: By exile or death, blood for blood. It was
Murder that brought the plague-wind on the city.
OEDIPUS: Murder of whom? Surely the god has named him?
CREON: My lord: long ago Laïos was our king,
Before you came to govern us.
OEDIPUS: I know;
I learned of him from others; I never saw him.
CREON: He was murdered; and Apollo commands us now
To take revenge upon whoever killed him.
OEDIPUS: Upon whom? Where are they? Where shall we find a clue
To solve that crime, after so many years?
CREON: Here in this land, he said.
If we make enquiry,
We may touch things that otherwise escape us.
OEDIPUS: Tell me: Was Laïos murdered in his house,
Or in the fields, or in some foreign country?
CREON: He said he planned to make a pilgrimage.
He did not come home again.
OEDIPUS: And was there no one,
No witness, no companion, to tell what happened?
CREON: They were all killed but one, and he got away
So frightened that he could remember one thing only.
OEDIPUS: What was that one thing? One may be the key
To everything, if we resolve to use it.
CREON: He said that a band of highwaymen attacked them,
Outnumbered them, and overwhelmed the King.
OEDIPUS: Strange, that a highwayman should be so daring—
Unless some faction here bribed him to do it.
CREON: We thought of that. But after Laïos' death
New troubles arose and we had no avenger.
OEDIPUS: What troubles could prevent your hunting down the killers?
CREON: The riddling Sphinx's song
Made us deaf to all mysteries but her own.
OEDIPUS: Then once more I must bring what is dark to light.
It is most fitting that Apollo shows,
As you do, this compunction for the dead.
You shall see how I stand by you, as I should,

To avenge the city and the city's god,
And not as though it were for some distant friend,
But for my own sake, to be rid of evil.
Whoever killed King Laïos might—who knows?—
Decide at any moment to kill me as well.
By avenging the murdered king I protect myself.

Come, then, my children: leave the altar steps,
Lift up your olive boughs!
                              One of you go
And summon the people of Kadmos to gather here.
I will do all that I can; you may tell them that.
    [Exit a PAGE.]
So, with the help of God,
We shall be saved—or else indeed we are lost.

PRIEST: Let us rise, children. It was for this we came,
And now the King has promised it himself.
Phoibos has sent us an oracle; may he descend
Himself to save us and drive out the plague.
    [Exeunt OEDIPUS *and* CREON *into the palace by the central door. The*
    PRIEST *and the* SUPPLIANTS *disperse R and L. After a short pause the*
    CHORUS *enters the orchestra.*]

PARODOS

CHORUS: What is God singing in his profound   [STROPHE 1]
    Delphi of gold and shadow?
What oracle for Thebes, the sunwhipped city?

Fear unjoints me, the roots of my heart tremble.

Now I remember, O Healer, your power, and wonder:
Will you send doom like a sudden cloud. or weave it
Like nightfall of the past?

Speak, speak to us, issue of holy sound:
Dearest to our expectancy: be tender!

Let me pray to Athenê, the immortal daughter of Zeus,   [ANTISTROPHE 1]
And to Artemis her sister
Who keeps her famous throne in the market ring,
And to Apollo, bowman at the far butts of heaven—

O gods, descend! Like three streams leap against
The fires of our grief, the fires of darkness;
Be swift to bring us rest!

As in the old time from the brilliant house
Of air you stepped to save us, come again!

Now our afflictions have no end,   [STROPHE 2]
Now all our stricken host lies down
And no man fights off death with his mind;

The noble plowland bears no grain,
And groaning mothers can not bear—

See, how our lives like birds take wing,
Like sparks that fly when a fire soars,
To the shore of the god of evening.

The plague burns on, it is pitiless,   [ANTISTROPHE 2]
Though pallid children laden with death
Lie unwept in the stony ways,

And old gray women by every path
Flock to the strand about the altars

There to strike their breasts and cry
Worship of Phoibos in wailing prayers:
Be kind, God's golden child!

There are no swords in this attack by fire,   [STROPHE 3]
No shields, but we are ringed with cries.
Send the besieger plunging from our homes
Into the vast sea-room of the Atlantic
Or into the waves that foam eastward of Thrace—

For the day ravages what the night spares—

Destroy our enemy, lord of the thunder!
Let him be riven by lightning from heaven!

Phoibos Apollo, stretch the sun's bowstring,   [ANTISTROPHE 3]
That golden cord, until it sing for us,
Flashing arrows in heaven!
                              Artemis, Huntress,
Race with flaring lights upon our mountains!

O scarlet god, O golden-banded brow,
O Theban Bacchos in a storm of Maenads,
     [*Enter* OEDIPUS, C.]
Whirl upon Death, that all the Undying hate!
Come with blinding torches, come in joy!

SCENE I

OEDIPUS: Is this your prayer? It may be answered. Come,
    Listen to me, act as the crisis demands,
    And you shall have relief from all these evils.

    Until now I was a stranger to this tale,
    As I had been a stranger to the crime.
    Could I track down the murderer without a clue?
    But now, friends,
    As one who became a citizen after the murder,
    I make this proclamation to all Thebans:
    If any man knows by whose hand Laïos, son of Labdakos,
    Met his death, I direct that man to tell me everything,
    No matter what he fears for having so long withheld it.
    Let it stand as promised that no further trouble
    Will come to him, but he may leave the land in safety.

    Moreover: If anyone knows the murderer to be foreign,
    Let him not keep silent: he shall have his reward from me.
    However, if he does conceal it; if any man
    Fearing for his friend or for himself disobeys this edict,
    Hear what I propose to do:

    I solemnly forbid the people of this country,
    Where power and throne are mine, ever to receive that man
    Or speak to him, no matter who he is, or let him
    Join in sacrifice, lustration, or in prayer.
    I decree that he be driven from every house,
    Being, as he is, corruption itself to us: the Delphic
    Voice of Zeus has pronounced this revelation.
    Thus I associate myself with the oracle
    And take the side of the murdered king.

    As for the criminal, I pray to God—
    Whether it be a lurking thief, or one of a number—
    I pray that that man's life be consumed in evil and wretchedness.
    And as for me, this curse applies no less
    If it should turn out that the culprit is my guest here,
    Sharing my hearth.
                You have heard the penalty.
    I lay it on you now to attend to this
    For my sake, for Apollo's, for the sick
    Sterile city that heaven has abandoned.
    Suppose the oracle had given you no command:
    Should this defilement go uncleansed for ever?

You should have found the murderer: your king,
A noble king, had been destroyed!
                                          Now I,
Having the power that he held before me,
Having his bed, begetting children there
Upon his wife, as he would have, had he lived—
Their son would have been my children's brother,
If Laïos had had luck in fatherhood!
(But surely ill luck rushed upon his reign)—
I say I take the son's part, just as though
I were his son, to press the fight for him
And see it won! I'll find the hand that brought
Death to Labdakos' and Polydoros' child,
Heir of Kadmos' and Agenor's line.
And as for those who fail me,
Many the gods deny them the fruit of the earth,
Fruit of the womb, and may they rot utterly!
Let them be wretched as we are wretched, and worse!

For you, for loyal Thebans, and for all
Who find my actions right, I pray the favor
Of justice, and of all the immortal gods.
CHORAGOS: Since I am under oath, my lord, I swear
    I did not do the murder, I can not name
    The murderer. Might not the oracle
    That has ordained the search tell where to find him?
OEDIPUS: An honest question. But no man in the world
    Can make the gods do more than the gods will.
CHORAGOS: There is one last expedient—
OEDIPUS: Tell me what it is.
    Though it seem slight, you must not hold it back.
CHORAGOS: A lord clairvoyant to the lord Apollo,
    As we all know, is the skilled Teiresias.
    One might learn much about this from him, Oedipus.
OEDIPUS: I am not wasting time:
    Creon spoke of this, and I have sent for him—
    Twice, in fact; it is strange that he is not here.
CHORAGOS: The other matter—that old report—seems useless.
OEDIPUS: Tell me. I am interested in all reports.
CHORAGOS: The King was said to have been killed by highwaymen.
OEDIPUS: I know. But we have no witnesses to that.
CHORAGOS: If the killer can feel a particle of dread,
    Your curse will bring him out of hiding!
OEDIPUS: No.
    The man who dared that act will fear no curse.
        [*Enter the blind seer* TEIRESIAS, *led by a* PAGE.]

CHORAGOS: But there is one man who may detect the criminal.
    This is Teiresias, this is the holy prophet
    In whom, alone of all men, truth was born.
OEDIPUS: Teiresias: seer: student of mysteries,
    Of all that's taught and all that no man tells,
    Secrets of Heaven and secrets of the earth:
    Blind though you are, you know the city lies
    Sick with plague; and from this plague, my lord,
    We find that you alone can guard or save us.

    Possibly you did not hear the messengers?
    Apollo, when we sent to him,
    Sent us back word that this great pestilence
    Would lift, but only if we established clearly
    The identity of those who murdered Laïos.
    They must be killed or exiled.
                         Can you use
    Birdflight or any art of divination
    To purify yourself, and Thebes, and me
    From this contagion? We are in your hands.
    There is no fairer duty
    Than that of helping others in distress.
TEIRESIAS: How dreadful knowledge of the truth can be
    When there's no help in truth! I knew this well,
    But made myself forget. I should not have come.
OEDIPUS: What is troubling you? Why are your eyes so cold?
TEIRESIAS: Let me go home. Bear your own fate, and I'll
    Bear mine. It is better so: trust what I say.
OEDIPUS: What you say is ungracious and unhelpful
    To your native country. Do not refuse to speak.
TEIRESIAS: When it comes to speech, your own is neither temperate
    Nor opportune. I wish to be more prudent.
OEDIPUS: In God's name, we all beg you—
TEIRESIAS: You are all ignorant.
    No; I will never tell you what I know.
    Now it is my misery; then, it would be yours.
OEDIPUS: What! You do know something, and will not tell us?
    You would betray us all and wreck the State?
TEIRESIAS: I do not intend to torture myself, or you.
    Why persist in asking? You will not persuade me.
OEDIPUS: What a wicked old man you are! You'd try a stone's
    Patience! Out with it! Have you no feeling at all?
TEIRESIAS: You call me unfeeling. If you could only see
    The nature of your own feelings . . .
OEDIPUS: Why,
    Who would not feel as I do? Who could endure
    Your arrogance toward the city?

TEIRESIAS: What does it matter!
Whether I speak or not, it is bound to come.
OEDIPUS: Then, if "it" is bound to come, you are bound to tell me.
TEIRESIAS: No, I will not go on. Rage as you please.
OEDIPUS: Rage? Why not!
                                    And I'll tell you what I think:
You planned it, you had it done, you all but
Killed him with your own hands: if you had eyes,
I'd say the crime was yours, and yours alone.
TEIRESIAS: So? I charge you, then,
Abide by the proclamation you have made:
From this day forth
Never speak again to these men or to me;
You yourself are the pollution of this country.
OEDIPUS: You dare say that! Can you possibly think you have
Some way of going free, after such insolence?
TEIRESIAS: I have gone free. It is the truth sustains me.
OEDIPUS: Who taught you shamelessness? It was not your craft.
TEIRESIAS: You did. You made me speak. I did not want to.
OEDIPUS: Speak what? Let me hear it again more clearly.
TEIRESIAS: Was it not clear before? Are you tempting me?
OEDIPUS: I did not understand it. Say it again.
TEIRESIAS: I say that you are the murderer whom you seek.
OEDIPUS: Now twice you have spat out infamy. You'll pay for it!
TEIRESIAS: Would you care for more? Do you wish to be really angry?
OEDIPUS: Say what you will. Whatever you say is worthless.
TEIRESIAS: I say you live in hideous shame with those
Most dear to you. You can not see the evil.
OEDIPUS: It seems you can go on mouthing like this for ever.
TEIRESIAS: I can, if there is power in truth.
OEDIPUS: There is:
But not for you, not for you,
You sightless, witless, senseless, mad old man!
TEIRESIAS: You are the madman. There is no one here
Who will not curse you soon, as you curse me.
OEDIPUS: You child of endless night! You can not hurt me
Or any other man who sees the sun.
TEIRESIAS: True: it is not from me your fate will come.
That lies within Apollo's competence.
As it is his concern.
OEDIPUS: Tell me.
Are you speaking for Creon, or for yourself?
TEIRESIAS: Creon is no threat. You weave your own doom.
OEDIPUS: Wealth, power, craft of statesmanship!
Kingly position, everywhere admired!
What savage envy is stored up against these,
If Creon, whom I trusted, Creon my friend,

For this great office which the city once
Put in my hands unsought—if for this power
Creon desires in secret to destroy me!

He has bought this decrepit fortune-teller, this
Collector of dirty pennies, this prophet fraud—
Why, he is no more clairvoyant than I am!

                                                                Tell us.
Has your mystic mummery ever approached the truth?
When that hellcat the Sphinx was performing here,
What help were you to these people?
Her magic was not for the first man who came along:
It demanded a real exorcist. Your birds—
What good were they? or the gods, for the matter of that?
But I came by,
Oedipus, the simple man, who knows nothing—
I thought it out for myself, no birds helped me!
And this is the man you think you can destroy,
That you may be close to Creon when he's king!
Well, you and your friend Creon, it seems to me,
Will suffer most. If you were not an old man,
You would have paid already for your plot.

CHORAGOS: We can not see that his words or yours
Have been spoken except in anger, Oedipus,
And of anger we have no need. How can God's will
Be accomplished best? That is what most concerns us.

TEIRESIAS: You are a king. But where argument's concerned
I am your man, as much a king as you.
I am not your servant, but Apollo's.
I have no need of Creon to speak for me.

Listen to me. You mock my blindness, do you?
But I say that you, with both your eyes, are blind:
You can not see the wretchedness of your life,
Nor in whose house you live, no, nor with whom.
Who are your father and mother? Can you tell me?
You do not even know the blind wrongs
That you have done them, on earth and in the world below.
But the double lash of your parents' curse will whip you
Out of this land some day, with only night
Upon your precious eyes.
Your cries then—where will they not be heard?
What fastness of Kithairon will not echo them?
And that bridal-descant of yours—you'll know it then,
The song they sang when you came here to Thebes
And found your misguided berthing.

All this, and more, that you can not guess at now,
Will bring you to yourself among your children.

Be angry, then. Curse Creon. Curse my words.
I tell you, no man that walks upon the earth
Shall be rooted out more horribly than you.
OEDIPUS: Am I to bear this from him?—Damnation
    Take you! Out of this place! Out of my sight!
TEIRESIAS: I would not have come at all if you had not asked me.
OEDIPUS: Could I have told that you'd talk nonsense, that
    You'd come here to make a fool of yourself, and of me?
TEIRESIAS: A fool? Your parents thought me sane enough.
OEDIPUS: My parents again!—Wait: who were my parents?
TEIRESIAS: This day will give you a father, and break your heart.
OEDIPUS: Your infantile riddles! Your damned abracadabra!
TEIRESIAS: You were a great man once at solving riddles.
OEDIPUS: Mock me with that if you like; you will find it true.
TEIRESIAS: It was true enough. It brought about your ruin.
OEDIPUS: But if it saved this town?
TEIRESIAS: [*to the* PAGE] Boy, give me your hand.
OEDIPUS: Yes, boy; lead him away.
                              —While you are here
    We can do nothing. Go; leave us in peace.
TEIRESIAS: I will go when I have said what I have to say.
    How can you hurt me? And I tell you again:
    The man you have been looking for all this time,
    The damned man, the murderer of Laïos,
    That man is in Thebes. To your mind he is foreign-born,
    But it will soon be shown that he is a Theban,
    A revelation that will fail to please.
                              A blind man,
    Who has his eyes now; a penniless man, who is rich now;
    And he will go tapping the strange earth with his staff
    To the children with whom he lives now he will be
    Brother and father—the very same; to her
    Who bore him, son and husband—the very same
    Who came to his father's bed, wet with his father's blood.

    Enough. Go think that over.
    If later you find error in what I have said,
    You may say that I have no skill in prophecy.
        [*Exit* TEIRESIAS, *led by his* PAGE. OEDIPUS *goes into the palace.*]

ODE I

CHORUS: The Delphic stone of prophecies   [STROPHE 1]
    Remembers ancient regicide
    And a still bloody hand.

That killer's hour of flight has come.
He must be stronger than riderless
Coursers of untiring wind,
For the son of Zeus armed with his father's thunder
Leaps in lightning after him;
And the Furies follow him, the sad Furies.

Holy Parnassos' peak of snow   [ANTISTROPHE 1]
Flashes and blinds that secret man,
That all shall hunt him down:
Though he may roam the forest shade
Like a bull wild from pasture
To rage through glooms of stone.
Doom comes down on him; flight will not avail him;
For the world's heart calls him desolate,
And the immortal Furies follow, for ever follow.

But now a wilder thing is heard   [STROPHE 2]
From the old man skilled at hearing Fate in the wingbeat of a bird.
Bewildered as a blown bird, my soul hovers and can not find
Foothold in this debate, or any reason or rest of mind.
But no man ever brought—none can bring
Proof of strife between Thebes' royal house,
Labdakos' line, and the son of Polybos;
And never until now has any man brought word
Of Laïos' dark death staining Oedipus the King.

Divine Zeus and Apollo hold   [ANTISTROPHE 2]
Perfect intelligence alone of all tales ever told;
And well though this diviner works, he works in his own night;
No man can judge that rough unknown or trust in second sight,
For wisdom changes hands among the wise.
Shall I believe my great lord criminal
At a raging word that a blind old man let fall?
I saw him, when the carrion woman faced him of old,
Prove his heroic mind! These evil words are lies.

SCENE II

CREON: Men of Thebes:
    I am told that heavy accusations
    Have been brought against me by King Oedipus.

    I am not the kind of man to bear this tamely.

    If in these present difficulties
    He holds me accountable for any harm to him
    Through anything I have said or done—why, then,

I do not value life in this dishonor.
It is not as though this rumor touched upon
Some private indiscretion. The matter is grave.
The fact is that I am being called disloyal
To the State, to my fellow citizens, to my friends.
CHORAGOS: He may have spoken in anger, not from his mind.
CREON: But did you not hear him say I was the one
　Who seduced the old prophet into lying?
CHORAGOS: The thing was said; I do not know how seriously.
CREON: But you were watching him! Were his eyes steady?
　Did he look like a man in his right mind?
CHORAGOS: I do not know.
　I can not judge the behavior of great men.
　But here is the King himself.
　　　　[*enter* OEDIPUS.]
OEDIPUS: So you dared come back.
　Why? How brazen of you to come to my house,
　You murderer!
　　　　　　　　Do you think I do not know
　That you plotted to kill me, plotted to steal my throne?
　Tell me, in God's name: am I coward, a fool,
　That you should dream you could accomplish this?
　A fool who could not see your slippery game?
　A coward, not to fight back when I saw it?
　You are the fool, Creon, are you not? hoping
　Without support or friends to get a throne?
　Thrones may be won or bought: you could do neither.
CREON: Now listen to me. You have talked; let me talk, too.
　You can not judge unless you know the facts.
OEDIPUS: You speak well: there is one fact; but I find it hard
　To learn from the deadliest enemy I have.
CREON: That above all I must dispute with you.
OEDIPUS: That above all I will not hear you deny.
CREON: If you think there is anything good in being stubborn
　Against all reason, then I say you are wrong.
OEDIPUS: If you think a man can sin against his own kind
　And not be punished for it, I say you are mad.
CREON: I agree. But tell me: what have I done to you?
OEDIPUS: You advised me to send for that wizard, did you not?
CREON: I did. I should do it again.
OEDIPUS: Very well. Now tell me:
　How long has it been since Laïos—
CREON: What of Laïos?
OEDIPUS: Since he vanished in that onset by the road?
CREON: It was long ago, a long time.
OEDIPUS: And this prophet,
　Was he practicing here then?
CREON: He was; and with honor, as now.

OEDIPUS: Did he speak of me at that time?
CREON: He never did;
    At least, not when I was present.
OEDIPUS: But . . . the enquiry?
    I suppose you held one?
CREON: We did, but we learned nothing.
OEDIPUS: Why did the prophet not speak against me then?
CREON: I do not know; and I am the kind of man
    Who holds his tongue when he has no facts to go on.
OEDIPUS: There's one fact that you know, and you could tell it.
CREON: What fact is that? If I know it, you shall have it.
OEDIPUS: If he were not involved with you, he could not say
    That it was I who murdered Laïos.
CREON: If he says that, you are the one that knows it!—
    But now it is my turn to question you.
OEDIPUS: Put your questions. I am no murderer.
CREON: First, then: You married my sister?
OEDIPUS: I married your sister.
CREON: And you rule the kingdom equally with her?
OEDIPUS: Everything that she wants she has from me.
CREON: And I am the third, equal to both of you?
OEDIPUS: That is why I call you a bad friend.
CREON: No. Reason it out, as I have done.
    Think of this first: Would any sane man prefer
    Power, with all a king's anxieties,
    To that same power and the grace of sleep?
    Certainly not I.
    I have never longed for the king's power—only his rights.
    Would any wise man differ from me in this?
    As matters stand, I have my way in everything
    With your consent, and no responsibilities.
    If I were king, I should be a slave to policy.

    How could I desire a scepter more
    Than what is now mine—untroubled influence?
    No, I have not gone mad; I need no honors,
    Except those with the perquisites I have now.
    I am welcome everywhere; every man salutes me,
    And those who want your favor seek my ear,
    Since I know how to manage what they ask.
    Should I exchange this ease for that anxiety?
    Besides, no sober mind is treasonable.
    I hate anarchy
    And never would deal with any man who likes it.

    Test what I have said. Go to the priestess
    At Delphi, ask if I quoted her correctly.
    And as for this other thing: if I am found

Guilty of treason with Teiresias,
Then sentence me to death! You have my word
It is a sentence I should cast my vote for—
But not without evidence!
              You do wrong
When you take good men for bad, bad men for good.
A true friend thrown aside—why, life itself
Is not more precious!
            In time you will know this well:
For time, and time alone, will show the just man,
Though scoundrels are discovered in a day.
CHORAGOS: This is well said, and a prudent man would ponder it.
    Judgments too quickly formed are dangerous.
OEDIPUS: But is he not quick in his duplicity?
    And shall I not be quick to parry him?
    Would you have me stand still, hold my peace, and let
    This man win everything, through my inaction?
CREON: And you want—what is it, then? To banish me?
OEDIPUS: No, not exile. It is your death I want,
    So that all the world may see what treason means.
CREON: You will persist, then? You will not believe me?
OEDIPUS: How can I believe you?
CREON: Then you are a fool.
OEDIPUS: To save myself?
CREON: In justice, think of me.
OEDIPUS: You are evil incarnate.
CREON: But suppose that you are wrong?
OEDIPUS: Still I must rule.
CREON: But not if you rule badly.
OEDIPUS: O city, city!
CREON: It is my city, too!
CHORAGOS: Now, my lords, be still. I see the Queen,
    Iocastê, coming from her palace chambers;
    And it is time she came, for the sake of you both.
    This dreadful quarrel can be resolved through her.
        [*enter* IOCASTE.]
IOCASTE: Poor foolish men, what wicked din is this?
    With Thebes sick to death, is it not shameful
    That you should rake some private quarrel up?
        [*to* OEDIPUS:]
    Come into the house.

            —And you, Creon, go now:
    Let us have no more of this tumult over nothing.
CREON: Nothing? No, sister: what your husband plans for me
    Is one of two great evils: exile or death.

OEDIPUS: He is right.
>Why, woman I have caught him squarely
>Plotting against my life.

CREON: No! Let me die
>Accurst if ever I have wished you harm!

IOCASTE: Ah, believe it, Oedipus!
>In the name of the gods, respect this oath of his
>For my sake, for the sake of these people here!

[STROPHE 1]

CHORAGOS: Open your mind to her, my lord. Be ruled by her, I beg you!

OEDIPUS: What would you have me do?

CHORAGOS: Respect Creon's word. He has never spoken like a fool,
>And now he has sworn an oath.

OEDIPUS: You know what you ask?

CHORAGOS: I do.

OEDIPUS: Speak on, then.

CHORAGOS: A friend so sworn should not be baited so,
>In blind malice, and without final proof.

OEDIPUS: You are aware, I hope, that what you say
>Means death for me, or exile at the least.

CHORAGOS: No, I swear by Helios, first in Heaven!   [STROPHE 2]
>May I die friendless and accurst,
>The worst of deaths, if ever I meant that!
>It is the withering fields
>That hurt my sick heart:
>Must we bear all these ills,
>And now your bad blood as well?

OEDIPUS: Then let him go. And let me die, if I must,
>Or be driven by him in shame from the land of Thebes.
>It is your unhappiness, and not his talk,
>That touches me.
>As for him—
>Wherever he goes, hatred will follow him.

CREON: Ugly in yielding, as you were ugly in rage!
>Natures like yours chiefly torment themselves.

OEDIPUS: Can you not go? Can you not leave me?

CREON: I can.
>You do not know me; but the city knows me,
>And in its eyes, I am just, if not in yours.
>[*Exit* CREON.]

[ANTISTROPHE 1]

CHORAGOS: Lady Iocastê, did you not ask the King to go to his chambers?

IOCASTE: First tell me what has happened.

CHORAGOS: There was suspicion without evidence; yet it rankled
>As even false charges will.

IOCASTE: On both sides?

CHORAGOS: On both.

IOCASTE: But what was said?
CHORAGOS: Oh let it rest, let it be done with!
     Have we not suffered enough?
OEDIPUS: You see to what your decency has brought you:
     You have made difficulties where my heart saw none.
CHORAGOS: Oedipus, it is not once only I have told you—   [ANTISTROPHE 2]
        You must know I should count myself unwise
     To the point of madness, should I now forsake you—
          You, under whose hand,
             In the storm of another time,
          Our dear land sailed out free.
          But now stand fast at the helm!
IOCASTE: In God's name, Oedipus, inform your wife as well:
     Why are you so set in this hard anger?
OEDIPUS: I will tell you, for none of these men deserves
     My confidence as you do. It is Creon's work,
     His treachery, his plotting against me.
IOCASTE: Go on, if you can make this clear to me.
OEDIPUS: He charges me with the murder of Laïos.
IOCASTE: Has he some knowledge? Or does he speak from hearsay?
OEDIPUS: He would not commit himself to such a charge,
     But he has brought in that damnable soothsayer
     To tell his story.
IOCASTE: Set your mind at rest.
     If it is a question of soothsayers, I tell you
     That you will find no man whose craft gives knowledge
     Of the unknowable.

                    Here is my proof:

     An oracle was reported to Laïos once
     (I will not say from Phoibos himself, but from
     His appointed ministers, at any rate)
     That his doom would be death at the hands of his own son—
     His son, born of his flesh and of mine!

     Now, you remember the story: Laïos was killed
     By marauding strangers where three highways meet.
     But his child had not been three days in this world
     Before the King had pierced the baby's ankles
     And left him to die on a lonely mountainside.

     Thus, Apollo never caused that child
     To kill his father, and it was not Laïos' fate
     To die at the hands of his son, as he had feared.
     This is what prophets and prophecies are worth!
     Have no dread of them.
                         It is God himself
     Who can show us what he wills, in his own way.

OEDIPUS: How strange a shadowy memory crossed my mind,
    Just now while you were speaking; it chilled my heart.
IOCASTE: What do you mean? What memory do you speak of?
OEDIPUS: If I understand you, Laïos was killed
    At a place where three roads meet.
IOCASTE: So it was said;
    We have no later story.
OEDIPUS: Where did it happen?
IOCASTE: Phokis, it is called: at a place where the Theban Way
    Divides into the roads toward Delphi and Daulia.
OEDIPUS: When?
IOCASTE: We had the news not long before you came
    And proved the right to your succession here.
OEDIPUS: Ah, what net has God been weaving for me?
IOCASTE: Oedipus! Why does this trouble you?
OEDIPUS: Do not ask me yet.
    First, tell me how Laïos looked, and tell me
    How old he was.
IOCASTE: He was tall, his hair just touched
    With white; his form was not unlike your own.
OEDIPUS: I think that I myself may be accurst
    By my own ignorant edict.
IOCASTE: You speak strangely.
    It makes me tremble to look at you, my King.
OEDIPUS: I am not sure that the blind man can not see.
    But I should know better if you were to tell me—
IOCASTE: Anything—though I dread to hear you ask it.
OEDIPUS: Was the King lightly escorted, or did he ride
    With a large company, as a ruler should?
IOCASTE: There were five men with him in all: one was a herald,
    And a single chariot, which he was driving.
OEDIPUS: Alas, that makes it plain enough!
                      But who—
    Who told you how it happened?
IOCASTE: A household servant,
    The only one to escape.
OEDIPUS: And is he still
    A servant of ours?
IOCASTE: No; for when he came back at last
    And found you enthroned in the place of the dead king,
    He came to me, touched my hand with his, and begged
    That I would send him away to the frontier district
    Where only the shepherds go—
    As far away from the city as I could send him.
    I granted his prayer; for although the man was a slave,
    He had earned more than this favor at my hands.
OEDIPUS: Can he be called back quickly?

IOCASTE: Easily.
    But why?
OEDIPUS: I have taken too much upon myself
    Without enquiry; therefore I wish to consult him.
IOCASTE: Then he shall come.
                  But am I not one also
    To whom you might confide these fears of yours?
OEDIPUS: That is your right; it will not be denied you,
    Now least of all; for I have reached a pitch
    Of wild foreboding. Is there anyone
    To whom I should sooner speak?

    Polybos of Corinth is my father.
    My mother is a Dorian: Meropê.
    I grew up chief among the men of Corinth
    Until a strange thing happened—
    Not worth my passion, it may be, but strange.

    At a feast, a drunken man maundering in his cups
    Cries out that I am not my father's son!

    I contained myself that night, though I felt anger
    And a sinking heart. The next day I visited
    My father and mother, and questioned them. They stormed,
    Calling it all the slanderous rant of a fool;
    And this relieved me. Yet the suspicion
    Remained always aching in my mind;
    I knew there was talk; I could not rest;
    And finally, saying nothing to my parents,
    I went to the shrine at Delphi.
    The god dismissed my question without reply;
    He spoke of other things.
                  Some were clear,
    Full of wretchedness, dreadful, unbearable:
    As, that I should lie with my own mother, breed
    Children from whom all men would turn their eyes;
    And that I should be my father's murderer.

    I heard all this, and fled. And from that day
    Corinth to me was only in the stars
    Descending in that quarter of the sky,
    As I wandered farther and farther on my way
    To a land where I should never see the evil
    Sung by the oracle. And I came to this country
    Where, so you say, King Laïos was killed.

    I will tell you all that happened there, my lady.

There were three highways
Coming together at a place I passed;
And there a herald came towards me, and a chariot
Drawn by horses, with a man such as you describe
Seated in it. The groom leading the horses
Forced me off the road at his lord's command;
But as this charioteer lurched over towards me
I struck him in my rage. The old man saw me
And brought his double goad down upon my head
As I came abreast.
             He was paid back, and more!
Swinging my club in this right hand I knocked him
Out of his car, and he rolled on the ground.
                       I killed him.

I killed them all.
Now if that stranger and Laïos were—kin,
Where is a man more miserable than I?
More hated by the gods? Citizen and alien alike
Must never shelter me or speak to me—
I must be shunned by all.
             And I myself
Pronounced this malediction upon myself!

Think of it: I have touched you with these hands,
These hands that killed your husband. What defilement!

Am I all evil, then? It must be so,
Since I must flee from Thebes, yet never again
See my own countrymen, my own country,
For fear of joining my mother in marriage
And killing Polybos, my father.
             Ah,
If I was created so, born to this fate,
Who could deny the savagery of God?

O holy majesty of heavenly powers!
May I never see that day! Never!
Rather let me vanish from the race of men
Than know the abomination destined me!
CHORAGOS: We too, my lord, have felt dismay at this.
     But there is hope: you have yet to hear the shepherd.
OEDIPUS: Indeed, I fear no other hope is left me.
IOCASTE: What do you hope from him when he comes?
OEDIPUS: This much:
     If his account of the murder tallies with yours,
     Then I am cleared.

IOCASTE: What was it that I said
    Of such importance?
OEDIPUS: Why, "marauders," you said,
    Killed the King, according to this man's story.
    If he maintains that still, if there were several,
    Clearly the guilt is not mine: I was alone.
    But if he says one man, singlehanded, did it,
    Then the evidence all points to me.
IOCASTE: You may be sure that he said there were several;
    And can he call back that story now? He cán not.
    The whole city heard it as plainly as I.
    But suppose he alters some detail of it:
    He can not ever show that Laïos' death
    Fulfilled the oracle: for Apollo said
    My child was doomed to kill him; and my child—
    Poor baby!—it was my child that died first.

    No. From now on, where oracles are concerned,
    I would not waste a second thought on any.
OEDIPUS: You may be right.
                But come: let someone go
    For the shepherd at once. This matter must be settled.
IOCASTE: I will send for him.
    I would not wish to cross you in anything,
    And surely not in this.—Let us go in.
      [*Exeunt into the palace.*]

ODE II

CHORUS: Let me be reverent in the ways of right,   [STROPHE 1]
    Lowly the paths I journey on;
    Let all my words and actions keep
    The laws of the pure universe
    From highest Heaven handed down.
    For Heaven is their bright nurse,
    Those generations of the realms of light;
    Ah, never of mortal kind were they begot,
    Nor are they slaves of memory, lost in sleep;
    Their Father is greater than Time, and ages not.

    The tyrant is a child of Pride   [ANTISTROPHE 1]
    Who drinks from his great sickening cup
    Recklessness and vanity,
    Until from his high crest headlong
    He plummets to the dust of hope.
    That strong man is not strong.
    But let no fair ambition be denied;

May God protect the wrestler for the State
In government, in comely policy,
Who will fear God, and on His ordinance wait.

Haughtiness and the high hand of disdain   [STROPHE 2]
Tempt and outrage God's holy law;
And any mortal who dares hold
No immortal Power in awe
Will be caught up in a net of pain:
The price for which his levity is sold.
Let each man take due earnings, then,
And keep his hands from holy things,
And from blasphemy stand apart—
Else the crackling blast of heaven
Blows on his head, and on his desperate heart;
Though fools will honor impious men,
In their cities no tragic poet sings.

Shall we lose faith in Delphi's obscurities,   [ANTISTROPHE 2]
We who have heard the world's core
Discredited, and the sacred wood
Of Zeus at Elis praised no more?
The deeds and the strange prophecies
Must make a pattern yet to be understood.
Zeus, if indeed you are lord of all,
Throned in light over night and day,
Mirror this in your endless mind:
Our masters call the oracle
Words on the wind, and the Delphic vision blind!
Their hearts no longer know Apollo,
And reverence for the gods has died away.

SCENE III

[*Enter* IOCASTE.]
IOCASTE: Princes of Thebes, it has occurred to me
    To visit the altars of the gods, bearing
    These branches as a suppliant, and this incense.
    Our King is not himself: his noble soul
    Is overwrought with fantasies of dread,
    Else he would consider
    The new prophecies in the light of the old.
    He will listen to any voice that speaks disaster,
    And my advice goes for nothing.
      [*She approaches the altar,* R.]
                To you, then, Apollo,
    Lycean lord, since you are nearest, I turn in prayer.

Receive these offerings, and grant us deliverance
From defilement. Our hearts are heavy with fear
When we see our leader distracted, as helpless sailors
Are terrified by the confusion of their helmsman.
      [*Enter* MESSENGER.]
MESSENGER: Friends, no doubt you can direct me:
Where shall I find the house of Oedipus,
Or, better still, where is the King himself?
CHORAGOS: It is this very place, stranger; he is inside.
This is his wife and mother of his children.
MESSENGER: I wish her happiness in a happy house,
Blest in all the fulfillment of her marriage.
IOCASTE: I wish as much for you: your courtesy
Deserves a like good fortune. But now, tell me:
Why have you come? What have you to say to us?
MESSENGER: Good news, my lady, for your house and your husband.
IOCASTE: What news? Who sent you here?
MESSENGER: I am from Corinth.
The news I bring ought to mean joy for you,
Though it may be you will find some grief in it.
IOCASTE: What is it? How can it touch us in both ways?
MESSENGER: The word is that the people of the Isthmus
Intend to call Oedipus to be their king.
IOCASTE: But old King Polybos—is he not reigning still?
MESSENGER: No. Death holds him in his sepulchre.
IOCASTE: What are you saying? Polybos is dead?
MESSENGER: If I am not telling the truth, may I die myself.
IOCASTE: [*to a* MAIDSERVANT:] Go in, go quickly; tell this to your master.

O riddlers of God's will, where are you now!
This was the man whom Oedipus, long ago,
Feared so, fled so, in dread of destroying him—
But it was another fate by which he died.
      [*Enter* OEDIPUS, *C.*]
OEDIPUS: Dearest Iocastê, why have you sent for me?
IOCASTE: Listen to what this man says, and then tell me
What has become of the solemn prophecies.
OEDIPUS: Who is this man? What is his news for me?
IOCASTE: He has come from Corinth to announce your father's death!
OEDIPUS: Is it true, stranger? Tell me in your own words.
MESSENGER: I can not say it more clearly: the King is dead.
OEDIPUS: Was it by treason? Or by an attack of illness?
MESSENGER: A little thing brings old men to their rest.
OEDIPUS: It was sickness, then?
MESSENGER: Yes, and his many years.
OEDIPUS: Ah!
Why should a man respect the Pythian hearth, or
Give heed to the birds that jangle above his head?

They prophesied that I should kill Polybos,
Kill my own father; but he is dead and buried,
And I am here—I never touched him, never,
Unless he died of grief for my departure,
And thus, in a sense, through me. No. Polybos
Has packed the oracles off with him underground.
They are empty words.

IOCASTE: Had I not told you so?

OEDIPUS: You had; it was my faint heart that betrayed me.

IOCASTE: From now on never think of those things again.

OEDIPUS: And yet—must I not fear my mother's bed?

IOCASTE: Why should anyone in this world be afraid,
    Since Fate rules us and nothing can be foreseen?
    A man should live only for the present day.

    Have no more fear of sleeping with your mother:
    How many men, in dreams, have lain with their mothers!
    No reasonable man is troubled by such things.

OEDIPUS: That is true; only—
    If only my mother were not still alive!
    But she is alive. I can not help my dread.

IOCASTE: Yet this news of your father's death is wonderful.

OEDIPUS: Wonderful. But I fear the living woman.

MESSENGER: Tell me, who is this woman that you fear?

OEDIPUS: It is Meropê, man; the wife of King Polybos.

MESSENGER: Meropê? Why should you be afraid of her?

OEDIPUS: An oracle of the gods, a dreadful saying.

MESSENGER: Can you tell me about it or are you sworn to silence?

OEDIPUS: I can tell you, and I will.
    Apollo said through his prophet that I was the man
    Who should marry his own mother, shed his father's blood
    With his own hands. And so, for all these years
    I have kept clear of Corinth, and no harm has come—
    Though it would have been sweet to see my parents again.

MESSENGER: And is this the fear that drove you out of Corinth?

OEDIPUS: Would you have me kill my father?

MESSENGER: As for that
    You must be reassured by the news I gave you.

OEDIPUS: If you could reassure me, I would reward you.

MESSENGER: I had that in mind, I will confess: I thought
    I could count on you when you returned to Corinth.

OEDIPUS: No: I will never go near my parents again.

MESSENGER: Ah, son, you still do not know what you are doing—

OEDIPUS: What do you mean? In the name of God tell me!

MESSENGER: —If these are your reasons for not going home.

OEDIPUS: I tell you, I fear the oracle may come true.

MESSENGER: And guilt may come upon you through your parents?

OEDIPUS: That is the dread that is always in my heart.

MESSENGER: Can you not see that all your fears are groundless?
OEDIPUS: How can you say that? They are my parents, surely?
MESSENGER: Polybos was not your father.
OEDIPUS: Not my father?
MESSENGER: No more your father than the man speaking to you.
OEDIPUS: But you are nothing to me!
MESSENGER: Neither was he.
OEDIPUS: Then why did he call me son?
MESSENGER: I will tell you:
    Long ago he had you from my hands, as a gift.
OEDIPUS: Then how could he love me so, if I was not his?
MESSENGER: He had no children, and his heart turned to you.
OEDIPUS: What of you? Did you buy me? Did you find me by chance?
MESSENGER: I came upon you in the crooked pass of Kithairon.
OEDIPUS: And what were you doing there?
MESSENGER: Tending my flocks.
OEDIPUS: A wandering shepherd?
MESSENGER: But your savior, son, that day.
OEDIPUS: From what did you save me?
MESSENGER: Your ankles should tell you that.
OEDIPUS: Ah, stranger, why do you speak of that childhood pain?
MESSENGER: I cut the bonds that tied your ankles together.
OEDIPUS: I have had the mark as long as I can remember.
MESSENGER: That was why you were given the name you bear.
OEDIPUS: God! Was it my father or my mother who did it?
    Tell me!
MESSENGER: I do not know. The man who gave you to me
    Can tell you better than I.
OEDIPUS: It was not you that found me, but another?
MESSENGER: It was another shepherd gave you to me.
OEDIPUS: Who was he? Can you tell me who he was?
MESSENGER: I think he was said to be one of Laïos' people.
OEDIPUS: You mean the Laïos who was king here years ago?
MESSENGER: Yes; King Laïos; and the man was one of his herdsmen.
OEDIPUS: Is he still alive? Can I see him?
MESSENGER: These men here
    Know best about such things.
OEDIPUS: Does anyone here
    Know this shepherd that he is talking about?
    Have you seen him in the fields, or in the town?
    If you have, tell me. It is time things were made plain.
CHORAGOS: I think the man he means is that same shepherd
    You have already asked to see. Iocastê perhaps
    Could tell you something.
OEDIPUS: Do you know anything
    About him, Lady? Is he the man we have summoned?
    Is that the man this shepherd means?

IOCASTE: Why think of him?
    Forget this herdsman. Forget it all.
    This talk is a waste of time.
OEDIPUS: How can you say that,
IOCASTE: For God's love, let us have no more questioning!
    Is your life nothing to you?
    My own is pain enough for me to bear.
OEDIPUS: You need not worry. Suppose my mother a slave,
    And born of slaves: no baseness can touch you.
IOCASTE: Listen to me, I beg you: do not do this thing!
OEDIPUS: I will not listen; the truth must be made known.
IOCASTE: Everything that I say is for your own good!
OEDIPUS: My own good
    Snaps my patience, then; I want none of it.
IOCASTE: You are fatally wrong! May you never learn who you are!
OEDIPUS: Go, one of you, and bring the shepherd here.
    Let us leave this woman to brag of her royal name.
IOCASTE: Ah, miserable!
    That is the only word I have for you now.
    That is the only word I can ever have.
       [*Exit into the palace.*]
CHORAGOS: Why has she left us, Oedipus? Why has she gone
    In such a passion of sorrow? I fear this silence:
    Something dreadful may come of it.
OEDIPUS: Let it come!
    However base my birth, I must know about it.
    The Queen, like a woman, is perhaps ashamed
    To think of my low origin. But I
    Am a child of Luck; I can not be dishonored.
    Luck is my mother; the passing months, my brothers,
    Have seen me rich and poor.
                    If this is so,
    How could I wish that I were someone else?
    How could I not be glad to know my birth?

ODE III

CHORUS: If ever the coming time were known   [STROPHE]
    To my heart's pondering,
    Kithairon, now by Heaven I see the torches
    At the festival of the next full moon,
    And see the dance, and hear the choir sing
    A grace to your gentle shade:
    Mountain where Oedipus was found,
    O mountain guard of a noble race!
    May the god who heals us lend his aid,

And let that glory come to pass
For our king's cradling-ground.

Of the nymphs that flower beyond the years,   [ANTISTROPHE]
Who bore you, royal child,
To Pan of the hills or the timberline Apollo,
Cold in delight where the upland clears,
Or Hermês for whom Kyllenê's heights are piled?
Or flushed as evening cloud,
Great Dionysos, roamer of mountains,
He—was it he who found you there,
And caught you up in his own proud
Arms from the sweet god-ravisher
Who laughed by the Muses' fountains?

SCENE IV

OEDIPUS: Sirs: though I do not know the man,
    I think I see him coming, this shepherd we want:
    He is old, like our friend here, and the men
    Bringing him seem to be servants of my house.
    But you can tell, if you have ever seen him.
        [*Enter* SHEPHERD *escorted by servants.*]
CHORAGOS: I know him, he was Laïos' man. You can trust him.
OEDIPUS: Tell me first, you from Corinth: is this the shepherd
    We were discussing?
MESSENGER: This is the very man.
OEDIPUS: [*to* SHEPHERD] Come here. No, look at me. You must answer
    Everything I ask.—You belonged to Laïos?
SHEPHERD: Yes: born his slave, brought up in his house.
OEDIPUS: Tell me: what kind of work did you do for him?
SHEPHERD: I was a shepherd of his, most of my life.
OEDIPUS: Where mainly did you go for pasturage?
SHEPHERD: Sometimes Kithairon, sometimes the hills near-by.
OEDIPUS: Do you remember ever seeing this man out there?
SHEPHERD: What would he be doing there? This man?
OEDIPUS: This man standing here. Have you ever seen him before?
SHEPHERD: No. At least, not to my recollection.
MESSENGER: And that is not strange, my lord. But I'll refresh
    His memory: he must remember when we two
    Spent three whole seasons together, March to September,
    On Kithairon or thereabouts. He had two flocks;
    I had one. Each autumn I'd drive mine home
    And he would go back with his to Laïos' sheepfold.—
    Is this not true, just as I have described it?
SHEPHERD: True, yes; but it was all so long ago.
MESSENGER: Well, then: do you remember, back in those days,
    That you gave me a baby boy to bring up as my own?

SHEPHERD: What if I did? What are you trying to say?
MESSENGER: King Oedipus was once that little child.
SHEPHERD: Damn you, hold your tongue!
OEDIPUS: No more of that!
   It is your tongue needs watching, not this man's.
SHEPHERD: My King, my Master, what is it I have done wrong?
OEDIPUS: You have not answered his question about the boy.
SHEPHERD: He does not know . . . He is only making trouble . . .
OEDIPUS: Come, speak plainly, or it will go hard with you.
SHEPHERD: In God's name, do not torture an old man!
OEDIPUS: Come here, one of you; bind his arms behind him.
SHEPHERD: Unhappy king! What more do you wish to learn?
OEDIPUS: Did you give this man the child he speaks of?
SHEPHERD: I did.
   And I would to God I had died that very day.
OEDIPUS: You will die now unless you speak the truth.
SHEPHERD: Yet if I speak the truth, I am worse than dead.
OEDIPUS: Very well; since you insist upon delaying—
SHEPHERD: No! I have told you already that I gave him the boy.
OEDIPUS: Where did you get him? From your house? From somewhere else?
SHEPHERD: Not from mine, no. A man gave him to me.
OEDIPUS: Is that man here? Do you know whose slave he was?
SHEPHERD: For God's love, my King, do not ask me any more!
OEDIPUS: You are a dead man if I have to ask you again.
SHEPHERD: Then . . . Then the child was from the palace of Laïos.
OEDIPUS: A slave child? or a child of his own line?
SHEPHERD: Ah, I am on the brink of dreadful speech!
OEDIPUS: And I of dreadful hearing. Yet I must hear.
SHEPHERD: If you must be told, then . . .
                           They said it was Laïos' child;
   But it is your wife who can tell you about that.
OEDIPUS: My wife!—Did she give it to you?
SHEPHERD: My lord, she did.
OEDIPUS: Do you know why?
SHEPHERD: I was told to get rid of it.
OEDIPUS: An unspeakable mother!
SHEPHERD: There had been prophecies . . .
OEDIPUS: Tell me.
SHEPHERD: It was said that the boy would kill his own father.
OEDIPUS: Then why did you give him over to this old man?
SHEPHERD: I pitied the baby, my King,
   And I thought that this man would take him far away
   To his own country.
                        He saved him—but for what a fate!
   For if you are what this man says you are,
   No man living is more wretched than Oedipus.

OEDIPUS: Ah God!
    It was true!
           All the prophecies!
                  —Now,
    O Light, may I look on you for the last time!
    I, Oedipus,
    Oedipus, damned in his birth, in his marriage damned,
    Damned in the blood he shed with his own hand!
        [*He rushes into the palace.*]

ODE IV

CHORUS: Alas for the seed of men.   [STROPHE 1]

    What measure shall I give these generations
    That breathe on the void and are void
    And exist and do not exist?

    Who bears more weight of joy
    Than mass of sunlight shifting in images,
    Or who shall make his thought stay on
    That down time drifts away?

    Your splendor is all fallen.

    O naked brow of wrath and tears,
    O change of Oedipus!
    I who saw your days call no man blest—
    Your great days like ghósts góne.

    That mind was a strong bow.   [ANTISTROPHE 1]

    Deep, how deep you drew it then, hard archer,
    At a dim fearful range,
    And brought dear glory down!

    You overcame the stranger—
    The virgin with her hooking lion claws—
    And though death sang, stood like a tower
    To make pale Thebes take heart.

    Fortress against our sorrow!

    True king, giver of laws,
    Majestic Oedipus!
    No prince in Thebes had ever such renown,
    No prince won such grace of power.

And now of all men ever known　　　　　　　　　　[STROPHE 2]
Most pitiful is this man's story:
His fortunes are most changed, his state
Fallen to a low slave's
Ground under bitter fate.

O Oedipus, most royal one!
The great door that expelled you to the light
Gave at night—ah, gave night to your glory:
As to the father, to the fathering son.

All understood too late.

How could that queen whom Laïos won,
The garden that he harrowed at his height,
Be silent when that act was done?

But all eyes fail before time's eye,　　　　　　　[ANTISTROPHE 2]
All actions come to justice there.
Though never willed, though far down the deep past,
Your bed, your dread sirings,
Are brought to book at last.
Child by Laïos doomed to die,
Then doomed to lose that fortunate little death,
Would God you never took breath in this air
That with my wailing lips I take to cry:

For I weep the world's outcast.

I was blind, and now I can tell why:
Asleep, for you had given ease of breath
To Thebes, while the false years went by.

ÉXODOS

　　　　　[Enter, from the palace, SECOND MESSENGER.]
SECOND MESSENGER: Elders of Thebes, most honored in this land,
　　What horrors are yours to see and hear, what weight
　　Of sorrow to be endured, if, true to your birth,
　　You venerate the line of Labdakos!
　　I think neither Istros nor Phasis, those great rivers,
　　Could purify this place of the corruption
　　It shelters now, or soon must bring to light—
　　Evil not done unconsciously, but willed.

　　The greatest griefs are those we cause ourselves.
CHORAGOS: Surely, friend, we have grief enough already;
　　What new sorrow do you mean?

SECOND MESSENGER: The Queen is dead.
CHORAGOS: Iocastê? Dead? But at whose hand?
SECOND MESSENGER: Her own.
    The full horror of what happened you can not know,
    For you did not see it; but I, who did, will tell you
    As clearly as I can how she met her death.

    When she had left us,
    In passionate silence, passing through the court,
    She ran to her apartment in the house,
    Her hair clutched by the fingers of both hands.
    She closed the doors behind her; then, by that bed
    Where long ago the fatal son was conceived—
    That son who should bring about his father's death—
    We hear her call upon Laïos, dead so many years,
    And heard her wail for the double fruit of her marriage,
    A husband by her husband, children by her child.

    Exactly how she died I do not know:
    For Oedipus burst in moaning and would not let us
    Keep vigil to the end: it was by him
    As he stormed about the room that our eyes were caught.
    From one to another of us he went, begging a sword,
    Cursing the wife who was not his wife, the mother
    Whose womb had carried his own children and himself.
    I do not know: it was none of us aided him,
    But surely one of the gods was in control!
    For with a dreadful cry
    He hurled his weight, as though wrenched out of himself,
    At the twin doors: the bolts gave, and he rushed in.
    And there we saw her hanging, her body swaying
    From the cruel cord she had noosed about her neck.
    A great sob broke from him, heartbreaking to hear,
    As he loosed the rope and lowered her to the ground.

    I would blot out from my mind what happened next!
    For the King ripped from her gown the golden brooches
    That were her ornament, and raised them, and plunged them down
    Straight into his own eyeballs, crying, "No more,
    No more shall you look on the misery about me,
    The horrors of my own doing! Too long you have known
    The faces of those whom I should never have seen,
    Too long been blind to those for whom I was searching!
    From this hour, go in darkness!;" And as he spoke,
    He struck at his eyes—not once, but many times;
    And the blood spattered his beard,
    Bursting from his ruined sockets like red hail.

So from the unhappiness of two this evil has sprung,
A curse on the man and woman alike. The old
Happiness of the house of Labdakos
Was happiness enough: where is it today?
It is all wailing and ruin, disgrace, death—all
The misery of mankind that has a name—
And it is wholly and for ever theirs.

CHORAGOS: Is he in agony still? Is there no rest for him?

SECOND MESSENGER: He is calling for someone to lead him to the gates
So that all the children of Kadmos may look upon
His father's murderer, his mother's—no,
I can not say it!

                    And then he will leave Thebes,
Self-exiled, in order that the curse
Which he himself pronounced may depart from the house.
He is weak, and there is none to lead him,
So terrible is his suffering.

                    But you will see:
Look, the doors are opening; in a moment
You will see a thing that would crush a heart of stone.

      [*The central door is opened;* OEDIPUS, *blinded, is led in.*]

CHORAGOS: Dreadful indeed for men to see.
Never have my own eyes
Looked on a sight so full of fear.

Oedipus!
What madness came upon you, what daemon
Leaped on your life with heavier
Punishment than a mortal man can bear?
No: I can not even
Look at you, poor ruined one.
And I would speak, question, ponder,
If I were able. No.
You make me shudder.

OEDIPUS: God.   God.
Is there a sorrow greater?
Where shall I find harbor in this world?
My voice is hurled far on a dark wind.
What has God done to me?

CHORAGOS: Too terrible to think of, or to see.

OEDIPUS: O cloud of night,   [STROPHE 1]
Never to be turned away: night coming on,
I can not tell how: night like a shroud!

My fair winds brought me here.
                    O God. Again
The pain of the spikes where I had sight,

The flooding pain
Of memory, never to be gouged out.
CHORAGOS: This is not strange.
    You suffer it all twice over, remorse in pain,
    Pain in remorse.
OEDIPUS: Ah dear friend   [ANTISTROPHE 1]
    Are you faithful even yet, you alone?
    Are you still standing near me, will you stay here,
    Patient, to care for the blind?
                The blind man!
    Yet even blind I know who it is attends me,
    By the voice's tone—
    Though my new darkness hide the comforter.
CHORAGOS: Oh fearful act!
    What god was it drove you to rake black
    Night across your eyes?
OEDIPUS: Apollo. Apollo. Dear   [STROPHE 2]
    Children, the god was Apollo.
    He brought my sick, sick fate upon me.
    But the blinding hand was my own!
    How could I bear to see
    When all my sight was horror everywhere?
CHORAGOS: Everywhere; that is true.
OEDIPUS: And now what is left?
    Images? Love? A greeting even,
    Sweet to the senses? Is there anything?
    Ah, no, friends: lead me away.
    Lead me away from Thebes.
                Lead the great wreck
    And hell of Oedipus, whom the gods hate.
CHORAGOS: Your fate is clear, you are not blind to that.
    Would God you had never found it out!
OEDIPUS: Death take the man who unbound   [ANTISTROPHE 2]
    My feet on that hillside
    And delivered me from death to life! What life?
    If only I had died,
    This weight of monstrous doom
    Could not have dragged me and my darlings down.
CHORAGOS: I would have wished the same.
OEDIPUS: Oh never to have come here
    With my father's blood upon me! Never
    To have been the man they call his mother's husband!
    Oh accurst! Oh child of evil,
    To have entered that wretched bed—
                the selfsame one!
    More primal than sin itself, this fell to me.

CHORAGOS: I do not know how I can answer you.
　　You were better dead than alive and blind.
OEDIPUS: Do not counsel me any more. This punishment
　　That I have laid upon myself is just.
　　If I had eyes,
　　I do not know how I could bear the sight
　　Of my father, when I came to the house of Death,
　　Or my mother: for I have sinned against them both
　　So vilely that I could not make my peace
　　By strangling my own life.
　　　　　　　　　　Or do you think my children,
　　Born as they were born, would be sweet to my eyes?
　　Ah never, never! Nor this town with its high walls,
　　Nor the holy images of the gods.
　　　　　　　　　　For I,
　　Thrice miserable!—Oedipus, noblest of all the line
　　Of Kadmos, have condemned myself to enjoy
　　These things no more, by my own malediction
　　Expelling that man whom the gods declared
　　To be a defilement in the house of Laïos.
　　After exposing the rankness of my own guilt,
　　How could I look men frankly in the eyes?
　　No, I swear it,
　　If I could have stifled my hearing at its source,
　　I would have done it and made all this body
　　A tight cell of misery, blank to light and sound:
　　So I should have been safe in a dark agony
　　Beyond all recollection.
　　　　　　　　　　Ah Kithairon!
　　Why did you shelter me? When I was cast upon you,
　　Why did I not die? Then I should never
　　Have shown the world my execrable birth.

　　Ah Polybos! Corinth, city that I believed
　　The ancient seat of my ancestors: how fair
　　I seemed, your child! And all the while this evil
　　Was cancerous within me!
　　　　　　　　　　For I am sick
　　In my daily life, sick in my origin.

　　O three roads, dark ravine, woodland and way
　　Where three roads met: you, drinking my father's blood,
　　My own blood, spilled by my own hand: can you remember
　　The unspeakable things I did there, and the things
　　I went on from there to do?
　　　　　　　　　　O marriage, marriage!
　　The act that engendered me, and again the act

Performed by the son in the same bed—
                              Ah, the net
Of incest, mingling fathers, brothers, sons,
With brides, wives, mothers: the last evil
That can be known by men: no tongue can say
How evil!
              No. For the love of God, conceal me
Somewhere far from Thebes; or kill me; or hurl me
Into the sea, away from men's eyes for ever.

Come, lead me. You need not fear to touch me.
Of all men, I alone can bear this guilt.
        [*Enter* CREON.]
CHORAGOS: We are not the ones to decide; but Creon here
        May fitly judge of what you ask. He only
        Is left to protect the city in your place.
OEDIPUS: Alas, how can I speak to him? What right have I
        To beg his courtesy whom I have deeply wronged?
CREON: I have not come to mock you, Oedipus,
        Or to reproach you, either.

        [*To* ATTENDANTS:]—You, standing there:
        If you have lost all respect for man's dignity,
        At least respect the flame of Lord Helios:
        Do not allow this pollution to show itself
        Openly here, an affront to the earth
        And Heaven's rain and the light of day. No, take him
        Into the house as quickly as you can.
        For it is proper
        That only the close kindred see his grief.
OEDIPUS: I pray you in God's name, since your courtesy
        Ignores my dark expectation, visiting
        With mercy this man of all men most execrable:
        Give me what I ask—for your good, not for mine.
CREON: And what is it that you would have me do?
OEDIPUS: Drive me out of this country as quickly as may be
        To a place where no human voice can ever greet me.
CREON: I should have done that before now—only,
        God's will had not been wholly revealed to me.
OEDIPUS: But his command is plain: the parricide
        Must be destroyed. I am that evil man.
CREON: That is the sense of it, yes; but as things are,
        We had best discover clearly what is to be done.
OEDIPUS: You would learn more about a man like me?
CREON: You are ready now to listen to the god.
OEDIPUS: I will listen. But it is to you
        That I must turn for help. I beg you, hear me.

The woman in there—
Give her whatever funeral you think proper:
She is your sister.
                        —But let me go, Creon!
Let me purge my father's Thebes of the pollution
Of my living here, and go out to the wild hills,
To Kithairon, that has won such fame with me,
The tomb my mother and father appointed for me,
And let me die there, as they willed I should.
And yet I know
Death will not ever come to me through sickness
Or in any natural way: I have been preserved
For some unthinkable fate. But let that be.

As for my sons, you need not care for them.
They are men, they will find some way to live.
But my poor daughters, who have shared my table,
Who never before have been parted from their father—
Take care of them. Creon; do this for me.
And will you let me touch them with my hands
A last time, and let us weep together?
Be kind, my lord,
Great prince, be kind!
                        Could I but touch them,
They would be mine again, as when I had my eyes.
        [*Enter* ANTIGONE *and* ISMENE, *attended.*]
Ah, God!
Is it my dearest children I hear weeping?
Has Creon pitied me and sent my daughters?
CREON: Yes, Oedipus: I knew that they were dear to you
    In the old days, and know you must love them still.
OEDIPUS: May God bless you for this—and be a friendlier
    Guardian to you than he has been to me!

Children, where are you?
Come quickly to my hands: they are your brother's—
Hands that have brought your father's once clear eyes
To this way of seeing—
                        Ah dearest ones,
I had neither sight nor knowledge then, your father
By the woman who was the source of his own life!
And I weep for you—having no strength to see you—,
I weep for you when I think of the bitterness
That men will visit upon you all your lives.
What homes, what festivals can you attend
Without being forced to depart again in tears?
And when you come to marriageable age,

Where is the man, my daughters, who would dare
Risk the bane that lies on all my children?
Is there any evil wanting? Your father killed
His father; sowed the womb of her who bore him;
Engendered you at the fount of his own existence!
That is what they will say of you.

                              Then, whom
Can you ever marry? There are no bridegrooms for you,
And your lives must wither away in sterile dreaming.

O Creon, son of Menoikeus!
You are the only father my daughters have,
Since we, their parents, are both of us gone for ever.
They are your own blood: you will not let them
Fall into beggary and loneliness;
You will keep them from the miseries that are mine!
Take pity on them; see, they are only children,
Friendless except for you. Promise me this,
Great Prince, and give me your hand in token of it.
        [CREON *clasps his right hand.*]
Children:
I could say much, if you could understand me,
But as it is, I have only this prayer for you:
Live where you can, be as happy as you can—
Happier, please God, than God has made your father!
CREON: Enough. You have wept enough. Now go within.
OEDIPUS: I must; but it is hard.
CREON: Time eases all things.
OEDIPUS: But you must promise—
CREON: Say what you desire.
OEDIPUS: Send me from Thebes!
CREON: God grant that I may!
OEDIPUS: But since God hates me . . .
CREON: No, he will grant your wish
OEDIPUS: You promise?
CREON: I can not speak beyond my knowledge.
OEDIPUS: Then lead me in.
CREON: Come now, and leave your children.
OEDIPUS: No! Do not take them from me!
CREON: Think no longer
        That you are in command here, but rather think
        How, when you were, you served your own destruction.
                [*Exeunt into the house all but the* CHORUS; *the* CHORAGOS
                chants directly to the audience:]
CHORAGOS: Men of Thebes: look upon Oedipus.

This is the king who solved the famous riddle
And towered up, most powerful of men.
No mortal eyes but looked on him with envy,
Yet in the end ruin swept over him.

Let every man in mankind's frailty
Consider his last day; and let none
Presume on his good fortune until he find
Life, at his death, a memory without pain.

PLAUTUS

THE MENAECHMI

Translated by
Richard W. Hyde
and Edward C. Weist

DRAMATIS PERSONAE

PROLOGUS
PENICULUS (SPONGE), *a Parasite*
MENAECHMUS I, *of Epidamnus*
EROTIUM, *a Courtesan*
CULINDRUS, *Cook of Erotium*
MENAECHMUS II (SOSICLES), *of Syracuse*
MESSENIO, *Slave of Menaechmus II*
MAID *of Erotium*
WIFE *of Menaechmus I*
FATHER-IN-LAW *of Menaechmus I*
DOCTOR
Sailors; DECIO *and other Slaves*

SCENE: *Epidamnus—a street, on which stand the houses of* MENAECHMUS I
(L.) *and* EROTIUM (R.).

PROLOGUE

PROLOGUS: Now first and above all, spectators, I'm bringing a few
    Of the best of good wishes to me—and then also to you;
    I'm bringing you Plautus—by mouth, of course, not in his person,
    And therefore I pray you receive him with kindliest ears.
    To the argument gird up your minds, as I babble my verse on,
    And I shall explain it—in briefest of terms, have no fears.
      Now, once an old merchant was living in Syracuse city,
    And he by some chance had a couple of twin sons,—yes, two of 'em—
    And they looked so alike that the nurse couldn't tell (more's the pity)
    Which one she gave suck to; no more could their mother, in lieu of whom
    The nurse was called in, no, not even their mother who'd borne 'em.
      Much later, the boys being now about seven years old,
    Their father filled up a big ship with a lot of his goods

And, putting one twin in safe-keeping with them in the hold,
Betook himself off to Tarentum to market, to turn 'em
To cash; and the other twin, having been naughty in moods,
Stayed home with his mother. Tarentum was holding some games
When they got there, and people were flocking to town, as they ever
Will do for the games; and the little boy strayed, as one never
Should do, from his father among all the crowds, and got lost.
He was found by a rich Epidamnian merchant (whose fame's
The worse for the story) who grabbed him and took him off home.
The father, however, by such a deep blow so star-crossed,
(That is, after the boy disappeared) was dejected at heart,
And only a little while later he died of despair.
Syracuse at last heard the bad news that the father was dead
And that some one had picked up the twin who had gone off to roam;
So the grandfather changed the remaining twin's name then and there,
Since the other had been so beloved (*he* could tell 'em apart);
The other one's name he bestowed on the twin safe at home,
And called him Menaechmus, the same as the one I have said.
And lest you get muddled, as I am, I'm free to confess,
I'll tell you both twins are the same in their name. What a mess!
    But now on the poet's rude feet I must seek Epidamnus,
To speed on my tale, or the *Transcript* critic will be slammin' us
For being so dull. The old merchant I told you about
Had no children whatever, unless you may count all his money.
He adopted the stolen young twin, so that neither made out
Much worse on the deal, for the man got a son, and the youth
At length got a wife and a dowry, and (this strikes me funny)
Came into the property after the old wretch's death.
For, wandering into the country—to tell you the truth—
Where torrents of rain had been falling, not far from the town, the
Epidamnian stepped in a freshet, and thought himself still able
To cross as of old. None the less, as he got out of breath,
The current caught quickly the kidnapper's feet, and pulled down the
Epidamnian—down to the place where they act his third syllable.
So from him the young man inherits a whale of a fortune,
And there is the house where the rich kidnapped twin is now dwelling.
    The other twin, living in Syracuse—pray don't importune,
For I've not forgotten it—comes with his slave now today
To seek out his twin brother here, as you've just heard me telling.
This town's Epidamnus in the present play,
In other plays the city's changed straightway;
So with the families in these two houses,
Where now Menaechmus dwells and now he souses.
The next incumbent may be beggar, thief,
Procurer, doctor, thug, or Indian chief.

ACT I

[*Enter* PENICULUS, L.   *He looks at houses, and finally notices audi-*
    ence.]

PENICULUS: My nickname's Sponge [Peniculus], because when I eat I wipe the
table clean.

　　Men who bind prisoners with chains and put shackles on runaway slaves
are very foolish, if you ask me. You see, if you add insult to injury, a poor
fellow is going to want all the more to escape and go wrong. They'll get
out of their chains somehow, you can be sure,—file away a link, or knock
out a nail with a stone.—That way's ridiculous.

　　If you really want to keep hold on somebody so he won't get away, you
want to tie him with food and drink; first hitch his beak to a full dinner-
pail. Give him all he wants to eat and drink every day, and he'll never
try to run away, not even if he's committed murder; you'll keep him all
right if you bind him this way. The bonds of food and drink are very
elastic, you know; the farther you stretch them, the tighter they hold you.
[*crosses towards house of* MENAECHMUS I]

　　I'm just going over to see my friend Menaechmus, with whom I've been
serving a long term: I'm going to let him bind me. He does more than
feed a man, you see; he reforms you and builds you up; there isn't a better
doctor alive. Just to show you what kind of man he is—he gives wonderful
feasts, regular Thanksgiving dinners: he builds such skyscrapers of dishes
that you have to stand on your couch to get anything off the top. But I
haven't been there for quite a few days; I've been confined at home with
my dear ones (I don't eat or buy anything but what is dear). But my army
of dear ones is deserting, and I must go see him. [*Approaches door. Enter*
MENAECHMUS I, *projected from doorway; the impulse evidently comes
from his wife. He wears cloak under his pallium.*] But the door is opening.
There's Menaechmus—he's coming out. [*Withdraws U. C.*]

MENAECHMUS I: [SONG]
　　　　　　　If you were not
　　　　　　　　　Stubborn, bad,
　　　　　　　　Stupid, and a
　　　　　　　　　Little mad,
　　　　　　　What your husband hates, you'd see
　　　　　　　And behave accordingly.
　　　　　　　Mind your manners—do you hear—
　　　　　　　Or home you go to "father dear."—
　　　　　　　When I say I'm going out,
　　　　　　　You're on hand to ask about
　　　　　　　Where I'm going,
　　　　　　　　What to do,
　　　　　　　What's my business,
　　　　　　　　What's for you.
　　　　　　　I can't get out anywhere,

But you want me to declare
All I've done and all I do,
Customs officer—that's you!
I've handled you with too much care;
Listen what I'm going to do:
Food I give you,
 Maids, indeed,
Gold and dresses—
 All you need;
Now you'll keep your spying eyes
Off your husband, if you're wise.

And besides that, so you won't have your watching for nothing, I'm going to invite a courtesan out to dinner somewhere, to spite you. [*Looks back into house.*]

PENICULUS: [*aside*] The man pretends he's cursing his wife, but he's really cursing me. It's me that he hurts by dining out, not his wife.

MENAECHMUS I: Can you beat it? I've finally scolded my wife away from the door. [*to audience*] Where are you philandering husbands? Why don't you come up and congratulate me, and reward me for my brave fight? [*shows cloak*] I've just stolen this cloak from my wife inside, and I'm going to take it to my mistress. This is a fine way to cheat my clever watchdog. It's

 An excellent job,
 An honest job,
 A gentleman's job,
 A workmanlike job.

I stole it from that shrew at my expense, and it's going to be a total loss. [*indicating house of* EROTIUM] But I got the spoils from the enemy without losing a man.

PENICULUS: [*accosting him*] Here, sir, is any of that haul for me?

MENAECHMUS I: [*retreating left and covering his head with his cloak*] The game's up. I've fallen into a trap.

PENICULUS: O no, sir, into a body guard, rather; don't be afraid.

MENAECHMUS I: Who are you?

PENICULUS: It's me.

MENAECHMUS I: [*grasping his hand*] O, my period of light-heartedness, my psychological moment, good morning!

PENICULUS: Good morning.

MENAECHMUS I: What are you up to?

PENICULUS: Why, holding my friend-in-need by the hand.

MENAECHMUS I: You couldn't have met me at a better time.

PENICULUS: That's my way: I am an expert in fitting occasions.

MENAECHMUS I: Want to see a rich treat?

PENICULUS: What cook cooked it? I'll know if the pan slipped when I see the leavings.

MENAECHMUS I: Say, did you ever see the painting in the temple where the eagle steals Ganymede, or Venus Adonis?

PENICULUS: Plenty of times. But what's that got to do with me?

MENAECHMUS I: [*revealing cloak*] Well, look at me. Do I look like that picture?

PENICULUS: What's that rig?

MENAECHMUS I: Say that I'm a gallant soul.

PENICULUS: When do we eat?

MENAECHMUS I: Say what I tell you.

PENICULUS: [*listlessly*] All right; gallant soul.

MENAECHMUS I: Won't you add anything of your own?

PENICULUS: [*with a sigh*] Well, gay dog.

MENAECHMUS I: Go on, go on.

PENICULUS: I will not go on until I know what I'm going to get. You've had a squabble with your wife and so I've got to be careful.

MENAECHMUS I: Suppose we find a place where we can have a funeral without my wife's knowing it—and then burn up the day?

PENICULUS: [*enthusiastically*] Wonderful, but go on—how soon can I light the pyre? The day's already dead up to the waist.

MENAECHMUS I: You'll wait, if you're going to contradict me.

PENICULUS: Knock my eye out, Menaechmus, if I say anything you don't tell me to.

MENAECHMUS I: Move over here away from the door. [*Pulls* PENICULUS *R., and twirls him around.*]

PENICULUS: Yes.

MENAECHMUS I: [*cautiously*] Come farther away. [*Twirling him around again.*]

PENICULUS: All right.

MENAECHMUS I: Come boldly away from the lion's den. [*Twirling him a third time.*]

PENICULUS: See here, I have an idea you'd make a good charioteer.

MENAECHMUS I: Why?

PENICULUS: Because you're always looking around to see that your wife is not following you.

MENAECHMUS I: But what do you say—

PENICULUS: What do I say? Any thing you want, sir.

MENAECHMUS I: Can you make a good guess from the odor of something if you smell it?

PENICULUS: Why, if you got the board of augurs,—

MENAECHMUS I: [*interrupting*] Come on, smell this cloak I've got. [*holds up the hem of the cloak*] What does it smell of? [PENICULUS *sniffs and draws back*] Why do you hang back?

PENICULUS: You ought to smell the top of a woman's dress, because the smell here is unforgettable.

MENAECHMUS I: Then smell here, Peniculus. [*Holding up another part.*] How dainty you are!

PENICULUS: [*smelling cautiously*] It smells.

MENAECHMUS I: Of what? What does it smell of?

PENICULUS: [*triumphantly*] A theft, a courtesan, and luncheon! And you—

MENAECHMUS I: You've said it. Now I'm going to take this to the courtesan Erotium here, and I'll have lunch prepared for us three.

PENICULUS: Great!

MENAECHMUS I: And after that we'll drink till tomorrow's morning star.

PENICULUS: You've said a mouthful! Shall I knock now?

MENAECHMUS I: Yes. [PENICULUS *crosses, and standing with his back to* EROTIUM's *door, raises one leg to knock*] But wait a minute.

PENICULUS: You've held up the drinking a mile.

MENAECHMUS I: Knock gently.

PENICULUS: I think you're afraid the door is made of Samian ware.

> [*Enter* EROTIUM *from her house. Music.*]

MENAECHMUS I: [*dragging* PENICULUS *to* C.] Wait, wait, please. She's coming out herself. See how the sun is blinded beside her body's splendor.

EROTIUM: Menaechmus, sweetheart, good morning.

PENICULUS: [*interrupting*] What about me?

EROTIUM: [*pushing* PENICULUS *away*] You don't count.

PENICULUS: That's what usually happens to the reserves in a regiment.

MENAECHMUS I: I'd like you to get ready for him and me today—a battle.

EROTIUM: So it shall be.

PENICULUS: [*pushing in*] Yes, and we'll drink in this battle, and the better fighter will be found by the bottle. You're at the head of the regiment, and you'll decide which of us shall spend the night with you.

MENAECHMUS I: [*pulling* PENICULUS *away from* EROTIUM] My heart's delight, how I hate my wife when I see you!

EROTIUM: [*spying the cloak*] Incidentally you can't keep from wearing her clothes. What's this? [*Examining the edge of the cloak.*]

MENAECHMUS I: Clothes for you from my wife, rosebud.

EROTIUM: You're an easy winner over every one of my other lovers. [*Crossing to her door and posing before it.*]

PENICULUS: [*aside*] The courtesan is flattering him now that she sees what he's stolen. [*looking towards* EROTIUM.] If you really loved him, you should have bitten his nose off with your kisses.

MENAECHMUS I: Take this, Peniculus. I want to make the offering I have vowed.

PENICULUS: Yes, [*holding* MENAECHMUS' *pallium*] but please, dance with that cloak on.

MENAECHMUS I: I dance? You must be mad.

PENICULUS: Either I or you. If you won't dance, take that thing off.

MENAECHMUS I: [*removing cloak*] I ran a great risk getting this.

PENICULUS: Yes, I think you ran a greater risk than Hercules when he stole the girdle of Hippolyta.

MENAECHMUS I: [*beckoning to* EROTIUM] Take this. [*He hands her the cloak.*] You are the only person who really understands me.

EROTIUM: That's the spirit that should inspire honest lovers.

PENICULUS: [*aside*] At least the ones that are on their way to the poorhouse.

MENAECHMUS I: [*taking cloak and holding it up*] I paid four minae for that last year for my wife. [*He teases* EROTIUM *by drawing away the cloak as she reaches for it, but finally hands it to her.*]

PENICULUS: [*aside*] Four minae gone up in smoke, as I foot up the account.

MENAECHMUS I: Do you know what I want you to do?

EROTIUM: Name it; I'll do anything you want.

MENAECHMUS I: Have a luncheon prepared for us at your house—

PENICULUS: [*Pushing him aside;* MENAECHMUS I *listens approvingly.*] And dainties bought at the market:

> The son of a glandule of pork,
>   Or the son of a fattened ham,
> Or the jowl of a hog—
>   Some food of that sort,
> Which set on the table,
> Will tickle my palate
> And give me the gorge of a kite.

And hurry up.

EROTIUM: Very good.

MENAECHMUS I: We'll go on to the forum but we'll be back soon. We'll pass the time when the lunch is being cooked in drinking.

EROTIUM: Come when you will. [*crossing to her door*] Things will be ready.

MENAECHMUS I: Hurry now. [*to* PENICULUS] You follow me.

PENICULUS: By Hercules, I'll watch over you and follow you, and I wouldn't take the wealth of heaven if I had to lose you. [*Exeunt* MENAECHMUS I *and* PENICULUS *at his heels, L.*]

EROTIUM [*calling inside*]: Call out my cook Culindrus in there at once. [*Enter* CULINDRUS.] Take a basket [*Exit* CULINDRUS, *who returns immediately with a market basket*] and some money. [*giving him coins*] There's three nummi.

CULINDRUS: Yes.

EROTIUM: Go and get some provisions, enough for three people—not too little, and not too much.

CULINDRUS: What sort of men will they be?

EROTIUM: I and Menaechmus and his parasite.

CULINDRUS: There's ten already, because a parasite easily does the work of eight men.

EROTIUM: I've told you the guests. You take care of the rest.

CULINDRUS: Yes indeed. [*running off, L.*] Everything's cooked. Tell them dinner is served.

EROTIUM: Hurry back. [*Exit into her house.*]

CULINDRUS: I'm back already. [*Exit, L.*]

ACT II

[*Enter* MENAECHMUS II, R., *and his slave* MESSENIO *carrying a bag, followed at a distance by sailors with baggage. Sailors cross to extreme L., where they deposit baggage and loll.*]

MENAECHMUS II: I think, Messenio, that there is no greater joy for sea travellers than sighting the distant land while still far out at sea.

MESSENIO: Frankly, it's a greater pleasure if it is your native land you're coming to. But, pray, why is it that we have now come to Epidamnus? Are we to be like the ocean, and go round all the islands?

MENAECHMUS II: [*sadly*] We are searching for my twin brother.

MESSENIO: Is there never to be an end to this search? This is the sixth year that we have spent on it: we have knocked about Histria, Spain, Massilia, Illyria, the whole Adriatic, all the Italian coast—every place that the sea touches; if you had been hunting a needle you'd have found it long ago, if there had been one. We're trying to find a dead man among the living; for if he were alive, we should have found him long ago.

MENAECHMUS II: Then, if you please, I am looking for some one who says he knows my brother is dead. Assured of this, I shall seek no further. But otherwise I shall never give up the search as long as I live; I know how dear he is to my heart.

MESSENIO: You might as well try to find a knot in a bulrush. Let's leave this place and go home.—Or are we, perhaps, going to write a book of travels?

MENAECHMUS II: [*angrily*] You had better stop making these witty remarks, unless you want to get into trouble. Don't provoke me; I am not carrying on this affair to suit you.

MESSENIO: [*aside*] Hey, now! That remark puts me in my place; he couldn't have put it more neatly and completely! But just the same I can't help talking. [*aloud*] Harkee, Menaechmus: when I look into the purse, it seems as though we were lightly clad for a summer journey! By heaven, if you don't go back home now, you'll be searching for that blessed brother of yours without a penny to bless *yourself* with. For Epidamnus is full of rakes and tremendous drinkers; a tremendous lot of swindlers and spongers live here, and their courtesans are called the most seductive in the whole world. That's why the place is called Epidamnus: scarcely anybody can come here without getting damned.

MENAECHMUS II: I'll be on my guard against that; just hand the purse over to me.

MESSENIO: What do you want with it?

MENAECHMUS II: I am worried about you, from what you have said.

MESSENIO: And why?

MENAECHMUS II: I am afraid you might get me damned in Epidamnus. You are very fond of the ladies, Messenio, and I am an irascible man of the most unmanageable disposition; with the money in my possession I shall be able to protect you doubly, both from any mishap and also from my anger.

MESSENIO: [*hands him purse*] Take it and keep it; I'm agreeable. [*Enter* CULIN-DRUS, *the cook, L., with his market basket of provisions.*]

CULINDRUS: [*to audience*] I have done a good job of marketing—just what I like myself! I'll set a fine lunch before the company.—Glory, there I see Menaechmus. Woe to my back! Here are the guests walking about at the door before I am back with the provisions. I'll go and speak to him. [*to* MENAECHMUS II] Good day, Menaechmus.

MENAECHMUS II: The lord love you, whoever you are. [*to* MESSENIO] This fellow seems to know my name. Do you know who he is?

MESSENIO: Not I, by heaven.

CULINDRUS: Where are the other guests?

MENAECHMUS II: What guests?

CULINDRUS: Why, your parasite.

MENAECHMUS II: My parasite? [*to* MESSENIO] Why, the man is mad.

MESSENIO: [*to* MENAECHMUS II] Didn't I tell you this place was full of swindlers?

MENAECHMUS II: What parasite of mine are you looking for, young man?

CULINDRUS: 'Sponge.'

MESSENIO: Nonsense, I have the sponge safe in the bag.

CULINDRUS: [*paying no attention to him*] You come too early for lunch,
Menaechmus; I've just got back from the marketing.

MENAECHMUS II: [*gently*] Young man, tell me: what is the price of pigs in
this town—unblemished ones, for sacrifice?

CULINDRUS: [*puzzled*] A drachma each.

MENAECHMUS II: Well, I'll give you a drachma; [*holds it out, but takes it
back*] go get yourself purified of your insanity at my expense. For really,
you must be perfectly mad, to be bothering a perfect stranger like me,—
whoever you are.

CULINDRUS: I am Culindrus. Don't you know my name?

MENAECHMUS II: The devil take you, whether your name is Cylinder or Col-
lander; I don't know you and I don't want to.

CULINDRUS: Your name is Menaechmus, I am sure of that much.

MENAECHMUS II: Now you're talking sense, since you call me by my right
name. But where have you known me?

CULINDRUS: Where have I known *you*, who keep my mistress Erotium as your
lady?

MENAECHMUS II: By heaven, I keep no such person, and I don't know you,
either.

CULINDRUS: You don't know me, who have so often filled your cup for you
here, when you have been drinking?

MESSENIO: O miserable me, not to have anything to break this fellow's head
with!

MENAECHMUS II: You used to be cup-bearer for me, who have never before
today been in Epidamnus or even seen it?

CULINDRUS: You deny it?

MENAECHMUS II: By heaven, I most certainly do deny it.

CULINDRUS: Don't you live in that house over there?

MENAECHMUS II: May the devil fly away with those that do!

CULINDRUS: [*aside*] Why, then, this man is mad too, calling the devil on his
own head. [*aloud*] Harkee, Menaechmus.

MENAECHMUS II: Well, what do you want?

CULINDRUS: If you should ask me, I should advise you to take that drachma
you promised me a minute ago and get a pig for yourself, because you are
most certainly mad if you bedevil yourself this way.

MENAECHMUS II: Gad, what a chatterer this man is; he makes me tired.

CULINDRUS: [*to audience*] He often jokes with me like this. How droll he is,
so long as his wife is not about! [*to* MENAECHMUS II, *showing his basket
of provisions*] What do you say to that?

MENAECHMUS II: What do you want now, you good for nothing?

CULINDRUS: Is what you see here enough provision for the three of you, or should I go buy some more for yourself, the parasite, and the lady?

MENAECHMUS II: What ladies, what parasites are you talking about?

MESSENIO: What's the matter with you? Why are you badgering the gentleman?

CULINDRUS: [*to* MESSENIO] What business is it of yours? I never saw you before. I am just having a talk with this gentleman, whom I know.

MENAECHMUS II: By the lord, you're no sane man, I'm sure of that.

CULINDRUS: These things shall be cooked, I promise you, and without delay. [*crossing to* EROTIUM's *door*] Don't go too far from the house! Do you wish anything more?

MENAECHMUS II: Yes. I wish you to go utterly and completely to the devil!

CULINDRUS: It would be better if you were to go—inside and take your place at table while I [*grandly*] am exposing these morsels to the violence of Vulcan! I'll go in and tell Erotium that you are out here, so that she can bring you in instead of your having to cool your heels outside. [*Exit into house.*]

MENAECHMUS II: Has he gone away? He has. Oh, Messenio, I see that your warning was far from being false.

MESSENIO: Yes, but watch out; I am sure that a courtesan lives here, just as that madman said who just went away.

MENAECHMUS II: All the same, I wonder how he knew my name.

MESSENIO: Nothing strange in that; it's just a way these courtesans have. They send their serving-boys and serving-girls down to the harbor; if a foreign ship comes in, they ask where it comes from and what the owner's name is, and then they immediately glue themselves to him. If he is taken in by them, he is sent home a ruined man. [*grandly*] Now in the harbor there [*pointing to* EROTIUM's *house*] rides a pirate craft, of which we must be wary.

MENAECHMUS II: By heaven, that is good advice.

MESSENIO: I'll soon know how good it is, if you'll only take it.

MENAECHMUS II: Be quiet a minute; I heard the door creak. Let's see who comes out.

MESSENIO: I'll set this bag down, then. [*to sailors*] Keep a sharp eye on those bundles, you toilers of the sea!

[*Enter* EROTIUM *from her house.*]

EROTIUM: [SONG]—[*to slaves within*]
Go in, and do not close the door,
   I want it left just so.
See what there is to do inside
   And do it all—now go.
The couches must be spread, and perfumes burned:
Neatness entices lovers, I have learned.
Splendor to lovers' loss, to our gain is turned. [*coming forward and looking about her*]
But where is the man they said was before my door? [*catching sight of* MENAECHMUS II] Ah, there he is: he's been of use before,

Yet is, as he deserves, my governor.
I'll go and speak to him myself.—My dear,
I am amazed to see you standing here;
Less wide your door than mine when you appear.
   Now all you ordered is prepared,
     The doors are opened wide,
   Your lunch is cooked, and when you like,
     Come take your place inside.

MENAECHMUS II: [*to* MESSENIO] Whom is this woman talking to?

ROTIUM: [*surprised*] Why, to whom but yourself?

MENAECHMUS II: What have you had to do with me, now or ever? Why do you speak to me?

EROTIUM: Because, in truth, it is the will of Love that I should exalt you of all others, and not beyond your desert, for it is you alone who make me flourish, by your kindness.

MENAECHMUS II: [*aside to* MESSENIO] Surely this woman is either insane or drunk, Messenio, to address an unknown man like me so familiarly.

MESSENIO: Didn't I tell you that was the way here? Why, these are just falling leaves compared to what will happen if we stay here a couple of days more: then it will be trees falling on you. All the courtesans here are just wheedlers of money. But let me speak to her a bit. [*to* EROTIUM, *who is looking into her house*] Harkee, my lady, I'm speaking to you.

EROTIUM: What is it?

MESSENIO: [*escaping her advances*] Where have you known this gentleman before?

EROTIUM: In the same place where he has known me for this long time, in Epidamnus.

MESSENIO: [*sarcastically*] In Epidamnus! A man who before this day has never set foot in the place?

EROTIUM: Ha, ha, you are joking.—Menaechmus, why don't you be a dear and come in? It will be nicer for you there.

MENAECHMUS II: [*aside to* MESSENIO] Great Scott, the woman has called me by my own name! I'd like very much to know the meaning of it all.

MESSENIO: She has got scent of that purse you have there.

MENAECHMUS II: That's a sound warning. Here, take it [*gives him purse*]; I'll soon find out which she loves better, me or my purse.

EROTIUM: [*attempting to draw* MENAECHMUS II *into her house*] Let us go inside to lunch.

MENAECHMUS II: You are very kind, but [*backing away*] no, thank you.

EROTIUM: But then why did you tell me just a little while ago to prepare a lunch for you?

MENAECHMUS II: *I* told you to prepare a lunch?

EROTIUM: Why of course, for you and your parasite.

MENAECHMUS II: Plague take it, what parasite? [*to* MESSENIO] Certainly this woman is not quite sane.

EROTIUM: 'Sponge.'

MENAECHMUS II: What is this sponge you all keep talking about? The kind you rub your shoes with?

EROTIUM: The one who came here with you a little while ago when you brought me the cloak you had stolen from your wife.

MENAECHMUS II: What? I gave you a cloak that I had stolen from my wife? Are you in your right senses? [*to* MESSENIO] Why, this woman dreams standing up, like a horse.

EROTIUM: Why do you enjoy making fun of me and denying what you have done?

MENAECHMUS II: Tell me what I have done, that I deny.

EROTIUM: That you gave me your wife's cloak today.

MENAECHMUS II: [*angrily*] I still deny it. I haven't a wife, never had one, and I have never in my life set foot in this place before. I had breakfast on board my ship, and from there I came by here and met you.

EROTIUM: Alack, I am a lost woman! What ship?

MENAECHUM II: [*grandiloquently*] A wooden one is she, often bruised and often busted, often smitten with sledge; like the furrier's furniture,—peg is paired with peg.

EROTIUM: Oh, my love, stop this joking and come inside with me at once.

MENAECHMUS II: [*beginning to weaken*] But, madam, you are looking for some other man, not me.

EROTIUM: Don't I know you,—Menaechmus, son of Moschus, who was born in Sicily, the story goes, at Syracuse where King Agathocles reigned, and after him Pintia, and then Liparo, who at his death left the kingdom to Hiero, who now is king?

MENAECHUM II: What you say is quite true.

MESSENIO: By heaven, the woman isn't from there herself, is she, to know you so well?

MENAECHMUS II: [*capitulating*] I don't think I can refuse. [*Moves toward* EROTIUM's *house*.]

MESSENIO: [*seizing his arm*] You are a lost man if you cross that threshold.

MENAECHMUS II: Be quiet. The affair goes well. I shall assent to anything she says, so long as it means entertainment. [*confidentially to* EROTIUM] I have been contradicting you for a purpose: I was afraid that this fellow might tell my wife about the cloak and the breakfast. Now, whenever you please, let us go indoors.

EROTIUM: Are you going to wait for the parasite any longer?

MENAECHMUS II: Certainly not. I don't care a straw about him, and if he comes, I don't want to have him let in.

EROTIUM: Goodness, that's quite agreeable to me.—But do you know what I should like to have you do for me?

MENAECHMUS II: Command me.

EROTIUM: I wish you would take that cloak you gave me just now to the embroiderer's to be repaired, and get them to add some new trimming that I want.

MENAECHMUS II: [*scenting booty*] By heaven, that's a good idea. It shall be so disguised that my wife wouldn't recognise it if she saw you wearing it in the street.

EROTIUM: You can take it with you presently, when you go.

MENAECHMUS II: Yes, certainly.

EROTIUM: Let us go inside.

MENAECHMUS II: I'll follow you; I just want to speak to this fellow. [*Exit* EROTIUM *into the house.* MENAECHMUS II *crosses* MESSENIO *to bag, R.*] Hi there, Messenio, come here.

MESSENIO: What for?

MENAECHMUS II: Pick up that bag.

MESSENIO: What for?

MENAECHMUS II: Never mind what for. [*shamefacedly*] I know what you are going to call me.

MESSENIO: So much the worse.

MENAECHMUS II: Hold your accursed tongue, you knave. I have the booty practically in my hands, such a siegework I have begun! You go as quickly as you can and take these porters immediately to an inn; then do you be sure to come back for me before sundown. [*Crosses to* EROTIUM's *door.*]

MESSENIO: Master, you don't know what these courtesans are!

MENAECHMUS II: Be quiet, I tell you, and go. It is my loss, not yours, if I do anything foolish. This woman is silly and inexperienced; and as far as I can judge, there is plunder for us here. [*Exit into* EROTIUM's *house.*]

MESSENIO: I am lost! Are you going? He is surely lost too. The pirate craft is leading the yacht straight to destruction. But I'm a fool to expect to rule my master. He brought me to obey, not to give him orders. [*to sailors*] You, follow me, so that I can come back in time to meet my master, as he ordered. [*Exeunt.*]

[*Enter* PENICULUS, *exasperated.*]

PENICULUS: More than thirty years old I am, but in all that time I have never done anything more mischievous or evil than I did to-day when, miserable me, I pushed into the middle of the assembly. While I stood there gaping, Menaechmus sneaked off from me and went away to see his lady friend, I suppose, and didn't want to take me.—May the devil take the men who invented the scurvy practice of holding assemblies to take up the time of busy men! Wouldn't it be better, now, to pick on unengaged people for that, and if they didn't appear when the roll was called, let *them* pay the fine on the spot? There are plenty of men who eat only once a day, who have nothing to do, who are never invited out to dine or give a dinner themselves; that's the sort of people who should have the job of sitting in the assembly and the law courts. If things were run that way, I shouldn't have missed my breakfast to-day; on my life, he was willing enough to give it to me.—I'll just go anyhow. I may still get some scraps, and the hope whets my appetite. [*Door opens, revealing* MENAECHMUS II *very drunk, with a garland on his head and wearing the cloak.*] But what's this? Menaechmus coming out of the house with a garland on? The dinner's over; I've just come in time to fetch him away, egad! I'll see what he's about, and then I'll go speak to him. [*Withdraws.*]

MENAECHMUS II: [*to* EROTIUM *within*] It will be so changed that you won't recognize it.

PENICULUS: [*to audience*] He is taking the mantle to an embroiderer's; the breakfast's eaten, the wine drunk, and the parasite shut outside. By heaven, I'll revenge myself handsomely for this trick, or my name's not Peniculus. Just watch how you'll catch it!

MENAECHMUS II: [*not seeing* PENICULUS] Ye gods! to whom did you ever in one day give more blessings, beyond all expectation? I've wined and dined with a courtesan, I've got me this [*indicating the cloak*], and she'll never have it again.

PENICULUS: [*aside*] From my hiding place I can't hear what he says. Now that he is full of dinner he is talking about me and my share.

MENAECHMUS II: [*still not noticing* PENICULUS] She says I stole this cloak from my wife and gave it to her. As soon as I saw she was mistaken, I began to assent, as though there had been something between us; whatever she said, I said too. Why waste words?—I have never had a better time at less expense.

PENICULUS: I'll go up to him. I'm just aching for a row.

MENAECHMUS II: Who is this coming towards me?

PENICULUS: [*violently*] What's that you say, you fellow lighter than a feather, you villain, you knave, you disgrace of humanity, you trickster, you cheap clown? What have I done to deserve ill of you? Sneak away from me in the forum a while ago and celebrate the funeral of the breakfast in my absence, would you? How did you dare do that, when I was entitled to it just as much as you were?

MENAECHMUS II: I beg you, young man, what have you to do with me, that you should ignorantly berate a stranger this way? Do you want to get a whipping for your insolence?

PENICULUS: Ha! you've given me that already.

MENAECHMUS II: Answer me, young man. What is your name?

PENICULUS: Are you mocking me too, pretending not to know my name?

MENAECHMUS II: As far as I can tell, I have never either seen or known you before this day. But, whoever you are, if you behave decently, we may get on together.

PENICULUS: You don't know me?

MENAECHMUS II: If I did, I should not deny it.

PENICULUS: Menaechmus, wake up! [*shakes him*]

MENAECHMUS II: By heaven, I *am* awake, I should think.

PENICULUS: Don't you know your own parasite?

MENAECHMUS II: I see that your head isn't sound, young man.

PENICULUS: Answer me: Did you not filch that cloak today from your wife and give it to Erotium?

MENAECHMUS II: Good Lord, I haven't any wife, I didn't give any mantle to Erotium, and I never stole it!

PENICULUS: Are *you* sane? [*aside*] This affair is done for. [*to* MENAECHMUS] Didn't I see you come out of that house with a woman's cloak on?

MENAECHMUS II:[*angry*] Plague take you! Do you think that everybody is an effeminate rogue simply because you are one? You declare that I had on a woman's cloak?

PENICULUS: I certainly do.

MENAECHMUS II: Go to the devil where you belong, or get yourself purified, you utter madman.

PENICULUS: [*furious*] By heaven, no one shall persuade me not to tell this whole affair, just as it happened, to your wife at once. All your abuse will fall back on your own head. I'll make you pay for hogging that breakfast. [*Exit into house of* MENAECHMUS I.]

MENAECHMUS II: What sort of a business is this? Is everybody going to make fun of me this way as soon as I meet them?—But I heard the door creak.
            [*Enter a servant-girl from house of* EROTIUM, *with a bracelet in her hand.*]

MAID: Menaechmus, Erotium says she would love to have you take this bracelet along to the goldsmith's and have an ounce of gold added and have it done over.

MENAECHMUS II: I promise to take care of this and anything else she wants attended to, anything at all. [*Takes it.*]

MAID: Do you know what bracelet this is?

MENAECHMUS II: Only that it's a gold one.

MAID: It is the one which you said you once stole from your wife's cupboard on the sly.

MENAECHMUS II: By all that's holy, I never did!

MAID: Don't you remember, pray? Give it back if you don't. [*Reaches for it.*]

MENAECHMUS II: [*keeping it out of reach*] Wait a moment. I do indeed remember it. [*lamely*] Why, it's the — one I gave her.

MAID: The very same.

MENAECHMUS II: Where are the armlets I gave her along with it?

MAID: You never gave her any.

MENAECHMUS II: I certainly did, along with the bracelet.

MAID: I'll say you will look after it?

MENAECHMUS I: Do. It shall be taken care of. I'll see that it's brought back — as soon as the cloak.

MAID: [*coaxingly*] Menaechmus, I'd love to have you give me some earrings. Have them made to weigh two drachmas each! Then I'd be glad to see you when you come here.

MENAECHMUS II: Certainly! Give me the gold, and I'll pay for working.

MAID: Oh, please, *you* give the gold. I'll repay you later.

MENAECHMUS II: No, you give it. Later I'll repay you double!

MAID: I haven't any.

MENAECHMUS II: [*no longer interested*] Well, when you get some, you can give it to me then.

MAID: [*turning to go*] Is there anything else, please? [*Exit.*]

MENAECHMUS II: Say I will take good care to sell these things for what they will bring! Has she gone inside? [*examines door to make sure*] Yes; the door is shut. The gods certainly aid me, prosper me, and love me. But why do I linger when now is the time and the chance to escape from these courtesan liars? Hasten, Menaechmus! Right foot forward, march! [*starts reeling off stage*] I'll take off this garland and throw it away over to the left [*throws it beyond house of* MENAECHMUS I], and then if they follow me they'll think I went that way. I'm off to find my slave, if I can, to tell himself about the blessings that the gods are sending me.

[*Exit, R.*]

ACT III

[*Enter* WIFE *from house of* MENAECHMUS I, *followed by* PENICULUS.]

WIFE: [*coming C.*] How can I put up with married life when my husband sneaks out of the house with anything he can lay his hands on and carries it off to his mistress?

PENICULUS: Keep quiet a minute. You'll catch him in the act — I'll warrant you that. Come here a minute. He was wearing a wreath, he was reeling drunk, he was taking the cloak he stole from you today to the dyers'. [*seeing wreath*] But look, here's the wreath he had on. Now am I a liar? See, this is the way he went, if you want to hunt him down. [*Looking off L. Enter* MENAECHMUS I, L.] For heaven's sake, there's the fellow himself coming back. What a piece of luck! But he hasn't got the cloak with him.

WIFE: What'll I do to him?

PENICULUS: The same as usual — treat him rough.

WIFE: All right.

PENICULUS: Let's step aside and catch him from ambush. [*Drawing her back between houses. Pantomine during* MENAECHMUS I's *song: they listen in vain for something that will betray him.* WIFE *gives up in disgust, and exit haughtily.* PENICULUS *sits dejected.* WIFE *returns in time to hear* MENAECHMUS I *tell of stealing of cloak.*]

MENAECHMUS I: [SONG]
It's very silly fashion and an awful nuisance, too,
That all of us obey, especially the titled few.
We want a lot of hangers-on — who may be good or bad:
Reputation doesn't matter when there's money to be had.
You may be poor and honest — as a fool you're sent away;
But if you're rich and wicked, you're a worthy protégé.
The lawless man, who when he's trusted with a thing, will swear
He never saw it — that's the man for whom we patrons care —
The contentious man, the trickster, who by means of perjury
Or bribes supports a life of law-suits, greed, and luxury.
But the patron has no holiday when law-days are decreed;
He must defend the guilty man and see that he is freed.
In just this way was I detained today by some poor sinner,
And now I've missed my mistress, to say nothing of the dinner.
I spoke before the aediles to allay their just suspicions,
And proposed a set of intricate and tortuous conditions,
Which, if we could have proved them, would have surely won the case.
But then this brainless fellow brought a bondsman to the place!

I'm sure I never saw a man more clearly caught than he:
Three witnesses were there, who swore to all his deviltry.
May heaven destroy the man who's made a ruin so complete
Of all my day — and me, who in the law-courts set my feet!
As soon as it was possible, I came directly here.
I've ordered lunch; I know she's waiting for me; yet I fear —
        She's mad at me now;
           But the cloak ought to move her,
        That I stole from my wife,
          And took to my lover.

PENICULUS: [*aside to wife*] What do you say to that?

WIFE: I'm blessed with a bad marriage and a bad husband.

PENICULUS: Can you hear what he's saying all right?

WIFE: I should say I could.

MENAECHMUS I: Now the best thing for me to do is to go in here, [*starting towards* EROTIUM's *door*] where I can have a good time.

PENICULUS: [*Suddenly blocking his way;* WIFE *steps forward on other side.*] Wait a minute; there's a bad time coming first.

MENAECHMUS I: [*to audience*] Who's this? What do I see? My wife and my parasite standing together in front of my house? She doesn't seem to be in good humor; I don't like it. I'll go up and speak to her, though. [*approaching* WIFE] Tell me, my dear, what's wrong with you?

PENICULUS: Soft soap!

MENAECHMUS I: [*pushing* PENICULUS *away*] Stop making a nuisance of yourself. Am I talking to you? [*He goes to* WIFE *and attempts to fondle her.*]

WIFE: [*resisting*] Take away your arm; cut out your pawing!

PENICULUS: Keep at him, madam!

MENAECHMUS I: Why are you so disagreeable to me?

WIFE: You ought to know.

PENICULUS: He does, the villain, but he's making out he doesn't.

MENAECHMUS I: Has one of the slaves been cutting up? Have the maids or menservants answered you back? Tell me; they'll be punished.

WIFE: Nonsense!

MENAECHMUS I: You must be angry with one of the servants.

WIFE: Nonsense!

MENAECHMUS I: Well, are you angry with me?

WIFE: Now that is not nonsense.

MENAECHMUS I: What the deuce! I haven't done anything.

WIFE: There you are — back where you started. Nonsense!

MENAECHMUS I: What is the trouble, wife?

WIFE: A fine question to ask me!

MENAECHMUS I: Do you want me to ask *him*, then? What's the trouble?

WIFE: [*emphatically*] A cloak.

MENAECHMUS I: [*taken aback*] A cloak? What about a cloak?

PENICULUS: What are you trembling for?

MENAECHMUS I: I'm not trembling —

PENICULUS: Except for one thing: the cloak's no joke. You won't sneak away from me again and eat dinner! [*to* WIFE] Go at the fellow!

MENAECHMUS I: Will you shut up?

PENICULUS: No, by George, I will not shut up. [*tattling to* WIFE] He's shaking his head at me to keep me from talking.

MENAECHMUS I: I am not, or winking either.

PENICULUS: That beats all: he says he's not doing a thing when you can see he's doing it.

MENAECHMUS I: [*loudly invoking*] By Jupiter and all the gods — is that enough for you, my dear? — I swear I did not shake my head at him.

PENICULUS: She'll believe that of you; get back to business.

MENAECHMUS I: What business?

PENICULUS: Oh, the dyers', I suppose. Come on now, give the cloak back.

MENAECHMUS I: What cloak are you talking about?

PENICULUS: I give up, if he can't remember his own affairs.

WIFE: So you thought you could get away with all this underhand business and me not know it, did you? You'll pay interest on what you stole, I'm sure of that. Take that! [*Slapping him down.*]

PENICULUS: [*echoing the triumph*] Take that! Now will you go and eat dinner behind my back? Now will you come out drunk and make fun of me in front of the house with a garland on your head?

MENAECHMUS I: I haven't had dinner or set foot in that house to-day.

PENICULUS: Do you mean to say that?

MENAECHMUS I: I guess I do!

PENICULUS: This fellow takes the cake! Didn't I see you standing here in front of the door just now, wearing a garland, and you said I was crazy and you didn't know me, and you insisted you were a foreigner?

MENAECHMUS I: Listen here, since I left you, this is the first time I've been home.

PENICULUS: Oh, I know you. You thought I didn't have any way of getting even with you. Now I've told everything to your wife.

MENAECHMUS I: What did you tell her?

PENICULUS: I don't know; ask her.

MENAECHMUS I: [*crossing to* WIFE] What is it, my dear? What stories has he been telling you? What is it? Why don't you say something? Why don't you tell me what it is?

WIFE: As if you didn't know! Oh dear, I am an unlucky woman!

MENAECHMUS I: Why unlucky? Explain yourself.

WIFE: What a thing for you to ask me!

MENAECHMUS I: Well, I wouldn't ask you if I knew, would I?

PENICULUS: What a man! Look how he makes believe. You can't hide it; she knows all about it. I told her everything.

MENAECHMUS I: What is it?

WIFE: Well, if you aren't ashamed and won't own up yourself, listen to me and keep your ears open. A cloak has been stolen from me out of the house.

MENAECHMUS I: A cloak stolen from me?

PENICULUS: See how the fellow is trying to catch you. It was stolen from her, not from you. If it had been stolen from you, it would be safe now.

MENAECHMUS I: [*pushing* PENICULUS *aside*] I'm not doing business with you. [*to* WIFE] What is it you're saying, madam?

WIFE: A cloak has disappeared from the house, I tell you.

MENAECHMUS I: Who stole it?

WIFE: I suppose the man that took it knows that.

MENAECHMUS I: Who is this man?

WIFE: A certain Menaechmus.

MENAECHMUS I: A rotten thing to do! But what Menaechmus do you mean? [*searching the stage*]

WIFE: You, I say!

MENAECHMUS I: Me?

WIFE: Yes, you, you!

MENAECHMUS I: Who accuses me?

WIFE: *I* do.

PENICULUS: *I* do, too; and you took the cloak over here to your mistress Erotium's.

MENAECHMUS I: What? I gave it to her?

WIFE: Yes, you — you [*like an owl*], I say!

PENICULUS: Do you want me to go and get an owl to say, "You, you!" to you? [*mocking her*] You see, we're tired of saying it.

MENAECHMUS I: By Jupiter and all the gods — is that enough for you, my dear? — I swear I didn't give —

PENICULUS: And we swear we're telling nothing but the truth.

MENAECHMUS I: But I didn't give it to her; I only lent it.

WIFE: Maybe you did, but I don't ever lend your dress-suit or your top-coat to anybody. [*By degrees she drives* MENAECHMUS I *and incidentally* PENICULUS, *R.*] It's the wife's business to lend her clothes, and the husband's to lend his. Now go and bring that cloak back home.

MENAECHMUS I: I'll see it's brought home.

WIFE: Well, you'd better, because you won't get into my house again unless you bring that cloak with you. [*marching to her door*] I'm going home.

PENICULUS: [*following* WIFE] What's to become of me after taking so much trouble for you?

WIFE: The trouble will be repaid when something is stolen from your house. [*Exit into house.*]

PENICULUS: That'll never be, because I haven't got anything at home to lose. Curse the husband and the wife, too! I'll go down to town; I can see I'm through with this family. [*Exit, L.*]

MENAECHMUS I: [*runs to door, peeks in, then turns laughing to audience*] My wife thinks she's punished me by shutting me out — as if I didn't have a better place where they'll let me in. If you don't like me, you've got to put up with me; Erotium here likes me. She won't shut me out from her: she'll shut me in *with* her. Well, I'll go and ask her to give me back the cloak I gave her this morning. I'll buy her a better one. [*knocking at* EROTIUM's *door*] Here, where's the doorman? Open up, and call Erotium out, somebody.

[*Enter* EROTIUM *from her house.*]

EROTIUM: Who wants me?

MENAECHMUS I: A greater enemy to himself than to your tender years.

EROTIUM: Menaechmus, my love, why do you stand out there? Come in.

MENAECHMUS I: By and by. Do you know why I've come to see you?

EROTIUM: Of course: to enjoy yourself with me.

MENAECHMUS I: No, it's that cloak I gave you a little while ago: give it back to me, that's a dear. My wife has found out about the whole thing. I'll buy you any cloak you want, worth twice as much.

EROTIUM: Why, I just gave it to you to take to the dyer's, and the bracelet, too, to take to the jeweler's to be done over.

MENAECHMUS I: You gave me the cloak and the bracelet? How could you, when I've just got back and seen you for the first time since I gave it to you and went to town?

EROTIUM: Oh, I get your idea. You're trying to cheat me out of what I let you take.

MENAECHMUS I: No, no, I don't want the cloak to cheat you; I tell you, my wife's found out about it.

EROTIUM: [*with mounting fury*] No, no, I didn't go out of my way to ask you to give it to me in the first place. You brought it to me yourself, and you gave it to me for a present. Now you want it back. All right. Have it. Take the old thing. Wear it yourself, or let your wife wear it, or lock it up in your trunk if you want to. After this you won't set foot inside this house again, you trifler with the affections of an innocent woman. [*changing her mood momentarily*] Unless you bring me money, you haven't got a chance. Go and find some other poor girl you can deceive. [*Exit into her house, slamming door.*]

MENAECHMUS I: By George, her temper's up! [*rushing to her door*] Here, woman, stop, say! Come back! Won't you wait? Won't you please come back for my sake? She's gone and closed the door. Now I'm the shut-outenest of men! They don't believe me at home or at my mistress's. I'll have to go and see what my friends advise me to do. [*Exit, L.*]

ACT IV

[*Enter* MENAECHMUS SOSICLES, R.]

MENAECHMUS II: That was a foolish thing I did a while ago when I handed over my purse and money to Messenio. He has got himself into a chop-house somewhere, I suppose.

[*Enter* WIFE, *from her house.*]

WIFE: I'll watch and see how soon my husband will get home. Ah ha, there he is. I'm saved! He is bringing back the cloak

MENAECHMUS II: [*to himself*] I wonder where Messenio can be rambling now.

WIFE: I'll go up to the fellow and welcome him as he deserves. [*to* MENAECHMUS II] You scoundrel, aren't you ashamed to come into my sight with that garment?

MENAECHMUS II: [*surprised*] What's this? What is troubling you, madam?

WIFE: You shameless wretch, do you dare say a single word to me? Do you dare to speak?

MENAECHMUS II: Pray, what have I done, that I shouldn't dare to speak to you?

WIFE: You ask me? Oh, the shameless impudence of the man!

MENAECHMUS II: [*mockingly*] I suppose you know, madam, why it was that the Greeks used to call Hecuba a bitch?

WIFE: No. I do *not*.

MENAECHMUS II: Because Hecuba used to act just the way you do now: she used to heap abuse on everybody that she saw. That's how she got to be called a bitch, and she deserved it, too.

WIFE: It's impossible to put up with such outrages. I'd rather be husbandless all my life than stand for such outrages!

MENAECHMUS II: Is it any of *my* business whether you can put up with the state of marriage or whether you are going to leave your husband? Or is it the custom here to babble to perfect strangers?

WIFE: Babble, you say? I swear I'll remain married not an instant longer — to put up with your ways!

MENAECHMUS II: For all of me, by heaven, you can be a widow as long as Jove sits on his throne.

WIFE: For that, by goodness, I'll call my father and tell him about your outrages. [*calls within the house to* SLAVE, *who comes at once*] Here, Decio, go find my father, and ask him to come with you to me. [SLAVE *runs off L.*] Tell him it's absolutely necessary. [*to* MENAECHMUS II] I'll tell him of all your outrages!

MENAECHMUS II: Are you mad? What outrages? [*mocking her*]

WIFE: You steal cloaks and money from your wife and take them to your mistress. Is that straight enough?

MENAECHMUS II: [*applauding*] Bravo, woman! You certainly are a bad one, and a bold one, too! Do you dare say that I stole this when I got it from another woman, who wanted me to have it repaired?

WIFE: A few minutes ago you didn't deny stealing it; and are you going to hold it now before my very eyes? Aren't you ashamed?

MENAECHMUS II: I beg of you, woman, tell me, if you can, what potion I can drink that will make me able to put up with your bad humor. I don't know whom you take me for. As for you, I don't know you any more than I know the man in the moon.

WIFE: You may make fun of me, but you won't be able to make fun of my father. He's coming now. [*pointing off L., where* FATHER *appears hobbling towards them*] Back there. Do you know *him*?

MENAECHMUS II: [*facetiously*] Yes, I knew him when I knew Methuselah. I met him the same day I met you.

WIFE: You deny that you know me? that you know my father?

MENAECHMUS II: Yes, and your grandfather too, if you want to lug *him* in. [*Stalks to extreme R.*]

WIFE: By heaven, that's the way you always are about everything.

[*Enter* FATHER.]

FATHER: [SONG]
    I'm getting along just as fast as my age will permit and this business requires.

But if some of you say that that's easy for me — very briefly I'll show that
  you're liars:
My body's a burden, my nimbleness gone, and of strength I've a notable
  lack,
I am quite overgrown with my years — oh, confounded old age is a curse
  on the back!
Why, if I were to tell all the terrible evils that age, when it comes, brings
  along,
I'm certain as certain can be that past suitable limits I'd lengthen this
  song.

However my mind is a little disturbed at this thing, for it seems a bit
  queer
That my daughter should suddenly send to my house with directions for
  me to come here.
And how the affair is related to me, she has not let me know up to now;
But I'm a good guesser, and feel pretty sure that her husband and she've
  had a row.
That's what usually happens when men are enslaved by their wives and
  must come when they call;
And then it's the wives who are mostly to blame, while the husbands
  aren't guilty at all.

And yet there are bounds, which we all must observe, to the things that a
  wife can endure,
And a woman won't call in her father unless the offense of her husband is
  sure.
But I think very soon the suspense will be over, and then I'll know what
  is the matter—
But look, there's my daughter in front of the door, and her husband; he's
  not looking at her.
        It's just as I suspected.

I'll speak to her.
WIFE: I'll go meet him [*meeting him* C.] I hope you are well, father.
FATHER: I hope you are well. Do I find you well? Are you well, that you sum-
  moned me? Why are you sad? Why does he [*pointing with staff*] stand
  apart from you, in anger? You have been quarreling about something. Tell
  me which of you is at fault, and be brief about it; no rigmarole.
WIFE: I am guilty of nothing on my part; I'll ease you on this point first, father.
  But I can't live here, and I can't stand it another minute. Take me away.
FATHER: Why, what's the matter?
WIFE: I'm made fun of, father.
FATHER: By whom?
WIFE: By *him*, to whom you gave me: my husband.
FATHER: [*to audience*] Look at that now! A squabble! [*to* WIFE] How many

times have I told you to see to it that neither of you come to me with
your complaints?

WIFE: [*tearfully*] But father, how could I help it? I think you could understand—unless you don't want to.

FATHER: How many times have I told you to humor your husband? Pay no
attention to what he does, or where he goes, or what he is about.

WIFE: Why, he has been making love to a courtesan who lives right next door.

FATHER: That's sensible enough. And I'll warrant he'll make love to her all the
more, with you spying on him this way.

WIFE: And he drinks there, too.

FATHER: Well, will he drink any the less on your account, here or anywhere
else that he chooses? Devil take it, why will you be so foolish? You might
as well expect to forbid him to accept dinner invitations or to entertain
guests at his own house. Do you want husbands to be slaves? You might
as well expect to give him a stint of work, and have him sit among the
slave-girls and card wool.

WIFE: [*resentfully*] Apparently I had you come here to defend my husband's
case, father, not mine! You're *my* attorney, but you plead *his* case.

FATHER: If he has been delinquent in any way, I'll be even more severe with
him than I was with you. But since he keeps you well supplied with gold
trinkets and clothes and gives you servants and provisions as he should
it is better for you, girl, to take a sane view of things.

WIFE: But he steals my gold and my cloaks from the cupboard. He robs me and
takes my trinkets to courtesans on the sly.

FATHER: He does wrong if he does; you do wrong if he doesn't: that's accusing
an innocent man.

WIFE: But he has the cloak right now, father, and the bracelet that he took to
the woman. He is bringing them back now because I have found out
about it.

FATHER: I'll find out from him just what has happened. I'll go speak to him.
[*goes over to* MENAECHMUS II *and taps him with staff*] Menaechmus, for
my enlightenment tells me what you are quarreling about. Why are you
sad? Why does she stand apart from you, in anger?

MENAECHMUS II: Whoever you are, whatever your name is, old man, I call as
my witnesses great Jupiter and the gods—

FATHER: Why? Wherefore? And for what?

MENAECHMUS II: That I have neither wronged this woman, who accuses me
of stealing this cloak from her house—

WIFE: Perjury, eh?

MENAECHMUS II: If I have ever set my foot inside the house in which she lives,
may I be the most accursedly accursed!

FATHER: Are you in your right mind, to make such a wish? Do you deny that
you have ever set foot in the house you live in, you utter madman?

MENAECHMUS II: Old man, do you say I live in that house?

FATHER: Do you deny it?

MENAECHMUS II: I' faith, I do deny it.

FATHER: No; you deny not "in faith" but in joke—unless, of course, you have moved out overnight. [*motions* WIFE *to* C.]—Come here, please, daughter. What do you say? You haven't moved from the house, have you?

WIFE: Why should we, or where should we move *to*, I ask you?

FATHER: By heaven, I don't know.

WIFE: It's clear that he is making fun of you. Don't you get that?

FATHER: Menaechmus, you have joked long enough; now attend to business.

MENAECHMUS II: I ask you, what business have I with you? Or who are you? Are you sane? And this woman, who has been plaguing me this way and that—is she sane? [*tears his hair in exasperation*]

WIFE: [*to* FATHER, *frightened*] Do you see the color of his eyes? See how a green color is coming over his temples and forehead! How his eyes shine!

MENAECHMUS II: [*to audience*] Alack, they say I'm crazy, whereas it is they who are really that way themselves. What could be better for me, since they say I am mad, than to pretend to be insane, to scare them off? [*begins to jump about madly*]

WIFE: How he stretches and gapes! What shall I do, father?

FATHER: Come over here, my child, as far as you can from him. [*Retreating L.*]

MENAECHMUS II: [*pretending madness*] Ho, Bacchus! Ho, Bromius! Where in this forest do you bid me to the hunt? I hear, but cannot leave this place, so closely am I guarded by that rabid bitch upon my left. And behind there is that bald goat, who often in his time has ruined innocent citizens by his false testimony.

FATHER: Curse you!

MENAECHMUS II: Lo, Apollo from his oracle bids me to burn out the eyes of that woman with flaming torches. [*Charges at* WIFE, *then immediately retreats*]

WIFE: I am lost, father! He threatens to burn out my eyes.

FATHER: [*to* WIFE, *aside*] Hist, daughter!

WIFE: What? What shall we do?

FATHER: Suppose I summon the slaves? I'll go bring some people to take this man away and chain him up indoors before he makes any more disturbance.

MENAECHMUS II: [*aside*] I'm stuck; if I don't hit upon a scheme, they'll take me into the house with them. [*aloud*] Apollo, you forbid me to spare her face with my fists unless she leaves my sight and goes utterly to the devil? [*advances threateningly*] I'll do your bidding, Apollo!

FATHER: Run home as fast as you can, before he thumps you.

WIFE: I am running. Watch him father; don't let him get away! Oh! am I not a miserable woman to have to listen to such things! [*Exit into her house.*]

MENAECHMUS II: [*aside*] I got rid of her rather well. [*aloud, threatening* FATHER] Now, Apollo, as for this most filthy wretch, this bearded tremulous Tithonus, who is called the son of Cygnus, you bid me break his limbs and bones and joints with that staff which he holds?

FATHER: [*retreats, shaking his staff*] You'll get a beating if you touch me or come any closer.

MENAECHMUS II: I'll do your bidding! I'll take a double-edged axe and chop the flesh of this old man to mince meat, down to the very bones!

FATHER: [*aside*] Well then, I must beware and take care of myself. Really, I am afraid, from the way he threatens, that he may do me harm. [MENAECHMUS *retreats C.*]

MENAECHMUS II: You give me many commands, Apollo! Now you bid me take my fierce untamed yoked horses and mount my chariot, to crush this old stinking toothless lion. Now I've mounted! [*business*] Now I hold the reins! Now the goad is in my hand! Forward, my steeds, make loud the clatter of your hooves! And in swift flight make undiminished the fleetness of your feet [*Gallops about the stage.*]

FATHER: Do you threaten me with yoked horses?

MENAECHMUS II: Lo, Apollo, again you bid me make a charge at him, this fellow who stands here, and slay him. [*rushes forward, then suddenly stops*] But who is this, who drags me from my chariot by the hair? He alters your commands, even the commands of Apollo! [*pretends to fall senseless to the ground*]

FATHER: [*advances cautiously*] Alas, by heaven, it is a severe disease! O gods, by your faith. what sudden changes do ye work! Take this madman—how strong he was a little while before. This disease has smitten him all of a sudden. I'll go get a doctor as quick as I can. [*Exit, L.*]

MENAECHMUS II: [*getting up*] Lord! These idiots who compel me, a sane man, to act like a madman! Have they got out of my sight now, I wonder? Why don't I go straight back to the ship while the going is good? [*as he starts to go, R., to audience*] I beg of all of you, if the old man comes back don't tell him what street I've taken. [*Exit, R.*]

ACT V

[*Enter FATHER.*]

FATHER: I've waited on the doctor's leisure until my limbs ache from sitting and my eyes from looking! I had a hard time persuading him to leave his patients. He says he set the broken leg of Aesculapius and the arm of Apollo, so that now I wonder whether I should say I am bringing a doctor or a joiner! [*glancing off L.*] Here he comes. Hurry up that ant's pace, will you!

[*Enter DOCTOR.*]

DOCTOR: What did you say was his disease? Tell me about it. sir. Has he a demoniacal affliction, or hallucinations? Explain. Is he lethargic, or has he a dropsical propensity?

FATHER: That's why I'm bringing you here; I want you to tell me just that and make him sound again.

DOCTOR: Ah, that is quite simple. He shall be sound as a nut, upon my honor.

FATHER: I want him cared for very carefully.

DOCTOR: I shall contrive a cure that will last a century; that is how carefully I shall care for him for you.

FATHER: There's the man himself.

DOCTOR: Let us observe what he does. [*They withdraw C.*]

[*Enter MENAECHMUS I.*]

MENAECHMUS I: [*to audience, while DOCTOR observes*] Good Lord, this has certainly been a perverse and adverse day for me! I thought I was acting on the sly, but that parasite has let everything out. He has filled me with fear and covered me with disgrace; he's my Ulysses. stirring up trouble for his master! As sure as I'm alive, I'll rid him of his life! But I'm a fool to call it *his*. It's mine; it was my food and money that gave him life. Well then, I'll take the breath out of him!—The courtesan acted true to form, in the regular courtesan way: because I asked for the cloak so that I could take it back to my wife, she said she had given it to me! [*sighs*] By heaven, I certainly lead a miserable life!

FATHER: Do you hear what he says?

DOCTOR: He says that he is miserable.

FATHER: I wish you'd go up to him.

DOCTOR: [*going up to* MENAECHMUS I] How do you do, Menaechmus. Please, why do you leave your arm uncovered? Do you not know how injurious that is to your present indisposition?

MENAECHMUS I: Go hang yourself!

FATHER: [*to* DOCTOR] Do you notice anything?

DOCTOR: Notice anything! This case cannot be cured with an acre of hellebore! But, Menaechmus,—

MENAECHMUS I: Well?

DOCTOR: Answer me this question: is it white or red wine that you drink?

MENAECHMUS I: And what is it to you? Go to the devil!

DOCTOR: Ah, the first symptoms of insanity.

MENAECHMUS I: Why not ask whether the bread I eat is crimson or purple or orange-colored? or whether I eat scaly birds and feathered fish?

FATHER: Dear me! Do you hear how he raves? Why don't you give him some kind of a potion before complete madness sets in?

DOCTOR: One moment. I wish to continue my diagnosis.

FATHER: You're killing me with your talk!

DOCTOR: [*to* MENAECHMUS I] Tell me this: do you ever notice a hardening of your eyes?

MENAECHMUS I: What! Do you take me for a lobster, you good-for-nothing?

DOCTOR: Tell me, are you subject to rumbling of the bowels—as far as you know?

MENAECHMUS I: When I've a full stomach, no. But when I go hungry, then there is a rumbling.

DOCTOR: [*to* FATHER] Dear me, that is no madman's answer! [*to* MENAECHMUS I] Do you sleep soundly at night? Do you go to sleep readily on retiring?

MENAECHMUS I: Yes, if I have paid my bills. [*angrily*] Jupiter and all the gods destroy you, you confounded busybody!

DOCTOR: The madness begins again. [*to* FATHER] You hear what he says; be on your guard.

FATHER: On the contrary, he talks like a perfect Nestor now, compared to what he was a while ago. Why, a few minutes ago he called his wife a rabid bitch.

MENAECHMUS I: I said *what?*

FATHER: You were raving, I say.

MENAECHMUS I: I raving?

FATHER: Yes, you. You threatened to trample me to death with a four-horse chariot. I myself saw you do it. I myself accuse you of it.

MENAECHMUS I: [*to* FATHER, *furiously, pushing* DOCTOR *aside*] Yes, and I know that you stole the sacred chaplet from the statue of Jupiter, and that you were clapped into jail for it; also that after you got out of prison you were strung up and flogged; also that you killed your father and sold your mother! Isn't that a sane man's retort? One flock of abuse deserves another.

FATHER: For God's sake, doctor, I beg of you; hurry! Whatever you are going to do, do it! Can't you see the man is raving?

DOCTOR: [*aside to* FATHER] It would be best if he were to be conveyed to my house.

FATHER: You think so?

DOCTOR: By all means. I shall be able to care for him there according to my own prescriptions.

FATHER: Just as you say.

DOCTOR: [*rubbing his hands, to* MENAECHMUS I] I shall set you to drinking hellebore for some twenty days!

MENAECHMUS I: [*savagely*] Yes, and I'll string you up and jab you with oxgoads for *thirty* days!

DOCTOR: [*aside to* FATHER] Go, fetch men to take him to my house.

FATHER: How many do we need?

DOCTOR: As I judge the extent of his madness, four; no less.

FATHER: They shall be here directly. [*starts to go*] Guard him, doctor!

DOCTOR: No, no! I shall go to my house and make the necessary preparations. Have the slaves bring him to me.

FATHER: I'll have him there immediately.

DOCTOR: Good. I leave you [*Exit L.*]

FATHER: [*calling after him*] Good-bye. [*Exit R. to get slaves.*]

MENAECHMUS I: [*watching them off*] Father-in-law gone; doctor gone; I'm alone. Great Jupiter! what makes all these people say that I'm insane? Since I was born I've never had a day's illness. I'm not mad; I don't brawl or pick fights in court. I'm sane, and I realize that others are, too. I recognize people, talk to them. These people who say falsely that I'm mad, perhaps they're mad themselves.—What shall I do? I want to go home, but my wife won't have it. Nobody will let me in here [*looking at* EROTIUM's *house*] either. What cursed luck! I'll be standing here forever! Well perhaps they'll let me into my house by evening. [*Withdraws U. C. to wait, where he sits and dozes.*]

[*Enter* MESSENIO L.; *does not observe* MENAECHMUS]

MESSENIO: [SONG]

> It's a proof of an excellent slave,
> If, his master's belongings to save,
>   He'll use as much care
>   When his master's not there
> As when master is watching the slave.

> For his back and his shins he must fear,
> The demands of his stomach not hear,
>   And the punishment know
>   Of the slothful and slow—
> This servant whose conscience is clear.
>
> There are beatings, and chains, and the mills,
> Hunger, weariness, terrible chills—
>   The reward of the lazy;
>   But since I'm not crazy,
> I'm good, and avoid all these ills.

I'm good at taking a tongue-lashing but a whip-lashing I don't like, and I very much prefer to eat the meal to turning the mill. Therefore I follow my master's orders properly and gravely. My principle is to consider my back; it's worth my while. Let others behave the way they think best suits them; I'll be what I should. If that's my rule, if I keep out of trouble so I can serve my master at all times, I've little to fear. The day's near when my master will reward me for my good services. I've left the baggage and the slaves at the inn, as he ordered, and now I've come to meet him. I'll knock on the door to let him know I'm here, and to get him safely out of this place of ruin. But I'm afraid that I'll be too late and get there after the battle is over. [*Goes to* EROTIUM's *door, but seeing slaves approach, withdraws to extreme R. to watch.*]

  [*Enter* FATHER *with a corporal's guard of four burly slaves.*]

FATHER: By all the gods and men I bid you take wise heed to my orders past and present. Pick up that man [*pointing to* MENAECHMUS] and fetch him to the doctor's at once, unless you care nothing for your shanks and sides. A straw for his threats, do you hear? Why do you stand there? Why do you hesitate? He should have been shoulder-high and hustled off already. I go to the doctor's; I'll be waiting there when you come. [*Exit L.*]

  [*Slaves advance towards* MENAECHMUS I.]

MENAECHMUS I: [*awakening and seeing himself surrounded*] I'm lost! What is this? Why do these men run at me? What do you want? What are you after? Why do you surround me? [*They raise him on their shoulders.*] Where are you taking me? Where are you carrying me? Murder! Help! Good folk of Epidamnus, help! Let me go!

MESSENIO: [*coming forward*] By the immortal gods, what's this I see? A gang of thugs carrying off my master bodily!

MENAECHMUS I: [*shouting*] Doesn's anybody dare to help me?

MESSENIO: [*dramatically*] I do, master. I dare most daringly! [*to audience, singing*]:

> Oh! what an outrageous crime I see!
> Epidamnians, this man was free,
> My master, when he came today:
> And now they're carrying him away,
> While you're at peace, by light of day!

[*cuffs one of the slaves*] Let go of him, you.

MENAECHMUS I: I implore you, whoever you are, help me: protect me from this outrage.

MESSENIO: [*acting the faithful slave*] Yes, yes, I'll help and defend and stand by you. I'll never let you be murdered. Sooner myself than you! [*general scuffle, in time with music*] Gouge the eye out of that fellow who has you by the shoulder. I'll plow these faces for the sowing of my fists! You shall smart to-day for trying to carry him off! Let go!

MENAECHMUS I: I've got him by the eye!

MESSENIO: Good; make us see the socket! You villains! You robbers! You bandits!

SLAVES: Murder! Stop, for God's sake!

MESSENIO: Let go then! [*They drop* MENAECHMUS I.]

MENAECHMUS I: [*to slaves*] Lay hands on me, will you? [*to* MESSENIO] Give 'em your fists!

MESSENIO: [*to slaves*] Go on, get out! Get out of here, devil take you! There's one for you [*gives a final kick to last slave*]; take it as a prize for being the last to go! [*Exeunt slaves; to* MENAECHMUS I:] I measured those faces pretty well, all right, and just to my taste. I came to your help in the nick of time then, master!

MENAECHMUS I: May the gods bless you forever, young man, whoever you may be: If it hadn't been for you, I should never have seen the sun set this day!

MESSENIO: Well then, by George, if you did the right thing you'd set me free.

MENAECHMUS I: I set you free?

MESSENIO: To be sure, master; because I saved your life.

MENAECHMUS I: What's this? There's some mistake, young man.

MESSENIO: [*worried*] What do you mean?

MENAECHMUS I: By father Jupiter I swear that I am not your master.

MESSENIO: What!

MENAECHMUS I: That's the truth. No slave of mine ever served me as you have.

MESSENIO: Well then, if you say I'm not your slave, let me go free.

MENAECHMUS I: By heaven, as far as I am concerned you can be free to go wherever you please.

MESSENIO: [*eagerly*] Those are really your orders?

MENAECHMUS I: Why yes, if I have any power over you.

MESSENIO: Hail, my patron! How happy I am that you have freed me!

MENAECHMUS I: [*dryly*] I can believe it!

MESSENIO: But, my patron, please do not command me any less now than when I was your slave. I shall live with you and go with you when you go back home.

MENAECHMUS I: [*aside*] I guess not!

MESSENIO: Wait for me. I'm off to the inn to bring the baggage and the money. The journey-money is safely sealed up in your bag. I'll have it here directly.

MENAECHMUS I: [*much interested*] Do, by all means.

MESSENIO: I'll give it back to you all safe, just as you gave it to me. Wait for me here. [*Exit L.*]

MENAECHMUS I: [*alone*] There certainly have been strange things happening to me today, and in strange ways! People denying that I am I, and that fellow whom I just freed, who said he was my slave! He says he will bring me a purse with money in it. If he does, I'll tell him he is free to go away wherever he wishes, so that when he comes to his senses he won't try to get the money back.—My father-in-law and the doctor said I was insane. Heaven only knows what it all means! It seems just like a dream.—Now I'll go in here to the courtesan, even though she is angry with me, and see if I can't get her to give me back the cloak, so I can take it home. [*Exit into the house of* EROTIUM.]

  MENAECHMUS II *enters* L. *looking about stage for* MESSENIO. *Exit* L., *but returns immediately with him.*]

MENAECHMUS II: [*angrily*] You brazen rascal, do you dare tell me that you have been with me to-day since the time I ordered you to meet me here?

MESSENIO:[*angrily. thinking that his master is trying to cheat him*] Why, I rescued you just a few minutes ago when four men were carrying you off bodily, before this very house. You were yelling for help to all of heaven and earth when I ran up and rescued you with my fists, in spite of them. Therefore, because I had saved your life, you set me free. When I said I was going to get the money and the luggage, you ran ahead to meet me, so you could deny what you had done!

MENAECHMUS II: I set you free?

MESSENIO: Yes.

MENAECHMUS II: [*emphatically*] I'd turn slave myself sooner than free you, and that's that!

  [*Enter* MENAECHMUS I *from the house of* EROTIUM.]

MENAECHMUS I: [*shouting into the house*] Swear by your eyes if you want to, but you can't make out that I took away the cloak and the armlet, you wantons!

MESSENIO: [*crossing towards* MENAECHMUS I] Immortal gods! what do I see!

MENAECHMUS II: What do you see?

MESSENIO: Your mirror.

MENAECHMUS II: What do you mean?

MESSENIO: He's your very image, as like you as can be.

MENAECHMUS II: [*comparing himself with the stranger*] Well! He's certainly not unlike me, now that I look at myself.

MENAECHMUS I: [*seeing* MESSENIO] The young man who saved me! Hail, whoever you are.

MESSENIO: Saving your presence, sir, tell me your name, for heaven's sake!

MENAECHMUS I: Well, by Apollo, you have not deserved so of me that I should object to your question. Menaechmus is my name.

MENAECHMUS II: [*surprised*] No, by Apollo, it's *mine!*

MENAECHMUS I: I'm a Sicilian, from Syracuse.

MENAECHMUS II: That's just where I came from!

MENAECHMUS I: What's that you say?

MENAECHMUS II: The truth.

MESSENIO: [*standing between them, indicating* MENAECHMUS I] This is the man I know, of course; *this* is my master. I'm *his* slave, though I thought

I was that fellow's. I thought he was you, and made a nuisance of myself to him. [*to* MENAECHMUS II] I beg your pardon, sir, if I said anything indiscreet to you.

MENAECHMUS II: [*angrily, to* MESSENIO] Why you're raving! Don't you remember coming off the ship with me today?

MESSENIO: [*hurriedly changing sides*] Yes, yes, you're quite right. You are my master. [*to* MENAECHMUS I] You can hunt for another slave. [*to* MENAECHMUS II] Good-day to you. [*to* MENAECHMUS I] Good-bye to you. I say that this man is Menaechmus.

MENAECHMUS I: Well, I say *I* am.

MENAECHMUS II: What's this nonsense! *You* Menaechmus?

MENAECHMUS I: Yes; Menaechmus, Son of Moschus.

MENAECHMUS II: *My* father's son?

MENAECHMUS I: No indeed, young man, not yours. [*dryly*] I've no wish to appropriate your father and tear him away from you.

MESSENIO: [*steps forward to audience*] Immortal gods! Fulfil this unhoped-for hope of mine! For unless my mind is playing me tricks, these two are the twin brothers! They both recall the same father and country. I'll speak to my master. [*aloud*] Menaechmus!

MENAECHMUS I *and* II: [*together*] What is it?

MESSENIO: I don't want both of you; just my master. Which of you came here in the ship with me?

MENAECHMUS I: Not I.

MENAECHMUS II: I did.

MESSENIO: [*aside to* MENAECHMUS II] This man is either a sycophant or your own twin brother. I've never seen anyone who looked so like you; water is not more like water, or milk like milk, than he is like you and you like him. Also, he says his father and his country are the same as yours. We'd better go up to him and investigate.

MENAECHMUS II: By heaven, that's good advice, and I'm grateful. Keep on helping me, for goodness' sake. If you prove he is my brother, you shall be free.

MESSENIO: I hope so.

MENAECHMUS II: And I hope so too.

MESSENIO: [*between them again; he assumes the dignity of a cross-questioner*] Let's see now. [*to* MENAECHMUS I] Menaechmus is your name, I believe you said?

MENAECHMUS I: Indeed it is.

MESSENIO: This man's name is Menaechmus, too. You are a Sicilian, from Syracuse. That's where he comes from. Moschus was your father, you said. His father, too. Now, both of you can help me, and yourselves as well.

MENAECHMUS I: You deserve to receive from me anything you ask. I'm your humble servant, as though you had bought me with money.

MESSENIO: [*dramatically*] I hope that I'll find you two to be twin brothers, born on the same day to the same mother and father.

MENAECHMUS I: This is a strange tale. I wish you could make your hope come true.

MESSENIO: I can. Come now, each of you, answer me some questions.

MENAECHMUS: Ask whenever you wish. I'll answer. I'll keep back nothing that I know.

MESSINO: [*interrogating each in turn*] Is your name Menaechmus?

MENAECHMUS I: It is.

MESSENIO: And it is yours too?

MENAECHMUS II: It is.

MESSENIO: Moschus, you say, was your father?

MENAECHMUS I: He was.

MENAECHMUS II: And mine too.

MESSENIO: Are you from Syracuse?

MENAECHMUS I: Yes.

MESSENIO: And you?

MENAECHMUS II: Yes, of course.

MESSENIO: So far the evidence agrees without a flaw. Give me your attention further. [*to* MENAECHMUS I] Tell me, what is the earliest thing that you remember in your native land?

MENAECHMUS I: I can remember going away with my father to the market at Tarentum. Then, in the crowd I strayed off from him, and after that I was carried off.

MENAECHMUS II: God save us!

MESSENIO: [*to* MENAECHMUS II] What are you shouting about? Won't you be still? [*to* MENAECHMUS I] How old were you when your father took you away from home?

MENAECHMUS I: I was seven at the time, for I was just beginning to lose my teeth. And from that time I never saw my father again.

MESSENIO: So. How many sons were there in the family at that time?

MENAECHMUS I: Two, if I am not mistaken.

MESSENIO: Which was the elder, you or your brother?

MENAECHMUS I: We were both the same age.

MESSENIO: How can that be so?

MENAECHMUS I: We were twins.

MENAECHMUS II: [*breaking in*] Thank Heaven!

MESSENIO: [*with finality*] If you interrupt again, I'll be still.

MENAECHMUS II: [*contritely*] No, I'll be still.

MESSENIO: Tell me, did you both have the same name?

MENAECHMUS I: Of course not. My name was Menaechmus, as it is now. My brother was called Sosicles.

MENAECHMUS II: That's enough proof. I can't keep from embracing him. My own twin brother, come to my arms! I am Sosicles. [*crosses and tries to embrace* MENAECHMUS I]

MENAECHMUS I: [*doubting*] Then how did your name become Menaechmus?

MENAECHMUS II: After we heard that you had been carried away and father was dead, grandfather changed my name and gave me yours.

MENAECHMUS I: [*still doubting*] I believe it happened just as you say. But answer me this.

MENAECHMUS II: What?

MENAECHMUS I: What was our mother's name?

MENAECHMUS II: Teuximarcha.

MENAECHMUS I: Everything fits together.—Let me embrace you, brother, unexpected sight after so many years. [*They embrace warmly.*]

MENAECHMUS II: And you, too, for whom till now I have been searching with so many trials and troubles, and at whose discovery I now rejoice.

MESSENIO: And this was why the courtesan here called you by his name: she mistook you for him, I suppose, when she invited you to lunch.

MENAECHMUS I: Why, of course. I ordered luncheon here (my wife didn't know) and gave her a cloak that I'd stolen from home.

MENAECHMUS II: Do you mean the cloak I have in my hand, brother?

MENAECHMUS I: How did you get it?

MENAECHMUS II: The courtesan who took me in to lunch here said I'd given it to her. I dined well, wined well, and had a glorious time with her. She gave me this cloak and jewelry.

MENAECHMUS I: I'm certainly glad if you've had any fun because of me. I think she thought you were I when she invited you in.

MESSENIO: [*hopefully*] Is there anything to prevent me from being free, as you promised?

MENAECHMUS I: A very good and fair request, brother. Grant it, for my sake.

MENAECHMUS II: Have your freedom. [MESSENIO *cuts a caper.*]

MENAECHMUS I: Congratulations on your freedom, Messenio.

MESSENIO: There ought to be a formal ceremony, so I'll be free forever.

MENAECHMUS II: Since we've had so much good fortune, brother, let's both return to our native land. [*They start R.*]

MENAECHMUS I: I'll do as you wish, brother, and I'll have an auction and sell all my property. But meanwhile, let's go in.

MENAECHMUS II: Very well.

[*They cross towards* MENAECHMUS' *house.*]

MESSENIO: [*to* MENAESCHMUS I] Will you do me a favor?

MENAECHMUS I: What is it?

MESSENIO: Give me the job of auctioneer.

MENAECHMUS I: Certainly.

MESSENIO: Do you want the auction cried at once?

MENAECHMUS I: Yes, for a week from today.

[*Exeunt* MENAECHMUS I *and* II *into house of* MENAECHMUS I]

MESSENIO: EXTRAORDINARY AUC—TION

WEEK—FROM TODAY

MENAECHMUS SELLS HIS PROPERTY

CASH AND NO DELAY

ALL MUST GO—HOUSE AND LOT

SLAVES AND FURNITURE

WIFE GOES TOO IF ANY ONE

TAKES A FANCY TO HER

[*aside*] I scarcely think he'll make a million out of the whole auction. [*to audience*] Now, spectators, fare you well, and lustily applaud us all. [*Exit, R.*]

THE WAKEFIELD CYCLE

THE SECOND SHEPHERDS' PLAY[1]

[*Anonymous*]
Editing and notes by Robert B. Heilman

CHARACTERS:

FIRST SHEPHERD
SECOND SHEPHERD
THIRD SHEPHERD
MAK
GILL, *his wife*
ANGEL
JESUS
MARY

[*Enter the* FIRST SHEPHERD.]
FIRST SHEPHERD: Lord! What these weathers are cold, and I am ill wrapped.
    My hands nearly numb, so long have I napped.
    My legs they fold, my fingers are chapped;
    It is not as I would, for I am all lapped
        In sorrow   5
    In storms and tempest,
    Now in the east, now in the west,
    Woe is him has never rest
        Midday nor morrow!

    But we poor shepherds that walk on the moor,   10
    In faith, we are near-hands out of the door;
    No wonder, as it stands, if we be poor,
    For the tilth of our lands lies fallow as the floor,
        As ye ken.
    We are so hamyd,   15
    For-taxed and ramyd[2],
    We are made hand-tamed
        By these gentlery-men.
    Thus they rob us of our rest. Our Lady them curse!
    These men that are lord-fast, they make the plough tarry.   20
    That, men say, is for the best; we find it contrary.
    Thus are husbandmen oppressed, in point to miscarry,
        In life.

---

[1] C. 1425–1450.
[2] Crippled, taxed to death, ruined.

Thus hold they us under;
Thus they bring us in blunder.   25
It were great wonder
     If ever should we thrive.

For may he get a painted sleeve, or a brooch, now-a-days,
Woe to him that him grieves, or one word gainsays!
Dare no man him reprove, what mastery he has.   30
And yet may no man believe one word that he says,
     No letter.
He can make purveyance[3],
With boast and arrogance;
And all is through maintenance   35
     Of men that are greater.

There shall come a swain as proud as a peacock,
He must borrow my wagon, my plough also,
That I am full fain to grant ere he go.
Thus live we in pain, anger, and woe   40
     By night and day.
He must have if he longéd;
If I should forgang[4] it,
I were better be hanged
     Than once say him nay.   45

It does me good, as I walk thus by mine own,
Of this world for to talk in manner of moan.
To my sheep will I stalk and hearken anon;
There abide on a ridge, or sit on a stone,
     Full soon.   50
For I trow, pardie,
True men if they be,
We get more company
     Ere it be noon. [*Moves aside.*]

[*Enter the* SECOND SHEPHERD.]
SECOND SHEPHERD: Ben'c'te[5] and Dominus! What may this bemean?   55
     Why, fares this world thus, oft have we not seen?
     Lord, these weathers are spiteful, and the winds full keen,
     And the frosts so hideous, they water my eyes,
          No lie.
     Now in dry, now in wet,   60
     Now in snow, now in sleet,
     When my shoes freeze to my feet,
          It is not all easy.

[3] Provision.
[4] Do without.
[5] Benedicite.

But as far as I ken, or yet as I go,
We poor wedded men endure much woe; 65
We have sorrow then and then, it falls oft so.
Silly Capel, our hen, both to and fro
    She cackles;
But begin she to croak,
To groan or to cluck, 70
Woe is him, is our cock,
    For he is in the shackles.

These men that are wed have not all their will.
When they are full hard bestead, they sigh full still.
God knows they are led full hard and full ill; 75
In bower nor in bed they say naught theretill,
    This tide.
My part have I found,
I know my lesson.
Woe is him that is bound, 80
    For he must abide.

But now late in our lives—a marvel to me,
That I think my heart rives such wonders to see,
What that destiny drives, it should so be—
Some men will have two wives, and some men three 85
    In store.
Some are woe that has any;
But so far ken I,
Woe is him that has many,
    For he feels sore. 90

But, young men, of wooing, for God that you bought,
Be well ware of wedding, and think in your thought,
"Had I known" is a thing it serves of naught.
Mickle still mourning has wedding home brought,
    And griefs, 95
With many a sharp shower;
For thou may catch in an hour
What shall seem full sour
    As long as thou lives.

For, as ever read I epistle[6], I have one to my fere[7], 100
As sharp as a thistle, as rough as a briar;
She is browed like a bristle, with a sour-laden cheer;
Had she once wet her whistle, she could sing full clear
    Her paternoster.

[6] In the Bible.
[7] Mate.

She is as great as a whale;   105
She has a gallon of gall;
By him that died for us all[8],
  I would I had run till I had lost her!

FIRST SHEPHERD: God, look over the row! Full deafly ye stand.
SECOND SHEPHERD: Yea, the devil in thy maw—so tarrying!   110
 Sawest thou anywhere Daw?
FIRST SHEPHERD: Yea, on a lea-land
 Heard I him blow. He comes here at hand,
  Not far.
 Stand still.
SECOND SHEPHERD: Why?
FIRST SHEPHERD: For he comes, hope I.   115
SECOND SHEPHERD: He will make us both a lie
 Unless we beware.
  [*Enter* THIRD SHEPHERD, *a boy*.]
THIRD SHEPHERD: Christ's cross me speed, and Saint Nicholas!
 Thereof had I need; it is worse than it was.
 Whoso could, take heed and let the world pass;   120
 It is ever in dread and brittle as glass,
  And slides.
 This world fared never so,
 With marvels more and moe,
 Now in weal, now in woe,   125
  And all things writhes.

 Was never since Noah's flood such floods seen,
 Winds and rains so rude, and storms so keen;
 Some stammered, some stood in doubt, as I ween.
 Now God turn all to good! I say as I mean,   130
  For ponder.
 These floods so they drown,
 Both in fields and in town,
 And bear all down,
  And that is a wonder.   135

 We that walk in the nights our cattle to keep,
 We see sudden sights when other men sleep.
 Yet methinks my heart lightens; I see shrews[9] peep.
 Ye are two tall wights! I will give my sheep
  A turn.   140
 But full ill have I meant;
 As I walk on this land,
 I may lightly repent,

[8] Note the many anachronisms in the play.
[9] Rogues.

My toes if I spurn.
[*To the other two.*]
Ah, sir, God you save, and master mine!   145
A drink fain would I have, and somewhat to dine.
FIRST SHEPHERD: Christ's curse, my knave, thou art an evil hind!
SECOND SHEPHERD: What! the boy likes to rave! Abide until syne[10]
      We have made it.
Ill thrift on thy pate!   150
Though the fellow came late,
Yet is he in state
      To dine—if he had it.

THIRD SHEPHERD: Such servants as I, that sweats and swinks[11],
      Eat our bread full dry. and that me forthinks[12].   155
We are oft wet and weary when master men winks;
Yet come full late both dinners and drinks.
      But neatly
Both our dame and our sire,
When we have run in the mire,   160
They can nip at our hire,
      And pay us full lately.

But hear my truth, master, for the fare that ye make:
I shall do, hereafter, work as I take[13];
I shall do a little, sir, and between times play,   165
For yet lay my supper never on my stomach
      In fields.
Whereto should I threap[14]?
With my staff can I leap;
And men say "Light cheap   170
      Badly for-yields[15]."

FIRST SHEPHERD: Thou were an ill lad, to ride a-wooing
With a man that had but little of spending.
SECOND SHEPHERD: Peace, boy! I bade; no more jangling,
Or I shall make thee a-feared, by the Heaven's King,   175
      With thy gawds[16].
Where are our sheep, boy? We scorn.
THIRD SHEPHERD: Sir, this same day at morn
      I them left in the corn,
      When they rang lauds[17].   180

---

[10] After.   [11] Labors.
[12] I regret.   [13] As I am paid.
[14] Talk back.   [15] An easy bargain badly pays back.
[16] Tricks.   [17] Early church service.

They have pasture good; they cannot go wrong.

FIRST SHEPHERD: That is right. By the rood, these nights are long!
　　Yet I would, ere we go, one gave us a song.

SECOND SHEPHERD: So I thought as I stood, for mirth us among.

THIRD SHEPHERD: I grant.   185

FIRST SHEPHERD: Let me sing the tenory.

SECOND SHEPHERD: And I the treble so high.

THIRD SHEPHERD: Then the mean falls to me.
　　　　Let see how ye chant.
　　　　[*Enter* MAK. *with a cloak thrown over his smock.*]

MAK: Now, Lord, for thy names seven, that made both moon and stars,   190
　　Well more than I can name; thy will, Lord, of me tharns[18].
　　I am all uneven; that moves oft my brains.
　　Now would God I were in heaven, for there weep no bairns
　　　　So still.

FIRST SHEPHERD: Who is that pipes so poor?   195

MAK: Would God ye knew how I fare!
　　Lo, a man that walks on the moor,
　　　　And has not all his will!

SECOND SHEPHERD: Mak, where hast thou gone? Tell us tidings.

THIRD SHEPHERD: Is he come? Then everyone take heed to his things.   200
　　　　[*Takes the cloak from* MAK.]

MAK: What! Ich be[19] a yeoman, I tell you, of the king;
　　The self and the same, sent from a great lording,
　　　　And such.
　　Fie on you! Go hence,
　　Out of my presence!   205
　　I must have reverence.
　　　　Why, who be ich?

FIRST SHEPHERD: Why make ye it so quaint? Mak, ye do wrong.

SECOND SHEPHERD: But Mak, list ye saint[20]? I trow for that you long.

THIRD SHEPHERD: I trow the shrew can paint! The devil might him hang!   210

MAK: Ich shall make complaint, and give you all a whang
　　　　At a word,
　　And tell even how ye doth.

FIRST SHEPHERD: But, Mak, is that truth?
　　Now take out that southern tooth,   215
　　　　And set in a turd.

SECOND SHEPHERD: Mak, the devil in your eye! A stroke would I lend you.

THIRD SHEPHERD: Mak, know ye not me? By God, I could 'tend to you.

MAK: God, look you all three! Methought I had seen you.
　　Ye are a fair company.

18 Finds me wanting.
19 Mak affects southern accent.
20 Do you like to show off?

FIRST SHEPHERD: · Can ye now mean you?[21]   220
SECOND SHEPHERD: Rascal, jape!
    Thus late as thou goes,
    What will men suppose?
    And thou hast an ill noise[22]
        Of stealing of sheep.   225

MAK: And I am true as steel, all men wot,
    But a sickness I feel that holds me full hot;
    My belly fares not well, it is out of state.
THIRD SHEPHERD: Seldom lies the devil dead by the gate.
MAK: Therefore   230
    Full sore am I and ill;
    If I stand stone still,
    I eat not a needle
        This month and more.

FIRST SHEPHERD: How fares thy wife? By my hood, how fares she?   235
MAK: Lies weltering, by the rood, by the fire, lo!
    And a house full of brood. She drinks well, too;
    Ill speed other good that she will do!
        But so,
    Eats as fast as she can;   240
    And every year that comes to man
    She brings forth a lakan[23],
        And some years two.

    Although I were more gracious and richer by far,
    I were eaten out of house and of harbor.   245
    Yet she is a foul dowse[24] if ye come near;
    There is none that trows nor knows a worse
        Than ken I.
    Now will ye see what I proffer—
    To give all in my coffer   250
    Tomorrow at next to offer
        Her head-mass penny.[25]
SECOND SHEPHERD: I wot so for-wakéd[26] is none in this shire.
    I would sleep, if I takéd less to my hire.
THIRD SHEPHERD: I am cold and naked, and would have a fire.   255
FIRST SHEPHERD: I am weary, for-rakéd[27], and run in the mire.
        Stay awake, thou!
SECOND SHEPHERD: Nay, I will lie down by,
    For I must sleep, truly.
THIRD SHEPHERD: As good a man's son was I   260
        As any of you.

---

[21] Identify yourself.   [22] Bad reputation.
[23] Plaything; i. e., child.   [24] Whore.
[25] He will gladly pay for her requiem mass.
[26] Worn out with watching.   [27] Worn out with walking.

But, Mak, come hither! Between shalt thou lie down.
MAK: Then might I stop you, certain, of that ye would rown[28].
      No dread.
    From my top to my toe,   265
    Manus tuas commendo,
    Pontio Pilato,
        Christ's cross me speed! [*Then he rises, the shepherds being asleep,*
        and says:]
Now were time for a man that lacks what he would
To stalk privily then unto a fold,   270
And nimbly to work then, and be not too bold,
For he might pay for the bargain, if it were told,
    At the ending.
Now were time for to begin,
But he needs good counsel   275
That fain would fare well,
    And has but little spending.

But about you a circle as round as a moon,
Till I have done that I will, till that it be noon,
That ye lie stone still till that I have done,   280
And I shall say thereto of good words a few.
    On height
Over your heads my hand I lift:
Out go your eyes, foredo your sight!
But yet I must make better shift   285
    If it be right.

Lord, how they sleep hard! That may ye all hear.
I never was a shepherd, but now will I learn.
If the flock be scared, yet shall I nip near.
How! Draw hitherward! Now mends our cheer   290
    From sorrow.
A fat sheep, I dare say;
A good fleece, dare I lay!
Pay back when I may,
    But this will I borrow.   295
    [MAK *crosses the stage to his house.*]
How, Gill, art thou in? Get us some light.
WIFE: Who makes such din this time of the night?
I am set for to spin; I hope[29] not I might
Rise a penny to win. I curse them on height.
    So fares   300
A housewife that has been
To be rushed thus between;
Here may no work be seen,
    Because of such chores.

[28] Whisper.
[29] Expect.

MAK: Good wife, open the hek[30]! Seest thou not what I bring?   305
WIFE: I may let thee draw the snek[31]. Ah, come in, my sweeting!
MAK: Yea, thou dost not reck of my long standing.
WIFE: By thy naked neck art thou like for to hang.
MAK: Go way:
   I am worthy of my meat,   310
   For in a pinch can I get
   More than they that swink and sweat
    All the long day.

   Thus it fell to my lot, Gill, I had such grace.
WIFE: It were a foul blot to be hanged for the case.   315
MAK: I have escaped, Gillot, often as hard a place.
WIFE: But so long goes the pot to the water, men say,
   At last
   Comes it home broken.
MAK: Well know I the token,   320
   But let it never be spoken;
    But come and help fast.

   I would he were slain; I like well to eat.
   This twelvemonth was I not so fain of one sheep's meat.
WIFE: Should they come ere he be slain, and hear the sheep bleat—   325
MAK: Then might I be ta'en! That were a cold sweat!
   Go bar
   The gate door.
WIFE: Yes, Mak,
   For if they come at thy back—
MAK: Then might I pay for all the pack!   330
   The devil of them warn.

WIFE: A good trick have I spied, since thou ken none.
   Here shall we him hide till they be gone—
   In my cradle abide. Let me alone,
   And I shall lie beside in childbed, and groan.   335
MAK: Thou hast said:
   And I shall say thou was light
   Of a male child this night.
WIFE: Now well is the day bright,
    That ever was I bred.   340

   This is a good disguise and a far cast;
   Yet a woman's advice helps at the last!
   I wot never who spies. Again go thou fast.
MAK: Unless I come ere they rise, there blows a cold blast!
   I will go sleep.   345
   [MAK *returns to the shepherds and resumes his place.*]

[30] Hatch.
[31] Latch.

Yet sleeps all this company;
And I shall go stalk privily,
As it never had been I
    That carried their sheep.

FIRST SHEPHERD: *Resurrex a mortruis!* Take hold of my hand.   350
    Judas carnas dominus! I may not well stand;
    My foot sleeps, by Jesus; and I walter fastand[32].
    I thought that we laid us full near England.
SECOND SHEPHERD: Ah, yea!
    Lord, but I have slept well.   355
    As fresh as an eel,
    As light I me feel
        As leaf on a tree.

THIRD SHEPHERD: Ben'c'te be herein! So my body shakes,
    My heart is out of skin, what so it quakes.   360
    Who makes all this din? So my brows blacks[33].
    To the door will I win. Hark, fellows, wake!
        We were four:
    See ye aught of Mak now?
FIRST SHEPHERD: We were up ere thou.   365
SECOND SHEPHERD: Man, I give God a vow,

    Yet went he nowhere.
THIRD SHEPHERD: Methought he was lapped in a wolf's skin.
FIRST SHEPHERD: So are many wrapped now—namely, within.
THIRD SHEPHERD: When we had long napped, methought with a gin[34]   370
    A fat sheep he trapped; but he made no din.
SECOND SHEPHERD: Be still!
    Thy dream makes thee mad;
    It is but phantom, by the rood.
FIRST SHEPHERD: Now God turn all to good,   375
        If it be his will!

SECOND SHEPHERD: Rise, Mak! For shame! Thou liest right long.
MAK: Now Christ's holy name be us among!
    What is this? By Saint James, I may not well gang!
    I think I be the same. Ah! my neck has lain wrong   380
        Enough.
        [*They help* MAK *up.*]
    Mickle thank! Since yester even,
    Now, by Saint Stephen,
    I was flayed with a dream
        That my heart of slough[35].   385

---

[32] Roll about famishing; cf. *wallow, welter*.
[33] Head aches (?).   [34] Trick.
[35] Slew my heart.

I thought Gill began to croak and travail full sad,
Well nigh at the first cock, of a young lad
For to mend our flock. Then be I never glad;
I have tow on my rock[36] more than ever I had.
    Ah, my head!   390
A house full of young tharnes[37]!
The devil knock out their brains!
Woe is him has many bairns,
    And thereto little bread!

I must go home, by your leave, to Gill, as I thought.   395
I pray you look in my sleeve that I steal naught;
I am loath you to grieve or from you take aught.
THIRD SHEPHERD: Go forth; ill might thou live! Now would I we sought,
    This morn.
That we had all our store.   400
FIRST SHEPHERD: But I will go before;
    Let us meet.
SECOND SHEPHERD: Where?
THIRD SHEPHERD: At the crooked thorn.
    [MAK *crosses to his cottage.*]
MAK: Undo this door! Who is here? How long shall I stand?
WIFE: Who makes such a stir? Now walk in the wenyand![38]   405
MAK: Ah, Gill, what cheer? It is I, Mak, your husband.
WIFE: Then may we see here the devil in a band,
    Sir Guile.
Lo, he comes with a lote[39]
As he were holden in the throat.   410
I may not sit at my note[40]
    A hand-long while.

MAK: Will ye hear what to-do she makes to get her a gloze[41]?
She does naught but plays, and wiggles her toes.
WIFE: Why, who wanders? Who wakes? Who comes? Who goes?   415
Who brews? Who bakes? What makes me thus do?
    And then,
It is ruth to behold,
Now in hot, now in cold,
Full woeful is the household   420
    That wants a woman.

But what end has thou made with the shepherds, Mak?
MAK: The last word that they said, when I turned my back,
They would look that they had their sheep, all the pack.

36 Distaff.   37 Bellies.
38 Waning (of the moon) — supposedly unlucky.
39 Noise, i. e., as if he were being hanged.   40 Work.
41 Lie, excuse.

I expect they will not be well paid when they their sheep lack,   425
    Perdie.
But how so the game goes,
To me they will suppose,
And make a foul noise,
       And cry out upon me.   430

But thou must do as thou hight[42].
WIFE: I accord me theretill;
    I shall swaddle him right in my cradle.
    If it were a greater plight, yet could I help till.
    I will lie down straight. Come, cover me.
MAK: I will.
WIFE: Behind!   435
    Come Coll and his maroo[43],
    They will nip us full narrow.
MAK: But I may cry "Out, harrow!"
       The sheep if they find.

WIFE: Hearken aye when they call; they will come anon.   440
    Come and make ready all, and sing by thine own;
    Sing lullaby thou shall, for I must groan
    And cry out by the wall on Mary and John,
       For sore.
    Sing lullaby fast   445
    When thou hears at the last;
    Unless I play a false cast,
       Trust me no more!
       [*The* SHEPHERDS *meet at the crooked hawthorne.*]
THIRD SHEPHERD: Ah, Coll, good morn! Why sleep thou not?
FIRST SHEPHERD: Alas, that ever was I born! We have a foul blot.   450
    A fat wether have we lorn.
THIRD SHEPHERD: Marry, God forbid!
SECOND SHEPHERD: Who should do us that scorn? That were a foul spot.
FIRST SHEPHERD: Some shrew.
    I have sought with my dogs
    All Horbury Shrogs,   455
    And of fifteen hogs[44]
       Found I but one ewe.

THIRD SHEPHERD: Now trust me if ye will; by Saint Thomas of Kent,
    Either Mak or Gill was at that assent.
FIRST SHEPHERD: Peace, man, be still! I saw when he went.   460
    Thou slanders him ill. Thou ought to repent,
       Good speed.

[42] Promised.
[43] Mate.
[44] Year-old sheep.

SECOND SHEPHERD: Now as ever might I thrive,
  If I should even here die,
  I would say it were he 465
    That did that same deed.
THIRD SHEPHERD: Go we thither, I rede, and run on our feet.
  I shall never eat bread the truth till I wit.
FIRST SHEPHERD: Nor drink, in my heed, with him I meet.
SECOND SHEPHERD: I will rest in no stead till that I him greet, 470
  My brother!
  One thing I will plight:
  Till I see him in sight
  Shall I never sleep one night
    Where I do another. 475
  [*At* MAK's *house they hear* GILL *groan and* MAK *sing a lullaby.*]
THIRD SHEPHERD: Will ye hear how they hack? Our sir likes to croon.
FIRST SHEPHERD: Heard I never one crack so clear out of tune!
  Call on him.
SECOND SHEPHERD: Mak! Undo your door soon.
MAK: Who is it that spake as it were noon
    On loft? 480
  Who is that, I say?
THIRD SHEPHERD: Good fellows, were it day—
MAK: As far as ye may,
    Good, speak soft,

Over a sick woman's head that is at malaise; 485
  I had liefer be dead e'er she had any dis-ease.
WIFE: Go to another place! I may not well wheeze.
  Each foot that ye tread goes through my nose,
    So high!
FIRST SHEPHERD: Tell us, Mak, if ye may, 490
  How fare ye, I say?
MAK: But are ye in this town today?
    How fare ye, I say?
  Ye have run in the mire, and are wet yet
  I shall make you a fire if ye will sit. 495
  .A nurse would I hire, think ye on it.
  Well paid is my hire; my dream—this is it,
    In season.
  I have bairns, if ye knew,
  Well more than enow. 500
  But we must drink as we brew,
    And that is but reason.

I would have ye dine ere ye go. Methinks that ye sweat.
SECOND SHEPHERD: Nay, neither mends our mood, drink nor meat.
MAK: Why, sir, ails you aught but good?

THIRD SHEPHERD: Yea, our sheep that we get   505
  Are stolen as they go. Our loss is great.
MAK: Sirs, drink!
  Had I been there,
  Some should have paid full sore.
FIRST SHEPHERD: Marry, some men think that ye were;
  And that makes us think.   510

SECOND SHEPHERD: Mak, some men trows that it should be ye.
THIRD SHEPHERD: Either ye or your spouse, so say we.
MAK: Now, if ye have suspicion of Gill or me,
  Come and rip our house, and then ye may see   515
    Who had her.
  If I any sheep got,
  Any cow or stott[45],
  And Gill, my wife, rose not
    Since here she laid her,   520
  As I am true and leal, to God here I pray
  That this be the first meal that I shall eat this day.
FIRST SHEPHERD: Mak, as have I weal, advise thee, I say:
  He learned timely to steal that could not say nay.
WIFE: I swelt[46]!   525
  Out, thieves, from my house!
  Ye come to rob us, for the nonce.
MAK: Hear ye not how she groans?
    Your hearts should melt.

WIFE: Out, thieves, from my bairn! Approach him not there!   530
MAK: Knew ye what she had borne, your hearts would be sore.
  Ye do wrong, I you warn, that thus come before
  To a woman that has farne[47]. But I say no more.
WIFE: Ah, my middle!
  I pray to God so mild,   535
  If ever I you beguiled,
  That I eat this child
    That lies in this cradle.

MAK: Peace, woman, for God's pain, and cry not so!
  Thou hurts thy brain, and makes me full of woe.   540
SECOND SHEPHERD: I think our sheep be slain. What find ye two?
THIRD SHEPHERD: All work we in vain; as well may we go.
    But, hatters[48],
  I can find no flesh,
  Hard nor nesh[49],   545
  Salt nor fresh,
    But two empty platters.

[45] Young steer.   [46] Faint.
[47] Fared; i. e., had a child.   [48] Confound it.
[49] Soft.

   Live cattle but this, tame nor wild,
   None, as have I bliss, so loud as he smelled.
WIFE: No, so God me bless, and give me joy of my child!   550
FIRST SHEPHERD: We have marked amiss; I hold us beguiled.
SECOND SHEPHERD: Sir, done.
   Sir, Our Lady him save!
   Is your child a knave⁵⁰?
MAK: Any lord might him have,   555
     This child as his son.

   When he wakens he skips, that joy is to see.
THIRD SHEPHERD: In good time to his hips, and in glee.
   Who were his godfathers, so soon ready?
MAK: So fair fall their lips!
FIRST SHEPHERD: Hark now, a lie!   560
MAK: So God them thank,
    Parkin and Gibbon Waller, I say,
    And gentle John Horn, in good faith,
    He made all the garray⁵¹
      With his great shank.   565

SECOND SHEPHERD: Mak, friends will we be, for we are all one.
MAK: We! Now I hold for me, for amends get I none.
   Farewell, all three! All glad were ye gone! [*Shepherds go out.*]
THIRD SHEPHERD: Fair words may there be, but love there is none
     This year.   570
FIRST SHEPHERD: Gave ye the child anything?
SECOND SHEPHERD: I trow, not one farthing!
THIRD SHEPHERD: Fast back will I fling;
    Abide ye me here.
    [SHEPHERDS *re-enter.*]
   Mak, take it to no grief, if I come to thy bairn.   575
MAK: Nay, thou does me great reproof; and foul has thou fared.
THIRD SHEPHERD: The child will it not grieve, that little daystar.
    Mak, with your leave, let me give your bairn
    But sixpence.
MAK: Nay, go 'way; he sleeps.   580
THIRD SHEPHERD: Methinks he peeps.
MAK: When he wakens he weeps;
    I pray you, go hence!

THIRD SHEPHERD: Give me leave him to kiss, and lift up the clout.
   What the devil is this? He has a long snout!   585
FIRST SHEPHERD: He is marked amiss. We wait ill about.
SECOND SHEPHERD: "Ill spun weft," ywis, "aye comes foul out."

⁵⁰ Boy.
⁵¹ Commotion.

    Aye, so!
He is like to our sheep!
THIRD SHEPHERD: How, Gib, may I peep?   590
FIRST SHEPHERD: I trow, nature will creep
    Where it may not go!

SECOND SHEPHERD: This was a quaint gawd[52] and a far cast!
    It was a high fraud!
THIRD SHEPHERD: Yea, sirs, was't.
    Let's burn this bawd, and bind her fast.   595
    Ah, false scold, hang at the last,
        So shall thou.
    Will ye see how they swaddle
    His four feet in the middle?
    Saw I never in a cradle   600
        A hornéd lad ere now.

MAK: Peace, bid I! What! Let be your fare!
    I am he that him begot, and yon woman him bare.
FIRST SHEPHERD: After what devil shall he be hatt[53]? "Mak"?
    Lo, God, Mak's heir!
SECOND SHEPHERD: Let be all that. Now God give him care, I say. 606
WIFE: A pretty child is he
    As sits on a woman's knee;
    A dilly-downe, perdie,
        To make a man laugh.   610

THIRD SHEPHERD: I know him by the ear-mark; that is a good token.
MAK: I tell you, sirs, hark! His nose was broken;
    Later told me a clerk that he was forespoken[54].
FIRST SHEPHERD: This is a false work; I would fain be wroken[55].
        Get a weapon.   615
WIFE: He was taken by an elf,
    I saw it myself;
    When the clock struck twelve
        Was he misshapen.

SECOND SHEPHERD: Ye two are well gifted, same in a stead.
THIRD SHEPHERD: Since they maintain their theft, let's do them to death. 621
MAK: If I trespass eft, gird off my head!
    With you will I be left.
FIRST SHEPHERD: Sirs, take my lead:

---

[52] Trick.   [53] Named.
[54] Enchanted.   [55] Avenged.

> For this trespass
> We will neither curse nor fight,   625
> Quarrel nor chide,
> But have done as tight[56],
>   And cast him in canvas.
>   [*They toss him and go back to the fields.*]

FIRST SHEPHERD: Lord, what! I am sore in point for to burst.
    In faith, I may no more; therefore will I rest.   630
SECOND SHEPHERD: As a sheep of seven score he weighed in my fist.
    For to sleep anywhere methinks that I list.
THIRD SHEPHERD: Now I pray you,
    Lie down on this green.
FIRST SHEPHERD: On these thieves yet I mind.   635
THIRD SHEPHERD: Whereto should ye strain
        So, I say you? [*They sleep.*]
        [*An* ANGEL *sings "Gloria in excelsis"; then let him say:*]
ANGEL: Rise, herd-men kind! For now is he born
    That shall take from the fiend what Adam had lorn:
    That devil to sheynd[57] this night is he born;   640
    God is made your friend now at this morn.
        He behests
    At Bethlehem go see,
    Where lies the Free
    In a crib full poorly   645
        Between two beasts.

FIRST SHEPHERD: This was a wise voice that ever yet I heard.
    It is a marvel to name, thus to be scared.
SECOND SHEPHERD: Of God's son of heaven he spake upward
    All the wood in a levin[58] methought that he made   650
        To appear.
THIRD SHEPHERD: He spake of a bairn
    In Bethlehem, I you warn.
FIRST SHEPHERD: That betokens yon star;
    Let us seek him there.   655

SECOND SHEPHERD: Say, what was his song? Heard ye not how he cracked it,
    Three briefs to a long?
THIRD SHEPHERD: Yea, marry, he hacked it;
    Was no crotchet wrong, nor nothing that lacked it.
FIRST SHEPHERD: For to sing us among, right as he knacked it, I can.   660
SECOND SHEPHERD: Let's see how ye croon.
    Can ye bark at the moon?
THIRD SHEPHERD: Hold your tongues, have done!
FIRST SHEPHERD: Hark after, then!

---

56 Quickly.
57 Destroy.
58 Lightning.

SECOND SHEPHERD: To Bethlehem he bade that we should gang;   665
    I am full afeared that we tarry too long.
THIRD SHEPHERD: Be merry and not sad; o mirth is our song;
    Everlasting glad our reward may we fang[59]
            Without noise.
FIRST SHEPHERD: Therefore thither hie we,   670
    If we be wet and weary,
    To that child and that lady.
            We have it not to lose.
SECOND SHEPHERD: We find by the prophecy—let be your din—
    Of David and Isaiah and more than I mind,   675
    They prophesied by clergy that in a virgin
    Should he light and lie, to slacken our sin
            And slake it,
    Our Race from woe.
    For Isaiah said so: 680
    "Ecce virgo
            Concipiet" a child that is naked.

THIRD SHEPHERD: Full glad may we be, and abide that day
    That lovely to see, that all mights may.
    Lord, well were me, for once and for aye,   685
    Might I kneel on my knee some word for to say
            To that child.
    But the angel said,
    In a crib was he laid;
    He was poorly arrayed,   690
            Both humble and mild.

FIRST SHEPHERD: Patriarchs that have been, and prophets before,
    They desired to have seen this child that is born.
    They are gone full clean; that have they lorn.
    We shall see him, I ween, ere it be morn,   695
            To token.
    When I see him and feel,
    Then know I full well
    It is true as steel
            That prophets have spoken: 700

    To so poor as we are that he would appear,
    First find, and declare by his messenger.
SECOND SHEPHERD: Go we now, let us fare; the place is us near.
THIRD SHEPHERD: I am ready, prepared; go we together
            To that bright.   705
    Lord, if thy will be—
    We are simple all three—

[59] Take.

Grant us some kind of glee
　　To comfort thy wight.
　　[*They enter the stable.*]
FIRST SHEPHERD: Hail, comely and clean! Hail, young child!
　　Hail, maker, as I mean, from a maiden so mild! 711
　　Thou has cursed, I ween, the devil so wild;
　　The false guiler of teen[60], now goes he beguiled.
　　　　Lo, he merry is!
　　Lo, he laughs, my sweeting! 715
　　A welfare meeting
　　I have holden my heting[61].
　　　　Have a bob of cherries!

SECOND SHEPHERD: Hail, sovereign Savior, for thou hast us sought!
　　Hail! noble child and flower, that all things has wrought!
　　Hail, full of favor, that made all of naught! 721
　　Hail! I kneel and I cower. A bird have I brought
　　　　To my bairn.
　　Hail, little tiny mop!
　　Of our creed thou art crop. 725
　　I would drink of thy cup,
　　　　Little day-star.

THIRD SHEPHERD: Hail, darling dear, full of godhead!
　　I pray thee be near when that I have need.
　　Hail! Sweet is thy cheer! My heart would bleed 730
　　To see thee sit here in so poor weed,
　　　　With no pennies.
　　Hail! Put forth thy dall[62]
　　I bring thee but a ball:
　　Have and play thee withal, 735
　　　　And go to the tennis.

MARY: The Father of Heaven, God omnipotent,
　　That set all in seven days, his Son has sent.
　　My name could he neven[63] and descend ere he went.
　　I conceived him full even, through might as he meant; 740
　　　　And now he is born.
　　Keep ye you from woe!
　　I shall pray him so.
　　Tell it forth as ye go,
　　　　And mind on this morn. 745

FIRST SHEPHERD: Farewell, lady, so fair to behold,
　　With thy child on thy knee!

[60] Contriver of evil. [61] Held to my promise.
[62] Hand. [63] Call.

SECOND SHEPHERD: But he lies full cold.
    Lord, well is me. Now we go, thou behold.
THIRD SHEPHERD: Forsooth, already it seems to be told
    Full oft.   750
FIRST SHEPHERD: What grace we have found!
SECOND SHEPHERD: Come forth; now are we won!
THIRD SHEPHERD: To sing are we bound:
    Let take aloft!
              EXPLICIT PAGINA PASTORUM

WILLIAM SHAKESPEARE

KING LEAR

Dramatis Personae

LEAR, *King of Britain*
KING OF FRANCE
DUKE OF BURGUNDY
DUKE OF CORNWALL
DUKE OF ALBANY
EARL OF KENT
EARL OF GLOUCESTER
EDGAR, *son of Gloucester*
EDMUND, *bastard son of Gloucester*
CURAN, *a courtier*
OSWALD, *steward to Goneril*
OLD MAN, *tenant of Gloucester*

DOCTOR
FOOL *to Lear*
A CAPTAIN, *under Edmund*
GENTLEMAN, *attendant on Cordelia*
HERALD
SERVANTS *to Cornwall*
GONERIL ⎫
REGAN ⎬ *daughters of Lear*
CORDELIA ⎭
KNIGHTS *attending on Lear,* GENTLE-MEN, MESSENGERS, SOLDIERS, *and* AT-TENDANTS.

SCENE——Britain.

ACT I

SCENE I——KING LEAR'S palace.

[*Enter* KENT, GLOUCESTER, *and* EDMUND.]

KENT: I thought the King had more affected the Duke of Albany than Cornwall.

GLOUCESTER: It did always seem so to us. But now in the division of the kingdom it appears not which of the dukes he values most, for equalities are so weighed, that curiosity in neither can make choice of either's moiety. 5

KENT: Is not this your son, my lord?

GLOUCESTER: His breeding sir, hath been at my charge. I have so often blushed to acknowledge him, that now I am brazed to't.

KENT: I cannot conceive you. 10

GLOUCESTER: Sir, this young fellow's mother could; whereupon she grew round-wombed, and had indeed, sir, a son for her cradle, ere she had a husband for her bed. Do you smell a fault?

KENT: I cannot wish the fault undone, the issue of it being so proper.

GLOUCESTER: But I have a son sir, by order of law, some year elder than this, who yet is no dearer in my account, though this knave came something saucily to the world before he was sent for. Yet was his mother fair; there was good sport at his making, and the whoreson must be acknowledged. Do you know this noble gentleman, Edmund? 15

20

99

EDMUND: No, my lord.

GLOUCESTER: My lord of Kent. Remember him hereafter as my honourable friend.

EDMUND: My services to your lordship.

KENT: I must love you, and sue to know you better.   25

EDMUND: Sir, I shall study deserving.

GLOUCESTER: He hath been out nine years, and away he shall again. The King is coming.

   [*Sennet. Enter one bearing a coronet,* LEAR, CORNWALL, AL-
   BANY, GONERIL, REGAN, CORDELIA, *and* ATTENDANTS.]

LEAR: Attend the Lords of France and Burgundy, Gloucester.

   [*Exeunt* GLOUCESTER *and* EDMUND.]

LEAR: Meantime we shall express our darker purpose.   30
  Give me the map there. Know that we have divided
  In three our kingdom; and 'tis our fast intent
  To shake all cares and business from our age,
  Conferring them on younger strengths, while we
  Unburdened crawl toward death. Our son of Cornwall,   35
  And you our no less loving son of Albany,
  We have this hour a constant will to publish
  Our daughters' several dowers, that future strife
  May be prevented now. The princes, France and Burgundy,
  Great rivals in our youngest daughter's love,   40
  Long in our Court have made their amorous sojourn,
  And here are to be answered. Tell me my daughters—
  Since now we will divest us both of rule,
  Interest of territory. cares of state—
  Which of you shall we say doth love us most,   45
  That we our largest bounty may extend
  Where nature doth with merit challenge. Goneril,
  Our eldest born, speak first.

GONERIL: Sir, I love you more than word can wield the matter,
  Dearer than eyesight, space, and liberty,   50
  Beyond what can be valued, rich or rare,
  No less than life, with grace, health, beauty, honour,
  As much as child e'er loved, or father found;
  A love that makes breath poor, and speech unable—
  Beyond all manner of so much I love you.   55

CORDELIA: [*aside*] What shall Cordelia speak? Love, and be silent.

LEAR: Of all these bounds, even from this line to this,
  With shadowy forests and with champains riched,
  With plenteous rivers, and wide-skirted meads,
  We make thee lady. To thine and Albany's issue   60
  Be this perpetual. What says our second daughter?
  Our dearest Regan, wife of Cornwall? Speak.

REGAN: I am made of that self metal as my sister,
  And prize me at her worth. In my true heart,

I find she names my very deed of love.   65
Only she comes too short, that I profess
Myself an enemy to all other joys,
Which the most precious square of sense possesses,
And find I am alone felicitate
In your dear Highness' love.   70
CORDELIA: [*aside*]   Then poor Cordelia—
And yet not so, since I am sure my love's
More ponderous than my tongue.
LEAR: To thee, and thine hereditary ever,
Remain this ample third of our fair kingdom,   75
No less in space, validity, and pleasure,
Than that conferred on Goneril. Now our joy,
Although our last and least, to whose young love
The vines of France and milk of Burgundy
Strive to be interest. What can you say, to draw   80
A third more opulent than your sisters? Speak.
CORDELIA: Nothing my lord.
LEAR: Nothing?
CORDELIA: Nothing.
LEAR: Nothing will come of nothing. Speak again.   85
CORDELIA: Unhappy that I am, I cannot heave
My heart into my mouth. I love your Majesty
According to my bond, no more nor less.
LEAR: How, how, Cordelia? Mend your speech a little,
Lest you may mar your fortunes.   90
CORDELIA: Good my lord,
You have begot me, bred me, loved me. I
Return those duties back as are right fit,
Obey you, love you, and most honour you.
Why have my sisters husbands, if they say   95
They love you all? Haply when I shall wed,
That lord whose hand must take my plight shall carry
Half my love with him, half my care, and duty.
Sure I shall never marry like my sisters,
To love my father all.   100
LEAR: But goes thy heart with this?
CORDELIA: Ay my good lord.
LEAR: So young, and so untender?
CORDELIA: So young my lord, and true.
LEAR: Let it be so, thy truth then be thy dower.   105
For by the sacred radiance of the sun,
The mysteries of Hecate and the night,
By all the operation of the orbs
From whom we do exist, and cease to be,
Here I disclaim all my paternal care,   110
Propinquity and property of blood,

And as a stranger to my heart and me
Hold thee from this for ever. The barbarous Scythian,
Or he that makes his generation messes
To gorge his appetite, shall to my bosom   115
Be as well neighboured, pitied, and relieved,
As thou my sometime daughter.

KENT: Good my liege—
LEAR: Peace Kent,
Come not between the dragon and his wrath.   120
I loved her most, and thought to set my rest
On her kind nursery.—Hence, and avoid my sight.—
So be my grave my peace, as here I give
Her father's heart from her. Call France. Who stirs?
Call Burgundy. Cornwall and Albany,   125
With my two daughters' dowers digest the third.
Let pride, which she calls plainness, marry her.
I do invest you jointly with my power,
Pre-eminence, and all the large effects
That troop with majesty. Ourself by monthly course,   130
With reservation of an hundred knights,
By you to be sustained, shall our abode
Make with you by due turn. Only we shall retain
The name, and all th' addition to a King.
The sway, revenue, execution of the rest,   135
Beloved sons, be yours, which to confirm,
This coronet part between you.

KENT: Royal Lear,
Whom I have ever honoured as my King,
Loved as my father, as my master followed,   140
As my great patron thought on in my prayers—
LEAR: The bow is bent and drawn, make from the shaft.
KENT: Let it fall rather, though the fork invade
The region of my heart. Be Kent unmannerly,
When Lear is mad. What wouldst thou do old man?   145
Think'st thou that duty shall have dread to speak,
When power to flattery bows? To plainness honour's **bound**,
When majesty fall to folly. Reserve thy state,
And in thy best consideration check
This hideous rashness. Answer my life my judgement;   150
Thy youngest daughter does not love thee least,
Nor are those empty-hearted whose low sounds
Reverb no hollowness.

LEAR: Kent, on thy life no more.
KENT: My life I never held but as a pawn   155
To wage against thine enemies; ne'er feared to lose it,
Thy safety being motive.
LEAR: Out of my sight!

KENT: See better, Lear, and let me still remain
    The true blank of thine eye. 160
LEAR: Now by Apollo—
KENT: Now by Apollo, King,
    Thou swear'st thy gods in vain.
LEAR: O vassal! Miscreant!
ALBANY *and* CORNWALL: Dear sir, forbear. 165
KENT: Kill thy physician, and the fee bestow
    Upon the foul disease. Revoke thy gift,
    Or whilst I can vent clamour from my throat,
    I'll tell thee thou dost evil.
LEAR: Hear me recreant, 170
    On thine allegiance hear me.
    That thou hast sought to make us break our vow,
    Which we durst never yet, and with strained pride
    To come between our sentence and our power,
    Which nor our nature nor our place can bear, 175
    Our potency made good, take thy reward.
    Five days we do allot thee for provision
    To shield thee from disasters of the world,
    And on the sixth to turn thy hated back
    Upon our kingdom. If on the tenth day following 180
    Thy banished trunk be found in our dominions,
    The moment is thy death. Away! By Jupiter,
    This shall not be revoked.
KENT: Fare thee well, King; sith thus thou wilt appear,
    Freedom lives hence, and banishment is here. 185
    [*to* CORDELIA] The gods to their dear shelter take thee, maid,
    That justly think'st, and hast most rightly said.
    [*to* REGAN *and* GONERIL] And your large speeches may your deeds
        approve,
    That good effects may spring from words of love.
    Thus Kent, o princes, bids you all adieu; 190
    He'll shape his old course in a country new. [*Exit.*]
        [*Flourish. Enter* GLOUCESTER, *with* KING OF FRANCE, BURGUNDY,
        and ATTENDANTS.]
GLOUCESTER: Here's France and Burgundy, my noble lord.
LEAR: My Lord of Burgundy,
    We first address toward you, who with this King
    Hath rivalled for our daughter. What in the least 195
    Will you require in present dower with her,
    Or cease your quest of love?
BURGUNDY: Most royal Majesty,
    I crave no more than hath your Highness offered,
    Nor will you tender less. 200
LEAR: Right noble Burgundy,
    When she was dear to us, we did hold her so,

But now her price is fallen. Sir, there she stands.
If aught within that little-seeming substance,
Or all of it, with our displeasure pieced,   205
And nothing more, may fitly like your Grace,
She's there, and she is yours.
BURGUNDY: I know no answer.
LEAR: Will you, with those infirmities she owes,
Unfriended, new adopted to our hate,   210
Dowered with our curse, and strangered with our oath,
Take her, or leave her?
BURGUNDY: Pardon me royal sir,
Election makes not up in such conditions.
LEAR: Then leave her sir, for by the power that made me,   215
I tell you all her wealth. [*to* FRANCE] For you, great King,
I would not from your love make such a stray,
To match you where I hate, therefore beseech you
T' avert your liking a more worthier way
Than on a wretch whom nature is ashamed   220
Almost t' acknowledge hers.
KING OF FRANCE: This is most strange,
That she whom even but now was your best object,
The argument of your praise, balm of your age,
The best, the dearest, should in this trice of time   225
Commit a thing so monstrous, to dismantle
So many folds of favour. Sure her offence
Must be of such unnatural degree,
That monsters it; or your fore-vouched affection
Fall into taint, which to believe of her,   230
Must be a faith that reason without miracle
Should never plant in me.
CORDELIA: I yet beseech your Majesty—
If for I want that glib and oily art,
To speak and purpose not; since what I well intend,   235
I'll do't before I speak—that you make known
It is no vicious blot, murder, or foulness,
No unchaste action, or dishonoured step,
That hath deprived me of your grace and favour;
But even for want of that for which I am richer,   240
A still-soliciting eye, and such a tongue
That I am glad I have not, though not to have it
Hath lost me in your liking.
LEAR: Better thou
Hadst not been born, than not t' have pleased me better.   245
KING OF FRANCE: Is it but this? A tardiness in nature
Which often leaves the history unspoke
That it intends to do? My Lord of Burgundy,
What say you to the lady? Love's not love
When it is mingled with regards that stands   250

Aloof from the entire point. Will you have her?
She is herself a dowry.
BURGUNDY: Royal King,
Give but that portion which yourself proposed,
And here I take Cordelia by the hand,   255
Duchess of Burgundy.
LEAR: Nothing. I have sworn, I am firm.
BURGUNDY: I am sorry then you have so lost a father,
That you must lose a husband.
CORDELIA: Peace be with Burgundy.   260
Since that respects of fortune are his love,
I shall not be his wife.
KING OF FRANCE: Fairest Cordelia, that art most rich being poor,
Most choice forsaken, and most loved despised,
Thee and thy virtues here I seize upon.   265
Be it lawful I take up what's cast away.
Gods, gods! 'Tis strange that from their cold'st neglect
My love should kindle to inflamed respect.
Thy dowerless daughter, King, thrown to my chance,
Is Queen of us, of ours, and our fair France.   270
Not all the dukes of wat'rish Burgundy
Can buy this unprized precious maid of me.
Bid them farewell Cordelia, though unkind;
Thou losest here, a better where to find.
LEAR: Thou hast her France, let her be thine, for we   275
Have no such daughter, nor shall ever see
That face of hers again. Therefore be gone,
Without our grace, our love, our benison.
Come noble Burgundy.
        [*Flourish. Exeunt* LEAR, BURGUNDY, CORNWALL, ALBANY, GLOU-
        CESTER, *and* ATTENDANTS.]
KING OF FRANCE: Bid farewell to your sisters.   280
CORDELIA: The jewels of our father, with washed eyes
Cordelia leaves you. I know you what you are,
And like a sister am most loth to call
Your faults as they are named. Love well our father.
To your professed bosoms I commit him,   285
But yet alas, stood I within his grace,
I would prefer him to a better place.
So farewell to you both.
REGAN: Prescribe not us our duty.
GONERIL: Let your study   290
Be to content your lord, who hath received you
At fortune's alms. You have obedience scanted,
And well are worth the want that you have wanted.
CORDELIA: Time shall unfold what plighted cunning hides,
Who covers faults, at last with shame derides.   295
Well may you prosper.

KING OF FRANCE: Come my fair Cordelia.
          [*Exeunt* KING OF FRANCE *and* CORDELIA.]
GONERIL: Sister, it is not little I have to say of what most nearly apper-
          tains to us both. I think our father will hence to-night.
REGAN: That's most certain, and with you; next month with us.   300
GONERIL: You see how full of changes his age is; the observation we have
          made of it hath not been little. He always loved our sister most, and
          with what poor judgement he hath now cast her off appears too
          grossly.
REGAN: 'Tis the infirmity of his age; yet he hath ever but slenderly known   305
          himself.
GONERIL: The best and soundest of his time hath been but rash, then
          must we look from his age to receive not alone the imperfections of
          long-ingrafted condition, but therewithal the unruly waywardness
          that infirm and choleric years bring with them.   310
REGAN: Such unconstant starts are we like to have from him, as this of
          Kent's banishment.
GONERIL: There is further compliment of leave-taking between France
          and him. Pray let us hit together; if our father carry authority with
          such disposition as he bears, this last surrender of his will but offend 315
          us.
REGAN: We shall further think of it.
GONERIL: We must do something, and i' th' heat. [*Exeunt.*]

                    SCENE II———GLOUCESTER's *castle.*

          [*Enter* EDMUND, *with a letter.*]
EDMUND: Thou, Nature, art my goddess, to thy law
          My services are bound. Wherefore should I
          Stand in the plague of custom, and permit
          The curiosity of nations to deprive me,
          For that I am some twelve or fourteen moonshines   5
          Lag of a brother? Why bastard? Wherefore base,
          When my dimensions are as well compact,
          My mind as generous, and my shape as true,
          As honest madam's issue? Why brand they us
          With base? With baseness? Bastardy? Base, base!   10
          Who in the lusty stealth of nature take
          More composition, and fierce quality,
          Than doth within a dull, stale, tired bed
          Go to th' creating a whole tribe of fops,
          Got 'tween asleep and wake? Well then,   15
          Legitimate Edgar, I must have your land.
          Our father's love is to the bastard Edmund
          As to th' legitimate. Fine word—legitimate!
          Well, my legitimate, if this letter speed,
          And my invention thrive, Edmund the base   20
          Shall to th' legitimate. I grow, I prosper.

Now gods, stand up for bastards.
[*Enter* GLOUCESTER.]
GLOUCESTER: Kent banished thus! And France in choler parted!
And the King gone to-night! Prescribed his power,
Confined to exhibition! All this done   25
Upon the gad. Edmund, how now! What news?
EDMUND: So please your lordship, none.
GLOUCESTER: Why so earnestly seek you to put up that letter?
EDMUND: I know no news, my lord.
GLOUCESTER: What paper were you reading?   30
EDMUND: Nothing my lord.
GLOUCESTER: No? What needed then that terrible dispatch of it into your
    pocket? The quality of nothing hath not such need to hide itself.
    Let's see. Come, if it be nothing, I shall not need spectacles.
EDMUND: I beseech you sir, pardon me; it is a letter from my brother, that   35
    I have not all o'er-read; and for so much as I have perused, I find it
    not fit for your o'er-looking.
GLOUCESTER: Give me the letter sir.
EDMUND: I shall offend either to detain or give it. The contents, as in
    part I understand them, are to blame.   40
GLOUCESTER: Let's see, let's see.
EDMUND: I hope, for my brother's justification, he wrote this but as an
    essay or taste of my virtue.
GLOUCESTER: [*reads*] *This policy, and reverence of age, makes the world*
    bitter to the best of our times; keeps our fortunes from us, till our   45
    oldness cannot relish them. I begin to find an idle and fond bondage
    in the oppression of aged tyranny, who sways not as it hath power,
    but as it is suffered. Come to me, that of this I may speak more. If
    our father would sleep till I waked him, you should enjoy half his
    revenue for ever, and live the beloved of your brother. Edgar.   50
    Hum! Conspiracy!—*Sleep till I waked him, you should enjoy half*
    his revenue—My son Edgar! Had he a hand to write this? A heart
    and brain to breed it in? When came this to you? Who brought it?
EDMUND: It was not brought me, my lord; there's the cunning of it. I
    found it thrown in at the casement of my closet.   55
GLOUCESTER: You know the character to be your brother's?
EDMUND: If the matter were good, my lord, I durst swear it were his; but
    in respect of that, I would fain think it were not.
GLOUCESTER: It is his.
EDMUND: It is his hand, my lord. But I hope his heart is not in the   60
    contents.
GLOUCESTER: Has he never before sounded you in this business?
EDMUND: Never my lord. But I have heard him oft maintain it to be fit,
    that sons at perfect age, and fathers declined, the father should be
    as ward to the son, and the son manage his revenue.   65
GLOUCESTER: O villain, villain—his very opinion in the letter. Abhorred
    villain, unnatural, detested, brutish villain; worse than brutish! Go

sirrah, seek him: I'll apprehend him. Abominable villain, where is he?

EDMUND: I do not well know my lord. If it shall please you to suspend   70
your indignation against my brother, till you can derive from him better testimony of his intent, you should run a certain course; where, if you violently proceed against him, mistaking his purpose, it would make a great gap in your own honour, and shake in pieces the heart of his obedience. I dare pawn down my life for him, that   75
he hath writ this to feel my affection to your honour, and to no other pretence of danger.

GLOUCESTER: Think you so?

EDMUND: If your honour judge it meet, I will place you where you shall hear us confer of this, and by an auricular assurance have your satis-   80
faction, and that without any further delay than this very evening.

GLOUCESTER: He cannot be such a monster.

EDMUND: Nor is not sure.

GLOUCESTER: To his father, that so tenderly and entirely loves him— heaven and earth! Edmund, seek him out; wind me into him, I pray   85
you. Frame the business after your own wisdom. I would unstate myself, to be in a due resolution.

EDMUND: I will seek him sir, presently; convey the business as I shall find means, and acquaint you withal.

GLOUCESTER: These late eclipses in the sun and moon portend no good   90
to us; though the wisdom of nature can reason it thus, and thus, yet nature finds itself scourged by the sequent effects. Love cools, friend-ship falls off, brothers divide. In cities, mutinies; in countries, dis-cord; in palaces, treason; and the bond cracked 'twixt son and father. This villain of mine comes under the prediction, there's son against   95
father; the King falls from bias of nature, there's father against child. We have seen the best of our time. Machinations, hollowness, treachery, and all ruinous disorders, follow us disquietly to our graves. Find out this villain, Edmund; it shall lose thee nothing, do it care-fully. And the noble and true-hearted Kent banished; his offence,   100
honesty. 'Tis strange. [*Exit.*]

EDMUND: This is the excellent foppery of the world, that when we are sick in fortune, often the surfeits of our own behavior, we make guilty of our disasters the sun, the moon, and stars, as if we were villains on necessity, fools by heavenly compulsion, knaves, thieves,   105
and treachers by spherical predominance; drunkards, liars, and adul-terers by an enforced obedience of planetary influence; and all that we are evil in, by a divine thrusting on. An admirable evasion of whoremaster man, to lay his goatish disposition on the charge of a star. My father compounded with my mother under the dragon's   110
tail, and my nativity was under ursa major, so that it follows, I am rough and lecherous. Fut, I should have been that I am, had the maidenliest star in the firmament twinkled on my bastardizing.

    [*Enter* EDGAR.]

Edgar! Pat. He comes like the catastrophe of the old comedy. My

cue is villainous melancholy, with a sigh like Tom o' Bedlam.—O   115
these eclipses do portend these divisions. Fa, sol, la, mi.

EDGAR: How now brother Edmund, what serious contemplation are you
in?

EDMUND: I am thinking, brother, of a prediction I read this other day,
what should follow these eclipses.   120

EDGAR: Do you busy yourself with that?

EDMUND: I promise you, the effects he writes of succeed unhappily; as of
unnaturalness between the child and the parent; death, dearth, dis-
solutions of ancient amities, divisions in state, menaces and maledic-
tions against king and nobles; needless diffidences, banishment of   125
friends, dissipation of cohorts, nuptial breaches, and I know not
what.

EDGAR: How long have you been a sectary astronomical?

EDMUND: Come, come, when saw you my father last?

EDGAR: The night gone by.   130

EDMUND: Spake you with him?

EDGAR: Ay, two hours together.

EDMUND: Parted you in good terms? Found you no displeasure in him, by
word, nor countenance?

EDGAR: None at all.   135

EDMUND: Bethink yourself wherein you may have offended him; and at
my entreaty forbear his presence until some little time hath qualified
the heat of his displeasure, which at this instant so rageth in him,
that with the mischief of your person it would scarcely allay.

EDGAR: Some villain hath done me wrong.   140

EDMUND: That's my fear. I pray you, have a continent forbearance till the
speed of his rage goes slower; and as I say, retire with me to my lodging, from whence I will fitly bring you to hear my lord speak. Pray
ye go,there's my key. If you do stir abroad, go armed.

EDGAR: Armed, brother?   145

EDMUND: Brother, I advise you to the best; I am no honest man if there
be any good meaning toward you. I have told you what I have seen,
and heard—but faintly—nothing like the image and horror of it.
Pray you away.

EDGAR: Shall I hear from you anon?   150

EDMUND: I do serve you in this business. [*Exit* EDGAR.]
A credulous father, and a brother noble,
Whose nature is so far from doing harms,
That he suspects none; on whose foolish honesty
My practices ride easy. I see the business.   155
Let me, if not by birth, have lands by wit;
All with me's meet, that I can fashion fit. [*Exit.*]

SCENE III——ALBANY's *palace.*

[*Enter* GONERIL *and* OSWALD.]

GONERIL: Did my father strike my gentleman for chiding of his fool?

OSWALD: Ay madam.

GONERIL: By day and night, he wrongs me; every hour
   He flashes into one gross crime or other,
     That sets us all at odds. I'll not endure it.   5
   His knights grow riotous, and himself upbraids us
   On every trifle. When he returns from hunting,
   I will not speak with him, say I am sick;
   If you come slack of former services,
   You shall do well; the fault of it I'll answer.   10
     [*Horns within.*]
OSWALD: He's coming madam, I hear him.
GONERIL: Put on what weary negligence you please,
   You and your fellows—I'd have it come to question.
   If he distaste it, let him to my sister,
   Whose mind and mine I know in that are one.   15
   Not to be over-ruled. Idle old man,
   That still would manage those authorities
   That he hath given away. Now by my life,
   Old fools are babes again, and must be used
   With checks as flatteries, when they are seen abused.   20
   Remember what I have said.
OSWALD: Well madam.
GONERIL: And let his knights have colder looks among you.
   What grows of it no matter, advise your fellows so.
   I would breed from hence occasions, and I shall,   25
   That I may speak. I'll write straight to my sister
   To hold my very course. Prepare for dinner. [*Exeunt.*]

SCENE IV——*The same.*

     [*Enter* KENT, *disguised.*]
KENT: If but as well I other accents borrow,
   That can my speech defuse, my good intent
   May carry through itself to that full issue
   For which I razed my likeness. Now banished Kent,
   If thou canst serve where thou dost stand condemned,   5
   So may it come, thy master whom thou lov'st
   Shall find thee full of labours.
     [*Horns within. Enter* LEAR, KNIGHTS, *and* ATTENDANTS.]
LEAR: Let me not stay a jot for dinner, go get it ready.
     [*Exit an* ATTENDANT.]
   How now, what art thou?
KENT: A man sir.   10
LEAR: What dost thou profess? What wouldst thou with us?
KENT: I do profess to be no less than I seem; to serve him truly that will
     put me in trust, to love him that is honest, to converse with him that
     is wise and says little, to fear judgement, to fight when I cannot
     choose, and to eat no fish.   15
LEAR: What art thou?

KENT: A very honest-hearted fellow, and as poor as the King.

LEAR: If thou beest as poor for a subject as he's for a King, thou are poor enough. What wouldst thou?

KENT: Service. 20

LEAR: Who wouldst thou serve?

KENT: You.

LEAR: Dost thou know me fellow?

KENT: No sir, but you have that in your countenance which I would fain call master. 25

LEAR: What's that?

KENT: Authority.

LEAR: What services canst thou do?

KENT: I can keep honest counsel, ride, run, mar a curious tale in telling it, and deliver a plain message bluntly. That which ordinary men are 30 fit for, I am qualified in, and the best of me, is diligence.

LEAR: How old art thou?

KENT: Not so young sir, to love a woman for singing, nor so old to dote on her for any thing. I have years on my back forty-eight.

LEAR: Follow me, thou shalt serve me; if I like thee no worse after dinner, 35 I will not part from thee yet. Dinner ho, dinner! Where's my knave? My fool? Go you and call my fool hither.
        [*Exit an* ATTENDANT. *Enter* OSWALD.]
        You, you sirrah, where's my daughter?

OSWALD: So please you—[*Exit.*]

LEAR: What says the fellow there? Call the clotpoll back. [*Exit a* KNIGHT.] 40 Where's my fool, ho? I think the world's asleep.
        [*Enter* KNIGHT.]
        How now? Where's that mongrel?

KNIGHT: He says, my lord, your daughter is not well.

LEAR: Why came not the slave back to me when I called him?

KNIGHT: Sir, he answered me in the roundest manner, he would not. 45

LEAR: He would not?

KNIGHT: My lord, I know not what the matter is, but to my judgement your Highness is not entertained with that ceremonious affection as you were wont; there's a great abatement of kindness appears as well in the general dependants, as in the duke himself also, and your 50 daughter.

LEAR: Ha! Sayest thou so?

KNIGHT: I beseech you pardon me my lord, if I be mistaken, for my duty cannot be silent, when I think your Highness wronged.

LEAR: Thou but rememberest me of mine own conception. I have per- 55 ceived a most faint neglect of late, which I have rather blamed as mine own jealous curiosity than as a very pretence and purpose of unkindness; I will look further into't. But where's my fool? I have not seen him this two days.

KNIGHT: Since my young lady's going into France sir, the fool hath much 60 pined away.

LEAR: No more of that, I have noted it well. Go you and tell my daughter
  I would speak with her. [*Exit an* ATTENDANT.] Go you, call hither
  my fool.
        [*Exit another* ATTENDANT. *Enter* OSWALD.]
  O you sir, you, come you hither sir. Who am I sir?   65
OSWALD: My lady's father.
LEAR: My lady's father? My lord's knave! You whoreson dog, you slave,
  you cur!
OSWALD: I am none of these my lord, I beseech your pardon.
LEAR: Do you bandy looks with me, you rascal? [*Strikes him.*]   70
OSWALD: I'll not be strucken my lord.
KENT: Nor tripped neither, you base football player. [*Trips up his heels.*]
LEAR: I thank thee fellow. Thou serv'st me, and I'll love thee.
KENT: Come sir, arise, away, I'll teach you differences. Away, away! If you
  will measure your lubber's length again, tarry. But away! Go to, have   75
  you wisdom? So. [*Pushes* OSWALD *out.*]
LEAR: Now my friendly knave I thank thee, there's earnest of thy service.
  [*Gives* KENT *money.*]
        [Enter Fool.]
FOOL: Let me hire him too, here's my coxcomb. [*Offers* KENT *his cap.*]
LEAR: How now my pretty knave, how dost thou?
FOOL: Sirrah, you were best take my coxcomb.   80
KENT: Why, fool?
FOOL: Why for taking one's part that's out of favour. Nay an thou canst
  not smile as the wind sits, thou'lt catch cold shortly; there, take my
  coxcomb. Why this fellow has banished two on's daughters, and did
  the third a blessing against his will; if thou follow him, thou must   85
  needs wear my coxcomb. How now nuncle? Would I had two cox-
  combs, and two daughters.
LEAR: Why, my boy?
FOOL: If I gave them all my living, I'd keep my coxcombs myself. There's
  mine, beg another of thy daughters.   90
LEAR: Take heed sirrah—the whip.
FOOL: Truth's a dog must to kennel; he must be whipped out, when the
  Lady Brach may stand by th'fire and stink.
LEAR: A pestilent gall to me.
FOOL: Sirrah, I'll teach thee a speech.   95
LEAR: Do.
FOOL: Mark it nuncle.
            Have more than thou showest,
            Speak less than thou knowest,
            Lend less than thou owest,   100
            Ride more than thou goest,
            Learn more than thou trowest,
            Set less than thou throwest;
            Leave thy drink and thy whore,
            And keep in-a-door,   105

> And thou shalt have more
> Than two tens to a score.

KENT: This is nothing, fool.

FOOL: Then 'tis the breath of an unfeed lawyer, you gave me nothing
for't. Can you make no use of nothing, nuncle? 110

LEAR: Why no boy, nothing can be made out of nothing.

FOOL: [*to* KENT] Prithee tell him, so much the rent of his land comes to;
he will not believe a fool.

LEAR: A bitter fool.

FOOL: Dost thou know the difference my boy, between a bitter fool, and a 115
sweet one?

LEAR: No lad, teach me.

FOOL: That lord that counselled thee
>   To give away thy land,
>   Come place him here by me, 120
>   Do thou for him stand.
>   The sweet and bitter fool
>   Will presently appear;
>   The one in motley here,
>   The other found out there. 125

LEAR: Dost thou call me fool boy?

FOOL: All thy other titles thou hast given away, that thou wast born with.

KENT: This is not altogether fool my lord.

FOOL: No faith, lords and great men will not let me; if I had a monopoly
out, they would have part an't; and ladies too, they will not let me 130
have all the fool to myself; they'll be snatching, Nuncle, give men an
egg. and I'll give thee two crowns.

LEAR: What two crowns shall they be?

FOOL: Why, after I have cut the egg i' th' middle and eat up the meat,
the two crowns of the egg. When thou clovest thy crown i' th' 135
middle, and gav'st way both parts, thou bor'st thine ass on thy back
o'er the dirt. Thou hadst little wit in thy bald crown, when thou
gav'st thy golden one away. If I speak like myself in this, let him be
whipped that first finds it so.

>   Fools had ne'er less grace in a year, 140
>   For wise men are grown foppish,
>   And know not how their wits to wear,
>   Their manners are so apish.

LEAR: When were you wont to be so full of songs sirrah?

FOOL: I have used it nuncle, ever since thou mad'st thy daughters thy 145
mothers, for when thou gav'st them the rod, and put'st down thine
own breeches—

>   Then they for sudden joy did weep,
>   And I for sorrow sung,
>   That such a king should play bo-peep, 150
>   And go the fools among.

Prithee nuncle keep a schoolmaster that can teach thy fool to lie—
I would fain learn to lie.

LEAR: An you lie sirrah, we'll have you whipped.

FOOL: I marvel what kin thou and thy daughters are, they'll have me   155
whipped for speaking true, thou'lt have me whipped for lying, and
sometimes I am whipped for holding my peace. I had rather be any
kind o' thing than a fool, and yet I would not be thee nuncle; thou
hast pared thy wit o' both sides, and left nothing i' th' middle—
[*Enter* GONERIL.]
here comes one o' the parings.   160

LEAR: How now daughter, what makes that frontlet on?
You are too much of late i' th' frown.

FOOL: Thou wast a pretty fellow when thou hadst no need to care for her
frowning; now thou art an O without a figure. I am better than thou
art now; I am a fool, thou art nothing. [*to* GONERIL] Yes forsooth, 165
I will hold my tongue; so your face bids me, though you say nothing.
Mum, mum.
He that keeps nor crust nor crumb,
Weary of all, shall want some.
That's a shealed peascod.   170

GONERIL: Not only sir, this your all-licensed fool,
But other of your insolent retinue
Do hourly carp and quarrel, breaking forth
In rank and not-to-be-endured riots. Sir,
I had thought by making this well known unto you,   175
To have found a safe redress, but now grow fearful,
By what yourself too late have spoke and done,
That you protect this course, and put it on
By your allowance; which if you should, the fault
Would not 'scape censure, nor the redresses sleep,   180
Which in the tender of a wholesome weal,
Might in their working do you that offence,
Which else were shame, that then necessity
Will call discreet proceeding.

FOOL: For you know nuncle,   185
The hedge-sparrow fed the cuckoo so long,
That it's had its head bit off by it young.
So out went the candle, and we were left darkling.

LEAR: Are you our daughter?

GONERIL: I would you would make use of your good wisdom,   190
Whereof I know you are fraught, and put away
These dispositions, which of late transport you
From what you rightly are.

FOOL: May not an ass know when the cart draws the horse? Whoop
Jug, I love thee.   195

LEAR: Does any here know me? This is not Lear.
Does Lear walk thus? Speak thus? Where are his eyes?

Either his notion weakens, his discernings
Are lethargied. Ha, waking? 'Tis not so.
Who is it that can tell me who I am? 200
FOOL: Lear's shadow.
LEAR: I would learn that, for by the marks of sovereignty, knowledge,
  and reason, I should be false persuaded I had daughters.
FOOL: Which they will make an obedient father.
LEAR: Your name fair gentlewoman? 205
GONERIL: This admiration sir, is much o' th' savour
  Of other your new pranks. I do beseech you
  To understand my purposes aright,
  As you are old, and reverend, should be wise.
  Here do you keep a hundred knights and squires, 210
  Men so disordered, so deboshed, and bold,
  That this our court infected with their manners,
  Shows like a riotous inn; epicurism and lust
  Makes it more like a tavern, or a brothel,
  Than a graced palace. The shame itself doth speak 215
  For instant remedy. Be then desired
  By her, that else will take the thing she begs,
  A little to disquantity your train;
  And the remainders that shall still depend,
  To be such men as may besort your age, 220
  Which know themselves and you.
LEAR: Darkness and devils!
  Saddle my horses; call my train together.
  Degenerate bastard, I'll not trouble thee.
  Yet have I left a daughter. 225
GONERIL: You strike my people, and your disordered rabble
  Make servants of their betters.
LEAR: Woe, that too late repents.
    [*Enter* ALBANY.]
  O sir, are you come?
  Is it your will? Speak sir. Prepare my horses. 230
  Ingratitude, thou marble-hearted fiend,
  More hideous when thou show'st thee in a child,
  Than the sea-monster.
ALBANY: Pray sir be patient.
LEAR: [*to* GONERIL] Detested kite, thou liest. 235
  My train are men of choice and rarest parts,
  That all particulars of duty know,
  And in the most exact regard support
  The worships of their name. O most small fault,
  How ugly didst thou in Cordelia show, 240
  Which like an engine wrenched my frame of nature
  From the fixed place; drew from my heart all love,
  And added to the gall. O Lear, Lear, Lear!

Beat at this gate that let thy folly in, [*strikes his head*]
And thy dear judgement out. Go, go, my people.   245
ALBANY: My lord, I am guiltless, as I am ignorant
Of what hath moved you.
LEAR: It may be so, my lord.
Hear Nature, hear, dear goddess hear.
Suspend thy purpose, if thou didst intend   250
To make this creature fruitful.
Into her womb convey sterility,
Dry up in her the organs of increase,
And from her derogate body never spring
A babe to honour her. If she must teem,   255
Create her child of spleen, that it may live
And be a thwart disnatured torment to her.
Let it stamp wrinkles in her brow of youth,
With cadent tears fret channels in her cheeks,
Turn all her mother's pains and benefits   260
To laughter, and contempt, that she may feel
How sharper than a serpent's tooth it is
To have a thankless child. Away, away! [*Exit.*]
ALBANY: Now gods that we adore, whereof comes this?
GONERIL: Never afflict yourself to know more of it;   265
But let his disposition have that scope
As dotage gives it.
        [*Enter* LEAR.]
LEAR: What, fifty of my followers at a clap?
        Within a fortnight?
ALBANY: What's the matter sir?   270
LEAR: I'll tell thee. [*to* GONERIL] Life and death, I am ashamed
That thou hast power to shake my manhood thus,
That these hot tears, which break from me perforce,
Should make thee worth them. Blasts and fogs upon thee!
Th' untented woundings of a father's curse   275
Pierce every sense about thee. Old fond eyes,
Beweep this cause again, I'll pluck ye out,
And cast you with the waters that you loose
To temper clay. Ha, is't come to this?
Let it be so, I have another daughter,   280
Who I am sure is kind and comfortable.
When she shall hear this of thee, with her nails
She'll flay thy wolvish visage. Thou shalt find,
That I'll resume the shape which thou dost think
I have cast off for ever.   285
        [*Exeunt* LEAR, KENT, *and* ATTENDANTS.]
GONERIL: Do you mark that?
ALBANY: I cannot be so partial Goneril,
To the great love I bear you—

GONERIL: Pray you, content. What Oswald, ho!

[*to* FOOL] You sir, more knave than fool, after your master.   290

FOOL: Nuncle Lear, nuncle Lear, tarry, take the fool with thee.

> A fox, when one has caught her,
> And such a daughter,
> Should sure to the slaughter,
> If my cap would buy a halter: 295
> So the fool follows after.   [*Exit.*]

GONERIL: This man hath had good counsel. A hundred knights!

> 'Tis politic, and safe, to let him keep
> At point a hundred knights—yes, that on every dream,
> Each buzz, each fancy, each complaint, dislike,   300
> He may enguard his dotage with their powers,
> And hold our lives in mercy. Oswald, I say!

ALBANY: Well, you may fear too far.

GONERIL: Safer than trust too far.

> Let me still take away the harms I fear,   305
> Not fear still to be taken. I know his heart.
> What he hath uttered I have writ my sister.
> If she sustain him, and his hundred knights,
> When I have showed th' unfitness—
>   [*Enter* OSWALD.]
>   How now Oswald?   310

What, have you writ that letter to my sister?

OSWALD: Ay madam.

GONERIL: Take you some company, and away to horse.

> Inform her full of my particular fear,
> And thereto add such reasons of your own,   315
> As may compact it more. Get you gone,
> And hasten your return. [*exit* OSWALD] No, no, my lord,
> This milky gentleness and course of yours,
> Though I condemn not, yet under pardon,
> You are much more ataxed for want of wisdom,   320
> Than praised for harmful mildness.

ALBANY: How far your eyes may pierce I cannot tell;

> Striving to better, oft we mar what's well.

GONERIL: Nay then—

ALBANY: Well, well, th' event.   [*Exeunt.*] 325

SCENE V——*Before* ALBANY's *palace.*

[*Enter* LEAR, KENT, *and* FOOL.]

LEAR: Go you before to Gloucester with these letters. Acquaint my daughter no further with any thing you know than comes from her demand out of the letter. If your diligence be not speedy, I shall be there afore you.

KENT: I will not sleep my lord, till I have delivered your letter.   [*Exit.*]   5

FOOL: If a man's brains were in's heels, were't not in danger of kibes?
LEAR: Ay boy.
FOOL: Then I prithee be merry, thy wit shall not go slipshod.
LEAR: Ha, ha, ha!
FOOL: Shalt see thy other daughter will use thee kindly, for though she's   10
    as like this, as a crab's like an apple, yet I can tell what I can tell.
LEAR: What canst tell boy?
FOOL: She will taste as like this as a crab does to a crab.
    Thou canst tell why one's nose stands i' th' middle on's face?
LEAR: No.   15
FOOL: Why to keep one's eyes of either side's nose, that what a man
    cannot smell out, he may spy into.
LEAR: I did her wrong.
FOOL: Canst tell how an oyster makes his shell?
LEAR: No.   20
FOOL: Nor I neither; but I can tell why a snail has a house.
LEAR: Why?
FOOL: Why to put's head in; not to give it away to his daughters, and
    leave his horns without a case.
LEAR: I will forget my nature. So kind a father. Be my horses ready?   25
FOOL: Thy asses are gone about 'em. The reason why the seven stars are
    no moe than seven, is a pretty reason.
LEAR: Because they are not eight?
FOOL: Yes indeed, thou wouldst make a good fool.
LEAR: To take't again perforce. Monster ingratitude.   30
FOOL: If thou wert my fool, nuncle, I'd have thee beaten for being old
    before thy time.
LEAR: How's that?
FOOL: Thou shouldst not have been old, till thou hadst been wise.
LEAR: O let me not be mad, not mad, sweet heaven.   35
    Keep me in temper, I would not be mad.
        [*Enter* GENTLEMAN.]
    How now, are the horses ready?
GENTLEMAN: Ready my lord.
LEAR: Come boy.
        [*Exeunt* LEAR *and* GENTLEMAN.]
FOOL: She that's a maid now, and laughs at my departure,   40
    Shall not be a maid long, unless things be cut shorter.   [*Exit.*]

ACT II

SCENE I——*Before* GLOUCESTER's *castle.*

[*Enter* EDMUND *and* CURAN, *at several doors.*]
EDMUND: Save thee Curan.
CURAN: And you sir. I have been with your father, and given him notice
    that the Duke of Cornwall, and Regan his duchess, will be here with
    him this night.

EDMUND: How comes that?   5
CURAN: Nay I know not. You have heard of the news abroad, I mean the
    whispered ones, for they are yet but ear-kissing arguments?
EDMUND: Not I. Pray you what are they?
CURAN: Have you heard of no likely wars toward, 'twixt the Dukes of
    Cornwall and Albany?   10
EDMUND: Not a word.
CURAN: You may do then in time. Fare you well sir.   [Exit.]
EDMUND: The duke be here to-night? The better. Best.
    This weaves itself perforce into my business.
    My father hath set guard to take my brother,   15
    And I have one thing of a queasy question
    Which I must act. Briefness and fortune work.
      [Enter EDGAR.]
    Brother, a word; descend. Brother I say!
    My father watches. O sir, fly this place,
    Intelligence is given where you are hid;   20
    You have now the good advantage of the night.
    Have you not spoken 'gainst the Duke of Cornwall?
    He's coming hither, now i' th' night, i' th' haste,
    And Regan with him; have you nothing said
    Upon his party 'gainst the Duke of Albany?   25
    Advise yourself.
EDGAR: I am sure on't, not a word.
EDMUND: I hear my father coming. Pardon me,
    In cunning, I must draw my sword upon you.
    Draw, seem to defend yourself; now quit you well—   30
    Yield, come before my father. Light ho, here!—
    Fly brother—Torches, torches!—So farewell.
      [Exit EDGAR.]
    Some blood drawn on me would beget opinion
    Of my more fierce endeavour. [stabs his arm]
      I have seen drunkards   35
    Do more than this in sport. Father, father!
    Stop, stop! No help?
      [Enter GLOUCESTER, and SERVANTS with torches.]
GLOUCESTER: Now, Edmund, where's the villain?
EDMUND: Here stood he in the dark, his sharp sword out,
    Mumbling of wicked charms, conjuring the moon   40
    To stand's auspicious mistress.
GLOUCESTER: But where is he?
EDMUND: Look sir, I bleed.
GLOUCESTER: Where is the villain, Edmund?
EDMUND: Fled this way sir. When by no means he could—   45
GLOUCESTER: Pursue him, ho! Go after. [exeunt SERVANTS] By no means
    what?

EDMUND: Persuade me to the murder of your lordship;
But that I told him the revenging gods
'Gainst parricides did all their thunders bend, 50
Spoke with how manifold and strong a bond
The child was bound to th' father; sir in fine,
Seeing how loathly opposite I stood
To his unnatural purpose, in fell motion,
With his prepared sword, he charges home 55
My unprovided body, latched mine arm;
And when he saw my best alarumed spirits
Bold in the quarrel's right, roused to th' encounter,
Or whether gasted by the noise I made,
Full suddenly he fled. 60
GLOUCESTER: Let him fly far.
Not in this land shall he remain uncaught;
And found—dispatch. The noble duke my master,
My worthy arch and patron, comes to-night.
By his authority I will proclaim it, 65
That he which finds him shall deserve our thanks,
Bringing the murderous coward to the stake;
He that conceals him, death.
EDMUND: When I dissuaded him from his intent,
And found him pight to do it, with curst speech 70
I threatened to discover him; he replied,
Thou unpossessing bastard, dost thou think,
If I would stand against thee, would the reposal
Of any trust, virtue, or worth in thee,
Make thy words faithed? No, what I should deny— 75
As this I would, ay though thou didst produce
My very character—I'd turn it all
To thy suggestion, plot, and damned practice.
And thou must make a dullard of the world,
If they not thought the profits of my death 80
Were very pregnant and potential spirits
To make thee seek it.
GLOUCESTER: O strange and fastened villain,
Would he deny his letter?—I never got him.
        [*Tucket within.*]
Hark, the duke's trumpets; I know not why he comes. 85
All ports I'll bar; the villain shall not 'scape,
The duke must grant me that. Besides, his picture
I will send far and near, that all the kingdom
May have due note of him; and of my land,
Loyal and natural boy, I'll work the means 90
To make thee capable.
        [*Enter* CORNWALL, REGAN *and* ATTENDANTS.]
CORNWALL: How now my noble friend. Since I came hither,
Which I can call but now—I have heard strange news.

REGAN: If it be true, all vengeance comes too short
    Which can pursue th' offender. How dost, my lord? 95
GLOUCESTER: O madam, my old heart is cracked, it's cracked.
REGAN: What, did my father's godson seek your life?
    He whom my father named, your Edgar?
GLOUCESTER: O lady, lady, shame would have it hid.
REGAN: Was he not companion with the riotous knights 100
    That tend upon my father?
GLOUCESTER: I know not madam; 'tis too bad, too bad.
EDMUND: Yes madam, he was of that consort.
REGAN: No marvel then, though he were ill affected.
    'Tis they have put him on the old man's death, 105
    To have th' expense and waste of his revenues.
    I have this present evening from my sister
    Been well informed of them, and with such cautions,
    That if they come to sojourn at my house,
    I'll not be there. 110
CORNWALL: Nor I, assure thee Regan.
    Edmund, I hear that you have shown your father
    A child-like office.
EDMOND: It was my duty sir.
GLOUCESTER: He did bewray his practice, and received 115
    This hurt you see, striving to apprehend him.
CORNWALL: Is he pursued?
GLOUCESTER: Ay my good lord.
CORNWALL: If he be taken, he shall never more
    Be feared of doing harm. Make your own purpose, 120
    How in my strength you please. For you Edmund,
    Whose virtue and obedience doth this instant
    So much commend itself, you shall be ours.
    Natures of such deep trust we shall much need.
    You we first seize on. 125
EDMUND: I shall serve you sir,
    Truly, however else.
GLOUCESTER: For him I thank your Grace.
CORNWALL: You know not why we came to visit you?
REGAN: Thus out of season, threading dark-eyed night. 130
    Occasions, noble Gloucester, of some poise,
    Wherein we must have use of your advice.
    Our father he hath writ, so hath our sister,
    Of differences, which I best thought it fit
    To answer from our home; the several messengers 135
    From hence attend dispatch. Our good old friend,
    Lay comforts to your bosom, and bestow
    Your needful counsel to our businesses,
    Which craves the instant use.
GLOUCESTER: I serve you madam. 140
    Your Graces are right welcome.   [*Exeunt.*]

SCENE II——*The same.*

[*Enter* KENT *and* OSWALD, *at several doors.*]
OSWALD: Good dawning to thee friend, art of this house?
KENT: Ay.
OSWALD: Where may we set our horses?
KENT: I' th' mire.
OSWALD: Prithee, if thou lov'st me, tell me.   5
KENT: I love thee not.
OSWALD: Why then I care not for thee.
KENT: If I had thee in Lipsbury pinfold, I would make thee care for me.
OSWALD: Why dost thou use me thus? I know thee not.
KENT: Fellow, I know thee.   10
OSWALD: What dost thou know me for?
KENT: A knave, a rascal, an eater of broken meats, a base, proud, shallow,
     beggarly, three-suited, hundred pound, filthy worsted-stocking knave,
     a lily-livered, action-taking, whoreson glass-gazing super-serviceable
     finical rogue, one trunk-inheriting slave, one that wouldst be a bawd   15
     in way of good service, and art nothing but the composition of a
     knave, beggar, coward, pandar, and the son and heir of a mongrel
     bitch; one whom I will beat into clamorous whining, if thou deny'st
     the least syllable of thy addition.
OSWALD: Why, what a monstrous fellow art thou, thus to rail on one that   20
     is neither known of thee, nor knows thee.
KENT: What a brazen-faced varlet art thou, to deny thou knowest me. Is
     it two days since I tripped up thy heels, and beat thee before the
     King? Draw you rogue, for though it be night, yet the moon shines;
     I'll make a sop o' th' moonshine of you, you whoreson cullionly   25
     barbermonger. Draw.   [*Draws his sword.*]
OSWALD: Away, I have nothing to do with thee.
KENT: Draw you rascal, you come with letters against the King, and take
     Vanity the puppet's part against the royalty of her father. Draw you
     rogue, or I'll so carbonado your shanks—draw you rascal, come your   30
     ways.
OSWALD: Help, ho, murder, help!
KENT: Strike, you slave; stand rogue, stand you neat slave, strike. [*Beats
     him.*]
OSWALD: Help ho! murder, murder!   35
          [*Enter* EDMUND, *with his rapier drawn,* GLOUCESTER, CORNWALL,
          REGAN *and* SERVANTS.]
EDMUND: How now, what's the matter? Part!
KENT: With you goodman boy, if you please; come,
     I'll flesh ye; come on young master.
GLOUCESTER: Weapons? Arms? What's the matter here?
CORNWALL: Keep peace upon your lives;   40
     He dies that strikes again. What is the matter?
REGAN: The messengers from our sister, and the King.

CORNWALL: What is your difference, speak.

OSWALD: I am scarce in breath my lord.

KENT: No marvel, you have so bestirred your valour. You cowardly rascal,   45
    nature disclaims in thee. A tailor made thee.

CORNWALL: Thou art a strange fellow. A tailor make a man?

KENT: A tailor sir; a stone-cutter, or a painter, could not have made him
    so ill, though they had been but two years o' th' trade.

CORNWALL: Speak yet, how grew your quarrel?   50

OSWALD: This ancient ruffian sir, whose life I have spared at suit of his
    gray beard—

KENT: Thou whoreson zed, thou unnecessary letter—my lord, if you will
    give me leave, I will tread this unbolted villain into mortar, and daub
    the wall of a jakes with him. Spare my gray beard, you wagtail?   55

CORNWALL: Peace sirrah!
    You beastly knave, know you no reverence?

KENT: Yes sir, but anger hath a privilege.

CORNWALL: Why art thou angry?

KENT: That such a slave as this should wear a sword,   60
    Who wears no honesty. Such smiling rogues as these
    Like rats oft bite the holy cords atwain
    Which are too intrinse t' unloose; smooth every passion
    That in the natures of their lords rebel,
    Bring oil to fire, snow to their colder moods;   65
    Renege, affirm, and turn their halcyon beaks
    With every gale and vary of their masters,
    Knowing naught, like dogs, but following.
    A plague upon your epileptic visage,
    Smile you my speeches, as I were a fool?   70
    Goose, if had you upon Sarum plain,
    I'd drive ye cackling home to Camelot.

CORNWALL: What, art thou mad old fellow?

GLOUCESTER: How fell you out, say that.

KENT: No contraries hold more antipathy   75
    Than I and such a knave.

CORNWALL: Why dost thou call him knave? What is his fault?

KENT: His countenance likes me not.

CORNWALL: No more perchance does mine, nor his, nor hers.

KENT: Sir, 'tis my occupation to be plain;   80
    I have seen better faces in my time
    Than stands on any shoulder that I see
    Before me, at this instant.

CORNWALL: This is some fellow,
    Who having been praised for bluntness, doth affect   85
    A saucy roughness, and constrains the garb
    Quite from his nature. He cannot flatter, he;
    An honest mind and plain; he must speak truth;
    An they will take it, so; if not, he's plain.

These kind of knaves I know, which in this plainness   90
Harbour more craft, and more corrupter ends,
Than twenty silly ducking observants
That stretch their duties nicely.
KENT: Sir, in good faith, in sincere verity,
Under th' allowance of your great aspect,   95
Whose influence like the wreath of radiant fire
On flickering Phœbus' front—
CORNWALL: What mean'st by this?
KENT: To go out of my dialect, which you discommend so much. I know
sir, I am no flatterer; he that beguiled you in plain accent was a plain 100
knave, which for my part I will not be, though I should win your dis-
pleasure to entreat me to't.
CORNWALL: What was th' offence you gave him?
OSWALD: I never gave him any.
It pleased the King his master very late   105
To strike at me, upon his misconstruction;
When he compact, and flattering his displeasure,
Tripped me behind; being down, insulted, railed,
And put upon him such a deal of man,
That worthied him, got praises of the King   110
For him attempting who was self-subdued,
And in the fleshment of this dread exploit,
Drew on me here again.
KENT: None of these rogues and cowards
But Ajax is their fool.   115
CORNWALL: Fetch forth the stocks.
You stubborn ancient knave, you reverend braggart,
We'll teach you.
KENT: Sir, I am too old to learn.
Call not your stocks for me; I serve the King,   120
On whose employment I was sent to you.
You shall do small respect, show too bold malice
Against the grace and person of my master,
Stocking his messenger.
CORNWALL: Fetch forth the stocks. As I have life and honour,   125
There shall he sit till noon.
REGAN: Till noon? Till night my lord, and all night too.
KENT: Why madam, if I were your father's dog,
You should not use me so.
REGAN: Sir, being his knave, I will. 130
CORNWALL: This is a fellow of the self-same colour
Our sister speaks of. Come, bring away the stocks.
        [*Stocks discovered in the inner stage.*]
GLOUCESTER: Let me beseech your Grace not to do so.
His fault is much, and the good King his master
Will check him for't; your purposed low correction   135

Is such as basest and contemned'st wretches
For pilferings and most common trespasses
Are punished with. The King must take it ill,
That he, so slightly valued in his messenger,
Should have him thus restrained.   140
CORNWALL: I'll answer that.
REGAN: My sister may receive it much more worse,
    To have her gentleman abused, assaulted,
    For following her affairs. Put in his legs.
    Come my good lord, away.   145
        [*Exeunt all but* GLOUSTER *and* KENT.]
GLOUCESTER: I am sorry for thee friend, 'tis the duke's pleasure,
    Whose disposition, all the world well knows,
    Will not be rubbed nor stopped. I'll entreat for thee.
KENT: Pray do not sir. I have watched, and travelled hard;
    Some time I shall sleep out, the rest I'll whistle.   150
    A good man's fortune may grow out at heels.
    Give you good morrow.
GLOUCESTER: The duke's to blame in this, 'twill be ill taken. [*Exit.*]
KENT: Good King, that must approve the common saw,
    Thou out of heaven's benediction com'st   155
    To the warm sun.
    Approach thou beacon to this under globe,
    That by thy comfortable beams I may
    Peruse this letter. Nothing almost sees miracles
    But misery. I know 'tis from Cordelia,   160
    Who hath most fortunately been informed
    Of my obscured course—[*reads*] *and shall find time*
    From this enormous state, seeking to give
    Losses their remedies.—All weary and o'erwatched,
    Take vantage heavy eyes, not to behold   165
    This shameful lodging.
    Fortune good night; smile once more, turn thy wheel.
        [*Sleeps. Curtains drawn.*]

                SCENE III——*The open country.*

        [*Enter* EDGAR.]
EDGAR: I heard myself proclaimed,
    And by the happy hollow of a tree
    Escaped the hunt. No port is free, no place,
    That guard, and most unusual vigilance,
    Does not attend my taking. Whiles I may 'scape,   5
    I will preserve myself; and am bethought
    To take the basest and most poorest shape
    That ever penury in contempt of man
    Brought near to beast; my face I'll grime with filth,

Blanket my loins, elf all my hairs in knots,   10
And with presented nakedness outface
The winds and persecutions of the sky.
The country gives me proof and precedent
Of Bedlam beggars, who with roaring voices,
Strike in their numbed and mortified bare arms   15
Pins, wooden pricks, nails, sprigs of rosemary;
And with this horrible object, from low farms,
Poor pelting villages, sheep cotes, and mills,
Sometime with lunatic bans, sometime with prayers,
Enforce their charity. Poor Turlygod, poor Tom!   20
That's something yet. Edgar I nothing am. [*Exit.*]

SCENE IV——*Before* GLOUCESTER'S *castle.*

[KENT *discovered in the stocks. Enter* LEAR, FOOL, *and* GENTLE-
MAN.]

LEAR: 'Tis strange that they should so depart from home,
And not send back my messenger.
GENTLEMAN: As I learned,
The night before there was no purpose in them
Of this remove.   5
KENT: Hail to thee noble master.
LEAR: Ha!
Mak'st thou this shame thy pastime?
KENT: No my lord.
FOOL: Ha, ha, he wears cruel garters. Horses are tied by the heads, dogs   10
and bears by th' neck, monkeys by th' loins, and men by th' legs.
When a man's over-lusty at legs, then he wears wooden netherstocks.
LEAR: What's he that hath so much thy place mistook
To set thee here?
KENT: It is both he and she,   15
Your son and daughter.
LEAR: No.
KENT: Yes.
LEAR: No I say.
KENT: I say yea.   20
LEAR: By Jupiter I swear, no.
KENT: By Juno I swear, ay.
LEAR: They durst not do't;
They could not, would not do't; 'tis worse than murder,
To do upon respect such violent outrage.   25
Resolve me with all modest haste, which way
Thou mightst deserve, or they impose this usage,
Coming from us.
KENT: My lord, when at their home
I did commend your Highness' letters to them,   30

Ere I was risen from the place that showed
My duty kneeling, came there a reeking post,
Stewed in his haste, half breathless, panting forth
From Goneril his mistress salutations;
Delivered letters, spite of intermission, 35
Which presently they read; on whose contents
They summoned up their meiny, straight took horse,
Commanded me to follow, and attend
The leisure of their answer, gave me cold looks;
And meeting here the other messenger, 40
Whose welcome I perceived had poisoned mine,
Being the very fellow which of late
Displayed so saucily against your Highness,
Having more man than wit about me, drew.
He raised the house, with loud and coward cries; 45
Your son and daughter found this trespass worth
The shame which here it suffers.
FOOL: Winter's not gone yet, if the wild geese fly that way.
                Fathers that wear rags
                Do make their children blind, 50
                But fathers that bear bags
                Shall see their children kind.
                Fortune, that arrant whore,
                Ne'er turns the key to th' poor
But for all this thou shalt have as many dolours for thy daughters as 55
thou canst tell in a year.
LEAR: O how this mother swells up toward my heart!
Hysterica passio, down thou climbing sorrow,
Thy element's below. Where is this daughter?
KENT: With the earl sir, here within. 60
LEAR: Follow me not;
Stay here.   [*Exit.*]
GENTLEMAN: Made you no more offence but what you speak of?
KENT: None.
How chance the King comes with so small a number? 65
FOOL: An thou hadst been set i' th' stocks for that question, thou'dst well
    deserved it.
KENT: Why fool?
FOOL: We'll set thee to school to an ant, to teach thee there's no labour-
    ing i' th' winter. All that follow their noses are led by their eyes but 70
    blind men, and there's not a nose among twenty but can smell him
    that's stinking. Let go thy hold when a great wheel runs down a hill,
    lest it break thy neck with following. But the great one that goes up-
    ward, let him draw thee after. When a wise man gives thee better
    counsel, give me mine again; I would have none but knaves follow 75
    it, since a fool gives it.

That sir, which serves and seeks for gain,
   And follows but for form
Will pack when it begins to rain,
   And leave thee in the storm.   80
But I will tarry, the fool will stay,
   And let the wise man fly.
The knave turns fool that runs away;
   The fool no knave perdy.

KENT: Where learned you this, fool?   85
FOOL: Not i' th' stocks, fool.
     [*Enter* LEAR *with* GLOUCESTER.]
LEAR: Deny to speak with me? They are sick, they are weary,
   They have travelled all the night! Mere fetches,
   The images of revolt and flying off.
   Fetch me a better answer.   90
GLOUCESTER: My dear lord,
   You know the fiery quality of the duke,
   How unremovable and fixed he is
   In his own course.
LEAR: Vengeance, plague, death, confusion!   95
   Fiery? What quality? Why Gloucester, Gloucester,
   I'd speak with the Duke of Cornwall, and his wife.
GLOUCESTER: Well my good lord, I have informed them so.
LEAR: Informed them? Dost thou understand me man?
GLOUCESTER: Ay my good lord.   100
LEAR: The King would speak with Cornwall; the dear father
   Would with his daughter speak, commands—tends—service.
   Are they informed of this? My breath and blood!
   Fiery? The fiery duke? Tell the hot duke that—
   No, but not yet, may be he is not well;   105
   Infirmity doth still neglect all office
   Whereto our health is bound; we are not ourselves,
   When nature being oppressed, commands the mind
   To suffer with the body; I'll forbear,
   And am fallen out with my more headier will,   110
   To take the indisposed and sickly fit
   For the sound man. Death on my state! Wherefore
   Should he sit here? This act persuades me,
   That this remotion of the duke and her
   Is practice only. Give me my servant forth.   115
   Go tell the duke and's wife I'd speak with them.
   Now, presently. Bid them come forth and hear me,
   Or at their chamber door I'll beat the drum,
   Till it cry sleep to death.
GLOUCESTER: I would have all well betwixt you.   [*Exit.*] 120
LEAR: O me my heart! My rising heart! But down.
FOOL: Cry to it nuncle, as the cockney did to the eels, when she put 'em

i' th' paste alive; she knapped 'em o' th' coxcombs with a stick, and
cried, down wantons, down. 'Twas her brother, that in pure kindness
to his horse buttered his hay.   125

[*Enter* CORNWALL, REGAN, GLOUCESTER, *and* SERVANTS.]

LEAR: Good morrow to you both.
CORNWALL: Hail to your Grace.

[KENT *is set at liberty.*]

REGAN: I am glad to see your Highness.
LEAR: Regan, I think you are. I know what reason
    I have to think so. If thou shouldst not be glad,   130
    I would divorce me from thy mother's tomb,
    Sepulchring an adultress. [*to* KENT] O are you free?
    Some other time for that.—Beloved Regan,
    Thy sister's naught. O Regan, she hath tied
    Sharp-toothed unkindness, like a vulture, here. [*points to his heart*] 135
    I can scarce speak to thee; thou'lt not believe
    Of how depraved a quality—O Regan.
REGAN: I pray you sir, take patience; I have hope
    You less know how to value her desert
    Than she to scant her duty.   140
LEAR: Say—how is that?
REGAN: I cannot think my sister in the least
    Would fail her obligation. If sir perchance
    She have restrained the riots of your followers,
    'Tis on such ground, and to such wholesome end,   145
    As clear her from all blame.
LEAR: My curses on her.
REGAN: O sir, you are old;
    Nature in you stands on the very verge
    Of his confine. You should be ruled, and led   150
    By some discretion that discerns your state
    Better than you yourself. Therefore I pray you,
    That to our sister you do make return;
    Say you have wronged her.
LEAR: Ask her forgiveness?   155
    Do you but mark how this becomes the house—
    Dear daughter, I confess that I am old;
    Age is unnecessary, on my knees I beg
    That you'll vouchsafe me raiment, bed, and food. [*Kneels.*]
REGAN: Good sir, no more; these are unsightly tricks.   160
    Return you to my sister.
LEAR: [*rises*]   Never, Regan.
    She hath abated me of half my train;
    Looked black upon me, struck me with her tongue
    Most serpent-like, upon the very heart.   165
    All the stored vengeances of heaven fall

      On her ingrateful top. Strike her young bones,
      You taking airs, with lameness.
CORNWALL: Fie sir, fie!
LEAR: You nimble lightnings, dart your blinding flames   170
      Into her scornful eyes. Infect her beauty,
      You fen-sucked fogs, drawn by the powerful sun,
      To fall and blister her.
REGAN: O the blessed gods,
      So will you wish on me when the rash mood—   175
LEAR: No Regan, thou shalt never have my curse.
      Thy tender-hefted nature shall not give
      Thee o'er to harshness. Her eyes are fierce, but thine
      Do comfort, and not burn. 'Tis not in thee
      To grudge my pleasures, to cut off my train,   180
      To bandy hasty words, to scant my sizes,
      And in conclusion, to oppose the bolt
      Against my coming in. Thou better know'st
      The offices of nature, bond of childhood,
      Effects of courtesy, dues of gratitude.   185
      Thy half o' th' kingdom hast thou not forgot,
      Wherein I thee endowed.
REGAN: Good sir, to th' purpose.
LEAR: Who put my man i' th' stocks?
        [*Tucket within.*]
CORNWALL: What trumpet's that?   190
        [*Enter* OSWALD.]
REGAN: I know't—my sister's. This approves her letter,
      That she would soon be here.—Is your lady come?
LEAR: This is a slave, whose easy-borrowed pride
      Dwells in the fickle grace of her he follows.
      Out varlet, from my sight.   195
CORNWALL: What means your Grace?
LEAR: Who stocked my servant? Regan, I have good hope
      Thou didst not know on't.
        [*Enter* GONERIL.]
                  Who comes here? O heavens,
      If you do love old men, if your sweet sway   200
      Allow obedience, if you yourselves are old,
      Make it your cause. Send down, and take my part.
      [*to* GONERIL] Art not ashamed to look upon this beard?
      O Regan, will you take her by the hand?
GONERIL: Why not by th' hand sir? How have I offended?   205
      All's not offence that indiscretion finds,
      And dotage terms so.
LEAR: O sides, you are too tough.
      Will you yet hold? How came my man i' th' stocks?
CORNWALL: I set him there, sir. But his own disorders   210
      Deserved much less advancement.

LEAR: You? Did you?
REGAN: I pray you father, being weak, seem so.
    If till the expiration of your month,
    You will return and sojourn with my sister,   215
    Dismissing half your train, come then to me.
    I am now from home, and out of that provision
    Which shall be needful for your entertainment.
LEAR: Return to her? And fifty men dismissed?
    No, rather I abjure all roofs, and choose   220
    To wage against the enmity o' th' air,
    To be a comrade with the wolf and owl,
    Necessity's sharp pinch. Return with her?
    Why the hot-blooded France, that dowerless took
    Our youngest born, I could as well be brought   225
    To knee his throne, and squire-like pension beg
    To keep base life afoot. Return with her?
    Persuade me rather to be slave and sumpter
    To this detested groom.
GONERIL: At your choice sir.   230
LEAR: I prithee daughter do not make me mad.
    I will not trouble thee my child; farewell.
    We'll no more meet, no more see one another.
    But yet thou art my flesh, my blood, my daughter;
    Or rather a disease that's in my flesh,   235
    Which I must needs call mine. Thou art a boil,
    A plague-sore, or embossed carbuncle
    In my corrupted blood. But I'll not chide thee;
    Let shame come when it will, I do not call it;
    I do not bid the thunder-bearer shoot,   240
    Nor tell tales of thee to high-judging Jove.
    Mend when thou canst, be better at thy leisure;
    I can be patient, I can stay with Regan,
    I and my hundred knights.
REGAN: Not altogether so;   245
    I looked not for you yet, nor am provided
    For your fit welcome. Give ear sir to my sister,
    For those that mingle reason with your passion
    Must be content to think you old, and so—
    But she knows what she does.   250
LEAR: Is this well spoken?
REGAN: I dare avouch it sir. What, fifty followers?
    Is it not well? What should you need of more?
    Yea or so many, sith that both charge and danger
    Speak 'gainst so great a number? How in one house   255
    Should many people, under two commands,
    Hold amity? 'Tis hard, almost impossible.
GONERIL: Why might not you my lord, receive attendance
    From those that she calls servants, or from mine?

REGAN: Why not my lord? If then they chanced to slack ye,   260
  We could control them. If you will come to me—
  For now I spy a danger—I entreat you
  To bring but five and twenty; to no more
  Will I give place or notice.
LEAR: I gave you all.   265
REGAN: And in good time you gave it.
LEAR: Made you my guardians, my depositaries,
  But kept a reservation to be followed
  With such a number. What, must I come to you
  With five and twenty? Regan, said you so?   270
REGAN: And speak't again my lord; no more with me.
LEAR: Those wicked creatures yet do look well-favoured,
  When others are more wicked; not being the worst
  Stands in some rank of praise. [*to* GONERIL] I'll go with thee;
  Thy fifty yet doth double five and twenty,   275
  And thou art twice her love.
GONERIL: Hear me my lord;
  What need you five and twenty? Ten? Or five?
  To follow in a house where twice so many
  Have a command to tend you?   280
REGAN: What need one?
LEAR: O reason not the need. Our basest beggars
  Are in the poorest thing superfluous.
  Allow not nature more than nature needs;
  Man's life is cheap as beast's. Thou art a lady;   285
  If only to go warm were gorgeous,
  Why nature needs not what thou gorgeous wear'st,
  Which scarcely keeps thee warm but for true need.
  You heavens, give me that patience, patience I need.
  You see me here, you gods, a poor old man,   290
  As full of grief as age, wretched in both.
  If it be you that stirs these daughters' hearts
  Against their father, fool me not so much
  To bear it tamely; touch me with noble anger,
  And let not women's weapons, water-drops,   295
  Stain my man's cheeks. No, you unnatural hags,
  I will have such revenges on you both,
  That all the world shall—I will do such things;
  What they are, yet I know not, but they shall be
  The terrors of the earth. You think I'll weep.   300
  No I'll not weep. [*storm and tempest*]
  I have full cause of weeping; but this heart
  Shall break into a hundred thousand flaws
  Or e'er I'll weep. O fool, I shall go mad.
      [*Exeunt* LEAR, GLOUCESTER, KENT, *and* FOOL.]
CORNWALL: Let us withdraw, 'twill be a storm.   305

REGAN: This house is little; the old man and's people
 Cannot be well bestowed.
GONERIL: 'Tis his own blame; hath put himself from rest,
 And must needs taste his folly.
REGAN: For his particular, I'll receive him gladly,   310
 But not one follower.
GONERIL: So am I purposed.
 Where is my Lord of Gloucester?
CORNWALL: Followed the old man forth—
  [*Enter* GLOUCESTER.]
           He is returned.   315
GLOUCESTER: The King is in high rage.
CORNWALL: Whither is he going?
GLOUCESTER: He calls to horse, but will I know not whither.
CORNWALL: 'Tis best to give him way, he leads himself.
GONERIL: My lord, entreat him by no means to stay.   320
GLOUCESTER: Alack, the night comes on, and the high winds
 Do sorely ruffle; for many miles about
 There's scarce a bush.
REGAN: O sir, to wilful men
 The injuries that they themselves procure   325
 Must be their schoolmasters. Shut up your doors,
 He is attended with a desperate train,
 And what they may incense him to, being apt
 To have his ear abused, wisdom bids fear.
CORNWALL: Shut up your doors my lord, 'tis a wild night.   330
 My Regan counsels well. Come out o' th' storm. [*Exeunt.*]

ACT III

SCENE I——*A heath. Storm still.*

   [*Enter* KENT *and* GENTLEMAN, *at several doors.*]
KENT: Who's there, besides foul weather?
GENTLEMAN: One minded like the weather, most unquietly.
KENT: I know you. Where's the King?
GENTLEMAN: Contending with the fretful elements;
 Bids the wind blow the earth into the sea,   5
 Or swell the curled waters 'bove the main,
 That things might change or cease; tears his white hair,
 Which the impetuous blasts with eyeless rage
 Catch in their fury, and make nothing of;
 Strives in his little world of man to outstorm   10
 The to and fro conflicting wind and rain.
 This night, wherein the cub-drawn bear would couch,
 The lion, and the belly-pinched wolf
 Keep their fur dry, unbonneted he runs,
 And bids what will take all.   15
KENT: But who is with him?

GENTLEMAN: None but the fool, who labours to outjest
     His heart-struck injuries.
KENT: Sir, I do know you,   20
     And dare upon the warrant of my note
     Commend a dear thing to you. There is division,
     Although as yet the face of it is covered
     With mutual cunning, 'twixt Albany and Cornwall;
     Who have—as who have not, that their great stars   25
     Throned and set high—servants, who seem no less,
     Which are to France the spies and speculations
     Intelligent of our state. What hath been seen,
     Either in snuffs and packings of the dukes,
     Or the hard rein which both of them hath borne
     Against the old kind King, or something deeper,   30
     Whereof perchance these are but furnishings—
     But true it is, from France there comes a power
     Into this scattered kingdom, who already,
     Wise in our negligence, have secret feet
     In some of our best ports, and are at point   35
     To show their open banner. Now to you.
     If on my credit you dare build so far
     To make your speed to Dover, you shall find
     Some that will thank you, making just report
     Of how unnatural and bemadding sorrow   40
     The King hath cause to plain.
     I am a gentleman of blood and breeding,
     And from some knowledge and assurance, offer
     This office to you.
GENTLEMAN: I will talk further with you.   45
KENT: No, do not.
     For confirmation that I am much more
     Than my out-wall, open this purse, and take
     What it contains. If you shall see Cordelia,
     As fear not but you shall, show her this ring,   50
     And she will tell you who that fellow is
     That yet you do not know. Fie on this storm!
     I will go seek the King.
GENTLEMAN: Give me your hand. Have you no more to say?
KENT: Few words, but to effect more than all yet,   55
     That when we have found the King—in which your pain
     That way, I'll this—he that first lights on him
     Holla the other.
          [*Exeunt at several doors.*]

          SCENE II——*The same. Storm still.*

     [*Enter* LEAR *and* FOOL.]
LEAR: Blow winds, and crack your cheeks. Rage, blow,
     You cataracts, and hurricanoes, spout

 Till you have drenched our steeples, drowned the cocks.
 You sulphurous and thought-executing fires,
 Vaunt-couriers of oak-cleaving thunderbolts,   5
 Singe my white head. And thou all-shaking thunder,
 Strike flat the thick rotundity o' th' world,
 Crack nature's moulds, all germens spill at once,
 That makes ingrateful man.
FOOL: O nuncle, Court holy water in a dry house is better than this rain-   10
  water out o' door. Good nuncle in, ask thy daughters' blessing; here's
  a night pities neither wise men, nor fools.
LEAR: Rumble thy bellyful. Spit fire, spout rain.
 Nor rain, wind, thunder, fire, are my daughters;
 I tax not you, you elements, with unkindness.   15
 I never gave you kingdom, called you children;
 You owe me no subscription. Then let fall
 Your horrible pleasure. Here I stand your slave,
 A poor, infirm, weak, and despised old man.
 But yet I call you servile ministers,   20
 That will with two pernicious daughters join
 Your high-engendered battles 'gainst a head
 So old and white. O, oho, 'tis foul.
FOOL: He that has a house to put's head in has a good head-piece.
    The codpiece that will house,   25
     Before the head has any,
    The head and he shall louse;
     So beggars marry many.
    The man that makes his toe,
     What he his heart should make,   30
    Shall of a corn cry woe,
     And turn his sleep to wake.
 For there was never yet fair woman, but she made mouths in a glass.
LEAR: No, I will be the pattern of all patience,
 I will say nothing.   35
   [*Enter* KENT.]
KENT: Who's there?
FOOL: Marry here's grace, and a codpiece; that's a wise man, and a fool.
KENT: Alas sir are you here? Things that love night
 Love not such nights as these. The wrathful skies
 Gallow the very wanderers of the dark,   40
 And make them keep their caves. Since I was man,
 Such sheets of fire, such bursts of horrid thunder,
 Such groans of roaring wind, and rain, I never
 Remember to have heard. Man's nature cannot carry
 Th' affliction, nor the fear.   45
LEAR: Let the great gods
 That keep this dreadful pudder o'er our heads
 Find out their enemies now. Tremble thou wretch.
 That hast within thee undivulged crimes,

Unwhipped of justice. Hide thee, thou bloody hand;   50
Thou perjured, and thou simular of virtue
That art incestuous. Caitiff, to pieces shake,
That under covert and convenient seeming
Has practised on man's life. Close pent-up guilts,
Rive your concealing continents, and cry   55
These dreadful summoners grace. I am a man
More sinned against, than sinning.
KENT: Alack, bare-headed!
Gracious my lord, hard by here is a hovel,
Some friendship will it lend you 'gainst the tempest.   60
Repose you there, while I to this hard house—
More harder than the stones whereof 'tis raised,
Which even but now, demanding after you,
Denied me to come in—return, and force
Their scanted courtesy.   65
LEAR: My wits begin to turn.
Come on my boy. How dost, my boy? Art cold?
I am cold myself. Where is this straw, my fellow?
The art of our necessities is strange
That can make vile things precious. Come, your hovel.   70
Poor fool and knave, I have one part in my heart
That's sorry yet for thee.
FOOL: [sings]
             He that has and a little tiny wit,
               With hey, ho, the wind and the rain,
             Must make content with his fortunes fit,   75
             Though the rain it raineth every day.
LEAR: True, boy. Come bring us to this hovel.
      [*Exeunt* LEAR *and* KENT.]
FOOL: This is a brave night to cool a courtezan. I'll speak a prophecy ere
    I go:
             When priests are more in word than matter;   80
             When brewers mar their malt with water;
             When nobles are their tailors' tutors;
             No heretics burned, but wenches' suitors;
             When every case in law is right;
             No squire in debt, nor no poor knight;   85
             When slanders do not live in tongues;
             Nor cutpurses come not to throng;
             When usurers tell their gold i' th' field,
             And bawds and whores do churches build,
             Then shall the realm of Albion   90
             Come to great confusion.
             Then comes the time, who lives to see't,
             That going shall be used with feet.
This prophecy Merlin shall make, for I live before his time. [*Exit.*]

SCENE III———GLOUCESTER'S *castle.*

[*Enter* GLOUCESTER *and* EDMUND.]

GLOUCESTER: Alack, alack Edmund, I like not this unnatural dealing.
When I desired their leave that I might pity him, they took from
me the use of mine own house, charged me on pain of perpetual
displeasure neither to speak of him, entreat for him, nor any way
sustain him.   5

EDMUND: Most savage and unnatural.

GLOUCESTER: Go to; say you nothing. There is division between the
dukes, and a worse matter than that. I have received a letter this
night—'tis dangerous to be spoken—I have locked the letter in my
closet; these injuries the King now bears will be revenged home.   10
There is part of a power already footed; we must incline to the
King. I will look him, and privily relieve him; go you and maintain
talk with the duke, that my charity be not of him perceived. If
he ask for me, I am ill, and gone to bed. If I die for it, as no less is
threatened me, the King my old master must be relieved. There   15
is strange things toward, Edmund, pray you be careful.   [*Exit.*]

EDMUND: This courtesy, forbid thee, shall the duke
Instantly know, and of that letter too.
This seems a fair deserving, and must draw me
That which my father loses—no less than all.   20
The younger rises when the old doth fall.   [*Exit.*]

SCENE IV———*The hearth, before a hovel.*

[*Enter* LEAR, KENT, *and* FOOL.]

KENT: Here is the place my lord; good my lord enter.
The tyranny of the open night's too rough
For nature to endure.   [*Storm still.*]
LEAR: Let me alone.
KENT: Good my lord enter here.   5
LEAR: Wilt break my heart?
KENT: I had rather break mine own. Good my lord enter.
LEAR: Thou think'st 'tis much that this contentious storm
Invades us to the skin; so 'tis to thee,
But where the greater malady is fixed,   10
The lesser is scarce felt. Thou'dst shun a bear,
But if thy flight lay toward the roaring sea,
Thou'dst meet the bear i' th' mouth. When the mind's free,
The body's delicate; this tempest in my mind
Doth from my senses take all feeling else   15
Save what beats there. Filial ingratitude,
Is it not as this mouth should tear this hand
For lifting food to't? But I will punish home.
No, I will weep no more. In such a night

To shut me out! Pour on, I will endure.   20
In such a night as this! O Regan, Goneril—
Your old kind father, whose frank heart gave all—
O that way madness lies, let me shun that.
No more of that.
KENT: Good my lord enter here.   25
LEAR: Prithee go in thyself, seek thine own ease.
This tempest will not give me leave to ponder
On things would hurt me more. But I'll go in.
In boy, go first.—You houseless poverty—
Nay get thee in. I'll pray, and then I'll sleep.   30
        [*Exit* FOOL *into the hovel.*]
Poor naked wretches, wheresoe'er you are,
That bide the pelting of this pitiless storm,
How shall your houseless heads, and unfed sides,
Your looped and windowed raggedness, defend you
From seasons such as these? O I have ta'en   35
Too little care of this! Take physic, pomp;
Expose thyself to feel what wretches feel,
That thou mayst shake the superflux to them,
And show the heavens more just.
EDGAR: [*within*] Fathom and half, fathom and half!   40
Poor Tom!
        [*Enter* FOOL *from the hovel.*]
FOOL: Come not in here nuncle, here's a spirit. Help me, help me.
KENT: Give me thy hand. Who's there?
FOOL: A spirit, a spirit, he says his name's poor Tom.
KENT: What art thou that dost grumble there i' th' straw? Come forth.   45
        [*Enter* EDGAR *from the hovel, disguised as a madman.*]
EDGAR: Away, the foul fiend follows me. Through the sharp hawthorn
    blow the winds. Hum, go to thy cold bed and warm thee.
LEAR: Didst thou give all to thy daughters? And art thou come to this?
EDGAR: Who gives any thing to poor Tom, whom the foul fiend hath
    led through fire, and through flame, through ford and whirlpool,   50
    o'er bog and quagmire, that hath laid knives under his pillow, and
    halters in his pew, set ratsbane by his porridge, made him proud of
    heart to ride on a bay trotting-horse over four-inched bridges, to
    course his own shadow for a traitor. Bless thy five wits, Tom's a-cold.
    O do, de, do, de, do, de. Bless thee from whirlwinds, star-blasting,   55
    and taking, do poor Tom some charity, whom the foul fiend vexes.
    There could I have him now—and there—and there again, and
    there.
        [*Storm still.*]
LEAR: What, has his daughters brought him to this pass?
    Couldst thou save nothing? Wouldst thou give 'em all?   60
FOOL: Nay, he reserved a blanket, else we had been all shamed.
LEAR: Now all the plagues that in the pendulous air
    Hang fated o'er men's faults light on thy daughters.

KENT: He hath no daughters sir.

LEAR: Death, traitor; nothing could have subdued nature 65
To such a lowness but his unkind daughters.
Is it the fashion, that discarded fathers
Should have thus little mercy on their flesh?
Judicious punishment; 'twas this flesh begot
Those pelican daughters. 70

EDGAR: Pillicock sat on Pillicock-hill. Alow; alow, loo, loo!

FOOL: This cold night will turn us all to fools, and madmen.

EDGAR: Take heed o' th' foul fiend, obey thy parents, keep thy words
justly, swear not, commit not with man's sworn spouse; set not thy
sweet heart on proud array. Tom's a-cold. 75

LEAR: What hast thou been?

EDGAR: A servingman, proud in heart and mind; that curled my hair,
wore gloves in my cap; served the lust of my mistress' heart, and
did the act of darkness with her; swore as many oaths as I spake
words, and broke them in the sweet face of heaven; one that slept 80
in the contriving of lust, and waked to do it. Wine loved I deeply,
dice dearly; and in woman out-paramoured the Turk. False of
heart, light of ear, bloody of hand; hog in sloth, fox in stealth,
wolf in greediness, dog in madness, lion in prey. Let not the creak-
ing of shoes, nor the rustling of silks, betray thy poor heart to 85
woman; keep thy foot out of brothels, thy hand out of plackets, thy
pen from lenders' books, and defy the foul fiend. Still through the
hawthorn blows the cold wind; says suum, mun, nonny. Dolphin
my boy, boy sessa, let him trot by.
[*Storm still.*]

LEAR: Thou wert better in a grave, than to answer with thy uncovered 90
body this extremity of the skies. Is man no more than this? Consider him well. Thou ow'st the worm no silk, the beast no hide, the
sheep no wool, the cat no perfume. Ha? Here's three on's are
sophisticated. Thou art the thing itself; unaccommodated man is
no more but such a poor, bare, forked animal as thou art. Off, off, 95
you lendings! Come, unbutton here.   [*Pulls at his clothes*]

FOOL: Prithee nuncle be contented, 'tis a naughty night to swim in.
Now a little fire in a wild field were like an old lecher's heart, a
small spark, all the rest on's body cold.
[*Enter* GLOUCESTER, *with a torch.*]
Look, here comes a walking fire. 100

EDGAR: This is the foul Flibbertigibbet; he begins at curfew, and walks
till the first cock; he gives the web and the pin, squints the eye,
and makes the hare-lip; mildews the white wheat, and hurts the
poor creature of earth.
        Swithold footed thrice the 'old; 105
        He met the night-mare, and her nine-fold;
            Bid her alight,
            And her troth plight,
        And, aroint thee, witch, aroint thee!

GLOUCESTER: How fares your Grace?   110
LEAR: What's he?
KENT: Who's there? What is't you seek?
GLOUCESTER: What are you there? Your names?
EDGAR: Poor Tom, that eats the swimming frog, the toad, the tadpole,
    the wall-newt and the water; that in the fury of his heart, when the   115
    foul fiend rages, eats cow-dung for sallets; swallows the old rat and
    the ditch-dog; drinks the green mantle of the standing pool; who is
    whipped from tithing to tithing, and stock-punished, and imprisoned;
    who hath had three suits to his back, six shirts to his body,
        Horse to ride, and weapons to wear;   120
        But mice, and rats, and such small deer,
        Have been Tom's food, for seven long year.
    Beware my follower. Peace Smulkin, peace thou fiend.
GLOUCESTER: What, hath your Grace no better company?
EDGAR: The prince of darkness is a gentleman. Modo he's called, and   125
    Mahu.
GLOUCESTER: Our flesh and blood, my lord, is grown so vile,
    That it doth hate what gets it.
EDGAR: Poor Tom's a-cold.
GLOUCESTER: Go in with me; my duty cannot suffer   130
    T' obey in all your daughters' hard commands.
    Though their injunction be to bar my doors,
    And let this tyrannous night take hold upon you,
    Yet have I ventured to come seek you out,
    And bring you where both fire and food is ready.   135
LEAR: First let me talk with this philosopher.
    What is the cause of thunder?
KENT: Good my lord take his offer, go into the house.
LEAR: I'll talk a word with this same learned Theban.
    What is your study?   140
EDGAR: How to prevent the fiend, and to kill vermin.
LEAR: Let me ask you one word in private.
KENT: Importune him once more to go, my lord,
    His wits begin t' unsettle.
    [*Storm still.*]
GLOUCESTER: Canst thou blame him?   145
    His daughters seek his death. Ah, that good Kent,
    He said it would be thus—poor banished man.
    Thou sayst the King grows mad; I'll tell thee friend,
    I am almost mad myself. I had a son,
    Now outlawed from my blood; he sought my life   150
    But lately, very late. I loved him, friend,
    No father his son dearer. True to tell thee,
    The grief hath crazed my wits. What a night's this!
    I do beseech your Grace—
LEAR: O cry you mercy, sir.   155
    Noble philosopher, your company.

EDGAR: Tom's a-cold.
GLOUCESTER: In fellow, there, into the hovel; keep thee warm.
LEAR: Come, let's in all.
KENT: This way, my lord.   160
LEAR: With him;
    I will keep still with my philosopher.
KENT: Good my lord, soothe him; let him take the fellow.
GLOUCESTER: Take him you on.
KENT: Sirrah, come on; go along with us.   165
LEAR: Come, good Athenian.
GLOUCESTER: No words, no words, hush.
EDGAR: Child Rowland to the dark tower came,
    His word was still, fie, foh, and fum,
    I smell the blood of a British man.   170
        [*Exeunt.*]

SCENE V——GLOUCESTER'S *castle*.

[*Enter* CORNWALL *and* EDMUND.]
CORNWALL: I will have my revenge ere I depart his house.
EDMUND: How, my lord, I may be censured, that nature thus gives way to
    loyalty, something fears me to think of.
CORNWALL: I now perceive, it was not altogether your brother's evil dis-
    position made him seek his death; but a provoking merit set awork   5
    by a reproveable badness in himself.
EDMUND: How malicious is my fortune, that I must repent to be just.
    This is the letter he spoke of, which approves him an intelligent
    party to the advantages of France. O heavens, that this treason were
    not, or not I the detector!   10
CORNWALL: Go with me to the duchess.
EDMUND: If the matter of this paper be certain, you have mighty business
    in hand.
CORNWALL: True or false, it hath made thee Earl of Gloucester. Seek out
    where thy father is, that he may be ready for our apprehension.   15
EDMUND: [*aside*] If I find him comforting the King, it will stuff his sus-
    picion more fully.—I will persevere in my course of loyalty, though
    the conflict be sore between that and my blood.
CORNWALL: I will lay trust upon thee; and thou shalt find a dearer father
    in my love.   [*Exeunt.*]   20

SCENE VI——*An outbuilding of the castle*.

[*Enter* KENT *and* GLOUCESTER.]
GLOUCESTER: Here is better than the open air, take it thankfully. I will
    piece out the comfort with what addition I can. I will not be long
    from you.
KENT: All the power of his wits have given way to his impatience. The
    gods reward your kindness.   5
    [*Exit* GLOUCESTER. *Enter* LEAR, EDGAR, *and* FOOL.]

EDGAR: Frateretto calls me, and tells me Nero is an angler in the lake of
darkness. Pray, innocent, and beware the foul fiend.

FOOL: Prithee nuncle tell me, whether a madman be a gentleman or a
yeoman?

LEAR: A king, a king.   10

FOOL: No, he's a yeoman that has a gentleman to his son; for he's a mad
yeoman that sees his son a gentleman before him.

LEAR: To have a thousand with red burning spits
Come hissing in upon 'em—

EDGAR: The foul fiend bites my back.   15

FOOL: He's mad that trusts in the tameness of a wolf, a horse's health, a
boy's love, or a whore's oath.

LEAR: It shall be done; I will arraign them straight.
[*to* EDGAR] Come sit thou here most learned Justice.
[*to the* FOOL] Thou sapient sir sit here.—Now, you she-foxes!   20

EDGAR: Look where he stands and glares.—Want'st thou eyes at trial,
madam?
Come o'er the bourn Bessy to me.

FOOL: Her boat hath a leak,
And she must not speak,   25
Why she dares not come over to thee.

EDGAR: The foul fiend haunts poor Tom in the voice of a nightingale.
Hopdance cries in Tom's belly for two white herring. Croak not
black angel, I have no food for thee:

KENT: How do you sir? Stand you not so amazed.   30
Will you lie down and rest upon the cushions?

LEAR: I'll see their trial first. Bring in their evidence.
Thou robed man of justice, take thy place;
And thou his yoke-fellow of equity,
Bench by his side. [*to* KENT] You are o' th' commission,   35
Sit you too.

EDGAR: Let us deal justly.
Sleepest or wakest thou, jolly shepherd?
Thy sheep be in the corn,
And for one blast of thy minikin mouth   40
Thy sheep shall take no harm.
Purr. The cat is gray.

LEAR: Arraign her first; 'tis Goneril. I here take my oath before this honourable assembly, she kicked the poor King her father.

FOOL: Come hither mistress. Is your name Goneril?   45

LEAR: She cannot deny it.

FOOL: Cry you mercy, I took you for a joint-stool.

LEAR: And here's another whose warped looks proclaim
What store her heart is made on. Stop her there!
Arms, arms, sword, fire! Corruption in the place!   50
False justicer, why hast thou let her 'scape?

EDGAR: Bless thy five wits.

KENT: O pity! Sir, where is the patience now
    That you so oft have boasted to retain?
EDGAR: [*aside*] My tears begin to take his part so much,   55
    They mar my counterfeiting.
LEAR: The little dogs and all,
    Tray, Blanch, and Sweetheart, see, they bark at me.
EDGAR: Tom will throw his head at them. Avaunt you curs!
                    Be thy mouth or black or white,   60
                    Tooth that poisons if it bite;
                    Mastiff, greyhound, mongrel grim,
                    Hound or spaniel, brach or lym,
                    Or bobtail tike or trundle-tail,
                    Tom will make him weep and wail;   65
                    For with throwing thus my head,
                    Dogs leapt the hatch, and all are fled.
    Do de, de, de. Sessa! Come, march to wakes and fairs and market
    towns. Poor Tom, thy horn is dry.
LEAR: Then let them anatomize Regan. See what breeds about her heart.   70
    Is there any cause in nature that makes these hard hearts? [*to* EDGAR]
    You sir, I entertain for one of my hundred; only I do not like the
    fashion of your garments. You will say they are Persian; but let them
    be changed.
KENT: Now good my lord, lie here, and rest awhile.   75
LEAR: Make no noise, make no noise, draw the curtains.
    So, so, we'll go to supper i' th' morning.
FOOL: And I'll go to bed at noon.
        [*Enter* GLOUCESTER.]
GLOUCESTER: Come hither friend. Where is the King my master?
KENT: Here sir, but trouble him not, his wits are gone.   80
GLOUCESTER: Good friend, I prithee take him in thy arms;
    I have o'erheard a plot of death upon him.
    There is a litter ready, lay him in't,
    And drive toward Dover, friend, where thou shalt meet
    Both welcome and protection. Take up thy master.   85
    If thou shouldst dally half an hour, his life,
    With thine, and all that offer to defend him,
    Stand in assured loss. Take up, take up;
    And follow me, that will to some provision
    Give thee quick conduct.   90
KENT: Oppressed nature sleeps.
    This rest might yet have balmed thy broken sinews,
    Which, if convenience will not allow,
    Stand in hard cure. [*to* FOOL] Come help to bear thy master;
    Thou must not stay behind.   95
GLOUCESTER: Come, come away.
        [*Exeunt* KENT, GLOUCESTER, *and* FOOL, *bearing off* LEAR.]

EDGAR: When we our betters see bearing our woes,
We scarcely think our miseries our foes.
Who alone suffers, suffers most i' th' mind,
Leaving free things and happy shows behind;   100
But then the mind much sufferance doth o'erskip,
When grief hath mates, and bearing fellowship.
How light and portable my pain seems now,
When that which makes me bend, makes the King bow—
He childed as I fathered. Tom, away!   105
Mark the high noises; and thy self bewray,
When false opinion, whose wrong thoughts defile thee,
In thy just proof repeals and reconciles thee.
What will hap more to-night, safe 'scape the King.
Lurk, lurk.   110
　　[*Exit.*]

SCENE VII——GLOUCESTER'S *castle.*

　　[*Enter* CORNWALL, REGAN, GONERIL, EDMUND, *and* SERVANTS.]
CORNWALL: Post speedily to my lord your husband; show him this letter
　　—the army of France is landed—seek out the traitor Gloucester.
REGAN: Hang him instantly.
GONERIL: Pluck out his eyes.
CORNWALL: Leave him to my displeasure. Edmund, keep you our sister   5
　　company; the revenges we are bound to take upon your traitorous
　　father are not fit for your beholding. Advise the duke where you are
　　going, to a most festinate preparation; we are bound to the like. Our
　　posts shall be swift and intelligent betwixt us. Farewell dear sister;
　　farewell my Lord of Gloucester.   10
　　[*Enter* OSWALD.]
　　How now? Where's the King?
OSWALD: My Lord of Gloucester hath conveyed him hence.
Some five or six and thirty of his knights,
Hot questrists after him, met him at gate,
Who with some other of the lords dependants,   15
Are gone with him toward Dover; where they boast
To have well armed friends.
CORNWALL:　　　　　　　　　　Get horses for your mistress.
GONERIL: Farewell sweet lord, and sister.
CORNWALL: Edmund farewell.   20
　　[*Exeunt* GONERIL, EDMUND, *and* OSWALD.]
　　　　　　　　　　Go seek the traitor Gloucester,
Pinion him like a thief, bring him before us.
　　[*Exeunt* SERVANTS.]
Though well we may not pass upon his life
Without the form of justice; yet our power

Shall do a court'sy to our wrath, which men   25
May blame, but not control.
    [*Enter* GLOUCESTER, *brought in by* SERVANTS.]
                    Who's there? The traitor?
REGAN: Ingrateful fox, 'tis he.
CORNWALL: Bind fast his corky arms.
GLOUCESTER: What means your Graces? Good my friends,   30
    consider
You are my guests. Do me no foul play, friends.
CORNWALL: Bind him I say.
REGAN: Hard, hard. [*She helps bind him.*] O filthy traitor!
GLOUCESTER: Unmerciful lady as you are, I'm none.   35
COBNWALL: To this chair bind him. Villain, thou shalt
    find—[REGAN *plucks his beard.*]
GLOUCESTER: By the kind gods, 'tis most ignobly done
    To pluck me by the beard.
REGAN: So white, and such a traitor!   40
GLOUCESTER: Naughty lady,
These hairs which thou dost ravish from my chin
Will quicken, and accuse thee. I am your host;
With robbers' hands my hospitable favours
You should not ruffle thus. What will you do?   45
CORNWALL: Come sir, what letters had you late from France?
REGAN: Be simple-answered, for we know the truth.
CORNWALL: And what confederacy have you with the traitors
    Late footed in the kingdom?
REGAN: To whose hands you have sent the lunatic King. Speak.   50
GLOUCESTER: I have a letter guessingly set down,
    Which came from one that's of a neutral heart,
    And not from one opposed.
CORNWALL: Cunning.
REGAN: And false.   55
CORNWALL: Where hast thou sent the King?
GLOUCESTER: To Dover.
REGAN: Wherefore to Dover? Wast thou not charged at peril—
CORNWALL: Wherefore to Dover? Let him answer that.
GLOUCESTER: I am tied to th' stake, and I must stand the course.   60
REGAN: Wherefore to Dover?
GLOUCESTER: Because I would not see thy cruel nails
    Pluck out his poor old eyes; nor thy fierce sister
    In his anointed flesh stick boarish fangs.
    The sea, with such a storm as his bare head   65
    In hell-black night endured, would have buoyed up
    And quenched the stelled fires;
    Yet, poor old heart, he holp the heavens to rain.
    If wolves had at thy gate howled that stern time,
    Thou shouldst have said, good porter turn the key.   70

All cruels else subscribe—but I shall see
The winged vengeance overtake such children.
CORNWALL: See't shalt thou never. Fellows hold the chair.
Upon these eyes of thine I'll set my foot.
GLOUCESTER: He that will think to live till he be old,   75
Give me some help!—O cruel!—O you gods!
REGAN: One side will mock another—th' other too.
CORNWALL: If you see vengeance—
FIRST SERVANT: Hold your hand, my lord.
I have served you ever since I was a child;   80
But better service have I never done you
Than now to bid you hold.
REGAN: How now, you dog!
FIRST SERVANT: If you did wear a beard upon your chin,
I'd shake it on this quarrel. What do you mean?   85
CORNWALL: My villain! [*Draws.*]
FIRST SERVANT: Nay then come on, and take the chance of anger.
[*Draws.* CORNWALL *is wounded.*]
REGAN: Give me thy sword. A peasant stand up thus?
[*Takes a sword from another* SERVANT *and stabs* FIRST SERVANT.]
FIRST SERVANT: O I am slain! My lord, you have one eye left   90
To see some mischief on him. O! [*Dies.*]
CORNWALL: Lest it see more, prevent it—out vile jelly!
Where is thy lustre now?
GLOUCESTER: All dark and comfortless. Where's my son Edmund?
Edmund, enkindle all the sparks of nature   95
To quit this horrid act.
REGAN: Out treacherous villain!
Thous call'st on him that hates thee. It was he
That made the overture of thy treasons to us;
Who is too good to pity thee.   100
GLOUCESTER: O my follies!
Then Edgar was abused.
Kind gods, forgive me that, and prosper him.
REGAN: Go thrust him out at gates, and let him smell
His way to Dover.   105
[*Exit* SERVANT *with* GLOUCESTER.] How is't my lord? How look
you?
CORNWALL: I have received a hurt. Follow me lady.
Turn out that eyeless villain. Throw this slave
Upon the dunghill. Regan, I bleed apace.   110
Untimely comes this hurt. Give me your arm.
[*Exit* CORNWALL, *led by Regan.*]
SECOND SERVANT: I'll never care what wickedness I do,
If this man come to good.
THIRD SERVANT: If she live long,

And in the end meet the old course of death, 115
Women will all turn monsters.
SECOND SERVANT: Let's follow the old earl, and get the bedlam
To lead him where he would; his roguish
madness
Allows itself to any thing. 120
THIRD SERVANT: Go thou. I'll fetch some flax and whites of eggs
To apply to his bleeding face. Now heaven help him.
[*Exeunt severally.*]

ACT IV

SCENE I——*The heath.*

[*Enter Edgar.*]
EDGAR: Yet better thus, and known to be contemned,
Than still contemned and flattered. To be worst,
The lowest and most dejected thing of fortune,
Stands still in esperance, lives not in fear.
The lamentable change is from the best: 5
The worst returns to laughter. Welcome then,
Thou unsubstantial air that I embrace.
The wretch that thou hast blown unto the worst
Owes nothing to thy blasts.
[*Enter* GLOUCESTER, *led by* OLD MAN.]
                    But who comes here? 10
My father, poorly led? World, world, o world!
But that thy strange mutations make us hate thee,
Life would not yield to age.
OLD MAN: O my good lord,
I have been your tenant, and your father's tenant, 15
These fourscore years.
GLOUCESTER: Away, get thee away; good friend be gone.
Thy comforts can do me no good at all;
Thee they may hurt.
OLD MAN: You cannot see your way. 20
GLOUCESTER: I have no way, and therefore want no eyes.
I stumbled when I saw. Full oft 'tis seen,
Our means secure us, and our mere defects
Prove our commodities. O dear son Edgar,
The food of thy abused father's wrath; 25
Might I but live to see thee in my touch,
I'd say I had eyes again.
OLD MAN: How now? Who's there?
EDGAR: [*aside*] O gods! Who is't can say, I am at the worst?
I am worse than e'er I was. 30
OLD MAN: 'Tis poor mad Tom.

EDGAR: [*aside*] And worse I may be yet. The worst is not
    So long as we can say, this is the worst.
OLD MAN: Fellow, where goest?
GLOUCESTER: Is it a beggar-man?   35
OLD MAN: Madman and beggar too.
GLOUCESTER: He has some reason, else he could not beg.
    I' th' last night's storm, I such a fellow saw;
    Which made me think a man a worm. My son
    Came then into my mind, and yet my mind   40
    Was then scarce friends with him. I have heard more since.
    As flies to wanton boys, are we to the gods;
    They kill us for their sport.
EDGAR: [*aside*]   How should this be?
    Bad is the trade that must play fool to sorrow,   45
    Ang'ring itself and others.—Bless thee master.
GLOUCESTER: Is that the naked fellow?
OLD MAN: Ay, my lord.
GLOUCESTER: Then prithee get thee away, if for my sake
    Thou wilt o'ertake us hence a mile or twain   50
    I' th' way toward Dover, do it for ancient love,
    And bring some covering for this naked soul,
    Which I'll entreat to lead me.
OLD MAN: Alack sir, he is mad.
GLOUCESTER: 'Tis the times' plague, when madmen lead the blind.   55
    Do as I bid thee, or rather do thy pleasure.
    Above the rest, be gone.
OLD MAN: I'll bring him the best 'parel that I have,
    Come on't what will.   [*Exit.*]
GLOUCESTER: Sirrah, naked fellow.   60
EDGAR: Poor Tom's a-cold. [*aside*] I cannot daub it further.
GLOUCESTER: Come hither fellow.
EDGAR: [*aside*] And yet I must. Bless thy sweet eyes, they bleed.
GLOUCESTER: Know'st thou the way to Dover?
EDGAR: Both stile, and gate; horse-way, and footpath. Poor Tom hath   65
    been scared out of his good wits. Bless thee good man's son from the
    foul fiend. Five fiends have been in poor Tom at once; of lust, as
    Obidicut; Hobbididence prince of dumbness; Mahu of stealing;
    Modo of murder; and Flibbertigibbet of mopping and mowing, who
    since possesses chambermaids and waiting-women. So, bless thee   70
    master.
GLOUCESTER: Here, take this purse, thou whom the heavens' plagues
    Have humbled to all strokes. That I am wretched
    Makes thee the happier. Heavens, deal so still.
    Let the superfluous and lust-dieted man,   75
    That slaves your ordinance, that will not see
    Because he does not feel, feel your power quickly;

So distribution should undo excess,
And each man have enough. Dost thou know Dover?
EDGAR: Ay master. 80
GLOUCESTER: There is a cliff, whose high and bending head
  Looks fearfully in the confined deep.
  Bring me but to the very brim of it,
  And I'll repair the misery thou dost bear
  With something rich about me. From that place 85
  I shall no leading need.
EDGAR: Give me thy arm;
  Poor Tom shall lead thee.   *[Exeunt.]*

SCENE II——*Before* ALBANY'S *palace.*

[Enter GONERIL *and* EDMUND.]
GONERIL: Welcome my lord, I marvel our mild husband
  Not met us on the way.
     [Enter OSWALD.]
             Now, where's your master?
OSWALD: Madam within; but never man so changed.
  I told him of the army that was landed; 5
  He smiled at it. I told him you were coming;
  His answer was, the worse. Of Gloucester's treachery,
  And of the loyal service of his son,
  When I informed him, then he called me sot,
  And told me I had turned the wrong side out. 10
  What most he should dislike, seems pleasant to him;
  What like, offensive.
GONERIL: *[to* EDMUND]   Then shall you go no further.
  It is the cowish terror of his spirit,
  That dares not undertake. He'll not feel wrongs, 15
  Which tie him to an answer. Our wishes on the way
  May prove effects. Back, Edmund, to my brother.
  Hasten his musters, and conduct his powers,
  I must change names at home, and give the distaff
  Into my husband's hands. This trusty servant 20
  Shall pass between us; ere long you are like to hear,
  If you dare venture in your own behalf,
  A mistress's command. Wear this; spare speech, *[gives a favour.]*
  Decline your head. This kiss, if it durst speak,
  Would stretch thy spirits up into the air. 25
  Conceive, and fare thee well.
EDMUND: Yours, in the ranks of death.
GONERIL: My most dear Gloucester.
    [Exit EDMUND.]
  O, the difference of man and man! To thee
  A woman's services are due; my fool 30
  Usurps my body.

OSWALD: Madam, here comes my lord. [*Exit.*]
    [*Enter Albany.*]
GONERIL: I have been worth the whistle.
ALBANY: O Goneril,
    You are not worth the dust which the rude wind   35
    Blows in your face. I fear your disposition.
    That nature which contemns its origin
    Cannot be bordered certain in itself;
    She that herself will sliver and disbranch
    From her material sap, perforce must wither,   40
    And come to deadly use.
GONERIL: No more; the text is foolish.
ALBANY: Wisdom and goodness to the vile seem vile,
    Filths savour but themselves. What have you done?
    Tigers, not daughters, what have you performed?   45
    A father, and a gracious aged man,
    Whose reverence even the head-lugged bear would lick,
    Most barbarous, most degenerate, have you madded.
    Could my good brother suffer you to do it?
    A man, a Prince, by him so benefited.   50
    If that the heavens do not their visible spirits
    Send quickly down to tame these vile offences,
    It will come,
    Humanity must perforce prey on itself,
    Like monsters of the deep.   55
GONERIL: Milk-livered man,
    That bear'st a cheek for blows, a head for wrongs,
    Who hast not in thy brows an eye discerning
    Thine honour from thy suffering, that not know'st
    Fools do those villains pity who are punished   60
    Ere they have done their mischief. Where's thy drum?
    France spreads his banners in our noiseless land
    With plumed helm. Thy state begins to threat,
    Whilst thou a moral fool sits still and cries,
    Alack why does he so?   65
ALBANY: See thyself, devil.
    Proper deformity shows not in the fiend
    So horrid as in woman.
GONERIL: O vain fool.
ALBANY: Thou changed and self-covered thing, for shame   70
    Be-monster not thy feature. Were't my fitness
    To let these hands obey my blood,
    They are apt enough to dislocate and tear
    Thy flesh and bones. Howe'er thou art a fiend,
    A woman's shape doth shield thee.   75
GONERIL: Marry, your manhood—mew!
    [*Enter* MESSENGER.]

ALBANY: What news?

MESSENGER: O my good lord, the Duke of Cornwall's dead,
Slain by his servant, going to put out
The other eye of Gloucester.   80

ALBANY: Gloucester's eyes!

MESSENGER: A servant that he bred, thrilled with remorse,
Opposed against the act; bending his sword
To his great master, who thereat enraged,
Flew on him, and amongst them felled him dead,   85
But not without that harmful stroke which since
Hath plucked him after.

ALBANY: This shows you are above,
You justicers, that these our nether crimes
So speedily can venge. But, o poor Gloucester,   90
Lost he his other eye?

MESSENGER: Both, both, my lord.
This letter, madam, craves a speedy answer;
'Tis from your sister.

GONERIL: [*aside*] One way I like this well.   95
But being widow, and my Gloucester with her,
May all the building in my fancy pluck
Upon my hateful life. Another way
The news is not so tart.—I'll read, and answer. [*Exit.*]

ALBANY: Where was his son, when they did take his eyes?   100

MESSENGER: Come with my lady hither.

ALBANY: He is not here.

MESSENGER: No my good lord, I met him back again.

ALBANY: Knows he the wickedness?

MESSENGER: Ay my good lord; 'twas he informed against him, 105
And quit the house on purpose, that their punishment
Might have the freer course.

ALBANY: Gloucester, I live
To thank thee for the love thou show'dst the King,
And to revenge thine eyes. Come hither friend,   110
Tell me what more thou know'st.   [*Exeunt.*]

SCENE III——*The French camp, near Dover.*

[*Enter* KENT *and* GENTLEMAN.]

KENT: Why the King of France is so suddenly gone back, know you no
reason?

GENTLEMAN: Something he left imperfect in the state, which since his
coming forth is thought of; which imports to the kingdom so much
fear and danger, that his personal return was most required and   5
necessary.

KENT: Who hath he left behind him general?

GENTLEMAN: The Marshal of France Monsieur La Far.

KENT: Did your letters pierce the Queen to any demonstration of grief?

GENTLEMAN: Ay sir, she took them, read them in my presence,   10
    And now and then an ample tear trilled down
    Her delicate cheek; it seemed she was a queen
    Over her passion, who most rebel-like,
    Sought to be king o'er her.
KENT: O then it moved her.   15
GENTLEMAN: Not to a rage; patience and sorrow strove
    Who should express her goodliest. You have seen
    Sunshine and rain at once; her smiles and tears
    Were like a better way; those happy smilets
    That played on her ripe lip seemed not to know   20
    What guests were in her eyes, which parted thence
    As pearls from diamonds dropped. In brief,
    Sorrow would be a rarity most beloved,
    If all could so become it.
KENT: Made she no verbal question?   25
GENTLEMAN: Faith once or twice she heaved the name of father
    Pantingly forth, as if it pressed her heart;
    Cried, sisters, sisters, shame of ladies, sisters!
    Kent! Father! Sisters! What, i' th' storm? I' th' night?
    Let pity not be believed. There she shook   30
    The holy water from her heavenly eyes,
    And clamour-moistened; then away she started
    To deal with grief alone.
KENT: It is the stars,
    The stars above us govern our conditions,   35
    Else one self mate and make could not beget
    Such different issues. You spoke not with her since?
GENTLEMAN: No.
KENT: Was this before the King returned?
GENTLEMAN: No, since.   40
KENT: Well sir, the poor distressed Lear's i' th' town,
    Who sometime in his better tune remembers
    What we are come about, and by no means
    Will yield to see his daughter.
GENTLEMAN: Why, good sir?   45
KENT: A sovereign shame so elbows him; his own unkindness
    That stripped her from his benediction, turned her
    To foreign casualties, gave her dear rights
    To his dog-hearted daughters, these things sting
    His mind so venomously that burning shame   50
    Detains him from Cordelia.
GENTLEMAN: Alack poor gentleman!
KENT: Of Albany's and Cornwall's powers you heard not?
GENTLEMAN: 'Tis so, they are afoot.
KENT: Well sir, I'll bring you to our master Lear,   55
    And leave you to attend him. Some dear cause
    Will in concealment wrap me up awhile;

When I am known aright you shall not grieve,
Lending me this acquaintance. I pray you go
Along with me. [*Exeunt.*] 60

SCENE IV——*The same.*

[*Enter, with drum and colours,* CORDELIA, DOCTOR, *and* SOL-
DIERS.]
CORDELIA: Alack, 'tis he; why he was met even now
As mad as the vexed sea, singing aloud,
Crowned with rank fumiter and furrow-weeds,
With hardocks, hemlock, nettles, cuckoo-flowers,
Darnel, and all the idle weeds that grow 5
In our sustaining corn. A century send forth;
Search every acre in the high-grown field,
And bring him to our eye. [*Exit* OFFICER.] What can man's wisdom
In the restoring his bereaved sense?
He that helps him take all my outward worth. 10
DOCTOR: There is means madam.
Our foster-nurse of nature is repose,
The which he lacks; that to provoke in him
Are many simples operative, whose power
Will close the eye of anguish. 15
CORDELIA: All blessed secrets,
All you unpublished virtues of the earth,
Spring with my tears, be aidant and remediate
In the good man's distress. Seek, seek for him,
Lest his ungoverned rage dissolve the life 20
That wants the means to lead it.
[*Enter* MESSENGER.]
MESSENGER: News madam;
The British powers are marching hitherward.
CORDELIA: 'Tis known before. Our preparation stands
In expectation of them. O dear father, 25
It is thy business that I go about;
Therefore great France
My mourning and importuned tears hath pitied.
No blown ambition doth our arms incite,
But love, dear love, and our aged father's right. 30
Soon may I hear, and see him. [*Exeunt.*]

SCENE V——GLOUCESTER'S *castle.*

[*Enter* REGAN *and* OSWALD.]
REGAN: But are my brother's powers set forth?
OSWALD: Ay madam.
REGAN: Himself in person there?

OSWALD: Madam, with much ado.
   Your sister is the better soldier.   5
REGAN: Lord Edmund spake not with your lord at home?
OSWALD: No madam.
REGAN: What might import my sister's letter to him?
OSWALD: I know not, lady.
REGAN: Faith, he is posted hence on serious matter.   10
   It was great ignorance, Gloucester's eyes being out,
   To let him live. Where he arrives, he moves
   All hearts against us. Edmund, I think, is gone,
   In pity of his misery, to dispatch
   His nighted life; moreover to descry   15
   The strength o' th' enemy.
OSWALD: I must needs after him, madam, with my letter.
REGAN: Our troops set forth to-morrow, stay with us.
   The ways are dangerous.
OSWALD: I may not madam.   20
   My lady charged my duty in this business.
REGAN: Why should she write to Edmund? Might not you
   Transport her purposes by word? Belike,
   Something, I know not what—I'll love thee much,
   Let me unseal the letter.   25
OSWALD: Madam, I had rather—
REGAN: I know your lady does not love her husband,
   I am sure of that; and at her late being here
   She gave strange œillades and most speaking looks
   To noble Edmund. I know you are of her bosom.   30
OSWALD: I, madam?
REGAN: I speak in understanding; y'are, I know't,
   Therefore I do advise you take this note.
   My lord is dead; Edmund and I have talked,
   And more convenient is he for my hand   35
   Than for your lady's. You may gather more.
   If you do find him, pray you give him this;
   And when your mistress hears thus much from you,
   I pray, desire her call her wisdom to her.
   So fare you well.   40
   If you do chance to hear of that blind traitor,
   Preferment falls on him that cuts him off.
OSWALD: Would I could meet him madam, I should show
   What party I do follow.
REGAN: Fare thee well.   [*Exeunt.*]   45

SCENE VI——*The country near Dover.*

[*Enter* GLOUCESTER, *and* EDGAR *dressed like a peasant.*]
GLOUCESTER: When shall I come to th' top of that same hill?
EDGAR: You do climb up it now. Look how we labour.

GLOUCESTER: Methinks the ground is even.

EDGAR: Horrible steep.
 Hark, do you hear the sea?   5

GLOUCESTER: No truly.

EDGAR: Why then your other senses grow imperfect
 By your eyes' anguish.

GLOUCESTER: So may it be indeed.
 Methinks thy voice is altered, and thou speak'st   10
 In better phrase and matter than thou didst.

EDGAR: Y'are much deceived. In nothing am I changed
 But in my garments.

GLOUCESTER: Methinks y'are better spoken.

EDGAR: Come on sir, here's the place; stand still. How fearful   15
 And dizzy 'tis, to cast one's eyes so low.
 The crows and choughs that wing the midway air
 Show scarce so gross as beetles. Half way down
 Hangs one that gathers samphire—dreadful trade.
 Methinks he seems no bigger than his head.   20
 The fishermen, that walk upon the beach,
 Appear like mice; and yond tall anchoring bark,
 Diminished to her cock; her cock, a buoy
 Almost too small for sight. The murmuring surge,
 That on th' unnumbered idle pebble chafes,   25
 Cannot be heard so high. I'll look no more,
 Lest my brain turn, and the deficient sight
 Topple down headlong.

GLOUCESTER: Set me where you stand.

EDGAR: Give me your hand. You are now within a foot   30
 Of th' extreme verge. For all beneath the moon
 Would I not leap upright.

GLOUCESTER: Let go my hand.
 Here friend's another purse; in it a jewel
 Well worth a poor man's taking. Fairies and gods   35
 Prosper it with thee. Go thou further off,
 Bid me farewell, and let me hear thee going.

EDGAR: Now fare ye well, good sir.

GLOUCESTER: With all my heart.

EDGAR: [*aside*] Why I do trifle thus with his despair,   40
 Is done to cure it.

GLOUCESTER: [*kneels*] O you mighty gods!
 This world I do renounce, and in your sights
 Shake patiently my great affliction off.
 If I could bear it longer, and not fall   45
 To quarrel with your great opposeless wills,
 My snuff and loathed part of nature should
 Burn itself out. If Edgar live, o bless him.
 Now fellow, fare thee well.

EDGAR: Gone sir—farewell.   50
　　　　[*Gloucester falls forward.*]
　　　　[*aside*] And yet I know not how conceit may rob
　　　　The treasury of life, when life itself
　　　　Yields to the theft. Had he been where he thought,
　　　　By this had thought been past. Alive or dead?—
　　　　Ho, you sir! Friend! Hear you sir, speak.   55
　　　　[*aside*] Thus might he pass indeed; yet he revives.—
　　　　What are you sir?
GLOUCESTER: Away, and let me die.
EDGAR: Hadst thou been aught but gossamer, feathers, air,
　　　　So many fathom down precipitating,   60
　　　　Thou'dst shivered like an egg; but thou dost breathe.
　　　　Hast heavy substance, bleed'st not, speak'st, art sound.
　　　　Ten masts at each make not the altitude
　　　　Which thou hast perpendicularly fell.
　　　　Thy life's miracle. Speak yet again.   65
GLOUCESTER: But have I fall'n or no?
EDGAR: From the dread summit of this chalky bourn.
　　　　Look up a height, the shrill-gorged lark so far
　　　　Cannot be seen or heard; do but look up.
GLOUCESTER: Alack, I have no eyes.   70
　　　　Is wretchedness deprived that benefit
　　　　To end itself by death? 'Twas yet some comfort,
　　　　When misery could beguile the tyrant's rage,
　　　　And frustrate his proud will.
EDGAR: Give me your arm.   75
　　　　Up. So. How is't? Feel you your legs? You stand.
GLOUCESTER: Too well, too well.
EDGAR: This is above all strangeness.
　　　　Upon the crown o' th' cliff, what thing was that
　　　　Which parted from you?   80
GLOUCESTER: A poor unfortunate beggar.
EDGAR: As I stood here below, methought his eyes
　　　　Were two full moons; he had a thousand noses,
　　　　Horns whelked and waved like the enridged sea.
　　　　It was some fiend. Therefore thou happy father,   85
　　　　Think that the clearest gods, who make them honours
　　　　Of men's impossibilities, have preserved thee.
GLOUCESTER: I do remember now; henceforth I'll bear
　　　　Affliction, till it do cry out itself,
　　　　Enough, enough, and die. That thing you speak of,   90
　　　　I took it for a man; often 'twould say,
　　　　The fiend, the fiend; he led me to that place.
EDGAR: Bear free and patient thoughts.
　　　　　　[*Enter* LEAR, *his hat bedecked with weeds and flowers.*]
　　　　　　　　　　　　But who comes here?

The safer sense will ne'er accommodate   95
   His master thus.
LEAR: No, they cannot touch me for coming; I am the King himself.
EDGAR: [*aside*] O thou side-piercing sight!
LEAR: Nature's above art in that respect. There's your press-money. That
   fellow handles his bow like a crow-keeper; draw me a clothier's yard.   100
   Look, look, a mouse! Peace, peace, this piece of toasted cheese will
   do't. There's my gauntlet, I'll prove it on a giant. Bring up the
   brown bills. O well flown, bird; i' th' clout, i' th' clout. Hewgh!
   Give the word.
EDGAR: Sweet marjoram.   105
LEAR: Pass.
GLOUCESTER: I know that voice.
LEAR: Ha! Goneril with a white beard! They flattered me like a dog, and
   told me I had white hairs in my beard, ere the black ones were there.
   To say ay, and no, to everything that I said! Ay, and no too, was no   110
   good divinity. When the rain came to wet me once, and the wind to
   make me chatter; when the thunder would not peace at my bidding;
   there I found 'em, there I smelt 'em out. Go to, they are not men
   o' their words; they told me I was every thing. 'Tis a lie, I am not
   ague-proof.   115
GLOUCESTER: The trick of that voice I do well remember;
   Is't not the King?
LEAR: Ay, every inch a King:
   When I do stare, see how the subject quakes.
   I pardon that man's life. What was thy cause?   120
   Adultery?
   Thou shalt not die. Die for adultery? No,
   The wren goes to't, and the small gilded fly
   Does lecher in my sight.
   Let copulation thrive; for Gloucester's bastard son   125
   Was kinder to his father than my daughters
   Got 'tween the lawful sheets.
   To't luxury pell-mell, for I lack soldiers.
   Behold yond simpering dame,
   Whose face between her forks presages snow,   130
   That minces virtue, and does shake the head
   To hear of pleasure's name—
   The fitchew nor the soiled horse goes to't
   With a more riotous appetite.
   Down from the waist they are centaurs,   135
   Though women all above;
   But to the girdle do the gods inherit,
   Beneath is all the fiends';
   There's hell, there's darkness, there is the sulphurous pit,
   Burning, scalding, stench, consumption. Fie, fie, fie; pah, pah! Give   140

me an ounce of civet; good apothecary sweeten my imagination.
There's money for thee.

GLOUCESTER: O let me kiss that hand.

LEAR: Let me wipe it first, it smells of mortality.

GLOUCESTER: O ruined piece of nature; this great world   145
    Shall so wear out to naught. Dost thou know me?

LEAR: I remember thine eyes well enough. Dost thou
    squint at me? No, do thy worst blind Cupid, I'll not love. Read thou
    this challenge; mark but the penning of it.

GLOUCESTER: Were all thy letters suns, I could not see one.   150

EDGAR: [aside] I would not take this from report—it is,
    And my heart breaks at it.

LEAR: Read.

GLOUCESTER: What, with the case of eyes?

LEAR: O ho, are you there with me? No eyes in your head, nor no money   155
    in your purse? Your eyes are in a heavy case, your purse in a light,
    yet you see how this world goes.

GLOUCESTER: I see it feelingly.

LEAR: What, art mad? A man may see how this world goes, with no eyes.
    Look with thine ears. See how yond justice rails upon yond simple   160
    thief. Hark in thine ear. Change places; and handy-dandy, which is
    the justice, which is the thief? Thou hast seen a farmer's dog bark
    at a beggar?

GLOUCESTER: Ay sir.

LEAR: An the creature run from the cur, there thou mightst behold the   165
    great image of authority—a dog's obeyed in office.
    Thou, rascal beadle, hold thy bloody hand;
    Why dost thou lash that whore? Strip thine own back;
    Thou hotly lusts to use her in that kind
    For which thou whipst her. The usurer hangs the cozener.   170
    Through tattered clothes small vices do appear;
    Robes and furred gowns hide all. Plate sin with gold,
    And the strong lance of justice hurtless breaks.
    Arm it in rags, a pigmy's straw does pierce it.
    None does offend, none—I say, none; I'll able 'em.   175
    Take that of me, my friend, who have the power
    To seal the accuser's lips. Get thee glass eyes,
    And like a scurvy politician, seem
    To see the things thou dost not.—Now, now, now, now.
    Pull off my boots; harder, harder; so.   180

EDGAR: [aside] O matter and impertinency mixed;
    Reason in madness.

LEAR: If thou wilt weep my fortunes, take my eyes.
    I know thee well enough, thy name is Gloucester.
    Thou must be patient; we came crying hither.   185
    Thou know'st, the first time that we smell the air
    We wawl, and cry. I will preach to thee. Mark. [*Takes off his hat.*]

GLOUCESTER: Alack, alack the day!
LEAR: When we are born, we cry that we are come
    To this great stage of fools.—This' a good block;   190
    It were a delicate stratagem to shoe
    A troop of horse with felt. I'll put't in proof,
    And when I have stol'n upon these son-in-laws,
    Then, kill, kill, kill, kill, kill, kill!
       [*Enter* GENTLEMAN, *with* ATTENDANTS.]
GENTLEMAN: O here he is; lay hand upon him. Sir,   195
    Your most dear daughter—
LEAR: No rescue? What, a prisoner? I am even
    The natural fool of fortune. Use me well,
    You shall have ransom. Let me have surgeons,
    I am cut to th' brains   200
GETLEMAN: You shall have any thing.
LEAR: No seconds? All myself?
    Why, this would make a man a man of salt,
    To use his eyes for garden water-pots,
    Ay and laying autumn's dust.   205
GENTLEMAN: Good sir—
LEAR: I will die bravely, like a smug bridegroom. What!
    I will be jovial. Come, come, I am a King
    My masters; know you that.
GENTLEMAN: You are a royal one, and we obey you.   210
LEAR: Then there's life in't. Come, an you get it, you shall get it by run-
    ning. Sa, sa, sa, sa. [*Exit running.* ATTENDANTS *follow.*]
GENTLEMAN: A sight most pitiful in the meanest wretch,
    Past speaking of in a King. Thou hast a daughter,
    Who redeems nature from the general curse   215
    Which twain have brought her to.
EDGAR: Hail gentle sir.
GENTLEMAN: Sir, speed you. What's your will?
EDGAR: Do you hear aught, sir, of a battle toward?
GENTLEMAN: Most sure, and vulgar. Every one hears that,   220
    Which can distinguish sound.
EDGAR: But by your favour;
    How near's the other army?
GENTLEMAN: Near, and on speedy foot; the main descry
    Stands on the hourly thought.   225
EDGAR: I thank you sir, that's all.
GENTLEMAN: Though that the Queen on special cause is here,
    Her army is moved on.
EDGAR: I thank you sir.
       [*Exit* GENTLEMAN.]
GLOUCESTER: You ever gentle gods, take my breath from me;   230
    Let not my worser spirit tempt me again
    To die before you please.

EDGAR: Well pray you, father.
GLOUCESTER: Now good sir, what are you?
EDGAR: A most poor man, made tame to fortune's blows;   235
    Who, by the art of known and feeling sorrows,
    Am pregnant to good pity. Give me your hand,
    I'll lead you to some biding.
GLOUCESTER: Hearty thanks.
    The bounty and the benison of heaven   240
    To boot, and boot.
      [*Enter* OSWALD.]
OSWALD: A proclaimed prize; most happy!
    That eyeless head of thine was first framed flesh
    To raise my fortunes. Thou old unhappy traitor,
    Briefly thyself remember—the sword is out   245
    That must destroy thee.
GLOUCESTER: Now let thy friendly hand
    Put strength enough to't.
      [EDGAR *interposes.*]
OSWALD: Wherefore, bold peasant,
    Dar'st thou support a published traitor? Hence,   250
    Lest that th' infection of his fortune take
    Like hold on thee. Let go his arm.
EDGAR: Chill not let go zir, without vurther 'casion.
OSWALD: Let go slave, or thou diest.
EDGAR: Good gentleman go your gait, and let poor volk pass. An chud ha'   255
    bin zwaggered out of my life, 'twould not ha' bin zo long as 'tis, by a
    vortnight. Nay, come not near th' old man; keep out che vor ye, or
    ise try whether your costard or my ballow be the harder; chill be
    plain with you.
OSWALD: Out dunghill! [*Thrusts at him.*]   260
EDGAR: Chill pick your teeth zir; come, no matter vor your foins.
      [*They fight.* OSWALD *falls.*]
OSWALD: Slave thou hast slain me. Villain, take my purse;
    If ever thou wilt thrive, bury my body,
    And give the letters which thou find'st about me
    To Edmund earl of Gloucester; seek him out   265
    Upon the English party. O untimely death!
    Death!   [*Dies.*]
EDGAR: I know thee well. A serviceable villain,
    As duteous to the vices of thy mistress
    As badness would desire.
GLOUCESTER: What, is he dead?   270
EDGAR: Sit down father; rest you.
    Let's see these pockets; the letters that he speaks of
    May be my friends. He's dead; I am only sorry
    He had no other deathsman. Let us see.
    Leave, gentle wax; and manners, blame us not.   275

To know our enemies' minds, we'd rip their hearts;
Their papers is more lawful. [*Reads.*]
   Let our reciprocal vows be remembered. You have many oppor-
tunities to cut him off: if your will want not, time and place will be
fruitfully offered. There is nothing done, if he return the conqueror: 280
then am I the prisoner and his bed my gaol; from the loathed
warmth whereof deliver me, and supply the place for your labour.
        Your—wife, so I would say—
          Affectionate servant,
              Goneril. 285
O indistinguished space of woman's will!
A plot upon her virtuous husband's life,
And the exchange my brother. Here in the sands,
Thee I'll rake up, the post unsanctified
Of murderous lechers; and in the mature time, 290
With this ungracious paper strike the sight
Of the death-practised duke. For him 'tis well,
That of thy death and business I can tell.
GLOUCESTER: The King is mad: how stiff is my vile sense,
That I stand up, and have ingenious feeling 295
Of my huge sorrows! Better I were distract;
So should my thoughts be severed from my griefs,
And woes, by wrong imaginations, lose
The knowledge of themselves.
    [*Drum afar off.*]
EDGAR: Give me your hand. 300
Far off methinks I hear the beaten drum.
Come father, I'll bestow you with a friend. [*Exeunt.*]

      SCENE VII——*Before a tent in the French camp.*

[*Enter* CORDELIA *and* KENT. DOCTOR *and* GENTLEMAN *follow.*]
CORDELIA: O thou good Kent, how shall I live and work,
To match thy goodness? My life will be too short,
And every measure fail me.
KENT: To be acknowledged madam, is o'erpaid.
All my reports go with the modest truth; 5
Nor more, nor clipped, but so.
CORDELIA: Be better suited;
These weeds are memories of those worser hours.
I prithee put them off.
KENT: Pardon dear madam,
Yet to be known shortens my made intent. 10
My boon I make it, that you know me not
Till time and I think meet.
CORDELIA: Then be't so my good lord. [*to* DOCTOR] How does the King?
DOCTOR: Madam, sleeps still.

CORDELIA: O you kind gods,   15
    Cure this great breach in his abused nature.
    Th' untuned and jarring senses, o wind up
    Of this child-changed father.
DOCTOR: So please your Majesty
    That we may wake the King? He hath slept long.   20
CORDELIA: Be governed by your knowledge, and proceed
    I' th' sway of your own will. Is he arrayed?
GENTLEMAN: Ay madam, in the heaviness of sleep
    We put fresh garments on him.
DOCTOR: Be by, good madam, when we do awake him.   25
    I doubt not of his temperance.
CORDELIA: Very well.
DOCTOR: Please you draw near.—Louder the music there.
       [*Music.* DOCTOR *draws curtains.* LEAR *discovered on a couch.*]
CORDELIA: O my dear father! Restoration hang
    Thy medicine on my lips, and let this kiss   30
    Repair those violent harms that my two sisters
    Have in thy reverence made.
KENT: Kind and dear Princess.
CORDELIA: Had you not been their father, these white flakes
    Did challenge pity of them. Was this a face   35
    To be opposed against the warring winds,
    To stand against the deep dread-bolted thunder,
    In the most terrible and nimble stroke
    Of quick, cross lightning, to watch—poor perdu—
    With this thin helm? Mine enemy's dog,   40
    Though he had bit me, should have stood that night
    Against my fire; and wast thou fain, poor father,
    To hovel thee with swine and rogues forlorn,
    In short and musty straw? Alack, alack,
    'Tis wonder that thy life and wits at once   45
    Had not concluded all. He wakes, speak to him.
DOCTOR: Madam do you, 'tis fittest.
CORDELIA: How does my royal lord? How fares your Majesty?
LEAR: You do me wrong to take me out o' th' grave.
    Thou art a soul in bliss, but I am bound   50
    Upon a wheel of fire, that mine own tears
    Do scald like molten lead.
CORDELIA: Sir, do you know me?
LEAR: You are a spirit, I know; where did you die?
CORDELIA: Still, still, far wide.   55
DOCTOR: He's scarce awake, let him alone awhile.
LEAR: Where have I been? Where am I? Fair daylight?
    I am mightily abused; I should e'en die with pity,
    To see another thus. I know not what to say.
    I will not swear these are my hands; let's see—   60

I feel this pin prick. Would I were assured
Of my condition.

CORDELIA: O look upon me sir.
And hold your hands in benediction o'er me—
No, sir, you must not kneel. 65

LEAR: Pray do not mock me.
I am a very foolish fond old man,
Fourscore and upward, not an hour more nor less;
And to deal plainly,
I fear I am not in my perfect mind. 70
Methinks I should know you, and know this man,
Yet I am doubtful. For I am mainly ignorant
What place this is; and all the skill I have
Remembers not these garments; nor I know not
Where I did lodge last night. Do not laugh at me, 75
For as I am a man, I think this lady
To be my child Cordelia.

CORDELIA: And so I am—I am.

LEAR: Be your tears wet? Yes faith. I pray weep not.
If you have poison for me, I will drink it. 80
I know you do not love me, for your sisters
Have, as I do remember, done me wrong.
You have some cause, they have not.

CORDELIA: No cause, no cause.

LEAR: Am I in France? 85

KENT: In your own kingdom sir.

LEAR: Do not abuse me.

DOCTOR: Be comforted good madam, the great rage,
You see, is killed in him: and yet it is danger
To make him even o'er the time he has lost. 90
Desire him to go in, trouble him no more
Till further settling.

CORDELIA: Will't please your Highness walk?

LEAR: You must bear with me.
Pray you now forget, and forgive; I am old and foolish. 95
[Exeunt all but KENT and GENTLEMAN.]

GENTLEMAN: Holds it true sir, that the Duke of Cornwall was so slain?

KENT: Most certain sir.

GENTLEMAN: Who is conductor of his people?

KENT: As 'tis said, the bastard son of Gloucester.

GENTLEMAN: They say Edgar his banished son is with the Earl of Kent in 100
Germany.

KENT: Report is changeable. 'Tis time to look about, the powers of the
kingdom approach apace.

GENTLEMAN: The arbitrement is like to be bloody. Fare you well sir. [Exit.]

KENT: My point and period will be thoroughly wrought, 105
Or well, or ill, as this day's battle's fought. [Exit]

ACT V.

SCENE I——*The British camp, near Dover.*

[*Enter, with drum and colours,* EDMUND, REGAN, GENTLEMEN, *and* SOLDIERS.]

EDMUND: Know of the duke if his last purpose hold,
    Or whether since he is advised by aught
    To change the course. He's full of alteration,
    And self-reproving. Bring his constant pleasure.
        [*Exit* GENTLEMAN.]

REGAN: Our sister's man is certainly miscarried.   5
EDMUND: 'Tis to be doubted madam.
REGAN: Now sweet lord,
    You know the goodness I intend upon you:
    Tell me—but truly—but then speak the truth—
    Do you not love my sister?   10
EDMUND: In honoured love.
REGAN: But have you never found my brother's way,
    To the forfended place?
EDMUND: That thought abuses you.
REGAN: I am doubtful that you have been conjunct   15
    And bosomed with her, as far as we call hers.
EDMUND: No by mine honour, madam.
REGAN: I never shall endure her. Dear my lord
    Be not familiar with her.
EDMUND: Fear me not,   20
    She and the duke her husband—
        [*Enter, with drum and colours,* ALBANY, GONERIL, *and* SOLDIERS.]
GONERIL: [*aside*] I had rather lose the battle, than that sister
    Should loosen him and me.
ALBANY: Our very loving sister, well be-met.
    Sir, this I heard, the King is come to his daughter,   25
    With others whom the rigour of our state
    Forced to cry out. Where I could not be honest,
    I never yet was valiant. For this business,
    It touches us, as France invades our land,
    Not bolds the King, with others whom I fear   30
    Most just and heavy causes make oppose.
EDMUND: Sir you speak nobly.
REGAN: Why is this reasoned?
GONERIL: Combine together 'gainst the enemy;
    For these domestic and particular broils   35
    Are not the question here.
ALBANY: Let's then determine
    With th' ancient of war on our proceeding.
EDMUND: I shall attend you presently at your tent.

REGAN: Sister, you'll go with us? 40
GONERIL: No.
REGAN: 'Tis most convenient, pray you go with us.
GONERIL: [*aside*] O ho, I know the riddle.—I will go.
       [*As they are going out, enter* EDGAR *disguised.*]
EDGAR: If e'er your Grace had speech with man so poor,
    Hear me one word. 45
ALBANY: I'll overtake you.—Speak.
       [*Exeunt all but* ALBANY *and* EDGAR.]
EDGAR: Before you fight the battle, ope this letter.
    If you have victory, let the trumpet sound
    For him that brought it. Wretched though I seem,
    I can produce a champion that will prove 50
    What is avouched there. If you miscarry,
    Your business of the world hath so an end,
    And machination ceases. Fortune love you.
ALBANY: Stay till I have read the letter.
EDGAR: I was forbid it. 55
    When time shall serve, let but the herald cry,
    And I'll appear again.
ALBANY: Why fare thee well, I will o'erlook thy paper.
       [*Exit* EDGAR. *Enter* EDMUND.]
EDMUND: The enemy's in view, draw up your powers.
    Here is the guess of their true strength and forces, 60
    By diligent discovery, but your haste
    Is now urged on you.
ALBANY: We will greet the time. [*Exit.*]
EDMUND: To both these sisters have I sworn my love;
    Each jealous of the other, as the stung 65
    Are of the adder. Which of them shall I take?
    Both? One? Or neither? Neither can be enjoyed,
    If both remain alive. To take the widow,
    Exasperates, makes mad her sister Goneril,
    And hardly shall I carry out my side, 70
    Her husband being alive. Now then, we'll use
    His countenance for the battle, which being done,
    Let her who would be rid of him devise
    His speedy taking off. As for the mercy
    Which he intends to Lear and to Cordelia, 75
    The battle done, and they within our power,
    Shall never see his pardon; for my state
    Stands on me to defend, not to debate. [*Exit.*]

SCENE II——*A field between the two camps.*

[*Alarum within. Enter, with drum and colours,* LEAR, CORDELIA,
and SOLDIERS *over the stage and exeunt. Enter* EDGAR *and*
GLOUCESTER.]

EDGAR: Here father, take the shadow of this tree
    For your good host; pray that the right may thrive.
    If ever I return to you again,
    I'll bring you comfort.
GLOUCESTER: Grace go with you sir.   5
    [*Exit* EDGAR. *Alarum and retreat within. Enter* EDGAR.]
EDGAR: Away old man, give me thy hand, away!
    King Lear hath lost, he and his daughter ta'en.
    Given me thy hand. Come on.
GLOUCESTER: No further sir, a man may rot even here.
EDGAR: What, in ill thoughts again? Men must endure   10
    Their going hence, even as their coming hither;
    Ripeness is all. Come on.
GLOUCESTER: And that's true too.   [*Exeunt.*]

SCENE III——*The British camp, near Dover.*

[*Enter, in conquest, with drum and colours,* EDMUND; LEAR *and*
    CORDELIA *as prisoners;* GENTLEMAN, CAPTAIN, *and* SOLDIERS.]
EDMUND: Some officers take them away; good guard,
    Until their greater pleasures first be known
    That are to censure them.
CORDELIA: We are not the first
    Who with best meaning have incurred the worst.   5
    For thee, oppressed King, am I cast down,
    Myself could else out-frown false fortune's frown.
    Shall we not see these daughters, and these sisters?
LEAR: No, no, no, no; come let's away to prison:
    We two alone will sing like birds i' th' cage.   10
    When thou dost ask me blessing, I'll kneel down,
    And ask of thee forgiveness. So we'll live,
    And pray, and sing, and tell old tales, and laugh
    At gilded butterflies; and hear poor rogues
    Talk of court news, and we'll talk with them too,   15
    Who loses, and who wins, who's in, who's out;
    And take upon's the mystery of things,
    As if we were God's spies. And we'll wear out
    In a walled prison, packs and sects of great ones,
    That ebb and flow by th' moon.   20
EDMUND: Take them away.
LEAR: Upon such sacrifices my Cordelia,
    The gods themselves throw incense. Have I caught thee?
    He that parts us shall bring a brand from heaven,
    And fire us hence like foxes. Wipe thine eyes;   25
    The good-years shall devour them, flesh and fell,
    Ere they shall make us weep. We'll see 'em starved first. Come.
    [*Exeunt* LEAR *and* CORDELIA, *guarded.*]

EDMUND: Come hither captain, hark.
   Take thou this note, go follow them to prison.
   One step I have advanced thee, if thou dost   30
   As this instructs thee, thou dost make thy way
   To noble fortunes. Know thou this, that men
   Are as the time is; to be tender-minded
   Does not become a sword. Thy great employment
   Will not bear question; either say thou'lt do't,   35
   Or thrive by other means.
CAPTAIN: I'll do't my lord.
EDMUND: About it, and write happy when th'hast done.
   Mark, I say instantly, and carry it so
   As I have set it down.   40
CAPTAIN: I cannot draw a cart, nor eat dried oats.
   If it be man's work, I'll do't.   *[Exit.]*
     [*Flourish. Enter* ALBANY, GONERIL, REGAN, GENTLEMEN, *and*
     SOLDIERS.]
ALBANY: Sir, you have showed to-day your valiant strain,
   And fortune led you well; you have the captives
   Who were the opposites of this day's strife.   45
   We do require them of you, so to use them
   As we shall find their merits and our safety
   May equally determine.
EDMUND: Sir, I thought it fit
   To send the old and miserable King   50
   To some retention and appointed guard;
   Whose age has charms in it, whose title more,
   To pluck the common bosom on his side,
   And turn our impressed lances in our eyes
   Which do command them. With him I sent the Queen;   55
   My reason all the same; and they are ready
   To-morrow, or at further space, t' appear
   Where you shall hold your session. At this time
   We sweat and bleed; the friend hath lost his friend,
   And the best quarrels in the heat are cursed   60
   By those that feel their sharpness.
   The question of Cordelia and her father
   Requires a fitter place.
ALBANY: Sir by your patience,
   I hold you but a subject of this war,   65
   Not as a brother.
REGAN: That's as we list to grace him.
   Methinks our pleasure might have been demanded,
   Ere you had spoke so far. He led our powers,
   Bore the commission of my place and person,   70
   The which immediately may well stand up
   And call itself your brother.

GONERIL: Not so hot.
In his own grace he doth exalt himself,
More than in your addition.   75
REGAN: In my rights
By me invested, he compeers the best.
GONERIL: That were the most, if he should husband you.
REGAN: Jesters do oft prove prophets.
GONERIL: Holla, holla!   80
That eye that told you so looked but a-squint.
REGAN: Lady, I am not well, else I should answer
From a full-flowing stomach. General,
Take thou my soldiers, prisoners, patrimony;
Dispose of them, of me, the walls is thine: 85
Witness the world, that I create thee here
My lord and master.
GONERIL: Mean you to enjoy him?
ALBANY: The let-alone lies not in your good will.
EDMUND: Nor in thine, lord.   90
ALBANY: Half-blooded fellow, yes.
REGAN: [*to* EDMUND] Let the drum strike, and prove my title thine.
ALBANY: Stay yet, hear reason. Edmund, I arrest thee
On capital treason; and in thy attaint,
This gilded serpent [*points to* GONERIL]. For your claim, fair sister,   95
I bar it in the interest of my wife;
'Tis she is sub-contracted to this lord,
And I her husband contradict your banns.
If you will marry, make your loves to me—
My lady is bespoke.   100
GONERIL: An interlude.
ALBANY: Thou art armed, Gloucester. Let the trumpet sound.
If none appear to prove upon thy person
Thy heinous, manifest, and many treasons,
There is my pledge [*throws down a glove*]. I'll make it on thy heart,   105
Ere I taste bread, thou art in nothing less
Than I have here proclaimed thee.
REGAN: Sick, o sick!
GONERIL: [*aside*] If not. I'll ne'er trust medicine.
EDMUND: There's my exchange [*throws down a glove*].
What in the world he is   110
That names me traitor, villain-like he lies.
Call by thy trumpet; he that dares approach,
On him, on you, who not, I will maintain
My truth and honour firmly.
ALBANY: A herald, ho!   115
EDMUND: A herald, ho, a herald!
ALBANY: Trust to thy single virtue, for thy soldiers,
All levied in my name, have in my name
Took their discharge.

REGAN: My sickness grows upon me.   120
ALBANY: She is not well, convey her to my tent.
    [*Exit* REGAN. *Enter* HERALD.]
    Come hither herald. Let the trumpet sound,
    And read out this.
    [*A trumpet sounds.*]
HERALD: [*reads*] *If any man of quality or degree, within the lists of the*
    army, will maintain upon Edmund, supposed Earl of Gloucester,   125
    that he is a manifold traitor, let him appear by the third sound of the
    trumpet: he is bold in his defence.
    [*First trumpet.*]
HERALD: Again!
    [*Second trumpet.*]
    Again!
    [*Third trumpet.*]
    [*Trumpet answers within.*]
    [*Enter* EDGAR, *armed, a trumpet before him.*]
ALBANY: Ask him his purposes, why he appears   130
    Upon this call o' th' trumpet.
HERALD: What are you?
    Your name, your quality, and why you answer
    This present summons?
EDGAR: Know, my name is lost,   135
    By treason's tooth bare-gnawn and canker-bit,
    Yet am I noble as the adversary
    I come to cope.
ALBANY: Which is that adversary?
EDGAR: What's he that speaks for Edmund Earl of Gloucester?   140
EDMUND: Himself—what sayest thou to him?
EDGAR: Draw thy sword,
    That if my speech offend a noble heart,
    Thy arm may do thee justice; here is mine.
    Behold, it is the privilege of mine honours,   145
    My oath, and my profession. I protest—
    Maugre thy strength, youth, place, and eminence,
    Despite thy victor sword and fire-new fortune,
    Thy valour and thy heart—thou art a traitor;
    False to thy gods, thy brother, and thy father,   150
    Conspirant 'gainst this high illustrious prince.
    And from th' extremest upward of thy head,
    To the descent and dust below thy foot,
    A most toad-spotted traitor. Say thou no,
    This sword, this arm, and my best spirits are bent   155
    To prove upon thy heart, whereto I speak,
    Thou liest.
EDMUND: In wisdom I should ask thy name,
    But since thy outside looks so fair and warlike,
    And that thy tongue some say of breeding breathes,   160

What safe and nicely I might well delay,
By rule of knighthood, I disdain and spurn.
Back do I toss these treasons to thy head;
With the hell-hated lie o'erwhelm thy heart;
Which—for they yet glance by, and scarcely bruise—   165
This sword of mine shall give them instant way,
Where they shall rest for ever. Trumpets speak!
    [*Alarums. They fight.* EDMUND *falls.*]
ALBANY: Save him, save him.
GONERIL: This is practice, Gloucester.
By the law of war, thou wast not bound to answer   170
An unknown opposite; thou art not vanquished,
But cozened, and beguiled.
ALBANY: Shut your mouth dame,
Or with this paper shall I stop it. Hold sir,
Thou worse than any name, read thine own evil.   175
No tearing, lady, I perceive you know it. [*Gives the letter to* EDMUND.]
GONERIL: Say if I do, the laws are mine, not thine.
Who can arraign me for't?
ALBANY: Most monstrous! O!
Know'st thou this paper?   180
GONERIL: Ask me not what I know.   [*Exit.*]
ALBANY: Go after her, she's desperate, govern her.
    [*Exit* GENTLEMAN.]
EDMUND: What you have charged me with, that have I done,
And more, much more; the time will bring it out.
'Tis past, and so am I. But what art thou   185
That hast this fortune on me? If thou'rt noble,
I do forgive thee.
EDGAR: Let's exchange charity.
I am no less in blood than thou art, Edmund;
If more, the more th'hast wronged me.   190
My name is Edgar, and thy father's son.
The gods are just, and of our pleasant vices
Make instruments to plague us.
The dark and vicious place where thee he got
Cost him his eyes.   195
EDMUND: Th'hast spoken right, 'tis true.
The wheel is come full circle; I am here.
ALBANY: Methought thy very gait did prophesy
A royal nobleness. I must embrace thee.
Let sorrow split my heart, if ever I   200
Did hate thee, or thy father.
EDGAR: Worthy prince,
I know't.
ALBANY: Where have you hid yourself?
How have you known the miseries of your father?   205

EDGAR: By nursing them, my lord. List a brief tale;
    And when 'tis told, o that my heart would burst.
    The bloody proclamation to escape,
    That followed me so near—o our lives' sweetness,
    That we the pain of death would hourly die   210
    Rather than die at once—taught me to shift
    Into a madman's rags, t' assume a semblance
    That very dogs disdained, and in this habit
    Met I my father with his bleeding rings,
    Their precious stones new lost; became his guide,   215
    Led him, begged for him, saved him from despair.
    Never—o fault—revealed myself unto him,
    Until some half hour past, when I was armed;
    Not sure, though hoping of this good success,
    I asked his blessing, and from first to last   220
    Told him my pilgrimage. But his flawed heart,
    Alack too weak the conflict to support,
    'Twixt two extremes of passion, joy and grief,
    Burst smilingly.
EDMUND: This speech of yours hath moved me,   225
    And shall perchance do good, but speak you on;
    You look as you had something more to say.
ALBANY: If there be more, more woeful, hold it in,
    For I am almost ready to dissolve,
    Hearing of this.   230
EDGAR: This would have seemed a period
    To such as love not sorrow; but another,
    To amplify too much, would make much more,
    And top extremity.
    Whilst I was big in clamour, came there in a man,   235
    Who having seen me in my worst estate,
    Shunned my abhorred society, but then finding
    Who 'twas that so endured, with his strong arms
    He fastened on my neck, and bellowed out
    As he'd burst heaven, threw him on my father,   240
    Told the most piteous tale of Lear and him
    That ever ear received: which in recounting
    His grief grew puissant, and the strings of life
    Began to crack. Twice then the trumpets sounded,
    And there I left him tranced.   245
ALBANY: But who was this?
EDGAR: Kent sir, the banished Kent, who in disguise
    Followed his enemy King and did him service
    Improper for a slave.
        [*Enter* GENTLEMAN *with a bloody knife.*]
GENTLEMAN: Help, help; o help!   250
EDGAR: What kind of help?

ALBANY: Speak man.
EDGAR: What means this bloody knife?
GENTLEMAN: 'Tis hot, it smokes,
     It came even from the heart of—o she's dead!   255
ALBANY: Who dead? speak man.
GENTLEMAN: Your lady sir, your lady; and her sister
     By her is poisoned; she confesses it.
EDMUND: I was contracted to them both. All three
     Now marry in an instant.   260
          [*Enter* KENT.]
EDGAR: Here comes Kent.
ALBANY: Produce the bodies, be they alive or dead.
          [*Exit* GENTLEMAN.]
     This judgement of the heavens, that makes us tremble,
     Touches us not with pity.—O is this he?
     The time will not allow the compliment   265
     Which very manners urges.
KENT: I am come
     To bid my King and master aye good night.
     Is he not here?
ALBANY: Great thing of us forgot.   270
     Speak Edmund, where's the King? And where's Cordelia?
          [*The bodies of* GONERIL *and* REGAN *are brought in.*]
     Seest thou this object Kent?
KENT: Alack, why thus?
EDMUND: Yet Edmund was beloved.
     The one the other poisoned for my sake,   275
     And after slew herself.
ALBANY: Even so. Cover their faces.
EDMUND: I pant for life. Some good I mean to do,
     Despite of mine own nature. Quickly send—
     Be brief in it—to the castle, for my writ   280
     Is on the life of Lear, and on Cordelia.
     Nay, send in time.
ALBANY: Run, run, o run.
EDGAR: To who my lord? Who has the office? Send
     Thy token of reprieve.   285
EDMUND: Well thought on, take my sword;
     Give it the captain.
ALBANY: Haste thee for thy life.
          [*Exit* EDGAR.]
EDMUND: He hath commission from thy wife and me
     To hang Cordelia in the prison, and   290
     To lay the blame upon her own despair,
     That she fordid herself.
ALBANY: The gods defend her. Bear him hence awhile.
          [EDMUND *is borne off.*]

[*Enter* LEAR, *with* CORDELIA *dead in his arms;* EDGAR, GENTLE-
MAN, *and others.*]

LEAR: Howl, howl, howl! O you are men of stones.
    Had I your tongues and eyes, I'd use them so   295
    That heaven's vault should crack. She's gone forever.
    I know when one is dead, and when one lives;
    She's dead as earth. Lend me a looking-glass;
    If that her breath will mist or stain the stone,
    Why then she lives.   300
KENT: Is this the promised end?
EDGAR: Or image of that horror?
ALBANY: Fall, and cease.
LEAR: This feather stirs, she lives; if it be so,
    It is a chance which does redeem all sorrows   305
    That ever I have felt.
KENT: O my good master.
LEAR: Prithee away.
EDGAR: 'Tis noble Kent your friend.
LEAR: A plague upon you, murderers. traitors all.   310
    I might have saved her; now she's gone for ever.
    Cordelia, Cordelia, stay a little. Ha!
    What is't thou sayst?—Her voice was ever soft,
    Gentle, and low, an excellent thing in woman.
    I killed the slave that was a-hanging thee.   315
GENTLEMAN: 'Tis true my lords, he did.
LEAR: Did I not fellow?
    I have seen the day, with my good biting falchion
    I would have made them skip. I am old now,
    And these same crosses spoil me. Who are you?   320
    Mine eyes are not o' th' best, I'll tell you straight.
KENT: If fortune brag of two she loved and hated.
    One of them we behold.
LEAR: This is a dull sight. Are you not Kent?
KENT: The same.   325
    Your servant Kent. Where is your servant Caius?
LEAR: He's a good fellow, I can tell you that.
    He'll strike, and quickly too—he's dead and rotten.
KENT: No my good lord, I am the very man—
LEAR: I'll see that straight.   330
KENT: That from your first of difference and decay,
    Have followed your sad steps.
LEAR: You are welcome hither.
KENT: Nor no man else. All's cheerless, dark, and deadly.
    Your eldest daughters have fordone themselves,   335
    And desperately are dead.
LEAR: Ay so I think.

ALBANY: He knows not what he says, and vain is it
    That we present us to him.
EDGAR: Very bootless.   340
    [*Enter* GENTLEMAN.] Edmund is dead my lord.
ALBANY: That's but a trifle here.
    You lords and noble friends, know our intent.
    What comfort to this great decay may come
    Shall be applied. For us, we will resign,   345
    During the life of this old Majesty,
    To him our absolute power—[*to* EDGAR *and* KENT] you to your rights,
    With boot, and such addition as your honours
    Have more than merited. All friends shall taste
    The wages of their virtue, and all foes   350
    The cup of their deservings. O see, see!
LEAR: And my poor fool is hanged. No, no, no life?
    Why should a dog, a horse, a rat, have life,
    And thou no breath at all? Thou'lt come no more,
    Never, never, never, never, never.   355
    Pray you undo this button. Thank you sir.
    Do you see this? Look on her, look her lips—
    Look there, look there—[*Dies*]
EDGAR: He faints. My lord, my lord!
KENT: Break heart, I prithee break.   360
EDGAR: Look up my lord.
KENT: Vex not his ghost. O let him pass. He hates him,
    That would upon the rack of this tough world
    Stretch him out longer.
EDGAR: He is gone indeed.   365
KENT: The wonder is, he hath endured so long;
    He but usurped his life.
ALBANY: Bear them from hence. Our present business
    Is general woe. [*to* KENT *and* EDGAR] Friends of my soul, you twain
    Rule in this realm, and the gored state sustain.   370
KENT: I have a journey sir, shortly to go.
    My master calls me, I must not say no.
EDGAR: The weight of this sad time we must obey,
    Speak what we feel, not what we ought to say.
    The oldest hath borne most; we that are young   375
    Shall never see so much, nor live so long.
        [*Exeunt, with a dead march.*]

MOLIÈRE

TARTUFFE OR THE IMPOSTER

Translated by
John Wood

CHARACTERS IN THE PLAY

MADAME PERNELLE, *mother of Orgon*
ORGON
ELMIRE, *his wife*
DAMIS, *his son*
MARIANE, *his daughter, in love with Valère*
VALÈRE, *in love with Mariane*
CLÉANTE, *brother-in-law of Orgon*
TARTUFFE, *a hypocrite*
DORINE, *maid to Mariane*
MR LOYAL, *a tipstaff*
FLIPOTE, *maid to Madame Pernelle*
AN OFFICER

THE SCENE *is* ORGON'S *house in Paris.*

ACT I

[*Enter* MADAME PERNELLE *and* FLIPOTE, ELMIRE, MARIANE, CLÉANTE, DAMIS, DORINE.]

MADAME PERNELLE: Come, Flipote, come along. Let me be getting away from them.

ELMIRE: You walk so fast one can hardly keep up with you.

MADAME PERNELLE: Never mind, my dear, never mind! Don't come any further. I can do without all this politeness.

ELMIRE: We are only paying you the respect that is due to you. Why must you be in such a hurry to go, mother?

MADAME PERNELLE: Because I can't bear to see the goings-on in this house and because there's no consideration shown to me at all. I have had a very unedifying visit indeed! All my advice goes for nothing here. There's no respect paid to anything. Everybody airs his opinions—the place is a veritable Bedlam!

DORINE: If . . .

175

MADAME PERNELLE: For a servant you have a good deal too much to say for yourself, my girl. You don't know your place. You give your opinion on everything.

DAMIS: But . . .

MADAME PERNELLE: You, my lad, are just a plain fool. I'm your grandmother and I'm telling you so! I warned your father a hundred times over that you showed all the signs of turning out badly and bringing him nothing but trouble.

MARIANE: I think . . .

MADAME PERNELLE: Oh Lord, yes! You are his little sister, and you put on your demure looks as if butter wouldn't melt in your mouth—but it's just as they say, 'Still waters run deep.' I hate to think of what you do on the sly.

ELMIRE: But mother . . .

MADAME PERNELLE: My dear, if you'll allow me to say so you go about these things in the wrong way entirely. You ought to set them an example. Their own mother did very much better. You are extravagant. It distresses me to see the way you go about dressed like a duchess. A woman who's concerned only with pleasing her husband has no need for so much finery, my dear.

CLÉANTE: Oh come, after all madam . . .

MADAME PERNELLE: As for you, sir, I have the greatest esteem, affection, and respect for you as the brother of Elmire but if I were in her husband's place I should entreat you never to set foot in the house. You keep on advocating a way of life which no respectable people should follow. If I speak a little bluntly—well, that's my way. I don't mince matters. I say what I think.

DAMIS: Your Mr Tartuffe is undoubtedly a very lucky man . . .

MADAME PERNELLE: He's a *good* man and people would do well to listen to him. It enrages me to hear him criticized by a dolt such as you.

DAMIS: What! Am I to allow a sanctimonious bigot to come and usurp tyrannical authority here in the very house? Are we to have no pleasure at all unless his lordship deigns to approve?

DORINE: If we took notice of him we should never be able to do anything without committing a sin. He forbids everything—pious busybody that he is!

MADAME PERNELLE: And whatever he forbids deserves to be forbidden. He means to lead you along the road to Salvation. My son ought to make you all love him.

DAMIS: No, grandmother, neither my father nor anyone else could make me have any liking for him. It would be hypocrisy for me to say anything else. His behaviour infuriates me at every turn. I can only see one end to it. It'll come to a row between this scoundrel and me. It's bound to.

DORINE: It really is a scandalous thing to see a mere nobody assuming a position of authority in the house, a beggar without shoes to his feet when he first came, all the clothes he had to his back not worth sixpence, and getting so far above himself as to interfere with everything and behave as if he were the master.

MADAME PERNELLE: Mercy on us! It would be a lot better if the whole place *were* under his pious instruction.

DORINE: You imagine he's a saint but believe me, he's nothing but a hypocrite!

MADAME PERNELLE: Listen to her talking!

DORINE: I wouldn't trust myself with him without good security or his man Laurence either.

MADAME PERNELLE: I don't know what the servant is really like, but the master's a good man, that I *will* warrant. The only reason you dislike him and are so set against him is that he tells you all the truth about yourselves: it's sin that rouses his wrath. Everything he does is done in the cause of the Lord.

DORINE: Hm! Then why is it—particularly just recently—that he can't bear to have anyone coming about the place? What is there sinful in calling on someone in an ordinary straightforward way that he should make such a hullabaloo about it? Shall I tell you what I think—between ourselves— [*she indicates* ELMIRE] I believe he's jealous on account of the mistress. Upon my word I do!

MADAME PERNELLE: Hold your tongue and mind what you are saying! He's not the only one who takes exception to visitors. All these people coming here and causing a disturbance, carriages for ever standing at the door, and swarms of noisy footmen and lackeys make a bad impression on the whole neighbourhood. I'm willing to believe that there's no harm in it really, but it sets people talking and that's not a good thing.

CLÉANTE: And do you propose, madam, to stop people talking? It would be a poor affair if we had to give up our best friends for fear of the silly things that people might say about us and even if we did, do you think you could shut everybody's mouth? There's no defence against malicious tongues, so let's pay no heed to their tittle-tattle; let us try to live virtuously and leave the gossips to say what they will.

DORINE: It's our neighbour, Daphne, and that little husband of hers who have been speaking ill of us, isn't it? Folk whose own behaviour is most ridiculous are always to the fore in slandering others. They never miss a chance of seizing on the least glimmering suspicion of an affair, of gleefully spreading the news and twisting things the way they want folk to believe. They think they can justify their own goings-on by painting other people's behaviour in the same colours as their own and so hope to give an air of innocence to their intrigues or throw on other people some share of the criticism their own actions only too well deserve.

MADAME PERNELLE: All this talk is beside the point. Everybody knows that Orante's life is an example to everybody. She's a God-fearing woman and I hear she strongly condemns the company that comes here.

DORINE:[1] She's a wonderful example—a really good woman! It's quite true that she leads a strict sort of life but it's age that has made her turn pious. We all know that she's virtuous only because she has no alternative. So long as she was able to attract men's attentions she enjoyed herself to the full, but now that she finds her eyes losing their lustre she resolves to renounce

---

[1] This is one of the speeches thought to have been originally given to Cléante.

the world which is slipping away from her and conceal the fading of her charms beneath an elaborate pretence of high principles. That's what coquettes come to in the end. It's hard for them to see their admirers desert them. Left alone and unhappy, the only course left to them is to turn virtuous. Their righteous severity condemns everything and forgives nothing. They rail against other people's way of life—not in the interests of righteousness but from envy—because they can't bear that anyone else should enjoy the pleasures which age had left them no power to enjoy.

MADAME PERNELLE: [*to* ELMIRE] These, daughter, are the sort of idle stories they serve up to please you. I have to hold my tongue when I'm at your house for Mistress Chatterbox here holds forth all day long. Nevertheless I will have my turn. What I say is that it was the wisest thing my son ever did to take into his house this holy man whom the Lord sent just when he was needed, to reclaim your minds from error. For the good of your souls you should hearken to him for he reproves nothing but what is deserving of reproof. This giddy round of balls, assemblies, and routs is all a device of the Evil One. In such places one never hears a word of godliness, nothing but idle chatter, singing, and nonsensical rigamaroles: often enough the neighbours come in for their share and slander and gossip go the rounds. Even sensible heads are turned in the turmoil of that sort of gathering, a thousand idle tongues get busy about nothing and, as a learned doctor said the other day, it becomes a veritable tower of Babylon where everybody babbles never-endingly—but to come to the point I was making. [*pointing to* CLÉANTE] What! The gentleman is sniggering already is he? Go find a laughing-stock elsewhere and don't—[*to* ELMIRE] Daughter, good-bye. I'll say no more, but I'd have you know I have even less opinion of this household than I had. It will be a long time before I set foot in here again. [*giving* FLIPOTE *a slap*] Hey you! What are you dreaming and gaping at? God bless my soul! I'll warm your ears for you. Come slut. Let's be off.

[*Exeunt all but* CLÉANTE *and* DORINE.]

CLÉANTE: I won't go out in case she starts on me again. How the old woman . . .

DORINE: It's a pity she can't hear you talking like that! She'd tell you what she thinks about you, and whether she's of an age that you can call her 'old woman' or not!

CLÉANTE: Didn't she get worked up against us—and all about nothing! How she dotes on her Tartuffe!

DORINE: Oh! It's nothing compared with her son. If you'd seen him you'd agree he was much worse. During the late disturbances he gained the reputation of being a reliable man and showed courage in the King's service, but since he took a fancy to Tartuffe he seems to have taken leave of his senses. He addresses him as brother and holds him a hundred times dearer than wife or mother, daughter or son. The man's the sole confidant of all his secrets and his trusted adviser in everything. He caresses and cossets him and he couldn't show more tenderness to a mistress. He insists on his taking the place of honour at table, and delights in seeing him devour enough for half a dozen. He has to have all the tit-bits and if he happens to belch it's 'Lord, preserve you!'[2] In short, he's crazy about him. He's his all in all, his hero: he admires everything he does, quotes him at every turn, his every trivial action is wonderful and every word he utters an oracle. As for Tartuffe, he knows his weakness and means to make use of it. He has a hundred ways of deceiving him, gets money out of him constantly by means of canting humbug, and assumes the right to take us to task. Even his lout of a servant has taken to instructing us, comes and harangues us with wild fanatical eyes, and throws away our ribbons, patches, and paint. The other day the dog tore up with his own hands a handkerchief he found in the *Flowers of Sanctity*. He said it was a dreadful thing to sully sacred things with the devil's trappings.

[*Re-enter* ELMIRE *and* MARIANE.]

ELMIRE: You are lucky to have missed the harangue she delivered at the gate. But I caught sight of my husband and as he didn't see me I'll go and wait for him upstairs.

CLÉANTE: I'll await him here to save time. I only want to say good morning.

[*Exeunt* ELMIRE *and* MARIANE.]

DAMIS: Have a word with him about my sister's marriage. I suspect that Tartuffe is opposing it and that it's he who is driving my father to these evasions. You know how closely concerned I am. Valère and my sister are in love and I, as you know, am no less in love with his sister, and if . . .

DORINE: Here he comes.

[*Enter* ORGON.]

ORGON: Ah, good morning, brother.

CLÉANTE: I was just going. I'm glad to see you back again. There isn't much life in the countryside just now.

ORGON: Dorine—[*to* CLÉANTE] a moment brother, please—excuse me if I ask the news of the family first and set my mind at rest. [*to* DORINE] Has everything gone well the few days I've been away? What have you been doing? How is everyone?

DORINE: The day before yesterday the mistress was feverish all day. She had a dreadful headache.

ORGON: And Tartuffe?

DORINE: Tartuffe? He's very well: hale and hearty; in the pink.

ORGON: Poor fellow!

DORINE: In the evening she felt faint and couldn't touch anything, her headache was so bad.

ORGON: And Tartuffe?

DORINE: He supped with her. She ate nothing but he very devoutly devoured a couple of partridges and half a hashed leg of mutton.

ORGON: Poor fellow!

DORINE: She never closed her eyes all through the night. She was too feverish to sleep and we had to sit up with her until morning.

ORGON: And Tartuffe?

[2] *Molière's note.* It is a servant speaking.

DORINE: Feeling pleasantly drowsy, he went straight to his room, jumped into a nice warm bed, and slept like a top until morning.

ORGON: Poor fellow!

DORINE: Eventually she yielded to our persuasions, allowed herself to be bled, and soon felt much relieved.

ORGON: And Tartuffe?

DORINE: He dutifully kept up his spirits, and took three or four good swigs of wine at breakfast to fortify himself against the worst that might happen and to make up for the blood the mistress had lost.

ORGON: Poor fellow!

DORINE: They are both well again now so I'll go ahead and tell the mistress how glad you are to hear that she's better.

      [*Exit.*]

CLÉANTE. She's laughing at you openly, brother, and, though I don't want to anger you, I must admit that she's right. Did anyone ever hear of such absurd behaviour? Can the man really have gained such influence over you as to make you forget everything else, so that after having rescued him from poverty you should be ready to . . .

ORGON: Enough brother! You don't know the man you are talking about.

CLÉANTE: I grant you I don't know him, but then, to see what sort of fellow he is, one need only . . .

ORGON: Brother, you would be charmed with him if you knew him. You would be delighted beyond measure . . . he's a man who . . . who . . . ah! a man . . . in short, a man! Whoever follows his precepts enjoys a profound peace of mind and looks upon the world as so much ordure. Yes, under his influence I'm becoming another man. He's teaching me how to forgo affection and free myself from all human ties. I could see brother, children, mother, wife, all perish without caring that much!

CLÉANTE: Very humane sentiments, I must say, brother!

ORGON: Ah! Had you seen how I first met him you would have come to feel for him as I do. Every day he used to come to church and modestly fall on his knees just beside me. He would draw the eyes of the whole congregation by the fervour with which he poured forth his prayers, sighing, groaning, kissing the ground in transports of humility. When I went out he would step in front of me to offer me the Holy water at the door. Having learned from his servant—a man who follows his example in every way—who he was and how needy his condition, I offered him alms, but he would always modestly return a part. 'Too much,' he'd say, 'too much by half. I'm not worthy of your pity.' When I wouldn't have it back he'd go and bestow it on the poor before my very eyes. At length Heaven inspired me to give him shelter in my house, since when all things seem to prosper here. He keeps a reproving eye upon everything and, mindful of my honour, his concern for my interests extends even to my wife. He warns me of those who make eyes at her and is ten times more jealous for her than I am myself. You wouldn't believe the lengths to which his piety extends: the most trivial failing on his own part he accounts a sin: the slightest thing may suffice to shock his conscience—so much so that the other day he was full of self-reproach for having caught a flea while at his prayers and killed it with too much vindictiveness.

CLÉANTE: Gad! You are crazy, brother, that's what I think—or are you trying to pull my leg with a tale like this? What do you intend all this foolery . . .

ORGON: Brother, what you are saying savours of atheism. You *are* somewhat tainted with it at heart. As I have warned you a dozen times you'll bring some serious trouble upon yourself.

CLÉANTE: That's the way your sort of people usually talk. You would have everyone as purblind as yourselves. If one sees things clearly one's an atheist: whoever doesn't bow the knee to pious flummery is lacking in faith and respect for sacred things. No, no! Your threats don't frighten me! I know what I'm talking about and Heaven sees what's in my heart. We are not all duped by humbugs. Devotion, like courage, may be counterfeit. Just as, when honour puts men to the test, the truly brave are not those who make the biggest noise, so the truly pious, whose example we should ever follow, are not those who make the greatest show. What! Would you make no distinction between hypocrisy and true religion? Would you class both together, describe them in the same terms, respect the mask as you would the face itself, treat artifice and sincerity alike, confound appearance and reality, accept the shadow for the substance, base coin for true? Men, in the main, are strangely made. They can never strike the happy mean: the bounds of reason seem too narrow for them: they must needs overact whatever part they play and often ruin the noblest things because they will go to extremes and push them too far. This, brother, is all by the way—

ORGON: Yes, yes, there's no doubt you are a most reverend doctor. You have a monopoly of knowledge, you are unique in wisdom and enlightenment, Sir Oracle, the Cato of our age. In comparison the rest of us are fools—

CLÉANTE: No brother. I'm no reverend doctor; I've no monopoly of knowledge. I merely claim to be able to discriminate between false and true. Just as I know no kind of man more estimable than those who are genuinely religious, nothing in the whole world nobler or finer than the holy fervour of true piety, so I know nothing more odious than those whited sepulchres of specious zeal, those charlatans, those professional zealots, who with sacrilegious and deceitful posturings abuse and mock to their heart's content everything which men hold most sacred and holy; men who put self-interest first, who trade and traffic in devotion, seek to acquire credit and dignities by turning up their eyes in transports of simulated zeal. I mean the people who tread with such extraordinary ardour the godly road to fortune, burning with devotion but seeking material advantage, preaching daily the virtues of solitude and retirement while following the life of courts, shaping their zeal to their vices, quick, revengeful, faithless, scheming, who when they wish to destroy, hide their vindictive pride under the cloak of religion. They are the more dangerous in that they turn against us in their bitter rage the very weapons which men revere and use the passion for which they are respected to destroy us with a consecrated blade. One sees all too much of falsehood such as this. Yet the truly devout are

easy to recognize. Our own age offers us many a glorious example,
brother. Look at Ariston, Periander, Oronte, Alcidamus, Polydore, Cli-
tander! Their claims no one can deny: theirs is no braggart virtue, no intolerable ostentation of piety; their religion is gentle and humane: they
don't censure our actions: they would consider such strictures arrogant:
leaving pride of eloquence to others they rebuke our conduct by their
own: they don't assume from appearances that others are in fault: they
are always ready to think well of people. No '*cabales*' for them, no intrigues! their whole concern is to live virtuously: they show no anger
against sinners: they reserve their hate for sin itself: nor do they take upon
themselves the interests of Heaven with a zeal beyond anything that
Heaven itself displays. These are my sort of men: this is how one should
conduct oneself: this is the example one should follow! Your man, however, is of another kind. You vaunt his zeal in all good faith but I think
you are deceived by false appearances.

ORGON: My dear brother-in-law, have you finished?

CLÉANTE: Yes.

ORGON: [*going*] I'm much obliged to you.

CLÉANTE: One word, brother, please. Let us leave this topic. You remember
that you promised Valère your daughter's hand?

ORGON: Yes.

CLÉANTE: And you named a day for the happy event.

ORGON: True.

CLÉANTE: Why then defer the ceremony?

ORGON: I don't know.

CLÉANTE: Have you something else in mind?

ORGON: Maybe.

CLÉANTE: Do you intend to break your word?

ORGON: I never said so.

CLÉANTE: There is nothing, I believe, to prevent your keeping your promise.

ORGON: That's as may be.

CLÉANTE: Why such circumspection in giving an answer? Valère has asked me
to come and see you.

ORGON: God be praised!

CLÉANTE: What am I to tell him?

ORGON: Whatever you please.

CLÉANTE: But I need to know your intentions. What do you mean to do?

ORGON: The will of Heaven.

CLÉANTE: But, speaking seriously, Valère has your promise—are you standing
to it or not?

ORGON: Good-bye. [*Exit.*]

CLÉANTE: I fear he is going to be disappointed in his love. I must warn him
of the way things are going.

ACT II

[ORGON, MARIANE]

ORGON: Mariane.

MARIANE: Yes, father.

ORGON: Come here. I want a word with you in private.

MARIANE: What are you looking for? [*He is looking into a closet.*]

ORGON: I'm looking to see that there's no one to overhear us. This little place is just right for eavesdropping. Now, we are all right. I've always known that you have an obedient disposition, Mariane, and you've always been very dear to me.

MARIANE: I am very grateful for your fatherly affection.

ORGON: I'm pleased to hear you say so, my girl—and if you want to deserve it you should be at pains to do what I want.

MARIANE: That is my most earnest wish.

ORGON: Very well. What have you to say about our guest, Tartuffe?

MARIANE: What have I to say?

ORGON: Yes, you! Mind how you answer.

MARIANE: Oh dear! I'll say anything you like about him.

[*Enter* DORINE, *unobserved; she takes up her position behind* ORGON.]

ORGON: That's very sensible. Then let me hear you say, my dear, that he is a wonderful man, that you love him, and you'd be glad to have me choose him for your husband. Eh?

[MARIANE *starts in surprise.*]

MARIANE: Eh?

ORGON: What's the matter?

MARIANE: *What* did you say?

ORGON: What?

MARIANE: I must have misheard you.

ORGON: How d'ye mean?

MARIANE: Who is it, father, I'm to say I love and be glad to have you choose as my husband?

ORGON: Tartuffe!

MARIANE: But, father, I assure you I don't feel like that at all. Why make me tell such an untruth?

ORGON: But I mean it to be the truth and it's sufficient for you that it's what I have decided.

MARIANE: What, father! You really want me to . . .

ORGON: My intention, my girl, is that you should marry Tartuffe and make him one of the family. He shall be your husband. I have made up my mind about that and it's for me to decide . . . [*seeing* DORINE] What are *you* doing here? You must be mighty curious, my lass, to come eavesdropping like that.

DORINE: I don't really know master how the rumour arose—whether it's guess-work or coincidence, but when I heard about this marriage I treated it as a joke.

ORGON: Why? Is it unbelievable?

DORINE: So much so that I *won't* believe it though you tell me yourself.

ORGON: I know how to make you believe it.

DORINE: Yes, yes, but you are telling us it as a joke.

ORGON: I'm telling you what's going to happen and before long too!

DORINE: Oh, rubbish!

ORGON: [*to* MARIANE] It's no joking matter I tell you!

DORINE: No! Don't you believe your Papa! He's teasing!

ORGON: I'm telling you . . .

DORINE: It's no good. We shan't believe you.

ORGON: If I once get annoyed.

DORINE: All right! We believe you then and so much the worse for you. Why! How can you, master! You with all the appearance of a sensible man—and a venerable beard like you have—how can you be so silly as to . . .

ORGON: Listen! You have got into the habit of taking liberties lately. I tell you, my girl, I don't like it at all!

DORINE: Do let us discuss it without getting cross, master, please. You really must have made it all up for a joke. Your daughter isn't at all the right person to marry a bigot and he ought to have other things to think about. Anyhow, what use is such an alliance to you? With all the money you have why go and choose a beggar for a son-in-law?

ORGON: Be quiet! If he's poor that's all the more reason for respecting him. Understand that! His is an honourable poverty. That's beyond question. It should raise him above material consequence for he's allowed himself to be deprived of his means by his indifference to temporal matters and his unswerving attachment to the things which are eternal. My help may be able to afford him the means to escape from embarrassment and enter into his own possessions again—lands which are quite well known in his part of the country. Moreover, whatever his present condition may appear to be, he's certainly a gentleman.

DORINE: Yes. That's what *he* says, but that kind of boasting doesn't go well with his piety. A man who chooses the saintly life shouldn't crack up his birth and family so much. The humble ways of piety don't go well with such-like ambitions. Why take pride in that sort of thing? But there, you'd rather not discuss that. Let's leave the question of his family and talk about the man himself! Could you really bear to hand over your daughter to a fellow like that? Shouldn't you consider what's due to her and what the consequences of such a marriage might be! Let me tell you that when a girl isn't allowed her own choice in marriage her virtue's in jeopardy: her resolve to live as a good woman depends on the qualities of the husband she's given. Those whose wives are unfaithful have often made them what they are. There are some husbands it's not easy to remain faithful to and whoever gives a girl a husband she detests is responsible to Heaven for the sins she commits. Just think then what perils this scheme of yours may involve you in!

ORGON: [*to* MARIANE] Well, I declare, I have to take lessons from her as to how to do my own business!

DORINE: You couldn't do better than follow my advice.

ORGON: Let's waste no more time on such nonsense, my girl. I'm your father and I know what's good for you. I had promised you to Valère, but apart from the fact that he's said to be a bit of a gambler I suspect him of being a free thinker. I don't see him at church much.

DORINE: I suppose you'd have him run there at the very moment you get there yourself like some folk who only go there to be noticed.

ORGON: I'm not asking for your opinion. [*to* MARIANE] Moreover Tartuffe stands well with Heaven and that surpasses all earthly riches. This marriage will give you everything you could wish for, a perpetual source of pleasure and delight. You'll live together loving and faithful just like two babes—like a pair of turtle doves. No differences will ever arise between you and you'll be able to do just what you like with him.

DORINE: Will she? She won't do anything with him but make him a cuckold, believe me!

ORGON: Sh! What a way to talk!

DORINE: I tell you he has all the looks of one—he's born to it, master, and all your daughter's virtue couldn't prevent it.

ORGON: Stop interrupting me! Just hold your tongue and don't be for ever putting your nose in where you have no business.

DORINE: I'm only telling you for your own good, master.

[*Every time he turns to speak to his daughter she interrupts.*]

ORGON: You don't need to trouble. Just be quiet!

DORINE: If it wasn't that I'm fond of you . . .

ORGON: I don't *want* you to be fond of me.

DORINE: Yes, but I'm *determined* to be fond of you—whether *you* like it or not.

ORGON: Tcha!

DORINE: I'm concerned for your good name, and I won't have you making yourself the butt of everyone's gibes.

ORGON: Will you never be quiet?

DORINE: I could never forgive myself if I let you make such an alliance.

ORGON: Will you be quiet, you reptile, with your impudent . . .

DORINE: Ah! Fancy a godly man like you getting angry!

ORGON: Yes! This ridiculous nonsense is more than my temper can stand. I insist on your holding your tongue.

DORINE: Right, but I shan't *think* any the less because I don't say anything.

ORGON: Think if you like but take care you don't talk or . . . that's enough. [*turning to* MARIANE] I've weighed everything carefully as a wise man should . . .

DORINE: It's maddening not to be able to speak. [*She stops as he turns his head.*]

ORGON: Without his being exactly a beauty Tartuffe's looks are . . .

DORINE: Yes! A lovely mug hasn't he?

ORGON: Such . . . that even if his other advantages don't appeal to you . . . [ORGON *turns and faces* DORINE, *looking at her with arms folded.*]

DORINE: She *would* be well off wouldn't she? If *I* were in her place no man would marry me against my will—not with impunity. I would show him, ay, and soon after the ceremony too, that a woman has always ways and means of getting her own back.

ORGON: So what I say hasn't any effect on you at all?

DORINE: What are you grumbling about? I'm not talking to you.

ORGON: Then what *are* you doing?

DORINE: I'm talking to myself.

ORGON: Very well. [*aside*] I shall have to give her a back-hander for her impudence yet. [*He stands ready to box her ears.* DORINE *every time he looks at her stands rigid and without speaking.*] You can't do otherwise, my girl, than approve what I have in mind for you . . . and believe that the husband . . . I have chosen for you . . . [*to* DORINE] Why aren't you talking to yourself now?

DORINE: I've nothing to say to myself.

ORGON: Not a word even?

DORINE: Not a word thank you!

ORGON: But I was waiting for you . . .

DORINE: I'm not so silly as that!

ORGON: Well now, my girl, you must show how obedient you are and fall in with my choice.

DORINE: [*running away*] I'd scorn to take such a husband! [*He takes a slap at her and misses.*]

ORGON: She's a thorough pest is that girl of yours! If I live with her any longer I shall do something I shall be sorry for. I'm in no state to go on now. I'm so incensed at her impudence I shall have to go outside to recover myself.

    [*Exit* ORGON.]

DORINE: Have you lost your tongue? Do I have to do all the talking for you? Fancy letting him put a ridiculous proposal like that to you and never saying a word in reply!

MARIANE: What would you have me do in face of the absolute power of my father?

DORINE: Whatever is needed to ward off the danger.

MARIANE: But what?

DORINE: Tell him one can't love at another's bidding; that you'll marry to suit yourself, not him; that *you* are the person concerned and therefore it's *you* the husband has to please not him; and that, if he has such a fancy for his precious Tartuffe, he can marry him himself and there's nothing to stop him.

MARIANE: I confess that a father's authority is such that I have never had the temerity to say anything.

DORINE: Well, let us get down to business. Valère has made proposals for you. I ask you, *do* you love him or don't you?

MARIANE: You do my love great injustice, Dorine. How can you ask such a question? Haven't I opened my heart to you many and many a time? Don't you know how much I love him?

DORINE: How do I know that you meant what you said or that the young man really appeals to you?

MARIANE: You do me grievous wrong to doubt it, Dorine. I've shown my true feelings all too clearly.

DORINE: So you *do* love him, then?

MARIANE: Indeed I do.

DORINE: And, so far as you know, he loves you too?

MARIANE: I believe so.

DORINE: And you both want to be married?

MARIANE: Assuredly!

DORINE: Then what do you mean to do about this other proposal?

MARIANE: To die by my own hand if they force me to submit to it.

DORINE: Splendid! That's something I never thought of! You only need die and you are finished with your troubles. There's no doubt that's a wonderful remedy. That sort of talk infuriates me!

MARIANE: Oh dear, you are tiresome, Dorine. You have no sympathy at all for other people's troubles.

DORINE: I've no sympathy with folk who talk nonsense and are as faint-hearted as you are when it comes to the point.

MARIANE: But what do you expect me to do? If I'm timid . . .

DORINE: What lovers need is determination.

MARIANE: And have I wavered in my love for Valère? Surely it's for him to deal with my father.

DORINE: What! If your father's the fantastic creature he is—if he's plumb crazy over his precious Tartuffe and breaks his promise about the marriage he had decided on, is your lover to be blamed?

MARIANE: But can I reveal by flat refusal and open defiance how much I'm in love? Can I, whatever Valère's qualities may be, abandon the modesty of my sex and my filial duty? Do you want me to expose my feelings for all the world to see and . . .

DORINE: No. No. *I* don't want anything. I see that you want to marry Mr Tartuffe and, now I come to think about it, it would be wrong of me to dissuade you from such an alliance. Why should I oppose your inclina- tions? It's a most suitable match. Mr Tartuffe! Ha! Ha! It's not an offer to be despised, is it? Come to think of it Mr Tartuffe's a fine fellow. It's no small honour to be his better half. Everybody defers to him already. He's a man of family—where he comes from, and a fine looking fellow to boot—with his red ears and his red face. You would be sure to live happily with a husband like that.

MARIANE: Heavens!

DORINE: How delightful to be married to such a fine-looking husband!

MARIANE: Oh, please stop talking like this, and suggest some means of avoiding the marriage. It's enough. I give in. I'm ready for anything.

DORINE: No. No, a daughter must do as her father tells her even if he wants her to marry a monkey. You are very lucky. What are you complaining of? You'll be carted off to his little provincial town, and find it swarming with his relations. What fun you'll have meeting them all! You'll be taken straight into local society, visit the bailiff's wife and the councillor's lady, and they'll accord you the honour of letting you sit down with them as an equal, perhaps! In carnival time you'll be able to look forward to a ball with a grand orchestra, to wit a couple of bagpipes, and now and again Fagotin the monkey, and a marionette show. If only your husband . . .

MARIANE: Oh! I can't endure it! Why don't you help me?

DORINE: No, you must excuse me!

MARIANE: Oh, Dorine, *please* . . .

DORINE: No it must go through now—you deserve it!

MARIANE: Dear Dorine . . .

DORINE: No.

MARIANE: If my confessions of love . . .

DORINE: No. Tartuffe is your man, you shall have your fill of him.

MARIANE: You know that I've always trusted in you. Help me to . . .

DORINE: No, no! I give you my word—you shall be thoroughly Tartuffed!

MARIANE: Very well, since my miserable lot doesn't move you, leave me alone with my despair. There my heart will find relief. I have one infallible remedy for my troubles. [*She makes to go.*]

DORINE: Hey there! Come back. I won't be angry any more. I must take pity on you in spite of everything.

MARIANE: I assure you, Dorine, if they put me to this cruel torment it will be the death of me.

DORINE: Don't distress yourself. We'll find some means of preventing it. But here comes your Valère.

[*Enter* VALÈRE.]

VALÈRE: I have just heard a fine piece of news. Something I was quite unaware of!

MARIANE: What is it?

VALÈRE: That you are to marry Tartuffe.

MARIANE: That is certainly my father's intention.

VALÈRE: But your father . . .

MARIANE: He's changed his mind. He has just put the new proposal to me now.

VALÈRE: What, seriously?

MARIANE: Yes, seriously. He's determined on the match.

VALÈRE: And what is your intention?

MARIANE: I don't know.

VALÈRE: That's a fine answer! You don't know?

MARIANE: No.

VALÈRE: No?

MARIANE: What do you advise me to do?

VALÈRE: What do I advise you to do? I advise you to take him!

MARIANE: *You* advise me to do that?

VALÈRE: Yes.

MARIANE: You really mean it?

VALÈRE: Of course. It's a splendid offer—one well worth considering.

MARIANE: Very well, sir. I'll take your advice.

VALÈRE: I don't doubt you'll find little difficulty in doing so.

MARIANE: No more than you in offering it.

VALÈRE: I gave it to please you.

MARIANE: And I'll follow it—to please you.

DORINE: [*aside*] We'll see what will come of this!

VALÈRE: So this is how you love me! You were deceiving me when . . .

MARIANE: Don't let us talk of that please! You told me frankly that I should accept the husband I was offered. Well then, that's just what I intend to do—since you give me such salutary advice.

VALÈRE: Don't make what I said your excuse! You had already made up your mind. You're just seizing on a frivolous pretext to justify breaking your word.

MARIANE: That's true. You put it very well.

VALÈRE: Of course! You never really loved me at all.

MARIANE: Alas! You may think so if you like.

VALÈRE: Yes, yes. I may indeed: but I may yet forestall your design. I know on whom to bestow both my hand and my affections.

MARIANE: Oh! I don't doubt that in the least, and the love which your good qualities inspire . . .

VALÈRE: Good Lord! Let's leave my good qualities out of it. They are slight enough and your behaviour is proof of it. But I know someone who will, I hope, consent to repair my loss once she knows I am free.

MARIANE: Your loss is little enough and, no doubt, you'll easily be consoled by the change.

VALÈRE: I shall do what I can you may be sure. To find oneself jilted is a blow to one's pride. One must do one's best to forget it and if one doesn't succeed, at least one must pretend to, for to love where one's love is scorned is an unpardonable weakness.

MARIANE: A very elevated and noble sentiment, I'm sure.

VALÈRE: Of course and one that everyone must approve. Would you have me languish for you indefinitely, see you throw yourself into the arms of another and yet not bestow elsewhere the heart that you spurn?

MARIANE: On the contrary, that is just what I want. I only wish it were done already.

VALÈRE: That's what you would like?

MARIANE: Yes.

VALÈRE: You have insulted me sufficiently. You shall have your wish . . . [*makes a move to go*] and immediately!

MARIANE: Very well.

VALÈRE: [*turning back*] At least remember that it is you yourself who are driving me to this extremity.

MARIANE: Yes.

VALÈRE: And that in what I am doing, I only am following your example.

MARIANE: My example, so be it!

VALÈRE: Very well! You shall have just what you asked for.

MARIANE: So much the better!

VALÈRE: You'll never see me again.

MARIANE: Capital!

VALÈRE: [*goes but when he reaches the door he returns*] Eh?

MARIANE: What?

VALÈRE: Didn't you call?

MARIANE: Me? You are dreaming.

VALÈRE: Good. I'm going then. Good-bye!

MARIANE: Good-bye!

DORINE: I think you must be out of your senses to behave in this absurd fashion. I've let you go on squabbling to see how far you would go. Here, Mr Valère! [*She takes him by the arm.* VALÈRE *pretends to resist.*]

VALÈRE: What do you want, Dorine?

DORINE: Come here!

VALÈRE: No, no. I'm too angry. Don't try to prevent me doing what she wants.

DORINE: Stop!

VALÈRE: No, no. It's all settled.

DORINE: Ah!

MARIANE: He can't bear the sight of me. He's going because I'm here. I'd better get out of his sight.

> [DORINE *leaves* VALÈRE *and runs to* MARIANE.]

DORINE: The other one now! Where are you off to?

MARIANE: Let me go!

DORINE: Come back!

MARIANE: No, no, Dorine. It's no good your trying to stop me.

VALÈRE: I can see that she hates the very sight of me. Far better I should spare her the embarrassment.

DORINE: [*leaving* MARIANE *and running to* VALÈRE] You again. The devil take you before I let you go. Stop this silly nonsense and come here both of you. [*She drags them both in.*]

VALÈRE: What are you trying to do?

MARIANE: What do you want?

DORINE: To bring you together again and get you out of this mess. [*to* VALÈRE] You must be crazy to quarrel like this!

VALÈRE: Didn't you hear how she spoke to me?

DORINE: You must be out of your mind to get so annoyed.

MARIANE: But didn't you see what happened? Didn't you see how he treated me?

DORINE: [*to* VALÈRE] Sheer silliness on both sides. She wants nothing better than to be yours—I can witness. [*to* MARIANE] He loves nobody but you and desires nothing better than to be your husband—I'll stake my life on it.

MARIANE: Then why did he give me the advice he did?

VALÈRE: Why did you ask me for advice on such a question?

DORINE: You are both quite mad. Here—give me your hands, both of you. [*to* VALÈRE] Come along, you.

VALÈRE: [*giving his hand to* DORINE] What good will that do?

DORINE: [*to* MARIANE] Now yours.

MARIANE: [*giving her hand*] What's the use?

DORINE: Heavens! Be quick. Come on! You love each other better than you think.

VALÈRE: [*to* MARIANE] Come, don't do it with such an ill grace. Don't look at a fellow as if you hated him. [MARIANE *turns toward* VALÈRE *and gives a little smile.*]

DORINE: The truth is all lovers are a bit touched!

VALÈRE: Ah! But hadn't I some cause for complaint? You must admit it was cruel of you to take such pleasure in giving me such a horrible piece of news.

MARIANE: But you—aren't you the most ungrateful of men?

DORINE: Let's leave the argument to another time and think how we can prevent this dreadful marriage . . .

MARIANE: Tell us what we are to do.

DORINE: We'll try everything we can. Your father can't be serious and it's all sheer rubbish, but you had better pretend to fall in with his nonsense and give the appearance of consenting so that if it comes to the point you'll more easily be able to delay the marriage. If we can only gain time we may set everything right. You can complain of a sudden illness that will necessitate delay; another time you can have recourse to bad omens—such as having met a corpse or broken a mirror or dreamt of muddy water. Finally, the great thing is that they can't make you his wife unless you answer 'I will'. But I think, as a precaution, you had better not be found talking together. [*to* VALÈRE] Off you go and get all your friends to use their influence with her father to stand by his promise. We must ask his brother to try once again, and see if we can get the stepmother on our side. Good-bye.

VALÈRE: [*to* MARIANE] Whatever schemes we may devise you are the one I really count on.

MARIANE: [*to* VALÈRE] I can't answer for what my father decides but I will never marry anyone but Valère.

VALÈRE: Ah, how happy you make me! Whatever they may venture to . . .

DORINE: Ah? Lovers are never tired of blathering! Be off, I tell you.

VALÈRE: [*making to go, then turning back*] Still . . .

DORINE: What a talker you are! [*pushing them both out*] You go this way and you that. Be off!

ACT III

DAMIS: May I be struck dead on the spot—call me the most miserable black-guard alive if I let either fear or favour prevent me—if I don't think out some master stroke!

DORINE: For goodness sake, don't get so excited! Your father has only just mentioned it. People don't do everything they intend to. There's a deal of difference between talking about a thing and doing it.

DAMIS: I must put a stop to the dog's machinations! I'll have something to say to him!

DORINE: Oh, go easy! Leave your stepmother to deal with both him and your father. She has some influence with Tartuffe. He takes notice of her. I'm not sure that he isn't sweet on her. I wish to Heaven he were! That would be a lark! As a matter of fact it's on your account that she's sent for him: she intends to sound him about this marriage you are so worried about: she means to find out what he has in mind and make him see what trouble it would cause in the family if he encouraged the idea. His servant said he was at his prayers so I wasn't able to see him, but he said he'd be coming down soon. So please go away and leave me to wait for him.

DAMIS: I'll be present at the interview.

DORINE: No. They must be alone.

DAMIS: I won't say a word.

DORINE: That's what *you* think! We all know how excitable you are and that's just the way to spoil everything. Off you go.

DAMIS: No I must see it. I won't lose my temper.

DORINE: How tiresome you are. Here he comes. Do go.

    [*Enter* TARTUFFE.]

TARTUFFE: [*seeing* DORINE] Laurent, put away my hair shirt and my scourge and continue to pray Heaven to send you grace. If anyone asks for me I'll be with the prisoners distributing alms.

DORINE: The impudent hypocrite!

TARTUFFE: What do you want?

DORINE: I'm to tell you . . .

TARTUFFE: For Heaven's sake! Before you speak, I pray you take this handkerchief. [*Takes handkerchief from his pocket.*]

DORINE: Whatever do you mean?

TARTUFFE: Cover your bosom. I can't bear to see it. Such pernicious sights give rise to sinful thoughts.

DORINE: You're mighty susceptible to temptation then! The flesh must make a great impression on you! I really don't know why you should get so excited. I can't say that I'm so easily roused. I could see you naked from head to foot and your whole carcass wouldn't tempt me in the least.

TARTUFFE: Pray, speak a little more modestly or I shall have to leave the room.

DORINE: No. No. *I'm* leaving *you*. All I have to say is that the mistress is coming down and would like a word with you.

TARTUFFE: Ah! Most willingly.

DORINE: [*aside*] That changes his tune. Upon my word I'm convinced there is something in what I said.

TARTUFFE: Will she be long?

DORINE: I think I hear her now. Yes, here she comes. I'll leave you together.

    [*Exit* DORINE. *Enter* ELMIRE.]

TARTUFFE: May the bounty of Heaven ever bestow on you health of body and of mind, and extend you blessings commensurate with the prayers of the most humble of its devotees!

ELMIRE: I'm very grateful for these pious wishes. Let us sit down. We shall be more comfortable.

TARTUFFE: Do you feel better of your indisposition?

ELMIRE: Very much. The feverishness soon left me.

TARTUFFE: My prayers have too little merit to have obtained this favour from on high; yet all the petitions I have addressed to Heaven have been concerned with your recovery.

ELMIRE: You are too solicitous on my behalf.

TARTUFFE: One cannot be too solicitous for your precious health. I would have sacrificed my own life for the sake of yours.

ELMIRE: That is carrying Christian charity rather far but I'm truly grateful for your kindness.

TARTUFFE: I do far less for you than you deserve.

ELMIRE: I wanted to speak to you in private on a certain matter. I'm pleased that no one can overhear us.

TARTUFFE: I too am delighted. I need hardly say how pleased I am to find myself alone with you. It's an opportunity which I have besought Heaven to accord me—vainly until this moment.

ELMIRE: What I want is that you should speak frankly and conceal nothing from me.

TARTUFFE: And my sole desire is that you should accord me the singular favour of allowing me to express all that is in my heart and assure you that anything I have said against those who were paying homage to your charms was not spoken in malice against you but rather that the intensity of my pious zeal and pure . . .

ELMIRE: I take it in that sense and believe that it arises from your concern for my salvation.

TARTUFFE: That is indeed so, madam, and such is the fervour of my . . . [*Squeezing her fingers.*]

ELMIRE: Oh! You're hurting me . . .

TARTUFFE: It comes from excess of devotion. I never intended to hurt you. [*Putting his hand upon her knee*] I would rather . . .

ELMIRE: What is your hand doing there?

TARTUFFE: I'm feeling your dress. How soft the material is!

ELMIRE: Please don't. I'm dreadfully ticklish.

[*She pushes back her chair.* TARTUFFE *brings his closer.*]

TARTUFFE: What marvellous lace! They do wonderful work nowadays. Things are so much better made than they used to be.

ELMIRE: Very true, but let us return to our business. They say my husband intends to break his promise to Valère and give his daughter to you. Tell me, is it true?

TARTUFFE: He did mention something about it, but to tell the truth, madam, that isn't the happiness I aspire to. All my hopes of felicity lie in another direction.

ELMIRE: That's because you have no interest in temporal things.

TARTUFFE: *My* breast does not enclose a heart of flint!

ELMIRE: I'm sure your thoughts are all turned Heavenward. Your desires are not concerned with anything here below.

TARTUFFE: A passion for the beauties which are eternal does not preclude a temporal love. Our senses can and do respond to those most perfect works of Heaven's creation, whose charms are exemplified in beings such as you and embodied in rarest measure in yourself. Heaven has lavished upon you a beauty that dazzles the eyes and moves the hearts of men. I never look upon your flawless perfections without adoring in you the great Author of all nature and feeling my heart filled with ardent love for that fair form in which He has portrayed Himself. At first I feared lest this secret passion which consumes me might be some subtle snare of the accursed one. I even resolved to avoid your sight, believing you to be an obstacle to my salvation; but at length I came to realize, O fairest among women, that there need be nothing culpable in my passion and that I could reconcile it with virtue. Since then I have surrendered to it heart and soul. It is, I admit, no small presumption on my part to address to you this offer of my love, but I rely upon your generosity and in no wise upon my own unworthy self: my hopes, my happiness, my peace are in your keeping: on you my bliss or future misery depends: my future hangs on your decree: make me for ever happy if such be your will, wretched if you would have it so.

ELMIRE: A very gallant declaration but a little surprising I must confess! It seems to me you ought to steel yourself more firmly against temptation and consider more deeply what you are about. A pious man like you, a holy man whom everyone . . .

TARTUFFE: Ah! But I'm not less a man for being devout! Confronted by your celestial beauty one can but let love have its way and make no demur. I realize that such a declaration coming from me may well seem strange but, after all, madam, I'm not an angel. If you condemn this declaration of mine you must lay the blame on your own enchanting loveliness. From the first moment that I beheld its more than mortal splendours you have ruled supreme in my affection. Those glances, goddess-like and gracious beyond all description, broke down my stubborn heart's resistance, surmounted every obstacle, prayers, fasting, tears, and turned all my thoughts to love of you. My eyes, my sighs, have told you a thousand times what I am now seeking to express in words. If you should turn a kindly eye upon the tribulations of your unworthy slave, if in your generosity you should choose to afford me consolation and deign to notice my insignificance, then I would offer you for ever, O miracle of loveliness, a devotion beyond compare. Moreover, your honour runs no risk with me; at my hands you need fear no danger of disgrace; these courtly gallants that women are so fond of noise their deeds abroad; they are for ever bragging of their conquests, never receiving a favour but they must divulge it, profaning with blabbing tongues (which folk still put their trust in) the altar to which they bring their offerings. But men of our sort burn with discreeter fires; our secrets are for ever sure; our concern for our own reputation is a safeguard for those we love, and to those who trust us we offer love without scandal, satisfaction without fear.

ELMIRE: I have listened to what you say and your eloquence has made your meaning sufficiently clear, but are you not afraid that I might take it into my head to tell my husband of this charming declaration of yours and that such a disclosure might impair his friendly feelings for you?

TARTUFFE: I know you are too kind, that you will pardon my temerity, condone as human frailty the transports of a passion which offends you, and, when you consult your glass, reflect that I'm not blind and that a man is but flesh and blood.

ELMIRE: Others might perhaps take a different course but I prefer to show discretion. I shall say nothing to my husband, but in return I must ask one thing of you—that you give your support openly and sincerely to the marriage of Valère and Mariane, renounce the exercise of that improper influence by which you have sought to promote your own hopes at the expense of another and . . .

DAMIS: [*coming out of the closet where he has been hidden*] No, no! This must be made known! I was in there and heard everything. Heaven's mercy has brought me here to confound the arrogance of a villain who intends me harm: it has offered me the opportunity to be revenged upon his insolence and hypocrisy, to undeceive my father, and lay bare the soul of this scoundrel who talks to you of love!

ELMIRE: No, Damis, it is sufficient that he should mend his ways and endeavour to deserve the pardon I have promised him. I have given my word so don't make me break it. I'm not one to make a fuss: a wife makes light of follies such as these and never troubles her husband with them.

DAMIS: You may have your reasons for doing this but I have mine for doing otherwise. Your wish to spare him is absurd. He has already triumphed sufficiently over my just resentment with his insolence and humbug and made enough trouble among us. The scoundrel has ruled my father long enough and thwarted my love as well as Valère's. My father must be shown what a perfidious wretch he is and Providence now offers a simple means of doing it. I'm answerable to Heaven for this opportunity and it's too favourable to be neglected. Not to make use of it would be to deserve to lose it.

ELMIRE: Damis . . .

DAMIS: No. Pardon me—I must trust to my own judgement. I'm overjoyed. Nothing you say can dissuade me from the pleasure of revenge. I'll finish the business without more ado, and [*seeing* ORGON] here comes the instrument of my satisfaction.

[*Enter* ORGON.]

DAMIS: We have interesting news for you father. Something has just occurred which will astonish you. You are well repaid for your kindness! The gentleman sets a very high value on the consideration you have shown for him! He has just been demonstrating his passionate concern for you and he stops at nothing less than dishonouring your bed. I have just overheard him making a disgraceful declaration of his guilty passion for your wife. She in kind-heartedness and over-anxiety to be discreet was all for keeping it secret but I can't condone such shameless behaviour. I consider it would be a gross injustice to you to keep it from you.

ELMIRE: Well, I still think a wife shouldn't disturb her husband's peace of mind by repeating such silly nonsense to him; one's honour is in no wise involved. It's sufficient that we women should know how to defend ourselves. That's what I think and if you had taken notice of me you would not have said anything at all. [*Exit.*]

ORGON: Oh Heavens! Can what they say be true?

TARTUFFE: Yes, brother, I am a guilty wretch, a miserable sinner steeped in iniquity, the greatest villain that ever existed; not a moment of my life but is sullied with some foul deed: it's a succession of wickedness and corruption. I see now that Heaven is taking this opportunity of chastising me for my sins. Whatever crime I may be charged with, far be it from me to take pride in denying it! Believe what they tell you. Set no bounds to your resentment! Hound me like a felon from your doors! Whatever shame is heaped upon me I shall have deserved much more.

ORGON: [*to his son*] Ah! Miscreant! How dare you seek to tarnish his unspotted virtue with this false accusation?

DAMIS: What! Can a pretence of meekness from this hypocrite make you deny . . .

ORGON: Silence! You accursed plague!

TARTUFFE: Ah, let him speak. You do wrong to accuse him. You would do better to believe what he tells you. Why should you take such a favourable view of me? After all, do you know what I am capable of? Why should you trust appearances? Do you think well of me because of what I seem to be? No, no, you are letting yourself be deceived by outward show. I am, alas, no better than they think; everyone takes me for a good man but the truth is I'm good for nothing. [*speaking to* DAMIS] Yes, my son, speak freely, call me deceitful, infamous, abandoned, thief, murderer, load me with names yet more detestable, I'll not deny them. I've deserved them all, and on my knees I'll suffer the ignominy, in expiation of my shameful life.

ORGON: [*to* TARTUFFE] Brother, this is too much. [*to his son*] Doesn't your heart relent, you dog!

DAMIS: What! Can what he says so far prevail with you that . . .

ORGON: [*raising up* TARTUFFE] Silence you scoundrel! [*to* TARTUFFE] Rise brother—I beg you. [*to his son*] You scoundrel!

DAMIS: He may—

ORGON: Silence!

DAMIS: This is beyond bearing! What! I'm to . . .

ORGON: Say another word and I'll break every bone in your body!

TARTUFFE: In God's name, brother, calm yourself. I would rather suffer any punishment than he should receive the slightest scratch on my account.

ORGON: [*to his son*] Ungrateful wretch!

TARTUFFE: Leave him in peace! If need be, I'll ask your pardon for him on my knees . . .

ORGON: [*to* TARTUFFE] Alas! What are you thinking of? [*to his son*] See how good he is to you, you dog!

DAMIS: Then . . .

ORGON: Enough!

DAMIS: What! Can't I . . .

ORGON: Enough, I say! I know too well why you attack him. You hate him. Every one of you, wife, children, servants, all are in full cry against him. You use every impudent means to drive this devout and holy person from my house: but the more you strive to banish him the more determined I am not to let him go. I'll hasten his marriage with my daughter and confound the pride of the whole family.

DAMIS: You mean to make her accept his hand?

ORGON: Yes, you scoundrel, and this very evening to spite you all. Ah! I defy the lot of you. I'll have you know that I'm the master and I'll be obeyed. Come, retract your accusation instantly, you wretch! Down on your knees and beg forgiveness!

DAMIS: Who? Me? Of a villain whose impostures . . .

ORGON: So you refuse, you scoundrel, do you? And abuse him too! A stick!

Give me a stick! [*to* TARTUFFE] Don't try to restrain me! [*to his son*] Out of my house this instant and never darken my doors again!

DAMIS: Yes, I'll go but . . .

ORGON: Out! Leave the house! Be off! I disinherit you, you dog! And take my curse into the bargain.

    [*Exit* DAMIS.]

ORGON: What a way to insult a holy man!

TARTUFFE: May Heaven forgive him the sorrow that he causes me! Ah, if you only knew how much it grieves me to see them try to blacken me in my brother's esteem—

ORGON: Alas!

TARTUFFE: The mere thought of such ingratitude is unbearable to me . . . it horrifies me . . . it wrings my heart so that I cannot speak . . . it will be the death of me.

ORGON: [*weeping, runs to the door through which he drove forth his son*] Scoundrel! I'm sorry I kept my hands off you and didn't fell you on the spot! [*to* TARTUFFE] Compose yourself brother. Don't give way to your feelings.

TARTUFFE: Let us put an end to these painful dissensions. When I see what troubles I cause here I feel that I must leave you, brother.

ORGON: What! Are you mad?

TARTUFFE: They hate me. I see now they are trying to make you doubt my sincerity.

ORGON: What does it matter? Do you think I listen to them?

TARTUFFE: But they'll not fail to try again. These same reports you have rejected now you may believe another time.

ORGON: No, brother, never!

TARTUFFE: Ah, brother, a wife can easily influence her husband's mind.

ORGON: No. No!

TARTUFFE: Let me go and by going hence remove all occasion for them to attack me.

ORGON: No. No. You shall stay. My very life depends upon it.

TARTUFFE: Well then if it be so, I must sacrifice myself. But if you would only . . .

ORGON: Yes?

TARTUFFE: Let it be so. We'll speak of it no more but I know now what I must do. Reputation is a brittle thing: friendship requires that I should forestall every whisper, every shadow of suspicion. I must forswear the company of your wife and you will never see . . .

ORGON: No! You *shall* see her in spite of them all. Nothing gives me greater joy than to annoy them. You shall appear with her constantly and—to show my defiance, I'll make you my sole heir. I'll make a gift to you in due form of all my goods here and now. My true, dear, friend whom I now take as my son-in-law, you are dearer to me than son or wife or kin. Will you not accept what I am offering you?

TARTUFFE: Heaven's will be done in all things.

ORGON: Poor fellow! Let us go and draft the document at once. And let the whole envious pack of them burst with their own vexation at the news!

ACT IV

[CLÉANTE, TARTUFFE]

CLÉANTE: Yes, everyone is talking about it and, believe me, the sensation the news has made has done your reputation no good. This is an opportune time to tell you briefly and bluntly what I think about it. I won't go into details of the reports that are going about; setting them on one side and taking the matter at its worst, let us suppose that Damis did behave badly and that you were accused unjustly. Wouldn't it be the Christian thing to pardon the offence and forgo your revenge? Can you allow a son to be turned out of his father's house because of your quarrel with him? I tell you again—and I'm speaking frankly—that everybody thinks it shocking —people of all sorts, high and low alike. If you'll take notice of me you'll come to terms and not push things to extremes. Sacrifice your resentment as a Christian should and reconcile the son to his father again.

TARTUFFE: Alas! For my own part, I would willingly do so. I harbour no resentment against him, sir. I forgive him everything. I don't blame him at all. I would do anything I could for him and gladly, but the interests of Heaven forbid it. If he comes back here, then I must go. After such unheard-of behaviour any further relations between us would create a scandal. God knows what people might think of it! They would impute it to purely material considerations on my part and say that, knowing I was guilty, I feigned a charitable concern for my accuser; that in my heart of hearts I was afraid of him, and sought an arrangement with him to keep his mouth shut.

CLÉANTE: That's just putting me off with specious excuses. Your arguments are all too far fetched. Why should you take upon yourself the interests of religion? Can't God punish the guilty without assistance from us? Leave Him to look after his own vengeance. Remember rather that He ordains that we should forgive those who offend against us. When you are following orders from on high why worry about human judgements? What! Lose the glory of doing a good deed for trivial considerations of what people may think! No. No. Let us just obey Heaven's commandᵉ and not bother our heads about anything else.

TARTUFFE: I have already said I forgive him. That's doing what Heaven commands, but Heaven doesn't command me to live with him after the scandal and the insults put on me today.

CLÉANTE: And does it command you to lend an ear to his father's fantastic caprices? Or to accept the gift of possessions to which you have no rightful claim?

TARTUFFE: People who know me will not suspect me of self-interest. Worldly wealth makes little appeal to me. Its tawdry glitter doesn't dazzle me. If I resolve to accept the gift the father insists on offering me it's only because I fear that such possessions may fall into unworthy hands or pass to people who will use them for evil purposes and not employ them as I intend to do, to the glory of God and the good of my neighbour.

CLÉANTE: My good sir, put aside these delicate scruples! They'll get you into trouble with the rightful heir. Let him enjoy his possessions at his own peril without worrying your head about it; consider how much better it would be that he should make ill use of them than that you should find yourself accused of defrauding him! I'm only surprised that you could permit such a proposal without embarrassment. Does any of the maxims of true piety enjoin one to plunder a lawful heir? If Heaven has really inspired you with an insurmountable inability to live in the same house as Damis, wouldn't it be better that you should prudently withdraw rather than let a son be hounded from his father's house on your account in the fact of all right and reason? Believe me, that would be showing some sense of decency and . . .

TARTUFFE: It is now half past three, sir. Certain pious obligations require my presence upstairs without delay. Excuse my leaving you so soon.

[*Exit* TARTUFFE.]

CLÉANTE: Ah!

[*Enter* ELMIRE, MARIANE, DORINE.]

DORINE: Please join with us in trying to help her, Sir. She's in dreadful distress. The betrothal her father has arranged for this evening has reduced her to despair. Here he comes. I beseech you, give us your help. Let us try by hook or crook to frustrate this wretched scheme which is worrying us all.

ORGON: Ah! I'm pleased to find you all here. [*to* MARIANE] I have something in this document to please you. You know what it is.

MARIANE: [*on her knees*] Father, in the name of Heaven which is witness to my unhappiness, and by everything that can move your heart, forgo your rights as a father and absolve me from the dire necessity of obeying you in this matter. Don't drive me, by harsh insistence on your rights, to complain to Heaven of being your daughter; don't condemn to misery the life you have bestowed upon me. If, contrary to the one dear hope I cherished, you now forbid me to give myself to the man I love, save me at least—on my knees I implore you—from the torment of belonging to a man I abhor! Don't drive me to some act of desperation by pushing your authority to the extreme.

ORGON: [*moved*] Steel your heart, man, now! No human weakness!

MARIANE: Your affection for him doesn't trouble me: show it to the full; give him your wealth and, if that's not enough, let him have mine. I consent with all my heart and freely give it to you, but at least don't include me with it. Rather let me spend such sad days as may remain to me within the austere walls of a convent.

ORGON: Oh yes! Of course, girls are all for going into convents as soon as their fathers' wishes conflict with their wanton designs! Get up! The harder you find it to accept him the better for your soul! Marry and mortify the flesh but don't plague me any more with your bawling and crying!

DORINE: But what . . .

ORGON: You be quiet! Mind your own business. I absolutely forbid you to say a single word.

CLÉANTE: If I might be allowed to offer you a word of advice . . .

ORGON: Brother, your advice is always excellent, most cogent, and I value it extremely, but I hope you will allow me to manage without it!

ELMIRE: [*to her husband*] I am at a loss to know what to say after what we have seen; I can only marvel at your blindness. You must be bewitched by the man—infatuated—to deny the truth of what we told you today.

ORGON: With all due deference to you I judge things as I see them. I know your indulgence for that worthless son of mine. You were afraid to admit that he had played a trick on this unfortunate man. But you took it too calmly for me to believe you. Had the accusation been true you would have been in a very different state of mind.

ELMIRE: Why should a woman have to behave as if her honour is imperilled by a mere declaration of love? Is there no answering but with blazing eyes and furious tongue? For my part I just laugh at such advances. I don't like all this fuss at all. I would rather we protected our good name by less violent means. I have no use for virtuous harridans who defend their honour with tooth and claw and scratch a man's eyes out at the slightest word. Heaven preserve me from that sort of rectitude! No woman need be a dragon of vindictiveness. A snub coolly and discreetly given is, I think, sufficiently effective in rebuffing advances.

ORGON: All the same, I know where I stand and I'm not going to be put off.

ELMIRE: I wonder more and more at this strange infatuation, but what would you say if I were actually to show you that we are telling you the truth.

ORGON: Show me?

ELMIRE: Yes.

ORGON: Rubbish!

ELMIRE: Supposing I could contrive a means of letting you see with your own eyes.

ORGON: The very idea!

ELMIRE: What a man you are! Do at least give an answer. I'm not asking you to take my word for it. Supposing that I arranged for you to see and hear everything from some point of vantage, what would you say then about this Godly man of yours?

ORGON: I should say nothing—because it just can't be done.

ELMIRE: This delusion has lasted too long. I have had enough of being accused of deceiving you. It's necessary now for my own satisfaction that I make you a witness to the truth of everything I have said and without more ado.

ORGON: Very well. I'll take you at your word. We'll see what you can do. Let me see how you make good your promise.

ELMIRE: [*to* DORINE] Ask him to come here.

DORINE: He's cunning. He may be difficult to catch.

ELMIRE: No. People are easily taken in by what they love and vanity predisposes them to deception. Have him come down. [*to* CLÉANTE *and* MARIANE] You two must retire.

    [*Exeunt.*]

ELMIRE: Help me to bring the table up. Now get under it.

ORGON: What!

ELMIRE: It's essential that you should be completely hidden.

ORGON: But why under the table?

ELMIRE: Oh, for Heaven's sake leave it to me! I know what I'm doing. You shall see in due course. Get under there and, mind now, take care that he doesn't see or hear you.

ORGON: You are asking a good deal of me, I must say, but I suppose I must see it through now.

ELMIRE: I don't think you'll have any cause to complain but I'm going to play a rather unusual role. Don't be shocked. [ORGON *is under the table.*] I must be allowed to say whatever I like—it will be to convince you as I promised. Since you reduce me to it, I intend to coax this hypocrite to drop his mask, to flatter his impudent desires and encourage his audacity. I shall lead him on merely for the purpose of opening your eyes and exposing him completely. I can stop as soon as you say you give in: things will only go so far as you wish them to go: it will be for you to call a halt to his insensate passion just as soon as you think he has gone far enough: you can spare your poor wife by exposing her to no more than is necessary to disabuse you. It's your affair, and it will be for you to decide . . . but here he comes. Keep in and take care not to be seen.

    [*Enter* TARTUFFE.]

TARTUFFE: I was informed that you wished to speak to me here.

ELMIRE: Yes, I have a secret to tell you—but shut the door before I begin and have a good look round in case we should be overheard. We don't want another business like this morning's. I was never so surprised in my life. Damis made me terribly frightened on your account. You must have seen what efforts I made to check him and quieten him down. The truth is I was so taken aback that it never entered my head to deny his accusations, but there—thank Heaven it all turned out for the best! We are much more secure now in consequence. Your reputation saved us. My husband is incapable of thinking ill of you. He insists on our being together to show his contempt for idle rumour. So now I can be in here with you without fear of reproach and can reveal to you that I'm perhaps only too ready to welcome your love.

TARTUFFE: I find it difficult to follow your meaning, madam. Only a while ago you spoke very differently.

ELMIRE: How little you know the heart of woman if such a rebuff has offended you! How little you understand what we mean to convey when we defend ourselves so feebly! At such moments our modesty and the tender sentiments you arouse in us are still in conflict. However compelling the arguments of passion may be we are still too diffident to confess it: we shrink from an immediate avowal but our manner sufficiently reveals that in our heart of hearts we surrender: though our lips must in honour deny our true feelings, such refusals in fact promise everything. I realize that I am making a very frank admission: it shows little regard for womanly modesty but since I *am* speaking—should I have been so anxious to restrain Damis, should I have listened so indulgently, do you think, to your declaration of love, should I have taken it as I did if I had not welcomed it? Moreover, when I sought to make you renounce the marriage which had just been announced what was that intended to convey to you, if not that I took an interest in you and regretted the conclusion of a marriage which would force me to share an affection I wanted entirely to myself?

TARTUFFE: Ah, Madam, it is indeed delightful to hear such words from the lips of one I love! The honey of your words sets coursing through my whole being sensations more delicious than I have ever known before. My supreme concern is to find favour in your eyes. My hopes of bliss lie in your love. Yet you must forgive me if my heart still dares to entertain some doubt of its own felicity. Suppose what you are saying proved to be no more than a virtuous stratagem to induce me to abandon this impending marriage. If I may be allowed to put the matter frankly, I'll never trust these promises until I have been vouchsafed some small foretaste of the favours for which I yearn—that alone will reassure me and give me absolute confidence in your intentions towards me.

ELMIRE: [*coughing to attract her husband's attention*] Why must you go so fast? Would you have me reveal at once all that I feel for you? I have overstepped the bounds of modesty in confessing my feelings and yet it isn't enough for you! Can there be no satisfying you without going to ultimate lengths?

TARTUFFE: The less one deserves the less one dares to hope, and words are poor assurances of love. One cannot but mistrust a prospect of felicity: one must enjoy it before one can believe in it. Knowing how little I deserve your favours I doubt the outcome of my own temerity. I'll believe nothing until you give me proofs tangible enough to satisfy my passion.

ELMIRE: Heavens! What an importunate lover you are! I just don't know where I am. You quite overwhelm me—is there no denying you? Is there no evading your demands? Won't you even allow me a breathing space? How can you be so insistent, so peremptory, so merciless? How can you take such advantage of one's fondness for you?

TARTUFFE: But if you look upon my advances with a favourable eye, why refuse me convincing proof?

ELMIRE: How can I consent to what you ask without offending Him whose name is ever on your lips?

TARTUFFE: If fear of Heaven is the only obstacle to my passion that is a barrier I can easily remove. That need not restrain you.

ELMIRE: But they threaten us with the wrath of Heaven.

TARTUFFE: I can dissipate these foolish fears for you. I know the way to remove such scruples. It is true that certain forms of indulgence[3] are forbidden but there are ways and means of coming to terms with Heaven, of easing the restraints of conscience according to the exigencies of the case, of redressing the evil of the action by the purity of the intention. I can instruct you in these secrets, Madam. Only allow yourself to be led by me. Satisfy my desires and have not the slightest fear. I will answer for everything and take the sin upon myself. You have a bad cough, Madam.

ELMIRE: Yes! I'm in great distress.

[3] *Molière's footnote:* "It is a scoundrel speaking"

TARTUFFE: Would you care for a little of this liquorice?

ELMIRE: It's a most obstinate cold. I fear that all the liquorice in the world won't help me now.

TARTUFFE: It is certainly very trying.

ELMIRE: More so than I can say.

TARTUFFE: As I was saying then, your scruples can easily be removed. You are assured of absolute secrecy with me and the harm of any action lies only in its being known. The public scandal is what constitutes the offence: sins sinned in secret are no sins at all.

ELMIRE: [*after coughing again*] Very well then, I see that I must make up my mind to yield and consent to accord you everything you wish. It's no use hoping that anything less will satisfy or convey conviction. It's hard indeed to go to such lengths: it's very much against my will that I do so but since, it seems, I *have* to do it, since I'm not believed in spite of all I've said, since proofs still more convincing are required—I must resign myself to doing what's required of me. But if in consenting I offend, so much the worse for him who forces me to such extremity. The fault can surely not be accounted mine.

TARTUFFE: Yes, Madam, upon me be it and . . .

ELMIRE: Just open the door a moment and make sure that my husband isn't in the gallery.

TARTUFFE: Why worry about him? Between ourselves—he's a fellow one can lead by the nose. He glories in our association. I've got him to the stage where though he saw everything with his own eyes he wouldn't believe it.

ELMIRE: All the same, do go out a moment, please, and have a good look round.

ORGON: [*coming out from under the table*] Yes! I must admit it! The man's an abominable scoundrel! I can't get over it! I'm in a daze.

ELMIRE: But why come out so soon? You can't mean what you say! Get under the table again! It's not time yet. Wait till the very end and make quite sure. Don't trust to mere conjecture.

ORGON: No! No! Hell itself never produced anything more wicked.

ELMIRE: Good Heavens! You mustn't believe as easily as that. Wait until you are utterly convinced before you give in. Don't be too hasty! You might be mistaken! [*She puts her husband behind her.*]

　　　　[*Re-enter* TARTUFFE.]

TARTUFFE: Everything favours me, Madam. I've looked in all the rooms. There's no one there and now my rapture . . .

ORGON: [*stopping him*] Steady! You are letting your amorous desires run away with you. You shouldn't get so excited! Ah ha, my godly friend, you would deceive me, would you? How you give way to temptation! You meant to marry my daughter and yet you coveted my wife! For a long time I couldn't believe that it was really true and thought to hear you change your tune: but the proof has gone far enough. I'm convinced, and, for my part, I ask nothing further.

ELMIRE: [*to* TARTUFFE] It was very disagreeable to me to do it. I was driven to treat you like this.

TARTUFFE: [*to* ORGON] What! You believe . . .

ORGON: Come, let's have no more of it, please. Get out of the house without more ado.

TARTUFFE: My intention . . .

ORGON: That sort of talk won't do now. You must leave the house forthwith.

TARTUFFE: You are the one who must leave the house—you who talk as if you were master. This house is mine and I'll have you realize it. What's more, I'll show you how vainly you resort to these devices for picking a quarrel with me. You little know what you are doing when you insult me. I have the means to confound and punish your imposture, avenge the affront to Heaven, and make those who talk of making me leave the house regret it.
[*Exit* TARTUFFE.]

ELMIRE: What is he talking about? What does he mean?

ORGON: Alas! I don't know what to do. This is no laughing matter.

ELMIRE: Why? What . . .

ORGON: What he said makes me realize my mistake. My deed of gift begins to worry me.

ELMIRE: Your deed of gift . . . ?

ORGON: Yes, there's no going back upon it now, but there's something else that worries me.

ELMIRE: What is it?

ORGON: I'll tell you everything but I must go at once and see whether a certain casket is still upstairs.

ACT V

[ORGON, CLÉANTE]

CLÉANTE: Where are you off to?

ORGON: Alas! How do I know?

CLÉANTE: The first thing is to consider what's to be done.

ORGON: It's the casket that's worrying me. I'm more concerned about that than anything else.

CLÉANTE: Is there some important secret about the casket?

ORGON: Argas, my lamented friend, left it with me for safe keeping. He put it into my hands himself in the greatest secrecy. He selected me for this when he fled the country. It contains documents on which, he told me, his life and property depended.

CLÉANTE: Then why did you trust them to someone else?

ORGON: Because of a scruple of conscience. I went straight to this scoundrel and took him into my confidence. He persuaded me that it was better to let him have the casket for safe keeping so that in case of inquiry I could deny that I had it, and yet safeguard my conscience so far as giving false testimony was concerned.

CLÉANTE: You're in a difficult position it seems to me. Both the deed of gift and your action in confiding the casket to him were, if I may say so, very ill considered; he's in a position to lead you a pretty dance! What's more it was most imprudent to provoke him when he has such a hold upon you. You ought to have been more conciliatory in dealing with him.

ORGON: What! A fellow who could hide such double dealing, such wickedness, under the outward semblance of ardent piety, a man whom I took into my house as a penniless beggar . . . No, that's finished with: I'll have no more to do with godly men. I'll hold them in utter abhorrence in future. I'll consider nothing too bad for them!

CLÉANTE: There you go again! No moderation in anything! You are incapable of being temperate and sensible; you seem to have no idea of behaving reasonably. You must always be rushing from one extreme to the other. You see your mistake now; you've learned that you were taken in by an assumed piety; but what's the good of correcting one error by an even greater one, and failing to make a distinction between a scoundrelly good for nothing and genuinely good men? Because an audacious rogue has deceived you by a pretentious assumption of virtue and piety must you go and think everybody is like him and that there are no truly devout people nowadays? Leave such foolish inferences to the unbelievers; distinguish between virtue and the outward appearance of it, don't be so hasty in bestowing your esteem, and keep a sense of proportion. Be on your guard if you can against paying deference to imposture but say nothing against true devotion, and if you must run to extremes, better err on the same side as you did before.

    [*Enter* DAMIS.]

DAMIS: Is it true, father, that this scoundrel is threatening you, that he's insensible to every benefit, and that in his wicked and outrageous pride he is turning your own generosity against you?

ORGON: It is, my son, and a dreadful grief it is to me too.

DAMIS: Leave it to me! I'll crop his ears for him. No half-measures with a rascal like that! I'll undertake to rid you of him without delay. I'll settle the business! I'll deal with him.

CLÉANTE: That's typical young man's talk. Moderate your feelings for goodness sake! We live in an age and under a government where it goes ill with those who resort to violence.

    [*Enter* MADAME PERNELLE.]

MADAME PERNELLE: What's all this? What are these strange goings-on I have been hearing about?

ORGON: Ay! Strange indeed and I've seen them with my own eyes too. This is the reward I get for my pains. In sheer kindness of heart I relieve a man in his misery, receive him into my house, treat him like a brother, load him with kindness, give him my daughter, everything I possess, and what does the infamous scoundrel do but foully endeavour to seduce my wife! Not content with that he has the audacity to turn my own benevolence against me and threatens to ruin me with the weapons my own unwise generosity has put into his hand, deprive me of my possessions, and reduce me to the beggary from which I rescued him.

DORINE: Poor fellow!

MADAME PERNELLE: My son, I just can't believe that he has been guilty of such wickedness.

ORGON: How d'ye mean?

MADAME PERNELLE: People are always envious of the righteous.

ORGON: Whatever are you talking about, mother?

MADAME PERNELLE: I mean that there are queer goings-on in this house and I know very well how much they hate him.

ORGON: What has their hatred to do with what I'm telling you?

MADAME PERNELLE: I told you a hundred times when you were a little boy.

> 'Virtue, on earth, is persecuted ever
> The envious die, but envy never.'

ORGON: But what has this to do with what has happened?

MADAME PERNELLE: They'll have made up a hundred idle tales about him.

ORGON: I've already told you that *I saw it all myself*.

MADAME PERNELLE: There are no limits to the malice of slanderous tongues.

ORGON: You'll make me swear, mother, I've told you I saw his wickedness with my own eyes.

MADAME PERNELLE: Malicious tongues spread their poison abroad and nothing here below is proof against them.

ORGON: This is ridiculous talk. I *saw* him, I tell you, *saw him* with my own eyes! When I say I saw him I mean I really did see it! Must I go on saying it? How many times am I to tell you? Must I bawl it at the top of my voice?

MADAME PERNELLE: Good Heavens, appearances can often be deceptive. One shouldn't judge by what one sees.

ORGON: You'll drive me mad!

MADAME PERNELLE: It's human nature to think evil of people. Goodness is often misinterpreted.

ORGON: Am I to interpret it as kindly solicitude when I see him trying to kiss my wife?

MADAME PERNELLE: One ought never to make accusations without just cause. You should have waited until you were quite certain of his intentions.

ORGON: What the devil! How was I to be more certain? I should have waited, should I, until he . . . You'll drive me to say something I shouldn't.

MADAME PERNELLE: No, no! He's far too good a man. I just can't imagine he meant to do what you are saying he did.

ORGON: Look here! If you weren't my mother—I don't know what I wouldn't say to you—I'm so angry.

DORINE: Serves you right, master; it's the way of the world. *You* refused to believe once and now she won't believe you.

CLÉANTE: We are wasting time with this nonsense which we ought to be using for making plans. We can't afford to go to sleep in face of the scoundrel's threats.

DAMIS: Why! Do you think he'll really have the audacity to carry them out?

ELMIRE: I can't think he would have a case. His ingratitude is too glaring.

CLÉANTE: I shouldn't rely on that. He'll find means to justify whatever he does to you. Intrigue has landed people in difficulties on less evidence than this before now. I repeat what I said before: when he was in so strong a position as he is, you should never have provoked him so far.

ORGON: True. But what could I do? The audacity of the villain was such that I wasn't master of my feelings.

CLÉANTE: I only wish we could patch up some sort of reconciliation.

ELMIRE: Had I known what a strong position he was in I would never have been a party to making such a fuss . . .

ORGON: [*to* DORINE] What does *this* fellow want? Go at once and see. I'm in a fine state for anyone to come to see me.

[*Enter* MR LOYAL.]

MR LOYAL: Good afternoon, dear sister. Pray let me speak with the master.

DORINE: He has company. I don't suppose he can see anyone just now.

MR LOYAL: I'm not for being troublesome. I don't think he'll find *my* visit unsatisfactory. He'll be pleased with what I've come about.

DORINE: Your name?

MR LOYAL: Just tell him that I'm here on behalf of Mr Tartuffe and for his own good.

DORINE: [*to* ORGON] It's a man who's come on behalf of Mr Tartuffe. He's very civil about it. He says that his business is something that you will be pleased to hear.

CLÉANTE: [*to* ORGON] We must see who the man is and what he wants.

ORGON: Perhaps he's come to reconcile us. How should I behave to him?

CLÉANTE: Don't show your resentment. If he's for coming to an agreement you must listen to him.

MR LOYAL: How d'ye do, sir. May Heaven bless you and confound all who seek to do you harm.

ORGON: [*aside to* CLÉANTE] This civil beginning confirms my impression. It means a reconciliation.

MR LOYAL: I have always been very devoted to your family. I was once in your father's service.

ORGON: I'm sorry not to recognize you. You must forgive me but I don't know your name.

MR LOYAL: Loyal's the name. Norman by birth and bailiff to the court; and let them envy me that want to. I can rightly claim to have discharged my duty with credit this forty year now, Heaven be praised, and now I've come, sir, to serve this writ upon you, excusing the liberty.

ORGON: What! You've come to . . .

MR LOYAL: Now take it quiet, sir. It's only a writ, an order to quit the house at once, you and yours, bag and baggage, and make way for others, without delay and without fail as herein provided.

ORGON: What, me? Leave the house?

MR LOYAL: That's it, sir, if you don't mind. This house is now, as you be duly aware, good Mr Tartuffe's and no argument about it. He's lord and master of your possessions from now on by virtue of the deed that I be the bearer of. It's in due form and there's no disputing it.

DAMIS: What marvellous impudence!

MR LOYAL: [*to* DAMIS] I want nothing to do with you, sir. It's this gentleman I'm dealing with. He's reasonable and good to deal with and he knows too well what a good man's duty is to want to interfere with the course of justice.

ORGON: But . . .

MR LOYAL: Yes sir. I know you'd never resist authority, not on any consideration. You'll allow me to carry out my orders as a gentleman should.

DAMIS: You may as easily find yourself getting a hiding for all your black gown, Mr Bailiff.

MR LOYAL: Ask your son to hold his tongue, sir, or retire. I should be very sorry to have to report you.

DORINE: He should be *Dis*loyal, not Loyal, by the look of him.

MR LOYAL: I have a soft spot for godly men, sir, and I only took service of this writ in consideration for you sir, and just to be helpful and to stop the job falling to anybody who mightn't have the same feeling for you that I have and wouldn't have gone about things so considerate-like.

ORGON: And what could be worse than ordering a man out of his own house?

MR LOYAL: We are giving you time. I'll give a stay of execution till tomorrow. I'll just come and pass the night here with a dozen or so of my men without fuss or scandal. I must ask for the keys as a matter of form, of course, before you go to bed. I'll take pains not to disturb your rest and I'll see that there's nothing that isn't as it should be. But tomorrow morning you'll have to look slippy and clear everything out of here down to the last article. My men will help you. I've picked a handy lot so that they can get everything out for you. Nobody could treat you fairer than that and, seeing as I'm showing you every consideration, I ask the same from you, sir—that is, that you won't do nothing to hinder me in discharge of my duty.

ORGON: [*aside*] I'd willingly give the last hundred louis I possess for the pleasure of landing him a punch on his ugly snout!

CLÉANTE: [*whispers to* ORGON] Steady. Don't do anything foolish.

DAMIS: I can hardly restrain myself before such unheard-of insolence. I'm itching to be at him.

DORINE: That broad back of yours could do with a good dusting, Mr Loyal.

MR LOYAL: I could get you into trouble for talking like that, my lass. The law applies to women as well, you know.

CLÉANTE: [*to* LOYAL] That's enough, sir. We'll leave it at that. Give us the document and go.

MR LOYAL: Good day then. The Lord be with you all.

     [*Exit* MR LOYAL.]

ORGON: Ay, and the Devil take you and him who sent you! Well mother, you see now whether I was right or not. On the other point you can judge from the writ. Do you realize now what a rascal he is?

MADAME PERNELLE: I don't know whether I'm on my head or my heels.

DORINE: You have no cause for complaint and no right to blame him. It all fits in with his pious intentions; it's all part of his love for his neighbour. He knows how possessions corrupt a man and it's pure charity on his part to rob you of everything that might stand in the way of your salvation.

ORGON: Be quiet! I'm always having to remind you!

CLÉANTE: Let us go and take counsel on what course to follow.

ELMIRE: Go and expose the ungrateful scoundrel! This last act of his must invalidate the deed of gift. His treachery must appear too obvious to permit him the success we fear.

[*Enter* VALÈRE.]

VALÈRE: I'm very sorry to bring you bad news, sis, but I'm obliged to do so because you are in most urgent danger. A very close friend who knows the interest I have reason to take in your welfare has violated the secrecy due to affairs of state and sent me intelligence, in confidence. The purport of it is that you must fly immediately. The scoundrel, who has so long imposed upon you, denounced you to the King an hour ago and, among various charges made against you, put into his hands a casket which belonged to a disaffected person whose secrets he contends you have kept in breach of your duty as a subject. I know no particulars of the offence with which you are charged but a warrant has been issued for your arrest and to ensure effective service of it Tartuffe himself is commanded to accompany the person who is to apprehend you.

CLÉANTE: And so he strengthens his hand! That's how he means to make himself master of your possessions.

ORGON: I must admit, the man really is a brute!

VALÈRE: The slightest delay may be fatal to you. I have my carriage at the door to take you away, and a thousand guineas which I have brought for you. We must lose no time: this is a shattering blow—there's no avoiding it except by flight. I offer you my services to conduct you to some place of safety. I'll stay with you until you are out of danger.

ORGON: Alas! How can I repay your kindness? But I must leave my thanks to another time. May Heaven allow me some day to return this service! Farewell! Take care all of you . . .

CLÉANTE: Go at once, brother. We'll see that everything necessary is done.

[*Enter* TARTUFFE *and an* OFFICER.]

TARTUFFE: Gently, sir, gently, don't run so fast. You don't need to go very far to find a lodging. You are a prisoner in the King's name.

ORGON: Villain! To keep this trick to the last! This is the blow whereby you finish me, the master stroke of all your perfidy!

TARTUFFE: Your insults are powerless to move me. I am schooled to suffer everything in the cause of Heaven.

CLÉANTE: Remarkable meekness indeed!

DAMIS: How impudently the dog makes mockery of Heaven.

TARTUFFE: Not all your rage can move me. I have no thought for anything but to fulfil my duty.

MARIANE: What credit can you hope to reap from this? How can you regard such employment as honourable?

TARTUFFE: Any employment must needs be honourable which proceeds from that authority which sent me hither.

ORGON: And do you not remember, ungrateful wretch, that it was my charitable hand which rescued you from indigence?

TARTUFFE: Yes, I am mindful of the assistance I received from you, but my first duty is to the interests of my King and that sacred obligation is so strong as to extinguish in me all gratitude to you. To that allegiance I would sacrifice friends, wife, kinsmen, and myself with them.

ELMIRE: Impostor!

DORINE: How cunningly he cloaks his villainies with the mantle of all that we most revere!

CLÉANTE: If this consuming zeal of which you boast is as great as you say, why didn't it come to light until he had caught you making love to his wife? Why didn't it occur to you to denounce him until your attempt to dishonour him had forced him to turn you out? If I mention the gift it isn't to deter you from doing your duty but, nevertheless, if you want to treat him as a criminal now, why did you consent to accept anything from him before?

TARTUFFE: Pray deliver me from this futile clamour, sir! Proceed to the execution of your orders.

OFFICER: Yes. I have indeed waited too long already and you do well to recall me to my duty. In fulfilment of my instructions I command you to accompany me forthwith to the prison in which you are to be lodged.

TARTUFFE: What? Me, sir?

OFFICER: Yes, you.

TARTUFFE: But why to prison?

OFFICER: I am not accountable to you. [*to* ORGON] Calm your fears, sir. We live under the rule of a prince inimical to fraud, a monarch who can read men's hearts, whom no impostor's art deceives. The keen discernment of that lofty mind at all times sees things in their true perspective; nothing can disturb the firm constancy of his judgement nor lead him into error. On men of worth he confers immortal glory but his favour is not shown indiscriminately: his love for good men and true does not preclude a proper detestation of those who are false. This man could never deceive him—he has evaded more subtle snares than his. From the outset he discerned to the full the baseness of the villain's heart and in coming to accuse you he betrayed himself and by a stroke of supreme justice revealed himself as a notorious scoundrel of whose activities under another name His Majesty was already informed. The long history of his dark crimes would fill volumes. In short, the King, filled with detestation for his base ingratitude and wickedness to you, added this to his other crimes and only put me under his orders to see to what lengths his impudence would go and to oblige him to give you full satisfaction. All documents he says he has of yours I am to take from him in your presence and restore them to you and His Majesty annuls by act of sovereign prerogative the deed of gift of your possessions that you made to him. Moreover, he pardons you that clandestine offence in which the flight of your friend involved you: this clemency he bestows upon you in recognition of your former loyal service and to let you see that he can reward a good action when least expected, that he is never insensible to true merit and chooses rather to remember good than ill.

DORINE: Heaven be praised!

MADAME PERNELLE: Now I can breathe again.

ELMIRE: A happy end to all our troubles!

MARIANE: Who could have foretold this?

ORGON: [*to* TARTUFFE] So you see, you villain, you . . .

CLÉANTE: Ah! Brother forbear. Do not stoop to such indignity. Leave the unhappy creature to his fate. Add nothing to the remorse which must now overwhelm him. Rather hope that he may henceforward return to the paths of virtue, reform his life, learn to detest his vices, and so earn some mitigation of the justice of the King. Meanwhile, for your own part, you must go on your knees and render appropriate thanks for the benevolence His Majesty has shown to you.

ORGON: Yes, that's well said. Let us go and offer him our humble thanks for all his generosity to us. Then, that first duty done, we have another to perform—to crown the happiness of Valère, a lover who has proved both generous and sincere.

RICHARD BRINSLEY SHERIDAN

THE SCHOOL FOR SCANDAL

CHARACTERS

SIR PETER TEAZLE	MOSES
SIR OLIVER SURFACE	TRIP
JOSEPH SURFACE	SIR HARRY BUMPER
CHARLES SURFACE	LADY TEAZLE
CARELESS	MARIA
SNAKE	LADY SNEERWELL
SIR BENJAMIN BACKBITE	MRS. CANDOUR
CRABTREE	*Gentlemen, Maid,*
ROWLEY	*and Servants*

THE SCENE *is London in the 1770's.*

PROLOGUE

[*Written by* MR. GARRICK]
[*Spoken by* SIR PETER TEAZLE.]

A School for Scandal! tell me, I beseech you,
Needs there a school this modish art to teach you?
No need of lessons now, the knowing think;
We might as well be taught to eat and drink.
Caused by a dearth of scandal, should the vapors
Distress our fair ones—let them read the papers;
Their powerful mixtures such disorders hit;
Crave what you will—there's *quantum sufficit.*
"Lord!" cries my Lady Wormwood (who loves tattle,
And puts much salt and pepper in her prattle),
Just risen at noon, all night at cards when threshing
Strong tea and scandal—"Bless me, how refreshing!
Give me the papers, Lisp—how bold and free! (*sips*)
Last night Lord L. (*sips*) *was caught with Lady D.*
For aching heads what charming sal volatile! (*sips*)
If Mrs. B. will still continue flirting,
We hope she'll DRAW, *or we'll* UNDRAW *the curtain.*
Fine satire, poz—in public all abuse it,
But, by ourselves (*sips*), our praise we can't refuse it.
Now, Lisp, read you—there at that dash and star."
"Yes, ma'am—*A certain Lord had best beware,*
Who lives not twenty miles from Grosvenor Square;

For should he Lady W. find willing,
Wormwood is bitter"—"Oh! that's me! the villian!
Throw it behind the fire, and never more
Let that vile paper come within my door."
Thus at our friends we laugh, who feel the dart;
To reach our feelings, we ourselves must smart.
Is our young bard so young, to think that he
Can stop the full spring-tide of calumny?
Knows he the world so little, and its trade?
Alas! the devil's sooner raised than laid.
So strong, so swift, the monster there's no gagging:
Cut Scandal's head off, still the tongue is wagging.
Proud of your smiles once lavishly bestowed,
Again our young Don Quixote takes the road;
To show his gratitude he draws his pen,
And seeks his hydra, Scandal, in his den.
For your applause all perils he would through—
He'll fight—thats *write*—a cavalliero true,
Till every drop of blood—that's *ink*—is spilt for you.

ACT I. SCENE I——LADY SNEERWELL's *dressing-room.*

[LADY SNEERWELL *at her dressing-table;* SNAKE *drinking chocolate.*]

LADY SNEERWELL: The paragraphs, you say, Mr. Snake, were all inserted?

SNAKE: They were, madam; and, as I copied them myself in a feigned hand, there can be no suspicion whence they came.

LADY SNEERWELL: Did you circulate the report of Lady Brittle's intrigue with Captain Boastall?

SNAKE: That's in as fine a train as your ladyship could wish. In the common course of things, I think it must reach Mrs. Clackitt's ears within four-and-twenty hours; and then, you know, the business is as good as done.

LADY SNEERWELL: Why, truly, Mrs. Clackitt has a very pretty talent, and a great deal of industry.

SNAKE: True, madam, and has been tolerably successful in her day. To my knowledge, she has been the cause of six matches being broken off, and three sons being disinherited; of four forced elopements, and as many close confinements; nine separate maintenances, and two divorces. Nay, I have more than once traced her causing a *tête-à-tête* in the *Town and Country Magazine*, when the parties, perhaps, had never seen each other's face before in the course of their lives.

LADY SNEERWELL: She certainly has talents, but her manner is gross.

SNAKE: 'Tis very true. She generally designs well, has a free tongue and a bold invention; but her coloring is too dark, and her outlines often extravagant. She wants that delicacy of tint, and mellowness of sneer, which distinguish your ladyship's scandal.

LADY SNEERWELL: You are partial, Snake.

SNAKE: Not in the least; everybody allows that Lady Sneerwell can do more with a word or look than many can with the most labored detail, even when they happen to have a little truth on their side to support it.

LADY SNEERWELL: Yes, my dear Snake; and I am no hypocrite to deny the satisfaction I reap from the success of my efforts. Wounded myself in the early part of my life, by the envenomed tongue of slander, I confess I have since known no pleasure equal to the reducing others to the level of my own injured reputation.

SNAKE: Nothing can be more natural. But, Lady Sneerwell, there is one affair in which you have lately employed me, wherein, I confess, I am at a loss to guess your motives.

LADY SNEERWELL: I conceive you mean with respect to my neighbor, Sir Peter Teazle, and his family?

SNAKE: I do. Here are two young men, to whom Sir Peter has acted as kind of guardian since their father's death; the eldest possessing the most amiable character, and universally well spoken of—the youngest, the most dissipated and extravagant young fellow in the kingdom, without friends or character: the former an avowed admirer of your ladyship, and apparently your favorite; the latter attached to Maria, Sir Peter's ward, and confessedly beloved by her. Now, on the face of these circumstances, it is utterly unaccountable to me why you, the widow of a city knight, with a good jointure, should not close with the passion of a man of such character and expectations as Mr. Surface; and more so, why you should be so uncommonly earnest to destroy the mutual attachment subsisting between his brother Charles and Maria.

LADY SNEERWELL: Then, at once to unravel this mystery, I must inform you that love has no share whatever in the intercourse between Mr. Surface and me.

SNAKE: No!

LADY SNEERWELL: His real attachment is to Maria or her fortune; but, finding in his brother a favorite rival, he has been obliged to mask his pretensions and profit by my assistance.

SNAKE: Yet still I am more puzzled why you should interest yourself in his success.

LADY SNEERWELL: Heavens! how dull you are! Cannot you surmise the weakness which I hitherto, through shame, have concealed even from you? Must I confess that Charles—that libertine, that extravagant, that bankrupt in fortune and reputation—that he it is for whom I am thus anxious and malicious, and to gain whom I would sacrifice everything?

SNAKE: Now, indeed, your conduct appears consistent; but how came you and Mr. Surface so confidential?

LADY SNEERWELL: For our mutual interest. I have found him out a long time since. I know him to be artful, selfish, and malicious—in short, a sentimental knave; while with Sir Peter, and indeed with all his acquaintance, he passes for a youthful miracle of prudence, good sense, and benevolence.

SNAKE: Yes! yet Sir Peter vows he has not his equal in England; and, above all, he praises him as a man of sentiment.

LADY SNEERWELL: True; and with the assistance of his sentiment and hypocrisy he has brought Sir Peter entirely into his interest with regard to Maria; while poor Charles has no friend in the house—though, I fear, he has a powerful one in Maria's heart, against whom we must direct our schemes.

    [*Enter* SERVANT.]

SERVANT: Mr. Surface.

LADY SNEERWELL: Show him up.

    [*Exit* SERVANT.]

He generally calls about this time. I don't wonder at people giving him to me for a lover.

    [*Enter* JOSEPH SURFACE.]

JOSEPH SURFACE: My dear Lady Sneerwell, how do you do today? Mr. Snake, your most obedient.

LADY SNEERWELL: Snake has just been rallying me on our mutual attachment; but I have informed him of our real views. You know how useful he has been to us; and, believe me, the confidence is not ill placed.

JOSEPH SURFACE: Madam, it is impossible for me to suspect a man of Mr. Snake's sensibility and discernment.

LADY SNEERWELL: Well, well, no compliments now; but tell me when you saw your mistress, Maria—or, what is more material to me, your brother.

JOSEPH SURFACE: I have not seen either since I left you; but I can inform you that they never meet. Some of your stories have taken a good effect on Maria.

LADY SNEERWELL: Ah, my dear Snake! the merit of this belongs to you. But do your brother's distresses increase?

JOSEPH SURFACE: Every hour. I am told he has had another execution in the house yesterday. In short, his dissipation and extravagance exceed anything I have ever heard of.

LADY SNEERWELL: Poor Charles!

JOSEPH SURFACE: True, madam; notwithstanding his vices one can't help feeling for him. Poor Charles! I'm sure I wish it were in my power to be of any essential service to him; for the man who does not share in the distresses of a brother, even though merited by his own misconduct, deserves—

LADY SNEERWELL: O Lud! you are going to be moral and forget that you are among friends.

JOSEPH SURFACE: Egad, that's true! I'll keep that sentiment till I see Sir Peter. However, it is certainly a charity to rescue Maria from such a libertine, who, if he is to be reclaimed, can be so only by a person of your ladyship's superior accomplishments and understanding.

SNAKE: I believe, Lady Sneerwell, here's company coming. I'll go and copy the letter I mentioned to you. Mr. Surface, your most obedient.

JOSEPH SURFACE: Sir, your very devoted.

    [*Exit* SNAKE.]

Lady Sneerwell, I am very sorry you have put any further confidence in that fellow.

LADY SNEERWELL: Why so?

JOSEPH SURFACE: I have lately detected him in frequent conference with old

Rowley, who was formerly my father's steward and has never, you know, been a friend of mine.

LADY SNEERWELL: And do you think he would betray us?

JOSEPH SURFACE: Nothing more likely: take my word for't, Lady Sneerwell, that fellow hasn't virtue enough to be faithful even to his own villainy. Ah, Maria!

[*Enter* MARIA.]

LADY SNEERWELL: Maria, my dear, how do you do? What's the matter?

MARIA: Oh! there's that disagreeable lover of mine, Sir Benjamin Backbite, has just called at my guardian's with his odious uncle, Crabtree; so I slipped out and ran hither to avoid them.

LADY SNEERWELL: Is that all?

JOSEPH SURFACE: If my brother Charles had been of the party, madam, perhaps you would not have been so much alarmed.

LADY SNEERWELL: Nay, now you are severe; for I dare swear the truth of the matter is, Maria heard you were here. But, my dear, what has Sir Benjamin done that you should avoid him so?

MARIA: Oh, he has done nothing—but 'tis for what he has said. His conversation is a perpetual libel on all his acquaintance.

JOSEPH SURFACE: Ay, and the worst of it is, there is no advantage in not knowing him, for he'll abuse a stranger just as soon as his best friend; and his uncle's as bad.

LADY SNEERWELL: Nay, but we should make allowance; Sir Benjamin is a wit and a poet.

MARIA: For my part, I own, madam, wit loses its respect with me when I see it in company with malice. What do you think, Mr. Surface?

JOSEPH SURFACE: Certainly, madam. To smile at the jest which plants a thorn in another's breast is to become a principal in the mischief.

LADY SNEERWELL: Psha! there's no possibility of being witty without a little ill nature. The malice of a good thing is the barb that makes it stick. What's your opinion, Mr. Surface?

JOSEPH SURFACE: To be sure, madam; that conversation, where the spirit of raillery is suppressed, will ever appear tedious and insipid.

MARIA: Well, I'll not debate how far scandal may be allowable; but in a man, I am sure, it is always contemptible. We have pride, envy, rivalship, and a thousand motives to depreciate each other; but the male slanderer must have the cowardice of a woman before he can traduce one.

[*Enter* SERVANT.]

SERVANT: Madam, Mrs. Candour is below, and, if your ladyship's at leisure, will leave her carriage.

LADY SNEERWELL: Beg her to walk in.

[*Exit* SERVANT.]

Now, Maria, here is a character to your taste; for, though Mrs. Candour is a little talkative, everybody knows her to be the best natured and best sort of woman.

MARIA: Yes, with a very gross affection of good nature and benevolence, she does more mischief than the direct malice of old Crabtree.

JOSEPH SURFACE: I'faith that's true, Lady Sneerwell: whenever I hear the current running against the characters of my friends, I never think them in such danger as when Candour undertakes their defence.

LADY SNEERWELL: Hush!—here she is!

[*Enter* MRS. CANDOUR.]

MRS. CANDOUR: My dear Lady Sneerwell, how have you been this century?—Mr. Surface, what news do you hear?—though indeed it is no matter, for I think one hears nothing else but scandal.

JOSEPH SURFACE: Just so, indeed, ma'am.

MRS. CANDOUR: Oh, Maria! child—what, is the whole affair off between you and Charles? His extravagance, I presume—the town talks of nothing else.

MARIA: I am very sorry, ma'am, the town has so little to do.

MRS. CANDOUR: True, true, child: but there's no stopping people's tongues. I own I was hurt to hear it, as I indeed was to learn, from the same quarter, that your guardian, Sir Peter, and Lady Teazle have not agreed lately as well as could be wished.

MARIA: 'Tis strangely impertinent for people to busy themselves so.

MRS. CANDOUR: Very true, child; but what's to be done? People will talk—there's no preventing it. Why, it was but yesterday I was told that Miss Gadabout had eloped with Sir Filagree Flirt. But, Lord! there's no minding what one hears; though, to be sure, I had this from very good authority.

MARIA: Such reports are highly scandalous.

MRS. CANDOUR: So they are, child—shameful, shameful! But the world is so censorious, no character escapes. Lord, now who would have suspected your friend, Miss Prim, of an indiscretion? Yet such is the ill nature of people that they say her uncle stopped her last week just as she was stepping into the York diligence with her dancing-master.

MARIA: I'll answer for't there are no grounds for that report.

MRS. CANDOUR: Ah, no foundation in the world, I dare swear: no more, probably, than for the story circulated last month, of Mrs. Festino's affair with Colonel Cassino—though, to be sure, that matter was never rightly cleared up.

JOSEPH SURFACE: The license of invention some people take is monstrous indeed.

MARIA: 'Tis so; but, in my opinion, those who report such things are equally culpable.

MRS. CANDOUR: To be sure they are; tale bearers are as bad as the tale makers—'tis an old observation and a very true one: but what's to be done, as I said before? how will you prevent people from talking? Today, Mrs. Clackitt assured me Mr. and Mrs. Honeymoon were at last become mere man and wife like the rest of their acquaintance. She likewise hinted that a certain widow in the next street had got rid of her dropsy and recovered her shape in a most surprising manner. And at the same time Miss Tattle, who was by, affirmed that Lord Buffalo had discovered his lady at a house of no extraordinary fame; and that Sir Harry Bouquet and Tom Saunter were to measure swords on a similar provocation. But, Lord, do you think

I would report these things! No, no! tale bearers, as I said before, are just as bad as the tale makers.

JOSEPH SURFACE: Ah! Mrs. Candour, if everybody had your forbearance and good nature!

MRS. CANDOUR: I confess, Mr. Surface, I cannot bear to hear people attacked behind their backs; and when ugly circumstances come out against our acquaintance, I own I always love to think the best. By-the-bye, I hope 'tis not true that your brother is absolutely ruined?

JOSEPH SURFACE: I am afraid his circumstances are very bad indeed, ma'am.

MRS. CANDOUR: Ah!—I heard so—but you must tell him to keep up his spirits; everybody almost is in the same way: Lord Spindle, Sir Thomas Splint, Captain Quinze, and Mr. Nickit—all up, I hear, within this week; so, if Charles is undone, he'll find half his acquaintance ruined too; and that, you know, is a consolation.

JOSEPH SURFACE: Doubtless, ma'am—a very great one.

[*Enter* SERVANT.]

SERVANT: Mr. Crabtree and Sir Benjamin Backbite.

[*Exit* SERVANT.]

LADY SNEERWELL: So, Maria, you see your lover pursues you; positively you shan't escape.

[*Enter* CRABTREE *and* SIR BENJAMIN BACKBITE.]

CRABTREE: Lady Sneerwell, I kiss your hand. Mrs. Candour, I don't believe you are acquainted with my nephew, Sir Benjamin Backbite? Egad, ma'am, he has a pretty wit and is a pretty poet too. Isn't he, Lady Sneerwell?

SIR BENJAMIN: Oh, fie, uncle!

CRABTREE: Nay, egad it's true: I back him at a rebus or a charade against the best rhymer in the kingdom. Has your ladyship heard the epigram he wrote last week on Lady Frizzle's feather catching fire?—Do, Benjamin, repeat it, or the charade you made last night extempore at Mrs. Drowzie's *conversazione*. Come now; your first is the name of a fish, your second a great naval commander, and—

SIR BENJAMIN: Uncle, now—prithee—

CRABTREE: I'faith, ma'am, 'twould surprise you to hear how ready he is at all these sort of things.

LADY SNEERWELL: I wonder, Sir Benjamin, you never publish anything.

SIR BENJAMIN: To say truth, ma'am, 'tis very vulgar to print; and, as my little productions are mostly satires and lampoons on particular people, I find they circulate more by giving copies in confidence to the friends of the parties. However, I have some love elegies, which, when favored with this lady's smiles, I mean to give the public.

CRABTREE: [*to* MARIA] 'Fore heaven, ma'am, they'll immortalize you—you will be handed down to posterity like Petrarch's Laura, or Waller's Sacharissa.

SIR BENJAMIN: [*to* MARIA] Yes, madam, I think you will like them when you shall see them on a beautiful quarto page, where a neat rivulet of text shall meander through a meadow of margin. 'Fore gad, they will be the most elegant things of their kind!

CRABTREE: But, ladies, that's true—have you heard the news?

MRS. CANDOUR: What, sir, do you mean the report of—

CRABTREE: No, ma'am, that's not it. Miss Nicely is going to be married to her own footman.

MRS. CANDOUR: Impossible!

CRABTREE: Ask Sir Benjamin.

SIR BENJAMIN: 'Tis very true, ma'am: everything is fixed and the wedding liveries bespoke.

CRABTREE: Yes—and they do say there were pressing reasons for it.

LADY SNEERWELL: Why, I have heard something of this before.

MRS. CANDOUR: It can't be—and I wonder any one should believe such a story of so prudent a lady as Miss Nicely.

SIR BENJAMIN: O lud! ma'am, that's the very reason 'twas believed at once. She has always been so cautious and so reserved, that everybody was sure there was some reason for it at bottom.

MRS. CANDOUR: Why, to be sure, a tale of scandal is as fatal to the credit of a prudent lady of her stamp as a fever is generally to those of the strongest constitution. But there is a sort of puny, sickly reputation, that is always ailing, yet will outlive the robuster characters of a hundred prudes.

SIR BENJAMIN: True, madam, there are valetudinarians in reputation as well as constitution, who, being conscious of their weak part, avoid the least breath of air and supply their want of stamina by care and circumspection.

MRS. CANDOUR: Well, but this may be all a mistake. You know, Sir Benjamin, very trifling circumstances often give rise to the most injurious tales.

CRABTREE: That they do, I'll be sworn, ma'am. Did you ever hear how Miss Piper came to lose her lover and her character last summer at Tunbridge? Sir Benjamin, you remember it?

SIR BENJAMIN: Oh, to be sure!—the most whimsical circumstance.

LADY SNEERWELL: How was it, pray?

CRABTREE: Why, one evening at Mrs. Ponto's assembly, the conversation happened to turn on the breeding Nova Scotia sheep in this country. Says a young lady in company, "I have known instances of it; for Miss Letitia Piper, a first cousin of mine, had a Nova Scotia sheep that produced her twins." "What!" cries the Lady Dowager Dundizzy [who you know is as deaf as a post], "has Miss Piper had twins?" This mistake, as you may imagine, threw the whole company into a fit of laughter. However, 'twas the next morning everywhere reported, and in a few days believed by the whole town, that Miss Letitia Piper had actually been brought to bed of a fine boy and a girl: and in less than a week there were some people who could name the father, and the farm-house where the babies were put to nurse.

LADY SNEERWELL: Strange, indeed!

CRABTREE: Matter of fact, I assure you. O lud! Mr. Surface, pray is it true that your uncle, Sir Oliver, is coming home?

JOSEPH SURFACE: Not that I know of, indeed, sir.

CRABTREE: He has been in the East Indies a long time. You can scarcely remember him, I believe? Sad comfort, whenever he returns, to hear how your brother has gone on!

JOSEPH SURFACE: Charles has been imprudent, sir, to be sure; but I hope no busy people have already prejudiced Sir Oliver against him. He may reform.

SIR BENJAMIN: To be sure he may. For my part I never believed him to be so utterly void of principle as people say; and though he has lost all his friends, I am told nobody is better spoken of by the Jews.

CRABTREE: That's true, egad, nephew. If the old Jewry was a ward, I believe Charles would be an alderman: no man more popular there, 'fore gad! I hear he pays as many annuities as the Irish tontine; and that whenever he is sick they have prayers for the recovery of his health in all the synagogues.

SIR BENJAMIN: Yet no man lives in greater splendor. They tell me, when he entertains his friends he will sit down to dinner with a dozen of his own securities, have a score of tradesmen in the ante-chamber, and an officer behind every guest's chair.

JOSEPH SURFACE: This may be entertainment to you gentlemen, but you pay very little regard to the feelings of a brother.

MARIA: [*aside*] Their malice is intolerable!—[*aloud*] Lady Sneerwell, I must wish you a good morning: I'm not very well.

[*Exit* MARIA.]

MRS. CANDOUR: O dear! she changes color very much.

LADY SNEERWELL: Do, Mrs. Candour, follow her; she may want assistance.

MRS. CONDOUR: That I will, with all my soul, ma'am. Poor dear girl, who knows what her situation may be!

[*Exit.*]

LADY SNEERWELL: 'Twas nothing but that she could not bear to hear Charles reflected on, notwithstanding their difference.

SIR BENJAMIN: The young lady's *penchant* is obvious.

CRABTREE: But, Benjamin, you must not give up the pursuit for that: follow her and put her into good humor. Repeat her some of your own verses. Come, I'll assist you.

SIR BENJAMIN: Mr. Surface, I did not mean to hurt you; but depend on't your brother is utterly undone.

CRABTREE: O lud, ay! undone as ever man was—can't raise a guinea!

SIR BENJAMIN: And everything sold, I'm told, that was movable.

CRABTREE: I have seen one that was at his house. Not a thing left but some empty bottles that were overlooked and the family pictures which I believe are framed in the wainscots.

SIR BENJAMIN: [*going*] And I'm very sorry also to hear some bad stories against him.

CRABTREE: Oh, he has done many mean things, that's certain.

SIR BENJAMIN: [*going*] But, however, as he's your brother—

CRABTREE: We'll tell you all another opportunity.

[*Exeunt* CRABTREE *and* SIR BENJAMIN.]

LADY SNEERWELL: Ha, ha! 'tis very hard for them to leave a subject they have not quite run down.

JOSEPH SURFACE: And I believe the abuse was no more acceptable to your ladyship than to Maria.

LADY SNEERWELL: I doubt her affections are further engaged than we imagine.

But the family are to be here this evening, so you may as well dine where you are and we shall have an opportunity of observing further. In the meantime, I'll go and plot mischief and you shall study sentiment.

SCENE II——SIR PETER TEAZLE's *House.*

SIR PETER: When an old bachelor marries a young wife, what is he to expect? 'Tis now six months since Lady Teazle made me the happiest of men—and I have been the most miserable dog ever since! We tiffed a little going to church and fairly quarrelled before the bells had done ringing. I was more than once nearly choked with gall during the honeymoon, and had lost all comfort in life before my friends had done wishing me joy. Yet I chose with caution—a girl bred wholly in the country, who never knew luxury beyond one silk gown, nor dissipation above the annual gala of a race ball. Yet she now plays her part in all the extravagant fopperies of fashion and the town, with as ready a grace as if she never had seen a bush or a grass-plot out of Grosvenor Square! I am sneered at by all my acquaintance and paragraphed in the newspapers. She dissipates my fortune, and contradicts all my humors; yet the worst of it is, I doubt I love her, or I should never bear all this. However, I'll never be weak enough to own it.

[*Enter* ROWLEY.]

ROWLEY: Oh! Sir Peter, your servant: how is it with you, sir?

SIR PETER: Very bad, Master Rowley, very bad. I meet with nothing but crosses and vexations.

ROWLEY: What can have happened to trouble you since yesterday?

SIR PETER: A good question to a married man!

ROWLEY: Nay, I'm sure, Sir Peter, your lady can't be the cause of your uneasiness.

SIR PETER: Why, has anybody told you she was dead?

ROWLEY: Come, come, Sir Peter, you love her, notwithstanding your tempers don't exactly agree.

SIR PETER: But the fault is entirely hers, Master Rowley. I am myself the sweetest tempered man alive, and hate a teasing temper; and so I tell her a hundred times a day.

ROWLEY: Indeed!

SIR PETER: Ay; and what is very extraordinary, in all our disputes she is always in the wrong! But Lady Sneerwell and the set she meets at her house encourage the perverseness of her disposition. Then, to complete my vexation, Maria, my ward, whom I ought to have the power of a father over, is determined to turn rebel too and absolutely refuses the man whom I have long resolved on for her husband; meaning, I suppose, to bestow herself on his profligate brother.

ROWLEY: You know, Sir Peter, I have always taken the liberty to differ with you on the subject of these two young gentlemen. I only wish you may not be deceived in your opinion of the elder. For Charles, my life on't! he will retrieve his errors yet. Their worthy father, once my honored master, was, at his years, nearly as wild a spark; yet, when he died, he did not leave a more benevolent heart to lament his loss.

SIR PETER: You are wrong, Master Rowley. On their father's death, you know, I acted as a kind of guardian to them both till their uncle Sir Oliver's liberality gave them an early independence. Of course no person could have more opportunity of judging of their hearts, and I was never mistaken in my life. Joseph is indeed a model for the young men of the age. He is a man of sentiment and acts up to the sentiments he professes; but, for the other, take my word for't, if he had any grain of virtue by descent, he has dissipated it with the rest of his inheritance. Ah! my old friend Sir Oliver will be deeply mortified when he finds how part of his bounty has been misapplied.

ROWLEY: I am sorry to find you so violent against the young man, because this may be the most critical period of his fortune. I came hither with news that will surprise you.

SIR PETER: What! let me hear.

ROWLEY: Sir Oliver is arrived, and at this moment in town.

SIR PETER: How! you astonish me! I thought you did not expect him this month.

ROWLEY: I did not: but his passage has been remarkably quick.

SIR PETER: Egad, I shall rejoice to see my old friend. 'Tis sixteen years since we met. We have had many a day together: but does he still enjoin us not to inform his nephews of his arrival?

ROWLEY: Most strictly. He means, before it is known, to make some trial of their dispositions.

SIR PETER: Ah! There needs no art to discover their merits—however, he shall have his way; but, pray, does he know I am married?

ROWLEY: Yes, and will soon wish you joy.

SIR PETER: What, as we drink health to a friend in consumption! Ah, Oliver will laugh at me. We used to rail at matrimony together, but he has been steady to his text. Well, he must be soon at my house, though—I'll instantly give orders for his reception. But, Master Rowley, don't drop a word that Lady Teazle and I ever disagree.

ROWLEY: By no means.

SIR PETER: For I should never be able to stand Noll's jokes; so I'll have him think, Lord forgive me! that we are a very happy couple.

ROWLEY: I understand you: but then you must be very careful not to differ while he is in the house with you.

SIR PETER: Egad, and so we must—and that's impossible. Ah! Master Rowley, when an old bachelor marries a young wife, he deserves—no—the crime carries its punishment along with it.

ACT II

SCENE I———SIR PETER TEAZLE'S *House.*

[SIR PETER *and* LADY TEAZLE.]

SIR PETER: Lady Teazle, Lady Teazle, I'll not bear it!

LADY TEAZLE: Sir Peter, Sir Peter, you may bear it or not as you please; but I ought to have my own way in everything, and what's more, I will too. What though I was educated in the country, I know very well that women of fashion in London are accountable to nobody after they are married.

SIR PETER: Very well, ma'am, very well; so a husband is to have no influence, no authority?

LADY TEAZLE: Authority! No, to be sure. If you wanted authority over me, you should have adopted me and not married me: I am sure you were old enough.

SIR PETER: Old enough! ay, there it is! Well, well, Lady Teazle, though my life may be made unhappy by your temper, I'll not be ruined by your extravagance!

LADY TEAZLE: My extravagance! I'm sure I'm not more extravagant than a woman of fashion ought to be.

SIR PETER: No, no, madam, you shall throw away no more sums on such unmeaning luxury. 'Slife! to spend as much to furnish your dressing-room with flowers in winter as would suffice to turn the Pantheon into a greenhouse, and give a *fête champêtre* at Christmas.

LADY TEAZLE: And am I to blame, Sir Peter, because flowers are dear in cold weather? You should find fault with the climate, and not with me. For my part, I'm sure I wish it was spring all the year round and that roses grew under our feet!

SIR PETER: Oons! madam—if you had been born to this, I shouldn't wonder at your talking thus; but you forget what your situation was when I married you.

LADY TEAZLE: No, no, I don't; 'twas a very disagreeable one, or I should never have married you.

SIR PETER: Yes, yes, madam, you were then in somewhat a humbler style—the daughter of a plain country squire. Recollect, Lady Teazle, when I saw you first sitting at your tambour in a pretty figured linen gown with a bunch of keys at your side, your hair combed smooth over a roll and your apartment hung round with fruits in worsted of your own working.

LADY TEAZLE: Oh, yes! I remember it very well, and a curious life I led. My daily occupation to inspect the dairy, superintend the poultry, make extracts from the family receipt-book, and comb my aunt Deborah's lapdog.

SIR PETER: Yes, yes, ma'am, 'twas so indeed.

LADY TEAZLE: And then, you know, my evening amusements! To draw patterns for ruffles, which I had not the materials to make up; to play Pope Joan with the Curate; to read a sermon to my aunt; or to be stuck down to an old spinet to strum my father to sleep after a fox-chase.

SIR PETER: I am glad you have so good a memory. Yes, madam, these were the recreations I took you from; but now you must have your coach—*vis-à-vis* —and three powdered footmen before your chair; and, in the summer, a pair of white cats to draw you to Kensington Gardens. No recollection, I suppose, when you were content to ride double, behind the butler, on a docked coach-horse?

LADY TEAZLE: No—I swear I never did that; I deny the butler and the coach-horse.

SIR PETER: This, madam, was your situation; and what have I done for you? I have made you a woman of fashion, of fortune, of rank—in short, I have made you my wife.

LADY TEAZLE: Well, then, and there is but one thing more you can make me to add to the obligation, that is—

SIR PETER: My widow, I suppose?

LADY TEAZLE: Hem! hem!

SIR PETER: I thank you, madam—but don't flatter yourself; for, though your ill-conduct may disturb my peace it shall never break my heart, I promise you. However, I am equally obliged to you for the hint.

LADY TEAZLE: Then why will you endeavor to make yourself so disagreeable to me and thwart me in every little elegant expense?

SIR PETER: 'Slife, madam, I say; had you any of these little elegant expenses when you married me?

LADY TEAZLE: Lud, Sir Peter! would you have me be out of the fashion?

SIR PETER: The fashion, indeed! what had you to do with the fashion before you married me?

LADY TEAZLE: For my part, I should think you would like to have your wife thought a woman of taste.

SIR PETER: Ay—there again—taste! Zounds! madam, you had no taste when you married me!

LADY TEAZLE: That's very true, indeed, Sir Peter! and after having married you, I should never pretend to taste again, I allow. But now, Sir Peter, since we have finished our daily jangle, I presume I may go to my engagement at Lady Sneerwell's?

SIR PETER: Ay, there's another precious circumstance—a charming set of acquaintance you have made there!

LADY TEAZLE: Nay, Sir Peter, they are all people of rank and fortune and remarkably tenacious of reputation.

SIR PETER: Yes, egad, they are tenacious of reputation with a vengeance; for they don't choose anybody should have a character but themselves! Such a crew! Ah! many a wretch has rid on a hurdle who has done less mischief than these utterers of forged tales, coiners of scandal, and clippers of reputation.

LADY TEAZLE: What, would you restrain the freedom of speech?

SIR PETER: Ah! they have made you just as bad as any one of the society.

LADY TEAZLE: Why, I believe I do bear a part with a tolerable grace. But I vow I bear no malice against the people I abuse: when I say an ill natured thing, 'tis out of pure good humor; and I take it for granted they deal exactly in the same manner with me. But, Sir Peter, you know you promised to come to Lady Sneerwell's too.

SIR PETER: Well, well, I'll call in just to look after my own character.

LADY TEAZLE: Then, indeed, you must make haste after me or you'll be too late. So goodbye to ye.

[*Exit* LADY TEAZLE.]

SIR PETER: So—I have gained much by my intended expostulation! Yet with what a charming air she contradicts everything I say, and how pleasantly she shows her contempt for my authority! Well, though I can't make her love me, there is great satisfaction in quarrelling with her; and I think she never appears to such advantage as when she is doing everything in her power to plague me.

SCENE II——LADY SNEERWELL'S *House.*

[LADY SNEERWELL, MRS. CANDOUR, CRABTREE, SIR BENJAMIN BACKBITE *and* JOSEPH SURFACE.]

LADY SNEERWELL: Nay, positively, we will hear it.

JOSEPH SURFACE: Yes, yes, the epigram, by all means.

SIR BENJAMIN: O plague on't, uncle! 'tis mere nonsense.

CRABTREE: No, no; 'fore gad, very clever for an extempore!

SIR BENJAMIN: But, ladies, you should be acquainted with the circumstance. You must know, that one day last week as Lady Betty Curricle was taking the dust in Hyde Park, in a sort of duodecimo phaeton, she desired me to write some verses on her ponies; upon which, I took out my pocket-book, and in one moment produced the following:—

Sure never we seen two such beautiful ponies;
Other horses are clowns, but these macaronies:
To give them this title I am sure can't be wrong.
Their legs are so slim, and their tails are so long.

CRABTREE: There, ladies, done in the smack of a whip, and on horseback too.

JOSEPH SURFACE: A very Phœbus mounted—indeed, Sir Benjamin!

SIR BENJAMIN: Oh dear, sir!—trifles—trifles.

[*Enter* LADY TEAZLE *and* MARIA.]

MRS. CANDOUR: I must have a copy.

LADY SNEERWELL: Lady Teazle, I hope we shall see Sir Peter?

LADY TEAZLE: I believe he'll wait on your ladyship presently.

LADY SNEERWELL: Maria, my love, you look grave. Come, you shall sit down to piquet with Mr. Surface.

MARIA: I take very little pleasure in cards—however, I'll do as your ladyship pleases.

LADY TEAZLE: [*aside*] I am surprised Mr. Surface should sit down with her; I thought he would have embraced this opportunity of speaking to me before Sir Peter came.

MRS. CANDOUR: Now, I'll die; but you are so scandalous, I'll forswear your society.

LADY TEAZLE: What's the matter, Mrs. Candour?

MRS. CANDOUR: They'll not allow our friend Miss Vermillion to be handsome.

LADY SNEERWELL: Oh, surely she is a pretty woman.

CRABTREE: I am very glad you think so, ma'am.

MRS. CANDOUR: She has a charming fresh color.

LADY TEAZLE: Yes, when it is fresh put on.

MRS. CANDOUR: Oh, fie! I'll swear her color is natural: I have seen it come and go!

LADY TEAZLE: I dare swear you have, ma'am: it goes off at night and comes again in the morning.

SIR BENJAMIN: True, ma'am, it not only comes and goes; but, what's more, egad, her maid can fetch and carry it!

MRS. CANDOUR: Ha! ha! ha! how I hate to hear you talk so! But surely, now, her sister is, or was, very handsome.

CRABTREE: Who? Mrs. Evergreen? O Lord! she's six-and-fifty if she's an hour!

MRS. CANDOUR: Now positively you wrong her; fifty-two or fifty-three is the utmost—and I don't think she looks more.

SIR BENJAMIN: Ah! there's no judging by her looks, unless one could see her face.

LADY SNEERWELL: Well, well, if Mrs. Evergreen does take some pains to repair the ravages of time, you must allow she effects it with great ingenuity; and surely that's better than the careless manner in which the widow Ochre caulks her wrinkles.

SIR BENJAMIN: Nay, now, Lady Sneerwell, you are severe upon the widow. Come, come, 'tis not that she paints so ill—but, when she has finished her face, she joins it on so badly to her neck, that she looks like a mended statue, in which the connoisseur may see at once that the head's modern, though the trunk's antique!

CRABTREE: Ha! ha! ha! well said, nephew!

MRS. CANDOUR: Ha! ha! ha! Well, you make me laugh; but I vow I hate you for it. What do you think of Miss Simper?

SIR BENJAMIN: Why, she has very pretty teeth.

LADY TEAZLE: Yes; and on that account, when she is neither speaking nor laughing [which very seldom happens], she never absolutely shuts her mouth, but leaves it always on ajar, as it were—thus.
    [*Shows her teeth.*]

MRS. CANDOUR: How can you be so ill natured?

LADY TEAZLE: Nay, I allow even that's better than the pains Mrs. Prim takes to conceal her losses in front. She draws her mouth till it positively resembles the aperture of a poor's-box, and all her words appear to slide out edgewise, as it were—thus: *How do you do, madam? Yes, madam.*

LADY SNEERWELL: Very well, Lady Teazle; I see you can be a little severe.

LADY TEAZLE: In defence of a friend it is but justice. But here comes Sir Peter to spoil our pleasantry.
    [*Enter* SIR PETER.]

SIR PETER: Ladies, your most obedient—[*aside*] Mercy on me, here is the whole set! a character dead at every word, I suppose.

MRS. CANDOUR: I am rejoiced you are come, Sir Peter. They have been so censorious—and Lady Teazle as bad as any one.

SIR PETER: That must be very distressing to you, Mrs. Candour, I dare swear.

MRS. CANDOUR: Oh, they will allow good qualities to nobody; not even good nature to our friend Mrs. Pursy.

LADY TEAZLE: What, the fat dowager who was at Mrs. Quadrille's last night?

MRS. CANDOUR: Nay, her bulk is her misfortune; and, when she takes so much pains to get rid of it, you ought not to reflect on her.

LADY SNEERWELL: That's very true, indeed.

LADY TEAZLE: Yes, I know she almost lives on acids and small whey; laces herself by pulleys; and often, in the hottest noon in summer, you may see her on a little squat pony, with her hair plaited up behind like a drummer's and puffing round the Ring on a full trot.

MRS. CANDOUR: I thank you, Lady Teazle, for defending her.

SIR PETER: Yes, a good defence, truly.

MRS. CANDOUR: Truly, Lady Teazle is as censorious as Miss Sallow.

CRABTREE: Yes, and she is a curious being to pretend to be censorious—an awkward gawky, without any one good point under heaven.

MRS. CANDOUR: Positively you shall not be so very severe. Miss Sallow is a near relation of mine by marriage, and, as for her person, great allowance is to be made; for, let me tell you, a woman labors under many disadvantages who tries to pass for a girl of six-and-thirty.

LADY SNEERWELL: Though, surely, she is handsome still—and for the weakness in her eyes, considering how much she reads by candlelight, it is not to be wondered at.

MRS. CANDOUR: True; and then as to her manner, upon my word, I think it is particularly graceful, considering she never had the least education; for you know her mother was a Welsh milliner, and her father a sugar-baker at Bristol.

SIR BENJAMIN: Ah! you are both of you too good natured!

SIR PETER: [aside] Yes, damned good natured! This their own relation! mercy on me!

MRS. CANDOUR: For my part, I own I cannot bear to hear a friend ill spoken of.

SIR PETER: No, to be sure.

SIR BENJAMIN: Oh! you are of a moral turn. Mrs. Candour and I can sit for an hour and hear Lady Stucco talk sentiment.

LADY TEAZLE: Nay, I vow Lady Stucco is very well with the dessert after dinner; for she's just like the French fruit one cracks for mottoes—made up of paint and proverb.

MRS. CANDOUR: Well, I will never join in ridiculing a friend; and so I constantly tell my cousin Ogle, and you all know what pretensions she has to be critical on beauty.

CRABTREE: Oh, to be sure! she has herself the oddest countenance that ever was seen; 'tis a collection of features from all the different countries of the globe.

SIR BENJAMIN: So she has, indeed—an Irish front—

CRABTREE: Caledonian locks—

SIR BENJAMIN: Dutch nose—

CRABTREE: Austrian lips—

SIR BENJAMIN: Complexion of a Spaniard—

CRABTREE: And teeth *à la Chinoise*—

SIR BENJAMIN: In short, her face resembles a *table d'hôte* at Spa—where no two guests are of a nation—

CRABTREE: Or a congress at the close of a general war—wherein all the members, even to her eyes, appear to have a different interest, and her nose and chin are the only parties likely to join issue.

MRS. CANDOUR: Ha! ha! ha!

SIR PETER: [*aside*] Mercy on my life!—a person they dine with twice a week!

LADY SNEERWELL: Go—go—you are a couple of provoking toads.

MRS. CANDOUR: Nay, but I vow you shall not carry the laugh off so—for give me leave to say, that Mrs. Ogle—

SIR PETER: Madam, madam, I beg your pardon—there's no stopping these good gentlemen's tongues. But when I tell you, Mrs. Candour, that the lady they are abusing is a particular friend of mine, I hope you'll not take her part.

LADY SNEERWELL: Ha! ha! ha! well said, Sir Peter! but you are a cruel creature —too phlegmatic yourself for a jest, and too peevish to allow wit in others.

SIR PETER: Ah, madam, true wit is more nearly allied to good nature than your ladyship is aware of.

LADY TEAZLE: True, Sir Peter: I believe they are so near akin that they can never be united.

SIR BENJAMIN: Or rather, madam, I suppose them man and wife because one seldom sees them together.

LADY TEAZLE: But Sir Peter is such an enemy to scandal, I believe he would have it put down by Parliament.

SIR PETER: 'Fore heaven, madam, if they were to consider the sporting with reputation of as much importance as poaching on manors, and pass an act for the preservation of fame, I believe many would thank them for the bill.

LADY SNEERWELL: O Lud! Sir Peter; would you deprive us of our privileges?

SIR PETER: Ay, madam; and then no person should be permitted to kill characters and run down reputations, but qualified old maids and disappointed widows.

LADY SNEERWELL: Go, you monster!

MRS. CANDOUR: But, surely, you would not be quite so severe on those who only report what they hear?

SIR PETER: Yes, madam, I would have law merchant for them too; and in all cases of slander currency, whenever the drawer of the lie was not to be found, the injured parties should have a right to come on any of the indorsers.

CRABTREE: Well, for my part, I believe there never was a scandalous tale without some foundation.

LADY SNEERWELL: Come, ladies, shall we sit down to cards in the next room?

[*Enter* SERVANT, *who whispers to* SIR PETER.]

SIR PETER: I'll be with them directly.

[*Exit* SERVANT.]

[*aside*] I'll get away unperceived.

LADY SNEERWELL: Sir Peter, you are not going to leave us?

SIR PETER: Your ladyships must excuse me: I'm called away by particular business. But I leave my character behind me.

[*Exit* SIR PETER.]

SIR BENJAMIN: Well—certainly, Lady Teazle, that lord of yours is a strange being. I could tell you some stories of him would make you laugh heartily if he were not your husband.

LADY TEAZLE: Oh, pray don't mind that; come, do let's hear them.

[*Exeunt all but* JOSEPH SURFACE *and* MARIA.]

JOSEPH SURFACE: Maria, I see you have no satisfaction in this society.

MARIA: How is it possible I should? If to raise malicious smiles at the infirmities or misfortunes of those who have never injured us be the province of wit or humor, Heaven grant me a double portion of dullness!

JOSEPH SURFACE: Yet they appear more ill natured than they are; they have no malice at heart.

MARIA: Then is their conduct still more contemptible; for in my opinion, nothing could excuse the intemperance of their tongues but a natural and uncontrollable bitterness of mind.

JOSEPH SURFACE: Undoubtedly, madam; and it has always been a sentiment of mine to propagate a malicious truth wantonly is more despicable than to falsify from revenge. But can you, Maria, feel thus for others, and be unkind to me alone? Is hope to be denied the tenderest passion?

MARIA: Why will you distress me by renewing this subject?

JOSEPH SURFACE: Ah, Maria! you would not treat me thus, and oppose your guardian, Sir Peter's will, but that I see that profligate Charles is still a favored rival.

MARIA: Ungenerously urged! But whatever my sentiments are for that unfortunate young man, be assured I shall not feel more bound to give him up, because his distresses have lost him the regard even of a brother.

JOSEPH SURFACE: Nay, but, Maria, do not leave me with a frown: by all that's honest, I swear—

    [*He kneels. Enter* LADY TEAZLE.]

    [*aside*] Gad's life, here's Lady Teasle.—[*aloud to* MARIA] You must not— no, you shall not—for, though I have the greatest regard for Lady Teazle—

MARIA: Lady Teazle!

JOSEPH SURFACE: Yet were Sir Peter to suspect—

LADY TEAZLE: [*coming forward*] What is this, pray? Do you take her for me?— Child, you are wanted in the next room.—

    [*Exit* MARIA.]

    What is all this, pray?

JOSEPH SURFACE: Oh, the most unlucky circumstance in nature! Maria has somehow suspected the tender concern I have for your happiness, and threatened to acquaint Sir Peter with her suspicions, and I was just endeavoring to reason with her when you came in.

LADY TEAZLE: Indeed! but you seemed to adopt a very tender mode of reasoning —do you usually argue on your knees?

JOSEPH SURFACE: Oh, she's a child and I thought a little bombast—but, Lady Teazle, when are you to give me your judgment on my library, as you promised?

LADY TEAZLE: No, no; I begin to think it would be imprudent, and you know I admit you as a lover no farther than fashion requires.

JOSEPH SURFACE: True—a mere Platonic cicisbeo, what every wife is entitled to.

LADY TEAZLE: Certainly, one must not be out of the fashion. However, I have so many of my country prejudices left that, though Sir Peter's ill humor may vex me ever so, it never shall provoke me to—

JOSEPH SURFACE: The only revenge in your power. Well, I applaud your moderation.

LADY TEAZLE: Go—you are an insinuating wretch! But we shall be missed—let us join the company.

JOSEPH SURFACE: But we had best not return together.

LADY TEAZLE: Well, don't stay; for Maria shan't come to hear any more of your reasoning, I promise you.

[*Exit.*]

JOSEPH SURFACE: A curious dilemma, truly, my politics have run me into! I wanted, at first, only to ingratiate myself with Lady Teazle, that she might not be my enemy with Maria; and I have, I don't know how, become her serious lover. Sincerely I begin to wish I had never made such a point of gaining so very good a character; for it has led me into so many cursed rogueries that I doubt I shall be exposed at last.

SCENE III——SIR PETER TEAZLE'S *House.*

[SIR OLIVER SURFACE *and* ROWLEY.]

SIR OLIVER: Ha! ha! ha! so my old friend is married, hey?—a young wife out of the country. Ha! ha! ha! that he should have stood bluff to old bachelor so long and sink into a husband at last!

ROWLEY: But you must not rally him on the subject, Sir Oliver; 'tis a tender point, I assure you, though he has been married only seven months.

SIR OLIVER: Then he has been just half a year on the stool of repentance!— Poor Peter! But you say he has entirely given up Charles—never sees him, hey?

ROWLEY: His prejudice against him is astonishing, and I am sure greatly increased by a jealousy of him with Lady Teazle, which he has industriously been led into by a scandalous society in the neighborhood, who have contributed not a little to Charles's ill name. Whereas the truth is, I believe, if the lady is partial to either of them, his brother is the favorite.

SIR OLIVER: Ay, I know there are a set of malicious, prating, prudent gossips, both male and female, who murder characters to kill time, and will rob a young fellow of his good name before he has years to know the value of it. But I am not to be prejudiced against my nephew by such, I promise you! No, no; if Charles has done nothing false or mean, I shall compound for his extravagance.

ROWLEY: Then, my life on't, you will reclaim him. Ah, sir, it gives me new life to find that your heart is not turned against him, and that the son of my good old master has one friend, however, left.

SIR OLIVER: What! shall I forget, Master Rowley, when I was at his years myself? Egad, my brother and I were neither of us very prudent youths; and yet, I believe, you have not seen many better men than your old master was?

ROWLEY: Sir, 'tis this reflection gives me assurance that Charles may yet be a credit to his family. But here comes Sir Peter.

SIR OLIVER: Egad, so he does! Mercy on me, he's greatly altered, and seems to have a settled married look! One may read *husband* in his face at this distance!

[*Enter* SIR PETER.]

SIR PETER: Ha! Sir Oliver—my old friend! Welcome to England a thousand times!

SIR OLIVER: Thank you, thank you, Sir Peter! and i'faith I am glad to find you well, believe me!

SIR PETER: Oh! 'tis a long time since we met—fifteen years, I doubt, Sir Oliver, and many a cross accident in the time.

SIR OLIVER: Ay, I have had my share. But, what! I find you are married, hey, my old boy? Well, well, it can't be helped; and so—I wish you joy with all my heart!

SIR PETER: Thank you, thank you, Sir Oliver.—Yes, I have entered into—the happy state; but we'll not talk of that now.

SIR OLIVER: True, true, Sir Peter; old friends should not begin on grievances at first meeting. No, no, no.

ROWLEY: [*aside to* SIR OLIVER] Take care, pray, sir.

SIR OLIVER: Well, so one of my nephews is a wild rogue, hey?

SIR PETER: Wild! Ah! my old friend. I grieve for your disappointment there; he's a lost young man, indeed. However, his brother will make you amends; Joseph is, indeed, what a youth should be—everyone in the world speaks well of him.

SIR OLIVER: I am sorry to hear it; he has too good a character to be an honest fellow. Everyone speaks well of him! Psha! then he has bowed as low to knaves and fools as to the honest dignity of genius and virtue.

SIR PETER: What, Sir Oliver! do you blame him for not making enemies?

SIR OLIVER: Yes, if he has merit enough to deserve them.

SIR PETER: Well, well—you'll be convinced when you know him. 'Tis edification to hear him converse; he professes the noblest sentiments.

SIR OLIVER: Oh, plague of his sentiments! If he salutes me with a scrap of morality in his mouth. I shall be sick directly. But, however, don't mistake me, Sir Peter; I don't mean to defend Charles's errors: but, before I form my judgment of either of them, I intend to make a trial of their hearts; and my friend Rowley and I have planned something for the purpose.

ROWLEY: And Sir Peter shall own for once he has been mistaken.

SIR PETER: Oh, my life on Joseph's honor!

SIR OLIVER: Well—come, give us a bottle of good wine, and we'll drink the lad's health and tell you our scheme.

SIR PETER: *Allons,* then!

SIR OLIVER: And don't, Sir Peter, be so severe against your old friend's son. Odds my life! I am not sorry that he has run out of the course a little. For my part, I hate to see prudence clinging to the green suckers of youth; 'tis like ivy round a sapling, and spoils the growth of the tree.

ACT III SCENE I——SIR PETER TEAZLE's *House.*

[SIR PETER TEAZLE, SIR OLIVER SURFACE, *and* ROWLEY.]

SIR PETER: Well, then, we will see this fellow first and have our wine afterwards. But how is this, Master Rowley? I don't see the jet of your scheme.

ROWLEY: Why, sir, this Mr. Stanley, whom I was speaking of, is nearly related to them by their mother. He was once a merchant in Dublin, but has been ruined by a series of undeserved misfortunes. He has applied, by letter, since his confinement, both to Mr. Surface and Charles. From the former he has received nothing but evasive promises of future service, while Charles has done all that his extravagance has left him power to do; and he is, at this time, endeavoring to raise a sum of money, part of which, in the midst of his own distresses, I know he intends for the service of poor Stanley.

SIR OLIVER: Ah, he is my brother's son.

SIR PETER: Well, but how is Sir Oliver personally to—

ROWLEY: Why, sir. I will inform Charles and his brother that Stanley has obtained permission to apply personally to his friends; and, as they have neither of them ever seen him, let Sir Oliver assume his character, and he will have a fair opportunity of judging, at least, of the benevolence of their dispositions; and believe me, sir, you will find in the youngest brother one who, in the midst of folly and dissipation, has still, as our immortal bard expresses it,—

> a tear for pity, and a hand
> Open as day, for melting charity.

SIR PETER: Psha! What signifies his having an open hand or purse either, when he has nothing left to give? Well, well, make the trial, if you please. But where is the fellow whom you brought for Sir Oliver to examine relative to Charles's affairs?

ROWLEY: Below, waiting his commands, and no one can give him better intelligence.—This, Sir Oliver, is a friendly Jew, who, to do him justice, has done everything in his power to bring your nephew to a proper sense of his extravagance.

SIR PETER: Pray let us have him in.

ROWLEY: [*calls to* SERVANT] Desire Mr. Moses to walk upstairs.

SIR PETER: But, pray, why should you suppose he will speak the truth?

ROWLEY: Oh, I have convinced him that he has no chance of recovering certain sums advanced to Charles but through the bounty of Sir Oliver, who he knows is arrived; so that you may depend on his fidelity to his own interests. I have also another evidence in my power, one Snake, whom I have detected in a matter little short of forgery and shall shortly produce to remove some of your prejudices, Sir Peter, relative to Charles and Lady Teazle.

SIR PETER: I have heard too much on that subject.

ROWLEY: Here comes the honest Israelite.

> [*Enter* MOSES.]

—This is Sir Oliver.

SIR OLIVER: Sir, I understand you have lately had great dealings with my nephew Charles.

MOSES: Yes, Sir Oliver, I have done all I could for him; but he was ruined before he came to me for assistance.

SIR OLIVER: That was unlucky, truly; for you have had no opportunity of showing your talents.

MOSES: None at all; I hadn't the pleasure of knowing his distresses till he was some thousands worse than nothing.

SIR OLIVER: Unfortunate, indeed! But I suppose you have done all in your power for him, honest Moses?

MOSES: Yes, he knows that. This very evening I was to have brought him a gentleman from the city, who does not know him, and will, I believe, advance him some money.

SIR PETER: What, one Charles has never had money from before?

MOSES: Yes, Mr. Premium, of Crutched Friars, formerly a broker.

SIR PETER: Egad, Sir Oliver, a thought strikes me!—Charles, you say, does not know Mr. Premium?

MOSES: Not at all.

SIR PETER: Now then, Sir Oliver, you may have a better opportunity of satisfying yourself than by an old romancing tale of a poor relation. Go with my friend Moses and represent Premium, and then, I'll answer for it, you'll see your nephew in all his glory.

SIR OLIVER: Egad, I like this idea better than the other and I may visit Joseph afterwards as old Stanley.

SIR PETER: True—so you may.

ROWLEY: Well, this is taking Charles rather at a disadvantage, to be sure. However, Moses, you understand Sir Peter, and will be faithful.

MOSES: You may depend upon me.—This is near the time I was to have gone.

SIR OLIVER: I'll accompany you as soon as you please, Moses—But hold! I have forgot one thing—how the plague shall I be able to pass for a Jew?

MOSES: There's no need—the principal is Christian.

SIR OLIVER: Is he? I'm very sorry to hear it. But, then again, an't I rather too smartly dressed to look like a money-lender?

SIR PETER: Not at all; 'twould not be out of character, if you went in your carriage—would it, Moses?

MOSES: Not in the least.

SIR OLIVER: Well, but how must I talk? there's certainly some cant of usury and mode of treating that I ought to know.

SIR PETER: Oh, there's not much to learn. The great point, as I take it, is to be exorbitant enough in your demands. Hey, Moses?

MOSES: Yes, that's a very great point.

SIR OLIVER: I'll answer for't I'll not be wanting in that. I'll ask him eight or ten per cent on the loan, at least.

MOSES: If you ask him no more than that, you'll be discovered immediately.

SIR OLIVER: Hey! what, the plague! how much then?

MOSES: That depends upon the circumstances. If he appears not very anxious for the supply, you should require only forty or fifty per cent; but if you find him in great distress, and want the moneys very bad, you may ask double.

SIR PETER: A good honest trade you're learning, Sir Oliver!

SIR OLIVER: Truly I think so—and not unprofitable.

MOSES: Then, you know, you haven't the moneys yourself, but are forced to borrow them for him of a friend.

SIR OLIVER: Oh! I borrow it of a friend, do I?

MOSES: And your friend is an unconscionable dog: but you can't help that.

SIR OLIVER: My friend an unconscionable dog, is he?

MOSES: Yes, and he himself has not the moneys by him, but is forced to sell stocks at a great loss.

SIR OLIVER: He is forced to sell stocks at a great loss, is he? Well, that's very kind of him.

SIR PETER: I'faith, Sir Oliver—Mr. Premium, I mean—you'll soon be master of the trade. But, Moses! would not you have him run out a little against the Annuity Bill? That would be in character, I should think.

MOSES: Very much.

ROWLEY: And lament that a young man now must be at years of discretion before he is suffered to ruin himself?

MOSES: Ay, great pity!

SIR PETER: And abuse the public for allowing merit to an act whose only object is to snatch misfortune and imprudence from the rapacious grip of usury, and give the minor a chance of inheriting his estate without being undone by coming into possession.

SIR OLIVER: So, so—Moses shall give me further instructions as we go together.

SIR PETER: You will not have much time, for your nephew lives hard by.

SIR OLIVER: Oh, never fear! my tutor appears so able, that though Charles lived in the next street, it must be my own fault if I am not a complete rogue before I turn the corner.

> [*Exit with* MOSES.]

SIR PETER: So, now, I think Sir Oliver will be convinced; you are partial, Rowley, and would have prepared Charles for the other plot.

ROWLEY: No, upon my word, Sir Peter.

SIR PETER: Well, go bring me this Snake, and I'll hear what he has to say presently. I see Maria and want to speak with her.

> [*Exit* ROWLEY.]

I should be glad to be convinced my suspicions of Lady Teazle and Charles were unjust. I have never yet opened my mind on this subject to my friend Joseph—I am determined I will do it—he will give me his opinion sincerely.

> [*Enter* MARIA.]

So, child, has Mr. Surface returned with you?

MARIA: No, sir; he was engaged.

SIR PETER: Well, Maria, do you not reflect, the more you converse with that amiable young man, what return his partiality for you deserves?

MARIA: Indeed, Sir Peter, your frequent importunity on this subject distresses me extremely—you compel me to declare, that I know no man who has ever paid me a particular attention whom I would not prefer to Mr. Surface.

SIR PETER: So—here's perverseness! No, no, Maria, 'tis Charles only whom you would prefer. 'Tis evident his vices and follies have won your heart.

MARIA: This is unkind sir. You know I have obeyed you in neither seeing nor corresponding with him: I have heard enough to convince me that he is unworthy my regard. Yet I cannot think it culpable, if, while my understanding severely condemns his vices, my heart suggests some pity for his distresses.

SIR PETER: Well, well, pity him as much as you please; but give your heart and hand to a worthier object.

MARIA: Never to his brother!

SIR PETER: Go, perverse and obstinate! But take care, madam; you have never yet known what the authority of a guardian is. Don't compel me to inform you of it.

MARIA: I can only say, you shall not have just reason. 'Tis true, by my father's will I am for a short period bound to regard you as his substitute; but must cease to think you so, when you would compel me to be miserable.

[*Exit* MARIA.]

SIR PETER: Was ever man so crossed as I am, everything conspiring to fret me! I had not been involved in matrimony a fortnight, before her father, a hale and hearty man, died, on purpose, I believe, for the pleasure of plaguing me with the care of his daughter.

[LADY TEAZLE *sings without.*]

But here comes my helpmate! She appears in great good humor. How happy I should be if I could tease her into loving me, though but a little!

[*Enter* LADY TEAZLE.]

LADY TEAZLE: Lud! Sir Peter, I hope you haven't been quarrelling with Maria? It is not using me well to be ill humored when I am not by.

SIR PETER: Ah, Lady Teazle, you might have the power to make me good humored at all times.

LADY TEAZLE: I am sure I wish I had; for I want you to be in a charming sweet temper at this moment. Do be good humored now, and let me have two hundred pounds, will you?

SIR PETER: Two hundred pounds; what, an't I to be in a good humor without paying for it! But speak to me thus, and i'faith there's nothing I could refuse you. You shall have it; but seal me a bond for the repayment.

LADY TEAZLE: Oh, no—there—my note of hand will do as well. [*Offering her hand.*]

SIR PETER: And you shall no longer reproach me with not giving you an independent settlement. I mean shortly to surprise you; but shall we always live thus, hey?

LADY TEAZLE: If you please; I'm sure I don't care how soon we leave off quarrelling, provided you'll own you were tired first.

SIR PETER: Well—then let our future contest be, who shall be most obliging.

LADY TEAZLE: I assure you, Sir Peter, good nature becomes you. You look now as you did before we were married, when you used to walk with me under the elms, and tell me stories of what a gallant you were in your youth, and chuck me under the chin, you would; and ask me if I thought I could love an old fellow who would deny me nothing—didn't you?

SIR PETER: Yes, yes, and you were as kind and attentive—

LADY TEAZLE: Ay, so I was, and would always take your part, when my acquaintance used to abuse you, and turn you into ridicule.

SIR PETER: Indeed!

LADY TEAZLE: Ay, and when my cousin Sophy has called you a stiff, peevish old bachelor, and laughed at me for thinking of marrying one who might be my father, I have always defended you, and said, I didn't think you so ugly by any means, and that I dared say you'd make a very good sort of a husband.

SIR PETER: And you prophesied right; and we shall now be the happiest couple—

LADY TEAZLE: And never differ again?

SIR PETER: No, never—though at the same time, indeed, my dear lady Teazle, you must watch your temper very seriously; for in all our little quarrels, my dear, if you recollect, my love, you always began first.

LADY TEAZLE: I beg your pardon, my dear Sir Peter: indeed, you always gave the provocation.

SIR PETER: Now, see, my angel! take care—contradicting isn't the way to keep friends.

LADY TEAZLE: Then, don't you begin it, my love!

SIR PETER: There now! you—you are going on. You don't perceive, my life, that you are just doing the very thing which you know always makes me angry.

LADY TEAZLE: Nay, you know if you will be angry without any reason, my dear—

SIR PETER: There! now you want to quarrel again.

LADY TEAZLE: No, I'm sure I don't; but, if you will be so peevish—

SIR PETER: There now! who begins first?

LADY TEAZLE: Why, you to be sure. I said nothing—but there's no bearing your temper.

SIR PETER: No, no madam: the fault's in your own temper.

LADY TEAZLE: Ay, you are just what my cousin Sophy said you would be.

SIR PETER: Your cousin Sophy is a forward, impertinent gypsy.

LADY TEAZLE: You are a great bear, I am sure, to abuse my relations.

SIR PETER: Now may all the plagues of marriage be doubled on me if ever I try to be friends with you any more!

LADY TEAZLE: So much the better.

SIR PETER: No, no, madam. 'Tis evident you never cared a pin for me, and I was a madman to marry you—a pert, rural coquette, that had refused half the honest squires in the neighborhood!

LADY TEAZLE: And I am sure I was a fool to marry you—an old dangling bachelor, who was single at fifty, only because he never could meet with any one who would have him.

SIR PETER: Ay, ay, madam; but you were pleased enough to listen to me: you never had such an offer before.

LADY TEAZLE: No! didn't I refuse Sir Tivy Terrier, who everybody said would have been a better match? for his estate is just as good as yours, and he has broke his neck since we have been married.

SIR PETER: I have done with you, madam! You are an unfeeling, ungrateful— but there's an end of everything. I believe you capable of everything that is bad. Yes, madam, I now believe the reports relative to you and Charles, madam. Yes, madam, you and Charles are, not without grounds—

LADY TEAZLE: Take care, Sir Peter! you had better not insinuate any such thing! I'll not be suspected without cause, I promise you.

SIR PETER: Very well, madam! very well! a separate maintenance as soon as you please. Yes, madam, or a divorce! I'll make an example of myself for the benefit of all old bachelors. Let us separate, madam.

LADY TEAZLE: Agreed! agreed! And now, my dear Sir Peter, we are of a mind once more, we may be the happiest couple, and never differ again, you know: ha! ha! ha! Well, you are going to be in a passion, I see, and I shall only interrupt you—so, bye! Bye!

[*Exit* LADY TEAZLE.]

SIR PETER: Plagues and tortures! can't I make her angry either! Oh, I am the most miserable fellow! But I'll not bear her presuming to keep her temper: no! she may break my heart, but she shan't keep her temper.

SCENE II——CHARLES SURFACE's *House.*

[TRIP, MOSES, *and* SIR OLIVER SURFACE.]

TRIP: Here, Master Moses! if you'll stay a moment; I'll try whether—what's the gentleman's name?

SIR OLIVER: [*aside to* MOSES] Mr. Moses, what is my name?

MOSES: Mr. Premium.

TRIP: Premium—very well.

[*Exit, taking snuff.*]

SIR OLIVER: To judge by the servants, one wouldn't believe the master was ruined. But what!—sure, this was my brother's house?

MOSES: Yes, sir; Mr. Charles bought it of Mr. Joseph, with the furniture, pictures, etc., just as the old gentleman left it. Sir Peter thought it a piece of extravagance in him.

SIR OLIVER: In my mind, the other's economy in selling it to him was more reprehensible by half.

[*Re-enter* TRIP.]

TRIP: My master says you must wait, gentlemen: he has company, and can't speak with you yet.

SIR OLIVER: If he knew who it was wanted to see him, perhaps he would not send a message?

TRIP: Yes, yes, sir; he knows you are here—I did not forget little Premium: no, no, no.

SIR OLIVER: Very well; and I pray, sir, what may be your name?

TRIP: Trip, sir; my name is Trip, at your service.

SIR OLIVER: Well, then, Mr. Trip, you have a pleasant sort of place here, I guess?

TRIP: Why, yes—here are three or four of us to pass our time agreeably enough; but then our wages are sometimes a little in arrear—and not very great either—but fifty pounds a year, and find our own bags and bouquets.

SIR OLIVER: [*aside*] Bags and bouquets! halters and bastinadoes!

TRIP: And *à propos*, Moses, have you been able to get me that little bill discounted?

SIR OLIVER: [*aside*] Wants to raise money, too!—mercy on me! Has his distresses too, I warrant, like a lord, and affects creditors and duns.

MOSES: 'Twas not to be done, indeed, Mr. Trip.

TRIP: Good lack, you surprise me! My friend Brush has indorsed it, and I thought when he put his name at the back of a bill 'twas the same as cash.

MOSES: No, 'twouldn't do.

TRIP: A small sum—but twenty pounds. Hark'ee, Moses, do you think you couldn't get it me by way of annuity?

SIR OLIVER: [*aside*] An annuity! ha! ha! a footman raise money by way of annuity. Well done, luxury, egad!

MOSES: Well, but you must insure your place.

TRIP: Oh, with all my heart! I'll insure my place and my life too, if you please.

SIR OLIVER: [*aside*] It's more than I would your neck.

MOSES: But is there nothing you could deposit?

TRIP: Why, nothing capital of my master's wardrobe has dropped lately; but I could give you a mortgage on some of his winter clothes, with equity of redemption before November—or you shall have the reversion of the French velvet, or a post-obit on the blue and silver. These, I should think, Moses, with a few pair of point ruffles, as a collateral security—hey, my little fellow?

MOSES: Well, well.
　　　[*Bell rings.*]

TRIP: Egad. I heard the bell! I believe, gentlemen, I can now introduce you. Don't forget the annuity, little Moses! This way gentlemen, I'll insure my place, you know.

SIR OLIVER: [*aside*] If the man be a shadow of the master, this is the temple of dissipation indeed!
　　　[*Exeunt.*]

SCENE III——*Another room.*

[CHARLES SURFACE, CARELESS, SIR HARRY BUMPER, *and Others, at a table with wine, etc.*]

CHARLES SURFACE: 'Fore heaven, 'tis true! there's the great degeneracy of the age. Many of our acquaintance have taste, spirit, and politeness; but plague on't they won't drink.

CARELESS: It is so, indeed, Charles! they give in to all the substantial luxuries of the table, and abstain from nothing but wine and wit. Oh, certainly society suffers by it intolerably! for now, instead of the social spirit of raillery that used to mantle over a glass of bright Burgundy, their conversation is become just like the Spa-water they drink, which has all the pertness and flatulency of champagne, without its spirit or flavor.

FIRST GENTLEMAN: But what are they to do who love play better than wine?

CARELESS: True! there's Sir Harry diets himself for gaming, and is now under a hazard regimen.

CHARLES SURFACE: Then he'll have the worst of it. What! you wouldn't train a horse for the course by keeping him from corn? For my part, egad, I'm never so successful as when I am a little merry. Let me throw on a bottle of champagne and I never lose—at least I never feel my losses, which is exactly the same thing.

SECOND GENTLEMAN: Ay, that I believe.

CHARLES SURFACE: And then, what man can pretend to be a believer in love who is an abjurer of wine? 'Tis the test by which the lover knows his own heart. Fill a dozen bumpers to a dozen beauties, and she that floats at the top is the maid that has bewitched you.

CARELESS: Now then, Charles, be honest, and give us your real favorite.

CHARLES SURFACE: Why, I have withheld her only in compassion to you. If I toast her, you must give her a round of her peers, which is impossible—on earth.

CARELESS: Oh, then we'll find some canonized vestals or heathen goddesses that will do, I warrant!

CHARLES SURFACE: Here then, bumpers, you rogues! bumpers! Maria! Maria—

SIR HARRY: Maria who?

CHARLES SURFACE: Oh, damn the surname—'tis too formal to be registered in Love's calendar—but now, Sir Harry, beware, we must have beauty superlative.

CARELESS: Nay, never study, Sir Harry: we'll stand to the toast, though your mistress should want an eye, and you know you have a song will excuse you.

SIR HARRY: Egad, so I have! and I'll give him the song instead of the lady. [*Sings.*]

Here's to the maiden of bashful fifteen;
    Here's to the widow of fifty;
Here's to the flaunting extravagant quean,
    And here's to the housewife that's thrifty.

Chorus   Let the toast pass,
          Drink to the lass,
I'll warrant she'll prove an excuse for a glass!

Here's to the charmer whose dimples we prize;
    Now to the maid who has none, sir;
Here's to the girl with a pair of blue eyes,
    And here's to the nymph with but one, sir.

Chorus   Let the toast pass,
          Drink to the lass,
I'll warrant she'll prove an excuse for a glass.

Here's to the maid with bosom of snow;
    Now to her that's as brown as a berry;
Here's to the wife with a face full of woe,
    And now to the damsel that's merry.

Chorus   Let the toast pass,
           Drink to the lass,
I'll warrant she'll prove an excuse for a glass.

For let 'em be clumsy, or let 'em be slim,
    Young or ancient, I care not a feather;
So fill a pint bumper quite up to the brim,
    And let us e'en toast them together.

Chorus   Let the toast pass,
           Drink to the lass,
I'll warrant she'll prove an excuse for a glass.

ALL: Bravo! Bravo!
    [*Enter* TRIP, *and whispers to* CHARLES SURFACE.]
CHARLES SURFACE: Gentlemen, you must excuse me a little. Careless, take the chair, will you?
CARELESS: Nay, prithee, Charles, what now? This is one of your peerless beauties, I suppose, has dropped in by chance?
CHARLES SURFACE: No, faith! To tell you the truth, 'tis a Jew and a broker, who are come by appointment.
CARELESS: Oh, damn it! let's have the Jew in.
FIRST GENTLEMAN: Ay, and the broker too, by all means.
SECOND GENTLEMAN: Yes, yes, the Jew, and the broker!
CHARLES SURFACE: Egad, with all my heart!— Trip, bid the gentlemen walk in.
    [*Exit* TRIP.]
Though there's one of them a stranger I can tell you.
CARELESS: Charles, let us give them some generous Burgundy and perhaps they'll grow conscientious.
CHARLES SURFACE: Oh, hang 'em, no! wine does but draw forth a man's natural qualities; and to make them drink would only be to whet their knavery.
    [*Enter* TRIP, *with* SIR OLIVER SURFACE *and* MOSES.]
CHARLES SURFACE: So, honest Moses; walk in, pray, Mr. Premium—that's the gentleman's name, isn't it, Moses?
MOSES: Yes, sir.
CHARLES SURFACE: Set chairs, Trip.—Sit down, Mr. Premium. Glasses, Trip.— Sit down, Moses.—Come, Mr. Premium, I'll give you a sentiment; here's *Success to usury!*—Moses, fill the gentleman a bumper.
MOSES: Success to usury! [*Drinks.*]
CARELESS: Right, Moses—usury is prudence and industry, and deserves to succeed.
SIR OLIVER: Then here's—all the success it deserves! [*Drinks.*]
CARELESS: No, no, that won't do! Mr. Premium, you have demurred at the toast, and must drink it in a pint bumper.
FIRST GENTLEMAN: A pint bumper, at least!
MOSES: Oh, pray, sir, consider—Mr. Premium's a gentleman.

CARELESS: And therefore loves good wine.

SECOND GENTLEMAN: Give Moses a quart glass—this is mutiny, and a high contempt for the chair.

CARELESS: Here now for't! I'll see justice done, to the last drop of my bottle.

SIR OLIVER: Nay, pray, gentlemen—I did not expect this usage.

CHARLES SURFACE: No, hang it, you shan't; Mr. Premium's a stranger.

SIR OLIVER: [aside] Odd! I wish I was well out of their company.

CARELESS: Plague on 'em then! if they won't drink, we'll not sit down with them. Come, Harry, the dice are in the next room.—Charles, you'll join us when you have finished your business with the gentlemen?

CHARLES SURFACE: I will! I will!

[Exeunt GENTLEMEN.]

Careless!

CARELESS: [returning] Well?

CHARLES SURFACE: Perhaps I may want you.

CARELESS: Oh, you know I am always ready: word, note, or bond. 'tis all the same to me. [Exit.]

MOSES: Sir, this is Mr. Premium, a gentleman of the strictest honor and secrecy; and always performs what he undertakes. Mr. Premium, this is—

CHARLES SURFACE: Psha! have done. Sir, my friend Moses is a very honest fellow, but a little slow at expression: he'll be an hour giving us our titles. Mr. Premium, the plain state of the matter is this: I am an extravagant young fellow who wants to borrow money; you I take to be a prudent old fellow, who has got money to lend. I am blockhead enough to give fifty per cent sooner than not have it! and you, I presume, are rogue enough to take a hundred if you can get it. Now, sir, you see we are acquainted at once, and may proceed to business without further ceremony.

SIR OLIVER: Exceeding frank, upon my word. I see, sir, you are not a man of many compliments.

CHARLES SURFACE: Oh, no, sir! plain dealing in business I always think best.

SIR OLIVER: Sir, I like you the better for it. However, you are mistaken in one thing. I have no money to lend, but I believe I could procure some of a friend; but then he's an unconscionable dog. Isn't he, Moses? And must sell stock to accommodate you. Mustn't he, Moses?

MOSES: Yes, indeed! You know I always speak the truth, and scorn to tell a lie!

CHARLES SURFACE: Right. People that speak truth generally do. But these are trifles, Mr. Premium. What! I know money isn't to be bought without paying for't!

SIR OLIVER: Well, but what security could you give? You have no land, I suppose?

CHARLES SURFACE: Not a mole-hill, nor a twig, but what's in the bough-pots out of the window!

SIR OLIVER: Nor any stock, I presume?

CHARLES SURFACE: Nothing but live stock—and that's only a few pointers and ponies. But pray, Mr. Premium, are you acquainted at all with any of my connections?

SIR OLIVER: Why, to say the truth, I am.

CHARLES SURFACE: Then you must know that I have a devilish rich uncle in the East Indies, Sir Oliver Surface, from whom I have the greatest expectations?

SIR OLIVER: That you have a wealthy uncle, I have heard; but how your expectations will turn out is more, I believe, than you can tell.

CHARLES SURFACE: Oh, no!—there can be no doubt. They tell me I'm a prodigious favorite, and that he talks of leaving me everything.

SIR OLIVER: Indeed! this is the first I've heard of it.

CHARLES SURFACE: Yes, yes, 'tis just so. Moses knows 'tis true; don't you, Moses?

MOSES: Oh, yes! I'll swear to't.

SIR OLIVER: [*aside*] Egad, they'll persuade me presently I'm at Bengal.

CHARLES SURFACE: Now I propose, Mr. Premium, if it's agreeable to you, a post-orbit on Sir Oliver's life: though at the same time the old fellow has been so liberal with me, that I give you my word, I should be very sorry to hear that anything had happened to him.

SIR OLIVER: Not more than I should, I assure you. But the bond you mention happens to be just the worst security you could offer me—for I might live to be a hundred and never see the principal.

CHARLES SURFACE: Oh, yes, you would! the moment Sir Oliver dies, you know, you would come on me for the money.

SIR OLIVER: Then I believe I should be the most unwelcome dun you ever had in your life.

CHARLES SURFACE: What! I suppose you're afraid that Sir Oliver is too good a life?

SIR OLIVER: No, indeed I am not; though I have heard he is as hale and healthy as any man of his years in Christendom.

CHARLES SURFACE: There again, now, you are misinformed. No, no, the climate has hurt him considerably, poor uncle Oliver. Yes, yes, he breaks apace, I'm told—and is so much altered lately that his nearest relations would not know him.

SIR OLIVER: No! Ha! ha ha! so much altered lately that his nearest relation would not know him! Ha! ha! ha! egad—ha! ha!

CHARLES SURFACE: Ha! ha!—you're glad to hear that, little Premium.

SIR OLIVER: No, no, I'm not.

CHARLES SURFACE: Yes, yes, you are—ha! ha! ha!—you know that mends your chance.

SIR OLIVER: But I'm told Sir Oliver is coming over; nay, some say he has actually arrived.

CHARLES SURFACE: Psha! sure I must know better than you whether he's come or not. No, no, rely on't he's at this moment at Calcutta. Isn't he, Moses?

MOSES: Oh, yes, certainly.

SIR OLIVER: Very true, as you say, you must know better than I, though I have it from a pretty good authority. Haven't I, Moses?

MOSES: Yes, most undoubted!

SIR OLIVER: But, sir, as I understand you want a few hundreds immediately, is there nothing you could dispose of?

CHARLES SURFACE: How do you mean?

SIR OLIVER: For instance, now, I have heard that your father left behind him a great quantity of massy old plate.

CHARLES SURFACE: O lud, that's gone long ago. Moses can tell you how better than I can.

SIR OLIVER: [*aside*] Good lack! all the family race-cups and corporation-bowls! [*aloud*] Then it was also supposed that his library was one of the most valuable and compact.

CHARLES SURFACE: Yes, yes, so it was—vastly too much for a private gentleman. For my part, I was always of a communicative disposition, so I thought it a shame to keep so much knowledge to myself.

SIR OLIVER: [*aside*] Mercy upon me! learning that had run in the family like an heirloom!—[*aloud*] Pray, what has become of the books?

CHARLES SURFACE: You must inquire of the auctioneer, Master Premium, for I don't believe even Moses can direct you.

MOSES: I know nothing of books.

SIR OLIVER: So, so, nothing of the family property left, I suppose?

CHARLES SURFACE: Not much, indeed; unless you have a mind to the family pictures. I have got a room full of ancestors above; and if you have a taste for old paintings, egad, you shall have 'em a bargain!

SIR OLIVER: Hey! what the devil! sure, you wouldn't sell your forefathers, would you?

CHARLES SURFACE: Every man of them, to the best bidder.

SIR OLIVER: What! your great-uncles and aunts?

CHARLES SURFACE: Ay, and my great-grandfathers and grandmothers too.

SIR OLIVER: [*aside*] Now I give him up!—[*aloud*] What the plague, have you no bowels for your own kindred? Odd's life! do you take me for Shylock in the play, that you would raise money of me on your own flesh and blood?

CHARLES SURFACE: Nay, my little broker, don't be angry. What need you care, if you have your money's worth?

SIR OLIVER: Well, I'll be the purchaser. I think I can dispose of the family canvas.—[*aside*] Oh, I'll never forgive him this! never!

[*Enter* CARELESS.]

CARELESS: Come, Charles, what keeps you?

CHARLES SURFACE: I can't come yet. I'faith, we are going to have a sale above stairs; here's little Premium will buy all my ancestors!

CARELESS: Oh, burn your ancestors!

CHARLES SURFACE: No, he may do that afterwards, if he pleases. Stay, Careless, we want you: egad, you shall be auctioneer—so come along with us.

CARELESS: Oh, have with you, if that's the case. I can handle a hammer as well as a dice box!

SIR OLIVER: [*aside*] Oh, the profligates!

CHARLES SURFACE: Come, Moses, you shall be appraiser, if we want one. Gad's life, little Premium, you don't seem to like the business?

SIR OLIVER: Oh, yes, I do, vastly! Ha! ha! ha! yes, yes, I think it a rare joke to sell one's family by auction—ha! ha!—[*aside*] Oh, the prodigal!

CHARLES SURFACE: To be sure! when a man wants money, where the plague should be get assistance if he can's make free with his own relations? [*Exeunt.*]

ACT IV

SCENE I———*Picture Room at* CHARLES'S.

[*Enter* CHARLES SURFACE, SIR OLIVER SURFACE, MOSES, *and* CARELESS.]

CHARLES SURFACE: Walk in, gentlemen, pray walk in—here they are, the family of the Surfaces up to the Conquest.

SIR OLIVER: And, in my opinion, a goodly collection.

CHARLES SURFACE: Ay, ay, these are done in the true spirit of portrait-painting; no *volontière grace* or expression. Not like the works of your modern Raphaels, who give you the strongest resemblance, yet contrive to make your portrait independent of you; so that you may sink the original and not hurt the picture. No, no; the merit of these is the inveterate likeness —all stiff and awkward as the originals, and like nothing in human nature besides.

SIR OLIVER: Ah! we shall never see such figures of men again.

CHARLES SURFACE: I hope not. Well, you see, Master Premium, what a domestic character I am; here I sit of an evening surrounded by my family. But come, get to your pulpit, Mr. Auctioneer; here's an old gouty chair of my grandfather's will answer the purpose.

CARELESS: Ay, ay, this will do. But, Charles, I haven't a hammer; and what's an auctioneer without his hammer?

CHARLES SURFACE: Egad, that's true. What parchment have we here? Oh, our genealogy in full. Here, Careless, you shall have no common bit of mahogany, here's the family tree for you, you rogue! This shall be your hammer, and now you may knock down my ancestors with their own pedigree.

SIR OLIVER: [*aside*] What an unnatural rogue!—an *ex post facto* parricide!

CARELESS: Yes, yes, here's a list of your generation indeed;—faith, Charles, this is the most convenient thing you could have found for the business, for 'twill not only serve as a hammer, but a catalogue into the bargain. Come, begin—A-going, a-going a-going!

CHARLES SURFACE: Bravo, Careless! Well, here's my great uncle, Sir Richard Raveline, a marvelous good general in his day, I assure you. He served in all the Duke of Marlborough's wars, and got that cut over his eye at the battle of Malplaquet. What say you, Mr. Premium? look at him—there's a hero! not cut out of his feathers, as your modern clipped captains are, but enveloped in wig and regimentals as a general should be. What do you bid?

MOSES: Mr. Premium would have you speak.

CHARLES SURFACE: Why, then he shall have him for ten pounds, and I'm sure that's not dear for a staff-officer.

SIR OLIVER: [*aside*] Heaven deliver me! his famous uncle Richard for ten pounds!—[*aloud*] Very well, sir. I take him at that.

CHARLES SURFACE: Careless, knock down my uncle Richard.—Here, now, is a maiden sister of his, my great-aunt Deborah, done by Kneller, in his best manner, and a very formidable likeness. There she is, you see, a shepherdess feeding her flock. You shall have her for five pounds ten—the sheep are worth the money.

SIR OLIVER: [*aside*] Ah! poor Deborah! a woman who set such a value on herself!—[*aloud*] Five pounds ten—she's mine.

CHARLES SURFACE: Knock down my aunt Deborah! Here, now, are two that were a sort of cousins of theirs—You see, Moses, these pictures were done some time ago, when beaux wore wigs, and the ladies their own hair.

SIR OLIVER: Yes, truly, head-dresses appear to have been a little lower in those days.

CHARLES SURFACE: Well, take that couple for the same.

MOSES: 'Tis a good bargain.

CHARLES SURFACE: Careless—this, now, is a grandfather of my mother's, a learned judge, well known on the western circuit.—What do you rate him at, Moses?

MOSES: Four guineas.

CHARLES SURFACE: Four guineas! Gad's life, you don't bid me the price of his wig.—Mr. Premium, you have more respect for the wool-sack, do let us knock his Lordship down at fifteen.

SIR OLIVER: By all means.

CARELESS: Gone!

CHARLES SURFACE: And there are two brothers of his, William and Walter Blunt, Esquires, both members of Parliament, and noted speakers; and, what's very extraordinary, I believe, this is the first time they were ever bought or sold.

SIR OLIVER: That is very extraordinary, indeed! I'll take them at your own price, for the honor of Parliament.

CARELESS: Well said, little Premium! I'll knock them down at forty.

CHARLES SURFACE: Here's a jolly fellow—I don't know what relation, but he was mayor of Manchester: take him at eight pounds.

SIR OLIVER: No, no, six will do for the mayor.

CHARLES SURFACE: Come, make it guineas, and I'll throw you the two aldermen there into the bargain.

SIR OLIVER: They're mine.

CHARLES SURFACE: Careless, knock down the mayor and aldermen. But, plague on't! we shall be all day retailing in this manner; do let us deal wholesale: what say you, little Premium? Give me three hundred pounds for the rest of the family in the lump.

CARELESS: Ay, ay, that will be the best way.

SIR OLIVER: Well, well, anything to accommodate you; they are mine. But there is one portrait which you have always passed over.

CARELESS: What, that ill-looking little fellow over the settee?

SIR OLIVER: Yes, sir, I mean that; though I don't think him so ill-looking a little fellow, by any means.

CHARLES SURFACE: What, that? Oh; that's my uncle Oliver! 'Twas done before he went to India.

CARELESS: Your uncle Oliver! Gad, then you'll never be friends, Charles. That, now, to me, is as stern a looking rogue as ever I saw; an unforgiving eye, and a damned disinheriting countenance! an inveterate knave, depend on't. Don't you think so little Premium?

SIR OLIVER: Upon my soul, sir, I do not; I think it is as honest a looking face as any in the room, dead or alive. But I suppose uncle Oliver goes with the rest of the lumber?

CHARLES SURFACE: No, hang it! I'll not part with poor Noll. The old fellow has been very good to me, and, egad, I'll keep his picture while I've a room to put it in.

SIR OLIVER: [*aside*] The rogue's my nephew after all!—[*aloud*] But, sir, I have somehow taken a fancy to that picture.

CHARLES SURFACE: I'm sorry for't, for you certainly will not have it. Oons, haven't you got enough of them?

SIR OLIVER: [*aside*] I forgive him everything!—[*aloud*] But, sir, when I take a whim in my head, I don't value money. I'll give you as much for that as for all the rest.

CHARLES SURFACE: Don't tease me, master broker; I tell you I'll not part with it, and there's an end of it.

SIR OLIVER: [*aside*] How like his father the dog is!—[*aloud*] Well, well, I have done.—[*aside*] I did not perceive it before, but I think I never saw such a striking resemblance.—[*aloud*] Here is a draught for your sum.

CHARLES SURFACE: Why, 'tis for eight hundred pounds!

SIR OLIVER: You will not let Sir Oliver go?

CHARLES SURFACE: Zounds! no! I tell you, once more.

SIR OLIVER: Then never mind the difference, we'll balance that another time. But give me your hand on the bargain; you are an honest fellow, Charles —I beg pardon, sir, for being so free.—Come, Moses.

CHARLES SURFACE: Egad, this is a whimsical old fellow!—But hark'ee, Premium, you'll prepare lodgings for these gentlemen.

SIR OLIVER: Yes, yes, I'll send for them in a day or two.

CHARLES SURFACE: But hold; do now send a genteel conveyance for them, for, I assure you, they were most of them used to ride in their own carriages.

SIR OLIVER: I will, I will—for all but Oliver.

CHARLES SURFACE: Ay, all but the little nabob.

SIR OLIVER: You're fixed on that?

CHARLES SURFACE: Peremptorily.

SIR OLIVER: [*aside*] A dear extravagant rogue!—[*aloud*] Good day!—Come, Moses.—[*aside*] Let me hear now who dares call him profligate!

[*Exeunt* SIR OLIVER *and* MOSES.]

CARELESS: Why, this is the oddest genius of the sort I ever met with!

CHARLES SURFACE: Egad, he's the prince of brokers, I think. I wonder how the devil Moses got acquainted with so honest a fellow.—Ha! here's Rowley. —Do, Careless, say I'll join the company in a few moments.

CARELESS: I will—but don't let that old blockhead persuade you to squander any of that money on old musty debts, or any such nonsense; for tradesmen, Charles, are the most exorbitant fellows.

CHARLES SURFACE: Very true, and paying them is only encouraging them.

CARELESS: Nothing else.

CHARLES SURFACE: Ay, ay, never fear.—

> [*Exit* CARELESS.]
>
> So! this was an odd old fellow, indeed. Let me see, two-thirds of this is mine by right: five hundred and thirty odd pounds. 'Fore heaven! I find one's ancestors are more valuable relations than I took them for!—Ladies and gentlemen, your most obedient and very grateful servant.
>
> [*Bows to the pictures. Enter* ROWLEY.]
>
> Ha! old Rowley! egad, you are just come in time to take leave of your old acquaintance.

ROWLEY: Yes, I heard they were a-going. But I wonder you can have such spirits under so many distresses.

CHARLES SURFACE: Why, there's the point! my distresses are so many that I can't afford to part with my spirits; but I shall be rich and splenetic, all in good time. However, I suppose you are surprised that I am not more sorrowful at parting with so many near relations; to be sure, 'tis very affecting; but you see they never move a muscle, so why should I?

ROWLEY: There's no making you serious a moment.

CHARLES SURFACE: Yes, faith, I am so now. Here, my honest Rowley, here, get me this changed directly and take a hundred pounds of it immediately to old Stanley.

ROWLEY: A hundred pounds! Consider only—

CHARLES SURFACE: Gad's life, don't talk about it! poor Stanley's wants are pressing, and, if you don't make haste, we shall have some one call that has a better right to the money.

ROWLEY: Ah! there's the point! I never will cease dunning you with the old proverb—

CHARLES SURFACE: "Be just before you're generous."—Why, so I would if I could; but Justice is an old lame, hobbling beldame, and I can't get her to keep pace with Generosity, for the soul of me.

ROWLEY: Yet, Charles, believe me, one hour's reflection—

CHARLES SURFACE: Ay, ay, it's very true; but, hark'ee, Rowley, while I have, by Heaven I'll give; so, damn your economy! and now for hazard. [*Exeunt.*]

SCENE II——*The parlor.*

[*Enter* SIR OLIVER SURFACE *and* MOSES.]

MOSES: Well, sir, I think, as Sir Peter said, you have seen Mr. Charles in high glory; 'tis great pity he's so extravagant.

SIR OLIVER: True, but he would not sell my picture.

MOSES: And loves wine and women so much.

SIR OLIVER: But he would not sell my picture.

MOSES: And games so deep.

SIR OLIVER: But he would not sell my picture. Oh, here's Rowley.

> [*Enter* ROWLEY.]

ROWLEY: So, Sir Oliver, I find you have made a purchase—

SIR OLIVER: Yes, yes, our young rake has parted with his ancestors like old tapestry.

ROWLEY: And here has he commissioned me to re-deliver you part of the purchase-money—I mean, though, in your necessitous character of old Stanley.

MOSES: Ah! there is the pity of all; he is so damned charitable.

ROWLEY: And I left a hosier and two tailors in the hall, who I'm sure, won't be paid, and this hundred would satisfy them.

SIR OLIVER: Well, well I'll pay his debts, and his benevolence too. But now I am no more a broker, and you shall introduce me to the elder brother as old Stanley.

ROWLEY: Not yet awhile; Sir Peter, I know, means to call there about this time.
[*Enter* TRIP.]

TRIP: Oh, gentlemen, I beg pardon for not showing you out; this way—Moses, a word.
[*Exit with* MOSES.]

SIR OLIVER: There's a fellow for you! Would you believe it, that puppy intercepted the Jew on our coming, and wanted to raise money before he got to his master!

ROWLEY: Indeed.

SIR OLIVER: Yes, they are now planning an annuity business. Ah, Master Rowley, in my days servants were content with the follies of their masters when they were worn a little threadbare; but now they have their vices, like their birthday clothes, with the gloss on. [*Exeunt.*]

SCENE III——A *Library in* JOSEPH SURFACE'S *House.*

JOSEPH SURFACE: No letter from Lady Teazle?

SERVANT: No, sir.

JOSEPH SURFACE: [*aside*] I am surprised she has not sent, if she is prevented from coming. Sir Peter certainly does not suspect me. Yet I wish I may not lose the heiress through the scrape I have drawn myself into with the wife. However, Charles's imprudence and bad character are great points in my favor.
[*Knocking.*]

SERVANT: Sir, I believe that must be Lady Teazle.

JOSEPH SURFACE: Hold! See whether it is or not before you go to the door. I have a particular message for you if it should be my brother.

SERVANT: 'Tis her ladyship, sir; she always leaves the chair at the milliner's in the next street.

JOSEPH SURFACE: Stay, stay! Draw that screen before the window—that will do. My opposite neighbor is a maiden lady of so curious a temper.
[*Servant draws the screen, and exits.*]
I have a difficult hand to play in this affair. Lady Teazle has lately suspected my views on Maria; but she must by no means be let into that secret—at least, till I have her more in my power.
[*Enter* LADY TEAZLE.]

LADY TEAZLE: What, sentiment in soliloquy now? Have you been very impatient? O lud! don't pretend to look grave. I vow I couldn't come before.

JOSEPH SURFACE: O madam, punctuality is a species of constancy very unfashionable in a lady of quality.

LADY TEAZLE: Upon my word, you ought to pity me. Do you know Sir Peter is grown so ill-natured to me of late, and so jealous of Charles too—that's the best of the story, isn't it?

JOSEPH SURFACE: [*aside*] I am glad my scandalous friends keep that up.

LADY TEAZLE: I am sure I wish he would let Maria marry him, and then perhaps he would be convinced; don't you, Mr. Surface?

JOSEPH SURFACE: [*aside*] Indeed I do not.—[*aloud*] Oh, certainly I do! for then my dear Lady Teazle would also be convinced how wrong her suspicions were of my having any design on the silly girl.

LADY TEAZLE: Well, well, I'm inclined to believe you. But isn't it provoking to have the most ill-natured things said at one? And there's my friend Lady Sneerwell has circulated I don't know how many scandalous tales of me, and all without any foundation, too; that's what vexes me.

JOSEPH SURFACE: Ay, madam, to be sure, that is the provoking circumstance—without foundation. Yes, yes, there's the mortification, indeed; for, when a scandalous story is believed against one, there certainly is no comfort like the consciousness of having deserved it.

LADY TEAZLE: No, to be sure, then I'd forgive their malice; but to attack me, who am really so innocent, and who never say an ill-natured thing of anybody—that is, of any friend; and then Sir Peter, too, to have him so peevish, and so suspicious, when I know the integrity of my own heart—indeed 'tis monstrous!

JOSEPH SURFACE: But, my dear Lady Teazle, 'tis your own fault if you suffer it. When a husband entertains a groundless suspicion of his wife, and withdraws his confidence from her, the original compact is broken, and she owes it to the honor of her sex to endeavor to outwit him.

LADY TEAZLE: Indeed! So that, if he suspects me without cause, it follows, that the best way of curing his jealousy is to give him reason for't?

JOSEPH SURFACE: Undoubtedly—for your husband should never be deceived in you: and in that case it becomes you to be frail in compliment to his discernment.

LADY TEAZLE: To be sure, what you say is very reasonable, and when the consciousness of my innocence—

JOSEPH SURFACE: Ah, my dear madam, there is the great mistake; 'tis this very conscious innocence that is of the greatest prejudice to you. What is it makes you negligent of forms, and careless of the world's opinion? why, the consciousness of your own innocence. What makes you thoughtless in your conduct and apt to run into a thousand little imprudences? why, the consciousness of your own innocence. What makes you impatient of Sir Peter's temper, and outrageous at his suspicions? why, the consciousness of your innocence.

LADY TEAZLE: 'Tis very true!

JOSEPH SURFACE: Now, my dear Lady Teazle, if you would but once make a trifling *faux pas*, you can't conceive how cautious you would grow, and how ready to humor and agree with your husband.

LADY TEAZLE: Do you think so?

JOSEPH SURFACE: Oh, I'm sure on't! and then you would find all scandal would cease at once, for—in short, your character at present is like a person in a plethora, absolutely dying from too much health.

LADY TEAZLE: So, so; then I perceive your prescription is that I must sin in my own defence, and part with my virtue to preserve my reputation?

JOSEPH SURFACE: Exactly so, upon my credit, ma'am.

LADY TEAZLE: Well, certainly this is the oddest doctrine, and the newest receipt for avoiding calumny.

JOSEPH SURFACE: An infallible one, believe me. Prudence, like experience, must be paid for.

LADY TEAZLE: Why, if my understanding were once convinced—

JOSEPH SURFACE: Oh, certainly, madam, your understanding should be convinced. Yes, yes—Heaven forbid I should persuade you to do anything you thought wrong. No, no, I have too much honor to desire it.

LADY TEAZLE: Don't you think we may as well leave honor out of the argument? [*rises*]

JOSEPH SURFACE: Ah, the ill effects of your country education, I see, still remain with you.

LADY TEAZLE: I doubt they do, indeed; and I will fairly own to you, that if I could be persuaded to do wrong, it would be by Sir Peter's ill usage sooner than your honorable logic, after all.

JOSEPH SURFACE: Then, by this hand, which he is unworthy of—[*taking her hand*]

[*Enter* SERVANT.]

'Sdeath, you blockhead—what do you want?

SERVANT: I beg your pardon, sir, but I thought you would not choose Sir Peter to come up without announcing him.

JOSEPH SURFACE: Sir Peter!—Oons—the devil!

LADY TEAZLE: Sir Peter! O lud! I'm ruined! I'm ruined!

SERVANT: Sir, 'twasn't I let him in.

LADY TEAZLE: Oh! I'm quite undone! What will become of me now, Mr. Logic?—Oh! mercy, he's on the stairs—I'll get behind here—and if ever I'm so imprudent again—[*Goes behind the screen.*]

JOSEPH SURFACE: Give me that book.

[*Sits down.* SERVANT *pretends to adjust his chair. Enter* SIR PETER TEAZLE.]

SIR PETER: Ay, ever improving himself. Mr. Surface, Mr. Surface—

JOSEPH SURFACE: Oh, my dear Sir Peter, I beg your pardon. [*Gaping, throws away the book.*] I have been dozing over a stupid book. Well, I am much obliged to you for this call. You haven't been here, I believe, since I fitted up this room. Books, you know, are the only things I am a coxcomb in.

SIR PETER: 'Tis very neat indeed. Well, well, that's proper; and you can make even your screen a source of knowledge—hung, I perceive, with maps.

JOSEPH SURFACE: Oh, yes, I find great use in that screen.

SIR PETER: I dare say you must, certainly, when you want to find anything in a hurry.

JOSEPH SURFACE: [*aside*] Ay, or to hide anything in a hurry either.

SIR PETER: Well, I have a little private business—

JOSEPH SURFACE: [*to* SERVANT] You need not stay.

SERVANT: No, sir.

      [*Exit* SERVANT.]

JOSEPH SURFACE: Here's a chair, Sir Peter—I beg—

SIR PETER: Well, now we are alone, there is a subject, my dear friend, on which I wish to unburden my mind to you—a point of the greatest moment to my peace; in short, my good friend, Lady Teazle's conduct of late has made me very unhappy.

JOSEPH SURFACE: Indeed! I am very sorry to hear it.

SIR PETER: Yes, 'tis but too plain she has not the least regard for me; but, what's worse, I have pretty good authority to suppose she has formed an attachment to another.

JOSEPH SURFACE: Indeed! you astonish me!

SIR PETER: Yes! and, between ourselves, I think I've discovered the person.

JOSEPH SURFACE: How! you alarm me exceedingly.

SIR PETER: Ay, my dear friend, I knew you would sympathize with me!

JOSEPH SURFACE: Yes, believe me, Sir Peter, such a discovery would hurt me just as much as it would you.

SIR PETER: I am convinced of it. Ah! it is a happiness to have a friend whom we can trust even with one's family secrets. But have you no guess who I mean?

JOSEPH SURFACE: I haven't the most distant idea. It can't be Sir Benjamin Backbite!

SIR PETER: Oh, no! what say you to Charles?

JOSEPH SURFACE: My brother! impossible!

SIR PETER: Oh, my dear friend, the goodness of your own heart misleads you. You judge of others by yourself.

JOSEPH SURFACE: Certainly, Sir Peter, the heart that is conscious of its own integrity is ever slow to credit another's treachery.

SIR PETER: True; but your brother has no sentiment—you never hear him talk so.

JOSEPH SURFACE: Yet I can't but think Lady Teazle herself has too much principle.

SIR PETER: Ay; but what is principle against the flattery of a handsome, lively young fellow?

JOSEPH SURFACE: That's very true.

SIR PETER: And then, you know, the difference of our ages makes it very improbable that she should have any great affection for me; and if she were to be frail, and I were to make it public, why the town would only laugh at me, the foolish old bachelor who had married a girl.

JOSEPH SURFACE: That's true, to be sure—they would laugh.

SIR PETER: Laugh! ay, and make ballads, and paragraphs, and the devil knows what of me.

JOSEPH SURFACE: No, you must never make it public.

SIR PETER: But then again—that the nephew of my old friend, Sir Oliver, should be the person to attempt such a wrong, hurts me more nearly.

JOSEPH SURFACE: Ay, there's the point. When ingratitude barbs the dart of injury, the wound has double danger in it.

SIR PETER: Ay—I that was, in a manner, left his guardian, in whose house he had been so often entertained, who never in my life denied him—my advice!

JOSEPH SURFACE: Oh, 'tis not to be credited! There may be a man capable of such baseness, to be sure; but, for my part, till you can give me positive proofs, I cannot but doubt it. However, if it should be proved on him, he is no longer a brother of mine—I disclaim kindred with him: for the man who can break the laws of hospitality and tempt the wife of his friend, deserves to be branded as the pest of society.

SIR PETER: What a difference there is between you! What noble sentiments!

JOSEPH SURFACE: Yet I cannot suspect Lady Teazle's honor.

SIR PETER: I am sure I wish to think well of her, and to remove all ground of quarrel between us. She has lately reproached me more than once with having made no settlement on her; and, in our last quarrel, she almost hinted that she should not break her heart if I was dead. Now, as we seem to differ in our ideas of expense, I have resolved she shall have her own way and be her own mistress in that respect for the future; and, if I were to die, she will find I have not been inattentive to her interest while living. Here, my friend, are the drafts of two deeds, which I wish to have your opinion on. By one, she will enjoy eight hundred a year independent while I live; and by the other, the bulk of my fortune at my death.

JOSEPH SURFACE: This conduct, Sir Peter, is indeed truly generous. [*aside*] I wish it may not corrupt my pupil.

SIR PETER: Yes, I am determined she shall have no cause to complain, though I would not have her acquainted with the latter instance of my affection yet awhile.

JOSEPH SURFACE: [*aside*] Nor I, if I could help it.

SIR PETER: And now, my dear friend, if you please, we will talk over the situation of your hopes with Maria.

JOSEPH SURFACE: [*softly*] Oh, no, Sir Peter; another time, if you please.

SIR PETER: I am sensibly chagrined at the little progress you seem to make in her affections.

JOSEPH SURFACE: [*softly*] I beg you will not mention it. What are my disappointments when your happiness is in debate! [*aside*] 'Sdeath, I shall be ruined every way!

SIR PETER: And though you are averse to my acquainting Lady Teazle with your passion, I'm sure she's not your enemy in the affair.

JOSEPH SURFACE: Pray, Sir Peter, now oblige me. I am really too much affected by the subject we have been speaking of to bestow a thought on my own

concerns. The man who is entrusted with his friend's distress can never—
[*Enter* SERVANT.]
Well, sir?

SERVANT: Your brother, sir, is speaking to a gentleman in the street, and says he knows you are within.

JOSEPH SURFACE: 'Sdeath, blockhead, I'm not within—I'm out for the day.

SIR PETER: Stay—hold—a thought has struck me: you shall be at home.

JOSEPH SURFACE: Well, well, let him up.
[*Exit* SERVANT.]
[*aside*] He'll interrupt Sir Peter, however.

SIR PETER: Now, my good friend, oblige me, I entreat you. Before Charles comes, let me conceal myself somewhere, then do you tax him on the point we have been talking, and his answer may satisfy me at once.

JOSEPH SURFACE: Oh, fie, Sir Peter! would you have me join in so mean a trick? —to trepan my brother too?

SIR PETER: Nay, you tell me you are sure he is innocent; if so, you do him the greatest service by giving him an opportunity to clear himself, and you will set my heart at rest. Come, you shall not refuse me: here, behind the screen will be—Hey! what the devil! there seems to be one listener here already—I'll swear I saw a petticoat!

JOSEPH SURFACE: Ha! ha! ha! Well, this is ridiculous enough. I'll tell you, Sir Peter, though I hold a man of intrigue to be a most despicable character, yet you know, it does not follow that one is to be an absolute Joseph either! Hark'ee, 'tis a little French milliner, a silly rogue that plagues me; and having some character to lose, on your coming, sir, she ran behind the screen.

SIR PETER: Ah, you rogue—But, egad, she has overheard all I have been saying of my wife.

JOSEPH SURFACE: Oh, 'twill never go any farther, you may depend upon it!

SIR PETER: No! then, faith, let her hear it out.—Here's a closet will do as well.

JOSEPH SURFACE: Well, go in there.

SIR PETER: Sly rogue; sly rogue! [*Goes into the closet.*]

JOSEPH SURFACE: A narrow escape, indeed! and a curious situation I'm in, to part man and wife in this manner.

LADY TEAZLE: [*peeping*] Couldn't I steal off?

JOSEPH SURFACE: Keep close, my angel.

SIR PETER: [*peeping*] Joseph, tax me home!

JOSEPH SURFACE: Back, my dear friend!

LADY TEAZLE: [*peeping*] Couldn't you lock Sir Peter in?

JOSEPH SURFACE: Be still, my life!

SIR PETER: [*peeping*] You're sure the little milliner won't blab?

JOSEPH SURFACE: In, in, my dear Sir Peter!—'Fore gad, I wish I had a key to the door!
[*Enter* CHARLES SURFACE.]

CHARLES SURFACE: Holla! brother, what has been the matter? Your fellow would not let me up at first. What! have you had a Jew or a wench with you?

JOSEPH SURFACE: Neither, brother, I assure you.

CHARLES SURFACE: But what has made Sir Peter steal off? I thought he had been with you.

JOSEPH SURFACE: He was, brother; but, hearing you were coming, he did not choose to stay.

CHARLES SURFACE: What! was the old gentleman afraid I wanted to borrow money of him!

JOSEPH SURFACE: No, sir: but I am sorry to find, Charles, you have lately given that worthy man grounds for great uneasiness.

CHARLES SURFACE: Yes, they tell me I do that to a great many worthy men. But how so, pray?

JOSEPH SURFACE: To be plain with you, brother, he thinks you are endeavoring to gain Lady Teazle's affections from him.

CHARLES SURFACE: Who, I? O lud! not I, upon my word.—Ha! ha! ha! ha! so the old fellow has found out that he has got a young wife, has he?—or, what's worse, Lady Teazle has found out she has an old husband?

JOSEPH SURFACE: This is no subject to jest on, brother. He who can laugh—

CHARLES SURFACE: True, true, as you were going to say—then, seriously, I never had the least idea of what you charge me with, upon my honor.

JOSEPH SURFACE: [*in a loud voice*] Well, it will give Sir Peter great satisfaction to hear this.

CHARLES SURFACE: To be sure, I once thought the lady seemed to have taken a fancy to me; but, upon my soul, I never gave her the least encouragement. Besides, you know my attachment to Maria.

JOSEPH SURFACE: But sure, brother, even if Lady Teazle had betrayed the fondest partiality for you—

CHARLES SURFACE: Why, look'ee, Joseph, I hope I shall never deliberately do a dishonorable action; but if a pretty woman were purposely to throw herself in my way—and that pretty woman married to a man old enough to be her father—

JOSEPH SURFACE: Well!

CHARLES SURFACE: Why, I believe I should be obliged to borrow a little of your morality, that's all. But, brother, do you know now that you surprise me exceedingly by naming me with Lady Teazle; for i'faith, I always understood you were her favorite.

JOSEPH SURFACE: Oh, for shame, Charles! This retort is foolish.

CHARLES SURFACE: Nay, I swear I have seen you exchange such significant glances—

JOSEPH SURFACE: Nay, nay, sir, this is no jest.

CHARLES SURFACE: Egad, I'm serious! Don't you remember one day when I called here—

JOSEPH SURFACE: Nay, prithee, Charles—

CHARLES SURFACE: And found you together—

JOSEPH SURFACE: Zounds, sir, I insist—

CHARLES SURFACE: And another time, when your servant—

JOSEPH SURFACE: Brother, brother, a word with you! [*aside*] Gad, I must stop him.

CHARLES SURFACE: Informed, I say, that—

JOSEPH SURFACE: Hush, I beg your pardon, but Sir Peter has overheard all we have been saying. I knew you would clear yourself, or I should not have consented.

CHARLES SURFACE: How, Sir Peter! Where is he?

JOSEPH SURFACE: Softly, there! [*Points to the closet.*]

CHARLES SURFACE: Oh, 'fore Heaven, I'll have him out. Sir Peter, come forth!

JOSEPH SURFACE: No, no—

CHARLES SURFACE: I say, Sir Peter, come into court. [*Pulls in* SIR PETER.]
What! my old guardian!—What! turn inquisitor and take evidence incog.?

SIR PETER: Give me your hand, Charles—I believe I have suspected you wrongfully; but you mustn't be angry with Joseph—'twas my plan!

CHARLES SURFACE: Indeed!

SIR PETER: But I acquit you. I promise you I don't think near so ill of you as I did. What I have heard has given me great satisfaction.

CHARLES SURFACE: Egad, then 'twas lucky you didn't hear any more. Wasn't it, Joseph?

SIR PETER: Ah! you would have retorted on him.

CHARLES SURFACE: Ah, ay, that was a joke.

SIR PETER: Yes, yes, I know his honor too well.

CHARLES SURFACE: But you might as well have suspected him as me in this matter, for all that. Mightn't he, Joseph?

SIR PETER: Well, well, I believe you.

JOSEPH SURFACE: [*aside*] Would they were both out of the room!

SIR PETER: And in future, perhaps, we may not be such strangers.

[*Enter* SERVANT *and whispers to* JOSEPH SURFACE.]

JOSEPH SURFACE: Gentlemen, I beg pardon—I must wait on you downstairs; here's a person come on particular business.

CHARLES SURFACE: Well, you can see him in another room. Sir Peter and I have not met a long time, and I have something to say to him.

JOSEPH SURFACE: [*aside*] They must not be left together—[*aloud*] I'll send Lady Sneerwell away, and return directly. [*aside to* SIR PETER] Sir Peter, not a word of the French milliner.

SIR PETER: [*aside to* JOSEPH SURFACE] I! not for the world!—

[*Exit* JOSEPH SURFACE.]
Ah, Charles, if you associated more with your brother, one might indeed hope for your reformation. He is a man of sentiment. Well, there is nothing in the world so noble as a man of sentiment.

CHARLES SURFACE: Psha! he is too moral by half; and so apprehensive of his good name, as he calls it, that I suppose he would as soon let a priest into his house as a wench.

SIR PETER: No, no—come, come,—you wrong him. No, no, Joseph is no rake, but he is no such saint either, in that respect. [*aside*] I have a great mind to tell him—we should have such a laugh at Joseph.

CHARLES SURFACE: Oh, hang him! he's a very anchorite, a young hermit!

SIR PETER: Hark'ee—you must not abuse him: he may chance to hear of it again I promise you.

CHARLES SURFACE: Why, you won't tell him?

SIR PETER: No—but—this way. [*aside*] Egad, I'll tell him. [*aloud*] Hark'ee, have you a mind to have a good laugh at Joseph?

CHARLES SURFACE: I should like it of all things.

SIR PETER: Then, i'faith, we will! I'll be quit with him for discovering me. He had a girl with him when I called.

CHARLES SURFACE: What! Joseph? you jest.

SIR PETER: Hush!—a little French milliner—and the best of the jest is—she's in the room now.

CHARLES SURFACE: The devil she is!

SIR PETER: Hush! I tell you. [*Points to the screen.*]

CHARLES SURFACE: Behind the screen! S'life, let's unveil her!

SIR PETER: No, no, he's coming. You shan't, indeed!

CHARLES SURFACE: Oh, egad, we'll have a peep at the little milliner!

SIR PETER: Not for the world!—Joseph will never forgive me.

CHARLES SURFACE: I'll stand by you—

SIR PETER: Odds, here he is!

[JOSEPH SURFACE *enters just as* CHARLES *throws down the screen.*]

CHARLES SURFACE: Lady Teazle, by all that's wonderful!

SIR PETER: Lady Teazle, by all that's damnable!

CHARLES SURFACE: Sir Peter, this is one of the smartest French milliners I ever saw. Egad, you seem all to have been diverting yourselves here at hide and seek, and I don't see who is out of the secret. Shall I beg your ladyship to inform me? Not a word!—Brother, will you be pleased to explain this matter? What! is Morality Dumb too?—Sir Peter, though I found you in the dark, perhaps you are not so now! All mute! Well—though I can make nothing of the affair, I suppose you perfectly understand one another; so I'll leave you to yourselves. [*going*] Brother, I'm sorry to find you have given that worthy man grounds for so much uneasiness.—Sir Peter! there's nothing in the world so noble as a man of sentiment.

[*Exit* CHARLES SURFACE. *They stand for some time looking at each other.*]

JOSEPH SURFACE: Sir Peter—notwithstanding—I confess—that appearances are against me—if you will afford me your patience—I make no doubt—but I shall explain everything to your satisfaction.

SIR PETER: If you please, sir.

JOSEPH SURFACE: The fact is, sir, that Lady Teazle, knowing my pretensions to your ward Maria—I say, sir, Lady Teazle, being apprehensive of the jealousy of your temper—and knowing my friendship to the family—she, sir, I say—called here—in order that—I might explain these pretensions—but on your coming—being apprehensive—as I said—of your jealousy—she withdrew—and this, you may depend on it, is the whole truth of the matter.

SIR PETER: A very clear account, upon my word; and I dare swear the lady will vouch for every article of it.

LADY TEAZLE: For not one word of it, Sir Peter!

SIR PETER: How! don't you think it worth while to agree in the lie?

LADY TEAZLE: There is not one syllable of truth in what that gentleman has told you.

SIR PETER: I believe you, upon my soul, ma'am!

JOSEPH SURFACE: [*aside to* LADY TEAZLE] 'Sdeath, madam, will you betray me?

LADY TEAZLE: Good Mr. Hypocrite, by your leave, I'll speak for myself.

SIR PETER: Ay, let her alone, sir; you'll find she'll make out a better story than you, without prompting.

LADY TEAZLE: Hear me, Sir Peter! I came here on no matter relating to your ward, and even ignorant of this gentleman's pretensions to her. But I came, seduced by his insidious arguments, at least to listen to his pretended passion, if not to sacrifice your honor to his baseness.

SIR PETER: Now, I believe, the truth is coming, indeed!

JOSEPH SURFACE: The woman's mad!

LADY TEAZLE: No, sir; she has recovered her senses, and your own arts have furnished her with the means. Sir Peter, I do not expect you to credit me —but the tenderness you express for me, when I am sure you could not think I was a witness to it, has penetrated so to my heart, that had I left the place without the shame of this discovery, my future life should have spoken the sincerity of my gratitude. As for that smooth-tongued hypocrite, who would have seduced the wife of his too credulous friend, while he affected honorable addresses to his ward—I behold him now in a light so truly despicable that I shall never again respect myself for having listened to him.

[*Exit* LADY TEAZLE.]

JOSEPH SURFACE: Notwithstanding all this, Sir Peter, Heaven knows—

SIR PETER: That you are a villain! and so I leave you to your conscience.

JOSEPH SURFACE: You are too rash, Sir Peter; you shall hear me. The man who shuts out conviction by refusing to—

[*Exeunt,* JOSEPH SURFACE *talking.*]

ACT V

SCENE I———*The Library in* JOSEPH SURFACE'S *House.*

[JOSEPH SURFACE *and* SERVANT.]

JOSEPH SURFACE: Mr. Stanley! and why should you think I would see him? you must know he comes to ask something.

SERVANT: Sir, I should not have let him in, but that Mr. Rowley came to the door with him.

JOSEPH SURFACE: Psha! blockhead! to suppose that I should now be in a temper to receive visits from poor relations!—Well, why don't you show the fellow up?

SERVANT: I will, sir.—Why, sir it was not my fault that Sir Peter discovered my lady—

JOSEPH SURFACE: Go, fool!

[*Exit* SERVANT.]

Sure fortune never played a man of my policy such a trick before! My character with Sir Peter, my hopes with Maria, destroyed in a moment!

I'm in a rare humor to listen to other people's distresses! I shan't be able to bestow even a benevolent sentiment on Stanley.—So! here he comes, and Rowley with him. I must try to recover myself, and put a little charity in my face, however.

[*Exit. Enter* SIR OLIVER SURFACE *and* ROWLEY.]

SIR OLIVER: What! does he avoid us? That was he, was it not?

ROWLEY: It was, sir. But I doubt you are coming a little too abruptly. His nerves are so weak that the sight of a poor relation may be too much for him. I should have gone first to break it to him.

SIR OLIVER: Oh, plague of his nerves! Yet this is he whom Sir Peter extols as a man of the most benevolent way of thinking!

ROWLEY: As to his way of thinking, I cannot pretend to decide; for, to do him justice, he appears to have as much speculative benevolence as any private gentleman in the kingdom, though he is seldom so sensual as to indulge himself in the exercise of it.

SIR OLIVER: Yet he has a string of charitable sentiments at his fingers' ends.

ROWLEY: Or, rather, at his tongue's end, Sir Oliver; for I believe there is no sentiment he has such faith in as that "Charity begins at home."

SIR OLIVER: And his, I presume, is of that domestic sort which never stirs abroad at all.

ROWLEY: I doubt you'll find it so;—but he's coming. I mustn't seem to interrupt you; and you know, immediately as you leave him, I come in to announce your arrival in your real character.

SIR OLIVER: True; and afterwards you'll meet me at Sir Peter's.

ROWLEY: Without losing a moment.

[*Exit* ROWLEY.]

SIR OLIVER: I don't like the complaisance of his features.

[*Enter* JOSEPH SURFACE.]

JOSEPH SURFACE: Sir, I beg you ten thousand pardons for keeping you a moment waiting.—Mr. Stanley, I presume.

SIR OLIVER: At your service.

JOSEPH SURFACE: Sir, I beg you will do me the honor to sit down—I entreat you, sir.

SIR OLIVER: Dear sir—there's no occasion. [*aside*] Too civil by half!

JOSEPH SURFACE: I have not the pleasure of knowing you, Mr. Stanley; but I am extremely happy to see you look so well. You were nearly related to my mother, I think, Mr. Stanley?

SIR OLIVER: I was, sir; so nearly that my present poverty, I fear, may do discredit to her wealthy children, else I should not have presumed to trouble you.

JOSEPH SURFACE: Dear sir, there needs no apology: he that is in distress, though a stranger, has a right to claim kindred with the wealthy. I am sure I wish I was one of that class, and had it in my power to offer you even a small relief.

SIR OLIVER: If your uncle, Sir Oliver, were here, I should have a friend.

JOSEPH SURFACE: I wish he was, sir, with all my heart: you should not want an advocate with him, believe me, sir.

SIR OLIVER: I should not need one—my distresses would recommend me. But I imagined his bounty would enable you to become the agent of his charity.

JOSEPH SURFACE: My dear sir, you were strangely misinformed. Sir Oliver is a worthy man, a very worthy man, but avarice, Mr. Stanley, is the vice of age. I will tell you, my good sir, in confidence, what he has done for me has been a mere nothing; though, people, I know, have thought otherwise; and, for my part, I never choose to contradict the report.

SIR OLIVER: What! has he never transmitted you bullion—rupees—pagodas?

JOSEPH SURFACE: Oh, dear sir, nothing of the kind; No, no; a few presents now and then—china, shawls, congou tea, avadavats,[1] and Indian crackers[2]—little more, believe me.

SIR OLIVER: [*aside*] Here's gratitude for twelve thousand pounds!—Avadavats and Indian crackers!

JOSEPH SURFACE: Then, my dear sir, you have heard, I doubt not, of the extravagance of my brother; there are very few would credit what I have done for that unfortunate young man.

SIR OLIVER: [*aside*] Not I, for one!

JOSEPH SURFACE: The sums I have lent him! Indeed I have been exceedingly to blame; it was an amiable weakness; however, I don't pretend to defend it—and now I feel it doubly culpable, since it has deprived me of the pleasure of serving you, Mr. Stanley, as my heart dictates.

SIR OLIVER: [*aside*] Dissembler! [*aloud*] Then, sir, you can't assist me?

JOSEPH SURFACE: At present, it grieves me to say, I cannot; but, whenever I have the ability, you may depend upon hearing from me.

SIR OLIVER: I am extremely sorry—

JOSEPH SURFACE: Not more than I, believe me; to pity, without the power to relieve, is still more painful than to ask and be denied.

SIR OLIVER: Kind sir, your most obedient humble servant.

JOSEPH SURFACE: You leave me deeply affected, Mr. Stanley.—William, be ready to open the door.

SIR OLIVER: Oh, dear sir, no ceremony.

JOSEPH SURFACE: Your very obedient.

SIR OLIVER: Sir, your most obsequious.

JOSEPH SURFACE: You may depend upon hearing from me, whenever I can be of service.

SIR OLIVER: Sweet sir, you are too good.

JOSEPH SURFACE: In the meantime I wish you health and spirits.

SIR OLIVER: Your ever grateful and perpetual humble servant.

JOSEPH SURFACE: Sir, yours as sincerely.

SIR OLIVER: [*aside*] Charles!—you are my heir.

[*Exit* SIR OLIVER.]

JOSEPH SURFACE: This is one bad effect of a good character; it invites application from the unfortunate, and there needs no small degree of address to gain the reputation of benevolence without incurring the expense. The

[1] *Avadavats:* Small songbirds from India.
[2] *Indian crackers:* firecrackers.

silver ore of pure charity is an expensive article in the catalogue of a man's good qualities; whereas the sentimental French plate I use instead of it makes just as good a show, and pays no tax.

[*Enter* ROWLEY.]

ROWLEY: Mr. Surface, your servant: I was apprehensive of interrupting you, though my business demands immediate attention, as this note will inform you.

JOSEPH SURFACE: Always happy to see Mr. Rowley.—[*reads*] Sir Oliver Surface! My uncle arrived!

ROWLEY: He is, indeed: we have just parted—quite well, after a speedy voyage, and impatient to embrace his worthy nephew.

JOSEPH SURFACE: I am astonished!—William! stop Mr. Stanley, if he's not gone.

ROWLEY: Oh, he's out of reach, I believe.

JOSEPH SURFACE: Why did you not let me know this when you came in together?

ROWLEY: I thought you had particular business. But I must be gone to inform your brother and appoint him here to meet your uncle. He will be with you in a quarter of an hour.

JOSEPH SURFACE: So he says. Well, I am strangely overjoyed at his coming.—[*aside*] Never, to be sure, was anything so damned unlucky!

ROWLEY: You will be delighted to see how well he looks.

JOSEPH SURFACE: Oh! I'm overjoyed to hear it. [*aside*]—Just at this time!

ROWLEY: I'll tell him how impatiently you expect him.

JOSEPH SURFACE: Do, do; pray give my best duty and affection. Indeed, I cannot express the sensations I feel at the thought of seeing him.

[*Exit* ROWLEY.]

Certainly his coming just at this time is the cruellest piece of ill fortune. [*Exit.*]

SCENE II———SIR PETER TEAZLE'S *House.*

[*Enter* MRS. CANDOUR *and* MAID.]

MAID: Indeed, ma'am, my lady will see nobody at present.

MRS. CANDOUR: Did you tell her it was her friend Mrs. Candour?

MAID: Yes, ma'am; but she begs you will excuse her.

MRS. CANDOUR: Do go again; I shall be glad to see her, if it be only for a moment, for I am sure she must be in great distress.

[*Exit* MAID.]

Dear heart, how provoking! I'm not mistress of half the circumstances! We shall have the whole affair in the newspapers, with the names of the parties at length, before I have dropped the story at a dozen houses.

[*Enter* SIR BENJAMIN BACKBITE.]

Oh, dear Sir Benjamin! you have heard, I suppose—

SIR BENJAMIN: Of Lady Teazle and Mr. Surface—

MRS. CANDOUR: And Sir Peter's discovery—

SIR BENJAMIN: Oh, the strangest piece of business, to be sure!

MRS. CANDOUR: Well, I never was so surprised in my life. I am so sorry for all parties, indeed.

SIR BENJAMIN: Now, I don't pity Sir Peter at all: he was so extravagantly partial to Mr. Surface.

MRS. CANDOUR: Mr. Surface! Why, 'twas with Charles Lady Teazle was detected.

SIR BENJAMIN: No, no, I tell you: Mr. Surface is the gallant.

MRS. CANDOUR: No such thing! Charles is the man. 'Twas Mr. Surface brought Sir Peter on purpose to discover them.

SIR BENJAMIN: I tell you I had it from one—

MRS. CANDOUR: And I have it from one—

SIR BENJAMIN: Who had it from one, who had it—

MRS. CANDOUR: From one immediately—But here comes Lady Sneerwell; perhaps she knows the whole affair.

[*Enter* LADY SNEERWELL.]

LADY SNEERWELL: So, my dear Mrs. Candour, here's a sad affair of our friend Lady Teazle!

MRS. CANDOUR: Ay, my dear friend, who would have thought—

LADY SNEERWELL: Well, there is no trusting to appearances; though indeed, she was always too lively for me.

MRS. CANDOUR: To be sure, her manners were a little too free; but then she was so young!

LADY SNEERWELL: And had, indeed, some good qualities.

MRS. CANDOUR: So she had, indeed. But have you heard the particulars?

LADY SNEERWELL: No; but everybody says that Mr. Surface—

SIR BENJAMIN: Ay, there; I told you Mr. Surface was the man.

MRS. CANDOUR: No, no: indeed the assignation was with Charles.

LADY SNEERWELL: With Charles! You alarm me, Mrs. Candour.

MRS. CANDOUR: Yes, yes: he was the lover. Mr. Surface, to do him justice, was only the informer.

SIR BENJAMIN: Well, I'll not dispute with you, Mrs Candour; but, be it which it may, I hope that Sir Peter's wound will not—

MRS. CANDOUR: Sir Peter's wound! Oh, mercy! I didn't hear a word of their fighting.

LADY SNEERWELL: Nor I, a syllable.

SIR BENJAMIN: No! what, no mention of the duel?

MRS. CANDOUR: Not a word.

SIR BENJAMIN: Oh yes: they fought before they left the room.

LADY SNEERWELL: Pray let us hear.

MRS. CANDOUR: Ay, do oblige us with the duel.

SIR BENJAMIN: "Sir," says Sir Peter, immediately after the discovery, "you are a most ungrateful fellow."

MRS. CANDOUR: Ay, to Charles—

SIR BENJAMIN: No, no—to Mr. Surface—"a most ungrateful fellow; and old as I am, sir," says he, "I insist on immediate satisfaction."

MRS. CANDOUR: Ay, that must have been to Charles; for 'tis very unlikely Mr. Surface should fight in his own house.

SIR BENJAMIN: 'Gad's life, ma'am, not at all—"giving me immediate satisfaction"—On this, ma'am, Lady Teazle, seeing Sir Peter in such danger, ran out of the room in strong hysterics, and Charles after her, calling out for hartshorn and water; then, madam, they began to fight with swords—
[*Enter* CRABTREE.]

CRABTREE: With pistols, nephew—pistols! I have it from undoubted authority.

MRS. CANDOUR: Oh, Mr. Crabtree, then it is all true!

CRABTREE: Too true, indeed, madam, and Sir Peter is dangerously wounded—

SIR BENJAMIN: By a thrust in *seconde* quite through his left side—

CRABTREE: By a bullet lodged in the thorax.

MRS. CANDOUR: Mercy on me! Poor Sir Peter!

CRABTREE: Yes, madam; though Charles would have avoided the matter, if he could.

MRS. CANDOUR: I knew Charles was the person.

SIR BENJAMIN: My uncle, I see, knows nothing of the matter.

CRABTREE: But Sir Peter taxed him with the basest ingratitude—

SIR BENJAMIN: That I told you, you know—

CRABTREE: Do, nephew, let me speak!—and insisted on immediate—

SIR BENJAMIN: Just as I said—

CRABTREE: Odds life, nephew, allow others to know something too! A pair of pistols lay on the bureau (for Mr. Surface, it seems, had come home the night before late from Salthill where he had been to see the Montem with a friend who has a son at Eton) so, unluckily, the pistols were left charged.

SIR BENJAMIN: I heard nothing of this.

CRABTREE: Sir Peter forced Charles to take one, and they fired, it seems, pretty nearly together. Charles's shot took effect, as I tell you, and Sir Peter's missed; but, what is very extraordinary, the ball struck against a little bronze Shakespeare that stood over the fireplace, grazed out of the window at a right angle, and wounded the postman who was just coming to the door with a double letter from Northamptonshire.

SIR BENJAMIN: My uncle's account is more circumstantial, I confess; but I believe mine is the true one for all that.

LADY SNEERWELL: [*aside*] I am more interested in this affair than they imagine, and must have better information.
[*Exit* LADY SNEERWELL.]

SIR BENJAMIN: Ah! Lady Sneerwell's alarm is very easily accounted for.

CRABTREE: Yes, yes, they certainly do say—but that's neither here nor there.

MRS. CANDOUR: But, pray, where is Sir Peter at present?

CRABTREE: Oh! they brought him home, and he is now in the house, though the servants are ordered to deny him.

MRS. CANDOUR: I believe so, and Lady Teazle, I suppose, attending him.

CRABTREE: Yes, yes; and I saw one of the faculty enter just before me.

SIR BENJAMIN: Hey! who comes here?

CRABTREE: Oh, this is he: the physician, depend on't.

MRS. CANDOUR: Oh, certainly; it must be the physician; and now we shall know.
[*Enter* SIR OLIVER SURFACE.]

CRABTREE: Well, doctor, what hopes?

MRS. CANDOUR: Ay, doctor, how's your patient?

SIR BENJAMIN: Now, doctor, isn't it a wound with a smallsword?

CRABTREE: A bullet lodged in the thorax, for a hundred!

SIR OLIVER: Doctor! a wound with a smallsword; and a bullet in the thorax?— Oons! are you mad, good people?

SIR BENJAMIN: Perhaps, sir, you are not a doctor?

SIR OLIVER: Truly, I am to thank you for my degree, if I am.

CRABTREE: Only a friend of Sir Peter's, then, I presume. But, sir, you must have heard of his accident?

SIR OLIVER: Not a word!

CRABTREE: Not of his being dangerously wounded?

SIR OLIVER: The devil he is!

SIR BENJAMIN: Run through the body—

CRABTREE: Shot in the breast—

SIR BENJAMIN: By one Mr. Surface—

CRABTREE: Ay, the younger.

SIR OLIVER: Hey! what the plague! you seem to differ strangely in your accounts: however, you agree that Sir Peter is dangerously wounded.

SIR BENJAMIN: Oh, yes, we agree there.

CRABTREE: Yes, yes, I believe there can be no doubt in that.

SIR OLIVER: Then, upon my word, for a person in that situation, he is the most imprudent man alive; for here he comes, walking as if nothing at all was the matter.

  [*Enter* SIR PETER TEAZLE.]

Odds heart, Sir Peter! you are come in good time, I promise you; for we had just given you over!

SIR BENJAMIN: [*aside to* CRABTREE] Egad, uncle, this is the most sudden recovery!

SIR OLIVER: Why, man! what do you do out of bed with a smallsword through your body and a bullet lodged in your thorax?

SIR PETER: A smallsword and a bullet?

SIR OLIVER: Ay; these gentlemen would have killed you without law or physic, and wanted to dub me a doctor, to make me an accomplice.

SIR PETER: Why, what is all this?

SIR BENJAMIN: We rejoice, Sir Peter, that the story of the duel is not true and are sincerely sorry for your other misfortune.

SIR PETER: [*aside*] So, so; all over the town already.

CRABTREE: Though, Sir Peter, you were certainly vastly to blame to marry at your years.

SIR PETER: Sir, what business is that of yours?

MRS. CANDOUR: Though, indeed, as Sir Peter made so good a husband, he's very much to be pitied.

SIR PETER: Plague on your pity, ma'am! I desire none of it.

SIR BENJAMIN: However, Sir Peter, you must not mind the laughing and jests you will meet with on the occasion.

SIR PETER: Sir, sir! I desire to be master in my own house.

CRABTREE: 'Tis no uncommon case, that's one comfort.

SIR PETER: I insist on being left to myself. Without ceremony, I insist on your leaving my house directly!

MRS. CANDOUR: Well, well, we are going; and depend on't, we'll make the best report of it we can.

[*Exit* MRS. CANDOUR.]

SIR PETER: Leave my house!

CRABTREE: And tell how hardly you've been treated!

[*Exit* CRABTREE.]

SIR PETER: Leave my house!

SIR BENJAMIN: And how patiently you bear it.

[*Exit* SIR BENJAMIN.]

SIR PETER: Fiends! vipers! furies! Oh! that their own venom would choke them!

SIR OLIVER: They are very provoking indeed, Sir Peter.

[*Enter* ROWLEY.]

ROWLEY: I heard high words: what has ruffled you, sir?

SIR PETER: Psha! what signifies asking? Do I ever pass a day without my vexations?

ROWLEY: Well, I'm not inquisitive.

SIR OLIVER: Well, Sir Peter, I have seen both my nephews in the manner we proposed.

SIR PETER: A precious couple they are!

ROWLEY: Yes, and Sir Oliver is convinced that your judgment was right, Sir Peter.

SIR OLIVER: Yes, I find Joseph is indeed the man, after all.

ROWLEY: Ay, as Sir Peter says, he is a man of sentiment.

SIR OLIVER: And acts up to the sentiments he professes.

ROWLEY: It certainly is edification to hear him talk.

SIR OLIVER: Oh, he's a model for the young men of the age! But how's this, Sir Peter? you don't join us in your friend Joseph's praise, as I expected.

SIR PETER: Sir Oliver, we live in a damned wicked world, and the fewer we praise the better.

ROWLEY: What! do you say so, Sir Peter, who were never mistaken in your life?

SIR PETER: Psha! plague on you both! I see by your sneering you have heard the whole affair. I shall go mad among you!

ROWLEY: Then, to fret you no longer, Sir Peter, we are indeed acquainted with it all. I met Lady Teazle coming from Mr. Surface's so humbled, that she deigned to request me to be her advocate with you.

SIR PETER: And does Sir Oliver know all this?

SIR OLIVER: Every circumstance.

SIR PETER: What, of the closet and the screen, hey?

SIR OLIVER: Yes, yes, and the little French milliner. Oh, I have been vastly diverted with the story! ha! ha! ha!

SIR PETER: 'Twas very pleasant.

SIR OLIVER: I never laughed more in my life, I assure you: ha! ha! ha!

SIR PETER: Oh, vastly diverting! ha! ha! ha!

ROWLEY: To be sure, Joseph with his sentiments! ha! ha! ha!

SIR PETER: Yes, yes, his sentiments! ha! ha! ha! Hyprocritical villain!

SIR OLIVER: Ay, and the rogue Charles to pull Sir Peter out of the closet: ha! ha! ha!

SIR PETER: Ha! ha! 'twas devilish entertaining, to be sure!

SIR OLIVER: Ha! ha! ha! Egad, Sir Peter, I should like to have seen your face when the screen was thrown down: ha! ha.

SIR PETER: Yes, yes, my face when the screen was thrown down: ha! ha! ha! Oh, I must never show my head again!

SIR OLIVER: But come, come, it isn't fair to laugh at you neither, my old friend; though, upon my soul, I can't help it.

SIR PETER: Oh, pray, don't restrain your mirth on my account: it does not hurt me at all! I laugh at the whole affair myself. Yes, yes, I think being a standing jest for all one's acquaintance a very happy situation. Oh, yes, and then of a morning to read the paragraphs about Mr. S—, Lady T—, and Sir P—, will be so entertaining!

ROWLEY: Without affection, Sir Peter, you may despise the ridicule of fools. But I see Lady Teazle going towards the next room, I am sure you must desire a reconciliation as earnestly as she does.

SIR OLIVER: Perhaps my being here prevents her coming to you. Well, I'll leave honest Rowley to mediate between you; but he must bring you all presently to Mr. Surface's where I am now returning, if not to reclaim a libertine, at least to expose hypocrisy.

SIR PETER: Ah, I'll be present at your discovering yourself there with all my heart; though 'tis a vile unlucky place for discoveries.

ROWLEY: We'll follow.

[*Exit* SIR OLIVER.]

SIR PETER: She is not coming here, you see, Rowley.

ROWLEY: No, but she has left the door of that room open, you perceive. See, she is in tears.

SIR PETER: Certainly a little mortification appears very becoming in a wife. Don't you think it will do her good to let her pine a little?

ROWLEY: Oh, this is ungenerous in you!

SIR PETER: Well, I know not what to think. You remember the letter I found of hers evidently intended for Charles!

ROWLEY: A mere forgery, Sir Peter! laid in your way on purpose. This is one of the points which I intend Snake shall give you conviction of.

SIR PETER: I wish I were once satisfied of that. She looks this way. What a remarkably elegant turn of the head she has! Rowley, I'll go to her.

ROWLEY: Certainly.

SIR PETER: Though, when it is known that we are reconciled, people will laugh at me ten times more.

ROWLEY: Let them laugh, and retort their malice only by showing them you are happy in spite of it.

SIR PETER: I'faith, so I will! and, if I'm not mistaken, we may yet be the happiest couple in the country.

ROWLEY: Nay, Sir Peter, he is who once lays aside suspicion—

SIR PETER: Hold, Master Rowley! if you have any regard for me, never let me hear you utter anything like a sentiment. I have had enough of them to serve me the rest of my life.

SCENE III——*The Library in* JOSEPH SURFACE'*s House.*

[JOSEPH SURFACE *and* LADY SNEERWELL.]

LADY SNEERWELL: Impossible! Will not Sir Peter immediately be reconciled to Charles, and of course no longer oppose his union with Maria? The thought is distraction to me.

JOSEPH SURFACE: Can passion furnish a remedy?

LADY SNEERWELL: No, nor cunning either. Oh, I was a fool, an idiot, to league with such a blunderer!

JOSEPH SURFACE: Sure, Lady Sneerwell, I am the greatest sufferer; yet you see I bear the accident with calmness.

LADY SNEERWELL: Because the disappointment doesn't reach your heart; your interest only attached you to Maria. Had you felt for her what I have for that ungrateful libertine, neither your temper nor hypocrisy could prevent your showing the sharpness of your vexation.

JOSEPH SURFACE: But why should your reproaches fall on me for this disappointment?

LADY SNEERWELL: Are you not the cause of it? Had you not a sufficient field for your roguery in imposing upon Sir Peter, and supplanting your brother, but you must endeavor to seduce his wife? I hate such an avarice of crimes; 'tis an unfair monopoly, and never prospers.

JOSEPH SURFACE: Well, I admit I have been to blame. I confess I deviated from the direct road of wrong, but I don't think we're so totally defeated neither.

LADY SNEERWELL: No?

JOSEPH SURFACE: You tell me you have made a trial of Snake since we met, and that you still believe him faithful to us?

LADY SNEERWELL: I do believe so.

JOSEPH SURFACE: And that he has undertaken, should it be necessary, to swear and prove that Charles is at this time contracted by vows and honor to your ladyship, which some of his former letters to you will serve to support?

LADY SNEERWELL: This, indeed, might have assisted.

JOSEPH SURFACE: Come, come; it is not too late yet.
    [*Knocking at the door.*]
    But hark! this is probably my uncle, Sir Oliver: retire to that room; we'll consult further when he's gone.

LADY SNEERWELL: Well, but if he should find you out too.

JOSEPH SURFACE: Oh, I have no fear of that. Sir Peter will hold his tongue for his own credit's sake—and you may depend on it I shall soon discover Sir Oliver's weak side!

LADY SNEERWELL: I have no diffidence of your abilities! only be constant to one roguery at a time.
    [*Exit* LADY SNEERWELL.]

JOSEPH SURFACE: I will, I will! So! 'tis confounded hard, after such bad fortune, to be baited by one's confederate in evil. Well, at all events, my character is so much better than Charles's that I certainly—hey!—what—this is not Sir Oliver, but old Stanley again. Plague on't that he should return to tease me just now! I shall have Sir Oliver come and find him here—and—

[*Enter* SIR OLIVER SURFACE.]

Gad's life, Mr. Stanley, why have you come back to plague me at this time? You must not stay now, upon my word.

SIR OLIVER: Sir, I hear your uncle Oliver is expected here, and though he has been so penurious to you, I'll try what he'll do for me.

JOSEPH SURFACE: Sir, 'tis impossible for you to stay now, so I must beg—Come any other time, and I promise you, you shall be assisted.

SIR OLIVER: No: Sir Oliver and I must be acquainted.

JOSEPH SURFACE: Zounds, sir! then I insist on your quitting the room directly.

SIR OLIVER: Nay, sir—

JOSEPH SURFACE: Sir, I insist on't!—Here, William! show this gentleman out. Since you compel me, sir not one moment—this is such insolence!

[*Going to push him out. Enter* CHARLES SURFACE.]

CHARLES SURFACE: Heyday! what's the matter now? What the devil have you got hold of my little broker here? Zounds, brother, don't hurt little Premium. What's the matter, my little fellow?

JOSEPH SURFACE: So! he has been with you, too, has he?

CHARLES SURFACE: To be sure he has. Why, he's as honest a little—But sure, Joseph, you have not been borrowing money too, have you?

JOSEPH SURFACE: Borrowing! no! But, brother, you know we expect Sir Oliver here every—

CHARLES SURFACE: O gad, that's true! Noll mustn't find the little broker here, to be sure.

JOSEPH SURFACE: Yet, Mr. Stanley insists—

CHARLES SURFACE: Stanley! why his name's Premium.

JOSEPH SURFACE: No, sir, Stanley.

CHARLES SURFACE: No, no, Premium.

JOSEPH SURFACE: Well, no matter which—but—

CHARLES SURFACE: Ay, ay, Stanley or Premium, 'tis the same thing, as you say; for I suppose he goes by half a hundred names, besides A.B. at the coffee-house.

[*Knocking.*]

JOSEPH SURFACE: 'Sdeath! here's Sir Oliver at the door. Now I beg, Mr. Stanley—

CHARLES SURFACE: Ay, ay, and I beg, Mr. Premium—

SIR OLIVER: Gentlemen—

JOSEPH SURFACE: Sir, by heaven you shall go!

CHARLES SURFACE: Ay, out with him, certainly!

SIR OLIVER: This violence—

JOSEPH SURFACE: Sir, 'tis your own fault.

CHARLES SURFACE: Out with him, to be sure!

[*Both forcing* SIR OLIVER *out. Enter* SIR PETER *and* LADY TEAZLE, MARIA, *and* ROWLEY.]

SIR PETER: My old friend, Sir Oliver—hey! What in the name of wonder!—here are dutiful nephews—assault their uncle at first visit!

LADY TEAZLE: Indeed, Sir Oliver, 'twas well we came in to rescue you.

ROWLEY: Truly it was; for I perceive, Sir Oliver, the character of old Stanley was no protection to you.

SIR OLIVER: Nor of Premium either: the necessities of the former could not extort a shilling from that benevolent gentleman; and now, egad, I stood a chance of faring worse than my ancestors and being knocked down without being bid for.

JOSEPH SURFACE: Charles!

CHARLES SURFACE: Joseph!

JOSEPH SURFACE: 'Tis now complete!

CHARLES SURFACE: Very!

SIR OLIVER: Sir Peter, my friend, and Rowley too—look on that elder nephew of mine. You know what he has already received from my bounty; and you also know how gladly I would have regarded half my fortune as held in trust for him? judge, then, my disappointment in discovering him to be destitute of truth, charity, and gratitude!

SIR PETER: Sir Oliver, I should be more surprised at this declaration, if I had not myself found him to be mean, treacherous, and hypocritical.

LADY TEAZLE: And if the gentleman pleads not guilty to these, pray let him call me to his character.

SIR PETER: Then, I believe, we need add no more: if he knows himself, he will consider it as the most perfect punishment that he is known to the world.

CHARLES SURFACE: [*aside*] If they talk this way to Honesty, what will they say to me, by-and-by?

SIR OLIVER: As for that prodigal, his brother, there—

CHARLES SURFACE: [*aside*] Ay, now comes my turn: the damned family pictures will ruin me!

JOSEPH SURFACE: Sir Oliver—uncle, will you honor me with a hearing?

CHARLES SURFACE: [*aside*] Now, if Joseph would make one of his long speeches, I might recollect myself a little.

SIR OLIVER: [*to* JOSEPH] I suppose you would undertake to justify yourself entirely?

JOSEPH SURFACE: I trust I could.

SIR OLIVER: [*to* CHARLES] Well, sir!—and you could justify yourself too, I suppose?

CHARLES SURFACE: Not that I know of, Sir Oliver.

SIR OLIVER: What!—Little Premium has been let too much into the secret, I suppose?

CHARLES SURFACE: True, sir; but they were family secrets, and should not be mentioned again, you know.

ROWLEY: Come, Sir Oliver, I know you cannot speak of Charles's follies with anger.

SIR OLIVER: Odd's heart, no more I can; nor with gravity either. Sir Peter, do you know the rogue bargained with me for all his ancestors; sold me judges and generals by the foot, and maiden aunts as cheap as broken china.

CHARLES SURFACE: To be sure, Sir Oliver, I did make a little free with the family canvas, that's the truth on't. My ancestors may rise in judgment against me, there's no denying it; but believe me sincere when I tell you —and upon my soul I would not say so if I was not—that if I do not appear mortified at the exposure of my follies, it is because I feel at this moment the warmest satisfaction at seeing you, my liberal benefactor.

SIR OLIVER: Charles, I believe you. Give me your hand again: the ill looking little fellow over the settee has made your peace.

CHARLES SURFACE: Then, sir, my gratitude to the original is still increased.

LADY TEAZLE: Yet, I believe, Sir Oliver, here is one whom Charles is still more anxious to be reconciled to.

[*Pointing to* MARIA.]

SIR OLIVER: Oh, I have heard of his attachment there; and, with the young lady's pardon, if I construe right—that blush—

SIR PETER: Well, child, speak your sentiments.

MARIA: Sir, I have little to say, but I shall rejoice to hear that he is happy; for me, whatever claim I had to his attention, I willingly resign to one who has a better title.

CHARLES SURFACE: How, Maria!

SIR PETER: Heyday! what's the mystery now? While he appeared an incorrigible rake, you would give your hand to no one else; and now that he is likely to reform I'll warrant you won't have him.

MARIA: His own heart and Lady Sneerwell know the cause.

CHARLES SURFACE: Lady Sneerwell!

JOSEPH SURFACE: Brother, it is with great concern I am obliged to speak on this point, but my regard to justice compels me, and Lady Sneerwell's injuries can no longer be concealed.

[*Opens the door. Enter* LADY SNEERWELL.]

SIR PETER: So! another French milliner! Egad, he has one in every room in the house, I suppose!

LADY SNEERWELL: Ungrateful Charles! Well may you be surprised, and feel for the indelicate situation your perfidy has forced me into.

CHARLES SURFACE: Pray, uncle, is this another plot of yours? For, as I have life, I don't understand it.

JOSEPH SURFACE: I believe, sir, there is but the evidence of one person more necessary to make it extremely clear.

SIR PETER: And that person, I imagine, is Mr. Snake. Rowley, you were perfectly right to bring him with us, and pray let him appear.

ROWLEY: Walk in, Mr. Snake.

[*Enter* SNAKE.]

I thought his testimony might be wanted; however, it happens unluckily, that he comes to confront Lady Sneerwell, not to support her.

LADY SNEERWELL: A villain! Treacherous to me at last! Speak, fellow, have you too conspired against me?

SNAKE: I beg your ladyship ten thousand pardons: you paid me extremely liberally for the lie in question; but I unfortunately have been offered double to speak the truth.

SIR PETER: Plot and counterplot, egad!

LADY SNEERWELL: The torments of shame and disappointment on you all!

LADY TEAZLE: Hold, Lady Sneerwell—before you go, let me thank you for the trouble you and that gentleman have taken in writing letters from me to Charles, and answering them yourself; and let me also request you to make my respects to the scandalous college, of which you are president, and inform them that Lady Teazle, licentiate, begs leave to return the diploma they granted her, as she leaves off practice and kills characters no longer.

LADY SNEERWELL: You too, madam!—provoking—insolent! May your husband live these fifty years!

[*Exit* LADY SNEERWELL.]

SIR PETER: Oons! what a fury!

LADY TEAZLE: A malicious creature, indeed!

SIR PETER: Hey! not for her last wish?

LADY TEAZLE: Oh, no!

SIR OLIVER: Well, sir, and what have you to say now?

JOSEPH SURFACE: Sir, I am so confounded, to find that Lady Sneerwell could be guilty of suborning Mr. Snake in this manner, to impose on us all, that I know not what to say: however, lest her revengeful spirit should prompt her to injure my brother, I had certainly better follow her directly.

[*Exit* JOSEPH SURFACE.]

SIR PETER: Moral to the last drop!

SIR OLIVER: Ay, and marry her, Joseph, if you can. Oil and vinegar—egad, you'll do very well together.

ROWLEY: I believe we have no more occasion for Mr. Snake at present?

SNAKE: Before I go, I beg pardon once for all, for whatever uneasiness I have been the humble instrument of causing to the parties present.

SIR PETER: Well, well, you have made atonement by a good deed at last.

SNAKE: But I must request of the company, that it shall never be known.

SIR PETER: Hey! what the plague! are you ashamed of having done a right thing once in your life?

SNAKE: Ah, sir, consider—I live by the badness of my character; I have nothing but my infamy to depend on; and, if it were once known that I had been betrayed into an honest action, I should lose every friend I have in the world.

SIR OLIVER: Well, well—we'll not traduce you by saying anything in your praise, never fear.

[*Exit* SNAKE.]

SIR PETER: There's a precious rogue!

LADY TEAZLE: See, Sir Oliver, there needs no persuasion now to reconcile your nephew and Maria.

SIR OLIVER: Ay, ay, that's as it should be; and, egad, we'll have the wedding tomorrow morning.

CHARLES SURFACE: Thank you, dear uncle.

SIR PETER: What, you rogue! don't you ask the girl's consent first?

CHARLES SURFACE: Oh, I have done that a long time—a minute ago—and she has looked yes.

MARIA: For shame, Charles!—I protest, Sir Peter, there has not been a word—

SIR OLIVER: Well, then, the fewer the better: may your love for each other never know abatement.

SIR PETER: And may you live as happily together as Lady Teazle and I intend to do!

CHARLES SURFACE: Rowley, my old friend, I am sure you congratulate me; and I suspect that I owe you much.

SIR OLIVER: You do, indeed, Charles.

ROWLEY: If my efforts to serve you had not succeeded, you would have been in my debt for the attempt—but deserve to be happy—and you overpay me.

SIR PETER: Ay, honest Rowley always said you would reform.

CHARLES SURFACE: Why as to reforming, Sir Peter, I'll make no promises, and that I take to be a proof that I intend to set about it. But here shall be my monitor—my gentle guide.—Ah! can I leave the virtuous path those eyes illumine?

> Though thou, dear maid, shouldst wave thy beauty's sway,
> Thou still must rule, because I will obey:
> An humble fugitive from Folly view,
> No sanctuary near but Love—and you: [*To the audience.*]
> *You* can, indeed, each anxious fear remove,
> For even Scandal dies, if you approve.

EPILOGUE

[*Written by* MR. COLMAN.]
[*Spoken by* LADY TEAZLE.]

> I, who was late so volatile and gay,
> Like a trade-wind must now blow all one way,
> Bend all my cares, my studies, and my vows,
> To one dull rusty weathercock—my spouse!
> So wills our virtuous bard—the motley Bayes   5
> Of crying epilogues and laughing plays!
> Old bachelors, who marry smart young wives—
> Learn from our play to regulate your lives:
> Each bring his dear to town, all faults upon her—
> London will prove the very source of honor.   10
> Plunged fairly in, like a cold bath it serves,
> When principles relax, to brace the nerves.
> Such is my case; and yet I must deplore
> That the gay dream of dissipation's o'er.
> And say, ye fair! was ever lively wife,   15
> Born with a genius for the highest life,

Like me untimely blasted in her bloom,
Like me condemned to such a dismal doom?
Save money—when I just knew how to waste it!
Leave London—just as I began to taste it!   20
Must I then watch the early-crowing cock,
The melancholy ticking of a clock;
In a lone rustic hall for ever pounded,
With dogs, cats, rats, and squalling brats surrounded?
With humble curate can I now retire,   25
(While good Sir Peter boozes with the squire,)
And at backgammon mortify my soul,
That pants for loo, or flutters at a vole.
Seven's the main! Dear sound that must expire,
Lost at hot cockles round a Christmas fire;   30
The transient hour of fashion too soon spent,
Farewell the tranquil mind, farewell content!
Farewell the pluméd head, the cushioned tête,
That takes the cushion from its proper seat!
That spirit-stirring drum—card drums I mean,   35
Spadille—odd trick—pam—basto—king and queen!
And you, ye knockers that with brazen throat
The welcome visitors' approach denote;
Farewell all quality of high renown,
Pride, pomp, and circumstance of glorious town!   40
Farewell! your revels I partake no more,
And Lady Teazle's occupation's o'er!
All this I told our bard; he smiled, and said 'twas clear,
I ought to play deep tragedy next year.
Meanwhile he drew wise morals from his play,   45
And in these solemn periods stalked away:—
"Blessed were the fair like you; her faults who stopped.
And closed her follies when the curtain dropped!
No more in vice or error to engage,
Or play the fool at large on life's great stage."   50

HENRIK IBSEN

THE WILD DUCK

Translated by
William Archer

PERSONS OF THE PLAY

WERLE, *a merchant*
GREGERS WERLE, *his son*
OLD EKDAL
HIALMAR EKDAL, *his son, a*
photographer
GINA EKDAL, *Hialmar's wife*
HEDVIG, *their daughter, a girl of*
fourteen
MRS SORBY, *Werle's housekeeper*
RELLING, *a doctor*

MOLVIK, *a student of theology*
GRABERG, *Werle's bookkeeper*
PETTERSEN, *Werle's servant*
JENSEN, *a hired waiter*
A FLABBY GENTLEMAN
A THIN-HAIRED GENTLEMAN
A SHORTSIGHTED GENTLEMAN
SIX OTHER GENTLEMEN, *guests at*
Werle's dinner party
SEVERAL HIRED WAITERS

The action takes place in the home of
WERLE *and the studio of* HIALMAR EKDAL.

ACT I

SCENE——*At* WERLE'S *house. A richly and comfortably furnished study; book-cases and upholstered furniture; a writing table, with papers and documents, in the center of the room; lighted lamps with green shades, giving a subdued light. At the back open folding doors with curtains drawn back. Within is seen a large and handsome room, brilliantly lighted with lamps and branching candlesticks. In front, on the right (in the study), a small baize door leads into* WERLE'S *office. On the left, in front, a fireplace with a glowing coal fire and farther back a double door leading into the dining room.*

[WERLE'S *servant,* PETTERSEN, *in livery, and* JENSEN, *the hired waiter, in black, are putting the study in order. In the large room two or three other hired waiters are moving about arranging things and lighting more candles. From the dining room the hum of conversation and laughter of many voices are heard; a glass is tapped with a knife; silence follows, and a toast is proposed; shouts of "Bravo!" and then again a buzz of conversation.*]

PETTERSEN: [*lights a lamp on the chimney place and places a shade over it*] Listen to them, Jensen! Now the old man's on his legs giving a long speech about Mrs Sorby.

JENSEN: [*pushing forward an armchair*] Is it true, what folks say, that they're— very good friends, eh?

PETTERSEN: Lord knows.

JENSEN: I've heard tell as he's been a lively customer in his day.

PETTERSEN: May be.

JENSEN: And he's giving this spread in honor of his son, they say.

PETTERSEN: Yes. His son came home yesterday.

JENSEN: This is the first time I ever heard as Mr Werle had a son.

PETTERSEN: Oh yes, he has a son right enough. But he's a fixture, as you might say, up at the Höidal works. He's never once come to town all the years I've been in service here.

A WAITER: [*in the doorway of the other room*] Pettersen, here's an old fellow wanting—

PETTERSEN: [*mutters*] The devil—who's this now?

[OLD EKDAL *appears from the right, in the inner room. He is dressed in a threadbare overcoat with a high collar; he wears woolen mittens and carries in his hand a stick and a fur cap. Under his arm a brown paper parcel. Dirty red-brown wig and small gray mustache.*]

PETTERSEN: [*goes toward him*] Good lord!—what do you want here?

EKDAL: [*in the doorway*] Must get into the office, Pettersen.

PETTERSEN: The office was closed an hour ago, and—

EKDAL: So they told me at the front door. But Graberg's in there still. Let me slip in this way, Pettersen; there's a good fellow. [*Points toward the baize door.*] It's not the first time I've come this way.

PETTERSEN: Well, you may pass. [*opens the door*] But mind you go out again the proper way, for we've got company.

EKDAL: I know, I know—h'm! Thanks, Pettersen, good old friend! Thanks! [*mutters softly*] Ass! [*He goes into the office;* PETTERSEN *shuts the door after him.*]

JENSEN: Is he one of the office people?

PETTERSEN: No, he's only an outside hand that does odd jobs of copying. But he's been a topnotcher in his day, has old Ekdal.

JENSEN: You can see he's been through a lot.

PETTERSEN: Yes; he was an army officer, you know.

JENSEN: You don't say so?

PETTERSEN: No mistake about it. But then he went into the timber trade or something of the sort. They say he once played Mr Werle a very nasty trick. They were partners in the Höidal works at the time. Oh, I know old Ekdal well, I do. Many a nip of bitters and bottle of ale we two have drunk at Madam Eriksen's.

JENSEN: He don't look as if he'd much to stand treat with.

PETTERSEN: Why, bless you, Jensen, it's me that stands treat. I always think there's no harm in being a bit civil to folks that have seen better days.

JENSEN: Did he go bankrupt then?

PETTERSEN: Worse than that. He went to jail.

JENSEN: To jail!

PETTERSEN: Or perhaps it was the penitentiary. [*listens*] Sh! They're leaving the table.

[*The dining-room door is thrown open from within by a couple of waiters.* MRS SORBY *comes out conversing with two gentlemen. Gradually the whole company follows, among them* WERLE. *Last come* HIALMAR EKDAL *and* GREGERS WERLE.]

MRS SORBY: [*in passing, to the servant*] Tell them to serve the coffee in the music room, Pettersen.

PETTERSEN: Very well, madam.

[*She goes with the two gentlemen into the inner room and thence out to the right.* PETTERSEN *and* JENSEN *go out the same way.*]

A FLABBY GENTLEMAN: [*to a* THIN-HAIRED GENTLEMAN] Whew! What a dinner! It was no joke to do it justice.

THE THIN-HAIRED GENTLEMAN: Oh, with a little good will one can get through a lot in three hours.

THE FLABBY GENTLEMAN: Yes, but afterward, afterward, my dear Chamberlain!

A THIRD GENTLEMAN: I hear the coffee and liqueur are to be served in the music room.

THE FLABBY GENTLEMAN: Bravo! Then perhaps Mrs Sorby will play us something.

THE THIN-HAIRED GENTLEMAN: [*in a low voice*] I hope Mrs Sorby doesn't play us a tune we don't like, one of these days!

THE FLABBY GENTLEMAN: Oh no, Bertha will never turn against her old friends.

[*They laugh and pass into the inner room.*]

WERLE: [*in a low voice, dejectedly*] I don't think anybody noticed it, Gregers.

GREGERS: [*looks at him*] Noticed what?

WERLE: Didn't you notice it either?

GREGERS: What do you mean?

WERLE: We were thirteen at table.

GREGERS: Really? Were there thirteen of us?

WERLE: [*glances toward* HIALMAR EKDAL] Our usual party is twelve. [*to the others*] This way, gentlemen!

[WERLE *and the others, all except* HIALMAR *and* GREGERS, *go out by the back, to the right.*]

HIALMAR: [*who has overheard the conversation*] You ought not to have invited me, Gregers.

GREGERS: What! Not ask my best and only friend to a party supposed to be in my honor?

HIALMAR: But I don't think your father likes it. You see, I am quite outside his circle.

GREGERS: So I hear. But I wanted to see you and have a talk with you, and I certainly shan't be staying long. Ah, we two old schoolfellows have drifted apart from each other. It must be sixteen or seventeen years since we met.

HIALMAR: Is it so long?

GREGERS: It is. Well, how goes it with you? You look well. You have put on flesh and grown almost stout.

HIALMAR: Well, "stout" is scarcely the word, but I daresay I look a little more of a man than I used to.

GREGERS: Yes, you do; your outer man is in first-rate condition.

HIALMAR: [*in a tone of gloom*] Ah, but the inner man! That is a very different matter, I can tell you! Of course you know of the terrible catastrophe that has befallen me since last we met.

GREGERS: [*more softly*] How are things going with your father now?

HIALMAR: Don't let us talk of it, old fellow. Of course my poor unhappy father lives with me. He hasn't another soul in the world to care for him. But you can understand that this is a miserable subject for me. Tell me, rather, how you have been getting on up at the works.

GREGERS: I have had a delightfully lonely time of it—plenty of leisure to think and think about things. Come over here; we may as well make ourselves comfortable.

[*He seats himself in an armchair by the fire and draws* HIALMAR *down into another alongside of it.*]

HIALMAR: [*sentimentally*] After all, Gregers, I thank you for inviting me to your father's table; for I take it as a sign that you have got over your feeling against me.

GREGERS: [*surprised*] How could you imagine I had any feeling against you?

HIALMAR: You had at first, you know.

GREGERS: How at first?

HIALMAR: After the great misfortune. It was natural enough that you should. Your father was within an ace of being drawn into that—well, that terrible business.

GREGERS: Why should that give me any feeling against you? Who can have put that into your head?

HIALMAR: I know it did, Gregers; your father told me so himself.

GREGERS: [*starts*] My father! Oh, indeed. H'm. Was that why you never let me hear from you?—not a single word.

HIALMAR: Yes.

GREGERS: Not even when you made up your mind to become a photographer?

HIALMAR: Your father said I had better not write to you at all, about anything.

GREGERS: [*looking straight before him*] Well, well, perhaps he was right. But tell me now, Hialmar: are you pretty well satisfied with your present position?

HIALMAR: [*with a little sigh*] Oh yes, I am; I have really no cause to complain. At first, as you may guess, I felt it a little strange. It was such a totally new state of things for me. But of course my whole circumstances were totally changed. Father's utter, irretrievable ruin—the shame and disgrace of it, Gregers—

GREGERS: [*affected*] Yes, yes; I understand.

HIALMAR: I couldn't think of remaining at college; there wasn't a shilling to spare; on the contrary, there were debts—mainly to your father, I be-lieve—

GREGERS: H'm.

HIALMAR: In short, I thought it best to break, once for all, with my old surroundings and associations. It was your father that specially urged me to it, and since he interested himself so much in me—

GREGERS: My father did?

HIALMAR: Yes, you surely knew that, didn't you? Where do you suppose I found the money to learn photography and to furnish a studio and make a start? All that costs money, I can tell you.

GREGERS: And my father provided it?

HIALMAR: Yes, my dear fellow, didn't you know? I understood him to say he had written to you about it.

GREGERS: Not a word about his part in the business. He must have forgotten it. Our correspondence has always been purely a business one. So it was my father that—

HIALMAR: Yes, certainly. He didn't wish it to be generally known, but he it was. And of course it was he, too, that put me in a position to marry. Don't you—don't you know about that either?

GREGERS: No, I haven't heard a word of it. [*shakes him by the arm*] But, my dear Hialmar, I can't tell you what pleasure all this gives me—pleasure and self-reproach. I have perhaps done my father injustice after all—in some things. This proves that he has a heart. It shows a sort of compunction—

HIALMAR: Compunction?

GREGERS: Yes, yes—whatever you like to call it. Oh, I can't tell you how glad I am to hear this of Father. So you are a married man, Hialmar! That is further than I shall ever get. Well, I hope you are happy in your married life?

HIALMAR: Yes, thoroughly happy. She is as good and capable a wife as any man could wish for. And she is by no means without culture.

GREGERS: [*rather surprised*] No, of course not.

HIALMAR: You see, life is itself an education. Her daily intercourse with me— And then we know one or two rather remarkable men who come a good deal about us. I assure you, you would hardly know Gina again.

GREGERS: Gina?

HIALMAR: Yes; had you forgotten that her name was Gina?

GREGERS: Whose name? I haven't the slightest idea—

HIALMAR: Don't you remember that she used to be in service here?

GREGERS: [*looks at him*] Is it Gina Hansen?

HIALMAR: Yes, of course it is Gina Hansen.

GREGERS: —who kept house for us during the last year of my mother's illness?

HIALMAR: Yes, exactly. But, my dear friend, I'm quite sure your father told you that I was married.

GREGERS: [*who has risen*] Oh yes, he mentioned it, but not that— [*walking about the room*] Stay—perhaps he did—now that I think of it. My father always writes such short letters. [*half seats himself on the arm of the chair*] Now tell me, Hialmar—this is interesting—how did you come to know Gina—your wife?

HIALMAR: The simplest thing in the world. You know Gina did not stay here long; everything was so much upset at that time, owing to your mother's illness and so forth, that Gina was not equal to it all; so she gave notice and left. That was the year before your mother died—or it may have been the same year.

GREGERS: It was the same year. I was up at the works then. But afterward?

HIALMAR: Well, Gina lived at home with her mother, Madam Hansen, an excellent, hard-working woman who kept a little eating house. She had a room to let too, a very nice comfortable room.

GREGERS: And I suppose you were lucky enough to secure it?

HIALMAR: Yes; in fact, it was your father that recommended it to me. So it was there, you see, that I really came to know Gina.

GREGERS: And then you got engaged?

HIALMAR: Yes. It doesn't take young people long to fall in love—h'm.

GREGERS: [*rises and moves about a little*] Tell me: was it after your engagement —was it then that my father— I mean was it then that you began to take up photography?

HIALMAR: Yes, precisely. I wanted to make a start and to set up house as soon as possible, and your father and I agreed that this photography business was the readiest way. Gina thought so too. Oh, and there was another thing in its favor, by the bye; it happened luckily, that Gina had learned to retouch.

GREGERS: That chimed in marvelously.

HIALMAR: [*pleased, rises*] Yes, didn't it? Don't you think it was a marvelous piece of luck?

GREGERS: Oh, unquestionably. My father seems to have been almost a kind of providence to you.

HIALMAR: [*with emotion*] He did not forsake his old friend's son in the hour of his need. For he has a heart, you see.

MRS SORBY: [*enters arm in arm with* WERLE] Nonsense, my dear Mr Werle; you mustn't stay there any longer staring at all the lights. It's very bad for you.

WERLE: [*lets go her arm and passes his hand over his eyes*] I daresay you are right.

[PETTERSEN *and* JENSEN *carry round refreshment trays.*]

MRS SORBY: [*to the guests in the other room*] This way, if you please, gentlemen. Whoever wants a glass of punch must be so good as to come in here.

THE FLABBY GENTLEMAN: [*comes up to* MRS SORBY] Surely it isn't possible that you have suspended our cherished right to smoke?

MRS SORBY: Yes, No smoking here, in Mr Werle's sanctum, Chamberlain.

THE THIN-HAIRED GENTLEMAN: When did you enact these stringent amendments on the cigar law, Mrs Sorby?

MRS SORBY: After the last dinner, Chamberlain, when certain persons permitted themselves to overstep the mark.

THE THIN-HAIRED GENTLEMAN: And may one never overstep the mark a little bit, Madame Bertha? Not the least little bit?

MRS SORBY: Not in any respect whatsoever, Mr Balle.

[*Most of the guests have assembled in the study; servants hand round glasses of punch.*]

WERLE: [*to* HIALMAR, *who is studying beside a table*] What are you studying so intently, Ekdal?

HIALMAR: Only an album, Mr Werle.

THE THIN-HAIRED GENTLEMAN: [*who is wandering about*] Ah, photographs! They are quite in your line of course.

THE FLABBY GENTLEMAN: [*in an armchair*] Haven't you brought any of your own with you?

HIALMAR: No, I haven't.

THE FLABBY GENTLEMAN: You ought to have; it's very good for the digestion to sit and look at pictures.

THE THIN-HAIRED GENTLEMAN: And it contributes to the entertainment, you know.

THE SHORTSIGHTED GENTLEMAN: And all contributions are thankfully received.

MRS SORBY: The chamberlains think that when one is invited out to dinner one ought to exert oneself a little in return, Mr Ekdal.

THE FLABBY GENTLEMAN: Where one dines so well, that duty becomes a pleasure.

THE THIN-HAIRED GENTLEMAN: And when it's a case of the struggle for existence, you know—

MRS SORBY: I quite agree with you!

[*They continue the conversation with laughter and joking.*]

GREGERS: [*softly*] You must join in, Hialmar.

HIALMAR: [*writhing*] What am I to talk about?

THE FLABBY GENTLEMAN: Don't you think, Mr Werle, that Tokay may be considered one of the more wholesome sorts of wine?

WERLE: [*by the fire*] I can answer for the Tokay you had today, at any rate; it's one of the very finest seasons. Of course you would notice that.

THE FLABBY GENTLEMAN: Yes, it had a remarkably delicate flavor.

HIALMAR: [*shyly*] Is there any difference between the seasons?

THE FLABBY GENTLEMAN: [*laughs*] Come! That's good!

WERLE: [*smiles*] It really doesn't pay to set fine wine before you.

THE THIN-HAIRED GENTLEMAN: Tokay is like photographs, Mr Ekdal; they both need sunshine. Am I not right?

HIALMAR: Yes, light is important, no doubt.

MRS SORBY: And it's exactly the same with the chamberlains—they, too, depend very much on sunshine, as the saying is.

THE THIN-HAIRED GENTLEMAN: Oh, shame! That's a very threadbare joke!

THE SHORTSIGHTED GENTLEMAN: Mrs Sorby is coming out—

THE FLABBY GENTLEMAN: —and at our expense too. [*holds up his finger reprovingly*] Oh, Madame Bertha, Madame Bertha!

MRS SORBY: Yes, and there's not the least doubt that the seasons differ greatly. The old vintages are the finest.

THE SHORTSIGHTED GENTLEMAN: Do you count me among the old vintages?

MRS SORBY: Oh, far from it.

THE THIN-HAIRED GENTLEMAN: There now! But me, dear Mrs Sorby—

THE FLABBY GENTLEMAN: Yes, and me? What vintage should you say that we belong to?

MRS SORBY: Why, to the sweet vintages, gentlemen. [*She sips a glass of punch. The gentlemen laugh and flirt with her.*]

WERLE: Mrs Sorby can always find a loophole—when she wants to. Fill your glasses, gentlemen! Pettersen, will you see to it? Gregers, suppose we have a glass together. [GREGERS *does not move.*] Won't you join us, Ekdal? I found no opportunity of drinking with you at table.

[GRABERG, *the bookkeeper, looks in at the baize door.*]

GRABERG: Excuse me, sir, but I can't get out.

WERLE: Have you been locked in again?

GRABERG: Yes, and Flakstad has carried off the keys.

WERLE: Well, you can pass out this way.

GRABERG: But there's someone else—

WERLE: All right; come through, both of you. Don't be afraid.

[GRABERG *and* OLD EKDAL *come out of the office.*]

WERLE: [*involuntarily*] Ugh!

[*The laughter and talk among the guests cease.* HIALMAR *starts at the sight of his father, puts down his glass and turns toward the fireplace.*]

EKDAL: [*does not look up but makes little bows to both sides as he passes, murmuring*] Beg pardon, come the wrong way. Door locked—door locked. Beg pardon.

[*He and* GRABERG *go out by the back, to the right.*]

WERLE: [*between his teeth*] That idiot Graberg.

GREGERS: [*open-mouthed and staring, to* HIALMAR] Why, surely that wasn't—

THE FLABBY GENTLEMAN: What's the matter? Who was it?

GREGERS: Oh, nobody; only the bookkeeper and someone with him.

THE SHORTSIGHTED GENTLEMAN: [*to* HIALMAR] Did you know that man?

HIALMAR: I don't know—I didn't notice—

THE FLABBY GENTLEMAN: What the devil has come over everyone? [*He joins another group who are talking softly.*]

MRS SORBY: [*whispers to the* SERVANT] Give him something to take with him—something good, mind.

PETTERSEN: [*nods*] I'll see to it.

[*Goes out.*]

GREGERS: [*softly and with emotion, to* HIALMAR] So that was really he!

HIALMAR: Yes.

GREGERS: And you could stand there and deny that you knew him.

HIALMAR: [*whispers vehemently*] But how could I—

GREGERS: —acknowledge your own father?

HIALMAR: [*with pain*] Oh, if you were in my place—

[*The conversation among the guests, which has been carried on in a low tone, now swells into constrained joviality.*]

THE THIN-HAIRED GENTLEMAN: [*approaching* HIALMAR *and* GREGERS *in a friendly manner*] Ah! Reviving old college memories, eh? Don't you smoke, Mr Ekdal? May I give you a light? Oh, by the bye, we mustn't—

HIALMAR: No, thank you, I won't—

THE FLABBY GENTLEMAN: Haven't you a nice little poem you could recite to us, Mr Ekdal? You used to recite so charmingly.

HIALMAR: I am sorry, I can't remember anything.

THE FLABBY GENTLEMAN: Oh, that's a pity. Well, what shall we do, Balle?

[*Both gentlemen move away and pass into the other room.*]

HIALMAR: [*gloomily*] Gregers—I am going! When a man has felt the crushing hand of Fate, you see— Say good-by to your father for me.

GREGERS: Yes, yes. Are you going straight home?

HIALMAR: Yes. Why?

GREGERS: Oh, because I may perhaps look in on you later.

HIALMAR: No, you mustn't do that. You must not come to my home. Mine is a melancholy abode, Gregers; especially after a splendid banquet like this. We can always arrange to meet somewhere in the town.

MRS SORBY: [*who has quietly approached*] Are you going, Ekdal?

HIALMAR: Yes.

MRS SORBY: Remember me to Gina.

HIALMAR: Thanks.

MRS SORBY: And say I am coming up to see her one of these days.

HIALMAR: Yes, thank you. [*to* GREGERS] Stay here; I will slip out unobserved.

[*He saunters away, then into the other room and so out to the right.*]

MRS SORBY: [*softly to the* SERVANT, *who has come back*] Well, did you give the old man something?

PETTERSEN: Yes; I sent him off with a bottle of brandy.

MRS SORBY: Oh, you might have thought of something better than that.

PETTERSEN: Oh no, Mrs Sorby; brandy is what he likes best in the world.

THE FLABBY GENTLEMAN: [*in the doorway with a sheet of music in his hand*] Shall we play a duet, Mrs Sorby?

MRS SORBY: Yes, suppose we do.

THE GUESTS: Bravo, bravo!

[*She goes with all the guests through the back room out to the right.* GREGERS *remains standing by the fire.* WERLE *is looking for something on the writing table and appears to wish that* GREGERS *would go; as* GREGERS *does not move* WERLE *goes toward the door.*]

GREGERS: Father, won't you stay a moment?

WERLE: [*stops*] What is it?

GREGERS: I must have a word with you.

WERLE: Can't it wait until we are alone?

GREGERS: No, it can't, for perhaps we shall never be alone together.

WERLE: [*drawing nearer*] What do you mean by that?

[*During what follows the pianoforte is faintly heard from the distant music room.*]

GREGERS: How has that family been allowed to go so miserably to the wall?

WERLE: You mean the Ekdals, I suppose.

GREGERS: Yes, I mean the Ekdals. Lieutenant Ekdal was once so closely associated with you.

WERLE: Much too closely; I have felt that to my cost for many a year. It is thanks to him that I—yes I—have had a kind of slur cast upon my reputation.

GREGERS: [*softly*] Are you sure that he alone was to blame?

WERLE: Who else do you suppose?

GREGERS: You and he acted together in that affair of the forests—

WERLE: But was it not Ekdal that drew the map of the tracts we had bought— that fraudulent map! It was he who felled all that timber illegally on government ground. In fact, the whole management was in his hands. I was quite in the dark as to what Lieutenant Ekdal was doing.

GREGERS: Lieutenant Ekdal himself seems to have been very much in the dark as to what he was doing.

WERLE: That may be. But the fact remains that he was found guilty and I acquitted.

GREGERS: Yes, I know that nothing was proved against you.

WERLE: Acquittal is acquittal. Why do you rake up these old miseries that turned my hair gray before its time? Is that the sort of thing you have been brooding over up there, all these years? I can assure you, Gregers, here in the town the whole story has been forgotten long ago—as far as *I* am concerned.

GREGERS: But that unhappy Ekdal family—

WERLE: What would you have me do for the people? When Ekdal came out of prison he was a broken-down being, past all help. There are people in the world who dive to the bottom the moment they get a couple of slugs in their body and never come to the surface again. You may take my word for it, Gregers, I have done all I could without positively laying myself open to all sorts of suspicion and gossip.

GREGERS: Suspicion? Oh, I see.

WERLE: I have given Ekdal copying to do for the office, and I pay him far, far more for it than his work is worth.

GREGERS: [*without looking at him*] H'm; that I don't doubt.

WERLE: You laugh? Do you think I am not telling you the truth? Well, I certainly can't refer you to my books, for I never enter payments of that sort.

GREGERS: [*smiles coldly*] No, there are certain payments it is best to keep no account of.

WERLE: [*taken aback*] What do you mean by that?

GREGERS: [*mustering up courage*] Have you entered what it cost you to have Hialmar Ekdal taught photography?

WERLE: I? How "entered" it?

GREGERS: I have learned that it was you who paid for his training. And I have learned, too, that it was you who enabled him to set up house so comfortably.

WERLE: Well, and yet you talk as though I had done nothing for the Ekdals! I can assure you these people have cost me enough in all conscience.

GREGERS: Have you entered any of these expenses in your books?

WERLE: Why do you ask?

GREGERS: Oh, I have my reasons. Now tell me: when you interested yourself so warmly in your old friend's son—it was just before his marriage, was it not?

WERLE: Why, deuce take it—after all these years how can I—

GREGERS: You wrote me a letter about that time—a business letter, of course—and in a postscript you mentioned—quite briefly—that Hialmar Ekdal had married a Miss Hansen.

WERLE: Yes, that was quite right. That was her name.

GREGERS: But you did not mention that this Miss Hansen was Gina Hansen—our former housekeeper.

WERLE: [*with a forced laugh of derision*] No; to tell the truth, it didn't occur to me that you were so particularly interested in our former housekeeper.

GREGERS: Nor was I. But [*lowers his voice*] there were others in this house who were particularly interested in her.

WERLE: What do you mean by that? [*flaring up*] You are not alluding to me, I hope?

GREGERS: [*softly but firmly*] Yes, I am alluding to you.

WERLE: And you dare— You presume to— How can that ungrateful hound—that photographer fellow—how dare he go making such insinuations!

GREGERS: Hialmar has never breathed a word about this. I don't believe he has the faintest suspicion of such a thing.

WERLE: Then where have you got it from? Who can have put such notions in your head?

GREGERS: My poor unhappy mother told me, the very last time I saw her.

WERLE: Your mother! I might have known as much! You and she—you always stuck together. It was she who turned you against me from the first.

GREGERS: No, it was all that she had to suffer and submit to, until she broke down and came to such a pitiful end.

WERLE: Oh, she had nothing to suffer or submit to; not more than most people, at all events. But there's no getting on with morbid, overstrained creatures —that I have learned to my cost. And you could go on nursing such a suspicion—burrowing into all sorts of slanders against your own father! I must say, Gregers, I really think at your age you might find something more useful to do.

GREGERS: Yes, it is high time.

WERLE: Then perhaps your mind would be easier than it seems to be now. What can be your object in remaining up at the works year out and year in, drudging away like a common clerk and not drawing a farthing more than the ordinary monthly wage? It is downright folly.

GREGERS: Ah, if I were only sure of that.

WERLE: I understand you well enough. You want to be independent; you won't be beholden to me for anything. Well, now there happens to be an opportunity for you to become independent, your own master in everything.

GREGERS: Indeed? In what way?

WERLE: When I wrote you insisting on your coming to town at once—h'm—

GREGERS: Yes, what is it you really want of me? I have been waiting all day to know.

WERLE: I want to propose that you should enter the firm as partner.

GREGERS: I! Join your firm? As partner?

WERLE: Yes. It would not involve our being constantly together. You could take over the business here in town, and I would move up to the works.

GREGERS: You would?

WERLE: The fact is, I am not so fit for work as I once was. I am obliged to spare my eyes, Gregers; they have begun to trouble me.

GREGERS: They have always been weak.

WERLE: Not as they are now. And besides, circumstances might possibly make it desirable for me to live up there—for a time, at any rate.

GREGERS: That is certainly quite a new idea to me.

WERLE: Listen, Gregers, there are many things that stand between us; but we are father and son after all. We ought surely to be able to come to some sort of understanding with each other.

GREGERS: Outwardly, you mean, of course?

WERLE: Well, even that would be something. Think it over, Gregers. Don't you think it ought to be possible? Eh?

GREGERS: [*looking at him coldly*] There is something behind all this.

WERLE: How so?

GREGERS: You want to make use of me in some way.

WERLE: In such a close relationship as ours the one can always be useful to the other.

GREGERS: Yes, so people say.

WERLE: I want very much to have you at home with me for a time. I am a lonely man, Gregers; I have always felt lonely all my life through, but most of all now that I am getting up in years. I feel the need of someone about me—

GREGERS: You have Mrs Sorby.

WERLE: Yes, I have her, and she has become, I may say, almost indispensable to me. She is lively and even tempered; she brightens up the house; and that is a very great thing for me.

GREGERS: Well, then, you have everything as you wish it.

WERLE: Yes, but I am afraid it can't last. A woman so situated may easily find herself in a false position in the eyes of the world. For that matter, it does a man no good either.

GREGERS: Oh, when a man gives such dinners as you give he can risk a great deal.

WERLE: Yes, but how about the woman, Gregers? I fear she won't accept the situation much longer, and even if she did—even if, out of attachment to me, she were to take her chance of gossip and scandal and all that—do you think, Gregers, you with your strong sense of justice—

GREGERS: [*interrupts him*] Tell me in one word: are you thinking of marrying her?

WERLE: Suppose I were thinking of it? What then?

GREGERS: That's what I say: What then?

WERLE: Should you be inflexibly opposed to it?

GREGERS: Not at all. Not by any means.

WERLE: I was not sure whether your devotion to your mother's memory—

GREGERS: I am not overstrained.

WERLE: Well, whatever you may or not be, at all events you have lifted a great weight from my mind. I am extremely pleased that I can reckon on your concurrence in this matter.

GREGERS: [*looking intently at him*] Now I see the use you want to put me to.

WERLE: Use to put you to? What an expression!

GREGERS: Oh, don't let us be nice in our choice of words—not when we are alone together, at any rate. [*with a short laugh*] Well, well. So this is what made it absolutely essential that I should come to town in person. For the sake of Mrs Sorby we are to get up a pretense at family life in the house—a tableau of filial affection. That will be something new, indeed.

WERLE: How dare you speak in that tone!

GREGERS: Was there ever any family life here? Never since I can remember. But now, your plans demand something of the sort. No doubt it will have an excellent effect when it is reported that the son has hastened home, on the wings of filial piety, to the gray-haired father's wedding feast. What will then remain of all the rumors as to the wrongs the poor dead mother had to submit to? Not a scrap. Her son annihilates them at one stroke.

WERLE: Gregers—I believe there is no one in the world you detest as you do me.

GREGERS: [*softly*] I have seen you at too close quarters.

WERLE: You have seen me with your mother's eyes. [*lowers his voice a little*] But you should remember that her eyes were—clouded now and then.

GREGERS: [*quivering*] I see what you are hinting at. But who was to blame for mother's unfortunate weakness? Why, you and all those— The last of them was this woman that you palmed off upon Hialmar Ekdal when you were— Ugh!

WERLE: [*shrugs his shoulders*] Word for word as if it were your mother speaking!

GREGERS: [*without heeding*] And there he is now, with his great, confiding childlike mind, compassed about with all this treachery—living under the same roof with such a creature and never dreaming that what he calls his home is built up on a lie! [*comes a step nearer*] When I look back upon your past I seem to see a battlefield with shattered lives on every hand.

WERLE: I begin to think that the chasm that divides us is too wide.

GREGERS: [*bowing with self-command*] So I have observed, and therefore I take my hat and go.

WERLE: You are going? Out of the house?

GREGERS: Yes. For at last I see my mission in life.

WERLE: What mission?

GREGERS: You would only laugh if I told you.

WERLE: A lonely man doesn't laugh so easily, Gregers.

GREGERS: [*pointing toward the background*] Look, Father—the chamberlains are playing blindman's buff with Mrs Sorby. Good night and good-by.

[*He goes out by the back to the right. Sound of laughter and merriment from the company, who are now visible in the outer room.*]

WERLE: [*muttering contemptuously after* GREGERS] Ha! Poor wretch—and he says he is not overstrained!

ACT II

SCENE——HIALMAR EKDAL'S *studio, a good-sized room, evidently in the top
story of the building. On the right a sloping roof of large panes of glass half
covered by a blue curtain. In the right-hand corner, at the back, the entrance
door; farther forward, on the same side, a door leading to the sitting room.
Two doors on the opposite side and between them an iron stove. At the back
a wide double sliding door. The studio is plainly but comfortably furnished.
Between the door on the right, standing out a little from the wall, a sofa with
a table and some chairs; on the table a lighted lamp with a shade; beside the
stove an old armchair. Photographic instruments and apparatus of different
kinds lying about the room. Against the back wall, to the left of the double
door, stands a bookcase containing a few books, boxes and bottles of chemi-
cals, instruments, tools and other objects. Photographs and small articles,
such as camel's-hair pencils, paper and so forth, lie on the table.*

> [GINA EKDAL *sits on a chair by the table, sewing.* HEDVIG *is sitting on
> the sofa, with her hands shading her eyes and her thumbs in her ears,
> reading a book.*]

GINA: [*glances once or twice at* HEDVIG, *as if with secret anxiety, then says*]
  Hedvig!

> [HEDVIG *does not hear.*]

GINA: [*repeats more loudly*] Hedvig!

HEDVIG: [*takes away her hands and looks up*] Yes, Mother?

GINA: Hedvig dear, you mustn't sit reading any longer now.

HEDVIG: Oh, Mother, mayn't I read a little more? Just a little bit?

GINA: No, no, you must put away your book now. Father doesn't like it; he
  never reads himself in the evening.

HEDVIG: [*shuts the book*] No, Father doesn't care much about reading.

GINA: [*puts aside her sewing and takes up a lead pencil and a little account book
  from the table*] Can you remember how much we paid for the butter
  today?

HEDVIG: It was one crown sixty-five.

GINA: That's right. [*puts it down*] It's terrible what a lot of butter we get
  through in this house. Then there was the smoked sausage and the cheese
  —let me see [*writes*]—and the ham. [*adds up*] Yes, that makes just—

HEDVIG: And then the beer.

GINA: Yes, to be sure.[*writes*] How it do mount up! But we can't manage with
  no less.

HEDVIG: And then you and I didn't need anything hot for dinner, as Father was
  out.

GINA: No, that was so much to the good. And then I took eight crowns fifty for
  the photographs.

HEDVIG: Really! As much as that?

GINA: Exactly eight crowns fifty.

> [*Silence.* GINA *takes up her sewing again;* HEDVIG *takes paper and
> pencil and begins to draw, shading her eyes with her left hand.*]

HEDVIG: Isn't it jolly to think that Father is at Mr Werle's big dinner party?

GINA: You know he's not really Mr Werle's guest. It was the son invited him. [*after a pause*] We have nothing to do with that Mr Werle.

HEDVIG: I'm longing for Father to come home. He promised to ask Mrs Sorby for something nice for me.

GINA: Yes, there's plenty of good things in that house, I can tell you.

HEDVIG: [*goes on drawing*] And I believe I'm a little hungry too.

[OLD EKDAL, *with the paper parcel under his arm and another parcel in his coat pocket, comes in by the entrance door.*]

GINA: How late you are today, Grandfather!

EKDAL: They had locked the office door. Had to wait in Graberg's room. And then they let me through—h'm.

HEDVIG: Did you get some more copying to do, Grandfather?

EKDAL: This whole packet. Just look.

GINA: That's fine.

HEDVIG: And you have another parcel in your pocket.

EKDAL: Eh? Oh, never mind, that's nothing. [*puts his stick away in a corner*] This work will keep me going a long time, Gina. [*opens one of the sliding doors in the back wall a little*] Hush! [*peeps into the room for a moment, then pushes the door carefully to again*] Hee-hee! They're fast asleep, all the lot of them. And she's gone into the basket herself. Hee-hee!

HEDVIG: Are you sure she isn't cold in that basket, Grandfather?

EKDAL: Not a bit of it! Cold? With all that straw? [*goes toward the farther door on the left*] There are matches in here, I suppose.

GINA: The matches is on the drawers.

[EKDAL *goes into his room.*]

HEDVIG: It's nice that Grandfather has got all that copying.

GINA: Yes, poor old Father; it means a bit of pocket money for him.

HEDVIG: And he won't be able to sit the whole forenoon down at that horrid Madam Eriksen's.

GINA: No more he won't. [*short silence*]

HEDVIG: Do you suppose they are still at the dinner table?

GINA: Goodness knows; as like as not.

HEDVIG: Think of all the delicious things Father is having to eat! I'm certain he'll be in splendid spirits when he comes. Don't you think so, Mother?

GINA: Yes; and if only we could tell him that we'd rented the room—

HEDVIG: But we don't need that this evening.

GINA: Oh, we'd be none the worst of it, I can tell you. It's no use to us as it is.

HEDVIG: I mean we don't need it this evening, for Father will be in good humor at any rate. It is best to keep the renting of the room for another time.

GINA: [*looks across at her*] You like having some good news to tell Father when he comes home in the evening?

HEDVIG: Yes, for then things are pleasanter somehow.

GINA: [*thinking to herself*] Yes, yes, there's something in that.

[OLD EKDAL *comes in again and is going out by the foremost door to the left.*]

GINA: [*half turning in her chair*] Do you want something in the kitchen, Grandfather?

EKDAL: Yes, yes, I do. Don't you trouble. [*Goes out.*]

GINA: He's not poking away at the fire, is he? [*waits a moment*] Hedvig, go and see what he's about.

[EKDAL *comes in again with a small jug of steaming hot water.*]

HEDVIG: Have you been getting some hot water, Grandfather?

EKDAL: Yes, hot water. Want it for something. Want to write, and the ink has got as thick as porridge—h'm.

GINA: But you'd best have your supper first, Grandfather. It's laid in there.

EKDAL: Can't be bothered with supper, Gina. Very busy, I tell you. No one's to come to my room. No one—h'm.

[*He goes into his room;* GINA *and* HEDVIG *look at each other.*]

GINA: [*softly*] Can you imagine where he's got money from?

HEDVIG: From Graberg, perhaps.

GINA: Not a bit of it. Graberg always sends the money to me.

HEDVIG: Then he must have got a bottle on credit somewhere.

GINA: Poor Grandfather, who'd give him credit?

[HIALMAR EKDAL, *in an overcoat and gray felt hat, comes in from the right.*]

GINA: [*throws down her sewing and rises*] Why, Ekdal, is that you already?

HEDVIG: [*at the same time jumping up*] Fancy your coming so soon, Father!

HIALMAR: [*taking off his hat*] Yes, most of the people were coming away.

HEDVIG: So early?

HIALMAR: Yes, it was a dinner party, you know. [*takes off his overcoat*]

GINA: Let me help you.

HEDVIG: Me too.

[*They draw off his coat;* GINA *hangs it up on the back wall.*]

HEDVIG: Were there many people there, Father?

HIALMAR: Oh no, not many. We had about twelve or fourteen at table.

GINA: And you had some talk with them all?

HIALMAR: Oh yes, a little; but Gregers took me up most of the time.

GINA: Is Gregers as ugly as ever?

HIALMAR: Well, he's not very much to look at. Hasn't the old man come home?

HEDVIG: Yes, Grandfather is in his room, writing.

HIALMAR: Did he say anything?

GINA: No, what should he say?

HIALMAR: Didn't he say anything about— I heard something about his having been with Graberg. I'll go in and see him for a moment.

GINA: No, no, better not.

HIALMAR: Why not? Did he say he didn't want me to go in?

GINA: I don't think he wants to see nobody this evening.

HEDVIG: [*making signs*] H'm—h'm!

GINA: [*not noticing*] He has been in to fetch hot water—

HIALMAR: Aha! Then he's—

GINA: Yes, I suppose so.

HIALMAR: Oh God! My poor old white-haired father! Well, well, there let him sit and get all the enjoyment he can.

[OLD EKDAL, *in an indoor coat and with a lighted pipe, comes from his room.*]

EKDAL: Got home? Thought it was you I heard talking.

HIALMAR: Yes, I have just come.

EKDAL: You didn't see me, did you?

HIALMAR: No, but they told me you had passed through—so I thought I would follow you.

EKDAL: H'm, good of you, Hialmar. Who were they, all those fellows?

HIALMAR: Oh, all sorts of people. There was Chamberlain Flor and Chamberlain Balle and Chamberlain Kaspersen and Chamberlain—this, that and the other—I don't know who all.

EKDAL: [*nodding*] Hear that, Gina! Chamberlains every one of them!

GINA: Yes, I hear as they're terrible genteel in that house nowadays.

HEDVIG: Did the chamberlains sing, Father? Or did they read aloud?

HIALMAR: No, they only talked nonsense. They wanted me to recite something for them, but I knew better than that.

EKDAL: You weren't to be persuaded, eh?

GINA: Oh, you might have done it.

HIALMAR: No; one mustn't be at everybody's beck and call. [*walks about the room*] That's not my way, at any rate.

EKDAL: No, no; Hialmar's not to be had for the asking, he isn't.

HIALMAR: I don't see why I should bother myself to entertain people on the rare occasions when I go into society. Let the others exert themselves. These fellows go from one great dinner table to the next and gorge and guzzle day out and day in. It's for them to bestir themselves and do something in return for all the good feeding they get.

GINA: But you didn't say that?

HIALMAR: [*humming*] Ho-ho-ho; I gave them a bit of my mind.

EKDAL: Not the chamberlains?

HIALMAR: Oh, why not? [*lightly*] After that we had a little discussion about Tokay.

EKDAL: Tokay! There's a fine wine for you!

HIALMAR: [*comes to a standstill*] It may be a fine wine. But of course you know the vintages differ; it all depends on how much sunshine the grapes have had.

GINA: Why, you know everything, Ekdal.

EKDAL: And did they argue that?

HIALMAR: They tried to, but they were requested to observe it was just the same with chamberlains—that with them, too, different batches were of different qualities.

GINA: What things you do think of!

EKDAL: Hee-hee! So they got that in their pipes too?

HIALMAR: Right in their teeth.

EKDAL: Do you hear that, Gina? He said it right in the very teeth of all the chamberlains.

GINA: Fancy! Right in their teeth!

HIALMAR: Yes, but I don't want it talked about. One doesn't speak of such things. The whole affair passed off quite amicably, of course. They were nice genial fellows; I didn't want to wound them—not I!

EKDAL: Right in their teeth, though!

HEDVIG: [*caressingly*] How nice it is to see you in a dress coat! It suits you so well, Father.

HIALMAR: Yes, don't you think so? And this one really fits to perfection. It fits almost as if it had been made for me—a little tight in the armholes, perhaps; help me, Hedvig. [*takes off the coat*] I think I'll put on my jacket. Where is my jacket, Gina?

GINA: Here it is. [*Brings the jacket and helps him.*]

HIALMAR: That's it! Don't forget to send the coat back to Molvik first thing tomorrow morning.

GINA: [*laying it away*] I'll be sure and see to it.

HIALMAR: [*stretching himself*] After all, there's a more homely feeling about this. A free-and-easy indoor costume suits my whole personality better. Don't you think so, Hedvig?

HEDVIG: Yes, Father.

HIALMAR: When I loosen my necktie into a pair of flowing ends—like this—eh?

HEDVIG: Yes, and that goes so well with your mustache and the sweep of your curls.

HIALMAR: I should not call them curls exactly; I should rather say locks.

HEDVIG: Yes, they are too big for curls.

HIALMAR: Locks describes them better.

HEDVIG: [*after a pause, twitching his jacket*] Father!

HIALMAR: Well, what is it?

HEDVIG: Oh, you know very well.

HIALMAR: No, really I don't.

HEDVIG: [*half laughing, half whispering*] Oh yes, Father; now don't tease me any longer!

HIALMAR: Why, what do you mean?

HEDVIG: [*shaking him*] Oh, what nonsense! Come, where are they, Father? All the good things you promised me, you know?

HIALMAR: Oh—if I haven't forgotten all about them!

HEDVIG: Now you're only teasing me, Father! Oh, it's too bad of you! Where have you put them?

HIALMAR: No, I positively forgot to get anything. But wait a little! I have something else for you, Hedvig.

[*Goes and searches in the pockets of the coat.*]

HEDVIG: [*skipping and clapping her hands*] Oh, Mother, Mother!

HIALMAR: [*with a paper*] Look, here it is.

GINA: There, you see; if you only give him time—

HEDVIG: That? Why, that's only a paper.

HIALMAR: That is the bill of fare, my dear; the whole bill of fare. Here you see "Menu"—that means bill of fare.

HEDVIG: Haven't you anything else?

HIALMAR: I forgot the other things, I tell you. But you may take my word for it, these dainties are very unsatisfying. Sit down at the table and read the bill of fare, and then I'll describe to you how the dishes taste. Here you are, Hedvig.

HEDVIG: [*gulping down her tears*] Thank you.

[*She seats herself but does not read;* GINA *makes signs to her;* HIALMAR *notices it.*]

HIALMAR: [*pacing up and down the room*] It's monstrous what absurd things the father of a family is expected to think of, and if he forgets the smallest trifle he is treated to sour faces at once. Well, well, one gets used to that too. [*stops near the stove by the old man's chair*] Have you peeped in there this evening, Father?

EKDAL: Yes, to be sure I have. She's gone into the basket.

HIALMAR: Ah, she has gone into the basket. Then she's beginning to get used to it.

EKDAL: Yes, just as I prophesied. But you know there are still a few little things—

HIALMAR: A few improvements, yes.

EKDAL: They've got to be made, you know.

HIALMAR: Yes, let us have a talk about the improvements, Father. Come, let us sit on the sofa.

EKDAL: All right. H'm—think I'll just fill my pipe first. Must clean it out too. H'm.

[*He goes into his room.*]

GINA: [*smiling to* HIALMAR] His pipe!

HIALMAR: Oh yes, yes, Gina; let him alone—the poor shipwrecked old man. Yes, these improvements—we had better get them out of the way tomorrow.

GINA: You'll hardly have time tomorrow, Ekdal.

HEDVIG: [*interposing*] Oh yes, he will, Mother!

GINA: —for remember them prints that has to be retouched; they've sent for them time after time.

HIALMAR: There now! Those prints again! I shall get them finished all right. Have any new orders come in?

GINA: No, worse luck; tomorrow I have nothing to do but those two sittings, you know.

HIALMAR: Nothing else? Oh no, if people won't set about things with a will—

GINA: But what more can I do? Don't I advertise in the papers as much as we can afford?

HIALMAR: Yes, the papers; you see how much good they do. And I suppose no one has been to look at the room either?

GINA: No, not yet.

HIALMAR: That was only to be expected. If people won't keep their eyes open— Nothing can be done without a real effort, Gina!

HEDVIG: [*going toward him*] Shall I fetch you the flute, Father?

HIALMAR: No; no flute for me; I want no pleasures in this world. [*pacing about*] Yes indeed, I will work tomorrow; you shall see if I don't. You may be sure I shall work as long as my strength holds out.

GINA: But, my dear good Ekdal, I didn't mean it in that way.

HEDVIG: Father, mayn't I bring in a bottle of beer?

HIALMAR: No, certainly not. I require nothing, nothing. [*comes to a standstill*] Beer? Was it beer you were talking about?

HEDVIG: [*cheerfully*] Yes, Father; beautiful fresh beer.

HIALMAR: Well—since you insist upon it, you may bring in a bottle.

GINA: Yes, do; and we'll be nice and cosy.

[HEDVIG *runs toward the kitchen door.*]

HIALMAR: [*by the stove, stops her, looks at her, puts his arm round her neck and presses her to him*] Hedvig, Hedvig!

HEDVIG: [*with tears of joy*] My dear, kind father!

HIALMAR: No, don't call me that. Here have I been feasting at the rich man's table—battening at the groaning board! And I couldn't even—

GINA: [*sitting at the table*] Oh, nonsense, nonsense, Ekdal.

HIALMAR: It's not nonsense! And yet you mustn't be too hard upon me. You know that I love you for all that.

HEDVIG: [*throwing her arms round him*] And we love you, oh, so dearly, Father!

HIALMAR: And if I am unreasonable once in a while—why, then—you must remember that I am a man beset by a host of cares. There, there! [*dries his eyes*] No beer at such a moment as this. Give me the flute.

[HEDVIG *runs to the bookcase and fetches it.*]

HIALMAR: Thanks! That's right. With my flute in my hand and you two at my side—ah!

[HEDVIG *seats herself at the table near* GINA; HIALMAR *paces backward and forward, pipes up vigorously and plays a Bohemian peasant dance, but in a slow plaintive tempo and with sentimental expression.*]

HIALMAR: [*breaking off the melody, holds out his left hand to* GINA *and says with emotion*] Our roof may be poor and humble, Gina, but it is home. And with all my heart I say: here dwells my happiness.

[*He begins to play again; almost immediately after a knocking is heard at the entrance door.*]

GINA: [*rising*] Hush, Ekdal—I think there's someone at the door.

HIALMAR: [*laying the flute on the bookcase*] There! Again!

[GINA *goes and opens the door.*]

GREGERS: [*in the passage*] Excuse me—

GINA: [*starting back slightly*] Oh!

GREGERS: —doesn't Mr Ekdal, the photographer, live here?

GINA: Yes, he does.

HIALMAR: [*going toward the door*] Gregers! You here after all? Well, come in then.

GREGERS: [*coming in*] I told you I would come and look you up.

HIALMAR: But this evening— Have you left the party?

GREGERS: I have left both the party and my father's house. Good evening, Mrs Ekdal. I don't know whether you recognize me?

GINA: Oh yes, it's not difficult to know young Mr Werle again.

GREGERS: No, I am like my mother, and no doubt you remember her.

HIALMAR: Left your father's house, did you say?

GREGERS: Yes, I have gone to a hotel.

HIALMAR: Indeed. Well, since you're here, take off your coat and sit down.

GREGERS: Thanks. [*He takes off his overcoat. He is now dressed in a plain gray suit of a countrified cut.*]

HIALMAR: Here on the sofa. Make yourself comfortable.

GREGERS: [*looking around him*] So these are your quarters, Hialmar—this is your home.

HIALMAR: This is the studio, as you see.

GINA: But it's the largest of our rooms, so we generally sit here.

HIALMAR: We used to live in a better place, but this flat has one great advantage: there are such capital outer rooms—

GINA: And we have a room on the other side of the passage that we can rent.

GREGERS: [*to* HIALMAR] Ah—so you have lodgers too?

HIALMAR: No, not yet. They're not so easy to find, you see; you have to keep your eyes open. [*to* HEDVIG] How about that beer, eh?

[HEDVIG *nods and goes out into the kitchen.*]

GREGERS: So that is your daughter?

HIALMAR: Yes, that is Hedvig.

GREGERS: And she is your only child?

HIALMAR: Yes, the only one. She is the joy of our lives, and [*lowering his voice*] at the same time our deepest sorrow, Gregers.

GREGERS: What do you mean?

HIALMAR: She is in serious danger of losing her eyesight.

GREGERS: Becoming blind?

HIALMAR: Yes. Only the first symptoms have appeared as yet, and she may not feel it much for some time. But the doctor has warned us. It is coming inexorably.

GREGERS: What a terrible misfortune! How do you account for it?

HIALMAR: [*sighs*] Hereditary, no doubt.

GREGERS: [*starting*] Hereditary?

GINA: Ekdal's mother had weak eyes.

HIALMAR: Yes, so my father says; I can't remember her.

GREGERS: Poor child! And how does she take it?

HIALMAR: Oh, you can imagine we haven't the heart to tell her of it. She dreams of no danger. Gay and careless and chirping like a little bird, she flutters onward into a life of endless night. [*overcome*] Oh, it is cruelly hard on me, Gregers.

[HEDVIG *brings a tray with beer and glasses which she sets upon the table.*]

HIALMAR: [*stroking her hair*] Thanks, thanks, Hedvig.

[HEDVIG *puts her arm around his neck and whispers in his ear.*]

HIALMAR: No, no bread and butter just now. [*looks up*] But perhaps you would like some, Gregers?

GREGERS: [*with a gesture of refusal*] No, no thank you.

HIALMAR: [*still melancholy*] Well, you can bring in a little all the same. If you have a crust, that is all I want. And plenty of butter on it, mind.

[HEDVIG *nods gaily and goes out into the kitchen again.*]

GREGERS: [*who has been following her with his eyes*] She seems quite strong and healthy otherwise.

GINA: Yes. In other ways there's nothing amiss with her, thank goodness.

GREGERS: She promises to be very like you, Mrs Ekdal. How old is she now?

GINA: Hedvig is close on fourteen; her birthday is the day after tomorrow.

GREGERS: She is pretty tall for her age then.

GINA: Yes, she's shot up wonderful this last year.

GREGERS: It makes one realize one's own age to see these young people growing up. How long is it now since you were married?

GINA: We've been married—let me see—just on fifteen years.

GREGERS: Is it so long as that?

GINA: [*becomes attentive, looks at him*] Yes, it is indeed.

HIALMAR: Yes, so it is. Fifteen years, all but a few months. [*changing his tone*] They must have been long years for you up at the works, Gregers.

GREGERS: They seemed long while I was living them; now they are over, I hardly know how the time has gone.

[OLD EKDAL *comes from his room without his pipe but with his old-fashioned uniform cap on his head; his gait is somewhat unsteady.*]

EKDAL: Come now, Hialmar, let's sit down and have a good talk about this— h'm—what was it again?

HIALMAR: [*going toward him*] Father, we have a visitor here—Gregers Werle— I don't know if you remember him.

EKDAL: [*looking at* GREGERS, *who has risen*] Werle? Is that the son? What does he want with me?

HIALMAR: Nothing! It's me he has come to see.

EKDAL: Oh! Then there's nothing wrong?

HIALMAR: No, no, of course not.

EKDAL: [*with a large gesture*] Not that I'm afraid, you know; but—

GREGERS: [*goes over to him*] I bring you a greeting from your old hunting grounds, Lieutenant Ekdal.

EKDAL: Hunting grounds?

GREGERS: Yes, up in Höidal, about the works, you know.

EKDAL: Oh, up there. Yes, I knew all those places well in the old days.

GREGERS: You were a great sportsman then.

EKDAL: So I was, I don't deny it. You're looking at my uniform cap. I don't ask anybody's leave to wear it in the house. So long as I don't go out in the streets with it—

[HEDVIG *brings a plate of bread and butter which she puts upon the table.*]

HIALMAR: Sit down, Father, and have a glass of beer. Help yourself, Gregers.

[EKDAL *mutters and stumbles over to the sofa.* GREGERS *seats himself on the chair nearest to him,* HIALMAR *on the other side of* GREGERS. GINA *sits a little way from the table, sewing;* HEDVIG *stands beside her father.*]

GREGERS: Can you remember, Lieutenant Ekdal, how Hialmar and I used to come up and visit you in the summer and at Christmas?

EKDAL: Did you? No, no, no; I don't remember it. But, sure enough, I've been a tidy bit of sportsman in my day. I've shot bears too. I've shot nine of 'em no less.

GREGERS: [*looking sympathetically at him*] And now you never get any shooting?

EKDAL: Can't say that, sir. Get a shot now and then, perhaps. Of course not in the old way. For the woods, you see—the woods, the woods— [*drinks*] Are the woods fine up there now?

GREGERS: Not so fine as in your time. They have been thinned out a good deal.

EKDAL: Thinned? [*more softly and as if afraid*] It's dangerous work, that. Bad things come of it. The woods revenge themselves.

HIALMAR: [*filling up his glass*] Come—a little more, Father.

GREGERS: How can a man like you—such a man for the open air—live in the midst of a stuffy town, boxed within four walls?

EKDAL: [*laughs quietly and glances at* HIALMAR] Oh, it's not so bad here. Not at all so bad.

GREGERS: But don't you miss all the things that used to be a part of your very being—the cool sweeping breezes, the free life in the woods and on the uplands, among beasts and birds?

EKDAL: [*smiling*] Hialmar, shall we let him see it?

HIALMAR: [*hastily and a little embarrassed*] Oh no, no, Father; not this evening.

GREGERS: What does he want to show me?

HIALMAR: Oh, it's only something—you can see it another time.

GREGERS: [*continues, to the old man*] You see, I have been thinking, Lieutenant Ekdal, that you should come up with me to the works; I am sure to be going back soon. No doubt you could get some copying there too. And here you have nothing on earth to interest you—nothing to liven you up.

EKDAL: [*stares in astonishment at him*] Have I nothing on earth to—

GREGERS: Of course you have Hialmar, but then he has his own family. And a man like you, who has always had such a passion for what is free and wild—

EKDAL: [*thumps the table*] Hialmar, he shall see it!

HIALMAR: Oh, do you think it's worth while, Father? It's all dark.

EKDAL: Nonsense; it's moonlight. [*rises*] He shall see it, I tell you. Let me pass! Come on and help me, Hialmar.

HEDVIG: Oh yes, do, Father!

HIALMAR: [*rising*] Very well then.

GREGERS: [*to* GINA] What is it?

GINA: Oh, nothing so wonderful after all.

[EKDAL *and* HIALMAR *have gone to the back wall and are each pushing back a side of the sliding door;* HEDVIG *helps the old man;* GREGERS *remains standing by the sofa;* GINA *sits still and sews. Through the open doorway a large, deep irregular garret is seen with odd nooks and corners, a couple of stovepipes running through it from rooms below. There are skylights through which clear moonbeams shine in on some parts of the great room; others lie in deep shadow.*]

EKDAL: [*to* GREGERS] You may come close up if you like.

GREGERS: [*going over to them*] Why, what is it?

EKDAL: Look for yourself, h'm.

HIALMAR: [*somewhat embarrassed*] This belongs to Father, you understand.

GREGERS: [*at the door, looks into the garret*] Why, you keep poultry, Lieutenant Ekdal.

EKDAL: Should think we did keep poultry. They've gone to roost now. But you should see our fowls by daylight, sir!

HEDVIG: And there's a—

EKDAL: Sh—sh! Don't say anything about it yet.

GREGERS: And you have pigeons too, I see.

EKDAL: Oh yes, haven't we just got pigeons! They have their nest boxes up there under the rooftree; for pigeons like to roost high, you see.

HIALMAR: They aren't all common pigeons.

EKDAL: Common! Should think not, indeed! We have tumblers and a pair of pouters too. But come here! Can you see that hutch down there by the wall?

GREGERS: Yes; what do you use it for?

EKDAL: That's where the rabbits sleep, sir.

GREGERS: Dear me, so you have rabbits too?

EKDAL: Yes, you may take my word for it, we have rabbits! He wants to know if we have rabbits, Hialmar! H'm! But now comes the thing, let me tell you! Here we have it! Move away, Hedvig. Stand here; that's right—and now look down there. Don't you see a basket with straw in it?

GREGERS: Yes. And I can see a fowl lying in the basket.

EKDAL: H'm—"a fowl"—

GREGERS: Isn't it a duck?

EKDAL: [*hurt*] Why, of course it's a duck.

HIALMAR: But what kind of a duck, do you think?

HEDVIG: It's not just a common duck.

EKDAL: Sh!

GREGERS: And it's not a Muscovy duck either.

EKDAL: No, Mr—Werle; it's not a Muscovy duck, for it's a wild duck!

GREGERS: Is it really? A wild duck?

EKDAL: Yes, that's what it is. That "fowl"—as you call it—is the wild duck. It's our wild duck, sir.

HEDVIG: My wild duck. It belongs to me.

GREGERS: And can it live up here in the garret? Does it thrive?

EKDAL: Of course it has a trough of water to splash about in, you know.

HIALMAR: Fresh water every other day.

GINA: [*turning toward* HIALMAR] But, my dear Ekdal, it's getting icy cold here.

EKDAL: H'm, we had better shut up then. It's as well not to disturb their night's rest too. Close up, Hedvig.

[HIALMAR *and* HEDVIG *push the garret doors together.*]

EKDAL: Another time you shall see her properly. [*seats himself in the armchair by the stove*] Oh, they're curious things, these wild ducks, I can tell you.

GREGERS: How did you manage to catch it, Lieutenant Ekdal?

EKDAL: *I* didn't catch it. There's a certain man in this town whom we have to thank for it.

GREGERS: [*starts slightly*] That man was not my father, was he?

EKDAL: You've hit it. Your father and no one else. H'm.

HIALMAR: Strange that you should guess that, Gregers.

GREGERS: You were telling me that you owed so many things to my father, and so I thought perhaps—

GINA: But we didn't get the duck from Mr Werle himself.

EKDAL: It's Hakon Werle we have to thank for her, all the same, Gina. [*to* GREGERS] He was shooting from a boat, you see, and he brought her down. But your father's sight is not very good now. H'm; she was only wounded.

GREGERS: Ah! She got a couple of slugs in her body, I suppose?

HIALMAR: Yes, two or three.

HEDVIG: She was hit under the wing so that she couldn't fly.

GREGERS: And I suppose she dived to the bottom, eh?

EKDAL: [*sleepily, in a thick voice*] Of course. Always do that, wild ducks do. They shoot to the bottom as deep as they can get, sir—and catch themselves in the tangle and seaweed—and all the devil's own mess that grows down there. And they never come up again.

GREGERS: But your wild duck came up again, Lieutenant Ekdal.

EKDAL: He had such an amazingly clever dog, your father had. And that dog— he dived in after the duck and fetched her up again.

GREGERS: [*who has turned to* HIALMAR] And then she was sent to you here?

HIALMAR: Not at once; at first your father took her home. But she wouldn't thrive there, so Pettersen was told to put an end to her.

EKDAL: [*half asleep*] H'm—yes—Pettersen—that ass—

HIALMAR: [*speaking more softly*] That was how we got her, you see; for Father knows Pettersen a little, and when he heard about the wild duck he got him to hand her over to us.

GREGERS: And now she thrives as well as possible in the garret there?

HIALMAR: Yes, wonderfully well. She has got fat. You see, she has lived in there so long now that she has forgotten her natural wild life, and it all depends on that.

GREGERS: You are right there, Hialmar. Be sure you never let her get a glimpse of the sky and the sea. But I mustn't stay any longer; I think your father is asleep.

HIALMAR: Oh, as for that—

GREGERS: But by the bye—you said you had a room to let—a spare room?

HIALMAR: Yes; what then? Do you know of anybody?

GREGERS: Can I have that room?

HIALMAR: You?

GINA: Oh no, Mr Werle, you—

GREGERS: May I have the room? If so, I'll take possession first thing tomorrow morning.

HIALMAR: Yes, with the greatest pleasure.

GINA: But, Mr Werle, I'm sure it's not at all the sort of room for you.

HIALMAR: Why, Gina! how can you say that?

GINA: Why, because the room's neither large enough nor light enough, and—

GREGERS: That really doesn't matter, Mrs Ekdal.

HIALMAR: I call it quite a nice room, and not at all badly furnished either.

GINA: But remember the pair of them underneath.

GREGERS: What pair?

GINA: Well, there's one as has been a tutor.

HIALMAR: That's Molvik—Mr Molvik, B.A.

GINA: And then there's a doctor by the name of Relling.

GREGERS: Relling? I know him a little; he practiced for a time up in Höidal.

GINA: They're a regular rackety pair, they are. As often as not they're out on the loose in the evenings, and then they come home at all hours, and they are not always just—

GREGERS: One soon gets used to that sort of thing. I daresay I shall be like the wild duck.

GINA: H'm; I think you ought to sleep upon it first, anyway.

GREGERS: You seem very unwilling to have me in the house, Mrs Ekdal.

GINA: Oh no! What makes you think that?

HIALMAR: Well, you really behave strangely about it, Gina. [*to* GREGERS] Then I suppose you intend to remain in town for the present?

GREGERS: [*putting on his overcoat*] Yes, now I intend to remain here.

HIALMAR: And yet not at your father's? What do you propose to do then?

GREGERS: Ah, if I only knew that, Hialmar, I shouldn't be so badly off! But when one has the misfortune to be called Gregers!—"Gregers"—and then "Werle" after it; did you ever hear of anything so hideous?

HIALMAR: Oh, I don't think so at all.

GREGERS: Ugh! Bah! I feel I should like to spit on the fellow that answers to such a name. But when a man is once for all doomed to be Gregers Werle —in this world—as I am—

HIALMAR: [*laughs*] Ha, ha! If you weren't Gregers Werle, what would you like to be?

GREGERS: If I should choose, I should like best to be a clever dog.

GINA: A dog!

HEDVIG: [*involuntarily*] Oh no!

GREGERS: Yes, an amazingly clever dog; one that goes to the bottom after wild ducks when they dive and catch themselves fast in tangle and seaweed down among the ooze.

HIALMAR: Upon my word now. Gregers—I don't in the least know what you are driving at.

GREGERS: Oh well, you might not be much the wiser if you did. It's understood, then, that I move in early tomorrow morning. [*to* GINA] I won't give you any trouble; I do everything for myself. [*to* HIALMAR] We will talk about the rest tomorrow. Good night, Mrs Ekdal. [*nods to* HEDVIG] Good night.

HEDVIG: Good night.

HIALMAR: [*who has lighted a candle*] Wait a moment; I must show you a light; the stairs are sure to be dark.

[GREGERS *and* HIALMAR *go out by the passage door.*]

GINA: [*looking straight before her with her sewing in her lap*] Wasn't that queer-like talk about wanting to be a dog?

HEDVIG: Do you know, Mother—I believe he meant something quite different by that.

GINA: Why, what should he mean?

HEDVIG: Oh, I don't know, but it seemed to me he meant something different from what he said—all the time.

GINA: Do you think so? Yes, it was sort of queer.

HIALMAR: [*comes back*] The lamp was still burning. [*puts out the candle and sets it down*] Ah, now one can get a mouthful of food at last. [*begins to eat the bread and butter*] Well, you see, Gina—if only you keep your eyes open—

GINA: How keep your eyes open?

HIALMAR: Why, haven't we at last had the luck to rent the room? And just think—to a person like Gregers—a good old friend.

GINA: Well, I don't know what to say about it.

HEDVIG: Oh, Mother, you'll see: it'll be such fun!

HIALMAR: You're very strange. You were so bent upon getting the room rented before, and now you don't like it.

GINA: Yes, I do, Ekdal; if it had only been to someone else. But what do you suppose Mr Werle will say?

HIALMAR: Old Werle? It doesn't concern him.

GINA: But surely you can see that there's something wrong between them again, or the young man wouldn't be leaving home. You know very well those two can't get on with each other.

HIALMAR: Very likely not, but—

GINA: And now Mr Werle may think it's you that has egged him on—

HIALMAR: Let him think so, then! Mr Werle has done a great deal for me; far be it from me to deny it. But that doesn't make me everlastingly dependent upon him.

GINA: But, my dear Ekdal, maybe Grandfather'll suffer for it. He may lose the little bit of work he gets from Graberg.

HIALMAR: I could almost say: so much the better! Is it not humiliating for a man like me to see his grayhaired father treated as a pariah? But now I believe the fullness of time is at hand. [*takes a fresh piece of bread and butter*] As sure as I have a mission in life, I mean to fulfill it now!

HEDVIG: Oh yes, Father, do!

GINA: Hush! Don't wake him!

HIALMAR: [*more softly*] I will fulfill it, I say. The day shall come when— And that is why I say it's a good thing we have rented the room, for that makes me more independent. The man who has a mission in life must be independent. [*by the armchair, with emotion*] Poor old white-haired Father! Rely on your Hialmar. He has broad shoulders—strong shoulders, at any rate. You shall yet wake up some fine day and— [*to* GINA] Do you not believe it?

GINA: [*rising*] Yes, of course I do, but in the meantime suppose we see about getting him to bed.

HIALMAR: Yes, come.

[*They take hold of the old man carefully.*]

ACT III

SCENE——HIALMAR EKDAL'S *studio. It is morning; the daylight shines through the large window in the slanting roof; the curtain is drawn back.*

> [HIALMAR *is sitting at the table, busy retouching a photograph; several others lie before him. Presently* GINA, *wearing her hat and cloak, enters by the passage door; she has a covered basket on her arm.*]

HIALMAR: Back already, Gina?

GINA: Oh yes, one can't let the grass grow under one's feet. [*Sets her basket on a chair and takes off her things.*]

HIALMAR: Did you look in at Gregers' room?

GINA: Yes, I did. It's a rare sight, I can tell you; he's made a pretty mess to start off with.

HIALMAR: How so?

GINA: He was determined to do everything for himself, he said; so he sets to work to light the stove, and what must he do but screw down the damper till the whole room is full of smoke. Ugh! There was a smell fit to—

HIALMAR: Well, really!

GINA: But that's not the worst of it; for then he thinks he'll put out the fire and goes and empties his water jug into the stove and so makes the whole floor one filthy puddle.

HIALMAR: How annoying!

GINA: I've got the porter's wife to clear up after him, the pig! But the room won't be fit to live in till the afternoon.

HIALMAR: What's he doing with himself in the meantime?

GINA: He said he was going out for a little while.

HIALMAR: I looked in upon him too, for a moment—after you had gone.

GINA: So I heard. You've asked him to lunch.

HIALMAR: Just to a little bit of early lunch, you know. It's his first day—we can hardly do less. You've got something in the house, I suppose?

GINA: I shall have to find something or other.

HIALMAR: And don't cut it too fine, for I fancy Relling and Molvik are coming up too. I just happened to meet Relling on the stairs, you see; so I had to—

GINA: Oh, are we to have those two as well?

HIALMAR: Good lord—a couple more or less can't make any difference.

OLD EKDAL: [*opens his door and looks in*] I say, Hialmar— [*sees* GINA] Oh!

GINA: Do you want anything, Grandfather?

EKDAL: Oh no, it doesn't matter. H'm! [*Retires again.*]

GINA: [*takes up the basket*] Be sure you see that he doesn't go out.

HIALMAR: All right, all right. And, Gina, a little herring salad wouldn't be a bad idea. Relling and Molvik were out on the loose again last night.

GINA: If only they don't come before I'm ready for them—

HIALMAR: No, of course they won't; take your own time.

GINA: Very well, and meanwhile you can be working a bit.

HIALMAR: Well, I am working! I am working as hard as I can!

GINA: Then you'll have that job off your hands, you see. [*She goes out to the kitchen with her basket.* HIALMAR *sits for a time penciling away at the photograph in an indolent and listless manner.*]

EKDAL: [*peeps in, looks round the studio and says softly*] Are you busy?

HIALMAR: Yes, I'm toiling at these wretched pictures.

EKDAL: Well, well, never mind—since you're so busy—h'm!
[*He goes out again; the door stands open.*]

HIALMAR: [*continues for some time in silence, then he lays down his brush and goes over to the door*] Are you busy, Father?

EKDAL: [*in a grumbling tone within*] If you're busy, I'm busy too. H'm!

HIALMAR: Oh, very well then. [*Goes to his work again.*]

EKDAL: [*presently coming to the door again*] H'm; I say Hialmar, I'm not so very busy, you know.

HIALMAR: I thought you were writing.

EKDAL: Oh, devil take it! Can't Graberg wait a day or two? After all, it's not a matter of life and death.

HIALMAR: No, and you're not his slave either.

EKDAL: And about that other business in there—

HIALMAR: Just what I was thinking of. Do you want to go in? Shall I open the door for you?

EKDAL: Well, it wouldn't be a bad notion.

HIALMAR: [*rises*] Then we'd have that off our hands.

EKDAL: Yes, exactly. It's got to be ready first thing tomorrow. It is tomorrow, isn't it? H'm?

HIALMAR: Yes, of course it's tomorrow.

[HIALMAR *and* EKDAL *push aside each his half of the sliding door. The morning sun is shining in through the skylights; some doves are flying about; others sit cooing upon the perches; the hens are heard clucking now and then further back in the garret.*]

HIALMAR: There; now you can get to work, Father.

EKDAL: [*goes in*] Aren't you coming too?

HIALMAR: Well, really, you know—I almost think—[*sees* GINA *at the kitchen door*] I? No; I haven't time; I must work— But now for our new contrivance—

[*He pulls a cord; a curtain slips down inside, the lower part consisting of a piece of old sailcloth, the upper part of a stretched fishing net. The floor of the garret is thus no longer visible.*]

HIALMAR: [*goes to the table*] So! Now perhaps I can sit in peace for a little while.

GINA: Is he rampaging in there again?

HIALMAR: Would you rather have him slip down to Madam Eriksen's? [*seats himself*] Do you want anything? You know you said—

GINA: I only wanted to ask if you think we can lay the table for lunch here?

HIALMAR: Yes; we have no early appointment, I suppose?

GINA: No, I expect no one today except those two sweethearts that are to be taken together.

HIALMAR: Why the devil couldn't they be taken together another day?

GINA: Don't you know, I told them to come in the afternoon, when you are having your nap.

HIALMAR: Oh, that's capital. Very well, let us have lunch here then.

GINA: All right, but there's no hurry about laying the cloth; you can have the table for a good while yet.

HIALMAR: Do you think I am not sticking to my work? I'm at it as hard as I can!

GINA: Then you'll be free later on, you know.

[*Goes out into the kitchen again. Short pause.*]

EKDAL: [*in the garret doorway, behind the net*] Hialmar!

HIALMAR: Well?

EKDAL: Afraid we shall have to move the water trough after all.

HIALMAR: What else have I been saying all along?

EKDAL: H'm—h'm—h'm.

[*Goes away from the door again.* HIALMAR *goes on working a little, glances toward the garret and half rises.* HEDVIG *comes in from the kitchen.*]

HIALMAR: [*sits down again hurriedly*] What do you want?

HEDVIG: I only wanted to come in beside you, Father.

HIALMAR: [*after a pause*] What makes you go prying around like that? Perhaps you are told to watch me?

HEDVIG: No, no.

HIALMAR: What is your mother doing out there?

HEDVIG: Oh, Mother's in the middle of making the herring salad. [*goes to the table*] Isn't there any little thing I could help you with, Father?

HIALMAR: Oh no. It is right that I should bear the whole burden—so long as my strength holds out. Set your mind at rest, Hedvig; if only your father keeps his health—

HEDVIG: Oh no, Father! You mustn't talk in that horrid way.

[*She wanders about a little, stops by the doorway and looks into the garret.*]

HIALMAR: Tell me, what is he doing?

HEDVIG: I think he's making a new path to the water trough.

HIALMAR: He can never manage that by himself! And here am I doomed to sit!

HEDVIG: [*goes to him*] Let me take the brush, Father; I can do it quite well.

HIALMAR: Oh, nonsense; you will only hurt your eyes.

HEDVIG: Not a bit. Give me the brush.

HIALMAR: [*rising*] Well, it won't take more than a minute or two.

HEDVIG: Pooh, what harm can it do then? [*takes the brush*] There! [*seats herself*] I can begin upon this one.

HIALMAR: But mind you don't hurt your eyes! Do you hear? I won't be answerable; you do it on your own responsibility—understand that.

HEDVIG: [*retouching*] Yes, yes, I understand.

HIALMAR: You are quite clever at it, Hedvig. Only a minute or two, you know.

[*He slips through by the edge of the curtain into the garret.* HEDVIG *sits at her work.* HIALMAR *and* EKDAL *are heard disputing inside.*]

HIALMAR: [*appears behind the net*] I say, Hedvig—give me those pliers that are lying on the shelf. And the chisel. [*turns away inside*] Now you shall see, Father. Just let me show you first what I mean!

> [HEDVIG *has fetched the required tools from the shelf and hands them to him through the net.*]

HIALMAR: Ah, thanks. I didn't come a moment too soon.

> [*Goes back from the curtain again; they are heard carpentering and talking inside.* HEDVIG *stands looking in at them. A moment later there is a knock at the passage door; she does not notice it.*]

GREGERS WERLE: [*bareheaded, in indoor dress, enters and stops near the door*] H'm!

HEDVIG: [*turns and goes toward him*] Good morning. Please come in.

GREGERS: Thank you. [*looking toward the garret*] You seem to have work-people in the house.

HEDVIG: No, it's only Father and Grandfather. I'll tell them you are here.

GREGERS: No, no, don't do that; I would rather wait a little. [*seats himself on the sofa.*]

HEDVIG: It looks so untidy here— [*Begins to clear away the photographs.*]

GREGERS: Oh, don't take them away. Are those prints that have to be finished off?

HEDVIG: Yes, they are a few I was helping Father with.

GREGERS: Please don't let me disturb you.

HEDVIG: Oh no.

> [*She gathers the things to her and sits down to work;* GREGERS *looks at her meanwhile in silence.*]

GREGORS: Did the wild duck sleep well last night?

HEDVIG: Yes, I think so, thanks.

GREGERS: [*turning toward the garret*] It looks quite different by day from what it did last night in the moonlight.

HEDVIG: Yes, it changes ever so much. It looks different in the morning and in the afternoon, and it's different on rainy days from what it is in fine weather.

GREGERS: Have you noticed it?

HEDVIG: Yes, how could I help it?

GREGERS: Are you too fond of being in there with the wild duck?

HEDVIG: Yes, when I can manage it.

GREGERS: But I suppose you haven't much spare time; you go to school, no doubt.

HEDVIG: No, not now; Father is afraid of my hurting my eyes.

GREGERS: Oh, then he reads with you himself?

HEDVIG: Father has promised to read with me, but he has never had time yet.

GREGERS: Then is there nobody else to give you a little help?

HEDVIG: Yes, there is Mr Molvik, but he is not always exactly—quite—

GREGERS: Sober?

HEDVIG: Yes, I suppose that's it!

GREGERS: Why, then, you must have any amount of time on your hands. And in there I suppose it is a sort of world by itself?

HEDVIG: Oh yes, quite. And there are such lots of wonderful things.

GREGERS: Indeed?

HEDVIG: Yes, there are big cupboards full of books, and a great many of the books have pictures in them.

GREGERS: Aha!

HEDVIG: And there's an old bureau with drawers and flaps and a big clock with figures that go out and in. But the clock isn't going now.

GREGERS: So time has come to a standstill in there—in the wild duck's world?

HEDVIG: Yes. And then there's an old paintbox and things of that sort, and all the books.

GREGERS: And you read the books, I suppose.

HEDVIG: Oh yes, when I get the chance. Most of them are English, though, and I don't understand English. But then I look at the pictures. There is one great book called *Harrison's History of London*. It must be a hundred years old, and there are such heaps of pictures in it. At the beginning there is Death with an hourglass and a woman. I think that is horrid. But then there are all the other pictures of churches and castles and streets and great ships sailing on the sea.

GREGERS: But tell me, where did all those wonderful things come from?

HEDVIG: Oh, an old sea captain once lived here, and he brought them home with him. They used to call him "The Flying Dutchman." That was curious, because he wasn't a Dutchman at all.

GREGERS: Was he not?

HEDVIG: No. But at last he was drowned at sea, and so he left all those things behind him.

GREGERS: Tell me now—when you are sitting in there looking at the pictures don't you wish you could travel and see the real world for yourself?

HEDVIG: Oh no! I mean always to stay at home and help Father and Mother.

GREGERS: To retouch photographs?

HEDVIG: No, not only that. I should love above everything to learn to engrave pictures like those in the English books.

GREGERS: H'm. What does your father say to that?

HEDVIG: I don't think Father likes it; Father is strange about such things. Only think, he talks of my learning basketmaking! But I don't think that would be much good.

GREGERS: Oh no, I don't think so either.

HEDVIG: But Father was right in saying that if I had learned basketmaking I could have made the new basket for the wild duck.

GREGERS: So you could; and it was you that ought to have done it, wasn't it?

HEDVIG: Yes, for it's my wild duck.

GREGERS: Of course it is.

HEDVIG: Yes, it belongs to me. But I lend it to Father and Grandfather as often as they please.

GREGERS: Indeed? What do they do with it?

HEDVIG: Oh, they look after it and build places for it and so on.

GREGERS: I see; for no doubt the wild duck is by far the most distinguished inhabitant of the garret?

HEDVIG: Yes, indeed she is; for she is a real wild fowl, you know. And then she is so much to be pitied; she has no one to care for, poor thing.

GREGERS: She has no family, as the rabbits have.

HEDVIG: No. The hens too, many of them, were chickens together; but she has been taken right away from all her friends. And then there is so much that is strange about the wild duck. Nobody knows her, and nobody knows where she came from either.

GREGERS: And she has been down in the depths of the sea.

HEDVIG: [*with a quick glance at him, represses a smile and asks*] Why do you say "depths of the sea"?

GREGERS: What else should I say?

HEDVIG: You could say "the bottom of the sea."

GREGERS: Oh, can't I just as well say the depths of the sea?

HEDVIG: Yes, but it sounds so strange to me when other people speak of the depths of the sea.

GREGERS: Why? Tell me why?

HEDVIG: No, I won't; it's so stupid.

GREGERS: Oh no, I am sure it's not. Do tell me why you smiled.

HEDVIG: Well, this is the reason: whenever I come to realize suddenly—in a flash—what is in there, it always seems to me that the whole room and everything in it should be called "the depths of the sea." But that is so stupid.

GREGERS: You mustn't say that.

HEDVIG: Oh yes, for you know it is only a garret.

GREGERS: [*looks fixedly at her*] Are you so sure of that?

HEDVIG: [*astonished*] That it's a garret?

GREGERS: Are you quite certain of it?

[HEDVIG *is silent and looks at him open-mouthed.* GINA *comes in from the kitchen with the table things.*]

GREGERS: [*rising*] I have come in upon you too early.

GINA: Oh, you must be somewhere, and we're nearly ready now anyway. Clear the table, Hedvig.

[HEDVIG *clears away her things; she and* GINA *lay the cloth during what follows.* GREGERS *seats himself in the armchair and turns over an album.*]

GREGERS: I hear you can retouch, Mrs Ekdal.

GINA: [*with a side glance*] Yes, I can.

GREGERS: That was exceedingly lucky.

GINA: How—lucky?

GREGERS: Since Ekdal took to photography, I mean.

HEDVIG: Mother can take photographs too.

GINA: Oh yes, I had to learn that.

GREGERS: So it is really you that carry on the business, I suppose?

GINA: Yes, when Ekdal hasn't time himself—

GREGERS: He is a great deal taken up with his old father, I daresay.

GINA: Yes; and then you can't expect a man like Ekdal to do nothing but take pictures of Dick, Tom and Harry.

GREGERS: I quite agree with you, but having once gone in for the thing—

GINA: You can surely understand, Mr Werle, that Ekdal's not like one of your common photographers.

GREGERS: Of course not, but still—
    [*A shot is fired within the garret.*]
GREGERS: [*starting up*] What's that?
GINA: Ugh! Now they're firing again!
GREGERS: Have they firearms in there?
HEDVIG: They are out shooting.
GREGERS: What! [*at the door of the garret*] Are you shooting, Hialmar?
HIALMAR: [*inside the net*] Are you there? I didn't know; I was so taken up—
    [*to* HEDVIG] Why did you not let us know? [*Comes into the studio.*]
GREGERS: Do you go shooting in the garret?
HIALMAR: [*showing a double-barreled pistol*] Oh, only with this thing.
GINA: Yes, you and Grandfather will hurt yourselves someday with that there pigstol.
HIALMAR: [*with irritation*] I believe I have told you that this kind of firearm is called a pistol.
GINA: Oh, that doesn't make it much better that I can see.
GREGERS: So you have become a sportsman too, Hialmar?
HIALMAR: Only a little rabbit shooting now and then. Mostly to please Father, you understand.
GINA: Men are strange beings; they must always have something to pervert theirselves with.
HIALMAR: [*snappishly*] Just so; we must always have something to divert ourselves with.
GINA: Yes, that's just what I say.
HIALMAR: H'm. [*to* GREGERS] You see, the garret is fortunately so situated that no one can hear us shooting. [*lays the pistol on the top shelf of the bookcase*] Don't touch the pistol, Hedvig! One of the barrels is loaded; remember that.
GREGERS: [*looking through the net*] You have a fowling piece too, I see.
HIALMAR: That is Father's old gun. It's of no use now. Something has gone wrong with the lock. But it's fun to have it all the same, for we can take it to pieces now and then and clean and grease it and screw it together again. Of course it's mostly Father that fiddles with all that sort of thing.
HEDVIG: [*beside* GREGERS] Now you can see the wild duck properly.
GREGERS: I was just looking at her. One of her wings seems to me to droop a bit.
HEDVIG: Well, no wonder; her wing was broken, you know.
GREGERS: And she trails one foot a little. Isn't that so?
HIALMAR: Perhaps a very little bit.
HEDVIG: Yes, it was by that foot the dog took hold of her.
HIALMAR: But otherwise she hasn't the least thing the matter with her, and that is simply marvelous for a creature that has a charge of shot in her body and has been between a dog's teeth—
GREGERS: [*with a glance at* HEDVIG] —and that has lain in the depths of the sea —so long.
HEDVIG: [*smiling*] Yes.
GINA: [*laying the table*] That blessed wild duck! What a lot of fuss you do make over her.

HIALMAR: H'm—will lunch soon be ready?

GINA: Yes, directly. Hedvig, you must come and help me now.

[GINA *and* HEDVIG *go out into the kitchen.*]

HIALMAR: [*in a low voice*] I think you had better not stand there looking in at Father; he doesn't like it. [GREGERS *moves away from the garret door.*] Besides, I may as well shut up before the others come. [*claps his hands to drive the fowls back*] Shh—shh, in with you! [*draws up the curtain and pulls the doors together*] All the contrivances are my own invention. Its really quite amusing to have things of this sort to potter with and to put to rights when they get out of order. And its absolutely necessary too, for Gina objects to having rabbits and fowls in the studio.

GREGERS: To be sure, and I suppose the studio is your wife's special department?

HIALMAR: As a rule I leave the everyday details of business to her, for then I can take refuge in the parlor and give my mind to more important things.

GREGERS: What things are they Hialmar?

HIALMAR: I wonder you have not asked that question sooner. But perhaps you haven't heard of the invention?

GREGERS: The invention? No.

HIALMAR: Really? Haven't you? Oh no, out there in the wilds—

GREGERS: So you have invented something, have you?

HIALMAR: It is not quite completed yet, but I am working at it. You can easily imagine that when I resolved to devote myself to photography it wasn't simply with the idea of taking likenesses of all sorts of commonplace people.

GREGERS: No; your wife was saying the same thing just now.

HIALMAR: I swore that if I concentrated my powers to this handicraft I would so exalt it that it should become both an art and a science. And to that end I determined to make this great invention.

GREGERS: And what is the nature of the invention? What purpose does it serve?

HIALMAR: Oh, my dear fellow, you mustn't ask for details yet. It takes time, you see. And you must not think that my motive is vanity. It is not for my own sake that I am working. Oh no; it is my life's mission that stands before me night and day.

GREGERS: What is your life's mission?

HIALMAR: Do you forget the old man with the silver hair?

GREGERS: Your poor father? Well, but what can you do for him?

HIALMAR: I can raise up his self-respect from the dead by restoring the name of Ekdal to honor and dignity.

GREGERS: Then that is your life's mission?

HIALMAR: Yes. I will rescue the shipwrecked man. For shipwrecked he was, by the very first blast of the storm. Even while those terrible investigations were going on he was no longer himself. That pistol there—the one we used to shoot rabbits with—has played its part in the tragedy of the house of Ekdal.

GREGERS: The pistol? Indeed?

HIALMAR: When the sentence of imprisonment was passed—he had the pistol in his hand.

GREGERS: Had he?

HIALMAR: Yes, but he dared not use it. His courage failed him. So broken, so demoralized was he even then! Oh, can you understand it? He, a soldier; he, who had shot nine bears and who was descended from two lieutenant colonels—one after the other, of course. Can you understand it, Gregers?

GREGERS: Yes, I understand it well enough.

HIALMAR: I cannot. And once more the pistol played a part in the history of our house. When he had put on the gray clothes and was under lock and key— oh, that was a terrible time for me, I can tell you. I kept the blinds drawn down over both my windows. When I peeped out I saw the sun shining as if nothing had happened. I could not understand it. I saw people going along the street, laughing and talking about indifferent things. I could not understand it. It seemed to me that the whole of existence must be at a standstill—as if under an eclipse.

GREGERS: I felt that too, when my mother died.

HIALMAR: It was in such an hour that Hialmar Ekdal pointed the pistol at his own breast.

GREGERS: You, too, thought of—

HIALMAR: Yes.

GREGERS: But you did not fire?

HIALMAR: No. At the decisive moment I won the victory over myself. I remained in life. But I can assure you it takes some courage to choose life under circumstances like those.

GREGERS: Well, that depends on how you look at it.

HIALMAR: Yes indeed, it takes courage. But I am glad I was firm, for now I shall soon perfect my invention; and Doctor Relling thinks, as I do myself, that Father may be allowed to wear his uniform again. I will demand that as my sole reward.

GREGERS: So that is what he meant about his uniform?

HIALMAR: Yes, that is what he most yearns for. You can't think how my heart bleeds for him. Every time we celebrate any little family festival—Gina's and my wedding day or whatever it may be—in comes the old man in the lieutenant's uniform of happier days. But if he only hears a knock at the door—for he daren't show himself to strangers, you know—he hurries back to his room again as fast as his old legs can carry him. Oh, it's heart-rending for a son to see such things!

GREGERS: How long do you think it will take you to finish your invention?

HIALMAR: Come now, you mustn't expect me to enter into particulars like that. An invention is not a thing completely under one's own control. It depends largely on inspiration—on intuition—and it is almost impossible to predict when the inspiration may come.

GREGERS: But it's advancing?

HIALMAR: Yes, certainly it is advancing. I turn it over in my mind every day; I am full of it. Every afternoon, when I have had my dinner, I shut myself up in the parlor where I can ponder undisturbed. But I can't be goaded to it; it's not a bit of good. Relling says so too.

GREGERS: And you don't think that all that business in the garret draws you off and distracts you too much?

HIALMAR: No, no, no; quite the contrary. You mustn't say that. I cannot be everlastingly absorbed in the same laborious train of thought. I must have something alongside of it to fill up the time of waiting. The inspiration, the intuition, you see—when it comes it comes, and there's an end of it.

GREGERS: My dear Hialmar, I almost think you have something of the wild duck in you.

HIALMAR: Something of the wild duck? How do you mean?

GREGERS: You have dived down and caught yourself fast in the undergrowth.

HIALMAR: Are you alluding to the almost fatal shot that has broken my father's wing—and mine too?

GREGERS: Not exactly to that. I don't say that your wing has been broken, but you have strayed into a poisonous marsh, Hialmar; an insidious disease has taken hold of you, and you have sunk down to die in the dark.

HIALMAR: I? To die in the dark? Look here, Gregers, you must really stop talking such nonsense.

GREGERS: Don't be afraid; I shall find a way to help you up again. I, too, have a mission in life now; I found it yesterday.

HIALMAR: That's all very well, but you will please leave me out of it. I can assure you that—apart from my very natural melancholy, of course—I am as contented as anyone can wish to be.

GREGERS: Your contentment is an effect of the marsh poison.

HIALMAR: Now, my dear Gregers, pray do not go on about disease and poison; I am not used to that sort of talk. In my house nobody ever speaks to me about unpleasant things.

GREGERS: Ah, that I can easily believe.

HIALMAR: It's not good for me, you see. And there are no marsh poisons here, as you express it. The poor photographer's roof is lowly, I know—and my circumstances are narrow. But I am an inventor, and I am the bread-winner of a family. That exalts me above my mean surroundings. Ah, here comes lunch!

> [GINA *and* HEDVIG *bring bottles of ale, a decanter of brandy, glasses, etc. At the same time* RELLING *and* MOLVIK *enter from the passage; they are both without hat or overcoat.* MOLVIK *is dressed in black.*]

GINA: [*placing the things upon the table*] Ah you two have come in the nick of time.

RELLING: Molvik got it into his head that he could smell herring salad, and then there was no holding him. Good morning again, Ekdal.

HIALMAR: Gregers, let me introduce you to Mr Molvik—Doctor— Oh, you know Relling, don't you?

GREGERS: Yes, slightly.

RELLING: Oh, Mr Werle junior! Yes, we two have had one or two little skirmishes up at the Höidal works. You've just moved in?

GREGERS: I moved in this morning.

RELLING: Molvik and I live right under you, so you haven't far to go for the doctor and the clergyman if you should need anything in that line.

GREGERS: Thanks; it's not quite unlikely, for yesterday we were thirteen at table.

HIALMAR: Oh, come now, don't let us get upon unpleasant subjects again!

RELLING: You may make your mind easy, Ekdal; I'll be hanged if the finger of fate points to you.

HIALMAR: I should hope not, for the sake of my family. But let us sit down now and eat and drink and be merry.

GREGERS: Shall we not wait for your father?

HIALMAR: No, his lunch will be taken in to him later. Come along!
[*The men seat themselves at table and eat and drink.* GINA *and* HEDVIG *go in and out and wait upon them.*]

RELLING: Molvik was frightfully drunk yesterday, Mrs Ekdal.

GINA: Really? Yesterday again?

RELLING: Didn't you hear him when I brought him home last night?

GINA: No, I can't say I did.

RELLING: That was a good thing, for Molvik was disgusting last night.

GINA: Is that true, Molvik?

MOLVIK: Let us draw a veil over last night's proceedings. That sort of thing is totally foreign to my better self.

RELLING: [*to* GREGERS] It comes over him like a sort of possession, and then I have to go out on the loose with him. Mr Molvik is demonic, you see.

GREGERS: Demonic?

RELLING: Molvik is demonic, yes.

GREGERS: H'm

RELLING: And demonic natures are not made to walk straight through the world; they must meander a little now and then. Well, so you still stay up there at those horrible grimy works?

GREGERS: I have stayed there until now.

RELLING: And did you ever manage to collect that claim you went about presenting?

GREGERS: Claim? [*understands him*] Ah, I see.

HIALMAR: Have you been presenting claims, Gregers?

GREGERS: Oh, nonsense.

RELLING: Faith, but he has, though! He went round to all the cotters' cabins presenting something he called "the claim of the ideal."

GREGERS: I was young then.

RELLING: You're right; you were very young. And as for the claim of the ideal— you never got it honored while *I* was up there.

GREGERS: Nor since either.

RELLING: Ah, then you've learned to knock a little discount off, I expect.

GREGERS: Never, when I have a true man to deal with.

HIALMAR: No, I should think not, indeed. A little butter, Gina.

RELLING: And a slice of bacon for Molvik.

MOLVIK: Ugh! not bacon!
[*A knock at the garret door.*]

HIALMAR: Open the door, Hedvig; Father wants to come out.
[HEDVIG *goes over and opens the door a little way;* EKDAL *enters with a fresh rabbitskin; she closes the door after him.*]

EKDAL: Good morning, gentlemen! Good sport today. Shot a big one.

HIALMAR: And you've gone and skinned it without waiting for me!

EKDAL: Salted it too. It's good tender meat, is rabbit; it's sweet; it tastes like sugar. Good appetite to you, gentlemen! [*Goes into his room.*]

MOLVIK: [*rising*] Excuse me—I can't—I must get downstairs immediately—

RELLING: Drink some soda water, man!

MOLVIK: [*hurrying away*] Ugh—ugh. [*Goes out by the passage door.*]

RELLING: [*to* HIALMAR] Let us drain a glass to the old hunter.

HIALMAR: [*clinks glasses with him*] To the undaunted sportsman who has looked death in the face!

RELLING: To the gray-haired— [*drinks*] By the bye. is his hair gray or white?

HIALMAR: Something between the two, I fancy; for that matter, he has very few hairs left of any color.

RELLING: Well, well, one can get through the world with a wig. After all, you are a happy man, Ekdal; you have your noble mission to labor for—

HIALMAR: And I do labor, I can tell you.

RELLING: And then you have your excellent wife, shuffling quietly in and out in her felt slippers, with that seesaw walk of hers, and making everything cosy and comfortable about you.

HIALMAR: Yes, Gina [*nods to her*] you've been a good helpmate on the path of life.

GINA: Oh, don't sit there cricketizing me.

RELLING: And your Hedvig too, Ekdal!

HIALMAR: [*affected*] The child, yes! The child before everything! Hedvig, come here to me. [*strokes her hair*] What day is it tomorrow, eh?

HEDVIG: [*shaking him*] Oh no, you're not to say anything, Father.

HIALMAR: It cuts me to the heart when I think what a poor affair it will be; only a little festivity in the garret.

HEDVIG: Oh, but that's just what I like!

RELLING: Just you wait till the wonderful invention sees the light, Hedvig!

HIALMAR: Yes indeed—then you shall see! Hedvig, I have resolved to make your future secure. You shall live in comfort all your days. I will demand something or other—on your behalf. That shall be the poor inventor's sole reward.

HEDVIG: [*whispering, with her arms round his neck*] Oh, you dear, kind father!

RELLING: [*to* GREGERS] Come now, don't you find it pleasant, for once, to sit at a well-spread table in a happy family circle?

HIALMAR: Ah yes, I really prize these social hours.

GREGERS: For my part, I don't thrive in marsh vapors.

RELLING: Marsh vapors?

HIALMAR: Oh, don't begin with that stuff again!

GINA: Goodness knows there's no vapors in this house, Mr Werle; I give the place a good airing every blessed day.

GREGERS: [*leaves the table*] No airing you can give will drive out the taint I mean.

HIALMAR: Taint!

GINA: Yes, what do you say to that, Ekdal!

RELLING: Excuse me—may it not be you yourself that have brought the taint from those mines up there?

GREGERS: It is like you to call what I bring into this house a taint.

RELLING: [*goes up to him*] Look here, Mr Werle junior: I have a strong suspicion that you are still carrying about that "claim of the ideal" large as life in your coattail pocket.

GREGERS: I carry it in my breast.

RELLING: Well, wherever you carry it, I advise you not to come dunning us with it here as long as *I* am on the premises.

GREGERS: And if I do so nonetheless?

RELLING: Then you'll go headfirst down the stairs; now I've warned you.

HIALMAR: [*rising*] Oh, but, Relling—

GREGERS: Yes, you may turn me out.

GINA: [*interposing between them*] We can't have that, Relling. But I must say, Mr Werle, it ill becomes you to talk about vapors and taints after all the mess you made with your stove.

[*A knock at the passage door.*]

HEDVIG: Mother, there's somebody knocking.

HIALMAR: There now, we're going to have a whole lot of people!

GINA: I'll go. [*goes over and opens the door, starts and draws back*] Oh—oh dear!

[WERLE, *in a fur coat, advances one step into the room.*]

WERLE: Excuse me, but I think my son is staying here.

GINA: [*with a gulp*] Yes.

HIALMAR: [*approaching him*] Won't you do us the honor to—

WERLE: Thank you, I merely wish to speak to my son.

GREGERS: What is it? Here I am.

WERLE: I want a few words with you in your room.

GREGERS: In my room? Very well. [*about to go*]

GINA: No, no, your room's not in a fit state.

WERLE: Well, then, out in the passage here; I want to have a few words with you alone.

HIALMAR: You can have them here, sir. Come into the parlor, Relling.

[HIALMAR *and* RELLING *go off to the right;* GINA *takes* HEDVIG *with her into the kitchen.*]

GREGERS: [*after a short pause*] Well, now we are alone.

WERLE: From something you let fall last evening, and from your coming to lodge with the Ekdals, I can't help inferring that you intend to make yourself unpleasant to me in one way or another.

GREGERS: I intend to open Hialmar Ekdal's eyes. He shall see his position as it really is—that is all.

WERLE: Is that the mission in life you spoke of yesterday?

GREGERS: Yes. You have left me no other.

WERLE: Is it I, then, that have crippled your mind, Gregers?

GREGERS: You have crippled my whole life. I am not thinking of all that about Mother—but it's thanks to you that I am continually haunted and harassed by a guilty conscience.

WERLE: Indeed! It is your conscience that troubles you, is it?

GREGERS: I ought to have taken a stand against you when the trap was set for

Lieutenant Ekdal. I ought to have cautioned him, for I had a misgiving as to what was in the wind.

WERLE: Yes, that was the time to have spoken.

GREGERS: I did not dare to, I was so cowed and spiritless. I was mortally afraid of you—not only then, but long afterward.

WERLE: You have got over that fear now, it appears.

GREGERS: Yes, fortunately. The wrong done to old Ekdal, both by me and by others, can never be undone; but Hialmar I can rescue from all the falsehood and deception that are bringing him to ruin.

WERLE: Do you think that will be doing him a kindness?

GREGERS: I have not the least doubt of it.

WERLE: You think our worthy photographer is the sort of man to appreciate such friendly offices?

GREGERS: Yes, I do.

WERLE: H'm—we shall see.

GREGERS: Besides, if I am to go on living, I must try to find some cure for my sick conscience.

WERLE: It will never be sound. Your conscience has been sickly from childhood. That is a legacy from your mother, Gregers—the only one she left you.

GREGERS: [*with a scornful half-smile*] Have you not yet forgiven her for the mistake you made in supposing she would bring you a fortune?

WERLE: Don't let us wander from the point. Then you hold to your purpose of setting young Ekdal upon what you imagine to be the right scent?

GREGERS: Yes, that is my fixed resolve.

WERLE: Well, in that case I might have spared myself this visit, for of course it is useless to ask whether you will return home with me?

GREGERS: Quite useless.

WERLE: And I suppose you won't enter the firm either?

GREGERS: No.

WERLE: Very good. But as I am thinking of marrying again, your share in the property will fall to you at once.

GREGERS: [*quickly*] No, I do not want that.

WERLE: You don't want it?

GREGERS: No, I dare not take it, for conscience' sake.

WERLE: [*after a pause*] Are you going up to the works again?

GREGERS: No; I consider myself released from your service.

WERLE: But what are you going to do?

GREGERS: Only fulfill my mission, nothing more.

WERLE: Well, but afterward? What are you going to live upon?

GREGERS: I have laid by a little out of my salary.

WERLE: How long will that last?

GREGERS: I think it will last my time.

WERLE: What do you mean?

GREGERS: I shall answer no more questions.

WERLE: Good-by, then, Gregers.

GREGORS: Good-by.

[WERLE *goes.*]

HIALMAR: [*peeping in*] He's gone, isn't he?

GREGERS: Yes.

[HIALMAR *and* RELLING *enter; also* GINA *and* HEDVIG *from the kitchen.*]

RELLING: That luncheon party was a failure.

GREGERS: Put on your coat, Hialmar; I want you to come for a long walk with me.

HIALMAR: With pleasure. What was it your father wanted? Had it anything to do with me?

GREGERS: Come along. We must have a talk. I'll go and put on my overcoat. [*Goes out by the passage door.*]

GINA: You shouldn't go out with him, Ekdal.

RELLING: No, don't you do it. Stay where you are.

HIALMAR: [*gets his hat and overcoat*] Oh, nonsense! When a friend of my youth feels impelled to open his mind to me in private—

RELLING: But devil take it—don't you see that the fellow's mad, cracked, demented!

GINA: There, what did I tell you! His mother before him had crazy fits like that sometimes.

HIALMAR: The more need for a friend's watchful eye. [*to* GINA] Be sure you have dinner ready in good time. Good-by for the present. [*Goes out by the passage door.*]

RELLING: It's a thousand pities the fellow didn't go to hell through one of the Höidal mines.

GINA: Good lord! What makes you say that?

RELLING: [*muttering*] Oh, I have my own reasons.

GINA: Do you think young Werle is really mad?

RELLING: No, worse luck; he's no madder than most other people. But one disease he has certainly got in his system.

GINA: What is it that's the matter with him?

RELLING: Well, I'll tell you, Mrs Ekdal. He is suffering from an acute attack of integrity.

GINA: Integrity?

HEDVIG: Is that a kind of disease?

RELLING: Yes, it's a national disease. but it only appears sporadically. [*nods to* GINA] Thanks for your hospitality. [*He goes out by the passage door.*]

GINA: [*moving restlessly to and fro*] Ugh, that Gregers Werle—he was always a wretched creature.

HEDVIG: [*standing by the table and looking searchingly at her*] I think all this is very strange.

ACT IV

SCENE——HIALMAR EKDAL'S *studio. A photograph has just been taken; a camera with the cloth over it, a pedestal, two chairs, a folding table, etc., are standing out in the room. Afternoon light; the sun is going down; a little later it begins to grow dusk.*

[*Gina stands in the passage doorway with a little box and a wet glass plate in her hand and is speaking to somebody outside.*]

GINA: Yes, certainly. When I make a promise I keep it. The first dozen will be ready on Monday. Good afternoon.

> [*Someone is heard going downstairs.* GINA *shuts the door, slips the plate into the box and puts it into the covered camera.*]

HEDVIG: [*comes in from the kitchen*] Are they gone?

GINA: [*tidying up*] Yes, thank goodness. I've got rid of them at last.

HEDVIG: But can you imagine why Father hasn't come home yet?

GINA: Are you sure he's not down in Relling's room?

HEDVIG: No, he's not; I ran down the kitchen stair just now and asked.

GINA: And his dinner standing and getting cold too.

HEDVIG: Yes, I can't understand it. Father's always so careful to be home for dinner!

GINA: Oh, he'll be here directly, you'll see.

HEDVIG: I wish he would come; everything seems so queer today.

GINA: [*calls out*] There he is!

> [HIALMAR EKDAL *comes in at the passage door.*]

HEDVIG: [*going to him*] Father! Oh, what a time we've been waiting for you!

GINA: [*glancing sidelong at him*] You've been out a long time, Ekdal.

HIALMAR: [*without looking at her*] Rather long, yes.

> [*He takes off his overcoat;* GINA *and* HEDVIG *go to help him; he motions them away.*]

GINA: Perhaps you've had dinner with Werle?

HIALMAR: [*hanging up his coat*] No.

GINA: [*going toward the kitchen door*] Then I'll bring some in for you.

HIALMAR: No; let the dinner alone. I want nothing to eat.

HEDVIG: [*going nearer to him*] Are you not well, Father?

HIALMAR: Well? Oh yes, well enough. We have had a tiring walk, Gregers and I.

GINA: You didn't ought to have gone so far, Ekdal; you're not used to it.

HIALMAR: H'm; there's many a thing a man must get used to in this world. [*wanders about the room*] Has anyone been here whilst I was out?

GINA: Nobody but the two sweethearts.

HIALMAR: No new orders?

GINA: No, not today.

HEDVIG: There will be some tomorrow, Father, you'll see.

HIALMAR: I hope there will, for tomorrow I am going to set to work in real earnest.

HEDVIG: Tomorrow! Don't you remember what day it is tomorrow?

HIALMAR: Oh yes, by the bye— Well, the day after, then. Henceforth I mean to do everything myself; I shall take all the work into my own hands.

GINA: Why, what can be the good of that. Ekdal? It'll only make your life a burden to you. I can manage the photography all right, and you can go on working at your invention.

HEDVIG: And think of the wild duck, Father. and all the hens and rabbits and—

HIALMAR: Don't talk to me of all that trash! From tomorrow I will never set foot in the garret again.

HEDVIG: Oh, but, Father, you promised that we should have a little party.

HIALMAR: H'm, true. Well, then, from the day after tomorrow. I should almost like to wring that cursed wild duck's neck!

HEDVIG: [*shrieks*] The wild duck!

GINA: Well, I never!

HEDVIG: [*shaking him*] Oh no, Father; you know it's my wild duck!

HIALMAR: That is why I don't do it. I haven't the heart to—for your sake, Hedvig. But in my inmost soul I feel that I ought to do it. I ought not to tolerate under my roof a creature that has been through those hands.

GINA: Why, good gracious, even if Grandfather did get it from that poor creature Pettersen—

HEDVIG: [*going after him*] But think of the wild duck—the poor wild duck!

HIALMAR: [*stops*] I tell you I will spare it—for your sake. Not a hair of its head shall be—I mean, it shall be spared. There are greater problems than that to be dealt with. But you should go out a little now, Hedvig, as usual; it is getting dusk enough for you now.

HEDVIG: No, I don't care about going out now.

HIALMAR: Yes, do; it seems to me your eyes are blinking a great deal; all these vapors in here are bad for you. The air is heavy under this roof.

HEDVIG: Very well then, I'll run down the kitchen stair and go for a little walk. My cloak and hat? Oh, they're in my own room. Father—be sure you don't do the wild duck any harm while I'm out.

HIALMAR: Not a feather of its head shall be touched. [*draws her to him*] You and I, Hedvig—we two—Well, go along.

   [HEDVIG *nods to her parents and goes out through the kitchen.*]

HIALMAR: [*walks about without looking up*] Gina.

GINA: Yes?

HIALMAR: From tomorrow—or say from the day after tomorrow—I should like to keep the household account book myself.

GINA: Do you want to keep the accounts too now?

HIALMAR: Yes; or to check the receipts at any rate.

GINA: Lord help us; that's soon done.

HIALMAR: One would hardly think so; at any rate you seem to make the money go a very long way. [*stops and looks at her*] How do you manage it?

GINA: It's because me and Hedvig, we need so little.

HIALMAR: Is it the case that Father is very liberally paid for the copying he does for Mr Werle?

GINA: I don't know as he gets anything out of the way. I don't know the rates for that sort of work.

HIALMAR: Well, what does he get, about? Let me hear!

GINA: Oh, it varies; I daresay it'll come to about as much as he costs us, with a little pocket money over.

HIALMAR: As much as he costs us! And you have never told me this before.

GINA: No, how could I tell you? It pleased you so much to think he got everything from you.

HIALMAR: And he gets it from Mr Werle.

GINA: Oh well, he has plenty and to spare, he has.

HIALMAR: Light the lamp for me, please!

GINA: [*lighting the lamp*] And of course we don't know as it's Mr Werle himself; it may be Graberg.

HIALMAR: Why attempt such an evasion?

GINA: I don't know; I only thought—

HIALMAR: H'm!

GINA: It wasn't me that got Grandfather that copying. It was Bertha, when she used to come about us.

HIALMAR: It seems to me your voice is trembling.

GINA: [*putting the lamp shade on*] Is it?

HIALMAR: And your hands are shaking, are they not?

GINA: [*firmly*] Come right out with it, Ekdal. What has he been saying about me?

HIALMAR: Is it true—can it be true that—that there was an—an understanding between you and Mr Werle while you were in service there?

GINA: That's not true. Not at that time. Mr Werle did come after me, that's a fact. And his wife thought there was something in it, and then she made such a hocus-pocus and hurly-burly, and she hustled me and bustled me about so that I left her service.

HIALMAR: But afterward, then?

GINA: Well. then I went home. And Mother—well, she wasn't the woman you took her for, Ekdal; she kept on worrying and worrying at me about one thing and another—for Mr Werle was a widower by that time.

HIALMAR: Well, and then?

GINA: I suppose you've got to know it. He gave me no peace until he'd had his way.

HIALMAR: [*striking his hands together*] And this is the mother of my child! How could you hide this from me?

GINA: Yes, it was wrong of me; I ought certainly to have told you long ago.

HIALMAR: You should have told me at the very first—then I should have known the sort of woman you were.

GINA: But would you have married me all the same?

HIALMAR: How can you dream that I would?

GINA: That's just why I didn't dare tell you anything then. For I'd come to care for you so much, you see, and I couldn't go and make myself utterly miserable.

HIALMAR: [*walks about*] And this is my Hedvig's mother! And to know that all I see before me [*kicks at chair*]—all that I call my home—I owe to a favored predecessor! Oh, that scoundrel Werle!

GINA: Do you repent of the fourteen—the fifteen years we've lived together?

HIALMAR: [*placing himself in front of her*] Have you not every day, every hour, repented of the spider's web of deceit you have spun around me? Answer me that! How could you help writhing with penitence and remorse?

GINA: Oh, my dear Ekdal, I've had all I could do to look after the house and get through the day's work.

HIALMAR: Then you never think of reviewing your past?

GINA: No; heaven knows I'd almost forgotten those old stories.

HIALMAR: Oh. this dull, callous contentment! To me there is something revolting about it. Think of it—never so much as a twinge of remorse!

GINA: But tell me, Ekdal—what would have become of you if you hadn't had a wife like me?

HIALMAR: Like you!

GINA: Yes; for you know I've always been a bit more practical and wide awake than you. Of course I'm a year or two older.

HIALMAR: What would have become of me!

GINA: You'd got into all sorts of bad ways when first you met me; that you can't deny.

HIALMAR: "Bad ways," do you call them? Little do you know what a man goes through when he is in grief and despair—especially a man of my fiery temperament.

GINA: Well, well, that may be so. And I've no reason to crow over you neither, for you turned a fine husband, that you did, as soon as ever you had a house and home of your own. And now we'd got everything so nice and cosy about us, and me and Hedvig was just thinking we'd soon be able to let ourselves go a bit in the way of both food and clothes.

HIALMAR: In the swamp of deceit, yes.

GINA: I wish to goodness that detestable thing had never set his foot inside our doors!

HIALMAR: And I, too, thought my home such a pleasant one. That was a delusion. Where shall I now find the elasticity of spirit to bring my invention into the world of reality? Perhaps it will die with me, and then it will be your past, Gina, that will have killed it.

GINA: [*nearly crying*] You mustn't say such things, Ekdal. Me, that has only wanted to do the best I could for you all my days!

HIALMAR: I ask you, what becomes of the breadwinner's dream? When I used to lie in there on the sofa and brood over my invention I had a clear enough presentiment that it would sap my vitality to the last drop. I felt even then that the day when I held the patent in my hand—that day— would bring my—release. And then it was my dream that you should live on after me, the dead inventor's well-to-do widow.

GINA: [*drying her tears*] No, you mustn't talk like that, Ekdal. May the Lord never let me see the day I am left a widow!

HIALMAR: Oh, the whole dream has vanished. It is all over now. All over!

[GREGERS WERLE *opens the passage door cautiously and looks in.*]

GREGERS: May I come in?

HIALMAR: Yes, come in.

GREGERS: [*comes forward, his face beaming with satisfaction, and holds out both his hands to them*] Well, dear friends! [*looks from one to the other and whispers to* HIALMAR] Have you not done it yet?

HIALMAR: [*aloud*] It is done.

GREGERS: It is?

HIALMAR: I have passed through the bitterest moments of my life.

GREGERS: But also, I trust, the most ennobling.

HIALMAR: Well, at any rate, we have got through it for the present.

GINA: God forgive you, Mr Werle.

GREGERS: [*in great surprise*] But I don't understand this.

HIALMAR: What don't you understand?

GREGERS: After so great a crisis—a crisis that is to be the starting point of an entirely new life—of a communion founded on truth and free from all taint of deception—

HIALMAR: Yes, yes, I know; I know that quite well.

GREGERS: I confidently expected, when I entered the room, to find the light of transfiguration shining upon me from both husband and wife. And now I see nothing but dullness, oppression, gloom—

GINA: Oh, is that it? [*takes off the lamp shade*]

GREGERS: You will not understand me, Mrs Ekdal. Ah well, you, I suppose, need time to— But you, Hialmar? Surely you feel a new consecration after the great crisis?

HIALMAR: Yes, of course I do. That is—in a sort of way.

GREGERS: For surely nothing in the world can compare with the joy of forgiving one who has sinned and raising her up to oneself in love.

HIALMAR: Do you think a man can so easily throw off the bitter cup I have drained?

GREGERS: No, not a common man, perhaps. But a man like you—

HIALMAR: Good God! I know that well enough. But you must keep me up to it, Gregers. It takes time, you know.

GREGERS: You have much of the wild duck in you, Hialmar.

[RELLING *has come in at the passage door.*]

RELLING: Oho! Is the wild duck to the fore again?

HIALMAR: Yes; Mr Werle's wing-broken victim.

RELLING: Mr Werle? So it's him you are talking about?

HIALMAR: Him and—ourselves.

RELLING: [*in an undertone to* GREGERS] May the devil take you!

HIALMAR: What is that you are saying?

RELLING: Only uttering a heartfelt wish that this quack would take himself off. If he stays here he is quite equal to making an utter mess of life for both of you.

GREGERS: These two will not make a mess of life, Mr Relling. Of course I won't speak for Hialmar—him we know. But she too, in her innermost heart, has certainly something loyal and sincere—

GINA: [*almost crying*] You might have let me alone for what I was then.

RELLING: [*to* GREGERS] Is it rude to ask what you really want in this house?

GREGERS: To lay the foundations of a true marriage.

RELLING: So you don't think Ekdal's marriage is good enough as it is?

GREGERS: No doubt it is as good a marriage as most others, worse luck. But a true marriage it has yet to become.

HIALMAR: You have never had eyes for the claims of the ideal, Relling.

RELLING: Rubbish, my boy! But excuse me, Mr Werle; how many—in round numbers—how many true marriages have you seen in the course of your life?

GREGERS: Scarcely a single one.

RELLING: Nor I either.

GREGERS: But I have seen innumerable marriages of the opposite kind. And it has been my fate to see at close quarters what ruin such a marriage can work in two human souls.

HIALMAR: A man's whole moral basis may give away beneath his feet; that is the terrible part of it.

RELLING: Well, I can't say I've ever been exactly married, so I don't pretend to speak with authority. But this I know, that the child enters into the marriage problem. And you must leave the child in peace.

HIALMAR: Oh—Hedvig! My poor Hedvig!

RELLING: Yes, you must be good enough to keep Hedvig outside of all this. You two are grown-up people; you are free, in God's name, to make what mess you please of your life. But you must deal cautiously with Hedvig, I tell you; otherwise you may do her a great injury.

HIALMAR: An injury!

RELLING: Yes, or she may do herself an injury—and perhaps others too.

GINA: How can you know that, Relling?

HIALMAR: Her sight is in no immediate danger, is it?

RELLING: I am not talking about her sight. Hedvig is at a critical age. She may be getting all sorts of mischief into her head.

GINA: That's true—I've noticed it already! She's taken to carrying on with the fire out in the kitchen. She calls it playing at house on fire. I'm often scared for fear she really sets fire to the house.

RELLING: You see, I thought as much.

GREGERS: [to RELLING] But how do you account for that?

RELLING: [sullenly] Her constitution's changing, sir.

HIALMAR: So long as the child has me—so long as I am above ground—
[A knock at the door.]

GINA: Hush, Ekdal, there's someone in the passage. [calls out] Come in!
[MRS SORBY, in walking dress, comes in.]

MRS SORBY: Good evening.

GINA: [going toward her] Is it really you, Bertha?

MRS SORBY: Yes, of course it is. But I'm disturbing you, I'm afraid.

HIALMAR: No, not at all; an emissary from that house—

MRS SORBY: [to GINA] To tell the truth, I hoped your menfolk would be out at this time. I just ran up to have a little chat with you and to say good-by.

GINA: Good-by? Are you going away then?

MRS SORBY: Yes, tomorrow morning—up to Höidal. Mr Werle started this afternoon. [lightly to GREGERS] He asked me to say good-by for him.

GINA: Only fancy!

HIALMAR: I say: beware!

GREGERS: I must explain the situation. My father and Mrs Sorby are going to be married.

HIALMAR: Going to be married!

GINA: Oh, Bertha! So it's come to that at last!

RELLING: [his voice quivering a little] This is surely not true?

MRS SORBY: Yes, my dear Relling, it's true enough.

RELLING: You are going to marry again?

MRS SORBY: Yes, it looks like it. Werle has got a special license, and we are going to be married quietly up at the works.

GREGERS: Then I must wish you all happiness, like a dutiful stepson.

MRS SORBY: Thank you very much—if you mean what you say. I certainly hope it will lead to happiness, both for Werle and for me.

RELLING: You have every reason to hope that. Mr Werle never gets drunk—so far as I know; and I don't suppose he's in the habit of thrashing his wives, like the late lamented horse doctor.

MRS SORBY: Come now, let Sorby rest in peace. He had his good points too.

RELLING: Mr Werle has better ones, I have no doubt.

MRS SORBY: He hasn't frittered away all that was good in him, at any rate. The man who does that must take the consequences.

RELLING: I shall go out with Molvik this evening.

MRS SORBY: You mustn't do that, Relling. Don't do it—for my sake.

RELLING: There's nothing else for it. [*to* HIALMAR] If you're going with us, come along.

GINA: No, thank you. Ekdal doesn't go in for that sort of dissertation.

HIALMAR: [*half aloud. in vexation*] Oh, do hold your tongue!

RELLING: Good-by, Mrs—Werle. [*Goes out through the passage door.*]

GREGERS: [*to* MRS SORBY] You seem to know Doctor Relling pretty intimately.

MRS SORBY: Yes, we have known each other for many years. At one time it seemed as if things might have gone further between us.

GREGERS: It was surely lucky for you that they did not.

MRS SORBY: You may well say that. But I have always been wary of acting on impulse. A woman can't afford absolutely to throw herself away.

GREGERS: Are you not in the least afraid that I may let my father know about this old friendship?

MRS SORBY: Why. of course I have told him all about it myself.

GREGERS: Indeed?

MRS SORBY: Your father knows every single thing that can, with any truth, be said about me. I have told him all; it was the first thing I did when I saw what was in his mind.

GREGERS: Then you have been franker than most people, I think.

MRS SORBY: I have always been frank. We women find that the best policy.

HIALMAR: What do you say to that, Gina?

GINA: Oh, we're not all alike, us women aren't. Some are made one way, some another.

MRS SORBY: Well, for my part, Gina, I believe it's wisest to do as I've done. And Werle has no secrets either, on his side. That's really the great bond between us, you see. Now he can talk to me as openly as a child. He has never had the chance to do that before. Fancy a man like him, full of health and vigor, passing his whole youth and the best years of his life in listening to nothing but penitential sermons! And very often the sermons had for their text the most imaginary offenses—at least so I understand.

GINA: That's true enough.

GREGERS: If you ladies are going to follow up this topic, I had better withdraw.

MRS SORBY: You can stay as far as that's concerned. I shan't say a word more. But I wanted you to know that I had done nothing secretly or in an underhand way. I may seem to have come in for a great piece of luck, and so I have, in a sense. But after all, I don't think I am getting any more than I am giving. I shall stand by him always, and I can tend and care for him as no one else can, now that he is getting helpless.

HIALMAR: Getting helpless?

GREGERS: [*to* MRS SORBY] Hush, don't speak of that here.

MRS SORBY: There is no disguising it any longer, however much he would like to. He is going blind.

HIALMAR: [*starts*] Going blind? That's strange. He, too, going blind!

GINA: Lots of people do.

MRS SORBY: And you can imagine what that means to a businessman. Well, I shall try as well as I can to make my eyes take the place of his. But I mustn't stay any longer; I have heaps of things to do. Oh, by the bye, Ekdal, I was to tell you that if there is anything Werle can do for you, you must just apply to Graberg.

GREGERS: That offer I am sure Hialmar Ekdal will decline with thanks.

MRS SORBY: Indeed? I don't think he used to be so—

GINA: No, Bertha, Ekdal doesn't need anything from Mr Werle now.

HIALMAR: [*slowly and with emphasis*] Will you present my compliments to your future husband and say that I intend very shortly to call upon Mr Graberg—

GREGERS: What! You don't really mean that?

HIALMAR: To call upon Mr Graberg, I say, and obtain an account of the sum I owe his principal. I will pay that debt of honor—ha, ha, ha! a debt of honor, let us call it! In any case I will pay the whole with five per cent interest.

GINA: But, my dear Ekdal, God knows we haven't got the money to do it.

HIALMAR: Be good enough to tell your future husband that I am working assiduously at my invention. Please tell him that what sustains me in this laborious task is the wish to free myself from a torturing burden of debt. That is my reason for proceeding with the invention. The entire profits shall be devoted to releasing me from my pecuniary obligations to your future husband.

MRS SORBY: Something has happened here.

HIALMAR: Yes, you are right.

MRS SORBY: Well, good-by. I had something else to speak to you about, Gina, but it must keep till another time. Good-by.

[HIALMAR *and* GREGERS *bow silently.* GINA *follows* MRS SORBY *to the door.*]

HIALMAR: Not beyond the threshold, Gina!

[MRS SORBY *goes;* GINA *shuts the door after her.*]

HIALMAR: There now, Gregers, I have got that burden of debt off my mind.

GREGERS: You soon will, at all events.

HIALMAR: I think my attitude may be called correct.

GREGERS: You are the man I have always taken you for.

HIALMAR: In certain cases it is impossible to disregard the claim of the ideal. Yet, as the breadwinner of a family, I cannot but writhe and groan under it. I can tell you it is no joke for a man without capital to attempt the repayment of a long-standing obligation over which, so to speak, the dust of oblivion has gathered. But it cannot be helped; the man in me demands his rights.

GREGERS: [*laying his hand on* HIALMAR's *shoulder*] My dear Hialmar—was it not a good thing I came?

HIALMAR: Yes.

GREGERS: Are you not glad to have had your true position made clear to you?

HIALMAR: [*somewhat impatiently*] Yes, of course I am. But there is one thing that is revolting to my sense of justice.

GREGERS: And what is that?

HIALMAR: It is that— But I don't know whether I ought to express myself so unreservedly about your father.

GREGERS: Say what you please so far as I am concerned.

HIALMAR: Well, then, is it not exasperating to think that it is not I, but he, who will realize the true marriage?

GREGERS: How can you say such a thing?

HIALMAR: Because it is clearly the case. Isn't the marriage between your father and Mrs Sorby founded upon complete confidence, upon entire and unreserved candor on both sides? They hide nothing from each other, they keep no secrets in the background; their relation is based, if I may put it so, on mutual confession and absolution.

GREGERS: Well, what then?

HIALMAR: Well, is not that the whole thing? Did you not yourself say that this was precisely the difficulty that had to be overcome in order to found a true marriage?

GREGERS: But this is a totally different matter, Hialmar. You surely don't compare either yourself or your wife with those two— Oh, you understood me well enough.

HIALMAR: Say what you like, there is something in all this that hurts and offends my sense of justice. It really looks as if there were no just Providence to rule the world.

GINA: Oh no, Ekdal; for God's sake don't say such things.

GREGERS: H'm; don't let us get upon those questions.

HIALMAR: And yet, after all, I cannot but recognize the guiding finger of Fate. He is going blind.

GINA: Oh, you can't be sure of that.

HIALMAR: There is no doubt about it. At all events there ought not to be, for in that very fact lies the righteous retribution. He has hoodwinked a confiding fellow creature in days gone by—

GREGERS: I fear he has hoodwinked many.

HIALMAR: And now comes inexorable, mysterious Fate and demands Werle's own eyes.

GINA: Oh, how dare you say such dreadful things! You make me quite scared.

HIALMAR: It is profitable, now and then, to plunge deep into the night side of existence.

[HEDVIG, *in her hat and cloak, comes in by the passage door. She is pleasurably excited and out of breath.*]

GINA: Are you back already?

HEDVIG: Yes, I didn't care to go any farther. It was a good thing, too, for I've just met someone at the door.

HIALMAR: It must have been that Mrs Sorby.

HEDVIG: Yes.

HIALMAR: [*walks up and down*] I hope you have seen her for the last time.

[*Silence.* HEDVIG, *discouraged, looks first at one and then at the other, trying to divine their frame of mind.*]

HEDVIG: [*approaching, coaxingly*] Father.

HIALMAR: Well—what is it, Hedvig?

HEDVIG: Mrs Sorby had something with her for me.

HIALMAR: [*stops*] For you?

HEDVIG: Yes. Something for tomorrow.

GINA: Bertha has always given you some little thing on your birthday.

HIALMAR: What is it?

HEDVIG: Oh, you mustn't see it now. Mother is to give it to me tomorrow morning before I'm up.

HIALMAR: What is all this hocus-pocus that I am to be in the dark about?

HEDVIG: [*quickly*] Oh no, you may see it if you like. It's a big letter. [*takes the letter out of her cloak pocket*]

HIALMAR: A letter too?

HEDVIG: Yes, it is only a letter. The rest will come afterward, I suppose. But fancy—a letter! I've never had a letter before. And there's "Miss" written upon it. [*reads*] "Miss Hedvig Ekdal." Only think—that's me!

HIALMAR: Let me see that letter.

HEDVIG: [*hands it to him*] There it is.

HIALMAR: That is Mr Werle's hand.

GINA: Are you sure of that, Ekdal?

HIALMAR: Look for yourself.

GINA: Oh, what do I know about suchlike things?

HIALMAR: Hedvig, may I open the letter—and read it?

HEDVIG: Yes, of course you may, if you want to.

GINA: No, not tonight, Ekdal; it's to be kept till tomorrow.

HEDVIG: [*softly*] Oh, can't you let him read it! It's sure to be something good, and then Father will be glad and everything will be nice again.

HIALMAR: I may open it then?

HEDVIG: Yes, do, Father. I'm so anxious to know what it is.

HIALMAR: Well and good. [*opens the letter, takes out a paper, reads it through and appears bewildered.*] What is this?

GINA: What does it say?

HEDVIG: Oh yes, Father—tell us!

HIALMAR: Be quiet. [*Reads it through again; he has turned pale but says with self-control.*] It is a deed of gift, Hedvig.

HEDVIG: Is it? What sort of gift am I to have?

HIALMAR: Read for yourself.

[HEDVIG *goes over and reads for a time by the lamp.*]

HIALMAR: [*half aloud, clenching his hands*] The eyes! The eyes—and then that letter!

HEDVIG: [*leaves off reading*] Yes, but it seems to me that it's Grandfather that's to have it.

HIALMAR: [*takes letter from her*] Gina—can you understand this?

GINA: I know nothing whatever about it; tell me what's the matter.

HIALMAR: Mr Werle writes to Hedvig that her old grandfather need not trouble himself any longer with the copying but that he can henceforth draw on the office for a hundred crowns a month—

GREGERS: Aha!

HEDVIG: A hundred crowns, Mother! I read that.

GINA: What a good thing for Grandfather!

HIALMAR: —a hundred crowns a month so long as he needs it—that means, of course, so long as he lives.

GINA: Well, so he's provided for, poor dear.

HIALMAR: But there is more to come. You didn't read that, Hedvig. Afterward this gift is to pass on to you.

HEDVIG: To me! The whole of it?

HIALMAR: He says that the same amount is assured to you for the whole of your life. Do you hear that, Gina?

GINA: Yes, I hear.

HEDVIG: Fancy—all that money for me! [*shakes him*] Father, Father, aren't you glad?

HIALMAR: [*eluding her*] Glad! [*walks about*] Oh, what vistas—what perspectives open up before me! It is Hedvig, Hedvig that he showers these benefactions upon!

GINA: Yes, because it's Hedvig's birthday.

HEDVIG: And you'll get it all the same, Father! You know quite well I shall give all the money to you and Mother.

HIALMAR: To Mother, yes! There we have it.

GREGERS: Hialmar, this is a trap he is setting for you.

HIALMAR: Do you think it's another trap?

GREGERS: When he was here this morning he said: Hialmar Ekdal is not the man you imagine him to be.

HIALMAR: Not the man—

GREGERS: That you shall see, he said.

HIALMAR: He meant you should see that I would let myself be bought off!

HEDVIG: Oh, Mother, what does all this mean?

GINA: Go and take off your things.

[HEDVIG *goes out by the kitchen door, half crying.*]

GREGERS: Yes, Hialmar—now is the time to show who was right, he or I.

HIALMAR: [*slowly tears the paper across, lays both pieces on the table and says*] Here is my answer.

GREGERS: Just what I expected.

HIALMAR: [*goes over to* GINA, *who stands by the stove and says in a low voice*] Now please make a clean breast of it. If the connection between you and him was quite over when you—came to care for me, as you call it—why did he place us in a position to marry?

GINA: I suppose he thought as he could come and go in our house.

HIALMAR: Only that? Was he not afraid of a possible contingency?

GINA: I don't know what you mean.

HIALMAR: I want to know whether—your child has the right to live under my roof.

GINA: [*draws herself up; her eyes flash*] You ask that!

HIALMAR: You shall answer me this one question: Does Hedvig belong to me—or—? Well?

GINA: [*looking at him with cold defiance*] I don't know.

HIALMAR: [*quivering a little*] You don't know!

GINA: How should I know. A creature like me—

HIALMAR: [*quietly turning away from her*] Then I have nothing more to do in this house.

GREGERS: Take care, Hialmar! Think what you are doing!

HIALMAR: [*puts on his overcoat*] In this case there is nothing for a man like me to think twice about.

GREGERS: Yes indeed, there are endless things to be considered. You three must be together if you are to attain the true frame of mind for self-sacrifice and forgiveness.

HIALMAR: I don't want to attain it. Never, never! My hat! [*takes his hat*] My home has fallen into ruins about me. [*bursts into tears*] Gregers, I have no child!

HEDVIG: [*who has opened the kitchen door*] What is that you're saying? [*coming to him*] Father, Father!

GINA: There, you see!

HIALMAR: Don't come near me, Hedvig! Keep far away. I cannot bear to see you. Oh! those eyes! Good-by.
    [*Makes for the door.*]

HEDVIG: [*clinging close to him and screaming loudly*] No! No! Don't leave me!

GINA: [*cries out*] Look at the child, Ekdal! Look at the child!

HIALMAR: I will not! I cannot! I must get out—away from all this! [*He tears himself away from* HEDVIG *and goes out by the passage door.*]

HEDVIG: [*with despairing eyes*] He is going away from us, Mother! He is going away from us! He will never come back again!

GINA: Don't cry, Hedvig. Father's sure to come back again.

HEDVIG: [*throws herself sobbing on the sofa*] No, no, he'll never come home to us any more.

GREGERS: Do you believe I meant all for the best, Mrs Ekdal?

GINA: Yes, I daresay you did, but God forgive you all the same.

HEDVIG: [*lying on the sofa*] Oh, this will kill me! What have I done to him? Mother, you must fetch him home again!

GINA: Yes, yes, yes; only be quiet, and I'll go out and look for him. [*puts on her outdoor things*] Perhaps he's gone into Relling's. But you mustn't lie there and cry. Promise me!

HEDVIG: [*weeping convulsively*] Yes, I'll stop, I'll stop; if only Father comes back!

GREGERS: [*to* GINA, *who is going*] After all, had you not better leave him to fight out his bitter fight to the end?

GINA: Oh, he can do that afterward. First of all we must get the child quieted. [*Goes out by the passage door.*]

HEDVIG: [*sits up and dries her tears*] Now you must tell me what all this means. Why doesn't Father want me any more?

GREGERS: You mustn't ask that till you are a big girl—quite grown up.

HEDVIG: [*sobs*] But I can't go on being as miserable as this till I'm grown up. I think I know what it is. Perhaps I'm not really Father's child.

GREGERS: [*uneasily*] How could that be?

HEDVIG: Mother might have found me. And perhaps Father has just found out; I've read of such things.

GREGERS: Well, but if it were so—

HEDVIG: I think he might be just as fond of me for all that. Yes, fonder almost. We got the wild duck as a present, you know, and I love it so dearly all the same.

GREGERS: [*turning the conversation*] Ah, the wild duck, by the bye! Let us talk about the wild duck a little, Hedvig.

HEDVIG: The poor wild duck! He doesn't want to see it any more either. Only think, he wanted to wring its neck!

GREGERS: Oh, he won't do that.

HEDVIG: No, but he said he would like to. And I think it was horrid of Father to say it, for I pray for the wild duck every night and ask that it may be preserved from death and all that is evil.

GREGERS: [*looking at her*] Do you say your prayers every night?

HEDVIG: Yes.

GREGERS: Who taught you to do that?

HEDVIG: I myself—one time when Father was very ill and said that death was staring him in the face.

GREGERS: Well?

HEDVIG: Then I prayed for him as I lay in bed, and since then I have always kept it up.

GREGERS: And now you pray for the wild duck too?

HEDVIG: I thought it best to bring in the wild duck, for she was so weak at first.

GREGERS: Do you pray in the morning too?

HEDVIG: No, of course not.

GREGERS: Why not in the morning as well?

HEDVIG: In the morning it's light, you know, and there's nothing in particular to be afraid of.

GREGERS: And your father was going to wring the neck of the wild duck that you love so dearly?

HEDVIG: No; he said he ought to wring its neck but he would spare it for my sake, and that was kind of Father.

GREGERS: [*coming a little nearer*] But suppose you were to sacrifice the wild duck of your own free will for his sake?

HEDVIG: [*rising*] The wild duck!

GREGERS: Suppose you were to make a free-will offering, for his sake, of the dearest treasure you have in the world?

HEDVIG: Do you think that would do any good?

GREGERS: Try it, Hedvig.

HEDVIG: [*softly, with flashing eyes*] Yes, I will try it.

GREGERS: Have you really the courage for it, do you think?

HEDVIG: I'll ask Grandfather to shoot the wild duck for me.

GREGERS: Yes, do. But not a word to your mother about it.

HEDVIG: Why not?

GREGERS: She doesn't understand us.

HEDVIG: The wild duck! I'll try it tomorrow morning.

[GINA *comes in by the passage door.*]

HEDVIG: [*going toward her*] Did you find him, Mother?

GINA: No, but I heard as he had called and taken Relling with him.

GREGERS: Are you sure of that?

GINA: Yes, the porter's wife said so. Molvik went with them too, she said.

GREGERS: This evening, when his mind so sorely needs to wrestle in solitude!

GINA: [*takes off her things*] Yes, men are strange creatures, so they are. The Lord only knows where Relling has dragged him to! I ran over to Madam Eriksen's, but they weren't there.

HEDVIG: [*struggling to keep back her tears*] Oh, if he should never come home any more!

GREGERS: He will come home again. I shall have news to give him tomorrow, and then you shall see how he comes home. You may rely upon that, Hedvig, and sleep in peace. Good night. [*He goes out by the passage door.*]

HEDVIG: [*throws herself sobbing on* GINA's *neck*] Mother, Mother!

GINA: [*pats her shoulder and sighs*] Ah yes, Relling was right, he was. That's what comes of it when crazy creatures go about presenting the claim of the—what-you-may-call-it.

ACT V

SCENE——HIALMAR EKDAL's *studio. Cold gray morning light. Wet snow lies upon the large panes of the sloping roof window.*

[GINA *comes from the kitchen with an apron and bib on and carrying a dusting brush and a duster; she goes toward the sitting-room door. At the same moment* HEDVIG *comes hurriedly in from the passage.*]

GINA: [*stops*] Well?

HEDVIG: Oh, Mother, I almost think he's down at Relling's—

GINA: There, you see!

HEDVIG: —because the porter's wife says she could hear that Relling had two people with him when he came home last night.

GINA: That's just what I thought.

HEDVIG: But it's no use his being there if he won't come up to us.

GINA: I'll go down and speak to him at all events.

[OLD EKDAL, *in dressing gown and slippers and with a lighted pipe, appears at the door of his room.*]

EKDAL: Hialmar—isn't Hialmar at home?

GINA: No, he's gone out.

EKDAL: So early? And in such a tearing snowstorm? Well, well, just as he pleases; I can take my morning walk alone.

[*He slides the garret door aside;* HEDVIG *helps him; he goes in; she closes it after him.*]

HEDVIG: [*in an undertone*] Only think, Mother, when poor Grandfather hears that Father is going to leave us.

GINA: Oh, nonsense; Grandfather mustn't hear anything about it. It was a heaven's mercy he wasn't at home yesterday in all that hurly-burly.

HEDVIG: Yes, but—

[GREGERS *comes in by the passage door.*]

GREGERS: Well, have you any news of him?

GINA: They say he's down at Relling's.

GREGERS: At Relling's! Has he really been out with those creatures?

GINA: Yes, like enough.

GREGERS: When he ought to have been yearning for solitude, to collect and clear his thoughts—

GINA: Yes you may well say so.

[RELLING *enters from the passage.*]

HEDVIG: [*going to him*] Is Father in your room?

GINA: [*at the same time*] Is he there?

RELLING: Yes, to be sure he is.

HEDVIG: And you never let us know!

RELLING: Yes, I'm a brute. But in the first place I had to look after the other brute; I mean our demonic friend, of course; and then I fell so dead asleep that—

GINA: What does Ekdal say today?

RELLING: He says nothing whatever.

HEDVIG: Doesn't he speak?

RELLING: Not a blessed word.

GREGERS: No, no; I can understand that very well.

GINA: But what's he doing then?

RELLING: He's lying on the sofa, snoring.

GINA: Oh, is he? Yes, Ekdal's a rare one to snore.

HEDVIG: Asleep? Can he sleep?

RELLING: Well, it certainly looks like it.

GREGERS: No wonder, after the spiritual conflict that has torn him—

GINA: And then he's never been used to gadding about out of doors at night.

HEDVIG: Perhaps it's a good thing that he's getting sleep, Mother.

GINA: Of course it is, and we must take care we don't wake him up too early. Thank you, Relling. I must get the house cleaned up a bit now, and then— Come and help me, Hedvig.

[GINA *and* HEDVIG *go into the sitting room.*]

GREGERS: [*turning to* RELLING] What is your explanation of the spiritual tumult that is now going on in Hialmar Ekdal?

RELLING: A lot of spiritual tumult I've noticed in him.

GREGERS: What! Not at such a crisis, when his whole life has been placed on a new foundation? How can you think that such an individuality as Hialmar's—

RELLING: Oh, individuality—he! If he ever had any tendency to the abnormal developments you call individuality, I can assure you it was rooted out of him while he was still in his teens.

GREGERS: That would be strange indeed—considering the loving care with which he was brought up.

RELLING: By those two high-flown, hysterical maiden aunts, you mean?

GREGERS: Let me tell you that they were women who never forgot the claim of the ideal—but of course you will only jeer at me again.

RELLING: No, I'm in no humor for that. I know all about those ladies, for he has ladled out no end of rhetoric on the subject of his "two soul mothers." But I don't think he has much to thank them for. Ekdal's misfortune is that in his own circle he has always been looked upon as a shining light.

GREGERS: Not without reason, surely. Look at the depth of his mind!

RELLING: I have never discovered it. That his father believed in it I don't so much wonder; the old lieutenant has been an ass all his days.

GREGERS: He has had a childlike mind all his days; that is what you cannot understand.

RELLING: Well, so be it. But then when our dear sweet Hialmar went to college he at once passed for the great light of the future amongst his comrades too! He was handsome, the rascal—red and white—a shopgirl's dream of manly beauty; and with his superficially emotional temperament and his sympathetic voice and his talent for declaiming other people's verses and other people's thoughts—

GREGERS: [*indignantly*] Is it Hialmar Ekdal you are talking about in this strain?

RELLING: Yes, with your permission; I am simply giving you an inside view of the idol you are groveling before.

GREGERS: I should hardly have thought I was quite stone-blind.

RELLING: Yes, you are—or not far from it. You are a sick man too, you see.

GREGERS: You are right there.

RELLING: Yes. Yours is a complicated case. First of all there is that plaguy integrity fever, and then—what's worse—you are always in a delirium of hero worship; you must always have something to adore, outside yourself.

GREGERS: Yes, I must certainly seek it outside myself.

RELLING: But you make such shocking mistakes about every new phoenix you think you have discovered. Here again you have come to a cotter's cabin with your claim of the ideal, and the people of the house are insolvent.

GREGERS: If you don't think better than that of Hialmar Ekdal, what pleasure can you find in being everlastingly with him?

RELLING: Well, you see, I'm supposed to be a sort of a doctor—God help me! I have to give a hand to the poor sick folk who live under the same roof with me.

GREGERS: Oh, indeed! Hialmar Ekdal is sick too, is he?

RELLING: Most people are, worse luck.

GREGERS: And what remedy are you applying in Hialmar's case?

RELLING: My usual one. I am cultivating the life illusion in him.

GREGERS: Life—illusion? I didn't catch what you said.

RELLING: Yes, I said illusion. For illusion, you know, is the stimulating principle.

GREGERS: May I ask with what illusion Hialmar is inoculated?

RELLING: No, thank you; I don't betray professional secrets to quacks. You would probably go and muddle his case still more than you have already. But my method is infallible. I have applied it to Molvik as well. I have made him "demonic." That's the treatment for him.

GREGERS: Is he not really demonic then?

RELLING: What the devil do you mean by demonic? It's only a piece of gibberish I've invented to keep up a spark of life in him. But for that, the poor harmless creature would have succumbed to self-contempt and despair many a long year ago. And then the old lieutenant! But he has hit upon his own cure, you see.

GREGERS: Lieutenant Ekdal? What of him?

RELLING: Just think of the old bear hunter shutting himself up in that dark garret to shoot rabbits! I tell you there is not a happier sportsman in the world than that old man pottering about in there among all that rubbish. The four or five withered Christmas trees he has saved up are the same to him as the whole great fresh Höidal forest; the cock and the hens are big game birds in the fir tops, and the rabbits that flop about the garret floor are the bears he has to battle with—the mighty hunter of the mountains!

GREGERS: Poor unfortunate old man! Yes, he has indeed had to narrow the ideals of his youth.

RELLING: While I think of it, Mr. Werle junior—don't use that foreign word: ideals. We have the excellent native word: lies.

GREGERS: Do you think the two things are related?

RELLING: Yes, just about as closely as typhus and putrid fever.

GREGERS: Doctor Relling, I shall not give up the struggle until I have rescued Hialmar from your clutches!

RELLING: So much the worse for him. Rob the average man of his life illusion and you rob him of his happiness at the same stroke. [*to* HEDVIG, *who comes in from the sitting room*] Well, little wild-duck mother. I'm just going down to see whether Papa is still lying meditating upon that wonderful invention of his.

[*Goes out by passage door.*]

GREGERS: [*approaches* HEDVIG] I can see by your face that you have not yet done it.

HEDVIG: What? Oh, that about the wild duck! No.

GREGERS: I suppose your courage failed when the time came?

HEDVIG: No, that wasn't it. But when I awoke this morning and remembered what we had been talking about it seemed so strange.

GREGERS: Strange?

HEDVIG: Yes, I don't know— Yesterday evening, at the moment, I thought there was something so delightful about it; but since I have slept and thought of it again, it somehow doesn't seem worth while.

GREGERS: Ah, I thought you could not have grown up quite unharmed in this house.

HEDVIG: I don't care about that, if only Father would come up—

GREGERS: Oh, if only your eyes had been opened to that which gives life its value—if you possessed the true, joyous, fearless spirit of sacrifice you would soon see how he would come up to you. But I believe in you still, Hedvig.

> [*He goes out by the passage door.* HEDVIG *wanders about the room for a time; she is on the point of going into the kitchen when a knock is heard at the garret door.* HEDVIG *goes over and opens it a little;* OLD EKDAL *comes out; she pushes the door to again.*]

EKDAL: H'm, it's not much fun to take a morning walk alone.

HEDVIG: Wouldn't you like to go shooting, Grandfather?

EKDAL: It's not the weather for it today. It's so dark there you can scarcely see where you're going.

HEDVIG: Do you never want to shoot anything besides the rabbits?

EKDAL: Do you think the rabbits aren't good enough?

HEDVIG: Yes, but what about the wild duck?

EKDAL: Ho-ho! Are you afraid I shall shoot your wild duck? Never in the world. Never!

HEDVIG: No, I suppose you couldn't; they say it's very difficult to shoot wild ducks.

EKDAL: Couldn't! Should rather think I could.

HEDVIG: How would you set about it, Grandfather? I don't mean with my wild duck, but with others.

EKDAL: I should take care to shoot them in the breast, you know; that's the surest place. And then you must shoot against the feathers, you see— not the way of the feathers.

HEDVIG: Do they die then, Grandfather?

EKDAL: Yes they die right enough—when you shoot properly. Well, I must go and brush up a bit. H'm—understand—h'm. [*Goes into his room.*]

> [HEDVIG *waits a little, glances toward the sitting-room door, goes over to the bookcase, stands on tiptoe, takes the double-barreled pistol down from the shelf and looks at it.* GINA, *with brush and duster, comes from the sitting room.* HEDVIG *hastily lays down the pistol unobserved.*]

GINA: Don't stand raking amongst Father's things, Hedvig.

HEDVIG: [*goes away from the bookcase*] I was only going to tidy up a little.

GINA: You'd better go into the kitchen and see if the coffee's still hot; I'll take his breakfast on a tray when I go down to him.

> [HEDVIG *goes out.* GINA *begins to sweep and clean up the studio. Presently the passage door is opened with hesitation and* HIALMAR EKDAL *looks in. He has on his overcoat but not his hat; he is unwashed, and his hair is disheveled and unkempt. His eyes are dull and heavy.*]

GINA: [*standing with the brush in her hand and looking at him*] Oh, there now, Ekdal—so you've come after all?

HIALMAR: [*comes in and answers in a toneless voice*] I come—only to depart immediately.

GINA: Yes, yes, I suppose so. But Lord help us! what a sight you are!

HIALMAR: A sight?

GINA: And your nice winter coat too! Well, that's done for.

HEDVIG: [*at the kitchen door*] Mother, hadn't I better—
　　　[*Sees* HIALMAR, *gives a loud scream of joy and runs to him*] Oh, Father, Father!

HIALMAR: [*turns away and makes a gesture of repulsion*] Away, away, away! [*to* GINA] Keep her away from me, I say!

GINA: [*in a low tone*] Go into the sitting room, Hedvig.
　　　[HEDVIG *does so without a word.*]

HIALMAR: [*fussily pulls out the table drawer*] I must have my books with me. Where are my books?

GINA: Which books?

HIALMAR: My scientific books, of course; the technical magazines I require for my invention.

GINA: [*searches in the bookcase*] Is it these here papercovered ones?

HIALMAR: Yes, of course.

GINA: [*lays a heap of magazines on the table*] Shan't I get Hedvig to cut them for you?

HIALMAR: I don't require to have them cut for me.
　　　[*Short silence.*]

GINA: Then you're still set on leaving us, Ekdal?

HIALMAR: [*rummaging amongst the books*] Yes, that is a matter of course, I should think.

GINA: Well, well.

HIALMAR: [*vehemently*] How can I live here, to be stabbed to the heart every hour of the day?

GINA: God forgive you for thinking such vile things of me.

HIALMAR: Prove—

GINA: I think it's you as has got to prove.

HIALMAR: After a past like yours? There are certain claims—I may almost call them claims of the ideal—

GINA: But what about Grandfather? What's to become of him, poor dear?

HIALMAR: I know my duty; my helpless father will come with me. I am going out into the town to make arrangements—H'm [*hesitatingly*]—has anyone found my hat on the stairs?

GINA: No. Have you lost your hat?

HIALMAR: Of course I had it on when I came in last night—there's no doubt about that—but I couldn't find it this morning.

GINA: Lord help us! Where have you been to with those two ne'er-do-wells?

HIALMAR: Oh, don't bother me about trifles. Do you suppose I am in the mood to remember details?

GINA: If only you haven't caught cold, Ekdal— [*Goes out into the kitchen.*]

HIALMAR: [*talks to himself in a low tone of irritation while he empties the table drawer*] You're a scoundrel, Relling! You're a low fellow! Ah, you shameless tempter! I wish I could get someone to stick a knife into you! [*He lays some old letters on one side, finds the torn document of yesterday, takes it up and looks at the pieces, puts it down hurriedly as* GINA *enters.*]

GINA: [*sets a tray with coffee, etc., on the table*] Here's a drop of something hot, if you'd fancy it. And there's some bread and butter and a snack of meat.

HIALMAR: [*glancing at the tray*] Meat? Never under this roof! It's true I have not had a mouthful of solid food for nearly twenty-four hours, but no matter. My memoranda! The commencement of my autobiography! What has become of my diary and all my important papers? [*opens the sitting-room door but draws back*] She is there too!

GINA: Good lord! the child must be somewhere!

HIALMAR: Come out.

[*He makes room;* HEDVIG *comes, scared, into the studio.*]

HIALMAR: [*with his hand on the door handle, says to* GINA] In these, the last moments I spend in my former home, I wish to be spared from interlopers. [*Goes into the room.*]

HEDVIG: [*with a bound toward her mother, asks softly, trembling*] Does that mean me?

GINA: Stay out in the kitchen, Hedvig; or, no—you'd best go into your own room. [*speaks to* HIALMAR *as she goes in to him*] Wait a bit, Ekdal; don't rummage so in the drawers. I know where everything is.

HEDVIG: [*stands a moment immovable, in terror and perplexity, biting her lips to keep the tears; then she clenches her hands convulsively and says softly*] The wild duck! [*She steals over and takes the pistol from the shelf, opens the garret door a little way, creeps in and draws the door to after her.* HIALMAR *and* GINA *can be heard disputing in the sitting room.*]

HIALMAR: [*comes in with some manuscript books and old loose papers which he lays upon the table*] That portmanteau is of no use! There are a thousand and one things I must drag with me.

GINA: [*following with the portmanteau*] Why not leave all the rest for the present and only take a shirt and a pair of woolen drawers with you?

HIALMAR: Whew! All these exhausting preparations! [*Pulls off his overcoat and throws it upon the sofa.*]

GINA: And there's the coffee getting cold.

HIALMAR: H'm. [*Drinks a mouthful without thinking of it and then another.*]

GINA: [*dusting the backs of the chairs*] A nice job you'll have to find such another big garret for the rabbits.

HIALMAR: What! Am I to drag all those rabbits with me too?

GINA: You don't suppose Grandfather can get on without his rabbits.

HIALMAR: He must just get used to doing without them. Have not *I* to sacrifice very much greater things than rabbits!

GINA: [*dusting the bookcase*] Shall I put the flute in the portmanteau for you?

HIALMAR: No. No flute for me. But give me the pistol!

GINA: Do you want to take the pistol with you?

HIALMAR: Yes. My loaded pistol.

GINA: [*searching for it*] It's gone. He must have taken it in with him.

HIALMAR: Is he in the garret?

GINA: Yes, of course he's in the garret.

HIALMAR: H'm—poor lonely old man. [*He takes a piece of bread and butter, eats it and finishes his cup of coffee.*]

GINA: And if we hadn't have let that room, you could have moved in there.

HIALMAR: And continued to live under the same roof with— Never—never!

GINA: But couldn't you put up with the sitting room for a day or two? You could have it all to yourself.

HIALMAR: Never within these walls!

GINA: Well, then, down with Relling and Molvik.

HIALMAR: Don't mention those wretches' names to me! The very thought of them almost takes away my appetite. Oh no, I must go out into the storm and the snowdrift—go from house to house and seek shelter for my father and myself.

GINA: But you've got no hat, Ekdal! You've gone and lost your hat, you know.

HIALMAR: Oh, those two brutes, those slaves of all the vices! A hat must be found. [*takes another piece of bread and butter*] Some arrangements must be made. For I have no mind to throw away my life either. [*looks for something on the tray*]

GINA: What are you looking for?

HIALMAR: Butter.

GINA: I'll get some at once. [*Goes out into the kitchen.*]

HIALMAR: [*calls after her*] Oh, it doesn't matter; dry bread is good enough for me.

GINA: [*brings a dish of butter*] Look here; this is fresh churned.

> [*She pours out another cup of coffee for him; he seats himself on the sofa, spreads more butter on the already buttered bread and eats and drinks a while in silence.*]

HIALMAR: Could I, without being subject to intrusion—intrusion of any sort— could I live in the sitting room there for a day or two?

GINA: Yes, to be sure you could, if you only would.

HIALMAR: For I see no possibility of getting all Father's things out in such a hurry.

GINA: And, besides, you've surely got to tell him first as you don't mean to live with us others no more.

HIALMAR: [*pushes away his coffee cup*] Yes, there is that too; I shall have to lay bare the whole tangled story to him— I must turn matters over; I must have breathing time. I cannot take all these burdens on my shoulders in a single day.

GINA: No, especially in such horrible weather as it is outside.

HIALMAR: [*touching* WERLE's *letter*] I see that paper still lying about here.

GINA: Yes, I haven't touched it.

HIALMAR: So far as I am concerned it is mere wastepaper—

GINA: Well, I have certainly no notion of making any use of it.

HIALMAR: —but we had better not let it get lost all the same, in all the upset when I move it might easily—

GINA: I'll take good care of it, Ekdal.

HIALMAR: The donation is in the first instance made to Father, and it rests with him to accept or decline it.

GINA: [*sighs*] Yes, poor old Father—

HIALMAR: To make quite safe—Where shall I find some glue?

GINA: [*goes to the bookcase*] Here's the glue pot.

HIALMAR: And a brush?

GINA: The brush is here too. [*brings him the things*]

HIALMAR: [*takes a pair of scissors*] Just a strip of paper at the back— [*clips and glues*] Far be it from me to lay hands upon what is not my own—and least of all upon what belongs to a destitute old man—and to—the other as well. There now! Let it lie there for a time, and when it is dry take it away. I wish never to see that document again. Never!

[GREGERS WERLE *enters from the passage.*]

GREGERS: [*somewhat surprised*] What—are you sitting here, Hialmar?

HIALMAR: [*rises hurriedly*] I had sunk down from fatigue.

GREGERS: You have been having breakfast, I see.

HIALMAR: The body sometimes makes its claims felt too.

GREGERS: What have you decided to do?

HIALMAR: For a man like me there is only one course possible. I am just putting my most important things together. But it takes time, you know.

GINA: [*with a touch of impatience*] Am I to get the room ready for you or am I to pack your suitcase?

HIALMAR: [*after a glance of annoyance at* GREGERS] Pack—and get the room ready!

GINA: [*takes the portmanteau*] Very well; then I'll put in the shirt and the other things. [*Goes into the sitting room and draws the door to after her.*]

GREGERS: [*after a short silence*] I never dreamed that this would be the end of it. Do you really feel it a necessity to leave house and home?

HIALMAR: [*wanders about restlessly*] What would you have me do? I am not fitted to bear unhappiness, Gregers. I must feel secure and at peace in my surroundings.

GREGERS: But can you not feel that here? Just try it. I should have thought you had firm ground to build upon now—if only you start afresh. And, remember, you have your invention to live for.

HIALMAR: Oh, don't talk about my invention. It's perhaps still in the dim distance.

GREGERS: Indeed!

HIALMAR: Why, great heavens, what would you have one invent? Other people have invented almost everything already. It becomes more and more difficult every day—

GREGERS: And you have devoted so much labor to it.

HIALMAR: It was that blackguard Relling that urged me to it.

GREGERS: Relling?

HIALMAR: Yes, it was he that first made me realize my aptitude for making some notable discovery in photography.

GREGERS: Aha—it was Relling!

HIALMAR: Oh, I have been so truly happy over it! Not so much for the sake of the invention itself as because Hedvig believed in it—believed in it with a child's whole eagerness of faith. At least I have been fool enough to imagine that she believed in it.

GREGERS: Can you really think Hedvig has been false toward you?

HIALMAR: I can think anything now. It is Hedvig that stands in my way. She will blot out the sunlight from my whole life.

GREGERS: Hedvig! Is it Hedvig you are talking of? How should she blot out your sunlight?

HIALMAR: [*without answering*] How unutterably I have loved that child! How unutterably happy I have felt every time I came home to my humble room and she flew to meet me with her sweet little blinking eyes. Oh, confiding fool that I have been! I loved her unutterably—and I yielded myself up to the dream, the delusion, that she loved me unutterably in return.

GREGER: Do you call that a delusion?

HIALMAR: How should I know? I can get nothing out of Gina; and besides, she is totally blind to the ideal side of these complications. But to you I feel impelled to open my mind, Gregers. I cannot shake off this frightful doubt—perhaps Hedvig has never really and honestly loved me.

GREGERS: What would you say if she were to give you a proof of her love? [*listens*] What's that? I thought I heard the wild duck—

HIALMAR: It's the wild duck quacking. Father's in the garret.

GREGERS: Is he? [*his face lights up with joy*] I say you may yet have proof that your poor misunderstood Hedvig loves you!

HIALMAR: Oh, what proof can she give me? I dare not believe in any assurance from that quarter.

GREGERS: Hedvig does not know what deceit means.

HIALMAR: Oh, Gregers, that is just what I cannot be sure of. Who knows what Gina and that Mrs Sorby may many a time have sat here whispering and tattling about? And Hedvig usually has her ears open, I can tell you. Perhaps the deed of gift was not such a surprise to her after all. In fact, I'm not sure but that I noticed something of the sort.

GREGERS: What spirit is this that has taken possession of you?

HIALMAR: I have had my eyes opened. Just you notice—you'll see, the deed of gift is only a beginning. Mrs Sorby has always been a good deal taken up with Hedvig, and now she has the power to do whatever she likes for the child. They can take her from me whenever they please.

GREGERS: Hedvig will never, never leave you.

HIALMAR: Don't be so sure of that. If only they beckon to her and throw out a golden bait— And oh! I have loved her so unspeakably! I would have counted it my highest happiness to take her tenderly by the hand and lead her, as one leads a timid child through a great dark empty room! I am cruelly certain now that the poor photographer in his humble attic has never really and truly been anything to her. She has only cunningly contrived to keep on a good footing with him until the time came.

GREGERS: You don't believe that yourself, Hialmar.

HIALMAR: That is just the terrible part of it— I don't know what to believe—

I never can know it. But can you really doubt that it must be as I say? Ho-ho, you have far too much faith in the claim of the ideal, my good Gregers! If those others came, with the glamour of wealth about them, and called to the child: "Leave him; come to us; here life awaits you—"

GREGERS: [*quickly*] Well, what then?

HIALMAR: If I then asked her: "Hedvig, are you willing to renounce that life for me?" [*laughs scornfully*] No, thank you! You would soon hear what answer I should get.

[*A pistol shot is heard from within the garret.*]

GREGERS: [*loudly and joyfully*] Hialmar!

HIALMAR: There now; he must needs go shooting too.

GINA: [*comes in*] Oh, Ekdal, I can hear Grandfather blazing away in the garret by himself.

HIALMAR: I'll look in—

GREGERS: [*eagerly, with emotion*] Wait a moment! Do you know what that was?

HIALMAR: Yes, of course I know.

GREGERS: No, you don't know. But *I* do. That was the proof!

HIALMAR: What proof?

GREGERS: It was a child's free-will offering. She has got your father to shoot the wild duck.

HIALMAR: To shoot the wild duck!

GINA: Oh, think of that!

HIALMAR: What was that for?

GREGERS: She wanted to sacrifice to you her most cherished possession, for then she thought you would surely come to love her again.

HIALMAR: [*tenderly, with emotion*] Oh, poor child!

GINA: What things she does think of!

GREGERS: She only wanted your love again, Hialmar. She could not live without it.

GINA: [*struggling with her tears*] There, you can see for yourself, Ekdal.

HIALMAR: Gina, where is she?

GINA: [*sniffs*] Poor dear, she's sitting out in the kitchen, I daresay.

HIALMAR: [*goes over, tears open the kitchen door and says*] Hedvig, come, come in to me! [*looks around*] No, she's not here.

GINA: Then she must be in her own little room.

HIALMAR: [*without*] No, she's not here either. [*comes in*] She must have gone out.

GINA: Yes, you wouldn't have her anywheres in the house.

HIALMAR: Oh, if she would only come home quickly, so that I can tell her— Everything will come right now, Gregers; now I believe we can begin life afresh.

GREGERS: [*quietly*] I knew it; I knew the child would make amends.

[OLD EKDAL *appears at the door of his room; he is in full uniform and is busy buckling on his sword.*]

HIALMAR: [*astonished*] Father! Are you there?

GINA: Have you been firing in your room?

EKDAL: [*resentfully, approaching*] So you go shooting alone, do you, Hialmar?

HIALMAR: [*excited and confused*] Then it wasn't you that fired that shot in the garret?

EKDAL: Me that fired? H'm.

GREGERS: [*calls out to* HIALMAR] She has shot the wild duck herself!

HIALMAR: What can it mean? [*hastens to the garret door, tears it aside, looks in and calls loudly*] Hedvig!

GINA: [*runs to the door*] Good God! what's that?

HIALMAR: [*goes in*] She's lying on the floor!

GREGERS: Hedvig! Lying on the floor! [*goes in to* HIALMAR]

GINA: [*at the same time*] Hedvig! [*inside the garret*] No, no, no!

EKDAL: Ho-ho! Does she go shooting too now?

> [HIALMAR, GINA *and* GREGERS *carry* HEDVIG *into the studio; in her dangling right hand she holds the pistol clasped in her fingers.*]

HIALMAR: [*distracted*] The pistol has gone off. She has wounded herself. Call for help! Help!

GINA: [*runs into the passage and calls down*] Relling! Relling! Doctor Relling, come up as quick as you can!

> [HIALMAR *and* GREGERS *lay* HEDVIG *down on the sofa.*]

EKDAL: [*quietly*] The woods avenge themselves.

HIALMAR: [*on his knees beside* HEDVIG] She'll soon come to now. She's coming to; yes, yes, yes.

GINA: [*who has come in again*] Where has she hurt herself? I can't see anything.

> [RELLING *comes hurriedly, and immediately after him* MOLVIK; *the latter without his waistcoat and necktie and with his coat open.*]

RELLING: What's the matter here?

GINA: They say Hedvig shot herself.

HIALMAR: Come and help us!

RELLING: Shot herself! [*He pushes the table aside and begins to examine her.*]

HIALMAR: [*kneeling and looking anxiously up at him*] It can't be dangerous? Speak, Relling! She is scarcely bleeding at all. It can't be dangerous?

RELLING: How did it happen?

HIALMAR: Oh, we don't know—

GINA: She wanted to shoot the wild duck.

RELLING: The wild duck?

HIALMAR: The pistol must have gone off.

RELLING: H'm. Indeed.

EKDAL: The woods avenge themselves. But I'm not afraid all the same. [*Goes into the garret and closes the door after him.*]

HIALMAR: Well, Relling, why don't you say something?

RELLING: The ball has entered the breast.

HIALMAR: Yes, but she's coming to!

RELLING: Surely you can see that Hedvig is dead.

GINA: [*bursts into tears*] Oh, my child, my child—

GREGERS: [*huskily*] In the depths of the sea—

HIALMAR: [*jumps up*] No, no, she must live! Oh, for God's sake, Relling—only a moment—only just till I can tell her how unspeakably I loved her all the time.

RELLING: The bullet has gone through her heart. Internal hemorrhage. Death must have been instantaneous.

HIALMAR: And I! I hunted her from me like an animal! And she crept terrified into the garret and died for love of me! [*sobbing*] I can never atone to her! I can never tell her— [*clenches his hands and cries upward*] Oh, Thou above—if Thou be indeed! Why hast Thou done this thing to me?

GINA: Hush, hush, you mustn't go on that awful way. We had no right to keep her, I suppose.

MOLVIK: The child is not dead but sleepeth.

RELLING: Bosh!

HIALMAR: [*becomes calm, goes over to the sofa, folds his arms and looks at* HEDVIG] There she lies so stiff and still.

RELLING: [*tries to loosen the pistol*] She's holding it so tight, so tight.

GINA: No, no, Relling; don't break her fingers; let the pistol be.

HIALMAR: She shall take it with her.

GINA: Yes, let her. But the child mustn't lie here for a show. She shall go to her own room, so she shall. Help me, Ekdal.

[HIALMAR *and* GINA *take* HEDVIG *between them.*]

HIALMAR: [*as they are carrying her*] Oh Gina, Gina, can you survive this?

GINA: We must help each other to bear it. For now, at least, she belongs to both of us.

MOLVIK: [*stretches out his arms and mumbles*] Blessed be the Lord; to earth thou shalt return; to earth thou shalt return—

RELLING: [*whispers*] Hold your tongue, you fool; you're drunk.

[HIALMAR *and* GINA *carry the body out through the kitchen door.* RELLING *shuts it after them.* MOLVIK *slinks out into the passage.*]

RELLING: [*goes over to* GREGERS *and says*] No one shall ever convince me that the pistol went off by accident.

GREGERS: [*who has stood terrified, with convulsive twitchings*] Who can say how the dreadful thing happened?

RELLING: The powder has burned the body of her dress. She must have pressed the pistol right against her breast and fired.

GREGERS: Hedvig has not died in vain. Did you not see how sorrow set free what is noble in him?

RELLING: Most people are ennobled by the actual presence of death. But how long do you suppose this nobility will last in him?

GREGERS: Why should it not endure and increase throughout his life?

RELLING: Before a year is over, little Hedvig will be nothing to him but a pretty theme for declamation.

GREGERS: How dare you say that of Hialmar Ekdal?

RELLING: We will talk of this again, when the grass has first withered on her grave. Then you'll hear him spouting about "the child too early torn from her father's heart"; then you'll see him steep himself in a syrup of sentiment and self-admiration and self-pity. Just you wait!

GREGERS: If you are right and I am wrong, then life is not worth living.

RELLING: Oh, life would be quite tolerable, after all, if only we could be rid of the confounded fools that keep on pestering us, in our poverty, with the claim of the ideal.

GREGERS: [*looking straight before him*] In that case I am glad that my destiny is what it is.

RELLING: May I inquire—what is your destiny?

GREGERS: [*going*] To be the thirteenth at table.

RELLING: The devil it is.

GEORG KAISER

FROM MORN TILL MIDNIGHT

Authorized Translation
by
Ulrich Weisstein

DRAMATIS PERSONAE

THE TELLER
HIS MOTHER
HIS WIFE
HIS TWO DAUGHTERS
THE BANK MANAGER
THE ASSISTANT
THE DOORMAN
FIRST *and* SECOND GENTLEMAN
MESSENGER BOY
HOUSEMAID
THE LADY
HER SON
THE WAITER AT THE HOTEL
JEWISH REFEREES
FOUR FEMALE MASKS
THEIR MALE COMPANIONS
WAITER *at the Dance Hall*
SALVATION ARMY LASS
OFFICERS *and* SOLDIERS *of the*
    Salvation Army
AUDIENCE *at a Meeting of the Salva-*
    tion Army: CLERK, SPORTSMEN,
    WORKER, CALL GIRL, *etc.*
POLICEMAN

Place of the Action: The little town W. and the big town B.
[W. stands for Weimar, B. for Berlin.]

342

PART I

SCENE I———*Lobby of a small bank. At left, the* TELLER's *window and a door marked "Manager". At center, a door marked "Vault". Entrance at right, behind a barrier. Next to it a wicker chair and a table with water pitcher and glass. At the window, the* TELLER; *at a desk, the* ASSISTANT, *writing. The wicker chair is occupied by the stout* GENTLEMAN, *who snorts audibly. Somebody exits at right. A* MESSENGER BOY *at the window follows him with his eyes.*

[TELLER *raps the window ledge.*]

[MESSENGER BOY *quickly places a note on the waiting hand.*]

[TELLER *writes, fetches money from underneath the ledge, counts it on his hand and, subsequently, on the counting board.*]

[MESSENGER BOY *moves aside with the counting board and pours the money into a linen bag.*]

GENTLEMAN: [*rises*] Now it's the turn of us stout ones [*He pulls a tightly stuffed leather bag from his coat pocket.*]

[*A* LADY *enters. Expensive fur, rustling silk.*]

[GENTLEMAN *stands perplexed.*]

LADY: [*opens the barrier with some effort, involuntarily smiles at the stout* GENTLEMAN] At last.

[GENTLEMAN *twists his mouth.*]

[TELLER *raps impatiently.*]

[LADY *gestures questioningly toward the* GENTLEMAN.]

GENTLEMAN: [*making room for her*] We stout ones always come last.

[LADY *bows slightly, steps up to the window.*]

[TELLER *raps.*]

LADY: [*opens her purse, removes an envelope and hands it to the* TELLER] Three thousand, please.

[TELLER *turns the envelope over in his hand and pushes it back.*]

LADY: [*comprehends*] Sorry. [*Takes the letter out of the envelope and offers it to the* TELLER.]

[TELLER *repeats the motion.*]

LADY: [*unfolds the letter*] Three thousand, please.

[TELLER *glances at the letter and hands it to the* ASSISTANT.]

[ASSISTANT *gets up and exits through the door marked "Manager".*]

GENTLEMAN: [*sitting down on the wicker chair*] I need more time. Stout ones always need more time.

[TELLER *busy with counting money.*]

LADY: Bills, please

[TELLER *remains hunched over.*]

MANAGER: [*young, plump, enters at left holding the letter*] Who is . . . [*Falls silent as he sees the* LADY.]

[ASSISTANT *writing at his desk.*]

GENTLEMAN: [*loudly*] Good morning, Sir.

MANAGER: [*paying little attention*] How do you do?

GENTLEMAN: [*patting his paunch*] The ball's rolling, Sir.

MANAGER: [*laughs curtly. To the* LADY] You wish to draw money on our bank?

LADY: Three thousand.

MANAGER: Three, yes, three thousand I would gladly pay . . .

LADY: Is anything wrong with the letter?

MANAGER: [*cloyingly polite*] The letter is fine. For twelve thousand. [*spelling the word*] B-A-N-K-O.

LADY: My bank in Florence assured me . . .

MANAGER: The letter was properly issued by the bank.

LADY: Then I don't see . . .

MANAGER: In Florence you asked for this letter to be issued.

LADY: Indeed.

MANAGER: Twelve thousand, payable in the cities . . .

LADY: Which I touch on my trip.

MANAGER: Your bank in Florence requested several signatures . . .

LADY: Which were sent to the banks designated in the letter, in order to prove my identity.

MANAGER: The note with your signature has not reached us.

GENTLEMAN: [*Coughs and winks slyly at the* MANAGER.]

LADY: I'll have to wait, then, until . . .

MANAGER: We have to have some sort of evidence.

[A GENTLEMAN *with fur cap and woollen scarf enters and goes to the window. He looks angrily at the* LADY.]

LADY: This comes so unexpected . . .

MANAGER: [*laughing coarsely*] We didn't expect it either.

LADY: I need the money so urgently.

GENTLEMAN IN THE WICKER CHAIR: [*laughs heartily.*]

MANAGER: We all do.

[GENTLEMAN IN THE WICKER CHAIR *roars with laughter.*]

MANAGER: [*seeking an audience*] I, for instance . . . [*to the* GENTLEMAN AT THE WINDOW] You have more time than I do. Don't you see that I am still talking to the lady?—My dear lady, did you think that I would pay merely on the basis of your . . .

[GENTLEMAN IN THE WICKER CHAIR *giggles.*]

LADY: [*quickly*] I'm staying at the Elephant.

[GENTLEMAN IN THE WICKER CHAIR *neighs.*]

MANAGER: I am glad to know your address. I am a frequent guest at the Elephant.

LADY: Couldn't the owner vouch for me?

MANAGER: Has he come to know you that well already?

[GENTLEMAN IN THE WICKER CHAIR *is greatly amused.*]

LADY: My luggage is in the hotel.

MANAGER: Should I search your trunks and suitcases?

LADY: This is a most embarrassing situation.

MANAGER: We're in the same boat, then. You are not in a position, I am not in a position. That's our position. [*He returns the letter to her*]

LADY: What would you advise me to do?

MANAGER: Our town is a nice place to be in, and the Elephant a well-known house. There's a special air about the area. You'll make one or the other interesting acquaintance; and the time passes, now day, now night, as the case may be.

LADY: I don't mind a brief delay.

MANAGER: The guests at the Elephant will be glad to contribute.

LADY: But today I urgently need three thousand.

MANAGER: [*to the* GENTLEMAN IN THE WICKER CHAIR] Does anyone here offer security for three thousand marks due to the lady from abroad?

LADY: I could not possibly accept such an offer. May I ask you to call me right away when the confirmation arrives from Florence? I can be reached in my room at the Elephant.

MANAGER: In person, if you so desire.

LADY: Whichever way is quicker. [*She returns the letter to the envelope and puts the latter into her pocket.*] I'll stop by in the afternoon.

MANAGER: I am at your service.

[LADY *greets curtly and exits.*]

[GENTLEMAN AT THE WINDOW *moves up and bangs a crumpled note on the ledge.*]

MANAGER: [*Pays no attention and looks amusedly at the* GENTLEMAN IN THE WICKER CHAIR.*]

GENTLEMAN IN THE WICKER CHAIR: [*Sniffs the air.*]

MANAGER: [*laughs*] All the fragrance of Italy—from the perfume bottle.

[GENTLEMAN IN THE WICKER CHAIR *fans himself with the palm of his hand.*]

MANAGER: Makes one hot, doesn't it?

GENTLEMAN IN THE WICKER CHAIR: [*pours water into a glass*] Three thousand is a bit much. [*drinks*] Three hundred wouldn't be bad either.

MANAGER: Perhaps you could bid lower—at the Elephant, in her room?

GENTLEMAN IN THE WICKER CHAIR: That's not for us stout ones.

MANAGER: With our moral paunch, we are legally protected.

GENTLEMAN AT THE WINDOW: [*Slams his fist on the ledge for the second time.*]

MANAGER: [*unruffled*] What do you want? [*He smooths the note and hands it to the teller.*]

[MESSENGER BOY, *who had stared first at the* LADY, *then at the speakers, misses the barrier and bumps into the* GENTLEMAN IN THE WICKER CHAIR.*]

GENTLEMAN IN THE WICKER CHAIR: [*snatches his money bag*] Yes, my boy, it's expensive to stare at pretty girls. Now your bag's gone.

[MESSENGER BOY *smiles at him sheepishly.*]

GENTLEMAN IN THE WICKER CHAIR: What are you going to do now when you get home?

[MESSENGER BOY *laughs.*]

GENTLEMAN IN THE WICKER CHAIR: [*returns the bag to him*] Keep that in mind. You're not the first one whose eyes run away with him, and the whole person follows.

[MESSENGER BOY *exits.*]

[TELLER *has counted out a few coins.*]

MANAGER: And they entrust money to such a rogue.

GENTLEMAN IN THE WICKER CHAIR: Stupidity is its own reward.

MANAGER: A boss should know better. Such a fellow bolts at the first occasion. The born embezzler. [*to the* GENTLEMAN AT THE WINDOW] Anything wrong?

[GENTLEMAN AT THE WINDOW *examines each coin.*]

MANAGER: This is a quarter. Makes a total of forty-five pfennigs. All that's coming to you.

[GENTLEMAN AT THE WINDOW *slowly pockets the money.*]

GENTLEMAN IN THE WICKER CHAIR: Why don't you deposit your capital in the vault? Now we stout ones unload.

[GENTLEMAN AT THE WINDOW *exits at right.*]

MANAGER: And what do you bring?

GENTLEMAN: [*who has risen, places a leather bag on the ledge and pulls out his billfold*] Your customers do inspire confidence. [*he shakes hands with the* MANAGER]

MANAGER: In business matters, at any rate, pretty eyes do not affect us.

GENTLEMAN: [*counting out his money*] How old was she? Guess.

MANAGER: I haven't seen her yet without make-up.

GENTLEMAN: What does she want here?

MANAGER: We'll find that out tonight at the Elephant.

GENTLEMAN: Whose turn do you think it will be?

MANAGER: In the long run, perhaps everybody's.

GENTLEMAN: What does she need the three thousand marks for?

MANAGER: She'll need them somehow.

GENTLEMAN: I wish her the best of luck.

MANAGER: In what?

GENTLEMAN: In scooping up her three thousand.

MANAGER: From me?

GENTLEMAN: It doesn't matter from whom.

MANAGER: I wonder when we'll get the note from Florence.

GENTLEMAN: If you get it.

MANAGER: If we get it at all, that's what I should like to know.

GENTLEMAN: We could make a collection to tide her over.

MANAGER: That's what she may have in mind.

GENTLEMAN: Exactly.

MANAGER: [*laughs*] Have you inherited a fortune?

GENTLEMAN: [*to the teller*] Put this away for me. [*to the* MANAGER] It doesn't matter whether we keep our cash or draw interest from you. Open an account for the Building Fund.

MANAGER: [*sharply to the* ASSISTANT] Account for the Building Fund.

GENTLEMAN: There's more to come.

MANAGER: Join the club, ladies and gentlemen. We can use you right now.

GENTLEMAN: Sixty thousand, then—fifty in bills and ten in gold coins.

[TELLER *counts.*]

MANAGER: [*after a pause*] How are things going with you otherwise?

GENTLEMAN: [*to the* TELLER] Yes, that bill is patched.

MANAGER: We'll take it, of course. We'll get rid of it. I'll keep it for our client from Florence. She, too, wore beauty patches.

GENTLEMAN: But this one hides a thousand marks.

MANAGER: Collector's item.[1]

GENTLEMAN: [*laughs uproariously*] Collector's item. That's great.

MANAGER: [*with tears in his eyes*] Collector's item. [*hands him the teller's receipt*] Your receipt. [*choking with laughter*] Sixty thou . . .

GENTLEMAN: [*takes the receipt, glances at it, repeats*] Sixty thou . . .

MANAGER: Collector's . . .

GENTLEMAN: Coll. . . . [*They shake hands.*]

MANAGER: Until tonight, then.

GENTLEMAN: [*nodding approvingly*] Collector's . . . [*He buttons up his coat and exits, shaking his head.*]

> [MANAGER *wipes off the tears that have collected behind his pince-nez, then exits at left.*]

> [TELLER *bundles the bills just received and stacks the coins.*]

MANAGER: [*returns*] This lady from Florence—who pretends to come from Florence—have you ever seen anybody like her? Fur—perfumed. The odor clings. One breathes adventures with the air. That's the grand style. Italy. That's stunning, fabulous. Riviera—Mentone—Bordighera—Nizza —Monte Carlo. Yes, where oranges grow, fraud also flourishes. Not a single square foot of soil down there is free from fraud. There's where the scheme was hatched. The gang disperses in all directions. They prefer the smaller towns, off the main highways. Then swimming in furs and silk. Women. These are the modern Sirens. Music from the Mediterranean— O bella Napoli. Seductive glances, and you are stripped to the shirt. Down to the skin, the naked, naked skin. [*he taps the* TELLER's *back with his pencil*] I am convinced that the bank in Florence, which has issued the letter, knows as little about it as—the Pope lives on the moon. The whole thing's a fraud, carefully contrived. And the masterminds don't sit in Florence but in Monte Carlo. That's my first guess. Believe me. She is one of those creatures who thrive in the morass of the gambling den. And I bet that we won't see her again. Since her first attempt failed, she won't try a second time. I may joke at times, but my eyes are sharp. We bankers. I should have dropped Lieutenant Werde a hint. But that's not my business. After all, a bank must keep its secrets. [*at the door*] Check the foreign papers. When you read about a confidence woman who has been clapped into jail, you'll know how right I was. Then we'll hear more about our friend from Florence than we shall see of her fur either today or tomorrow. [*Exits.*]

> [TELLER *seals rolls of coins.*]

DOORMAN: [*enters at right with letters, hands them to the assistant*] I'll need a receipt for this registered letter.

> [ASSISTANT *stamps the paper and returns it to the* DOORMAN.]

---

[1] "Collector's item" (In German, a word play, *Liebhaberwert* meaning both the value attached to certain objects by collectors and, literally translated, lover's value).

    [DOORMAN *arranges water pitcher and glass on the table, then exits.*]

    [ASSISTANT *takes the letters to the director's office, returns.*]

LADY: [*returns and hurries to the window*] Excuse me.

    [TELLER *extends the palm of his hand.*]

LADY: [*with greater emphasis*] Excuse me.

    [TELLER *raps the ledge.*]

LADY: I would hate to bother the director once more.

    [TELLER *raps the ledge.*]

LADY: [*smiling in despair*] Please tell me. Isn't it possible for me to leave the whole letter of credit with the bank and receive an advance payment of three thousand?

    [TELLER *raps the ledge impatiently.*]

LADY: I would even be willing to offer my diamonds as security. Any jeweller in town will price them for you. [*she slips off one glove and busies herself with her bracelet*]

    [HOUSEMAID *enters quickly at right, sits down on the wicker chair and rummages through her shopping basket.*]

    [LADY *turns around, slightly flustered. As she seeks support for her arm, her hand touches that of the* TELLER.]

    [TELLER *bends over the hand in his hand. Now the lenses of his glasses shoot upward along the wrist.*]

    [HOUSEMAID, *greatly relieved, finds the bill.*]

    [LADY *nods approvingly in her direction.*]

    [HOUSEMAID *arranges things in her basket.*]

    [LADY, *turning to the* TELLER, *meets his face.*]

    [TELLER *smiles.*]

LADY: [*withdraws her hand*] I don't want the bank to violate its rules. [*she puts on her bracelet, trying to fix the clasp. Offering her arm to the* TELLER] Would you be kind enough? I can't manage with one hand.

    [TELLER, *as the bushes of his beard sway, his glances sink into the blooming sockets of wide open eyes.*]

LADY: [*to the* HOUSEMAID] Would you help me, Miss?

    [HOUSEMAID *complies.*]

LADY: Now the safety catch. [*with a slight exclamation of pain*] You're pinching my naked flesh. This will do. Thank you, Miss. [*She greets the* TELLER *and exits.*]

    [HOUSEMAID, *at the window, presents her bill.*]

    [TELLER, *takes it with flowing hands, gropes under the ledge and dishes out money.*]

HOUSEMAID: [*looks at the money and exclaims*] That's not what I get.

    [TELLER *writes.*]

    [ASSISTANT *begins to pay attention.*]

HOUSEMAID: [*to the assistant*] It's too much.

    [ASSISTANT *looks at the* TELLER.]

    [TELLER *scoops in part of the money.*]

HOUSEMAID: Still too much.

    [TELLER *writes.*]

    [HOUSEMAID *shakes her head and puts the money away, then exits.*]

TELLER: [*the sound writhing up through hoarseness*] Fetch—glass of water!
>   [ASSISTANT *goes to the table.*]
TELLER: That's stale. Fresh water—from the tap.
>   [ASSISTANT *takes the glass to the vault.*]
>   [TELLER *reaches for the bell button and pushes it.*]
>   [DOORMAN *enters.*]
TELLER: Get me some fresh water!
DOORMAN: I can't leave the door.
TELLER: For my sake. That's disgusting. I want water from the tap.
>   [DOORMAN *takes the pitcher to the vault.*]
>   [TELLER *rapidly pockets the bills and coins he has just handled. Then
>   he takes his coat from the rack and throws it over his arm. The hat
>   as well. He leaves the window and exits at right.*]
MANAGER: [*enters, reading a letter*] Here's the note from Florence.
>   [ASSISTANT *enters with the glass of water.*]
>   [DOORMAN *enters with the pitcher of water.*]
MANAGER: [*catching sight of them*] For Pete's sake, what's the matter?

SCENE II——*The writing room of a hotel. At rear, a glass door. At left, a desk
with a telephone. At right, a couch, an easy chair, a table with newspapers,
etc.*

>   [LADY *writes.*]
>   [SON *enters, wearing hat and coat. He carries a large, flat object
>   wrapped in a cloth.*]
LADY: [*surprised*] You have it?
SON: The wine dealer is downstairs. The stupid fellow is afraid I might bolt.
LADY: And this morning he was glad to get rid of it.
SON: He may suspect something.
LADY: You must have alerted him.
SON: I looked pleased.
LADY: That would make the blind see.
SON: Let them open their eyes. But don't worry, mother, the price is still the
>   same.
LADY: Is he waiting?
SON: Let him wait.
LADY: I am sorry to have to tell you . . .
SON: [*kisses her*] Quiet now. Don't look until I ask you to. [*he removes his hat
>   and coat, places the picture on an easy chair and removes the cloth*]
LADY: Not yet?
SON: [*very gently*] Mother!
>   [LADY *turns around in her chair.*]
SON: [*comes up and embraces her*] Well?
LADY: That's hardly fit for a wine cellar.
SON: It was turned to the wall. The man had pasted his picture on the back.
LADY: Did you buy that, too?
SON: [*laughs*] How do you like it?

LADY: I find it—very naive.

SON: Splendid, isn't it? Marvellous, for a Cranach.

LADY: Do you think of it so highly as a picture?

SON: As a picture, of course. But notice also the strange conception. Strange for Cranach and for the treatment of this subject in general. Is there anything like it in the Pitti, the Uffizi, the Vatican gallery? There is nothing of the kind in the Louvre. This is surely the first and only erotic presentation of Adam and Eve. The apple is still lying in the grass, and the snake peeps out of the ineffable foliage. The event, then, occurs in Paradise itself, and not after the expulsion. That is the true fall. A rarity. Cranach has painted a dozen Adams and Eves, stiff, the branch between them and separating them. It says there: they know each other. Here, for the first time, is the blissful gospel of humanity: they loved each other. Here a German master shows himself an erotic painter of the most southerly passion. [*close to the picture*] And this control despite the ecstasy. This line of the male arm intersects the female hip. The horizontal formed by one pair of thighs, and the vertical by the other. The observer's eye is never strained. The painting radiates love. The flesh tone, naturally, enhances this effect. Don't you feel the same way?

LADY: You are as naive as your picture.

SON: What do you mean?

LADY: May I ask you to hide the picture in your room?

SON: At home, it will touch me even more strongly. Florence and this Cranach. The conclusion of my book will have to be delayed. I shall have to digest the new experience. It has to enter his bloodstream, or the art historian commits a sacrilege.—Right now, I am rather exhausted. To find the picture on the first stop of our journey!

LADY: But you were sure that you would find it here.

SON: The event still staggers me. It's fabulous. Mother, I am a child of luck.

LADY: You reap the fruits of your thorough research.

SON: And without your help, without your kindness?

LADY: I share your happiness.

SON: You are so patient with me. I tear you away from your quiet, pleasant life in Fiesole. You are Italian, and I rush you through Germany in midwinter. You spend the nights in sleeping cars or second rate hotels and are forced to bicker with all sorts of people.

LADY: Indeed, I have had my share of that.

SON: I promise to hurry. I am just as impatient to stow away my treasure. Let's leave at three P.M. Would you give me the three thousand?

LADY: I don't have them.

SON: The owner of the picture is waiting.

LADY: The bank refused to pay. The letter from Florence must have been delayed.

SON: I have promised to pay.

LADY: You will have to return the picture until the bank receives the order.

SON: Can't that be expedited?

LADY: I have composed a telegram and shall now dispatch it. We have travelled fast . . .

> [WAITER *knocks.*]

LADY: Come in.

WAITER: A gentleman from the bank wishes to see the lady.

LADY: [*to her* SON] They are sending the money. [*to the* WAITER] Let him enter.

> [WAITER *exits.*]

SON: You call me when you have the money. I should hate to see the man leave.

LADY: I'll phone you.

SON: I'll be downstairs. [*Exits.*]

> [LADY *closes the writing pad. The* WAITER *and the* TELLER *appear behind the glass door. The* TELLER *overtakes the* WAITER *and opens the door. The* WAITER *turns around and exits.*]
>
> [TELLER, *the coat still on his arm, enters.*]
>
> [LADY *points to an easy chair and sits down on the couch.*]
>
> [TELLER *sits down, still holding his coat.*]

LADY: The bank has . . .

> [TELLER *sees the picture.*]

LADY: The picture is closely connected with my visit to the bank.

TELLER: Your portrait?

LADY: Do you see a resemblance?

TELLER: [*smiling*] At the wrist.

LADY: Are you an expert?

TELLER: I wish to know more.[2]

LADY: You like these pictures?

TELLER: I am in on the picture.

LADY: Are there other works like it in this town? You would do me a favor. That matters more than the money.

TELLER: I have money.

LADY: Perhaps the sum mentioned in the letter of credit will be too small.

TELLER: [*produces the bills and rolls of coins*] This is sufficient.

LADY: Twelve thousand is the limit.

TELLER: Sixty thousand.

LADY: How so?

TELLER: That's my business.

LADY: How shall I . . . ?

TELLER: We travel.

LADY: Where?

TELLER: Across the border. Pack your suitcase, if you have one. You leave from the local station. I'll walk to the next one and board the train there. We spend the first night . . . Time table? [*He finds one on the table*]

LADY: Are you bringing more than three thousand from the bank?

---

[2] "Expert . . ." (In German, a word play: "Sind Sie Kenner?—"Ich wünsche mehr kennenzulernen").

TELLER: [*busy*] I pocketed sixty thousand. Fifty thousand in bills and ten thousand in gold coins.

LADY: My share amounts to . . . ?

TELLER: [*opens a roll of coins, counts the pieces expertly on his hand and then on the table*] Take them. Put them away. We may be overheard. The door has glass panes. Five hundred in coins.

LADY: Five hundred?

TELLER: There's more to come. When we are safe. We must not let anything be seen. Quickly. Put it away. This hour is not fit for caresses. The wheel turns rapidly, and woe to the arm that tries to stop it. [*He rises quickly*]

LADY: I need three thousand.

TELLER: If the police find it in your pocket, you go to jail.

LADY: What do the police have to do with it?

TELLER: You suffused the bank office. Suspicion will fall on you, and our complicity is revealed.

LADY: I entered the bank.

TELLER: Boldly.

LADY: I asked . . .

TELLER: You tried . . .

LADY: I sought . . .

TELLER: To defraud the bank when you presented your forged letter.

LADY: [*taking the letter from her purse*] This letter is forged?

TELLER: As false as your jewels.

LADY: I offered my jewels as security. Why are my diamonds false?

TELLER: Ladies like you seek to impress.

LADY: What am I like? Blackhaired. Dark complexion. I am from the South. Toscana.

TELLER: Monte Carlo.

LADY: No, Florence.

TELLER: [*suddenly noticing the* SON's *hat and coat*] Am I too late?

LADY: Too late?

TELLER: Where is he? I shall negotiate with him. He will not refuse a deal. I have the money. How much shall I offer? What compensation would seem to be adequate? How much shall I stuff into his pocket? I'll go up to fifteen thousand.—Is he asleep? Stretching on his bed? Where is your room? Twenty thousand—five thousand for immediate cessation. [*He picks up the* SON's *hat and coat*] I'll take him his things.

LADY: [*puzzled*] The gentleman is in the hall.

TELLER: That's too dangerous. It's too busy downstairs. Ask him to come up here. I'll checkmate him here. Ring the bell. The waiter must hurry. Twenty thousand—in bills. [*he counts them out*]

LADY: Can my son vouch for me?

TELLER: [*shrinks back*] Your—son?

LADY: I am his travelling companion. We are on a study trip that takes us from Florence to Germany. My son is collecting material for a study in art history.

TELLER: [*stares at her*] Son?

LADY: Is that so strange?

TELLER: [*confused*] This picture?

LADY: Is his lucky find. It costs him three thousand. The money I need so urgently. A wholesale wine dealer, whose name will be familiar to you, sells it for that amount.

TELLER: Fur—silk—it shimmered and rustled—the air was heavy with perfumes.

LADY: It is winter. I am not extravagantly dressed.

TELLER: The forged letter.

LADY: I was about to send my bank a telegram.

TELLER: Your bare wrist—around which I was to wreathe the bracelet?!

LADY: By itself, the left hand is clumsy.

TELLER: [*dully*] I have—taken the money.

LADY: [*amused*] Are you and the police satisfied now? My son is well known in scholarly circles.

TELLER: Now—at this moment my absence will be noticed. I had asked for water, in order to get rid of the assistant. For two glasses, to get rid of the doorman as well. The bills and coins are gone. I have embezzled. I cannot let myself be seen in the streets and on the square.[3] I can't enter the station. The police have been alerted. Sixty thousand—I have to run cross country, through the snow, before the alarm is sounded.

LADY: [*aghast*] Be quiet, for heaven's sake.

TELLER: I took all the money. You suffused the bank. You shimmered and rustled. You lowered your naked hand into mine. Your scent overwhelmed, your mouth smelled . . .

LADY: I am a lady.

TELLER: [*insistently*] And now you must . . .

LADY: [*controlling herself*] Are you married? [*in response to his roving gesture*] I think that means a lot. Unless I am to regard the whole thing as a joke. You have acted rashly. You repair the damage by returning to the bank and pretending that you suddenly fell ill. You still have the full amount?

TELLER: I have robbed the bank.

LADY: [*abruptly*] That is none of my business.

TELLER: I have stolen money.

LADY: You annoy me, Sir.

TELLER: Now you must . . .

LADY: What I should do . . .

TELLER: You really must . . .

LADY: Ridiculous.

TELLER: I have robbed and stolen. I have given myself away. I have ruined my life. All the bridges are burned. I am a thief, a robber. [*leaning over the table*] You really must, you really must . . .

LADY: I'll call my son; perhaps . . .

---

3 In German "Ich darf mich nicht in den Strassen—auf dem Markt sehen lassen," an allusion to *Faust*, where Margarete says, with reference to the jewelry which Mephisto has furnished at Faust's request: "Darf mich, leider, nicht auf der Gassen, noch in der Kirche mit sehen lassen."

TELLER: [*changed, nimbly*] Call somebody? Tom, Dick, and Harry? Rouse people? Marvellous!—Foolish. Inept. They won't catch me. I won't fall into that trap. I, too, have brains, ladies and gentlemen. Your wit is slower; I am always ten miles ahead. Don't move. Sit still until . . . [*he puts the money away, pulls his hat down, presses the coat to his chest*] Until I . . . [*Exits lithely and quietly through the glass door.*]

    [LADY *stays behind, confused.*]

SON: [*enters*] The gentleman from the bank has left the hotel. You seem to be upset, mother. Has the money . . .

LADY: The conversation was strenuous. Financial matters, my son. You know such things always upset me a little.

SON: Are there any further delays in the payment.

LADY: Perhaps I had better tell you.

SON: Must I return the picture?

LADY: It is not the picture I am thinking of.

SON: But that's what matters most to us.

LADY: I think I shall have to notify the police immediately.

SON: Notify of what?

LADY: Dispatch the telegram! I must have a confirmation from my bank.

SON: Your letter of credit won't do, then?

LADY: No. Not quite. Go to the telegraph office. I don't want to send the doorman.

SON: And when shall we get the money?

    [*The telephone rings.*]

LADY: There's the call. [*at the phone*] Has arrived. I am to fetch it myself? Gladly. Not at all, Sir. Florence is far away. The Italian mail service. What? Why? I see. Via Berlin; that's round about. Not in the least, Sir. In ten minutes. Good bye. [*to the* SON] It's all settled. No need for the telegram. [*she tears up the form*] The picture is yours. Your wine dealer can join us. He'll get his money at the bank. Wrap up your treasure. From the bank we'll go directly to the station. [*at the phone, while her* SON *covers the picture*] May I have the bill, please? Rooms fourteen and sixteen. Right away please.

SCENE III——*A snow-covered field with a tree whose branches hang down in great profusion. The sun casts blueish shadows.*

TELLER: [*enters, walking backwards. He shovels snow with his hands, in order to cover up his track*] What a splendid mechanism is man. How everything moves on its hinges—noiselessly. Suddenly one discovers new abilities and puts them to use. How do my hands act? Where did they shovel snow? Now they heave the masses so that the flakes scatter. And my track across the snow-field is wiped out. My incognito is perfect. [*he removes his wet cuffs*] Moisture and frost are conducive to severe colds. Fever suddenly erupts and clouds one's mind. One loses control over one's actions and, stretched out on the sickbed, gives oneself away. [*he removes the links and throws the cuffs away*] Done your duty. Lie there. You'll be missed in the wash. Lament croaks through the kitchen: a pair of cuffs are missing. Catastrophe in the washing tub. Twilight of the gods. [*he picks up the cuffs and stuffs them into his coat pockets*] Stupendous. My brain's going full speed. With utmost precision. I wrestle with the snow and betray myself through two carelessly dropped items of clothing. Usually it is a trifle, an oversight, something hastily done that gives away the culprit. Hoopla. [*looking for a comfortable seat in the crook of the tree*] I am really curious. The tension has greatly increased. I have reason to expect great discoveries. Rapidly gained experiences will aid me. In the morning, a loyal employee. Sizeable fortunes are entrusted to me. The Building Fund deposits enormous sums. At noon, an arch scoundrel. Knowing all the tricks. The technique of flight perfected in detail. The deed done and over with. Stunning feat. And the day only half gone. [*he rests his chin on the back of his fist.*]

I am ready to face whatever is in store for me. I have sure signs that I can meet all demands. I'm on the march, and there's no turning back. I march. Let's play the trumps. I have staked sixty thousand and am waiting for the ace. I am playing too high to lose. No excuses, then, show your cards and see. Is that clear? [*he laughs hoarsely*]

Now you will have to, my pretty lady. Your cue, my silken lady. Let me have it, shimmering lady. Why, you're scratching the whole scene. Silly goose. What a poor actress. Women like you should fulfill their natural duty by breeding children rather than bother the prompter.—Excuse me, you've got a son. That sets the record straight. I liquidate my suspicions. Fare well and give my regards to the manager. His frog's eyes will cover you with slime, but never mind. The man is poorer by sixty thousand. But the Building Fund will repair the damage. That stinks. I release you from all obligations towards me. You are fired, you may go.— Stop. Take my thanks along with you, into the train. What? Nothing to thank you for? I should think, a lot. Not worth mentioning?—I am deeply indebted to you. For heaven's sake. I owe you my life. I exaggerate? Rustling, you have instilled new life into me. A leap after you places me in the center of incredible happenings. And with this freight in my pocket I pay cash for all favors. [*with a nonchalant gesture*] Slink off, now. A higher bid has been made, and with your slender means—you should think of your son—you won't be able to top it. [*he removes the bundle of bills from his pocket and slams it on his hand*] I pay cash. The amount is handy. The payment precedes the offer. Let's see now what's in the offing. [*he scans the field*] Snow, snow, sun, silence. [*he shakes his head and puts the money away*] It would be a poor deal to buy snow at that price. I withdraw the offer. No decent business. [*raising his arms*] I have to pay. I have the cash. Where's the merchandise bought with the whole self? With sixty thousand, and the buyer, flesh and bones, into the bargain? [*shouting*] You must supply. You must match value with value. [*The sun is hidden by clouds. He descends from the crook.*] The earth labors—spring storms. That clicks, that clicks. I knew I hadn't called in vain. The request was urgent. The chaos is offended. It does not want to be put to shame by my resolute deed of this morning. I knew all along that in such cases one must persist. Fight close to the bull and without protection.[4] That's what I call pluck. Who is it to whom I raise my hat so politely?

[*His hat is snatched away by the wind. The storm has lashed the snow from the branches. What remains in the crown has the shape of a human skeleton with grinning jaws. A bony hand holds the hat.*]

Did you sit behind me all this time to spy on me? Are you an agent of the police? Not in this ridiculously narrow sense. Broadly speaking: the police of existence. Are you the final answer to my urgent questions? Do you want to imply, by your shabby appearance, that this is the final outcome? That's rather meager. Very meager, that is to say, nothing. I reject the answer as incomplete. That doesn't do me any good. Close your old bones shop. I am not that easily deceived. That process would be incredibly simple. You save one further complications. But I like complications. Fare well—if that is possible in your condition. There are a few things I want to do first. When one travels, one can't stop at every door, not even when cordially invited. Before nightfall, I'll have to meet a number of obligations. You can't be the first one. Perhaps the last. But even that only for lack of anything better. We'll see. Call me up around midnight. The exchange will give you my new number. Excuse me for addressing you so formally. We are buddies, after all, as one can easily see. I even think that you're inside me. Unravel yourself from the branches that pierce you from all sides, and slide into me. In my compromising situation I hate to leave any traces. But first return my hat to me. [*he removes the hat from the branch, which the storm bends toward him, and bows*] I see we have come to some kind of understanding. Such a beginning inspires confidence and provides much needed support in the turmoil of coming adventures. I certainly appreciate that. Sincerely yours . . . [*The thunder rolls. A final gust of wind blows the phantom skeleton to pieces. The sun breaks through. It is as bright as at the beginning of the scene.*] I knew right away that the apparition would pass.

[*He claps on his hat, raises the collar of his coat and trots off through the spraying snow.*]

PART II

SCENE I——*The living room of the* TELLER's *home. Windows with geraniums past their bloom. Two doors at rear, one at right. Table and chairs. A piano. The* MOTHER *sits at the window. The* FIRST DAUGHTER *embroiders at the table. The* SECOND DAUGHTER *practices the* Tannhäuser *overture. The wife comes and goes through the door at right rear.*

MOTHER: What are you playing now?
FIRST DAUGHTER: It's the *Tannhäuser* overture.

4 "das Mäntelchen vom Leib": another reference to *Faust*.

MOTHER: The *White Lady*[5] is nice, too.

1. DAUGHTER: She hasn't subscribed to it this week.

WIFE: [*enters*] It's time to fix the steaks.

1. DAUGHTER: There's plenty of time left.

WIFE: Yes, there's plenty of time left to fix the steaks. [*Exits.*]

MOTHER: What are you embroidering now?

1. DAUGHTER: The sleeves.

WIFE: [*approaches the* MOTHER] We have steaks today.

MOTHER: Are you fixing them now?

WIFE: There's plenty of time until lunch.

1. DAUGHTER: It's not yet twelve o'clock.

WIFE: No, it's not yet twelve o'clock.

MOTHER: When he comes, it's twelve o'clock.

WIFE: He isn't coming yet.

1. DAUGHTER: When father comes, it's twelve o'clock.

WIFE: Yes. [*Exits.*]

2. DAUGHTER: [*stops playing and listens*] Father?

1. DAUGHTER: [*stops embroidering*] Father?

WIFE: [*enters*] My husband?

MOTHER: My son?

2. DAUGHTER: [*opens the door at right*] Father!

1. DAUGHTER: [*has risen*] Father!

WIFE: The husband.

MOTHER: The son.

[TELLER *enters at right, hangs up his coat and hat.*]

WIFE: Where have you been?

TELLER: At the cemetery.

MOTHER: Did somebody die suddenly?

TELLER: [*pats her back*] One can die suddenly, but one can't be buried suddenly.

WIFE: Where are you coming from?

TELLER: From the grave. I have pushed through clods of earth. There's still ice on my brow. It was exceedingly difficult to break through. Exceedingly difficult. I dirtied my hands a bit. One gets dirty hands when one tries to reach out. One lies so deeply buried. A life like ours really ploughs one under. There are mountains piled on top of one. Trash, garbage—it's a huge dump. The dead lie exactly three feet deep under the ground, but the living sink deeper and deeper.

WIFE: You look frozen—from top to toe.

TELLER: Thawed. Shaken by spring-like storms. It roared and whistled. I tell you, it tore my flesh away, and my bones lay bare. Bones—bleached in a matter of minutes. A real Golgotha. The sun, finally, melted me together again. Thus I became a totally new man. And there I am.

MOTHER: Have you been outdoors?

TELLER: In horrible dungeons, mother. Deeply buried under abysmal towers. Rattling chains deafened my ear. My eyes were pierced by utter darkness.

---

[5] Boeïldieu's opera "La Dame blanche".

WIFE: The bank is closed. The manager invited you for a drink. Has his wife had a baby?

TELLER: He's after a new mistress. An Italian girl. Fur—silk—where the oranges bloom. Polished wrists. Black hair. A dark complexion. Genuine diamonds. Tos- Tos- the end sounds like Canaan. Get a map. Tos- Canaan. Is there such a thing? Is it an island? A mountain range? A morass? Geography tells everything. But he'll be out of luck. Dropped—brushed off like a speck of dust. There he lies, wriggling on the rug, legs up in the air, our fat little boss.

WIFE: The bank isn't closed?

TELLER: Never, wife. Prisons never close. There are always newcomers. The pilgrimage knows no end. They jump in—like sheep into the stockyards. They crowd over each other. No escape is possible—unless one boldly leaps over their backs.

MOTHER: The back of your coat is torn.

TELLER: Look at my hat. A tramp.

2. DAUGHTER: The lining is torn.

TELLER: Search my pockets—left—right!

> [1. DAUGHTER *pulls out a cuff.*]
> [2. DAUGHTER *pulls out the second cuff.*]

TELLER: Result?

BOTH DAUGHTERS: Your cuffs.

TELLER: Without links. The links are here. Triumph of coldbloodedness. Hat— coat. Things get torn when one jumps over backs. They try to grab you, scratch you. Fences and barriers. Order must prevail. Equality for all. But a daring ruthless leap, and you have cleared the fence. A *tour de force*, and here I am. Nothing behind me—and before me? [*he looks around in the room*]

> [WIFE *stares at him.*]

MOTHER: [*mutters*] He is ill.

WIFE: [*walks resolutely toward the door at right.*]

TELLER: [*stops her. To one daughter*] Get my jacket. [DAUGHTER *exits through the door at left rear and returns with a braided velvet vest. He puts it on.*] My slippers [*The other* DAUGHTER *brings them.*] My skull cap. [DAUGHTER *brings a braided one.*] My pipe.

MOTHER: You shouldn't smoke if you are . . .

WIFE: [*interrupts her*] Shall I light it?

TELLER: [*in domestic garb, relaxes at the table*] Light it!

WIFE: [*eagerly concerned*] Does it burn?

TELLER: [*busy with his pipe*] I'll have to have it thoroughly cleaned. Tobacco must have collected in the stem. I'm meeting some internal resistance. I shouldn't have to pull so hard.

WIFE: Shall I have it fixed immediately?

TELLER: No. Stay here. [*exhaling large puffs of smoke*] It's all right. [*to the* SECOND DAUGHTER] Play!

> [2. DAUGHTER, *at the wife's signal, sits down at the piano and plays.*]

TELLER: What piece is that?

2. DAUGHTER: [*out of breath*] Wagner.

TELLER: [*nods approvingly. To the* FIRST DAUGHTER] And you sew—darn —patch?

1. DAUGHTER: [*sitting down hastily*] I embroider sleeves.

TELLER: How practical! And you, mother?

MOTHER: [*gripped by the general fear*] I was nodding a wink.

TELLER: How peaceful!

MOTHER: Yes, my life is peaceful.

TELLER: [*to his* WIFE] You?

WIFE: I'll fix the steaks.

TELLER: [*nods approvingly*] The kitchen.

WIFE: I'll fix yours now.

TELLER: [*as before*] The kitchen.

> [WIFE *exits.*]

TELLER: [*to the* FIRST DAUGHTER] Open the doors!

> [1. DAUGHTER *opens the doors at rear. The* WIFE *is seen busying herself at the stove. At left, the bedroom with the two beds.*]

WIFE: [*in the door*] Are you very hot? [*returns to the stove*]

TELLER: [*looking around*] Old mother at the window. Daughters embroidering at the table—playing Wagner. Wife fixing lunch. Hedged in by four walls. Family life. Sweet pleasure of togetherness. Mother—son—child are gathered.[6] Cozy home. Enchanting. A room with table and floor lamp. Piano at right. Tile stove. Kitchen, daily bread. Coffee in the morning, steaks at lunch. Bedroom, beds. In, out. Cozy home. At last—on one's back—stiff and pale. The table is moved close to the wall. A yellow coffin, with screw lid. Some crepe around the lamp. The piano closed for a year.

> [2. DAUGHTER *stops playing and, sobbing, runs into the kitchen.*]

WIFE: [*on the threshold, panting*] She's still practicing the new piece.

MOTHER: Why doesn't she subscribe to the *White Lady*?

> [TELLER *puts out his pipe and starts to dress in his street clothes.*]

WIFE: Are you going to the bank? On an errand?

TELLER: To the bank—errand—No.

WIFE: Where are you going, then?

TELLER: Hardest question, wife. To find an answer, I have climbed down from swaying trees. This was my first stop. It was my duty. Everything's nice. I won't deny the obvious advantages. But it does not pass the final test. It isn't here, and that points the way. The answer is clearly No. [*he is fully dressed*]

WIFE: [*distressed*] Husband, how strange you look!

TELLER: Tramp. That's what I said. Don't scold. Better a tramp on the road— than roads without tramps.

WIFE: We'll eat lunch now.

TELLER: Steaks, I smell them.

---

[6] Allusion to the opening line of Gustav Schwab's poem "Das Gewitter," which runs: "Urahne, Grossmutter, Mutter und Kind/In dumpfer Stube beisammen sind."

MOTHER: Before lunch you want to . . . ?

TELLER: A full stomach makes one sleepy.

[MOTHER *waves her arms wildly and collapses.*]

1. DAUGHTER: The grandmother.

2. DAUGHTER: [*from the kitchen*] Grandmother.

[*They fall on their knees.*]

[WIFE *stands immobile.*]

TELLER: [*by the easy chair*] She dies because I leave before lunch. [*he looks at the dead woman*] Pain? Sadness? A flood of tears? Are the ties so closely knit that pain overwhelms when they are severed?[7] Mother—Son. [*He takes the bills from his pockets and weighs them on the palm of his hand. Then he shakes his head and puts them back.*] No total paralysis in pain, no welling up of tears. The eyes are dry, the mind continues to work. I must hurry if I want to reach my goal. [*He places his worn billfold on the table*] Spend it wisely. It's hard-earned money. Keep that well in mind. Take care. [*Exits at right.*]

[WIFE *remains immobile.*]

MANAGER: [*enters through the open door at right*] Is your husband at home? Has your husband been here? I am sorry to have to tell you that he has robbed the bank. We found out a couple of hours ago. The sum in question amounts to sixty thousand marks deposited by the Building Fund. I have not reported the theft, in the hope that he would come to his senses. This is my last attempt. I have come in person. Your husband hasn't been here? [*he looks around and notices the jacket, the pipe, the open doors, etc.*] Apparently . . . [*his attention is caught by the group at the window*] I see, things have come to this point already. In that case . . . [*he shrugs his shoulders and puts on his hat*] Although, personally, I regret, we have to draw the consequences. [*Exits.*]

BOTH DAUGHTERS: [*approach the* WIFE] Mother . . .

WIFE: [*losing control of herself*] Don't shout at me. Don't stare at me. What do you want from me? Who are you? Grimaces—monkey faces. What do I care! [*leaning over the table, dramatically*] My husband has left me.

[BOTH DAUGHTERS *shyly holding hands.*]

SCENE II——*Sports arena. Tandem race. Arc lights. In the mist that fills the hall, a roughly hewn, unsupported wooden bridge is visible. The* JEWISH GENTLEMEN, *who act as referees, come and go. They all look alike: small, agile creatures in tuxedos and silk hats tilted back, with binoculars fastened to their belts. Thundering noise of wheels on wooden planks. Whistles, screams, catcalls issuing from the densely packed crowd above and below. Bands are playing.*[8]

[7] An untranslatable, typically Expressionistic phrase. In German: "Sind die Bande so eng geknüpft, dass, wenn sie zerrissen, in geballtem Leid es sich erfüllt?"

[8] The reader should realize that, since Kaiser treats the referees not as individuals but as perfectly identical-looking members of a group, and since he wants them to come and go continuously, they are not generally identified as speakers.

A REFEREE: [*enters*] Everything ready?

REFEREE: Look for yourself.

REFEREE: [*using his binoculars*] The evergreens . . .

REFEREE: What's wrong with the evergreens?

REFEREE: No doubt.

REFEREE: What's the matter with them?

REFEREE: Who has arranged them that way?

REFEREE: You're right.

REFEREE: That's crazy.

REFEREE: Did nobody supervise the arrangement?

REFEREE: Simply ridiculous.

REFEREE: The man must have been blind.

REFEREE: Or asleep.

REFEREE: That's the only possible explanation.

REFEREE: What do you say—asleep? This is only the fourth night.

REFEREE: The pots must be pushed aside.

REFEREE: Will you take care of it?

REFEREE: Close to the walls.

REFEREE: We must be able to see the whole track.

REFEREE: The box must be visible.

REFEREE: I'll come along.

> [*All exeunt.*]
>
> REFEREE enters and fires a pistol. Exits.
>
> [TWO REFEREES *enter with a red megaphone.*]

1. REFEREE: How large is the prize?

2. REFEREE: Eighty marks. Fifty for the winner, thirty for the runner-up.

1. REFEREE: Three laps, and no more; or we'll exhaust the riders.

2. REFEREE: [*speaking through the megaphone*] Donation of a prize by a gentleman in the bar. To be run immediately over three laps. Fifty marks for the winner, thirty for the runner-up. [*applause*]

> [SEVERAL REFEREES *enter, one of them carrying a red flag.*]

REFEREE: You give the signal.

REFEREE: Not yet. Team No. 7 is changing riders.

REFEREE: Let's go.

> [REFEREE *lowers the flag. Growing noise, followed by applause and catcalls.*]

REFEREE: The underdogs, too, must get a chance.

REFEREE: I'm glad the bigshots bide their time.

REFEREE: There'll be plenty of work for them tonight.

REFEREE: The riders are terribly excited.

REFEREE: No wonder.

REFEREE: I tell you: this night will bring the decision.

REFEREE: [*shrugging his shoulders*] The Americans are still fresh.

REFEREE: Our Germans will put them to the test.

REFEREE: The audience will get its money's worth.

REFEREE: [*through the glass*] Now the box is visible.

> [*All, except the* REFEREE *with the megaphone, exeunt.*]

REFEREE: [*enters with a note*] The result.

REFEREE: [*through the megaphone*] Prize from the bar: fifty marks for number eleven, thirty marks for number four.

> [*Flourish. Applause and catcalls. The bridge is empty. A* REFEREE *enters with the* TELLER. *The latter wears a tuxedo, cloak, top hat and suede gloves. He has a goatee, and his hair is parted in the middle.*]

TELLER: Tell me what this is all about.

REFEREE: I'll introduce you.

TELLER: My name doesn't matter.

REFEREE: You ought to be introduced to the managers.

TELLER: I prefer to remain incognito.

REFEREE: You patronize our sport.

TELLER: I don't know a thing about it. What are the fellows doing down there? I see a circle and the colorful serpentine. Sometimes one rider joins in while another drops out. Why?

REFEREE: The riders race in pairs. While one partner rides . . .

TELLER: The other fellow takes a nap?

REFEREE: He gets a massage.

TELLER: And you call that a tandem race?

REFEREE: What do you mean?

TELLER: It might just as well be called a tandem sleep, since one partner always sleeps.

REFEREE: [*enters*] The bridge is reserved for referees.

1. REFEREE: The gentleman offers a prize of one thousand marks.

2. REFEREE: May I introduce myself?

TELLER: By no means.

1. REFEREE: The gentleman wants to remain incognito.

TELLER: Impenetrably.

1. REFEREE: I've explained the races.

TELLER: Isn't it funny?

2. REFEREE: In what respect?

TELLER: The tandem sleep.

2. REFEREE: A thousand marks for how many laps?

TELLER: As you see fit.

2. REFEREE: How much for the winner?

TELLER: As you please.

2. REFEREE: Eight hundred and two hundred. [*through the megaphone*] Prize donated by a gentleman who wants to remain incognito. To be decided immediately over ten rounds. Eight hundred for the winner, two hundred for the runner-up. A total of one thousand marks.

> [*Thundering noise*]

1. REFEREE: Tell me, if you don't take the matter seriously, why do you offer a prize of one thousand marks?

TELLER: Because the effect is fabulous.

1. REFEREE: On the speed of the riders?

TELLER: Nonsense.

A REFEREE: [*enters*] Are you the gentleman who offered the prize of one thousand marks?

TELLER: In gold.

REFEREE: That takes too much time to count.

TELLER: That's your business. [*he pulls out a roll of coins, opens it, pours the contents on his hand, examines the empty wrapper, throws it away, and skillfully counts the coins in the palm of his hand*] It'll also relieve my pockets.

REFEREE: You seem to be an expert in this matter.

TELLER: A mere trifle, Sir. [*he hands over the money*] Accept it.

REFEREE: Gratefully acknowledged.

TELLER: In keeping with the circumstances.

A REFEREE: [*enters*] Where's the gentleman? May I . . .

TELLER: Certainly not.

REFEREE: [*with the red flag*] I'll give the signal.

REFEREE: Now the bigshots will show their mettle.

REFEREE: The sprinters are in the race now.

REFEREE: [*waving the flag*] The start. [*He lowers the flag. An earsplitting noise is heard.*]

TELLER: [*grabbing two referees by the neck and bending their heads backwards*] Now I'll answer your questions. Raise your eyes.

REFEREE: You should watch the various phases of the contest on the track.

TELLER: Childish. Somebody has to be first. Up there comes the revelation. In three rings placed on top of each other, bursting with spectators—the magic works. In the first gallery, discipline is maintained by the higher class audience. Mere glances, but wide, round, gazing eyes. Higher up, the bodies begin to move. Exclamations are heard. Second gallery. At the very top, all restraint is abandoned. Fanatic shouts. Naked screams. The gallery of passion. Look at that group: Fivefold entanglement. Five heads on one shoulder. Five pairs of arms embracing a howling chest. One forms the core. It is squashed, pushed to the rim. The bowler hat tumbles, sluggishly dropping in the mist, into the second gallery. On a lady's bosom. She doesn't understand. There it rests grandly. Splendid. She'll never notice the hat. She'll go to bed with it. All her life, she'll wear the bowler hat on her bosom.

REFEREE: The Belgian starts to sprint.

TELLER: The middle gallery starts to howl. That hat has fashioned a link. The lady has squashed it against the balustrade. Her bosom shows broad stripes. Pretty lady, you must press against the balustrade and tattoo your breasts.[9] You must inevitably. You can't possibly resist. Hopelessly entangled, you are pushed against the wall and have to yield yourself altogether. Altogether, without complaints.

REFEREE: Do you know the lady?

TELLER: Look now: The five up there push their core over the balustrade. He hangs suspended, falls and sails into the first gallery. Where is he? Where

---

[9] A word play. In German: "Du musst hier an die Brüstung and Deine Brüste brandmarken."

does he suffocate? Extinguished. Buried without a trace. Indifferently. A spectator—a diver—a coincidence, no more, among many thousands.[10]

REFEREE: The German catches up.

TELLER: The first gallery seethes. The fellow has closed the chain. All restraint is gone. The tuxedos quiver. The shirts tear. Buttons burst everywhere. Beards are moved by parted lips. Teeth rattle. Above and center and below are fused. A howling from all three rings alike. No more distinction. It has been accomplished.

REFEREE: [*turning around*] The German did it. What do you say?

TELLER: Silly twaddle.

       [*wild applause*]

REFEREE: A marvellous sprint.

TELLER: Marvellous nonsense.

REFEREE: We'll verify the outcome in the office. [*All exeunt.*]

TELLER: [*holding a* REFEREE *back*] Can you still doubt?

REFEREE: The Germans will win the race.

TELLER: That, too, if you wish. [*pointing upwards*] That's what I mean. Factually overwhelming. The utmost concentration of fact. Here fact does the impossible. Fusion of all rings. Utter dissolution of the individual results in the densest core: passion. To reach that point is the greatest experience. Doors and gates dissolve in mist. Trumpets sound and walls crumble. No resistance, no chastity, no maternal feelings, no love between parent and child. Passion. That's what I mean. That is worth one's while. That justifies my deed, that multiplies the gain.

REFEREE: [*enters*] The Red Cross works efficiently.

TELLER: Was the fellow crushed in the fall?

REFEREE: Squashed under foot.

TELLER: There must be victims where life brims over.

REFEREE: [*through the megaphone*] Result of the race for the prize donated by the gentleman who wants to stay anonymous: eight hundred marks won by number two, two hundred by number one. [*Frenetic applause. Flourish.*]

REFEREE: The teams are exhausted.

REFEREE: They're getting slower and slower.

REFEREE: We have to tell the managers to restore order in the field.

TELLER: Another prize!

REFEREE: Later on, Sir.

TELLER: No interruption at this point.

REFEREE: It's getting risky for the drivers.

TELLER: I don't care about those fellows. The audience boils with excitement. That must be exploited. The heat must reach a hitherto unknown degree. Fifty thousand marks.

REFEREE: Actually?

REFEREE: How much?

TELLER: I stake everything.

---

[10] "A spectator—a diver—a coincidence." (In German: "Ein Zuschauer, ein Zufall, ein Zufallender.")

REFEREE: Fantastic.

TELLER: I want the effect to be fantastic. Alert the Red Cross columns in all rings.

REFEREE: We accept the donation. We shall start the race when the box is occupied.

REFEREE: Splendid.

REFEREE: Marvellous.

REFEREE: That justifies the visit.

TELLER: What do you mean: when the box is occupied?

REFEREE: We'll settle the details in the office. Thirty thousand for the winner, fifteen thousand for the runner-up, five thousand for the third.

REFEREE: The field will break up tonight.

REFEREE: That's the end of the race.

REFEREE: At any rate: when the box is occupied.

[*All exeunt.*]

[A *Salvation Army* LASS *enters. Laughter, catcalls, exclamations.*]

LASS: [*offering her pamphlets*] The War Cry, ten pfennigs, Sir.

TELLER: Another time.

LASS: The War Cry, Sir.

TELLER: What kind of tearsheet are you peddling there?

LASS: The War Cry, Sir.

TELLER: You come too late. The battle is in full swing.

LASS: [*shaking her metal collection box*] Ten pfennigs, Sir.

TELLER: You want to start a war with ten pfennigs?

LASS: Ten pfennigs, Sir.

TELLER: The war cost me fifty thousand.

LASS: Ten pfennigs.

TELLER: I have nothing but gold coins on me.

LASS: Ten pfennigs.

TELLER: Gold . . .

LASS: Ten . . .

TELLER: [*shouts at her through the megaphone*] Gold, gold, gold.

[LASS *exits. The spectators laugh uproariously. Applause. Many* REFEREES *enter.*]

REFEREE: Would you like to announce your own donation?

TELLER: I wish to stay in the background. [*he hands the megaphone to him*] You speak. You deal the final blow.

REFEREE: [*through the megaphone*] A new donation by the same gentleman who wants to remain anonymous. [*applause*] Total value: fifty thousand marks. [*deafening roar*] Five thousand marks for the third. [*shouts*] Fifteen thousand marks for the runner-up. [*greater enthusiasm*] Thirty thousand marks for the winner. [*ecstasy*]

TELLER: [*near the* REFEREE, *nods approval*] That will do the trick. That will bring it out. Those are fulfillments. The roaring blasts of the spring storm. The rushing stream of humanity. Unchained—free. Curtains up—pretensions down. Humanity, free humanity. High and low—man. No rings, no levels, no classes. Work and wages replaced by unbounded passion. Not pure, but free. Thus my daring is rewarded. [*he pulls out the bundle of bills*] Gladly offered—freely given.

>   [*The crowd falls suddenly silent. The national anthem is heard. The* REFEREES *have removed their hats and bow.*]

REFEREE: [*to the* TELLER] Give me the money, so that the race can be run immediately.

TELLER: What does that mean?

REFEREE: What, Sir?

TELLER: This sudden silence above and below.

REFEREE: By no means sudden. His Highness has entered the box.

TELLER: His Highness—the box.

REFEREE: All the more timely is your gift.

TELLER: I do not want to waste my money.

REFEREE: What do you mean?

TELLER: That I consider it too expensive to spend that much on feeding servile slaves.

REFEREE: Would you explain.

TELLER: This fire, raging even now, quenched by a boot on the leg of His Highness. Are you mad to think me crazy enough to toss ten pfennigs to the swine? Even that would be too much. A kick in the rear, that's what they need.

REFEREE: The prize has been announced. His Highness is waiting in the box. The audience waits respectfully. What does it mean?

TELLER: If you don't believe what I say, you'll see the light if I enlighten you with one blow.

>   [*He crushes the* REFEREE's *silk hat and exits. The national anthem continues. Silence. The* REFEREES *still bow.*]

SCENS III——*Dance hall. A chambre separée. It is dark. In the background, the muffled sound of an orchestra playing dance tunes.*

>   [WAITER *opens the door and turns on red light.*]
>   [TELLER, *tuxedo, dress coat, scarf, bamboo cane with gold button enters.*]

WAITER: Suitable?

TELLER: Completely.

>   [WAITER *takes his coat.*]
>   [TELLER *looks at himself in the mirror.*]

WAITER: How many places shall I set?

TELLER: Twenty-four. I expect my grandma, my ma, my wife, and several aunts. Today's my daughter's confirmation.

>   [WAITER *is perplexed.*]

TELLER: [*to him, through the mirror*] Ass. Two. Or why do you pad these discreetly lighted booths?

WAITER: What brand do you prefer, Sir?

TELLER: Old pander. I decide myself which flower I shall pick, bud or rose, fat or thin. I don't want to tax your abilities unduly. Do you have fixed prices for that, too?

WAITER: The brand of champagne, I mean.

TELLER: [*hems*] Grand Marnier.

WAITER: That's the cognac after the champagne.

TELLER: Then I'll follow your advice.

WAITER: Two bottles of Pommery. Dry?[11]

TELLER: Two, as you say.

WAITER: Extra dry?

TELLER: Two will do for a start. Or do you mean three bottles extra for discreet service? Granted.

WAITER: [*with the menu*] The dinner?

TELLER: Peaks, peaks.

WAITER: Oeufs pochés Bergère? Poulet grillé? Steak de veau truffé? Parfait de foie gras en croûte? Salade coeur de laitue?

TELLER: Peaks, nothing but peaks from beginning to end.

WAITER: Excuse me?

TELLER: [*poking his nose*] Peaks are the utmost concentrations in everything. Even of what comes out of your pots and pans. The dainty of dainties. The meal of meals. To crown important events. Your business, my friend. I'm not the cook.

WAITER: [*places a larger menu on the table*] Ready for serving in twenty minutes [*He arranges the glasses, etc.*]

[*Heads with silk masks appear in the partly open door.*]

TELLER: [*threatening them, through the mirror, with his finger*] Wait, you moths. I'll soon hold you under the lamplight. We'll discuss the matter when you join me.[12] [*He nods approvingly.*]

[*The giggling masks depart.*]

[WAITER *fastens a sign "Reserved" to the door. Exits.*]

TELLER: [*pushes back his top hat, takes cigarettes from a golden case and lights one*] Into the fray, Toreador. Funny things I'm saying. I am charged. Everything, simply everything. Toreador. Carmen. Caruso. Read that stuff somewhere. Remembered it. Stored it. Right now, I feel capable of giving a detailed account of our negotiations with the Bagdad railroad. The Crown Prince of Rumania marries the second daughter of the Tsar. Tatjana. Go ahead. Let her marry. Pleasant honeymoon. The people need kings. Tat- Tat- jana. [*Exits, swinging his bamboo cane.*]

[WAITER *enters with bottles and a champagne bucket. He uncorks a bottle and pours. Exits.*]

TELLER: [*enters with a female* MASK, *a harlequin in tightly fitting costume with red and yellow squares*] Hello, moth!

MASK: [*running around the table*] Champagne. [*she empties both glasses of champagne and drops on the couch*] Champagne.

TELLER: [*fills the glasses*] Liquid powder. Recharge your checkered body.

---

11 "The teller takes "dry" to mean "drei" (three).

12 "We'll discuss the matter when you join me". In German: "Wir werden uns über den Gegenstand auseinandersetzen, wenn wir beieinandersitzen").

MASK: [*drinks*] Champagne.
TELLER: Move in batteries and prepare the charge.
MASK: Champagne.
TELLER: [*removing the bottles*] Empty. [*he joins the* MASK *on the couch*] Ready for the charge.
      [MASK *leans over tipsily.*]
TELLER: [*shakes her limp arms*] Stir yourself, moth.
      [MASK *does not move.*]
TELLER: Collect your wits, butterfly. You have sipped the bubbling yellow honey. Unfold your wings. Overpower me. Bury me. Cover me up. I have thrown away my past—throw yourself at me.
MASK: [*speaking with heavy tongue*] Champagne.
TELLER: No, my bird of Paradise. You are sufficiently charged. You are full.
MASK: Champagne.
TELLER: Not a drop, or you'll get dizzy. You'll rob me of nice opportunities.
MASK: Champagne.
TELLER: Or don't you offer any? Let's get to the heart of the matter. What do you have?
MASK: Champagne.
TELLER: You certainly do. From me, that is to say. What do I get in exchange?
      [MASK *goes to sleep.*]
TELLER: Want to take a nap here? Little fool. Today I have no time for such time-consuming jokes. [*he rises, fills a glass and pours the contents into her face*] At sunrise, when the cocks do crow . . .[13]
MASK: [*jumps up*] Pig.
TELLER: A pretty name. Unfortunately, I am not in the position to introduce myself. You member of the common snout family, make yourself rare.
MASK: You'll pay for that.
TELLER: That's only fair since I've paid for your drinks.
      [MASK *exits.*]
      [TELLER *drinks champagne and exits.*]
      [WAITER *enters, bringing caviar and removing the empty bottles.*]
      [TELLER *enters with two black* MASKS.]
1. MASK: Reserved.
2. MASK: [*at the table*] Caviar.
1. MASK: [*joining her*] Caviar.
TELLER: Just as black as you are. Gobble it up. Stuff yourselves. [*He sits down on the couch between the two*] Talk caviar, sing champagne. I don't need your brains. [*he pours champagne and fills the plates*] I don't want you to talk. Not a word, not a sound. Dumb like the fish who spawned this black caviar across the Black Sea. Giggle, laugh, but don't talk. That doesn't get you anywhere, except perhaps up from the couch. I've cleaned out once before.
      [MASKS, *giggling, look at each other.*]
TELLER: [*grabbing the* FIRST MASK] What's the color of your eyes? Green, or yellow? [*to the* SECOND MASK] And yours? Blue or red? How nicely you

---

[13] Allusion to the opening line of Eduard Mörike's poem 'Das verlassene Mägdlein'

ogle. That's tempting. Out with the truth. A prize for the prettiest one.
[MASKS *laugh.*]

TELLER: [*to the* FIRST MASK] You are more beautiful. You're mighty shy. Wait,
I'll open the curtain and view the picture.

[1. MASK *moves away from him.*]

TELLER: [*to the* FIRST MASK] Must you hide? Your bashfulness makes you
irresistible. You have strayed into this dance hall. You are looking for
adventures. You have found your adventure. Down with the mask on
your dainty face.

[MASK *moves away from him.*]

TELLER: I've reached the goal. I sit trembling—my blood boils. The moment
has come. And now the payment. [*he pulls out the bundle of bills and
divides them*] Pretty mask, because you are pretty. Pretty mask, because
you are pretty. [*he covers his face with his hands*] One—two—three.

[MASKS *lift their masks.*]

TELLER: [*looks at them and laughs*] Cover up—cover up. [*he runs around the
table*] Monster—monster. Hurry up, clear out, or . . . [*he lifts his
bamboo cane.*]

1. MASK: Would you . . .
2. MASK: You would . . .
TELLER: I would indeed.

[MASKS *exeunt.*]

TELLER: [*shakes himself and drinks champagne*] Old hags. [*Exits.*]

[WAITER *enters with fresh bottles. Exits.*]

TELLER: [*opens the door. He is dancing with a female Pierrot, whose skirt
reaches down to her ankles. He breaks away from her in the center of
the room and plumps down on the couch*] Dance.

[MASK *does not move.*]

TELLER: Dance. Whirl around. Dance, dance. Brains don't count. Beauty
doesn't count. Dancing counts, turning, twisting. Dance, dance, dance.

[MASK *approaches the table.*]

TELLER: [*impatiently*] No break. No interruption. Dance.

[MASK *does not move.*]

TELLER: Why don't you jump? Ever heard of Dervishes? Dancing men. Men
when dancing, corpses when resting. Death and dance, erected at the
corners of life. In between . . . [*The Salvation Army* LASS *enters.*] Hallelujah.

LASS: The War Cry.
TELLER: Ten pfennigs.

[LASS *offers her collection box.*]

TELLER: When, do you think, I will jump into your box?
LASS: The War Cry.
TELLER: You seem to be so sure of it.
LASS: Ten pfennigs.
TELLER: But when?
LASS: Ten pfennigs.
TELLER: You cling to my heels.

[LASS, *shaking her box.*]

TELLER: But I'll shake you off.
  [LASS, *shaking her box.*]
TELLER: Now. [*to the* MASK] Dance.
  [LASS *exits.*]
  [MASK *on the couch.*]
TELLER: Why do you sit in the corners of the hall instead of dancing in the
  center? You caught my attention. Everybody jumps and you stand still.
  Why do you wear skirts while the others dress lightly like slender youths.
MASK: I don't dance.
TELLER: You don't dance like the others?
MASK: I can't dance.
TELLER: Not in step with the music. That's silly, anyway. You know other
  dances. You hide something under your clothes—your special leaps, not
  to be squeezed into a pattern of bars and steps. Quicker turns are your
  specialty. [*removes everything from the table*] Here is your dance floor.
  Jump onto it. Leap up from the rug. Effortless. Lifted by springs that
  bounce in your knuckles. Jump. Brace your heels. Round your thighs. Let
  your skirt billow around your legs.
MASK: [*nestles up to him on the couch*] I can't dance.
TELLER: You sharpen my curiosity. You don't know what is at stake. I'll tell
  you. [*he shows her the bills*] Everything.
MASK: [*guides his hand down her leg*] I can't.
TELLER: [*rises quickly*] A wooden leg. [*he grabs the champagne bucket and
  puts it over her head*] May it grow buds. I'll water it.
MASK: Now you are in for something.
TELLER: That suits me well.
MASK: Wait for me. [*Exits.*]
   [TELLER *puts a bill on the table, takes his coat and hat and hurries
   off.* GENTLEMEN *in tuxedos enter.*]
GENTLEMAN: Where is the lout?
GENTLEMAN: Let's have a close look at him.
GENTLEMAN: To take our girls away . . .
GENTLEMAN: Splurge caviar and champagne . . .
GENTLEMAN: Offend them afterwards . . .
GENTLEMAN: We'll show the fellow.
GENTLEMAN: Where is he?
GENTLEMAN: Cleared out.
GENTLEMAN: Bolted.
GENTLEMAN: The gentleman smelled a rat.
GENTLEMAN: [*discovering the bill*] A thousand bucks.
GENTLEMAN: My gosh.
GENTLEMAN: He must be stinking with money.
GENTLEMAN: Is that how he paid his bill?
GENTLEMAN: Never mind. He has bolted. We'll render this greenback in-
  visible. [*He puts it in his pocket.*]
GENTLEMAN: That's our compensation.
GENTLEMAN: He's stolen our girls.

GENTLEMAN: Never mind the girls.

GENTLEMAN: They're drunk anyway.

GENTLEMAN: They'll soil our clothes.

GENTLEMAN: Let's go to a brothel and rent the whole joint for half a week.

SEVERAL GENTLEMEN: Splendid. Let's go. Watch out, the waiter's coming.

> [WAITER *enters with a heavily loaded tray. He stands perplexed at the table.*]

GENTLEMAN: Are you looking for somebody?

GENTLEMAN: Why don't you serve supper under the table? [*The* GENTLEMEN *laugh*]

WAITER: [*frantically*] The champagne—the dinner—the reserved room—nothing is paid for. Four bottles of Pommery, two portions of caviar, two special menus. I have to make it up. I have a wife and children. I've been unemployed for four months, on account of my lungs. You won't ruin me, gentlemen?

GENTLEMAN: What do we care about your lungs. We all have families. What do you expect us to do? Are we the ones who haven't paid their bills? Tell me.

GENTLEMAN: What kind of joint is this anyway? Where are we? A place where people don't pay their bills. And you lure guests into such company? We are honest fellows who pay for their drinks. Or don't we?

GENTLEMAN: [*turning the key in the lock*] Look around. It's our turn to pay. [*He pushes the* WAITER, *who has turned around, so that he staggers and falls down on the rug. The* GENTLEMEN *exeunt.*]

WAITER: [*rises, runs to the door and finds it closed. Beating the wood with his fists*] Let me out. You needn't pay. I'll drown myself.

SCENE IV——*A hall owned by the Salvation Army. Deep and narrow, it terminates in a yellow curtain on which a black cross, large enough to hold a human being, is sewn. On the platform, at right, the penitential bench. At left, the trumpets and kettle drums. The hall is closely packed. Suspended from the ceiling is a luster with a tangle of wires for the light bulbs. The door of the hall is upstage. Music of trumpets and kettle drums. Applause and laughter issuing from one corner.*

> [SOLDIER (*girl*) *goes to the corner and sits down by the heckler, a clerk. She takes his hand and whispers into his ear.*]

SOMEBODY: [*in another corner*] Cuddle up.

> [SOLDIER (*girl*) *approaches the speaker, a youthful worker.*]

THE WORKER: What do you want?

> [SOLDIER (*girl*) *looks at him and shakes her head. Laughter.*]

OFFICER (woman): [*appears on the podium*] I wish to ask you a question.

> [*Some members of the audience clamor for silence, others, amused, shout:* "Speak louder, don't talk, music, drum, trumpet angels."]

A MEMBER OF THE CROWD: Go ahead.

ANOTHER: Stop.

OFFICER: Why are you sitting on the benches down there?

A VOICE: Why shouldn't we?

OFFICER: You fill the hall to the bursting point. You nudge each other. And yet one bench remains empty.

A VOICE: Nothing doing.

OFFICER: Why do you stay down there, where you are so tightly packed? Isn't it disgusting to be jostled by the crowd? Who knows his neighbor? You brush your knees against his, and perhaps he is a sick man. You look in his face, and perhaps he harbors murderous thoughts. I know there are many invalids and criminals in this hall. Criminals and invalids enter and mingle with you. That's why I warn you. Beware of your neighbors on the benches. The benches down there hold criminals and invalids.

A VOICE: Are you talking about me?

OFFICER: I know it and urge you to part with your neighbor. Crime and disease abound in this asphalt city. Who among you is free of blemish? Your skin may be white and smooth, but your looks betray you. You don't have eyes to see, but your looks betray you. You betray yourself. The disease has already touched you. The contagion spreads. Too long you have endured evil neighbors. And if you don't want to be like your neighbors in this asphalt city, step forward. This is the last warning. Do penance. Do penance. Come up, come to the penitential bench. Come to the penitential bench.

> [*The trumpets and drums begin to sound.*]
> [LASS *ushers in the* TELLER.]
> [TELLER, *still formally dressed, attracts attention.*]
> [LASS *shows him to his seat, sits down at his side and furnishes explanations.*]
> [TELLER *looks around amusedly. The music stops. Loud, but frankly ironic, applause.*]

OFFICER: [*appears on the platform*] Let our comrade tell you how he found his way to the penitential bench.

> [SOLDIER (*a fairly young man*) *appears.*]

A VOICE: Is that how you look?[14]

SOLDIER: I will tell you about my sin. I lived without thinking of my soul. I thought only of the body. I used it as a screen for my soul and made it grow bigger and stronger, so that the soul was completely hidden. I sought fame with my body and did not know that I was merely lengthening the shadow in which my soul withered. Sport was my sin. I practiced it without stopping to think. I was proud of the speed of my feet on the pedals, of the strength of my arms on the handle bar. When the spectators raged, I forgot everything. I doubled my efforts and won all competitions fought with the body. My name appeared on all the bulletin boards, and on millions of leaflets. I became world champion. Finally, my soul raised its voice. It had lost patience. I fell during a race. I was only slightly injured.

---

14 "Is that how you look". (A word play on "aussehen." In German, "so siehst du aus", when used colloquially, means something like "you won't have any luck with that.")

The soul wanted to give me time to change my ways. I exchanged the benches in the hall for the penitential bench. Here my soul can talk to me in peace. I cannot tell you what it says to me; for that is too beautiful, and my words are too weak to describe it. You must come up here and listen to it speaking inside you. [*He steps aside.*]

 [A VOICE *laughs obscenely.*]

 [SEVERAL OTHER VOICES *hush it.*]

LASS: [*softly to the* TELLER] Do you hear him?

TELLER: Leave me alone.

OFFICER: You have heard our comrade's story. Is it not tempting? Is there a greater prize to be won than one's soul? And how easy it is; for the soul is inside you. All you need to do is to rest. It wants to be quiet within you. It prefers to sit on this bench. There must be someone among you who sinned the way our comrade sinned. Our comrade wants to help him. He has opened the way for him. Come now, come to the penitential bench.

 [*Silence throughout the hall. A sturdy* YOUNG MAN, *with a bandaged arm, rises in one corner, moves forward with an embarrassed smile, and mounts the platform. Somebody makes an obscene joke.*]

A VOICE: Who is that boor?

 [*The man who has made the joke rises and shamefacedly hastens to the door.*]

A VOICE: There's the lout.

 [SOLDIER (*girl*) *hurries up to him and leads him back to his seat.*]

A VOICE: Don't be so gentle.

SEVERAL VOICES: Bravo.

THE YOUNG MAN: [*on the platform, starting to speak falteringly*] The asphalt city has built a hall. I raced in the sports palace. I am a cyclist. I participated in the tandem races. On the second night, I collided with another rider. I broke my arm and had to quit the race. The race continues but I am at rest. I can reflect in peace. All my life I raced heedlessly. I want to think—about everything. [*emphatically*] On the penitential bench I want to think about my sins. [*Led by the* SOLDIER, *he sinks down on the bench. The* SOLDIER *remains at his side.*]

OFFICER: A soul has been won.

 [*Flourish of drums and trumpets. The* SOLDIERS, *scattered throughout the hall, have risen and cheer with raised arms. The music stops.*]

LASS: [*to the* TELLER] Do you see him?

TELLER: The tandem race.

LASS: What is it you whisper?

TELLER: *Mea res, mea res.*

LASS: Are you ready?

TELLER: Be quiet.

OFFICER: [*appears on the podium*] Now this comrade wants to speak to you.

 [*Somebody in the audience hisses. Others cry "Silence!"*]

SOLDIER (*girl*): [*appears on the platform*] Whose sin is my sin? I will tell you all about myself. The home in which I grew up was disorderly. The man

—he was not my father—drank. My mother slept with gentleman callers. She gave me all the money I wanted. The man all the blows I wanted. [*laughter*] Nobody watched me, I least of all. Thus I became a lost woman. For at that time I did not know that the conditions at home were to alert me to my soul and remind me of devoting myself entirely to it. I found out one night. A gentleman who was with me wanted me to turn the light out. I turned off the light, although I wasn't used to that. Later, when we were together, I understood the reason. For I felt only the trunk of a man without legs. I wasn't to see that beforehand. He had wooden legs, which he had unfastened secretly. Terror gripped me then and did not leave me. I hated my body. Only my soul I was still able to love. Now I love my soul alone. It is so perfect that it is the most beautiful thing I know. I know too much about it to tell you all. If you ask your soul, it will tell you everything. [*She steps aside. Silence in the hall.*]

OFFICER: [*appears on the platform*] You have heard this comrade's story. Her soul offered itself to her. She did not turn it away. Now she talks about it joyously. Does the soul now offer itself to one of you? Let it come to you. Let it talk and tell. It will be undisturbed on this bench. Come to the penitential bench, come to the penitential bench.

    [*Commotion in the hall. People in the audience turn around.*]

CALLGIRL: [*elderly, in the front row, begins to address the crowd*] What do you think of me, ladies and gentlemen? I have sought shelter here, because I was tired of walking the streets. I'm not in the least ashamed. I don't know this place. I haven't been here before. I'm here by pure chance. [*she has reached the platform*] But you are mistaken, ladies and gentlemen, if you think that I should wait to be asked a second time. I would regard this as an imposition. As you see me here—scrutinize me from top to toe—look at me closely. That doesn't bother me at all. I'm not in the least embarrassed. You won't be able to enjoy the same spectacle a second time. You'll be sorely disappointed if you think that my soul, too, is for sale. I have never sold it yet, no matter how much was offered. I thank you, ladies and gentlemen, for your compliments. You'll no longer meet me on the streets. I don't have a single moment to spare for you. My soul does not give me any peace. Thank you kindly, gentlemen. I'm not in the least embarrassed. [*She has taken off her hat. The* SOLDIER *who has spoken before leads her to the penitential bench.*]

OFFICER: A soul has been won.

    [*Drums and trumpets. The* SOLDIERS *cheer.*]

LASS: [*to the* TELLER] Did you hear everything?

TELLER: *Mea res, mea res.*

LASS: What is it you are humming there?

TELLER: The wooden leg.

LASS: Are you ready?

TELLER: Not yet, not yet.

A MEMBER OF THE AUDIENCE: [*has risen in the center of the hall*] What is my sin? I want to know my sin.

OFFICER: [*appears on the platform*] Our comrade wants to tell you.

SEVERAL VOICES: [*excitedly*] Sit down. Silence. Go ahead.

SOLDIER: [*elderly man*] Let me tell you about myself. It's a common story, indeed. This is why it became my sin. I had a cozy apartment, a loving family, an easy job—our life passed complacently. When at night, surrounded by my family, I sat at the table under the lamp, smoking my pipe, I was satisfied. I did not want my life to change. And yet it changed. I don't know how it happened—perhaps I never knew. The soul manifests itself even without special provocation. It knew its hour and used it wisely. I could not miss its admonition. My inertia initially blocked the way, but the soul was stronger. I became increasingly aware of this. Only the soul was able to give me lasting satisfaction. And satisfaction I had desired all my life. Now I do no longer find it sitting at the table under the lamp, smoking my pipe, but on the penitential bench. That is my common story. [*He steps aside.*]

OFFICER: [*appears on the platform*] Our comrade has . . .

A MEMBER OF THE AUDIENCE: [*walking forward*] My sin. [*on the platform*] I have a family. I have two daughters. I have a wife. I have a mother. We live in three rooms. It's quite pleasant at home. My daughters—one of them plays the piano, the other embroiders. My wife cooks. My mother waters the flowers on the window sill. It's so pleasant at home. Couldn't be more so. It is splendid, exemplary, practical, inimitable. [*With a change of tone*] It is disgusting, abominable, ghastly, pitiful, with all the piano playing, embroidering, cooking, watering of flowers. [*Frantically*] I have a soul. I have a soul. I have a soul. [*He staggers to the penitential bench.*]

OFFICER: A soul has been won.

[*Drums and trumpets. The hall is in an uproar.*]

MANY MEMBERS OF THE AUDIENCE: [*have risen as the drums and trumpets sound. Some are standing on the benches*] What is my sin? What is my sin? I want to know my sin.

OFFICER: [*appears on the platform*] Our comrade wants to tell you his story. [*Silence.*]

LASS: Do you see him?

TELLER: My daughters. My wife. My mother.

LASS: What is it you are humming and whispering?

TELLER: *Mea res, mea res, mea res.*

LASS: Are you ready?

TELLER: Not yet, not yet, not yet.

SOLDIER: [*middle-aged, on the platform*] It wasn't easy for my soul to triumph. It had to grip me hard and shake me violently. In the end, it used its strongest means. It sent me to prison. I had taken money in my keeping and embezzled a large sum. I was caught and sentenced. Then I found peace in my cell. That's what the soul had waited for. Now it could freely talk to me. I had to listen to it. The lonely weeks I spent in the cell were the best time of my life. And when I was discharged, I only wanted to live with my soul. I looked for a quiet place for it. I found it on the penitential bench and find it daily when I want to enjoy a pleasant hour. [*He steps aside.*]

OFFICER: [*appears on the platform*] Our comrade has told you about the pleasant hours he spends on the penitential bench. Who among you is there who wants to shed his sin? Whose sin is the one from which he recovers so joyously? Here is peace for him. Come to the penitential bench.

THE CROWD: [*in the hall shouting and waving*] That is nobody's sin here. That is nobody's sin here. I want to know my sin. My sin. My sin. My sin. My sin.

LASS: What are you shouting?

TELLER: The money.

LASS: [*urgently*] Are you ready?

TELLER: I am ready now.

LASS: [*hanging on to his arm*] I'll lead you there. I'll assist you. I'll always help you. [*ecstatically into the hall*] A soul wants to make itself known. I have found this soul. I have found this soul.

[*The noise subsides. Silence hums.*]

TELLER: [*on the platform, close to the* LASS] I began my search this morning. Something caused me to search. It was a real awakening, without possible retreat. A burning of bridges. Thus I've been on the march since this morning. I don't want to bore you with listing all the stations at which I did not stop. They did not justify the awakening. I marched on resolutely, probing, testing and choosing. Station after station faded behind me. It was neither this one nor that one nor the other one. What is it? What is it now that justifies the risk of the total self? This hall, replete with mighty sounds, filled with benches. This hall. It rises from these benches, promises fulfillment. Free from dross, it mounts in praise, purified in these two redhot crucibles: confession and penance. There it stands like a shining tower, firm and bright: confession and penance. You call for it. To you I will tell my story.

LASS: Speak. I'm at your side. I'm always at your side.

TELLER: I've been on the march since this morning. I confess having stolen money in my keeping. I'm a teller. A large sum: sixty thousand. I fled with it to the asphalt city. They're hunting me now. A reward will have been posted for my apprehension. I no longer hide. I confess. No money from all the banks in the world can buy anything of value. One always buys less than one pays for. And the more one pays, the poorer is the ware. Money reduces the value. Money hides all true values. Money is the worst of all evils. [*he takes the money out of his pockets*] This hall is the hot furnace heated by your contempt for all mean things. I'll throw it among you and you quickly trample it underfoot. Thus some of the evil is done away with. I walk through the rows of benches and report to the nearest policeman. After confession I seek penance. Thus everything is made perfect.

[*He scatters bills and coins through the hall. The bills drift down to the stunned audience. The coins roll among their feet. A fierce struggle for the money ensues. The crowd is hopelessly entangled. The* SOLDIERS *on the platform desert their instruments to join the fight. The benches are being turned over, hoarse screams are uttered, fists hammer on bodies. The crowd finally moves toward the door and rolls out of the hall. The* LASS, *who has not joined in the fight, stands alone in the midst of the overturned benches.*]

TELLER: [*smiles at her*] You are at my side. You are always at my side. [*he notices the deserted drums and picks up two sticks*] Onward [*brief drum roll*] From station to station. [*individual drum beats corresponding with units of meaning*] Crowds back there. Mass dispersed. Extended void. Space created. Space. Space. [*drum roll*] A girl stands there—as the waters recede. Upright. [*drum roll*] Loyal. Woman and Man. Primeval gardens unlocked. Cloudless sky. A voice from the silent treetops. Peace on earth. [*drum roll*] Woman and man. Eternally faithful. Woman and man, wealth in poverty. Woman and man, promise fulfilled. Woman and man, seed and fruit. Woman and man, aim, meaning, and goal. [*repeated drum beats, ending in a prolonged roll*]

[LASS *sneaks to the door and disappears.*]

[TELLER, *fading drum roll.*]

LASS: [*opens the door. To the policeman, pointing at the* TELLER] There he is. I showed him to you. I've earned the reward.

TELLER: [*dropping the drum sticks*] Here I stand. Up here I stand. Two are too many. The space holds but one. Loneliness is space. Space is loneliness. Coldness is sun. Sun is coldness. The body bleeds feverishly. The body shivers feverishly. Fields deserted. Ice is growing. Who escapes? Where's a way out?

POLICEMAN: Are there other exits?

LASS: No.

[TELLER *searches in his pocket.*]

POLICEMAN: He's got his hand in his pocket. Turn out the lights. We offer a target.

[*The* LASS *does as she is bidden. The light of the chandelier fades, with the exception of one bulb. That bulb lights up the bright wires of the chandelier in such a way that they seem to form a human skeleton.*]

TELLER: [*buries his left hand in his breast pocket and, grabbing a trumpet with the other hand, blows in the direction of the chandelier*] Discovered. [*trumpet blast*] Ridiculed in snow-covered branches, now welcomed in the tangled wires of the chandelier. [*trumpet blasts*] I report my arrival. [*trumpet blast*] I have completed my journey. I climb up breathlessly along steep curves. I have used my strength. I have not spared myself. [*trumpet blast*] I have made it hard for myself and could have found an easy way out—up there in the snow tree when we sat on *one* branch together. You should have persuaded me a little more strongly. A spark of insight would have saved me all this trouble. That requires so very little brains. [*trumpet blasts*] Why did I get down from the tree? Why did I march on? Where am I going? [*trumpet blasts*] Then he sat there—

bareboned, now he sits here—bareboned. From morn till midnight I race in a circle. Now his finger shows a way—toward what goal? [*He shoots the answer into his breast. The trumpet dies at his mouth with diminishing sound.*]

POLICEMAN: Turn on the lights. [LASS *does so. At this moment, the bulbs explode violently. The* TELLER, *with outstretched arms, has fallen against the cross sewn on to the curtains. His sighs hack like an Ecce, his breath hums like a Homo.*] We've had a short circuit. [*The stage is completely dark.*]

THE END

BERTOLT BRECHT

THE GOOD WOMAN OF SETZUAN

Revised English Version by
Eric Bentley

CHARACTERS

WONG, *a water seller*
THREE GODS
SHEN TE, *a prostitute, later a shopkeeper*
MRS. SHIN, *former owner of Shen Te's shop*
A FAMILY OF EIGHT (*husband, wife, brother, sister-in-law, grandfather, nephew, niece, boy*)
AN UNEMPLOYED MAN
A CARPENTER

MRS. MI TZU, *Shen Te's landlady*
YANG SUN, *an unemployed pilot, later a factory manager*
AN OLD WHORE
A POLICEMAN
AN OLD MAN
AN OLD WOMAN, *his wife*
MR. SHU FU, *a barber*
MRS. YANG, *mother of Yang Sun*
GENTLEMEN, VOICES, CHILDREN (*three*), *etc.*

PROLOGUE

At the gates of the half-Westernized city of Setzuan. Evening.

[WONG *the water seller introduces himself to the audience.*]
WONG: I sell water here in the city of Setzuan. It isn't easy. When water is scarce, I have long distances to go in search of it, and when it is plentiful, I have no income. But in our part of the world there is nothing unusual about poverty. Many people think only the gods can save the situation. And I hear from a cattle merchant—who travels a lot—that some of the highest gods are on their way at this very moment. Informed sources have it that heaven is quite disturbed at all the complaining. I've been coming out here to the city gates for three days now to bid these gods welcome. I want to be the first to greet them. What about those fellows over there? No, no, they *work*. And that one there has ink on his fingers, he's no god, he must be a clerk from the cement factory. *Those* two are another story. They look as though they'd like to beat you. But gods don't need to beat you, do they?
[THREE GODS *appear.*]
What about those three? Old-fashioned clothes—dust on their feet—

they *must be gods!* [*he throws himself at their feet*] Do with me what
    you will, illustrious ones!
FIRST GOD: [*with an ear trumpet*] Ah! [*he is pleased*] So we are expected?
WONG: [*giving them water*] Oh, yes. And I *knew* you'd come.
FIRST GOD: We need somewhere to stay the night. You know of a place?
WONG: The whole town is at your service, illustrious ones! What sort of a
    place would you like?
        [*The* GODS *eye each other.*]
FIRST GOD: Just try the first house you come to, my son.
WONG: That would be Mr. Fo's place.
FIRST GOD: Mr. Fo.
WONG: One moment! [*He knocks at the first house.*]
VOICE FROM MR. FO'S: No!
        [WONG *returns a little nervously.*]
WONG: It's too bad. Mr. Fo isn't in. And his servants don't dare do a thing
    without his consent. He'll have a fit when he finds out who they turned
    away, won't he?
FIRST GOD: [*smiling*] He will, won't he?
WONG: One moment! The next house is Mr. Cheng's. Won't he be thrilled!
FIRST GOD: Mr. Cheng.
        [WONG *knocks.*]
VOICE FROM MR. CHENG'S: Keep your gods. We have our own troubles!
WONG: [*back with the* GODS] Mr. Cheng is very sorry, but he has a houseful of
    relations. I think some of them are a bad lot, and naturally, he wouldn't
    like you to see them.
THIRD GOD: Are we so terrible?
WONG: Well, only with bad people, of course. Everyone knows the province of
    Kwan is always having floods.
SECOND GOD: Really? How's that?
WONG: Why, because they're so irreligious.
SECOND GOD: Rubbish. It's because they neglected the dam.
FIRST GOD: [*to* SECOND] Sh! [*to* WONG] You're still in hopes, aren't you, my
    son?
WONG: Certainly. All Setzuan is competing for the honor! What happened up
    to now is pure coincidence. I'll be back. [*He walks away, but then stands
    undecided.*]
SECOND GOD: What did I tell you?
THIRD GOD: It *could* be pure coincidence.
SECOND GOD: The same coincidence in Shun, Kwan, and Setzuan? People just
    aren't religious any more, let's face the fact. Our mission has failed!
FIRST GOD: Oh come, we might run into a good person any minute.
THIRD GOD: How did the resolution read? [*unrolling a scroll and reading from
    it*] "The world can stay as it is if enough people are found [*at the word
    "found" he unrolls it a little more*] living lives worthy of human beings.*"
    Good people, that is. Well, what about this water seller himself? *He's*
    good, or I'm very much mistaken.
SECOND GOD: You're very much mistaken. When he gave us a drink, I had the

impression there was something odd about the cup. Well, look! [*He shows the cup to the* FIRST GOD.]

FIRST GOD: A false bottom!

SECOND GOD: The man is a swindler.

FIRST GOD: Very well, count *him* out. That's one man among millions. And as a matter of fact, we only need one on *our* side. These atheists are saying, "The world must be changed because no one can *be* good and *stay* good." No one, eh? I say: let us find one—just one—and we have those fellows where we want them!

THIRD GOD: [*to* WONG] Water seller, is it so hard to find a place to stay?

WONG: Nothing could be easier. It's just me. I don't go about it right.

THIRD GOD: Really?

[*He returns to the others. A* GENTLEMAN *passes by.*]

WONG: Oh dear, they're catching on. [*he accosts the* GENTLEMAN] Excuse the intrusion, dear sir, but three gods have just turned up. Three of the very highest. They need a place for the night. Seize this rare opportunity—to have real gods as your guests!

GENTLEMAN: [*laughing*] A new way of finding free rooms for a gang of crooks. [*Exit* GENTLEMAN.]

WONG: [*shouting at him*] Godless rascal! Have you no religion, gentleman of Setzuan? [*pause*] Patience, illustrious ones! [*pause*] There's only one person left. Shen Te, the prostitute. She *can't* say no. [*Calls up to a window*] Shen Te!

[SHEN TE *opens the shutters and looks out.*]

WONG: Shen Te, it's Wong. *They're* here, and nobody wants them. Will you take them?

SHEN TE: Oh, no, Wong, I'm expecting a gentleman.

WONG: Can't you forget about him for tonight?

SHEN TE: The rent has to be paid by tomorrow or I'll be out on the street.

WONG: This is no time for calculation, Shen Te.

SHEN TE: Stomachs rumble even on the Emperor's birthday, Wong.

WONG: Setzuan is one big dung hill!

SHEN TE: Oh, very well! I'll hide till my gentleman has come and gone. Then I'll take them. [*She disappears.*]

WONG: They mustn't see her gentleman or they'll know what she is.

FIRST GOD: [*who hasn't heard any of this*] I think it's hopeless.

[*They approach* WONG.]

WONG: [*jumping, as he finds them behind him*] A room has been found, illustrious ones! [*He wipes sweat off his brow.*]

SECOND GOD: Oh, good.

THIRD GOD: Let's see it.

WONG: [*nervously*] Just a minute. It has to be tidied up a bit.

THIRD GOD: Then we'll sit down here and wait.

WONG: [*still more nervous*] No, no! [*holding himself back*] Too much traffic, you know.

THIRD GOD: [*with a smile*] Of course, if you *want* us to move.

[*They retire a little. They sit on a doorstep.* WONG *sits on the ground.*]

WONG: [*after a deep breath*] You'll be staying with a single girl—the finest human being in Setzuan!

THIRD GOD: That's nice.

WONG: [*to the audience*] They gave me such a look when I picked up my cup just now.

THIRD GOD: You're worn out, Wong.

WONG: A little, maybe.

FIRST GOD: Do people here have a hard time of it?

WONG: The good ones do.

FIRST GOD: What about yourself?

WONG: You mean I'm not good. That's true. And I don't have an easy time either!

> [*During this dialogue, a* GENTLEMAN *has turned up in front of Shen Te's house, and has whistled several times. Each time* WONG *has given a start.*]

THIRD GOD: [*to* WONG, *softly*] Psst! I think he's gone now.

WONG: [*confused and surprised*] Ye-e-es.

> [*The* GENTLEMAN *has left now, and* SHEN TE *has come down to the street.*]

SHEN TE: [*softly*] Wong!

> [*Getting no answer, she goes off down the street.* WONG *arrives just too late, forgetting his carrying pole.*]

WONG: [*softly*] Shen Te! Shen Te! [*to himself*] So she's gone off to earn the rent. Oh dear, I can't go to the gods *again* with no room to offer them. Having failed in the service of the gods, I shall run to my den in the sewer pipe down by the river and hide from their sight!

> [*He rushes off.* SHEN TE *returns, looking for him, but finding the* GODS. *She stops in confusion.*]

SHEN TE: You are the illustrious ones? My name is Shen Te. It would please me very much if my simple room could be of use to you.

THIRD GOD: Where is the water seller, Miss . . . Shen Te?

SHEN TE: I missed him, somehow.

FIRST GOD: Oh, he probably thought you weren't coming, and was afraid of telling us.

THIRD GOD: [*picking up the carrying pole*] We'll leave this with you. He'll be needing it.

> [*Led by* SHEN TE, *they go into the house. It grows dark, then light. Dawn. Again escorted by* SHEN TE, *who leads them through the half-light with a little lamp, the* GODS *take their leave.*]

FIRST GOD: Thank you, thank you, dear Shen Te, for your elegant hospitality! We shall not forget! And give our thanks to the water seller—he showed us a good human being.

SHEN TE: Oh, *I'm* not good. Let me tell you something: when Wong asked me to put you up, I hesitated.

FIRST GOD: It's all right to hesitate if you then go ahead! And in giving us that room you did much more than you knew. You proved that good people still exist, a point that has been disputed of late—even in heaven. Farewell!

SECOND GOD: Farewell!

THIRD GOD: Farewell!

SHEN TE: Stop, illustrious ones! I'm not sure you're right. I'd like to be good, it's true, but there's the rent to pay. And that's not all: I sell myself for a living. Even so I can't make ends meet, there's too much competition. I'd like to honor my father and mother and speak nothing but the truth and not covet my neighbor's house. I should love to stay with one man. But how? How is it done? Even breaking a few of your commandments, I can hardly manage.

FIRST GOD: [*clearing his throat*] These thoughts are but, um, the misgivings of an unusually good woman!

THIRD GOD: Good-bye, Shen Te! Give our regards to the water seller!

SECOND GOD: And above all: be good! Farewell!

FIRST GOD: Farewell!

THIRD GOD: Farewell!

    [*They start to wave good-bye.*]

SHEN TE: But everything is so expensive. I don't feel sure I can do it!

SECOND GOD: That's not in our sphere. We never meddle with economics.

THIRD GOD: One moment. [*They stop.*] Isn't it true she might do better if she had more money?

SECOND GOD: Come, come! How could we ever account for it Up Above?

FIRST GOD: Oh, there are ways. [*They put their heads together and confer in dumb show. To* SHEN TE, *with embarrassment:*] As you say you can't pay your rent, well, um, we're not paupers, so of course we *insist* on paying for our room. [*awkwardly thrusting money into her hand.*] There! [*quickly*] But don't tell anyone! The incident is open to misinterpretation.

SECOND GOD: It certainly is!

FIRST GOD: [*defensively*] But there's no law against it! It was never decreed that a god mustn't pay hotel bills!

    [*The* GODS *leave.*]

SCENE I——*A small tobacco shop. The shop is not as yet completely furnished and hasn't started doing business.*

SHEN TE: [*to the audience*] It's three days now since the gods left. When they wanted to pay for the room, I looked down at my hand, and there was more than a thousand silver dollars! I bought a tobacco shop with the money, and moved in yesterday. I don't own the building, of course, but I can pay the rent, and I hope to do a lot of good here. Beginning with Mrs. Shin, who's just coming across the square with her pot. She had the shop before me, and yesterday she dropped in to ask for rice for her children. [*Enter* MRS. SHIN. *Both women bow.*] How do you do, Mrs. Shin.

MRS. SHIN: How do you do, Miss Shen Te. You like your new home?

SHEN TE: Indeed, yes. Did your children have a good night?

MRS. SHIN: In that hovel? The youngest is coughing already.

SHEN TE: Oh, dear!

MRS. SHIN: You're going to learn a thing or two in these slums.

SHEN TE: Slums? That's not what you said when you sold me the shop!

MRS. SHIN: Now don't start nagging! Robbing me and my innocent children of their home and then calling it a slum! That's the limit! [*She weeps.*]

SHEN TE: [*tactfully*] I'll get your rice.

MRS. SHIN: And a little cash while you're at it.

SHEN TE: I'm afraid I haven't sold anything yet.

MRS. SHIN: [*screeching*] I've got to have it. Strip the clothes from my back and then cut my throat, will you? I know what I'll do: I'll dump my children on your doorstep! [*She snatches the pot out of* SHEN TE'*s hands.*]

SHEN TE: Please don't be angry. You'll spill the rice.

　　　[*Enter an elderly* HUSBAND *and* WIFE *with their shabbily dressed* NEPHEW.]

WIFE: Shen Te, dear! You've come into money, they tell me. And we haven't a roof over our heads! A tobacco shop. We had one too. But it's gone. Could we spend the night here, do you think?

NEPHEW: [*appraising the shop*] Not bad!

WIFE: He's our nephew. We're inseparable!

MRS. SHIN: And who are these . . . ladies and gentlemen?

SHEN TE: They put me up when I first came in from the country. [*to the audience*] Of course, when my small purse was empty, they put me out on the street, and they may be afraid I'll do the same to them. [*to the newcomers, kindly*] Come in, and welcome, though I've only one little room for you— it's behind the shop.

HUSBAND: That'll do. Don't worry.

WIFE: [*bringing* SHEN TE *some tea*] We'll stay over here, so we won't be in your way. Did you make it a tobacco shop in memory of your first real home? We can certainly give you a hint or two! That's one reason we came.

MRS. SHIN: [*to* SHEN TE] Very nice! As long as you have a few customers too!

HUSBAND: Sh! A customer!

　　　[*Enter an* UNEMPLOYED MAN, *in rags.*]

UNEMPLOYED MAN: Excuse me. I'm unemployed.

　　　[MRS. SHIN *laughs.*]

SHEN TE: Can I help you?

UNEMPLOYED MAN: Have you any damaged cigarettes? I thought there might be some damage when you're unpacking.

WIFE: What nerve, begging for tobacco! [*rhetorically*] Why don't they ask for bread?

UNEMPLOYED MAN: Bread is expensive. One cigarette butt and I'll be a new man.

SHEN TE: [*giving him cigarettes*] That's very important—to be a new man. You'll be my first customer and bring me luck.

　　　[*The* UNEMPLOYED MAN *quickly lights a cigarette, inhales, and goes off, coughing.*]

WIFE: Was that right, Shen Te, dear?

MRS. SHIN: If this is the opening of a shop, you can hold the closing at the end of the week.

HUSBAND: I bet he had money on him.

SHEN TE: Oh, no, he said he hadn't!

NEPHEW: How d'you know he wasn't lying?

SHEN TE: [*angrily*] How do you know he was?

WIFE: [*wagging her head*] You're too good, Shen Te, dear. If you're going to keep this shop, you'll have to learn to say no.

HUSBAND: Tell them the place isn't yours to dispose of. Belongs to . . . some relative who insists on all accounts being strictly in order . . .

MRS. SHIN: That's right! What do you think you are—a philanthropist?

SHEN TE: [*laughing*] Very well, suppose I ask you for my rice back, Mrs. Shin?

WIFE: [*combatively, at* MRS. SHIN] So that's *her* rice?

[*Enter the* CARPENTER, *a small man.*]

MRS. SHIN: [*who, at the sight of him, starts to hurry away*] See you tomorrow, Miss Shen Te! [*Exit* MRS. SHIN.]

CARPENTER: Mrs. Shin, it's you I want!

WIFE: [*to* SHEN TE] Has she some claim on you?

SHEN TE: She's hungry. That's a claim.

CARPENTER: Are you the new tenant? And filling up the shelves already? Well, they're not yours till they're paid for, ma'am. I'm the carpenter, so I should know.

SHEN TE: I took the shop "furnishings included."

CARPENTER: You're in league with that Mrs. Shin, of course. All right. I demand my hundred silver dollars.

SHEN TE: I'm afraid I haven't got a hundred silver dollars.

CARPENTER: Then you'll find it. Or I'll have you arrested.

WIFE: [*whispering to* SHEN TE] That relative: make it a cousin.

SHEN TE: Can't it wait till next month?

CARPENTER: No!

SHEN TE: Be a little patient, Mr. Carpenter, I can't settle all claims at once.

CARPENTER: Who's patient with me? [*he grabs a shelf from the wall*] Pay up— or I take the shelves back!

WIFE: Shen Te! Dear! Why don't you let your . . . cousin settle this affair? [*to* CARPENTER] Put your claim in writing. Shen Te's cousin will see you get paid.

CARPENTER: [*derisively*] Cousin, eh?

HUSBAND: Cousin, yes.

CARPENTER: I know these cousins!

NEPHEW: Don't be silly. He's a personal friend of mine.

HUSBAND: What a man! Sharp as a razor!

CARPENTER: All right. I'll put my claim in writing. [*puts shelf on floor, sits on it, writes out bill*]

WIFE: [*to* SHEN TE] He'd tear the dress off your back to get his shelves. Never recognize a claim. That's my motto.

SHEN TE: He's done a job, and wants something in return. It's shameful that I can't give it to him. What will the gods say?

HUSBAND: You did your bit when you took *us* in.

[*Enter the* BROTHER, *limping, and the* SISTER-IN-LAW, *pregnant.*]

BROTHER: [*to* HUSBAND *and* WIFE] So this is where you're hiding out! There's family feeling for you! Leaving us on the corner!

WIFE: [*embarrassed, to* SHEN TE] It's my brother and his wife. [*to them*] Now stop grumbling, and sit quietly in that corner. [*to* SHEN TE] It can't be helped. She's in her fifth month.

SHEN TE: Oh yes. Welcome!

WIFE: [*to the couple*] Say thank you. [*They mutter something.*] The cups are there. [*to* SHEN TE] Lucky you bought this shop when you did!

SHEN TE: [*laughing and bringing tea*] Lucky indeed!
    [*Enter* MRS. MI TZU, *the landlady.*]

MRS. MI TZU: Miss Shen Te? I am Mrs. Mi Tzu, your landlady. I hope our relationship will be a happy one. I like to think I give my tenants modern, personalized service. Here is your lease. [*to the others, as* SHEN TE *reads the lease*] There's nothing like the opening of a little shop, is there? A moment of true beauty! [*she is looking around*] Not very much on the shelves, of course. But everything in the gods' good time! Where are your references, Miss Shen Te?

SHEN TE: Do I *have* to have references?

MRS. MI TZU: After all, I haven't a notion who you are!

HUSBAND: Oh, *we'd* be glad to vouch for Miss Shen Te! We'd go through fire for her!

MRS. MI TZU: And who may *you* be?

HUSBAND: [*stammering*] Ma Fu, tobacco dealer.

MRS. MI TZU: Where is your shop, Mr. . . . Ma Fu?

HUSBAND: Well, um, I haven't got a shop—I've just sold it.

MRS. MI TZU: I see. [*to* SHEN TE] Is there no one else that knows you?

WIFE: [*whispering to* SHEN TE] Your cousin! Your cousin!

MRS. MI TZU: This is a respectable house, Miss Shen Te. I never sign a lease without certain assurances.

SHEN TE: [*slowly, her eyes downcast*] I have . . . a cousin.

MRS. MI TZU: On the square? Let's go over and see him. What does he do?

SHEN TE: [*as before*] He lives . . . in another city.

WIFE: [*prompting*] Didn't you say he was in Shung?

SHEN TE: That's right. Shung.

HUSBAND: [*prompting*] I had his name on the tip of my tongue. Mr. . . .

SHEN TE: [*with an effort*] Mr. . . . Shui . . . Ta.

HUSBAND: That's it! Tall, skinny fellow!

SHEN TE: Shui Ta!

NEPHEW: [*to* CARPENTER] *You* were in touch with him, weren't you? About the shelves?

CARPENTER: [*surlily*] Give him this bill. [*He hands it over.*] I'll be back in the morning. [*Exit* CARPENTER.]

NEPHEW: [*calling after him, but with his eyes on* MRS. MI TZU] Don't worry! Mr. Shui Ta pays on the nail!

MRS. MI TZU: [*looking closely at* SHEN TE] I'll be happy to make his acquaintance, Miss Shen Te. [*Exit* MRS. MI TZU.]
    [*Pause.*]

WIFE: By tomorrow morning she'll know more about you than you do yourself.

SISTER-IN-LAW: [*to* NEPHEW] This thing isn't built to last.
    [*Enter* GRANDFATHER.]
WIFE: It's Grandfather! [*to* SHEN TE] Such a good old soul!
    [*The* BOY *enters.*]
BOY: [*over his shoulder*] Here they are!
WIFE: And the boy, how he's grown! But he always could eat enough for ten.
    [*Enter the* NIECE.]
WIFE: [*to* SHEN TE] Our little niece from the country. There are more of us
    now than in your time. The less we had, the more there were of us; the
    more there were of us, the less we had. Give me the key. We must protect
    ourselves from unwanted guests. [*she takes the key and locks the door*]
    Just make yourself at home. I'll light the little lamp.
NEPHEW: [*a big joke*] I hope her cousin doesn't drop in tonight! The strict Mr.
    Shui Ta!
    [SISTER-IN-LAW *laughs.*]
BROTHER: [*reaching for a cigarette*] One cigarette more or less . . .
HUSBAND: One cigarette more or less.
    [*They pile into the cigarettes. The* BROTHER *hands a jug of wine
    round.*]
NEPHEW: Mr. Shui Ta'll pay for it!
GRANDFATHER: [*gravely, to* SHEN TE] How do you do?
    [SHEN TE, *a little taken aback by the belatedness of the greeting, bows.
    She has the carpenter's bill in one hand, the landlady's lease in the
    other.*]
WIFE: How about a bit of a song? To keep Shen Te's spirits up?
NEPHEW: Good idea. Grandfather: you start!

SONG OF THE SMOKE

GRANDFATHER:
        I used to think (before old age beset me)
          That brains could fill the pantry of the poor.
        But where did all my cerebration get me?
          I'm just as hungry as I was before.
            So what's the use?
              See the smoke float free
            Into ever colder coldness!
              It's the same with me.
HUSBAND:
        The straight and narrow path leads to disaster
          And so the crooked path I tried to tread.
        That got me to disaster even faster.
          (They say we shall be happy when we're dead.)
            So what's the use?
              See the smoke float free
            Into ever colder coldness!
              It's the same with me.

NIECE:

> You older people, full of expectation,
>> At any moment now you'll walk the plank!
> The future's for the younger generation!
>> Yes, even if that future is a blank.
>>> So what's the use?
>>>> See the smoke float free
>>>> Into ever colder coldness!
>>>> It's the same with me.

NEPHEW: [*to the* BROTHER] Where'd you get that wine?

SISTER-IN-LAW: [*answering for the* BROTHER] He pawned the sack of tobacco.

HUSBAND: [*stepping in*] What? That tobacco was all we had to fall back on! You pig!

BROTHER: *You'd* call a man a pig because your wife was frigid! Did you refuse to drink it?

> [*They fight. The shelves fall over.*]

SHEN TE: [*imploringly*] Oh don't! Don't break everything! Take it, take it, take it all, but don't destroy a gift from the gods!

WIFE: [*disparagingly*] This shop isn't big enough. I should never have mentioned it to Uncle and the others. When *they* arrive, it's going to be disgustingly overcrowded.

SISTER-IN-LAW: And did you hear our gracious hostess? She cools off quick!

> [*Voices outside. Knocking at the door.*]

UNCLE'S VOICE: Open the door!

WIFE: Uncle! Is that you, Uncle?

UNCLE'S VOICE: Certainly, it's me. Auntie says to tell you she'll have the children here in ten minutes.

WIFE: [*to* SHEN TE] I'll have to let him in.

SHEN TE: [*who scarcely hears her*]

> The little lifeboat is swiftly sent down
> Too many men too greedily
> Hold on to it as they drown.

SCENE IA——WONG's *den in a sewer pipe.*

WONG: [*crouching there*] All quiet! It's four days now since I left the city. The gods passed this way on the second day. I heard their steps on the bridge over there. They must be a long way off by this time, so I'm safe. [*Breathing a sigh of relief, he curls up and goes to sleep. In his dream the pipe becomes transparent, and the* GODS *appear. Raising an arm, as if in self-defense:*] I know, I know, illustrious ones! I found no one to give you a room—not in all Setzuan! There, it's out. Please continue on your way!

FIRST GOD: [*mildly*] But you did find someone. Someone who took us in for the night, watched over us in our sleep, and in the early morning lighted us down to the street with a lamp.

WONG: It was . . . Shen Te that took you in?

THIRD GOD: Who else?

WONG: And I ran away! "She isn't coming," I thought, "she just can't afford it."

GODS: [*singing*]
> O you feeble, well-intentioned, and yet feeble chap
> Where there's need the fellow thinks there is no goodness!
> When there's danger he thinks courage starts to ebb away!
> Some people only see the seamy side!
> What hasty judgment! What premature desperation!

WONG: I'm *very* ashamed, illustrious ones.

FIRST GOD: Do us a favor, water seller. Go back to Setzuan. Find Shen Te, and give us a report on her. We hear that she's come into a little money. Show interest in her goodness—for no one can be good for long if goodness is not in demand. Meanwhile we shall continue the search, and find other good people. After which, the idle chatter about the impossibility of goodness will stop!

[*The* GODS *vanish.*]

SCENE II

[*A knocking.*]

WIFE: Shen Te! Someone at the door. Where is she anyway?

NEPHEW: She must be getting the breakfast. Mr. Shui Ta will pay for it.

[*The* WIFE *laughs and shuffles to the door. Enter* MR. SHUI TA *and the* CARPENTER.]

WIFE: Who is it?

SHUI TA: I am Miss Shen Te's cousin.

WIFE: What?

SHUI TA: My name is Shui Ta.

WIFE: Her cousin?

NEPHEW: Her cousin?

NIECE: But that was a joke. She hasn't got a cousin.

HUSBAND: So early in the morning?

BROTHER: What's all the noise?

SISTER-IN-LAW: This fellow says he's her cousin.

BROTHER: Tell him to prove it.

NEPHEW: Right. If you're Shen Te's cousin, prove it by getting the breakfast.

SHUI TA: [*whose regime begins as he puts out the lamp to save oil; loudly, to all present, asleep or awake*] Would you all please get dressed! Customers will be coming! I wish to open my shop!

HUSBAND: *Your* shop? Doesn't it belong to our good friend Shen Te?

[SHUI TA *shakes his head.*]

SISTER-IN-LAW: So we've been cheated. Where *is* the little liar?

SHUI TA: Miss Shen Te has been delayed. She wishes me to tell you there will be nothing she can do—now I am here.

WIFE: [*bowled over*] I thought she was good!

NEPHEW: Do you have to believe *him?*

HUSBAND: I don't.

NEPHEW: Then do something.

HUSBAND: Certainly! I'll send out a search party at once. You, you, you, and you, go out and look for Shen Te. [*as the* GRANDFATHER *rises and makes for the door*] Not you, Grandfather, you and I will hold the fort.

SHUI TA: You won't find Miss Shen Te. She has suspended her hospitable activity for an unlimited period. There are too many of you. She asked me to say: this is a tobacco shop, not a gold mine.

HUSBAND: Shen Te never said a thing like that. Boy, food! There's a bakery on the corner. Stuff your shirt full when they're not looking!

SISTER-IN-LAW: Don't overlook the raspberry tarts.

HUSBAND: And don't let the policeman see you.

[*The* BOY *leaves.*]

SHUI TA: Don't you depend on this shop now? Then why give it a bad name by stealing from the bakery?

NEPHEW: Don't listen to him. Let's find Shen Te. She'll give him a piece of her mind.

SISTER-IN-LAW: Don't forget to leave us some breakfast.

[BROTHER, SISTER-IN-LAW, *and* NEPHEW *leave.*]

SHUI TA: [*to the* CARPENTER] You see, Mr. Carpenter, nothing has changed since the poet, eleven hundred years ago, penned these lines:

A governor was asked what was needed
To save the freezing people in the city.
He replied:
"A blanket ten thousand feet long
to cover the city and all its suburbs."

[*He starts to tidy up the shop.*]

CARPENTER: Your cousin owes me money. I've got witnesses. For the shelves.

SHUI TA: Yes, I have your bill. [*he takes it out of his pocket*] Isn't a hundred silver dollars rather a lot?

CARPENTER: No deductions! I have a wife and children.

SHUI TA: How many children?

CARPENTER: Three.

SHUI TA: I'll make you an offer. Twenty silver dollars.

[*The* HUSBAND *laughs.*]

CARPENTER: You're crazy. Those shelves are real walnut.

SHUI TA: Very well. Take them away.

CARPENTER: What?

SHUI TA: They cost too much. Please take them away.

WIFE: Not bad! [*And she, too, is laughing.*]

CARPENTER: [*a little bewildered*] Call Shen Te, someone! [*to* SHUI TA] She's good!

SHUI TA: Certainly. She's ruined.

CARPENTER: [*provoked into taking some of the shelves*] All right, you can keep your tobacco on the floor.

SHUI TA: [*to the* HUSBAND] Help him with the shelves.

HUSBAND: [*grins and carries one shelf over to the door where the* CARPENTER *now is*] Good-bye, shelves!

CARPENTER: [*to the* HUSBAND] You dog! You want my family to starve?

SHUI TA: I repeat my offer. I have no desire to keep my tobacco on the floor. Twenty silver dollars.

CARPENTER: [*with desperate aggressiveness*] One hundred!

[SHUI TA *shows indifference, looks through the window. The* HUSBAND *picks up several shelves.*]

CARPENTER: [*to* HUSBAND] You needn't smash them against the doorposts, you idiot! [*to* SHUI TA] These shelves were made to measure. They're no use anywhere else!

SHUI TA: Precisely.

[*The* WIFE *squeals with pleasure.*]

CARPENTER: [*giving up, sullenly*] Take the shelves. Pay what you want to pay.

SHUI TA: [*smoothly*] Twenty silver dollars.

[*He places two large coins on the table. The* CARPENTER *picks them up.*]

HUSBAND: [*brings the shelves in*] And quite enough too!

CARPENTER: [*slinking off*] Quite enough to get drunk on.

HUSBAND: [*happily*] Well, we got rid of *him!*

WIFE: [*weeping with fun, gives a rendition of the dialogue just spoken*] "Real walnut," says he. "Very well, take them away," says his lordship. "I have three children," says he. "Twenty silver dollars," says his lordship. "They're no use anywhere else," says he. "Pre-cisely," said his lordship! [*she dissolves into shrieks of merriment*]

SHUI TA: And now: go!

HUSBAND: What's that?

SHUI TA: You're thieves, parasites. I'm giving you this chance. Go!

HUSBAND: [*summoning all his ancestral dignity*] That sort deserves no answer. Besides, one should never shout on an empty stomach.

WIFE: Where's that boy?

SHUI TA: Exactly. The boy. I want no stolen goods in this shop. [*very loudly*] I strongly advise you to leave! [*But they remain seated, noses in the air. Quietly.*] As you wish. [SHUI TA *goes to the door. A* POLICEMAN *appears.* SHUI TA *bows.*] I am addressing the officer in charge of this precinct?

POLICEMAN: That's right, Mr., um, what was the name, sir?

SHUI TA: Mr. Shui Ta.

POLICEMAN: Yes, of course, sir.

[*They exchange a smile.*]

SHUI TA: Nice weather we're having.

POLICEMAN: A little on the warm side, sir.

SHUI TA: Oh, a little on the warm side.

HUSBAND: [*whispering to the* WIFE] If he keeps it up till the boy's back, we're done for. [*Tries to signal* SHUI TA.]

SHUI TA: [*ignoring the signal*] Weather, of course, is one thing indoors, another out on the dusty street!

POLICEMAN: Oh, quite another, sir!

WIFE: [*to the* HUSBAND] It's all right as long as he's standing in the doorway—the boy will see him.

SHUI TA: Step inside for a moment! It's quite cool indoors. My cousin and I have just opened the place. And we attach the greatest importance to being on good terms with the, um, authorities.

POLICEMAN: [*entering*] Thank you, Mr. Shui Ta. It *is* cool.

HUSBAND: [*whispering to the* WIFE] And now the boy *won't* see him.

SHUI TA: [*showing* HUSBAND *and* WIFE *to the* POLICEMAN] Visitors, I think my cousin knows them. They were just leaving.

HUSBAND: [*defeated*] Ye-e-es, we were . . . just leaving.

SHUI TA: I'll tell my cousin you couldn't wait.

[*Noise from the street. Shouts of "Stop, Thief!"*]

POLICEMAN: What's that?

[*The* BOY *is in the doorway with cakes and buns and rolls spilling out of his shirt. The* WIFE *signals desperately to him to leave. He gets the idea.*]

POLICEMAN: No, you don't! [*he grabs the* BOY *by the collar*] Where's all this from?

BOY: [*vaguely pointing*] Down the street.

POLICEMAN: [*grimly*] So that's it. [*Prepares to arrest the* BOY.]

WIFE: [*stepping in*] And *we* knew nothing about it. [*to the* BOY] Nasty little thief!

POLICEMAN: [*dryly*] Can you clarify the situation, Mr. Shui Ta?

[SHUI TA *is silent.*]

POLICEMAN: [*who understands silence*] Aha. You're all coming with me—to the station.

SHUI TA: I can hardly say how sorry I am that my establishment . . .

WIFE: Oh, he saw the boy leave not ten minutes ago!

SHUI TA: And to conceal the theft asked a policeman in?

POLICEMAN: Don't listen to her, Mr. Shui Ta, I'll be happy to relieve you of their presence one and all! [*to all three*] Out! [*He drives them before him.*]

GRANDFATHER: [*leaving last, gravely*] Good morning!

POLICEMAN: Good morning!

[SHUI TA, *left alone, continues to tidy up.* MRS. MI TZU *breezes in.*]

MRS. MI TZU: You're her cousin, are you? Then have the goodness to explain what all this means—police dragging people from a respectable house! By what right does your Miss Shen Te turn my property into a house of assignation? Well, as you see, I know all!

SHUI TA: Yes. My cousin has the worst possible reputation: that of being poor.

MRS. MI TZU: No sentimental rubbish, Mr. Shui Ta. Your cousin was a common . . .

SHUI TA: Pauper. Let's use the uglier word.

MRS. MI TZU: I'm speaking of her conduct, not her earnings. But there must have *been* earnings, or how did she buy all this? Several elderly gentlemen took care of it, I suppose. I repeat: this is a respectable house! I have tenants who prefer not to live under the same roof with such a person.

SHUI TA: [*quietly*] How much do you want?

MRS. MI TZU: [*he is ahead of her now*] I beg your pardon.

SHUI TA: To reassure yourself. To reassure your tenants. How much will it cost?

MRS. MI TZU: You're a cool customer.

SHUI TA: [*picking up the lease*] The rent is high. [*he reads on*] I assume it's payable by the month?

MRS. MI TZU: Not in her case.

SHUI TA: [*looking up*] What?

MRS. MI TZU: Six months' rent payable in advance. Two hundred silver dollars.

SHUI TA: Six . . . ! Sheer usury! And where am I to find it?

MRS. MI TZU: You should have thought of that before.

SHUI TA: Have you no heart, Mrs. Mi Tzu? It's true Shen Te acted foolishly, being kind to all those people, but she'll improve with time. I'll see to it she does. She'll work her fingers to the bone to pay her rent, and all the time be as quiet as a mouse, as humble as a fly.

MRS. MI TZU: Her social background . . .

SHUI TA: Out of the depths! She came out of the depths! And before she'll go back there, she'll work, sacrifice, shrink from nothing. . . . Such a tenant is worth her weight in gold, Mrs. Mi Tzu.

MRS. MI TZU: It's silver dollars we were talking about, Mr. Shui Ta. Two hundred silver dollars or . . .

[*Enter the* POLICEMAN.]

POLICEMAN: Am I intruding, Mr. Shui Ta?

MRS. MI TZU: This tobacco shop is well known to the police, I see.

POLICEMAN: Mr. Shui Ta has done us a service, Mrs. Mi Tzu. I am here to present our official felicitations!

MRS. MI TZU: That means less than nothing to me, sir. Mr. Shui Ta, all I can say is: I hope your cousin will find my terms acceptable. Good day, gentlemen. [*Exit.*]

SHUI TA: Good day, ma'am.

[*Pause.*]

POLICEMAN: Mrs. Mi Tzu a bit of a stumbling block, sir?

SHUI TA: She wants six months' rent in advance.

POLICEMAN: And you haven't got it, eh? [SHUI TA *is silent.*] But surely you can get it, sir? A man like you?

SHUI TA: What about a woman like Shen Te?

POLICEMAN: You're not staying, sir?

SHUI TA: No, and I won't be back. Do you smoke?

POLICEMAN: [*taking two cigars, and placing them both in his pocket*] Thank you, sir—I see your point. Miss Te—let's mince no words—Miss Shen Te lived by selling herself. "What else could she have done?" you ask. "How else was she to pay the rent?" True. But the fact remains, Mr. Shui Ta, it is not respectable. Why not? A very deep question. But, in the first place, love—love isn't bought and sold like cigars, Mr. Shui Ta. In the second place, it isn't respectable to go waltzing off with someone that's paying his way, so to speak—it must be for love! Thirdly and lastly, as the proverb has it: not for a handful of rice but for love! [*Pause. He is thinking hard.*]

"Well," you may say, "and what good is all this wisdom if the milk's already spilt?" Miss Shen Te is what she is. Is *where* she is. We have to face the fact that if she doesn't get hold of six months' rent pronto, she'll be back on the streets. The question then as I see it—everything in this world is a matter of opinion—the question as I see it is: *how* is she to get hold of this rent? How? Mr. Shui Ta: I don't know. [*Pause.*] I take that back, sir. It's just come to me. A husband. We must find her a husband!

[*Enter a little* OLD WOMAN.]

OLD WOMAN: A good cheap cigar for my husband, we'll have been married forty years tomorrow and we're having a little celebration.

SHUI TA: Forty years? And you still want to celebrate?

OLD WOMAN: As much as we can afford to. We have the carpet shop across the square. We'll be good neighbors, I hope?

SHUI TA: I hope so too.

POLICEMAN: [*who keeps making discoveries*] Mr. Shui Ta, you know what we need? We need capital. And how do we acquire capital? We get married.

SHUI TA: [*to* OLD WOMAN] I'm afraid I've been pestering this gentleman with my personal worries.

POLICEMAN: [*lyrically*] We can't pay six months' rent, so what do we do? We marry money.

SHUI TA: That might not be easy.

POLICEMAN: Oh, I don't know. She's a good match. Has a nice, growing business. [*to the* OLD WOMAN] What do you think?

OLD WOMAN: [*undecided*] Well—

POLICEMAN: Should she put an ad in the paper?

OLD WOMAN: [*not eager to commit herself*] Well, if *she* agrees—

POLICEMAN: I'll write it for her. *You* lend us a hand, and *we* write an ad for you! [*He chuckles away to himself, takes out his notebook, wets the stump of a pencil between his lips, and writes away.*]

SHUI TA: [*slowly*] Not a bad idea.

POLICEMAN: "What . . . *respectable* . . . man . . . with small capital . . . widower . . . not excluded . . . desires . . . marriage . . . into flourishing . . . tobacco shop?" And now let's add: "Am . . pretty . . ." No! . . . "Prepossessing appearance."

SHUI TA: If you don't think that's an exaggeration?

OLD WOMAN: Oh, not a bit. I've seen her.

[*The* POLICEMAN *tears the page out of his notebook, and hands it over to* SHUI TA.]

SHUI TA: [*with horror in his voice*] How much luck we need to keep our heads above water! How many ideas! How many friends! [*to the* POLICEMAN] Thank you, sir, I think I see my way clear.

SCENE III——*Evening in the municipal park. Noise of a plane overhead.*

[YANG SUN, *a young man in rags, is following the plane with his eyes: one can tell that the machine is describing a curve above the park.* YANG SUN *then takes a rope out of his pocket, looking anxiously about him as he does so. He moves toward a large willow. Enter two prosti-*

tutes, one the OLD WHORE, *the other the* NIECE *whom we have already met.*]

NIECE: Hello. Coming with me?

YANG SUN: [*taken aback*] If you'd like to buy me a dinner.

OLD WHORE: Buy you a dinner! [*to the* NIECE] Oh, we know him—it's the un-employed pilot. Waste no time on him!

NIECE: But he's the only man left in the park. And it's going to rain.

OLD WHORE: Oh, how do you know?

[*And they pass by.* YANG SUN *again looks about him, again takes his rope, and this time throws it round a branch of the willow tree. Again he is interrupted. It is the two prostitutes returning—and in such a hurry they don't notice him.*]

NIECE: It's going to pour!

[*Enter* SHEN TE.]

OLD WHORE: There's that *gorgon* Shen Te! That *drove* your family out into the cold!

NIECE: It wasn't her. It was that cousin of hers. She offered to pay for the cakes. I've nothing against her.

OLD WHORE: I have, though. [*so that* SHEN TE *can hear*] Now where would the little lady be off to? She may be rich now but that won't stop her snatch-ing our young men, will it?

SHEN TE: I'm going to the tearoom by the pond.

NIECE: Is it true what they say? You're marrying a widower—with three chil-dren?

SHEN TE: Yes. I'm just going to see him.

YANG SUN: [*his patience at breaking point*] Move on there! This is a park, not a whorehouse!

OLD WHORE: Shut your mouth!

[*But the two prostitutes leave.*]

YANG SUN: Even in the farthest corner of the park, even when it's raining, you can't get rid of them! [*he spits*]

SHEN TE: [*overhearing this*] And what right have you to scold them? [*but at this point she sees the rope*] Oh!

YANG SUN: Well, what are you staring at?

SHEN TE: That rope. What is it for?

YANG SUN: Think! Think! I haven't a penny. Even if I had, I wouldn't spend it on you. I'd buy a drink of water.

[*The rain starts.*]

SHEN TE: [*still looking at the rope*] What is the rope for? You mustn't!

YANG SUN: What's it to you? Clear out!

SHEN TE: [*irrelevantly*] It's raining.

YANG SUN: Well, don't try to come under this tree.

SHEN TE: Oh, no. [*She stays in the rain.*]

YANG SUN: Now go away. [*pause*] For one thing, I don't like your looks, you're bowlegged.

SHEN TE: [*indignantly*] That's not true!

YANG SUN: Well, don't show 'em to me. Look, it's raining. You better come under this tree.

    [*Slowly, she takes shelter under the tree.*]

SHEN TE: Why did you want to do it?

YANG SUN: You really want to know? [*pause*] To get rid of you! [*pause*] You know what a flyer is?

SHEN TE: Oh yes, I've met a lot of pilots. At the tearoom.

YANG SUN: You call *them* flyers? Think they know what a machine is? Just 'cause they have leather helmets? They gave the airfield director a bribe, that's the way *those* fellows got up in the air! Try one of them out sometime. "Go up to two thousand feet," tell them, "then let it fall, then pick it up again with a flick of the wrist at the last moment." Know what he'll say to that? "It's not in my contract." Then again, there's the landing problem. It's like landing on your own backside. It's no different, planes are human. Those fools don't understand. [*pause*] And I'm the biggest fool for reading the book on flying in the Peking school and skipping the page where it says: "We've got enough flyers and we don't need you." I'm a mail pilot with no mail. You understand that?

SHEN TE: [*shyly*] Yes. I do.

YANG SUN: No, you don't. You'd never understand that.

SHEN TE: When we were little we had a crane with a broken wing. He made friends with us and was very good-natured about our jokes. He would strut along behind us and call out to stop us going too fast for him. But every spring and autumn when the cranes flew over the villages in great swarms, he got quite restless. [*pause*] I understand that. [*She bursts out crying.*]

YANG SUN: Don't!

SHEN TE: [*quieting down*] No.

YANG SUN: It's bad for the complexion.

SHEN TE: [*sniffing*] I've stopped.

    [*She dries her tears on her big sleeve. Leaning against the tree, but not looking at her, he reaches for her face.*]

YANG SUN: You can't even wipe your own face. [*He is wiping it for her with his handkerchief. Pause.*]

SHEN TE: [*still sobbing*] I don't know *anything!*

YANG SUN: You interrupted me! What for?

SHEN TE: It's such a rainy day. You only wanted to do . . . *that* because it's such a rainy day. [*To the audience:*]

    In our country
    The evenings should never be somber
    High bridges over rivers
    The gray hour between night and morning
    And the long, long winter:
    Such things are dangerous
    For, with all the misery,
    A very little is enough
    And men throw away an unbearable life.

    [*Pause.*]

YANG SUN: Talk about yourself for a change.

SHEN TE: What about me? I have a shop.

YAN SUN: [*incredulous*] You have a shop, have you? Never thought of walking the streets?

SHEN TE: I did walk the streets. Now I have a shop.

YANG SUN: [*ironically*] A gift of the gods, I suppose!

SHEN TE: How did you know?

YANG SUN: [*even more ironical*] One fine evening the gods turned up saying: here's some money!

SHE TE: [*quickly*] One fine morning.

YANG SUN: [*fed up*] This isn't much of an entertainment.
    [*Pause.*]

SHEN TE: I can play the zither a little. [*pause*] And I can mimic men. [*pause*] I got the shop, so the first thing I did was to give my zither away. So I can be as stupid as a fish now, I said to myself, and it won't matter.

I'm rich now, I said
I walk alone, I sleep alone
For a whole year, I said
I'll have nothing to do with a man.

YANG SUN: And now you're marrying one! The one at the tearoom by the pond?
    [SHEN TE *is silent.*]

YANG SUN: What do you know about love?

SHEN TE: Everything.

YANG SUN: Nothing. [*pause*] Or d'you just mean you enjoyed it?

SHEN TE: No.

YANG SUN: [*again without turning to look at her, he strokes her cheek with his hand*] You like that?

SHEN TE: Yes.

YANG SUN: [*breaking off*] You're easily satisfied, I must say. [*pause*] What a town!

SHEN TE: You have no friends?

YANG SUN: [*defensively*] Yes, I have! [*change of tone*] But they don't want to hear I'm still unemployed. "What?" they ask. "Is there still water in the sea?" You have friends?

SHEN TE: [*hesitating*] Just a . . . cousin.

YANG SUN: Watch him carefully.

SHEN TE: He only came once. Then he went away. He won't be back. [YANG SUN *is looking away.*] But to be without hope, they say, is to be without goodness!
    [*Pause.*]

YANG SUN: Go on talking. A voice is a voice.

SHEN TE: Once, when I was a little girl, I fell, with a load of brushwood. An old man picked me up. He gave me a penny too. Isn't it funny how people who don't have very much like to give some of it away? They must like to show what they can do, and how could they show it better than by being kind? Being wicked is just like being clumsy. When we sing a song, or build a machine, or plant some rice, we're being kind. You're kind.

YANG SUN: You make it sound easy.

SHEN TE: Oh, no. [*little pause*] Oh! A drop of rain!

YANG SUN: Where'd you feel it?

SHEN TE: Right between the eyes.

YANG SUN: Near the right eye? Or the left?

SHEN TE: Near the left eye.

YANG SUN: Oh, good. [*he is getting sleepy*] So you're through with men, eh?

SHEN TE: [*with a smile*] But I'm not bowlegged.

YANG SUN: Perhaps not.

SHE TE: Definitely not.

    [*Pause.*]

YANG SUN: [*leaning wearily against the willow*] I haven't had a drop to drink all day, I haven't eaten anything for *two* days. I couldn't love you if I tried.

    [*Pause.*]

SHEN TE: I like it in the rain.

    [*Enter* WONG *the water seller, singing.*]

      THE SONG OF THE WATER SELLER IN THE RAIN

"Buy my water," I am yelling
And my fury restraining
For no water I'm selling
'Cause it's raining, 'cause it's raining!
    I keep yelling: "Buy my water!"
    But no one's buying
    Athirst and dying
    And drinking and paying!
    Buy water!
    Buy water, you dogs!

Nice to dream of lovely weather!
Think of all the consternation
Were there no precipitation
Half a dozen years together!
    Can't you hear them shrieking: "Water!"
    Pretending they adore me?
    They all would go down on their knees
        before me!
    Down on your knees!
    Go down on your knees, you dogs!

What are lawns and hedges thinking?
What are fields and forests saying?
"At the cloud's breast we are drinking!
And we've no idea who's paying!"
    I keep yelling: "Buy my water!"

But no one's buying
Athirst and dying
And drinking and paying!
Buy water
Buy water, you dogs!

[*The rain has stopped now,* SHEN TE *sees* WONG *and runs toward him.*]

SHEN TE: Wong! You're back! Your carrying pole's at the shop.

WONG: Oh, thank you, Shen Te. And how is life treating *you?*

SHEN TE: I've just met a brave and clever man. And I want to buy him a cup of your water.

WONG: [*bitterly*] Throw back your head and open your mouth and you'll have all the water you need—

SHEN TE: [*tenderly*]

I want *your* water, Wong
The water that has tired you so
The water that you carried all this way
The water that is hard to sell because
      it's been raining.

I need it for the young man over there—he's a flyer!
A flyer is a bold man:
Braving the storms
In company with the clouds
He crosses the heavens
And brings to friends in faraway lands
The friendly mail!

[*She pays* WONG, *and runs over to* YANG SUN *with the cup. But* YANG SUN *is fast asleep.*]

SHEN TE: [*calling to* WONG, *with a laugh*] He's fallen asleep! Despair and rain and I have worn him out!

SCENE IIIA——WONG'S *den.*

[*The sewer pipe is transparent, and the* GODS *again appear to* WONG *in a dream.*]

WONG: [*radiant*] I've seen her, illustrious ones! And she hasn't changed!

FIRST GOD: That's good to hear.

WONG: She loves someone.

FIRST GOD: Let's hope the experience gives her the strength to stay good!

WONG: It does. She's doing good deeds all the time.

FIRST GOD: Ah? What sort? What sort of good deeds, Wong?

WONG: Well, she has a kind word for everybody.

FIRST GOD: [*eagerly*] And then?

WONG: Hardly anyone leaves her shop without tobacco in his pocket—even if he can't pay for it.

FIRST GOD: Not bad at all. Next?

WONG: She's putting up a family of eight.

FIRST GOD: [*gleefully, to the* SECOND GOD] Eight! [*to* WONG] And that's not all, of course!

WONG: She bought a cup of water from me even though it was raining.

FIRST GOD: Yes, yes, yes, all these smaller good deeds!

WONG: Even they run into money. A little tobacco shop doesn't make so much.

FIRST GOD: [*sententiously*] A prudent gardener works miracles on the smallest plot.

WONG: She hands out rice every morning. That eats up half her earnings.

FIRST GOD: [*a little disappointed*] Well, as a beginning . . .

WONG: They call her the Angel of the Slums—whatever the carpenter may say!

FIRST GOD: What's this? A carpenter speaks ill of her?

WONG: Oh, he only says her shelves weren't paid for in full.

SECOND GOD: [*who has a bad cold and can't pronounce his n's and m's*] What's this? Not paying a carpenter? Why was that?

WONG: I suppose she didn't have the money.

SECOND GOD: [*severely*] One pays what one owes, that's in our book of rules! First the letter of the law, then the spirit.

WONG: But it wasn't Shen Te, illustrious ones, it was her cousin. She called *him* in to help.

SECOND GOD: Then her cousin must never darken her threshold again!

WONG: Very well, illustrious ones! But in fairness to Shen Te, let me say that her cousin is a businessman.

FIRST GOD: Perhaps we should inquire what is customary? I find business quite unintelligible. But everybody's doing it. Business! Did the Seven Good Kings do business? Did Kung the Just sell fish?

SECOND GOD: In any case, such a thing must not occur again!

[*The* GODS *start to leave.*]

THIRD GOD: Forgive us for taking this tone with you, Wong, we haven't been getting enough sleep. The rich recommend us to the poor, and the poor tell us they haven't enough room.

SECOND GOD: Feeble, feeble, the best of them!

FIRST GOD: No great deeds! No heroic daring!

THIRD GOD: On such a *small* scale!

SECOND GOD: Sincere, yes, but what is actually *achieved?*

[*One can no longer hear them.*]

WONG: [*calling after them*] I've thought of something, illustrious ones: Perhaps you shouldn't ask—too—much—all—at—once!

SCENE IV——*The square in front of* SHEN TE's *tobacco shop. Besides Shen Te's place, two other shops are seen: the carpet shop and a barber's. Morning.*

[*Outside Shen Te's the* GRANDFATHER, *the* SISTER-IN-LAW, *the* UNEMPLOYED MAN, *and* MRS. SHIN *stand waiting.*]

SISTER-IN-LAW: She's been out all night again.

MRS. SHIN: No sooner did we get rid of that crazy cousin of hers than Shen Te herself starts carrying on! Maybe she does give us an ounce of rice now and then, but can you depend on her? Can you depend on her?

[*Loud voices from the barber's.*]

VOICE OF SHU FU: What are you doing in my shop? Get out—at once!

VOICE OF WONG: But sir. They all let me sell . . .

[WONG *comes staggering out of the barber's shop pursued by* MR.
SHU FU, *the barber, a fat man carrying a heavy curling iron.*]

SHU FU: Get out, I said! Pestering my customers with your slimy old water! Get
out! Take your cup!

[*He holds out the cup.* WONG *reaches out for it.* MR. SHU FU *strikes his
hand with the curling iron, which is hot.* WONG *howls.*]

SHU FU: You had it coming, my man!

[*Puffing, he returns to his shop. The* UNEMPLOYED MAN *picks up the
cup and gives it to* WONG.]

UNEMPLOYED MAN: You can report that to the police.

WONG: My hand! It's smashed up!

UNEMPLOYED MAN: Any bones broken?

WONG: I can't move my fingers.

UNEMPLOYED MAN: Sit down. I'll put some water on it.

[WONG *sits.*]

MRS. SHIN: The water won't cost you anything.

SISTER-IN-LAW: You might have got a bandage from Miss Shen Te till she took
to staying out all night. It's a scandal.

MRS. SHIN: [*despondently*] If you ask me, she's forgotten we ever existed!

[*Enter* SHEN TE *down the street, with a dish of rice.*]

SHEN TE: [*to the audience*] How wonderful to see Setzuan in the early morning!
I always used to stay in bed with my dirty blanket over my head afraid to
wake up. This morning I saw the newspapers being delivered by little boys,
the streets being washed by strong men, and fresh vegetables coming in
from the country on ox carts. It's a long walk from where Yang Sun lives,
but I feel lighter at every step. They say you walk on air when you're in
love, but it's even better walking on the rough earth, on the hard cement.
In the early morning, the old city looks like a great heap of rubbish! Nice,
though, with all its little lights. And the sky, so pink, so transparent, before
the dust comes and muddies it! What a lot you miss if you never see your
city rising from its slumbers like an honest old craftsman pumping his
lungs full of air and reaching for his tools as the poet says! [*cheerfully, to
her waiting guests*] Good morning, everyone, here's your rice! [*Distributing
the rice, she comes upon* WONG.] Good morning, Wong, I'm quite lightheaded today. On my way over, I looked at myself in all the shop windows.
I'd love to be beautiful.

[*She slips into the carpet shop.* MR. SHU FU *has just emerged from his
shop.*]

SHU FU: [*to the audience*] It surprises me how beautiful Miss Shen Te is looking
today! I never gave her a passing thought before. But now I've been gazing
upon her comely form for exactly three minutes! I begin to suspect I am
in love with her. She is overpoweringly attractive! [*crossly, to* WONG] Be
off with you, rascal!

[*He returns to his shop.* SHEN TE *comes back out of the carpet shop
with the* OLD MAN, *its proprietor, and his wife—whom we have al-*

ready met—the OLD WOMAN. SHEN TE *is wearing a shawl. The* OLD
MAN *is holding up a looking glass for her.*]

OLD WOMAN: Isn't it lovely? We'll give you a reduction because there's a little
hole in it.

SHEN TE: [*looking at another shawl on the* OLD WOMAN'S *arm*] The other one's
nice too.

OLD WOMAN: [*smiling*] Too bad there's no hole in that!

SHEN TE: That's right. My shop doesn't make very much.

OLD WOMAN: And your good deeds eat it all up! Be more careful, my dear. . . .

SHEN TE: [*trying on the shawl with the hole*] Just now, I'm lightheaded! Does
the color suit me?

OLD WOMAN: You'd better ask a man.

SHEN TE: [*to the* OLD MAN] Does the color suit me?

OLD MAN: You'd better ask your young friend.

SHEN TE: I'd like to have your opinion.

OLD MAN: It suits you very well. But wear it this way: the dull side out.

        [SHEN TE *pays up.*]

OLD WOMAN: If you decide you don't like it, you can exchange it. [*She pulls*
SHEN TE *to one side.*] Has he got money?

SHEN TE: [*with a laugh*] Yang Sun? Oh, no.

OLD WOMAN: Then how're you going to pay your rent?

SHEN TE: I'd forgotten about that.

OLD WOMAN: And next Monday is the first of the month! Miss Shen Te, I've
got something to say to you. After we [*indicating her husband*] got to
know you, we had our doubts about that marriage ad. We thought it
would be better if you'd let *us* help you. Out of our savings. We reckon we
could lend you two hundred silver dollars. We don't need anything in
writing—you could pledge us your tobacco stock.

SHEN TE: You're prepared to lend money to a person like me?

OLD WOMAN: It's folks like you that need it. We'd think twice about lending
anything to your cousin.

OLD MAN: [*coming up*] All settled, my dear?

SHEN TE: I wish the gods could have heard what your wife was just saying, Mr.
Ma. They're looking for good people who're happy—and helping me
makes you happy because you know it was love that got me into
difficulties!

        [*The* OLD COUPLE *smile knowingly at each other.*]

OLD MAN: And here's the money, Miss Shen Te.

        [*He hands her an envelope.* SHEN TE *takes it. She bows. They bow
        back. They return to their shop.*]

SHEN TE: [*holding up her envelope*] Look, Wong, here's six months' rent! Don't
you believe in miracles now? And how do you like my new shawl?

WONG: For the young fellow I saw you with in the park?

        [SHEN TE *nods.*]

MRS. SHIN: Never mind all that. It's time you took a look at his hand!

SHEN TE: Have you hurt your hand?

MRS. SHIN: That barber smashed it with his hot curling iron. Right in front of
our eyes.

SHEN TE: [*shocked at herself*] And I never noticed! We must get you to a doctor this minute or who knows what will happen?

UNEMPLOYED MAN: It's not a doctor he should see, it's a judge. He can ask for compensation. The barber's filthy rich.

WONG: You think I have a chance?

MRS. SHIN: [*with relish*] If it's really good and smashed. But is it?

WONG: I think so. It's very swollen. Could I get a pension?

MRS. SHIN: You'd need a witness.

WONG: Well, you all saw it. You could all testify.

> [*He looks round. The* UNEMPLOYED MAN, *the* GRANDFATHER, *and the* SISTER-IN-LAW *are all sitting against the wall of the shop eating rice. Their concentration on eating is complete.*]

SHEN TE: [*to* MRS. SHIN] You saw it yourself.

MRS. SHIN: I want nothing to do with the police. It's against my principles.

SHEN TE: [*to* SISTER-IN-LAW] What about you?

SISTER-IN-LAW: Me? I wasn't looking.

SHEN TE: [*to the* GRANDFATHER, *coaxingly*] Grandfather, *you'll* testify, won't you?

SISTER-IN-LAW: And a lot of good that will do. He's simple-minded.

SHEN TE: [*to the* UNEMPLOYED MAN] You seem to be the only witness left.

UNEMPLOYED MAN: My testimony would only hurt him. I've been picked up twice for begging.

SHEN TE: Your brother is assaulted, and you shut your eyes?
He is hit, cries out in pain, and you are silent?
The beast prowls, chooses and seizes his victim, and you say:
"Because we showed no displeasure, he has spared us."

If no one present will be a witness, I will. I'll say
I saw it.

MRS. SHIN: [*solemnly*] The name for that is perjury.

WONG: I don't know if I can accept that. Though maybe I'll have to. [*looking at his hand*] Is it swollen enough, do you think? The swelling's not going down?

UNEMPLOYED MAN: No, no. The swelling's holding up well.

WONG: Yes. It's *more* swollen if anything. Maybe my wrist is broken after all. I'd better see a judge at once.

> [*Holding his hand very carefully, and fixing his eyes on it, he runs off.* MRS. SHIN *goes quickly into the barber's shop.*]

UNEMPLOYED MAN: [*seeing her*] She is getting on the right side of Mr. Shu Fu.

SISTER-IN-LAW: You and I can't change the world, Shen Te.

SHEN TE: Go away! Go away all of you!

> [*The* UNEMPLOYED MAN, *the* SISTER-IN-LAW, *and the* GRANDFATHER *stalk off, eating and sulking.*]

[*to the audience*]
They've stopped answering
They stay put
They do as they're told
They don't care

Nothing can make them look up
But the smell of food.
[*Enter* MRS. YANG, *Yang Sun's mother, out of breath.*]

MRS. YANG: Miss Shen Te. My son has told me everything. I am Mrs. Yang, Sun's mother. Just think. He's got an offer. Of a job as a pilot. A letter has just come. From the director of the airfield in Peking!

SHEN TE: So he can fly again? Isn't that wonderful!

MRS. YANG: [*less breathlessly all the time*] They won't give him the job for nothing. They want five hundred silver dollars.

SHEN TE: We can't let money stand in his way, Mrs. Yang!

MRS. YANG: If only you could help him out!

SHEN TE: I have the shop. I can try! [*she embraces* MRS. YANG] I happen to have two hundred with me now. Take it. [*she gives her the old couple's money*] It was a loan but they said I could repay it with my tobacco stock.

MRS. YANG: And they were calling Sun the Dead Pilot of Setzuan! A friend in need!

SHEN TE: We must find another three hundred.

MRS. YANG: How?

SHEN TE: Let me think. [*slowly*] I know someone who can help. I didn't want to call on his services again, he's hard and cunning. But a flyer must fly. And I'll make this the last time.
[*Distant sound of a plane.*]

MRS. YANG: If the man you mentioned can do it. . . . Oh, look, there's the morning mail plane, heading for Peking!

SHEN TE: The pilot can see us, let's wave!
[*They wave. The noise of the engine is louder.*]

MRS. YANG: You know that pilot up there?

SHEN TE: Wave, Mrs. Yang! I know the pilot who will be up there. He gave up hope. But he'll do it now. One man to raise himself above the misery, above us all. [*To the audience:*]
Yang Sun, my lover:
Braving the storms
In company with the clouds
Crossing the heavens
And bringing to friends in faraway lands
The friendly mail!

SCENE IVA——*In front of the inner curtain.*
[*Enter* SHEN TE, *carrying Shui Ta's mask. She sings:*]

THE SONG OF DEFENSELESSNESS

In our country
A useful man needs luck
Only if he finds strong backers
Can he prove himself useful.
The good can't defend themselves and
Even the gods are defenseless.

Oh, why don't the gods have their own ammunition
And launch against badness their own expedition
Enthroning the good and preventing sedition
And bringing the world to a peaceful condition?

Oh, why don't the gods do the buying and selling
Injustice forbidding, starvation dispelling
Give bread to each city and joy to each dwelling?
Oh, why don't the gods do the buying and selling?
[*She puts on* SHUI TA's *mask and sings in his voice.*]
You can only help one of your luckless brothers
By trampling down a dozen others.

Why is it the gods do not feel indignation
And come down in fury to end exploitation
Defeat all defeat and forbid desperation
Refusing to tolerate such toleration?

Why is it?

SCENE V——SHEN TE's *tobacco shop.*

[*Behind the counter,* MR. SHUI TA, *reading the paper.* MRS. SHIN *is cleaning up. She talks and he takes no notice.*]

MRS. SHIN: And when certain rumors get about, what *happens* to a little place like this? It goes to pot. *I* know. So, if you want my advice, Mr. Shui Ta, find out just what has been going on between Miss Shen Te and that Yang Sun from Yellow Street. And remember: a certain interest in Miss Shen Te has been expressed by the barber next door, a man with twelve houses and only one wife, who, for that matter, is likely to drop off at any time. A certain interest has been expressed. He was even inquiring about her means and, if *that* doesn't prove a man is getting serious, what would? [*Still getting no response, she leaves with her bucket.*]

YANG SUN'S VOICE: Is that Miss Shen Te's tobacco shop?

MRS. SHIN'S VOICE: Yes, it is, but it's Mr. Shui Ta who's here today.

[SHUI TA *runs to the mirror with the short, light steps of* SHEN TE, *and is just about to start primping, when he realizes his mistake, and turns away, with a short laugh. Enter* YANG SUN. MRS. SHIN *enters behind him and slips into the back room to eavesdrop.*]

YANG SUN: I am Yang Sun. [SHUI TA *bows*] Is Shen Te in?

SHUI TA: No.

YANG SUN: I guess you know our relationship? [*he is inspecting the stock*] Quite a place! And I thought she was just talking big. I'll be flying again, all right. [*He takes a cigar, solicits and receives a light from* SHUI TA.] You think we can squeeze the other three hundred out of the tobacco stock?

SHUI TA: May I ask if it is your intention to sell at once?

YANG SUN: It was decent of her to come out with the two hundred but they aren't much use with the other three hundred still missing.

SHUI TA: Shen Te was overhasty promising so much. She might have to sell the shop itself to raise it. Haste, they say, is the wind that blows the house down.

YANG SUN: Oh, she isn't a girl to keep a man waiting. For one thing or the other, if you take my meaning.

SHUI TA: I take your meaning.

YANG SUN: [*leering*] Uh, huh.

SHUI TA: Would you explain what the five hundred silver dollars are for?

YANG SUN: Want to sound me out? Very well. The director of the Peking airfield is a friend of mine from flying school. I give him five hundred: he gets me the job.

SHUI TA: The price is high.

YANG SUN: Not as these things go. He'll have to fire one of the present pilots— for negligence. Only the man he has in mind isn't negligent. Not easy, you understand. You needn't mention that part of it to Shen Te.

SHUI TA: [*looking intently at* YANG SUN] Mr. Yang Sun, you are asking my cousin to give up her possessions, leave her friends, and place her entire fate in your hands. I presume you intend to marry her?

YANG SUN: I'd be prepared to.

> [*Slight pause.*]

SHUI TA: Those two hundred silver dollars would pay the rent here for six months. If you were Shen Te wouldn't you be tempted to continue in business?

YANG SUN: What? Can you imagine Yang Sun the flyer behind a counter? [*in an oily voice*] "A strong cigar or a mild one, worthy sir?" Not in this century!

SHUI TA: My cousin wishes to follow the promptings of her heart, and, from her own point of view, she may even have what is called the right to love. Accordingly, she has commissioned me to help you to this post. There is nothing here that I am not empowered to turn immediately into cash. Mrs. Mi Tzu, the landlady, will advise me about the sale.

> [*Enter* MRS. MI TZU.]

MRS. MI TZU: Good morning, Mr. Shui Ta, you wish to see me about the rent? As you know it falls due the day after tomorrow.

SHUI TA: Circumstances have changed, Mrs. Mi Tzu: my cousin is getting married. Her future husband here, Mr. Yang Sun, will be taking her to Peking. I am interested in selling the tobacco stock.

MRS. MI TZU: How much are you asking, Mr. Shui Ta?

YANG SUN: Three hundred sil—

SHUI TA: Five hundred silver dollars.

MRS. MI TZU: How much did she pay for it, Mr. Shui Ta?

SHUI TA: A thousand. And very little has been sold.

MRS. MI TZU: She was robbed. But I'll make you a special offer if you'll promise to be out by the day after tomorrow. Three hundred silver dollars.

YANG SUN: [*shrugging*] Take it, man, take it.

SHUI TA: It is not enough.

YANG SUN: Why not? Why not? Certainly, it's enough.

SHUI TA: Five hundred silver dollars.

YANG SUN: But why? We only need three!

SHUI TA: [*to* MRS. MI TZU] Excuse me. [*takes* YANG SUN *on one side*] The tobacco stock is pledged to the old couple who gave my cousin the two hundred.

YANG SUN: Is it in writing?

SHUI TA: No.

YANG SUN: [*to* MRS. MI TZU] Three hundred will do.

MRS. MI TZU: Of course, I need an assurance that Miss Shen Te is not in debt.

YANG SUN: Mr. Shui Ta?

SHUI TA: She is not in debt.

YANG SUN: When can you let us have the money?

MRS. MI TZU: The day after tomorrow. And remember: I'm doing this because I have a soft spot in my heart for young lovers! [*Exit.*]

YANG SUN: [*calling after her*] Boxes, jars and sacks—three hundred for the lot and the pain's over! [*to* SHUI TA] Where else can we raise money by the day after tomorrow?

SHUI TA: Nowhere. Haven't you enough for the trip and the first few weeks?

YANG SUN: Oh, certainly.

SHUI TA: How much, exactly.

YANG SUN: Oh, I'll dig it up, even if I have to steal it.

SHUI TA: I see.

YANG SUN: Well, don't fall off the roof. I'll get to Peking somehow.

SHUI TA: Two people can't travel for nothing.

YANG SUN: [*not giving* SHUI TA *a chance to answer*] I'm leaving *her* behind. No millstones round *my* neck!

SHUI TA: Oh.

YANG SUN: Don't look at me like that!

SHUI TA: How precisely is my cousin to live?

YANG SUN: Oh, you'll think of something.

SHUI TA: A small request, Mr. Yang Sun. Leave the two hundred silver dollars here until you can show me two tickets for Peking.

YANG SUN: You learn to mind your own business, Mr. Shui Ta.

SHUI TA: I'm afraid Miss Shen Te may not wish to sell the shop when she discovers that . . .

YANG SUN: You don't know women. She'll want to. Even then.

SHUI TA: [*a slight outburst*] She is a human being, sir! And not devoid of common sense!

YANG SUN: Shen Te is a woman: she *is* devoid of common sense. I only have to lay my hand on her shoulder, and church bells ring.

SHUI TA: [*with difficulty*] Mr. Yang Sun!

YANG SUN: Mr. Shui Whatever-it-is!

SHUI TA: My cousin is devoted to you . . . because . . .

YANG SUN: Because I have my hands on her breasts. Give me a cigar. [*He takes one for himself, stuffs a few more in his pocket, then changes his mind and takes the whole box.*] Tell her I'll marry her, then bring me the three hundred. Or let her bring it. One or the other. [*Exit.*]

MRS. SHIN: [*sticking her head out of the back room*] Well, he has your cousin under his thumb, and doesn't care if all Yellow Street knows it!

SHUI TA: [*crying out*] I've lost my shop! And he doesn't love me! [*He runs berserk through the room, repeating these lines incoherently. Then stops suddenly, and addresses* MRS. SHIN.] Mrs. Shin, you grew up in the gutter, like me. Are we lacking in hardness? I doubt it. If you steal a penny from me, I'll take you by the throat till you spit it out! You'd do the same to me. The times are bad, this city is hell, but we're like ants, we keep coming, up and up the walls, however smooth! Till bad luck comes. Being in love, for instance. One weakness is enough, and love is the deadliest.

MRS. SHIN: [*emerging from the back room*] You should have a little talk with Mr. Shu Fu, the barber. He's a real gentleman and just the thing for your cousin. [*She runs off.*]

SHUI TA: A caress becomes a stranglehold
A sigh of love turns to a cry of fear
Why are there vultures circling in the air?
A girl is going to meet her lover.

[SHUI TA *sits down and* MR. SHU FU *enters with* MRS. SHIN.]

SHUI TA: Mr. Shu Fu?

SHU FU: Mr. Shui Ta.

[*They both bow.*]

SHUI TA: I am told that you have expressed a certain interest in my cousin Shen Te. Let me set aside all propriety and confess: she is at this moment in grave danger.

SHU FU: Oh, dear!

SHUI TA: She has lost her shop, Mr. Shu Fu.

SHU FU: The charm of Miss Shen Te, Mr. Shui Ta, derives from the goodness, not of her shop, but of her heart. Men call her the Angel of the Slums.

SHUI TA: Yet her goodness has cost her two hundred silver dollars in a single day: we must put a stop to it.

SHU FU: Permit me to differ, Mr. Shui Ta. Let us, rather, open wide the gates to such goodness! Every morning, with pleasure tinged by affection, I watch her charitable ministrations. For they are hungry, and she giveth them to eat! Four of them, to be precise. Why only four? I ask. Why not four hundred? I hear she has been seeking shelter for the homeless. What about my humble cabins behind the cattle run? They are at her disposal. And so forth. And so on. Mr. Shui Ta, do you think Miss Shen Te could be persuaded to listen to certain ideas of mine? Ideas like these?

SHUI TA: Mr. Shu Fu, she would be honored.

[*Enter* WONG *and the* POLICEMAN. MR. SHU FU *turns abruptly away and studies the shelves.*]

WONG: Is Miss Shen Te here?

SHUI TA: No.

WONG: I am Wong the water seller. You are Mr. Shui Ta?

SHUI TA: I am.

WONG: I am a friend of Shen Te's.

SHUI TA: An intimate friend, I hear.

WONG: [*to the* POLICEMAN] You see? [*to* SHUI TA] It's because of my hand.

POLICEMAN: He hurt his hand, sir, that's a fact.

SHUI TA: [*quickly*] You need a sling, I see. [*He takes a shawl from the back room, and throws it to* WONG.]

WONG: But that's her new shawl!

SHUI TA: She has no more use for it.

WONG: But she bought it to please someone!

SHUI TA: It happens to be no longer necessary.

WONG: [*making the sling*] She is my only witness.

POLICEMAN: Mr. Shui Ta, your cousin is supposed to have seen the barber hit the water seller with a curling iron.

SHUI TA: I'm afraid my cousin was not present at the time.

WONG: But she was, sir! Just ask her! Isn't she in?

SHUI TA: [*gravely*] Mr. Wong, my cousin has her own troubles. You wouldn't wish her to add to them by committing perjury?

WONG: But it was she that told me to go to the judge!

SHUI TA: Was the judge supposed to heal your hand?

[MR. SHU FU *turns quickly around.* SHUI TA *bows to* SHU FU, *and vice versa.*]

WONG: [*taking the sling off, and putting it back*] I see how it is.

POLICEMAN: Well, I'll be on my way. [*to* WONG] And you be careful. If Mr. Shu Fu wasn't a man who tempers justice with mercy, as the saying is, you'd be in jail for libel. Be off with you!

[*Exit* WONG, *followed by* POLICEMAN.]

SHUI TA: Profound apologies, Mr. Shu Fu.

SHU FU: Not at all, Mr. Shui Ta. [*pointing to the shawl*] The episode is over?

SHUI TA: It may take her time to recover. There are some fresh wounds.

SHU FU: We shall be discreet. Delicate. A short vacation could be arranged. . . .

SHUI TA: First of course, you and she would have to talk things over.

SHU FU: At a small supper in a small, but high-class, restaurant.

SHUI TA: I'll go and find her. [*Exit into back room.*]

MRS. SHIN: [*sticking her head in again*] Time for congratulations, Mr. Shu Fu?

SHU FU: Ah, Mrs. Shin! Please inform Miss Shen Te's guests they may take shelter in the cabins behind the cattle run!

[MRS. SHIN *nods, grinning.*]

SHU FU: [*to the audience*] Well? What do you think of me, ladies and gentlemen? What could a man do more? Could he be less selfish? More farsighted A small supper in a small but . . . Does that bring rather vulgar and clumsy thoughts into your mind? Ts, ts, ts. Nothing of the sort will occur. She won't even be touched. Not even accidentally while passing the salt. An exchange of ideas only. Over the flowers on the table—white chrysanthemums, by the way [*he writes down a note of this*]—yes, over the white chrysanthemums, two young souls will . . . shall I say "find each other"? We shall NOT exploit the misfortune of others. Understanding? Yes. An offer of assistance? Certainly. But quietly. Almost inaudibly. Perhaps with a single glance. A glance that could also—also mean more.

MRS. SHIN: [*coming forward*] Everything under control, Mr. Shu Fu?

SHU FU: Oh, Mrs. Shin, what do you know about this worthless rascal Yang Sun?

MRS. SHIN: Why, he's the most worthless rascal . . .

SHU FU: Is he really? You're sure? [*as she opens her mouth*] From now on, he doesn't exist! Can't be found anywhere!

[*Enter* YANG SUN.]

YANG SUN: What's been going on here?

MRS. SHIN: Shall I call Mr. Shui Ta, Mr. Shu Fu? He wouldn't want strangers in here!

SHU FU: Mr. Shui Ta is in conference with Miss Shen Te. Not to be disturbed.

YANG SUN: Shen Te here? I didn't see her come in. What kind of conference?

SHU FU: [*not letting him enter the back room*] Patience, dear sir! And if by chance I have an inkling who you are, pray take note that Miss Shen Te and I are about to announce our engagement.

YANG SUN: What?

MRS SHIN: You didn't expect that, did you?

[YANG SUN *is trying to push past the barber into the back room when* SHEN TE *comes out.*]

SHU FU: My dear Shen Te, ten thousand apologies! Perhaps you . . .

YANG SUN: What is it, Shen Te? Have you gone crazy?

SHEN TE: [*breathless*] My cousin and Mr. Shu Fu have come to an understanding. They wish me to hear Mr. Shu Fu's plans for helping the poor.

YANG SUN: Your cousin wants to part us.

SHEN TE: Yes.

YANG SUN: And you've agreed to it?

SHEN TE: Yes.

YANG SUN: They told you I was bad. [SHEN TE *is silent.*] And suppose I am. Does that make me need you less? I'm low, Shen Te, I have no money, I don't do the right thing but at least I put up a fight! [*He is near her now, and speaks in an undertone.*] Have you no eyes? Look at him. Have you forgotten already?

SHEN TE: No.

YANG SUN: How it was raining?

SHEN TE: No.

YANG SUN: How you cut me down from the willow tree? Bought me water? Promised me money to fly with?

SHEN TE: [*shakily*] Yang Sun, what do you want?

YANG SUN: I want you to come with me.

SHEN TE: [*in a small voice*] Forgive me, Mr. Shu Fu, I want to go with Mr. Yang Sun.

YANG SUN: We're lovers you know. Give me the key to the shop. [SHEN TE *takes the key from around her neck.* YANG SUN *puts it on the counter. To* MRS. SHIN:] Leave it under the mat when you're through. Let's go, Shen Te.

SHU FU: But this is rape! Mr. Shui Ta!!

YANG SUN: [*to* SHEN TE] Tell him not to shout.

SHEN TE: Please don't shout for my cousin, Mr. Shu Fu. He doesn't agree with me, I know, but he's wrong. [*to the audience*]
I want to go with the man I love

I don't want to count the cost
I don't want to consider if it's wise
I don't want to know if he loves me
I want to go with the man I love.
YANG SUN: That's the spirit.
[*And the couple leave.*]

SCENE va———*In front of the inner curtain.*

[SHEN TE *in her wedding clothes, on the way to her wedding.*]
SHEN TE: Something terrible has happened. As I left the shop with Yang Sun,
I found the old carpet dealer's wife waiting on the street, trembling all
over. She told me her husband had taken to his bed sick with all the worry
and excitement over the two hundred silver dollars they lent me. She said
it would be best if I gave it back now. Of course, I had to say I would.
She said she couldn't quite trust my cousin Shui Ta or even my fiancé
Yang Sun. There were tears in her eyes. With my emotions in an uproar,
I threw myself into Yang Sun's arms, I couldn't resist him. The things
he'd said to Shui Ta had taught Shen Te nothing. Sinking into his arms,
I said to myself:

To let no one perish, not even oneself
To fill everyone with happiness, even oneself
Is so good

How could I have forgotten those two old people? Yang Sun swept me
away like a small hurricane. But he's not a bad man, and he loves me.
He'd rather work in the cement factory than owe his flying to a crime.
Though, of course, flying *is* a great passion with Sun. Now, on the way
to my wedding, I waver between fear and joy.

SCENE VI———*The "private dining room" on the upper floor of a cheap restaurant
in a poor section of town.*

[*With* SHEN TE: *the* GRANDFATHER, *the* SISTER-IN-LAW, *the* NIECE,
MRS. SHIN, *the* UNEMPLOYED MAN. *In a corner, alone, a* PRIEST. *A*
WAITER *pouring wine. Downstage,* YANG SUN *talking to his* MOTHER.
He wears a dinner jacket.]
YANG SUN: Bad news, Mamma. She came right out and told me she can't sell
the shop for me. Some idiot is bringing a claim because he lent her the
two hundred she gave you.
MRS. YANG: What did you say? Of course, you can't marry her now.
YANG SUN: It's no use saying anything to *her*. I've sent for her cousin, Mr. Shui
Ta. He said there was nothing in writing.
MRS. YANG: Good idea. I'll go and look for him. Keep an eye on things.
[*Exit* MRS. YANG. SHEN TE *has been pouring wine.*]

SHEN TE: [*to the audience, pitcher in hand*] I wasn't mistaken in him. He's bearing up well. Though it must have been an awful blow—giving up flying. I do love him so. [*calling across the room to him*] Sun, you haven't drunk a toast with the bride!

YANG SUN: What do we drink to?

SHEN TE: Why, to the future!

YANG SUN: When the bridegroom's dinner jacket won't be a hired one!

SHEN TE: But when the bride's dress will still get rained on sometimes!

YANG SUN: To everything we ever wished for!

SHEN TE: May all our dreams come true!

    [*They drink.*]

YANG SUN: [*with loud conviviality*] And now, friends, before the wedding gets under way, I have to ask the bride a few questions. I've no idea what kind of wife she'll make, and it worries me. [*wheeling on* SHEN TE] For example. Can you make five cups of tea with three tea leaves?

SHEN TE: No.

YANG SUN: So I won't be getting very much tea. Can you sleep on a straw mattress the size of that book? [*He points to the large volume the* PRIEST *is reading.*]

SHEN TE: The two of us?

YANG SUN: The one of you.

SHEN TE: In that case, no.

YANG SUN: What a wife! I'm shocked!

    [*While the audience is laughing, his* MOTHER *returns. With a shrug of her shoulders, she tells* YANG SUN *the expected guest hasn't arrived. The* PRIEST *shuts the book with a bang, and makes for the door.*]

MRS. YANG: Where are *you* off to? It's only a matter of minutes.

PRIEST: [*watch in hand*] Time goes on, Mrs. Yang, and I've another wedding to attend to. Also a funeral.

MRS. YANG: [*irately*] D'you think we planned it this way? I was hoping to manage with one pitcher of wine, and we've run through two already. [*points to empty pitcher. Loudly*] My dear Shen Te, I don't know where your cousin can be keeping himself!

SHEN TE: My cousin?!

MRS. YANG: Certainly. I'm old-fashioned enough to think such a close relative should attend the wedding.

SHEN TE: Oh, Sun, is it the three hundred silver dollars?

YANG SUN: [*not looking her in the eye*] Are you deaf? Mother says she's old-fashioned. And I say I'm considerate. We'll wait another fifteen minutes.

HUSBAND: Another fifteen minutes.

MRS. YANG: [*addressing the company*] Now you all know, don't you, that my son is getting a job as a mail pilot?

SISTER-IN-LAW: In Peking, too, isn't it?

MRS. YANG: In Peking, too! The two of us are moving to Peking!

SHEN TE: Sun, tell your mother Peking is out of the question now.

YANG SUN: Your cousin'll tell her. If he agrees. I don't agree.

SHEN TE: [*amazed, and dismayed*] Sun!

YANG SUN: I hate this godforsaken Setzuan. What people! Know what they look like when I half close my eyes? Horses! Whinnying, fretting, stamping, screwing their necks up! [*loudly*] And what is it the thunder says? They are su-per-flu-ous! [*he hammers out the syllables*] They've run their last race! They can go trample themselves to death! [*pause*] I've got to get out of here.

SHEN TE: But I've promised the money to the old couple.

YANG SUN: And since you always do the wrong thing, it's lucky your cousin's coming. Have another drink.

SHEN TE: [*quietly*] My cousin can't be coming.

YANG SUN: How d'you mean?

SHEN TE: My cousin can't be where I am.

YANG SUN: Quite a conundrum!

SHEN TE: [*desperately*] Sun, I'm the one that loves you. Not my cousin. He was thinking of the job in Peking when he promised you the old couple's money—

YANG SUN: Right. And that's why he's bringing the three hundred silver dollars. Here—to my wedding.

SHEN TE: He is not bringing the three hundred silver dollars.

YANG SUN: Huh? What makes you think that?

SHEN TE: [*looking into his eyes*] He says you only bought one ticket to Peking. [*Short pause.*]

YANG SUN: That was yesterday. [*He pulls two tickets part way out of his inside pocket, making her look under his coat.*] Two tickets. I don't want Mother to know. She'll get left behind. I sold her furniture to buy these tickets, so you see . . .

SHEN TE: But what's to become of the old couple?

YANG SUN: What's to become of me? Have another drink. Or do you believe in moderation? If I drink, I fly again. And if you drink, you may learn to understand me.

SHEN TE: You want to fly. But I can't help you.

YANG SUN: "Here's a plane, my darling—but it's only got one wing!"
[*The* WAITER *enters.*]

WAITER: Mrs. Yang!

MRS. YANG: Yes?

WAITER: Another pitcher of wine, ma'am?

MRS. YANG: We have enough, thanks. Drinking makes me sweat.

WAITER: Would you mind paying, ma'am?

MRS. YANG: [*to everyone*] Just be patient a few moments longer, everyone, Mr. Shui Ta is on his way over! [*to the* WAITER] Don't be a spoilsport.

WAITER: I can't let you leave till you've paid your bill, ma'am.

MRS. YANG: But they know me here!

WAITER: That's just it.

PRIEST: [*ponderously getting up*] I humbly take my leave. [*And he does.*]

MRS. YANG: [*to the others, desperately*] Stay where you are, everybody! The priest says he'll be back in two minutes!

YANG SUN: It's no good, Mamma. Ladies and gentlemen, Mr. Shui Ta still hasn't arrived and the priest has gone home. We won't detain you any longer.

[*They are leaving now.*]

GRANDFATHER: [*in the doorway, having forgotten to put his glass down*] To the bride! [*He drinks, puts down the glass, and follows the others.*]

[*Pause.*]

SHEN TE: Shall I go too?

YANG SUN: You? Aren't you the bride? Isn't this your wedding? [*he drags her across the room, tearing her wedding dress*] If we can wait, you can wait. Mother calls me her falcon. She wants to see me in the clouds. But I think it may be St. Nevercome's Day before she'll go to the door and see my plane thunder by. [*Pause. He pretends the guests are still present.*] Why such a lull in the conversation, ladies and gentlemen? Don't you like it here? The ceremony is only slightly postponed—because an important guest is expected at any moment. Also because the bride doesn't know what love is. While we're waiting, the bridegroom will sing a little song. [*He does so:*]

[THE SONG OF ST. NEVERCOME'S DAY]

On a certain day, as is generally known,
    One and all will be shouting: Hooray, hooray!
For the beggar maid's son has a solid-gold throne
    And the day is St. Nevercome's Day
On St. Nevercome's, Nevercome's, Nevercome's Day
    He'll sit on his solid-gold throne

Oh, hooray, hooray! That day goodness will pay!
    That day badness will cost you your head!
And merit and money will smile and be funny
    While exchanging salt and bread
On St. Nevercome's, Nevercome's, Nevercome's Day
    While exchanging salt and bread

And the grass, oh, the grass will look down at the sky
    And the pebbles will roll up the stream
And all men will be good without batting an eye
    They will make of our earth a dream
On St. Nevercome's, Nevercome's, Nevercome's Day
    They will make of our earth a dream

And as for me, that's the day I shall be
    A flyer and one of the best
Unemployed man, you will have work to do
    Washerwoman, you'll get your rest
On St. Nevercome's, Nevercome's, Nevercome's Day
    Washerwoman, you'll get your rest

MRS. YANG: It looks like he's not coming.

[*The three of them sit looking at the door.*]

SCENE VIa——WONG's *den.*

[*The sewer pipe is again transparent and again the* GODS *appear to* WONG *in a dream.*]

WONG: I'm so glad you've come, illustrious ones. It's Shen Te. She's in great trouble from following the rule about loving thy neighbor. Perhaps she's *too* good for this world!

FIRST GOD: Nonsense! You are eaten up by lice and doubts!

WONG: Forgive me, illustrious one, I only meant you might deign to intervene.

FIRST GOD: Out of the question! My colleague here intervened in some squabble or other only yesterday. [*He points to the* THIRD GOD *who has a black eye*] The results are before us!

WONG: She had to call on her cousin again. But not even he could help. I'm afraid the shop is done for.

THIRD GOD: [*a little concerned*] Perhaps we should help after all?

FIRST GOD: The gods help those that help themselves.

WONG: What if we *can't* help ourselves, illustrious ones?

[*Slight pause.*]

SECOND GOD: Try, anyway! Suffering ennobles!

FIRST GOD: Our faith in Shen Te is unshaken!

THIRD GOD: We certainly haven't found any *other* good people. You can see where we spend our nights from the straw on our clothes.

WONG: You might help her find her way by—

FIRST GOD: The good man finds his own way here below!

SECOND GOD: The good woman too.

FIRST GOD: The heavier the burden, the greater her strength!

THIRD GOD: We're only onlookers, you know.

FIRST GOD: And everything will be all right in the end, O ye of little faith!

[*They are gradually disappearing through these last lines.*]

SCENE VII——*The yard behind* SHEN TE's *shop. A few articles of furniture on a cart.*

[SHEN TE *and* MRS. SHIN *are taking the washing off the line.*]

MRS. SHIN: If you ask me, you should fight tooth and nail to keep the shop.

SHEN TE: How can I? I have to sell the tobacco to pay back the two hundred silver dollars today.

MRS. SHIN: No husband, no tobacco, no house and home! What are you going to live on?

SHEN TE: I can work. I can sort tobacco.

MRS. SHIN: Hey, look, Mr. Shui Ta's trousers! He must have left here stark naked!

SHEN TE: Oh, he may have another pair, Mrs. Shin.

MRS. SHIN: But if he's gone for good as you say, why has he left his pants behind?

SHEN TE: Maybe he's thrown them away.

MRS. SHIN: Can I take them?

SHEN TE: Oh, no.

[*Enter* MR. SHU FU, *running.*]

SHU FU: Not a word! Total silence! I know all. You have sacrificed your own love and happiness so as not to hurt a dear old couple who had put their trust in you! Not in vain does this district—for all its malevolent tongues —call you the Angel of the Slums! That young man couldn't rise to your level, so you left him. And now, when I see you closing up the little shop, that veritable haven of rest for the multitude, well, I cannot, I cannot let it pass. Morning after morning I have stood watching in the doorway not unmoved—while you graciously handed out rice to the wretched. Is that never to happen again? Is the good woman of Setzuan to disappear? If only you would allow *me* to assist you! Now don't say anything! No assurances, no exclamations of gratitude! [*He has taken out his checkbook*] Here! A blank check. [*He places it on the cart.*] Just my signature. Fill it out as you wish. Any sum in the world. I herewith retire from the scene, quietly, unobtrusively, making no claims, on tiptoe, full of veneration, absolutely selflessly . . . [*He has gone.*]

MRS. SHIN: Well! You're saved. There's always some idiot of a man. . . . Now hurry! Put down a thousand silver dollars and let me fly to the bank before he comes to his senses.

SHEN TE: I can pay you for the washing without any check.

MRS. SHIN: What? You're not going to cash it just because you might have to marry him? Are you crazy? Men like him *want* to be led by the nose! Are you still thinking of that flyer? All Yellow Street knows how he treated you!

SHEN TE: When I heard his cunning laugh, I was afraid
But when I saw the holes in his shoes, I loved him dearly.

MRS. SHIN: Defending that good-for-nothing after all that's happened!

SHEN TE: [*staggering as she holds some of the washing*] Oh!

MRS. SHIN: [*taking the washing from her, dryly*] So you feel dizzy when you stretch and bend? There couldn't be a little visitor on the way? If that's it, you can forget Mr. Shu Fu's blank check: it wasn't meant for a christening present!

[*She goes to the back with a basket.* SHEN TE's *eyes follow* MRS. SHIN *for a moment. Then she looks down at her own body, feels her stomach, and a great joy comes into her eyes.*]

SHEN TE: O joy! A new human being is on the way. The world awaits him. In the cities the people say: he's got to be reckoned with, this new human being! [*She imagines a little boy to be present, and introduces him to the audience.*] This is my son, the well-known flyer!

Say: Welcome
To the conqueror of unknown mountains and unreachable regions
Who brings us our mail across the impassable deserts!

[*She leads him up and down by the hand.*]

Take a look at the world, my son. That's a tree. Tree, yes. Say: "Hello, tree!" And bow. Like this. [*She bows.*] Now you know each other. And, look, here comes the water seller. He's a friend, give him your hand. A cup of fresh water for my little son, please. Yes, it *is* a warm day. [*handing the cup*] Oh dear, a policeman, we'll have to make a circle round *him*. Perhaps we can pick a few cherries over there in the rich Mr. Pung's garden. But we mustn't be seen. You want cherries? Just like children with fathers. No, no, you can't go straight at them like that. Don't pull. We must learn to be reasonable. Well, have it your own way. [*She has let him make for the cherries.*] Can you reach? Where to put them? Your mouth is the best place. [*She tries one herself.*] Mmm, they're good. But the policeman, we must run! [*They run.*] Yes, back to the street. Calm now, so no one will notice us. [*Walking the street with her child, she sings.*]

> Once a plum—'twas in Japan—
> Made a conquest of a man
> But the man's turn soon did come
> For he gobbled up the plum

[*Enter* WONG, *with a* CHILD *by the hand. He coughs.*]

SHEN TE: Wong!

WONG: It's about the carpenter, Shen Te. He's lost his shop, and he's been drinking. His children are on the streets. This is one. Can you help?

SHEN TE: [*to the* CHILD] Come here, little man. [*Takes him down to the footlights. To the audience:*]

> You there! A man is asking you for shelter!
> A man of tomorrow says: what about today?
> His friend the conqueror, whom you know,
> Is his advocate!

[*to* WONG] He can live in Mr. Shu Fu's cabins. I may have to go there myself. I'm going to have a baby. That's a secret—don't tell Yang Sun—we'd only be in his way. Can you find the carpenter for me?

WONG: I knew you'd think of something. [*to the* CHILD] Good-bye, son, I'm going for your father.

SHEN TE: What about your hand, Wong? I wanted to help, but my cousin . . .

WONG: Oh, I can get along with one hand, don't worry. [*He shows how he can handle his pole with his left hand alone.*]

SHEN TE: But your right hand! Look, take this cart, sell everything that's on it, and go to the doctor with the money . . .

WONG: She's still good. But first I'll bring the carpenter. I'll pick up the cart when I get back. [*Exit* WONG.]

SHEN TE: [*to the* CHILD] Sit down over here, son, till your father comes.

[*The* CHILD *sits cross-legged on the ground. Enter the* HUSBAND *and* WIFE, *each dragging a large, full sack.*]

WIFE: [*furtively*] You're alone, Shen Te, dear?

[SHEN TE *nods. The* WIFE *beckons to the* NEPHEW *offstage. He comes on with another sack.*]

WIFE: Your cousin's away? [SHEN TE *nods.*] He's not coming back?

SHEN TE: No. I'm giving up the shop.

WIFE: That's why we're here. We want to know if we can leave these things in your new home. Will you do us this favor?

SHEN TE: Why, yes, I'd be glad to.

HUSBAND: [*cryptically*] And if anyone asks about them, say they're yours.

SHEN TE: Would anyone ask?

WIFE: [*with a glance back at her husband*] Oh, someone might. The police, for instance. They don't seem to like us. Where can we put it?

SHEN TE: Well, I'd rather not get in any more trouble . . .

WIFE: Listen to her. The good woman of Setzuan!

    [SHEN TE *is silent.*]

HUSBAND: There's enough tobacco in those sacks to give us a new start in life. We could have our own tobacco factory!

SHEN TE: [*slowly*] You'll have to put them in the back room.

    [*The sacks are taken offstage, while the* CHILD *is alone. Shyly glancing about him, he goes to the garbage can, starts playing with the contents, and eating some of the scraps. The others return.*]

WIFE: We're counting on you, Shen Te!

SHEN TE: Yes. [*She sees the* CHILD *and is shocked.*]

HUSBAND: We'll see you in Mr. Shu Fu's cabins.

NEPHEW: The day after tomorrow.

SHEN TE: Yes. Now, go. Go! I'm not feeling well.

    [*Exeunt all three, virtually pushed off.*]

    He is eating the refuse in the garbage can!

    Only look at his little gray mouth!

    [*Pause. Music.*]

    As this is the world *my* son will enter

    I will study to defend him.

    To be good to you, my son,

    I shall be a tigress to all others

    If I have to.

    And I shall have to.

    [*She starts to go.*]

    One more time, then. I hope really the last.

    [*Exit* SHEN TE, *taking* SHUI TA's *trousers.* MRS. SHIN *enters and watches her with marked interest. Enter the* SISTER-IN-LAW *and the* GRAND-FATHER.]

SISTER-IN-LAW: So it's true, the shop has closed down. And the furniture's in the back yard. It's the end of the road!

MRS. SHIN: [*pompously*] The fruit of high living, selfishness, and sensuality! Down the primrose path to Mr. Shu Fu's cabins—with you!

SISTER-IN-LAW: Cabins? Rat holes! He gave them to us because his soap supplies only went moldy there!

    [*Enter the* UNEMPLOYED MAN.]

UNEMPLOYED MAN: Shen Te is moving?

SISTER-IN-LAW: Yes. She was sneaking away.

MRS. SHIN: She's ashamed of herself, and no wonder!

UNEMPLOYED MAN: Tell her to call Mr. Shui Ta or she's done for this time!

SISTER-IN-LAW: Tell her to call Mr. Shui Ta or *we're* done for this time.

    [*Enter* WONG *and* CARPENTER, *the latter with a* CHILD *on each hand.*]

CARPENTER: So we'll have a roof over our heads for a change!

MRS. SHIN: Roof? Whose roof?

CARPENTER: Mr. Shu Fu's cabins. And we have little Feng to thank for it. [FENG, *we find, is the name of the* CHILD *already there; his* FATHER *now takes him. To the other two*] Bow to your little brother, you two!

[*The* CARPENTER *and the two new arrivals bow to* FENG. *Enter* SHUI TA.]

UNEMPLOYED MAN: Sst! Mr. Shui Ta!

[*Pause.*]

SHUI TA: And what is this crowd here for, may I ask?

WONG: How do you do, Mr. Shui Ta. This is the carpenter. Miss Shen Te promised him space in Mr. Shu Fu's cabins.

SHUI TA: That will not be possible.

CARPENTER: We can't go there after all?

SHUI TA: All the space is needed for other purposes.

SISTER-IN-LAW: You mean we have to get out? But we've got nowhere to go.

SHUI TA: Miss Shen Te finds it possible to provide employment. If the proposition interests you, you may stay in the cabins.

SISTER-IN-LAW: [*with distaste*] You mean *work*? Work for Miss Shen Te?

SHUI TA: Making tobacco, yes. There are three bales here already. Would you like to get them?

SISTER-IN-LAW: [*trying to bluster*] We have our own tobacco! We were in the tobacco business before you were born!

SHUI TA: [*to the* CARPENTER *and the* UNEMPLOYED MAN] You *don't* have your own tobacco. What about you?

[*The* CARPENTER *and the* UNEMPLOYED MAN *get the point, and go for the sacks. Enter* MRS. MI TZU.]

MRS. MI TZU: Mr. Shui Ta? I've brought you your three hundred silver dollars.

SHUI TA: I'll sign your lease instead. I've decided not to sell.

MRS. MI TZU: What? You don't need the money for that flyer?

SHUI TA: No.

MRS. MI TZU: And you can pay six months' rent?

SHUI TA: [*takes the barber's blank check from the cart and fills it out*] Here is a check for ten thousand silver dollars. On Mr. Shu Fu's account. Look! [*He shows her the signature on the check.*] Your six months' rent will be in your hands by seven this evening. And now, if you'll excuse me.

MRS. MI TZU: So it's Mr. Shu Fu now. The flyer has been given his walking papers. These modern girls! In my day they'd have said she was flighty. That poor, deserted Mr. Yang Sun!

[*Exit* MRS. MI TZU. *The* CARPENTER *and the* UNEMPLOYED MAN *drag the three sacks back on the stage.*]

CARPENTER: [*to* SHUI TA] I don't know why I'm doing this for you.

SHUI TA: Perhaps your children want to eat, Mr. Carpenter.

SISTER-IN-LAW: [*catching sight of the sacks*] Was my brother-in-law here?

MRS. SHIN: Yes, he was.

SISTER-IN-LAW: I thought as much. I know those sacks! That's our tobacco!

SHUI TA: Really? I thought it came from my back room! Shall we consult the police on the point?

SISTER-IN-LAW: [*defeated*] No.

SHUI TA: Perhaps you will show me the way to Mr. Shu Fu's cabins?
> [*Taking* FENG *by the hand,* SHUI TA *goes off, followed by the* CAR-
> PENTER *and his two older children, the* SISTER-IN-LAW, *the* GRAND-
> FATHER, *and the* UNEMPLOYED MAN. *Each of the last three drags a
> sack. Enter* OLD MAN *and* OLD WOMAN.]

MRS. SHIN: A pair of pants—missing from the clothesline one minute—and
next minute on the honorable backside of Mr. Shui Ta.

OLD WOMAN: We thought Miss Shen Te was here.

MRS. SHIN: [*preoccupied*] Well, she's not.

OLD MAN: There was something she was going to give us.

WONG: She was going to help me too. [*looking at his hand*] It'll be too late
soon. But she'll be back. This cousin has never stayed long.

MRS. SHIN: [*approaching a conclusion*] No, he hasn't, has he?

SCENE VIIa————*The Sewer Pipe*

> [WONG *asleep. In his dream, he tells the* GODS *his fears. The* GODS
> *seem tired from all their travels. They stop for a moment and look
> over their shoulders at the water seller.*]

WONG: Illustrious ones. I've been having a bad dream. Our beloved Shen Te
was in great distress in the rushes down by the river—the spot where the
bodies of suicides are washed up. She kept staggering and holding her
head down as if she was carrying something and it was dragging her down
into the mud. When I called out to her, she said she had to take your
Book of Rules to the other side, and not get it wet, or the ink would all
come off. You had talked to her about the virtues, you know, the time
she gave you shelter in Setzuan.

THIRD GOD: Well, but what do you suggest, my dear Wong?

WONG: Maybe a little relaxation of the rules, Benevolent One, in view of the
bad times.

THIRD GOD: As for instance?

WONG: Well, um, good will, for instance, might do instead of love?

THIRD GOD: I'm afraid that would create new problems.

WONG: Or, instead of justice, good sportsmanship?

THIRD GOD: That would only mean more work.

WONG: Instead of honor, outward propriety?

THIRD GOD: Still more work! No, no! The rules will have to stand, my dear
Wong!
> [*Wearily shaking their heads, all three journey on.*]

SCENE VIII————*Shui Ta's tobacco factory in Shu Fu's cabins.*

> [*Huddled together behind bars, several families, mostly women and
> children. Among these people the* SISTER-IN-LAW, *the* GRANDFATHER,
> *the* CARPENTER, *and his* THREE CHILDREN. *Enter* MRS. YANG *followed
> by* YANG SUN.]

MRS. YANG: [*to the audience*] There's something I just *have* to tell you:

strength and wisdom are wonderful things. The strong and wise Mr. Shui Ta has transformed my son from a dissipated good-for-nothing into a model citizen. As you may have heard, Mr. Shui Ta opened a small tobacco factory near the cattle runs. It flourished. Three months ago—I shall never forget it—I asked for an appointment, and Mr. Shui Ta agreed to see us—me and my son. I can see him now as he came through the door to meet us. . . .

[*Enter* SHUI TA *from a door.*]

SHUI TA: What can I do for you, Mrs. Yang?

MRS. YANG: This morning the police came to the house. We find you've brought an action for breach of promise of marriage. In the name of Shen Te. You also claim that Sun came by two hundred silver dollars by improper means.

SHUI TA: That is correct.

MRS. YANG: Mr. Shui Ta, the money's all gone. When the Peking job didn't materialize, he ran through it all in three days. I know he's a good-for-nothing. He sold my furniture. He was moving to Peking without me. Miss Shen Te thought highly of him at one time.

SHUI TA: What do *you* say, Mr. Yang Sun?

YANG SUN: The money's gone.

SHUI TA: [*to* MRS. YANG] Mrs. Yang, in consideration of my cousin's incomprehensible weakness for your son, I am prepared to give him another chance. He can have a job—here. The two hundred silver dollars will be taken out of his wages.

YANG SUN: So it's the factory or jail?

SHUI TA: Take your choice.

YANG SUN: May I speak with Shen Te?

SHUI TA: You may not.

[*Pause.*]

YANG SUN: [*sullenly*] Show me where to go.

MRS. YANG: Mr. Shui Ta, you are kindness itself: the gods will reward you! [*to* YANG SUN] And honest work will make a man of you, my boy. [YANG SUN *follows* SHUI TA *into the factory.* MRS. YANG *comes down again to the footlights.*] Actually, honest work didn't agree with him—at first. And he got no opportunity to distinguish himself till—in the third week—when the wages were being paid . . .

[SHUI TA *has a bag of money. Standing next to his foreman—the former* UNEMPLOYED MAN—*he counts out the wages. It is* YANG SUN's *turn.*]

UNEMPLOYED MAN: [*reading*] Carpenter, six silver dollars. Yang Sun, six silver dollars.

YANG SUN: [*quietly*] Excuse me, sir. I don't think it can be more than five. May I see? [*He takes the foreman's list.*] It says six working days. But that's a mistake, sir. I took a day off for court business. And I won't take what I haven't earned, however miserable the pay is!

UNEMPLOYED MAN: Yang Sun. Five silver dollars. [*to* SHUI TA] A rare case, Mr. Shui Ta!

SHUI TA: How is it the book says six when it should say five?

UNEMPLOYED MAN: I must've made a mistake, Mr. Shui Ta. [*with a look at* YANG SUN] It won't happen again.

SHUI TA: [*taking* YANG SUN *aside*] You don't hold back, do you? You give your all to the firm. You're even honest. Do the foreman's mistakes always favor the workers?

YANG SUN: He does have . . . friends.

SHUI TA: Thank you. May I offer you any little recompense?

YANG SUN: Give me a trial period of one week, and I'll prove my intelligence is worth more to you than my strength.

MRS. YANG: [*still down at the footlights*] Fighting words, fighting words! That evening, I said to Sun: "If you're a flyer, then fly, my falcon! Rise in the world!" And he got to be foreman. Yes, in Mr. Shui Ta's tobacco factory, he worked real miracles.

[*We see* YANG SUN *with his legs apart standing behind the workers who are handing along a basket of raw tobacco above their heads.*]

YANG SUN: Faster! Faster! You, there, d'you think you can just stand around, now you're not foreman any more? It'll be your job to lead us in song. Sing!

[UNEMPLOYED MAN *starts singing. The others join in the refrain.*]

[SONG OF THE EIGHTH ELEPHANT]

Chang had seven elephants—all much the same—
   But then there was Little Brother
The seven, they were wild, Little Brother, he was tame
   And to guard them Chang chose Little Brother
      Run faster!
      Mr. Chang has a forest park
      Which must be cleared before tonight
      And already it's growing dark!

When the seven elephants cleared that forest park
   Mr. Chang rode high on Little Brother
While the seven toiled and moiled till dark
   On his big behind sat Little Brother
      Dig faster!
      Mr. Chang has a forest park
      Which must be cleared before tonight
      And already it's growing dark!

And the seven elephants worked many an hour
   Till none of them could work another
Old Chang, he looked sour, on the seven he did glower
   But gave a pound of rice to Little Brother
      What was that?
      Mr. Chang has a forest park
      Which must be cleared before tonight
      And already it's growing dark!

And the seven elephants hadn't any tusks
    The one that had the tusks was Little Brother
Seven are no match for one, if the one has a gun!
    How old Chang did laugh at Little Brother!
        Keep on digging!
        Mr. Chang has a forest park
        Which must be cleared before tonight
        And already it's growing dark!

[*Smoking a cigar,* SHUI TA *strolls by.* YANG SUN, *laughing, has joined in the refrain of the third stanza and speeded up the tempo of the last stanza by clapping his hands.*]

MRS. YANG: And that's why I say: strength and wisdom are wonderful things. It took the strong and wise Mr. Shui Ta to bring out the best in Yang Sun. A real superior man is like a bell. If you ring it, it rings, and if you don't, it don't, as the saying is.

SCENE IX——*Shen Te's shop, now an office with club chairs and fine carpets. It is raining.*

[SHUI TA, *now fat, is just dismissing the* OLD MAN *and* OLD WOMAN. MRS. SHIN, *in obviously new clothes, looks on, smirking.*]

SHUI TA: No! I can NOT tell you when we expect her back.

OLD WOMAN: The two hundred silver dollars came today. In an envelope. There was no letter, but it must be from Shen Te. We want to write and thank her. May we have her address?

SHUI TA: I'm afraid I haven't got it.

OLD MAN: [*pulling* OLD WOMAN's *sleeve*] Let's be going.

OLD WOMAN: She's got to come back some time!

[*They move off, uncertainly, worried.* SHUI TA *bows.*]

MRS. SHIN: They lost the carpet shop because they couldn't pay their taxes. The money arrived too late.

SHUI TA: They could have come to me.

MRS. SHIN: People don't like coming to you.

SHUI TA: [*sits suddenly, one hand to his head*] I'm dizzy.

MRS. SHIN: After all, you *are* in your seventh month. But old Mrs. Shin will be there in your hour of trial! [*She cackles feebly*]

SHUI TA: [*in a stifled voice*] Can I count on that?

MRS. SHIN: We all have our price, and mine won't be too high for the great Mr. Shui Ta! [*She opens* SHUI TA's *collar.*]

SHUI TA: It's for the child's sake. All of this.

MRS. SHIN: "All for the child," of course.

SHUI TA: I'm so fat. People must notice.

MRS. SHIN: Oh no, they think it's 'cause you're rich.

SHUI TA: [*more feelingly*] What will happen to the child?

MRS. SHIN: You ask that nine times a day. Why, it'll have the best that money can buy!

SHUI TA: He must never see Shui Ta.

MRS. SHIN: Oh, no. Always Shen Te.

SHUI TA: What about the neighbors? There are rumors, aren't there?

MRS. SHIN: As long as Mr. Shu Fu doesn't find out, there's nothing to worry about. Drink this.

> [*Enter* YANG SUN *in a smart business suit, and carrying a business-man's briefcase.* SHUI TA *is more or less in* MRS. SHIN'S *arms.*]

YANG SUN: [*surprised*] I guess I'm in the way.

SHUI TA: [*ignoring this, rises with an effort*] Till tomorrow, Mrs. Shin.

> [MRS. SHIN *leaves with a smile, putting her new gloves on.*]

YANG SUN: Gloves now! She couldn't be fleecing you? And since when did *you* have a private life? [*taking a paper from the briefcase*] You haven't been at your desk lately, and things are getting out of hand. The police want to close us down. They say that at the most they can only permit twice the lawful number of workers.

SHUI TA: [*evasively*] The cabins are quite good enough.

YANG SUN: For the workers maybe, not for the tobacco. They're too damp. We must take over some of Mrs. Mi Tzu's buildings.

SHUI TA: Her price is double what I can pay.

YANG SUN: Not unconditionally. If she has me to stroke her knees she'll come down.

SHUI TA: I'll never agree to that.

YANG SUN: What's wrong? Is it the rain? You get so irritable whenever it rains.

SHUI TA: Never! I will never . . .

YANG SUN: Mrs. Mi Tzu'll be here in five minutes. *You* fix it. And Shu Fu will be with her. . . . What's all that noise?

> [*During the above dialogue,* WONG *is heard offstage, calling:* "The good Shen Te, where is she? Which of you has seen Shen Te, good people? Where is Shen Te?" *A knock. Enter* WONG.]

WONG: Mr. Shui Ta, I've come to ask when Miss Shen Te will be back, it's six months now. . . . There are rumors. People say something's happened to her.

SHUI TA: I'm busy. Come back next week.

WONG: [*excited*] In the morning there was always rice on her doorstep—for the needy. It's been there again lately!

SHUI TA: And what do people conclude from this?

WONG: That Shen Te is still in Setzuan! She's been . . . [*He breaks off.*]

SHUI TA: She's been what? Mr. Wong, if you're Shen Te's friend, talk a little less about her, that's my advice to you.

WONG: I don't want your advice! Before she disappeared, Miss Shen Te told me something very important—she's pregnant!

YANG SUN: What? What was that?

SHUI TA: [*quickly*] The man is lying.

WONG: A good woman isn't so easily forgotten, Mr. Shui Ta.

> [*He leaves.* SHUI TA *goes quickly into the back room.*]

YANG SUN: [*to the audience*] Shen Te pregnant? So that's why. Her cousin sent her away, so I wouldn't get wind of it. I have a son, a Yang appears on the scene, and what happens? Mother and child vanish into thin air! That scoundrel, that unspeakable . . . [*The sound of sobbing is heard from the back room.*] What was that? Someone sobbing? Who was it? Mr. Shui Ta the Tobacco King doesn't weep his heart out. And where does the rice come from that's on the doorstep in the morning? [SHUI TA *returns. He goes to the door and looks out into the rain.*] Where is she?

SHUI TA: Sh! It's nine o'clock. But the rain's so heavy, you can't hear a thing.

YANG SUN: What do you want to hear?

SHUI TA: The mail plane.

YANG SUN: What?!

SHUI TA: I've been told *you* wanted to fly at one time. Is that all forgotten?

YANG SUN: Flying mail is night work. I prefer the daytime. And the firm is very dear to me—after all it belongs to my ex-fiancée, even if she's not around. And she's not, is she?

SHUI TA: What do you mean by that?

YANG SUN: Oh, well, let's say I haven't altogether—lost interest.

SHUI TA: My cousin might like to know that.

YANG SUN: I might not be indifferent—if I found she was being kept under lock and key.

SHUI TA: By whom?

YANG SUN: By you.

SHUI TA: What could you do about it?

YANG SUN: I could submit for discussion—my position in the firm.

SHUI TA: You are now my manager. In return for a more . . . appropriate position, you might agree to drop the inquiry into your ex-fiancée's whereabouts?

YANG SUN: I might.

SHUI TA: What position *would* be more appropriate?

YANG SUN: The one at the top.

SHUI TA: My own? [*silence*] And if I preferred to throw you out on your neck?

YANG SUN: I'd come back on my feet. With suitable escort.

SHUI TA: The police?

YANG SUN: The police.

SHUI TA: And when the police found no one?

YANG SUN: I might ask them not to overlook the back room. [*ending the pretense*] In short, Mr. Shui Ta, my interest in this young woman has not been officially terminated. I should like to see more of her. [*into* SHUI TA'S *face*] Besides, she's pregnant and needs a friend. [*He moves to the door.*] I shall talk about it with the water seller.

[*Exit.* SHUI TA *is rigid for a moment, then he quickly goes into the back room. He returns with Shen Te's belongings: underwear, etc. He takes a long look at the shawl of the previous scene. He then wraps the things in a bundle, which, upon hearing a noise, he hides under the table. Enter* MRS. MI TZU *and* MR. SHU FU. *They put away their umbrellas and galoshes.*]

MRS. MI TZU: I thought your manager was here, Mr. Shui Ta. He combines charm with business in a way that can only be to the advantage of all of us.

SHU FU: You sent for us, Mr. Shui Ta?

SHUI TA: The factory is in trouble.

SHU FU: It always is.

SHUI TA: The police are threatening to close us down unless I can show that the extension of our facilities is imminent.

SHU FU: Shui Ta, I'm sick and tired of your constantly expanding projects. I place cabins at your cousin's disposal; you make a factory of them. I hand your cousin a check; you present it. Your cousin disappears; you find the cabins too small and start talking of yet more—

SHUI TA: Mr. Shu Fu, I'm authorized to inform you that Miss Shen Te's return is now imminent.

SHU FU: Imminent? It's becoming his favorite word.

MRS. MI TZU: Yes, what does it mean?

SHUI TA: Mrs. Mi Tzu, I can pay you exactly half what you asked for your buildings. Are you ready to inform the police that I am taking them over?

MRS. MI TZU: Certainly, if I can take over your manager.

SHU FU: What?

MRS. MI TZU: He's so efficient.

SHUI TA: I'm afraid I need Mr. Yang Sun.

MRS. MI TZU: So do I.

SHUI TA: He will call on you tomorrow.

SHU FU: So much the better. With Shen Te likely to turn up at any moment, the presence of that young man is hardly in good taste.

SHUI TA: So we have reached a settlement. In what was once the good Shen Te's little shop we are laying the foundations for the great Mr. Shui Ta's twelve magnificent super tobacco markets. You will bear in mind that though they call me the Tobacco King of Setzuan, it is my cousin's interests that have been served . . .

VOICES: [off] The police, the police! Going to the tobacco shop! Something must have happened!

[Enter YANG SUN, WONG *and the* POLICEMAN.]

POLICEMAN: Quiet there, quiet, quiet! [They quiet down.] I'm sorry, Mr. Shui Ta, but there's a report that you've been depriving Miss Shen Te of her freedom. Not that I believe all I hear, but the whole city's in an uproar.

SHUI TA: That's a lie.

POLICEMAN: Mr. Yang Sun has testified that he heard someone sobbing in the back room.

SHU FU: Mrs. Mi Tzu and myself will testify that no one here has been sobbing.

MRS. MI TZU: We have been quietly smoking our cigars.

POLICEMAN: Mr. Shui Ta, I'm afraid I shall have to take a look at that room. [He does so. The room is empty.] No one there, of course, sir.

YANG SUN: But I heard sobbing. What's that? [He finds the clothes.]

WONG: Those are Shen Te's things. [to crowd] Shen Te's clothes are here!

VOICES: [off, in sequence]

—Shen Te's clothes!

—They've been found under the table!

—Body of murdered girl still missing!

—Tobacco King suspected!

POLICEMAN: Mr. Shui Ta, unless you can tell us where the girl is, I'll have to ask you to come along.

SHUI TA: I do not know.

POLICEMAN: I can't say how sorry I am, Mr. Shui Ta. [*He shows him the door.*]

SHUI TA: Everything will be cleared up in no time. There are still judges in Setzuan.

YANG SUN: I heard sobbing!

SCENE IXa——WONG's *den.*

[*For the last time, the* GODS *appear to the water seller in his dream. They have changed and show signs of a long journey, extreme fatigue, and plenty of mishaps. The* FIRST *no longer has a hat; the* THIRD *has lost a leg; all three are barefoot.*

WONG: Illustrious ones, at last you're here. Shen Te's been gone for months and today her cousin's been arrested. They think he murdered her to get the shop. But I had a dream and in this dream Shen Te said her cousin was keeping her prisoner. You must find her for us, illustrious ones!

FIRST GOD: We've found very few good people anywhere, and even they didn't keep it up. Shen Te is still the only one that stayed good.

SECOND GOD: If she *has* stayed good.

WONG: Certainly she has. But she's vanished.

FIRST GOD: That's the last straw. All is lost!

SECOND GOD: A little moderation, dear colleague!

FIRST GOD: [*plaintively*] What's the good of moderation now? If she can't be found, we'll have to resign! The world is a terrible place! Nothing but misery, vulgarity, and waste! Even the countryside isn't what it used to be. The trees are getting their heads chopped off by telephone wires, and there's such a noise from all the gunfire, and I can't stand those heavy clouds of smoke, and—

THIRD GOD: The place is absolutely unlivable! Good intentions bring people to the brink of the abyss, and good deeds push them over the edge. I'm afraid our book of rules is destined for the scrap heap—

SECOND GOD: It's people! They're a worthless lot!

THIRD GOD: The world is too cold!

SECOND GOD: It's people! They're too weak!

FIRST GOD: Dignity, dear colleagues, dignity! Never despair! As for this world, didn't we agree that we only have to find one human being who can stand the place? Well, we found her. True, we lost her again. We must find her again, that's all. And at once!

[*They disappear.*]

SCENE X——*Courtroom.*

[*Groups:* SHU FU *and* MRS. MI TZU; YANG SUN *and* MRS. YANG; WONG, *the* CARPENTER, *the* GRANDFATHER, *the* NIECE, *the* OLD MAN, *the* OLD WOMAN; MRS. SHIN, *the* POLICEMAN; *the* UNEMPLOYED MAN, *the* SISTER-IN-LAW.]

OLD MAN: So much power isn't good for one man.

UNEMPLOYED MAN: And he's going to open twelve super tobacco markets!

WIFE: One of the judges is a friend of Mr. Shu Fu's.

SISTER-IN-LAW: Another one accepted a present from Mr. Shui Ta only last night. A great fat goose.

OLD WOMAN: [*to* WONG] And Shen Te is nowhere to be found.

WONG: Only the gods will ever know the truth.

POLICEMAN: Order in the court! My lords the judges!

> [*Enter the* THREE GODS *in judges' robes. We overhear their conversation as they pass along the footlights to their bench.*]

THIRD GOD: We'll never get away with it, our certificates were so badly forged.

SECOND GOD: My predecessor's "sudden indigestion" will certainly cause comment.

FIR~T GOD: But he *had* just eaten a whole goose.

UNEMPLOYED MAN: Look at that! *New* judges.

WONG: New judges. And what good ones!

> [*The* THIRD GOD *hears this, and turns to smile at* WONG. *The* GODS *sit. The* FIRST GOD *beats on the bench with his gavel. The* POLICEMAN *brings in* SHUI TA *who walks with lordly steps. He is whistled at.*]

POLICEMAN: [*to* SHUI TA] Be prepared for a surprise. The judges have been changed.

> [SHUI TA *turns quickly round, looks at them, and staggers.*]

NIECE: What's the matter now?

WIFE: The great Tobacco King nearly fainted.

HUSBAND: Yes, as soon as he saw the new judges.

WONG: Does *he* know who they are?

> [SHUI TA *picks himself up, and the proceedings open.*]

FIRST GOD: Defendant Shui Ta, you are accused of doing away with your cousin Shen Te in order to take possession of her business. Do you plead guilty or not guilty?

SHUI TA: Not guilty, my lord.

FIRST GOD: [*thumbing through the documents of the case*] The first witness is the policeman. I shall ask him to tell us something of the respective reputations of Miss Shen Te and Mr. Shui Ta.

POLICEMAN: Miss Shen Te was a young lady who aimed to please, my lord. She liked to live and let live, as the saying goes. Mr. Shui Ta, on the other hand, is a man of principle. Though the generosity of Miss Shen Te forced him at times to abandon half measures, unlike the girl he was always on the side of the law, my lord. One time, he even unmasked a gang of thieves to whom his too trustful cousin had given shelter. The evidence, in short, my lord, proves that Mr. Shui Ta was *incapable* of the crime of which he stands accused!

FIRST GOD: I see. And are there others who could testify along, shall we say, the same lines?

> [SHU FU *rises.*]

POLICEMAN: [*whispering to* GODS] Mr. Shu Fu—a very important person.

FIRST GOD: [*inviting him to speak*] Mr. Shu Fu!

SHU FU: Mr. Shui Ta is a businessman, my lord. Need I say more?

FIRST GOD: Yes.

SHU FU: Very well, I will. He is Vice President of the Council of Commerce and is about to be elected a Justice of the Peace. [*He returns to his seat.*]

[MRS. MI TZU *rises.*]

WONG: Elected! *He* gave him the job!

[*With a gesture the* FIRST GOD *asks who* MRS. MI TZU *is.*]

POLICEMAN: Another very important person. Mrs. Mi Tzu.

MRS. MI TZU: My lord, as Chairman of the Committee on Social Work, I wish to call attention to just a couple of eloquent facts: Mr. Shui Ta not only has erected a model factory with model housing in our city, he is a regular contributor to our home for the disabled. [*She returns to her seat.*]

POLICEMAN: [*whispering*] And she's a great friend of the judge that ate the goose!

FIRST GOD: [*to the* POLICEMAN] Oh, thank you. What next? [*to the Court, genially*] Oh, yes. We should find out if any of the evidence is less favorable to the defendant.

[WONG, *the* CARPENTER, *the* OLD MAN, *the* OLD WOMAN, *the* UNEMPLOYED MAN, *the* SISTER-IN-LAW, *and the* NIECE *come forward.*]

POLICEMAN: [*whispering*] Just the riffraff, my lord.

FIRST GOD: [*addressing the "riffraff"*] Well, um, riffraff—do you know anything of the defendant, Mr. Shui Ta?

WONG: Too much, my lord.

UNEMPLOYED MAN: What don't we know, my lord.

CARPENTER: He ruined us.

SISTER-IN-LAW: He's a cheat.

NIECE: Liar.

WIFE: Thief.

BOY: Blackmailer.

BROTHER: Murderer.

FIRST GOD: Thank you. We should now let the defendant state his point of view.

SHUI TA: I only came on the scene when Shen Te was in danger of losing what I had understood was a gift from the gods. Because I did the filthy jobs which someone had to do, they hate me. My activities were restricted to the minimum, my lord.

SISTER-IN-LAW: He had us arrested!

SHUI TA: Certainly. You stole from the bakery!

SISTER-IN-LAW: Such concern for the bakery! You didn't want the shop for yourself, I suppose!

SHUI TA: I didn't want the shop overrun with parasites.

SISTER-IN-LAW: We had nowhere else to go.

SHUI TA: There were too many of you.

WONG: What about this old couple: Were *they* parasites?

OLD MAN: We lost our shop because of you!

OLD WOMAN: And we gave your cousin money!

SHUI TA: My cousin's fiancé was a flyer. The money had to go to *him*.

WONG: Did you care whether he flew or not? Did you care whether she married him or not? You wanted her to marry someone else! [*He points at* SHU FU.]

SHUI TA: The flyer unexpectedly turned out to be a scoundrel.

YANG SUN: [*jumping up*] Which was the reason you made him your manager?

SHUI TA: Later on he improved.

WONG: And when he improved, you sold him to her? [*he points out* MRS. TZU]

SHUI TA: She wouldn't let me have her premises unless she had him to stroke her knees!

MRS. MI TZU: What? The man's a pathological liar. [*to him*] Don't mention my property to me as long as you live! Murderer! [*She rustles off, in high dudgeon.*]

YANG SUN: [*pushing in*] My lord, I wish to speak for the defendant.

SISTER-IN-LAW: Naturally. He's your employer.

UNEMPLOYED MAN: And the worst slave driver in the country.

MRS. YANG: That's a lie! My lord, Mr. Shui Ta is a great man. He . . .

YANG SUN: He's this and he's that, but he is not a murderer, my lord. Just fifteen minutes before his arrest I heard Shen Te's voice in his own back room.

FIRST GOD: Oh? Tell us more!

YANG SUN: I heard sobbing, my lord!

FIRST GOD: But lots of women sob, we've been finding.

YANG SUN: Could I fail to recognize her voice?

SHU FU: No, you made her sob so often yourself, young man!

YANG SUN: Yes. But I also made her happy. Till he [*pointing at* SHUI TA] decided to sell her to you!

SHUI TA: Because you didn't love her.

WONG: Oh, no: it was for the money, my lord!

SHUI TA: And what was the money for, my lord? For the poor! And for Shen Te so she could go on being good!

WONG: For the poor? That he sent to his sweatshops? And why didn't you let Shen Te be good when you signed the big check?

SHUI TA: For the child's sake, my lord.

CARPENTER: What about *my* children? What did he do about them?

[SHUI TA *is silent.*]

WONG: The shop was to be a fountain of goodness. That was the gods' idea. You came and spoiled it!

SHUI TA: If I hadn't, it would have run dry!

MRS. SHIN: There's a lot in that, my lord.

WONG: What have you done with the good Shen Te, bad man? She *was* good, my lords, she was, I swear it! [*He raises his hand in an oath.*]

THIRD GOD: What's happened to your hand, water seller?

WONG: [*pointing to* SHUI TA] It's all his fault, my lord, *she* was going to send me to a doctor—[*to* SHUI TA] You were her worst enemy!

SHUI TA: I was her only friend!

WONG: Where is she then? Tell us where your good friend is!

[*The excitement of this exchange has run through the whole crowd.*]

ALL: Yes, where is she? Where is Shen Te? [*etc.*]

SHUI TA: Shen Te . . . had to go.

WONG: Where? Where to?

SHUI TA: I cannot tell you! I cannot tell you!

ALL: Why? Why did she have to go away? [*etc.*]

WONG: [*into the din with the first words, but talking on beyond the others*] Why not, why not? Why did she have to go away?

SHUI TA: [*shouting*] Because you'd all have torn her to shreds, that's why! My lords, I have a request. Clear the court! When only the judges remain, I will make a confession.

ALL: [*except* WONG, *who is silent, struck by the new turn of events*] So he's guilty? He's confessing! [*etc.*]

FIRST GOD: [*using the gavel*] Clear the court!

POLICEMAN: Clear the court!

WONG: Mr. Shui Ta has met his match this time.

MRS. SHIN: [*with a gesture toward the judges*] You're in for a little surprise.

[*The court is cleared. Silence.*]

SHUI TA: Illustrious ones!

[*The* GODS *look at each other, not quite believing their ears.*]

SHUI TA: Yes, I recognize you!

SECOND GOD: [*taking matters in hand, sternly*] What have you done with our good woman of Setzuan?

SHUI TA: I have a terrible confession to make: I am she! [*He takes off his mask, and tears away his clothes.* SHEN TE *stands there.*]

SECOND GOD: Shen Te!

SHEN TE: Shen Te, yes. Shui Ta *and* Shen Te. Both.

Your injunction
To be good and yet to live
Was a thunderbolt:
It has torn me in two
I can't tell how it was
But to be good to others
And myself at the same time
I could not do it
Your world is not an easy one, illustrious ones!
When we extend our hand to a begger, he tears it off for us
When we help the lost, we are lost ourselves
And so
Since not to eat is to die
Who can long refuse to be bad?
As I lay prostrate beneath the weight of good intentions
Ruin stared me in the face
It was when I was unjust that I ate good meat
And hobnobbed with the mighty
Why?
Why are bad deeds rewarded?
Good ones punished?

I enjoyed giving
I truly wished to be the Angel of the Slums
But washed by a foster mother in the water of the gutter
I developed a sharp eye
The time came when pity was a thorn in my side
And, later, when kind words turned to ashes in my mouth
And anger took over
I became a wolf
Find me guilty, then, illustrious ones,
But know:
All that I have done I did
To help my neighbor
To love my lover
And to keep my little one from want
For your great, godly deeds, I was too poor, too small.
> [*Pause.*]

FIRST GOD: [*shocked*] Don't go on making yourself miserable, Shen Te! We're overjoyed to have found you!

SHEN TE: I'm telling you I'm the bad man who committed all those crimes!

FIRST GOD: [*using—or failing to use—his ear trumpet*] The good woman who did all those good deeds?

SHEN TE: Yes, but the bad man too!

FIRST GOD: [*as if something had dawned*] Unfortunate coincidences! Heartless neighbors!

THIRD GOD: [*shouting in his ear*] But how is she to continue?

FIRST GOD: Continue? Well, she's a strong, healthy girl . . .

SECOND GOD: You didn't hear what she said!

FIRST GOD: I heard every word! She is confused, that's all! [*He begins to bluster.*] And what about this book of rules—we can't renounce our rules, can we? [*more quietly*] Should the world be changed? How? By whom? The world should *not* be changed! [*At a sign from him, the lights turn pink, and music plays.*]¹
And now the hour of parting is at hand.
Dost thou behold, Shen Te, yon fleecy cloud?
It is our chariot. At a sign from me
'Twill come and take us back from whence we came
Above the azure vault and silver stars. . . .

SHEN TE: No! Don't go, illustrious ones!

FIRST GOD: Our cloud has landed now in yonder field
From which it will transport us back to heaven.
Farewell, Shen Te, let not thy courage fail thee. . . .
> [*Exeunt* GODS.]

SHEN TE: What about the old couple? They've lost their shop! What about the water seller and his hand? And I've got to defend myself against the

---

¹ The rest of this scene has been adapted for the many American theatres that do not have "fly-space" to lower things from ropes.

barber, because I don't love him! And against Sun, because I do love him! How? How?

> [SHEN TE's *eyes follow the* GODS *as they are imagined to step into a cloud which rises and moves forward over the orchestra and up beyond the balcony.*]

FIRST GOD: [*from on high*] We have faith in you, Shen Te!

SHEN TE: There'll be a child. And he'll have to be fed. I can't stay here. Where shall I go?

FIRST GOD: Continue to be good, good woman of Setzuan!

SHEN TE: I need my bad cousin!

FIRST GOD: But not very often!

SHEN TE: Once a wcek at least!

FIRST GOD: Once a month will be quite enough!

SHEN TE: [*shrieking*] No, no! Help!

> [*But the cloud continues to recede as the* GODS *sing.*]

VALEDICTORY HYMN

What rapture, oh, it is to know
    A good thing when you see it
And having seen a good thing, oh,
    What rapture 'tis to flee it

Be good, sweet maid of Setzuan
    Let Shui Ta be clever
Departing, we forget the man
    Remember your endeavor

Because through all the length of days
    Her goodness faileth never
Sing hallelujah! Make Shen Te's
    Good name live on forever!

SHEN TE: Help!

EPILOGUE

You're thinking, aren't you, that this is no right
Conclusion to the play you've seen tonight?[2]
After a tale, exotic, fabulous,
A nasty ending was slipped up on us.
We feel deflated too. We too are nettled
To see the curtain down and nothing settled.
How could a better ending be arranged?
Could one change people? Can the world be changed?
Would new gods do the trick? Will atheism?
Moral rearmament? Materialism?

---

[2] At *afternoon performances:*
  We quite agree, our play this afternoon
  Collapsed upon us like a pricked balloon.

It is for you to find a way, my friends,
To help good men arrive at happy ends.
You write the happy ending to the play!
There must, there must, there's got to be a way![3]

[3] When I first received the German manuscript of *Good Woman* from Brecht in
1945 it had no Epilogue. He wrote it a little later, influenced by misunderstandings of
the ending in the press on the occasion of the Viennese première of the play. I believe
that the Epilogue has sometimes been spoken by the actress playing Shen Te, but the
actor playing Wong might be a shrewder choice, since the audience has already accepted him as a kind of chorus. On the other hand, it is not *Wong* who should
deliver the Epilogue: whichever actor delivers it should drop the character he has been
playing.—E. B.

ARTHUR MILLER

DEATH OF A SALESMAN

CHARACTERS

WILLY LOMAN
LINDA, *his wife*
BIFF
HAPPY } *his sons*
UNCLE BEN
CHARLEY
BERNARD
THE WOMAN
HOWARD WAGNER
JENNY
STANLEY
MISS FORSYTHE
LETTA

The action takes place in WILLY LOMAN'S *house and yard and in various places he visits in the New York and Boston of today.*

ACT I

A melody is heard, played upon a flute. It is small and fine, telling of grass and trees and the horizon. The curtain rises.

Before us is the Salesman's house. We are aware of towering, angular shapes behind it, surrounding it on all sides. Only the blue light of the sky falls upon the house and forestage; the surrounding area shows an angry glow of orange. As more light appears, we see a solid vault of apartment houses around the small, fragile-seeming home. An air of the dream clings to the place, a dream rising out of reality. The kitchen at center seems actual enough, for there is a kitchen table with three chairs, and a refrigerator. But no other fixtures are seen. At the back of the kitchen there is a draped entrance, which leads to the living-room. To the right of the kitchen, on a level raised two feet, is a bedroom furnished only with a brass bedstead and a straight chair. On a shelf over the bed a silver athletic trophy stands. A window opens onto the apartment house at the side.

Behind the kitchen, on a level raised six and a half feet, is the boys' bedroom, at present barely visible. Two beds are dimly seen, and at the back of the room a dormer window. (This bedroom is above the unseen living-room.) At the left a stairway curves up to it from the kitchen.

The entire setting is wholly or, in some places, partially transparent. The roof-line of the house is one-dimensional; under and over it we see the apartment buildings. Before the house lies an apron, curving beyond the forestage into the orchestra. This forward area serves as the back yard as well as the locale of all Willy's imaginings and of his city scenes. Whenever the action is in the present the actors observe the imaginary wall-lines, entering the house only through its door at the left. But in the scenes of the past these boundaries are broken, and characters enter or leave a room by stepping "through" a wall onto the forestage.

> [*From the right,* WILLY LOMAN, *the Salesman, enters, carrying two large sample cases. The flute plays on. He hears but is not aware of it. He is past sixty years of age, dressed quietly. Even as he crosses the stage to the doorway of the house, his exhaustion is apparent. He unlocks the door, comes into the kitchen, and thankfully lets his burden down, feeling the soreness of his palms. A word-sigh escapes his lips—it might be "Oh, boy, oh, boy." He closes the door, then carries his cases out into the living-room, through the draped kitchen doorway.*]
>
> LINDA, *his wife, has stirred in her bed at the right. She gets out and puts on a robe, listening. Most often jovial, she has developed an iron repression of her exceptions to Willy's behavior—she more than loves him, she admires him, as though his mercurial nature, his temper, his massive dreams and little cruelties, served her only as sharp reminders of the turbulent longings within him, longings which she shares but lacks the temperament to utter and follow to their end.*]

LINDA: [*hearing* WILLY *outside the bedroom, calls with some trepidation*] Willy!

WILLY: It's all right. I came back.

LINDA: Why? What happened? [*slight pause*] Did something happen, Willy?

WILLY: No, nothing happened.

LINDA: You didn't smash the car, did you?

WILLY: [*with casual irritation*] I said nothing happened. Didn't you hear me?

LINDA: Don't you feel well?

WILLY: I'm tired to the death. [*The flute has faded away. He sits on the bed beside her, a little numb.*] I couldn't make it. I just couldn't make it, Linda.

LINDA: [*very carefully, delicately*] Where were you all day? You look terrible.

WILLY: I got as far as a little above Yonkers. I stopped for a cup of coffee. Maybe it was the coffee.

LINDA: What?

WILLY: [*after a pause*] I suddenly couldn't drive any more. The car kept going off onto the shoulder, y'know?

LINDA: [*helpfully*] Oh. Maybe it was the steering again. I don't think Angelo knows the Studebaker.

WILLY: No, it's me, it's me. Suddenly I realize I'm goin' sixty miles an hour and I don't remember the last five minutes. I'm—I can't seem to—keep my mind to it.

LINDA: Maybe it's your glasses. You never went for your new glasses.

WILLY: No, I see everything. I came back ten miles an hour. It took me nearly four hours from Yonkers.

LINDA: [*resigned*] Well, you'll just have to take a rest, Willy, you can't continue this way.

WILLY: I just got back from Florida.

LINDA: But you didn't rest your mind. Your mind is overactive, and the mind is what counts, dear.

WILLY: I'll start out in the morning. Maybe I'll feel better in the morning. [*She is taking off his shoes.*] These goddam arch supports are killing me.

LINDA: Take an aspirin. Should I get you an aspirin? It'll soothe you.

WILLY: [*with wonder*] I was driving along, you understand? And I was fine. I was even observing the scenery. You can imagine, me looking at scenery, on the road every week of my life. But it's so beautiful up there, Linda, the trees are so thick, and the sun is warm. I opened the windshield and just let the warm air bathe over me. And then all of a sudden I'm goin' off the road! I'm tellin' ya, I absolutely forgot I was driving. If I'd've gone the other way over the white line I might've killed somebody. So I went on again—and five minutes later I'm dreamin' again, and I nearly— [*He presses two fingers against his eyes.*] I have such thoughts, I have such strange thoughts.

LINDA: Willy, dear. Talk to them again. There's no reason why you can't work in New York.

WILLY: They don't need me in New York. I'm the New England man. I'm vital in New England.

LINDA: But you're sixty years old. They can't expect you to keep traveling every week.

WILLY: I'll have to send a wire to Portland. I'm supposed to see Brown and Morrison tomorrow morning at ten o'clock to show the line. Goddammit, I could sell them! [*He starts putting on his jacket.*]

LINDA: [*taking the jacket from him*] Why don't you go down to the place tomorrow and tell Howard you've simply got to work in New York? You're too accommodating, dear.

WILLY: If old man Wagner was alive I'd a been in charge of New York now! That man was a prince, he was a masterful man. But that boy of his, that Howard, he don't appreciate. When I went north the first time, the Wagner Company didn't know where New England was!

LINDA: Why don't you tell those things to Howard, dear?

WILLY: [*encouraged*] I will, I definitely will. Is there any cheese?

LINDA: I'll make you a sandwich.

WILLY: No, go to sleep. I'll take some milk. I'll be up right away. The boys in?

LINDA: They're sleeping. Happy took Biff on a date tonight.

WILLY: [*interested*] That so?

LINDA: It was so nice to see them shaving together, one behind the other, in the bathroom. And going out together. You notice? The whole house smells of shaving lotion.

WILLY: Figure it out. Work a lifetime to pay off a house. You finally own it, and there's nobody to live in it.

LINDA: Well, dear, life is a casting off. It's always that way.

WILLY: No, no, some people—some people accomplish something. Did Biff say anything after I went this morning?

LINDA: You shouldn't have criticized him, Willy, especially after he just got off the train. You mustn't lose your temper with him.

WILLY: When the hell did I lose my temper? I simply asked him if he was making any money. Is that a criticism?

LINDA: But, dear, how could he make any money?

WILLY: [worried and angered] There's such an undercurrent in him. He became a moody man. Did he apologize when I left this morning?

LINDA: He was crestfallen, Willy. You know how he admires you. I think if he finds himself, then you'll both be happier and not fight any more.

WILLY: How can he find himself on a farm? Is that a life? A farmhand? In the beginning, when he was young, I thought, well, a young man, it's good for him to tramp around, take a lot of different jobs. But it's more than ten years now and he has yet to make thirty-five dollars a week!

LINDA: He's finding himself, Willy.

WILLY: Not finding yourself at the age of thirty-four is a disgrace!

LINDA: Shh!

WILLY: The trouble is he's lazy, goddammit!

LINDA: Willy, please!

WILLY: Biff is a lazy bum!

LINDA: They're sleeping. Get something to eat. Go on down.

WILLY: Why did he come home? I would like to know what brought him home.

LINDA: I don't know. I think he's still lost, Willy. I think he's very lost.

WILLY: Biff Loman is lost. In the greatest country in the world a young man with such—personal attractiveness, gets lost. And such a hard worker. There's one thing about Biff—he's not lazy.

LINDA: Never.

WILLY: [with pity and resolve] I'll see him in the morning; I'll have a nice talk with him. I'll get him a job selling. He could be big in no time. My God! Remember how they used to follow him around in high school? When he smiled at one of them their faces lit up. When he walked down the street . . . [He loses himself in reminiscences.]

LINDA: [trying to bring him out of it] Willy, dear, I got a new kind of American-type cheese today. It's whipped.

WILLY: Why do you get American when I like Swiss?

LINDA: I just thought you'd like a change—

WILLY: I don't want a change! I want Swiss cheese. Why am I always being contradicted?

LINDA: [with a covering laugh] I thought it would be a surprise.

WILLY: Why don't you open a window in here, for God's sake?

LINDA: [with infinite patience] They're all open, dear.

WILLY: The way they boxed us in here. Bricks and windows, windows and bricks.

LINDA: We should've bought the land next door.

WILLY: The street is lined with cars. There's not a breath of fresh air in the neighborhood. The grass don't grow any more, you can't raise a carrot in the back yard. They should've had a law against apartment houses. Remember those two beautiful elm trees out there? When I and Biff hung the swing between them?

LINDA: Yeah, like being a million miles from the city.

WILLY: They should've arrested the builder for cutting those down. They massacred the neighborhood. [*lost*] More and more I think of those days, Linda. This time of year it was lilac and wisteria. And then the peonies would come out, and the daffodils. What fragrance in this room!

LINDA: Well, after all, people had to move somewhere.

WILLY: No, there's more people now.

LINDA: I don't think there's more people. I think—

WILLY: There's more people! That's what's ruining this country! Population is getting out of control. The competition is maddening! Smell the stink from that apartment house! And another one on the other side . . . How can they whip cheese?

[*On Willy's last line,* BIFF *and* HAPPY *raise themselves up in their beds, listening.*]

LINDA: Go down, try it. And be quiet.

WILLY: [*turning to* LINDA, *guiltily*] You're not worried about me, are you, sweetheart?

BIFF: What's the matter?

HAPPY: Listen!

LINDA: You've got too much on the ball to worry about.

WILLY: You're my foundation and my support, Linda.

LINDA: Just try to relax, dear. You make mountains out of molehills.

WILLY: I won't fight with him any more. If he wants to go back to Texas, let him go.

LINDA: He'll find his way.

WILLY: Sure. Certain men just don't get started till later in life. Like Thomas Edison, I think. Or B. F. Goodrich. One of them was deaf. [*He starts for the bedroom doorway.*] I'll put my money on Biff.

LINDA: And Willy—if it's warm Sunday we'll drive in the country. And we'll open the windshield, and take lunch.

WILLY: No, the windshields don't open on the new cars.

LINDA: But you opened it today.

WILLY: Me? I didn't. [*He stops.*] Now isn't that peculiar! Isn't that a remarkable— [*He breaks off in amazement and fright as the flute is heard distantly.*]

LINDA: What, darling?

WILLY: That is the most remarkable thing.

LINDA: What, dear?

WILLY: I was thinking of the Chevvy. [*slight pause*] Nineteen twenty-eight . . . when I had that red Chevvy— [*breaks off*] That funny? I coulda sworn I was driving that Chevvy today.

LINDA: Well, that's nothing. Something must've reminded you.

WILLY: Remarkable. Ts. Remember those days? The way Biff used to simonize that car? The dealer refused to believe there was eighty thousand miles on it. [*He shakes his head.*] Heh! [*to* LINDA] Close your eyes, I'll be right up. [*He walks out of the bedroom.*]

HAPPY: [*to* BIFF] Jesus, maybe he smashed up the car again!

LINDA: [*calling after* WILLY] Be careful on the stairs, dear! The cheese is on the middle shelf! [*She turns, goes over to the bed, takes his jacket, and goes out of the bedroom.*]

> [*Light has risen on the boys' room. Unseen,* WILLY *is heard talking to himself, "Eighty thousand miles," and a little laugh.* BIFF *gets out of bed, comes downstage a bit, and stands attentively.* BIFF *is two years older than his brother* HAPPY, *well built, but in these days bears a worn air and seems less self-assured. He has succeeded less, and his dreams are stronger and less acceptable than Happy's.* HAPPY *is tall, powerfully made. Sexuality is like a visible color on him, or a scent that many women have discovered. He, like his brother, is lost, but in a different way, for he has never allowed himself to turn his face toward defeat and is thus more confused and hard-skinned, although seemingly more content.*]

HAPPY: [*getting out of bed*] He's going to get his license taken away if he keeps that up. I'm getting nervous about him, y'know, Biff?

BIFF: His eyes are going.

HAPPY: No, I've driven with him. He sees all right. He just doesn't keep his mind on it. I drove into the city with him last week. He stops at a green light and then it turns red and he goes. [*He laughs.*]

BIFF: Maybe he's color-blind.

HAPPY: Pop? Why he's got the finest eye for color in the business. You know that.

BIFF: [*sitting down on his bed*] I'm going to sleep.

HAPPY: You're not still sour on Dad, are you, Biff?

BIFF: He's all right, I guess.

WILLY: [*underneath them, in the living-room*] Yes, sir, eighty thousand miles—eighty-two thousand!

BIFF: You smoking?

HAPPY: [*holding out a pack of cigarettes*] Want one?

BIFF: [*taking a cigarette*] I can never sleep when I smell it.

WILLY: What a simonizing job, heh!

HAPPY: [*with deep sentiment*] Funny, Biff, y'know? Us sleeping in here again? The old beds. [*He pats his bed affectionately*] All the talk that went across those two beds, huh? Our whole lives.

BIFF: Yeah. Lotta dreams and plans.

HAPPY: [*with a deep and masculine laugh*] About five hundred women would like to know what was said in this room.

> [*They share a soft laugh.*]

BIFF: Remember that big Betsy something—what the hell was her name—over on Bushwick Avenue?

HAPPY: [*combing his hair*] With the collie dog!

BIFF: That's the one. I got you in there, remember?

HAPPY: Yeah, that was my first time—I think. Boy, there was a pig! [*They laugh, almost crudely.*] You taught me everything I know about women. Don't forget that.

BIFF: I bet you forgot how bashful you used to be. Especially with girls.

HAPPY: Oh, I still am, Biff.

BIFF: Oh, go on.

HAPPY: I just control it, that's all. I think I got less bashful and you got more so. What happened, Biff? Where's the old humor, the old confidence? [*He shakes Biff's knee.* BIFF *gets up and moves restlessly about the room.*] What's the matter?

BIFF: Why does Dad mock me all the time?

HAPPY: He's not mocking you, he—

BIFF: Everything I say there's a twist of mockery on his face. I can't get near him.

HAPPY: He just wants you to make good, that's all. I wanted to talk to you about Dad for a long time, Biff. Something's— happening to him. He— talks to himself.

BIFF: I noticed that this morning. But he always mumbled.

HAPPY: But not so noticeable. It got so embarrassing I sent him to Florida. And you know something? Most of the time he's talking to you.

BIFF: What's he say about me?

HAPPY: I can't make it out.

BIFF: What's he say about me?

HAPPY: I think the fact that you're not settled, that you're still kind of up in the air . . .

BIFF: There's one or two other things depressing him, Happy.

HAPPY: What do you mean?

BIFF: Never mind. Just don't lay it all to me.

HAPPY: But I think if you just got started—I mean—is there any future for you out there?

BIFF: I tell ya, Hap, I don't know what the future is. I don't know—what I'm supposed to want.

HAPPY: What do you mean?

BIFF: Well, I spent six or seven years after high school trying to work myself up. Shipping clerk, salesman, business of one kind or another. And it's a measly manner of existence. To get on that subway on the hot mornings in summer. To devote your whole life to keeping stock, or making phone calls, or selling or buying. To suffer fifty weeks of the year for the sake of a two-week vacation, when all you really desire is to be outdoors, with your shirt off. And always to have to get ahead of the next fella. And still— that's how you build a future.

HAPPY: Well, you really enjoy it on a farm? Are you content out there?

BIFF: [*with rising agitation*] Hap, I've had twenty or thirty different kinds of jobs since I left home before the war, and it always turns out the same. I just realized it lately. In Nebraska when I herded cattle, and the Dakotas, and Arizona, and now in Texas. It's why I came home now, I guess, because I realized it. This farm I work on, it's spring there now, see? And they've got about fifteen new colts. There's nothing more inspiring or— beautiful than the sight of a mare and a new colt. And it's cool there now, see? Texas is cool now, and it's spring. And whenever spring comes to where I am, I suddenly get the feeling, my God, I'm not gettin' anywhere! What the hell am I doing, playing around with horses, twenty-eight dollars a week! I'm thirty-four years old, I oughta be makin' my future. That's when I come running home. And now, I get here, and I don't know what to do with myself. [*after a pause*] I've always made a point of not wasting my life, and everytime I come back here I know that all I've done is to waste my life.

HAPPY: You're a poet, you know that, Biff? You're a—you're an idealist!

BIFF: No, I'm mixed up very bad. Maybe I oughta get married. Maybe I oughta get stuck into something. Maybe that's my trouble. I'm like a boy. I'm not married, I'm not in business, I just—I'm like a boy. Are you content, Hap? You're a success, aren't you? Are you content?

HAPPY: Hell, no!

BIFF: Why? You're making money, aren't you?

HAPPY: [*moving about with energy, expressiveness*] All I can do now is wait for the merchandise manager to die. And suppose I get to be merchandise manager? He's a good friend of mine, and he just built a terrific estate on Long Island. And he lived there about two months and sold it, and now he's building another one. He can't enjoy it once it's finished. And I know that's just what I would do. I don't know what the hell I'm workin' for. Sometimes I sit in my apartment—all alone. And I think of the rent I'm paying. And it's crazy. But then, it's what I always wanted. My own apartment, a car, and plenty of women. And still, goddammit, I'm lonely.

BIFF: [*with enthusiasm*] Listen, why don't you come out West with me?

HAPPY: You and I, heh?

BIFF: Sure, maybe we could buy a ranch. Raise cattle, use our muscles. Men built like we are should be working out in the open.

HAPPY: [*avidly*] The Loman Brothers, heh?

BIFF: [*with vast affection*] Sure, we'd be known all over the counties!

HAPPY: [*enthralled*] That's what I dream about, Biff. Sometimes I want to just rip my clothes off in the middle of the store and outbox that goddam merchandise manager. I mean I can outbox, outrun, and outlift anybody in that store, and I have to take orders from those common, petty sons-of-bitches till I can't stand it any more.

BIFF: I'm tellin' you, kid, if you were with me I'd be happy out there.

HAPPY: [*enthused*] See, Biff, everybody around me is so false that I'm constantly lowering my ideals . . .

BIFF: Baby, together we'd stand up for one another, we'd have someone to trust.

HAPPY: If I were around you—

BIFF: Hap, the trouble is we weren't brought up to grub for money. I don't know how to do it.

HAPPY: Neither can I!

BIFF: Then let's go!

HAPPY: The only thing is—what can you make out there?

BIFF: But look at your friend. Builds an estate and then hasn't the peace of mind to live in it.

HAPPY: Yeah, but when he walks into the store the waves part in front of him. That's fifty-two thousand dollars a year coming through the revolving door, and I got more in my pinky finger than he's got in his head.

BIFF: Yeah, but you just said—

HAPPY: I gotta show some of those pompous, self-important executives over there that Hap Loman can make the grade. I want to walk into the store the way he walks in. Then I'll go with you, Biff. We'll be together yet, I swear. But take those two we had tonight. Now weren't they gorgeous creatures?

BIFF: Yeah, yeah, most gorgeous I've had in years.

HAPPY: I get that any time I want, Biff. Whenever I feel disgusted. The only trouble is, it gets like bowling or something. I just keep knockin' them over and it doesn't mean anything. You still run around a lot?

BIFF: Naa. I'd like to find a girl—steady, somebody with substance.

HAPPY: That's what I long for.

BIFF: Go on! You'd never come home.

HAPPY: I would! Somebody with character, with resistance! Like Mom, y'know? You're gonna call me a bastard when I tell you this. That girl Charlotte I was with tonight is engaged to be married in five weeks. [*He tries on his new hat.*]

BIFF: No kiddin'!

HAPPY: Sure, the guy's in line for the vice-presidency of the store. I don't know what gets into me, maybe I just have an overdeveloped sense of competition or something, but I went and ruined her, and furthermore I can't get rid of her. And he's the third executive I've done that to. Isn't that a crummy characteristic? And to top it all, I go to their weddings! [*indignantly, but laughing*] Like I'm not supposed to take bribes. Manufacturers offer me a hundred-dollar bill now and then to throw an order their way. You know how honest I am, but it's like this girl, see. I hate myself for it. Because I don't want the girl, and, still, I take it and—I love it!

BIFF: Let's go to sleep.

HAPPY: I guess we didn't settle anything, heh?

BIFF: I just got one idea that I think I'm going to try.

HAPPY: What's that?

BIFF: Remember Bill Oliver?

HAPPY: Sure, Oliver is very big now. You want to work for him again?

BIFF: No, but when I quit he said something to me. He put his arm on my shoulder, and he said, "Biff, if you ever need anything, come to me."

HAPPY: I remember that. That sounds good.

BIFF: I think I'll go to see him. If I could get ten thousand or even seven or eight thousand dollars I could buy a beautiful ranch.

HAPPY: I bet he'd back you. 'Cause he thought highly of you, Biff. I mean, they all do. You're well liked, Biff. That's why I say to come back here, and we both have the apartment. And I'm tellin' you, Biff, any babe you want . . .

BIFF: No, with a ranch I could do the work I like and still be something. I just wonder though. I wonder if Oliver still thinks I stole that carton of basketballs.

HAPPY: Oh, he probably forgot that long ago. It's almost ten years. You're too sensitive. Anyway, he didn't really fire you.

BIFF: Well, I think he was going to. I think that's why I quit. I was never sure whether he knew or not. I know he thought the world of me, though. I was the only one he'd let lock up the place.

WILLY: [*below*] You gonna wash the engine, Biff?

HAPPY: Shh!

[BIFF *looks at* HAPPY, *who is gazing down, listening.* WILLY *is mumbling in the parlor.*]

HAPPY: You hear that?

[*They listen.* WILLY *laughs warmly.*]

BIFF: [*growing angry*] Doesn't he know Mom can hear that?

WILLY: Don't get your sweater dirty, Biff!

[*A look of pain crosses* BIFF'*s face.*]

HAPPY: Isn't that terrible? Don't leave again, will you? You'll find a job here. You gotta stick around. I don't know what to do about him, it's getting embarrassing.

WILLY: What a simonizing job!

BIFF: Mom's hearing that!

WILLY: No kiddin', Biff, you got a date? Wonderful!

HAPPY: Go on to sleep. But talk to him in the morning, will you?

BIFF: [*reluctantly getting into bed*] With her in the house. Brother!

HAPPY: [*getting into bed*] I wish you'd have a good talk with him.

[*The light on their room begins to fade.*]

BIFF: [*to himself in bed*] That selfish, stupid . . .

HAPPY: Sh . . . Sleep, Biff.

[*Their light is out. Well before they have finished speaking,* WILLY'*s form is dimly seen below in the darkened kitchen. He opens the refrigerator, searches in there, and takes out a bottle of milk. The apartment houses are fading out, and the entire house and surroundings become covered with leaves. Music insinuates itself as the leaves appear.*]

WILLY: Just wanna be careful with those girls, Biff, that's all. Don't make any promises. No promises of any kind. Because a girl, y'know, they always believe what you tell 'em, and you're very young, Biff, you're too young to be talking seriously to girls.

[*Light rises on the kitchen.* WILLY, *talking, shuts the refrigerator door and comes downstage to the kitchen table. He pours milk into a glass. He is totally immersed in himself, smiling faintly.*]

WILLY: Too young entirely, Biff. You want to watch your schooling first. Then when you're all set, there'll be plenty of girls for a boy like you. [*He smiles broadly at a kitchen chair.*] That so? The girls pay for you? [*He laughs.*] Boy, you must really be makin' a hit.

[WILLY *is gradually addressing—physically—a point offstage, speaking through the wall of the kitchen, and his voice has been rising in volume to that of a normal conversation.*]

WILLY: I been wondering why you polish the car so careful. Ha! Don't leave the hubcaps, boys. Get the chamois to the hubcaps. Happy, use newspaper on the windows, it's the easiest thing. Show him how to do it, Biff! You see, Happy? Pad it up, use it like a pad. That's it, that's it, good work. You're doin' all right, Hap. [*he pauses, then nods in approbation for a few seconds, then looks upward*] Biff, first thing we gotta do when we get time is clip that big branch over the house. Afraid it's gonna fall in a storm and hit the roof. Tell you what. We get a rope and sling her around, and then we climb up there with a couple of saws and take her down. Soon as you finish the car, boys, I wanna see ya. I got a surprise for you, boys.

BIFF: [*offstage*] Whatta ya got, Dad?

WILLY: No, you finish first. Never leave a job till you're finished—remember that. [*looking toward the "big trees"*] Biff, up in Albany I saw a beautiful hammock. I think I'll buy it next trip, and we'll hang it right between those two elms. Wouldn't that be something? Just swingin' there under those branches. Boy, that would be . . .

[YOUNG BIFF *and* YOUNG HAPPY *appear from the direction* WILLY *was addressing.* HAPPY *carries rags and a pail of water.* BIFF, *wearing a sweater with a block "S," carries a football.*]

BIFF: [*pointing in the direction of the car offstage*] How's that, Pop, professional?

WILLY: Terrific. Terrific job, boys. Good work, Biff.

HAPPY: Where's the surprise, Pop?

WILLY: In the back seat of the car.

HAPPY: Boy! [*He runs off.*]

BIFF: What is it, Dad? Tell me, what'd you buy?

WILLY: [*laughing, cuffs him*] Never mind, something I want you to have.

BIFF: [*turns and starts off*] What is it, Hap?

HAPPY: [*offstage*] It's a punching bag!

BIFF: Oh, Pop!

WILLY: It's got Gene Tunney's signature on it!

[HAPPY *runs onstage with a punching bag.*]

BIFF: Gee, how'd you know we wanted a punching bag?

WILLY: Well, it's the finest thing for the timing.

HAPPY: [*lies down on his back and pedals with his feet*] I'm losing weight, you notice, Pop?

WILLY: [*to* HAPPY] Jumping rope is good too.

BIFF: Did you see the new football I got?

WILLY: [*examining the ball*] Where'd you get a new ball?

BIFF: The coach told me to practice my passing.

WILLY: That so? And he gave you the ball, heh?

BIFF: Well, I borrowed it from the locker room. [*He laughs confidentially.*]

WILLY: [*laughing with him at the theft*] I want you to return that.

HAPPY: I told you he wouldn't like it!

BIFF: [*angrily*] Well, I'm bringing it back!

WILLY: [*stopping the incipient argument, to* HAPPY] Sure, he's gotta practice with a regulation ball, doesn't he? [*to* BIFF] Coach'll probably congratulate you on your initiative!

BIFF: Oh, he keeps congratulating my initiative all the time, Pop.

WILLY: That's because he likes you. If somebody else took that ball there'd be an uproar. So what's the report, boys, what's the report?

BIFF: Where'd you go this time, Dad? Gee we were lonesome for you.

WILLY: [*pleased, puts an arm around each boy and they come down to the apron*] Lonesome, heh?

BIFF: Missed you every minute.

WILLY: Don't say? Tell you a secret, boys. Don't breathe it to a soul. Someday I'll have my own business, and I'll never have to leave home any more.

HAPPY: Like Uncle Charley, heh?

WILLY: Bigger than Uncle Charley! Because Charley is not—liked. He's liked, but he's not—well liked.

BIFF: Where'd you go this time, Dad?

WILLY: Well, I got on the road, and I went north to Providence. Met the Mayor.

BIFF: The Mayor of Providence!

WILLY: He was sitting in the hotel lobby.

BIFF: What'd he say?

WILLY: He said, "Morning!" And I said, "You got a fine city here, Mayor." And then he had coffee with me. And then I went to Waterbury. Waterbury is a fine city. Big clock city, the famous Waterbury clock. Sold a nice bill there. And then Boston—Boston is the cradle of the Revolution. A fine city. And a couple of other towns in Mass., and on to Portland and Bangor and straight home!

BIFF: Gee, I'd love to go with you sometime, Dad.

WILLY: Soon as summer comes.

HAPPY: Promise?

WILLY: You and Hap and I, and I'll show you all the towns. America is full of beautiful towns and fine, upstanding people. And they know me, boys, they know me up and down New England. The finest people. And when I bring you fellas up, there'll be open sesame for all of us, 'cause one thing, boys: I have friends. I can park my car in any street in New England, and the cops protect it like their own. This summer, heh?

BIFF and HAPPY: [*together*] Yeah! You bet!

WILLY: We'll take our bathing suits.

HAPPY: We'll carry your bags, Pop!

WILLY: Oh, won't that be something! Me comin' into the Boston stores with you boys carryin' my bags. What a sensation!

[BIFF *is prancing around, practicing passing the ball.*]

WILLY: You nervous, Biff, about the game?

BIFF: Not if you're gonna be there.

WILLY: What do they say about you in school, now that they made you captain?

HAPPY: There's a crowd of girls behind him everytime the classes change.

BIFF: [*taking* WILLY's *hand*] This Saturday, Pop, this Saturday—just for you, I'm going to break through for a touchdown.

HAPPY: You're supposed to pass.

BIFF: I'm takin' one play for Pop. You watch me, Pop, and when I take off my helmet, that means I'm breakin' out. Then you watch me crash through that line!

WILLY: [*kisses* BIFF] Oh, wait'll I tell this in Boston!

[BERNARD *enters in knickers. He is younger than* BIFF, *earnest and loyal, a worried boy.*]

BERNARD: Biff, where are you? You're supposed to study with me today.

WILLY: Hey, looka Bernard. What're you lookin' so anemic about, Bernard?

BERNARD: He's gotta study, Uncle Willy. He's got Regents next week.

HAPPY: [*tauntingly, spinning* BERNARD *around*] Let's box, Bernard!

BERNARD: Biff! [*He gets away from* HAPPY.] Listen, Biff, I heard Mr. Birnbaum say that if you don't start studyin' math he's gonna flunk you, and you won't graduate. I heard him!

WILLY: You better study with him, Biff. Go ahead now.

BERNARD: I heard him!

BIFF: Oh, Pop, you didn't see my sneakers! [*He holds up a foot for* WILLY *to look at.*]

WILLY: Hey, that's a beautiful job of printing!

BERNARD: [*wiping his glasses*] Just because he printed University of Virginia on his sneakers doesn't mean they've got to graduate him, Uncle Willy!

WILLY: [*angrily*] What're you talking about? With scholarships to three universities they're gonna flunk him?

BERNARD: But I heard Mr. Birnbaum say—

WILLY: Don't be a pest, Bernard! [*to his boys*] What an anemic!

BERNARD: Okay, I'm waiting for you in my house, Biff.

[BERNARD *goes off. The* LOMANS *laugh.*]

WILLY: Bernard is not well liked, is he?

BIFF: He's liked, but he's not well liked.

HAPPY: That's right, Pop.

WILLY: That's just what I mean. Bernard can get the best marks in school, y'understand, but when he gets out in the business world, y'understand, you are going to be five times ahead of him. That's why I thank Almighty God you're both built like Adonises. Because the man who makes an appearance in the business world, the man who creates personal interest, is the man who gets ahead. Be liked and you will never want. You take me, for instance. I never have to wait in line to see a buyer. "Willy Loman is here!" That's all they have to know, and I go right through.

BIFF: Did you knock them dead, Pop?

WILLY: Knocked 'em cold in Providence, slaughtered 'em in Boston.

HAPPY: [*on his back, pedaling again*] I'm losing weight, you notice, Pop?

[LINDA *enters, as of old, a ribbon in her hair, carrying a basket of washing.*]

LINDA: [*with youthful energy*] Hello, dear!

WILLY: Sweetheart!

LINDA: How'd the Chevvy run?

WILLY: Chevrolet, Linda, is the greatest car ever built. [*to the boys*] Since when do you let your mother carry wash up the stairs?

BIFF: Grab hold there, boy!

HAPPY: Where to, Mom?

LINDA: Hang them up on the line. And you better go down to your friends, Biff. The cellar is full of boys. They don't know what to do with themselves.

BIFF: Ah, when Pop comes home they can wait!

WILLY: [*laughs appreciatively*] You better go down and tell them what to do, Biff.

BIFF: I think I'll have them sweep out the furnace room.

WILLY: Good work, Biff.

BIFF: [*goes through wall-line of kitchen to doorway at back and calls down*] Fellas! Everybody sweep out the furnace room! I'll be right down!

VOICES: All right! Okay, Biff.

BIFF: George and Sam and Frank, come out back! We're hangin' up the wash! Come on, Hap, on the double! [*He and* HAPPY *carry out the basket.*]

LINDA: The way they obey him!

WILLY: Well, that's training, the training. I'm tellin' you, I was sellin' thousands and thousands, but I had to come home.

LINDA: Oh, the whole block'll be at that game. Did you sell anything?

WILLY: I did five hundred gross in Providence and seven hundred gross in Boston.

LINDA: No! Wait a minute, I've got a pencil. [*She pulls pencil and paper out of her apron pocket.*] That makes your commission . . . Two hundred— my God! Two hundred and twelve dollars!

WILLY: Well, I didn't figure it yet, but . . .

LINDA: How much did you do?

WILLY: Well, I—I did—about a hundred and eighty gross in Providence. Well, no—it came to—roughly two hundred gross on the whole trip.

LINDA: [*without hesitation*] Two hundred gross. That's . . . [*She figures.*]

WILLY: The trouble was that three of the stores were half closed for inventory in Boston. Otherwise I woulda broke records.

LINDA: Well, it makes seventy dollars and some pennies. That's very good.

WILLY: What do we owe?

LINDA: Well, on the first there's sixteen dollars on the refrigerator—

WILLY: Why sixteen?

LINDA: Well, the fan belt broke, so it was a dollar eighty.

WILLY: But it's brand new.

LINDA: Well, the man said that's the way it is. Till they work themselves in, y'know.

[*They move through the wall-line into the kitchen.*]

WILLY: I hope we didn't get stuck on that machine.

LINDA: They got the biggest ads of any of them!

WILLY: I know, it's a fine machine. What else?

LINDA: Well, there's nine-sixty for the washing machine. And for the vacuum cleaner there's three and a half due on the fifteenth. Then the roof, you got twenty-one dollars remaining.

WILLY: It don't leak, does it?

LINDA: No, they did a wonderful job. Then you owe Frank for the carburetor.

WILLY: I'm not going to pay that man! That goddam Chevrolet, they ought to prohibit the manufacture of that car!

LINDA: Well, you owe him three and a half. And odds and ends, comes to around a hundred and twenty dollars by the fifteenth.

WILLY: A hundred and twenty dollars! My God, if business don't pick up I don't know what I'm gonna do!

LINDA: Well, next week you'll do better.

WILLY: Oh, I'll knock 'em dead next week. I'll go to Hartford. I'm very well liked in Hartford. You know, the trouble is, Linda, people don't seem to take to me.

[*They move onto the forestage.*]

LINDA: Oh, don't be foolish.

WILLY: I know it when I walk in. They seem to laugh at me.

LINDA: Why? Why would they laugh at you? Don't talk that way, Willy.

[WILLY *moves to the edge of the stage.* LINDA *goes into the kitchen and starts to darn stockings.*]

WILLY: I don't know the reason for it, but they just pass me by. I'm not noticed.

LINDA: But you're doing wonderful, dear. You're making seventy to a hundred dollars a week.

WILLY: But I gotta be at it ten, twelve hours a day. Other men—I don't know —they do it easier. I don't know why—I can't stop myself—I talk too much. A man oughta come in with a few words. One thing about Charley. He's a man of few words, and they respect him.

LINDA: You don't talk too much, you're just lively.

WILLY: [*smiling*] Well, I figure, what the hell, life is short, a couple of jokes. [*to himself*] I joke too much! [*The smile goes.*]

LINDA: Why? You're—

WILLY: I'm fat. I'm very—foolish to look at, Linda. I didn't tell you, but Christmas time I happened to be calling on F. H. Stewarts, and a salesman I know, as I was going in to see the buyer I heard him say something about —walrus. And I—I cracked him right across the face. I won't take that. I simply will not take that. But they do laugh at me. I know that.

LINDA: Darling . . .

WILLY: I gotta overcome it. I know I gotta overcome it. I'm not dressing to advantage, maybe.

LINDA: Willy, darling, you're the handsomest man in the world—

WILLY: Oh, no, Linda.

LINDA: To me you are. [*slight pause*] The handsomest.

[*From the darkness is heard the laughter of a woman.* WILLY *doesn't turn to it, but it continues through* LINDA's *lines.*]

LINDA: And the boys, Willy. Few men are idolized by their children the way you are.

[*Music is heard as behind a scrim, to the left of the house,* THE WOMAN, *dimly seen, is dressing.*]

WILLY: [*with great feeling*] You're the best there is, Linda, you're a pal, you know that? On the road—on the road I want to grab you sometimes and just kiss the life outa you.

[*The laughter is loud now, and he moves into a brightening area at the left, where* THE WOMAN *has come from behind the scrim and is standing, putting on her hat, looking into a "mirror" and laughing.*]

WILLY: 'Cause I get so lonely—especially when business is bad and there's nobody to talk to. I get the feeling that I'll never sell anything again, that I won't make a living for you, or a business, a business for the boys. [*He talks through* THE WOMAN's *subsiding laughter;* THE WOMAN *primps at the "mirror."*] There's so such I want to make for—

THE WOMAN: Me? You didn't make me, Willy. I picked you.

WILLY: [*pleased*] You picked me?

THE WOMAN: [*who is quite proper-looking,* Willy's *age*] I did. I've been sitting at that desk watching all the salesmen go by, day in, day out. But you've got such a sense of humor, and we do have such a good time together, don't we?

WILLY: Sure, sure. [*He takes her in his arms.*] Why do you have to go now?

THE WOMAN: It's two o'clock . . .

WILLY: No, come on in! [*He pulls her.*]

THE WOMAN: . . . my sisters'll be scandalized. When'll you be back?

WILLY: Oh, two weeks about. Will you come up again?

THE WOMAN: Sure thing. You do make me laugh. It's good for me. [*She squeezes his arm, kisses him.*] And I think you're a wonderful man.

WILLY: You picked me, heh?

THE WOMAN: Sure. Because you're so sweet. And such a kidder.

WILLY: Well, I'll see you next time I'm in Boston.

THE WOMAN: I'll put you right through to the buyers.

WILLY: [*slapping her bottom*] Right. Well, bottoms up!

THE WOMAN: [*slaps him gently and laughs*] You just kill me, Willy. [*He suddenly grabs her and kisses her roughly.*] You kill me. And thanks for the stockings. I love a lot of stockings. Well, good night.

WILLY: Good night. And keep your pores open!

THE WOMAN: Oh, Willy!

[THE WOMAN *bursts out laughing, and* LINDA's *laughter blends in.* THE WOMAN *disappears into the dark. Now the area at the kitchen table brightens.* LINDA *is sitting where she was at the kitchen table, but now is mending a pair of her silk stockings.*]

LINDA: You are, Willy. The handsomest man. You've got no reason to feel that—

WILLY: [*coming out of* THE WOMAN's *dimming area and going over to* LINDA] I'll make it all up to you, Linda, I'll—

LINDA: There's nothing to make up, dear. You're doing fine, better than—

WILLY: [*noticing her mending*] What's that?

LINDA: Just mending my stockings. They're so expensive—

WILLY: [*angrily, taking them from her*] I won't have you mending stockings in this house! Now throw them out!

[LINDA *puts the stockings in her pocket.*]

BERNARD: [*entering on the run*] Where is he? If he doesn't study!

WILLY: [*moving to the forestage, with great agitation*] You'll give him the answers!

BERNARD: I do, but I can't on a Regents! That's a state exam! They're liable to arrest me!

WILLY: Where is he? I'll whip him, I'll whip him!

LINDA: And he'd better give back that football, Willy, it's not nice.

WILLY: Biff! Where is he? Why is he taking everything?

LINDA: He's too rough with the girls, Willy. All the mothers are afraid of him!

WILLY: I'll whip him!

BERNARD: He's driving the car without a license!

[THE WOMAN'*s laugh is heard.*]

WILLY: Shut up!

LINDA: All the mothers—

WILLY: Shut up!

BERNARD: [*backing quietly away and out*] Mr. Birnbaum says he's stuck up.

WILLY: Get outa here!

BERNARD: If he doesn't buckle down he'll flunk math! [*He goes off.*]

LINDA: He's right, Willy, you've gotta—

WILLY: [*exploding at her*] There's nothing the matter with him! You want him to be a worm like Bernard? He's got spirit, personality . . .

[As he speaks, LINDA, *almost in tears, exits into the living-room.* WILLY *is alone in the kitchen, wilting and staring. The leaves are gone. It is night again, and the apartment houses look down from behind.*]

WILLY: Loaded with it. Loaded! What is he stealing? He's giving it back, isn't he? Why is he stealing? What did I tell him? I never in my life told him anything but decent things.

[HAPPY *in pajamas has come down the stairs;* WILLY *suddenly becomes aware of* HAPPY'*s presence.*]

HAPPY: Let's go now, come on.

WILLY: [*sitting down at the kitchen table*] Huh! Why did she have to wax the floors herself? Everytime she waxes the floors she keels over. She knows that!

HAPPY: Shh! Take it easy. What brought you back tonight?

WILLY: I got an awful scare. Nearly hit a kid in Yonkers. God! Why didn't I go to Alaska with my brother Ben that time! Ben! That man was a genius, that man was success incarnate! What a mistake! He begged me to go.

HAPPY: Well, there's no use in—

WILLY: You guys! There was a man started with the clothes on his back and ended up with diamond mines!

HAPPY: Boy, someday I'd like to know how he did it.

WILLY: What's the mystery? The man knew what he wanted and went out and got it! Walked into a jungle, and comes out, the age of twenty-one, and he's rich! The world is an oyster, but you don't crack it open on a mattress!

HAPPY: Pop, I told you I'm gonna retire you for life.

WILLY: You'll retire me for life on seventy goddam dollars a week? And your women and your car and your apartment, and you'll retire me for life! Christ's sake, I couldn't get past Yonkers' today! Where are you guys, where are you? The woods are burning! I can't drive a car!

[CHARLEY *has appeared in the doorway. He is a large man, slow of speech, laconic, immovable. In all he says, despite what he says, there is pity, and, now, trepidation. He has a robe over pajamas, slippers on his feet. He enters the kitchen.*]

CHARLEY: Everything all right?

HAPPY: Yeah, Charley, everything's . . .

WILLY: What's the matter?

CHARLEY: I heard some noise. I thought something happened. Can't we do something about the walls? You sneeze in here, and in my house hats blow off.

HAPPY: Let's go to bed, Dad. Come on.

[CHARLEY *signals to* HAPPY *to go.*]

WILLY: You go ahead, I'm not tired at the moment.

HAPPY: [*to* WILLY] Take it easy, huh? [*He exits.*]

WILLY: What're you doin' up?

CHARLEY: [*sitting down at the kitchen table opposite* WILLY] Couldn't sleep good. I had a heartburn.

WILLY: Well, you don't know how to eat.

CHARLEY: I eat with my mouth.

WILLY: No, you're ignorant. You gotta know about vitamins and things like that.

CHARLEY: Come on, let's shoot. Tire you out a little.

WILLY: [*hesitantly*] All right. You got cards?

CHARLEY: [*taking a deck from his pocket*] Yeah, I got them. Someplace. What is it with those vitamins?

WILLY: [*dealing*] They build up your bones. Chemistry.

CHARLEY: Yeah, but there's no bones in a heartburn.

WILLY: What are you talkin' about? Do you know the first thing about it?

CHARLEY: Don't get insulted.

WILLY: Don't talk about something you don't know anything about.

[*They are playing. Pause.*]

CHARLEY: What're you doin' home?

WILLY: A little trouble with the car.

CHARLEY: Oh. [*pause*] I'd like to take a trip to California.

WILLY: Don't say.

CHARLEY: You want a job?

WILLY: I got a job, I told you that. [*after a slight pause*] What the hell are you offering me a job for?

CHARLEY: Don't get insulted.

WILLY: Don't insult me.

CHARLEY: I don't see no sense in it. You don't have to go on this way.

WILLY: I got a good job. [*slight pause*] What do you keep comin' in here for?

CHARLEY: You want me to go?

WILLY: [*after a pause, withering*] I can't understand it. He's going back to Texas again. What the hell is that?

CHARLEY: Let him go.

WILLY: I got nothin' to give him, Charley, I'm clean, I'm clean.

CHARLEY: He won't starve. None a them starve. Forget about him.

WILLY: Then what have I got to remember?

CHARLEY: You take it too hard. To hell with it. When a deposit bottle is broken you don't get your nickel back.

WILLY: That's easy enough for you to say.

CHARLEY: That ain't easy for me to say.

WILLY: Did you see the ceiling I put up in the living-room?

CHARLEY: Yeah, that's a piece of work. To put up a ceiling is a mystery to me. How do you do it?

WILLY: What's the difference?

CHARLEY: Well, talk about it.

WILLY: You gonna put up a ceiling?

CHARLEY: How could I put up a ceiling?

WILLY: Then what the hell are you bothering me for?

CHARLEY: You're insulted again.

WILLY: A man who can't handle tools is not a man. You're disgusting.

CHARLEY: Don't call me disgusting, Willy.

[UNCLE BEN, *carrying a valise and an umbrella, enters the forestage from around the right corner of the house. He is a stolid man, in his sixties, with a mustache and an authoritative air. He is utterly certain of his destiny, and there is an aura of far places about him. He enters exactly as* WILLY *speaks.*]

WILLY: I'm getting awfully tired, Ben.

[*Ben's music is heard.* BEN *looks around at everything.*]

CHARLEY: Good, keep playing; you'll sleep better. Did you call me Ben?

[BEN *looks at his watch.*]

WILLY: That's funny. For a second there you reminded me of my brother Ben.

BEN: I only have a few minutes. [*He strolls, inspecting the place.* WILLY *and* CHARLEY *continue playing.*]

CHARLEY: You never heard from him again, heh? Since that time?

WILLY: Didn't Linda tell you? Couple of weeks ago we got a letter from his wife in Africa. He died.

CHARLEY: That so.

BEN: [*chuckling*] So this is Brooklyn, eh?

CHARLEY: Maybe you're in for some of his money.

WILLY: Naa, he had seven sons. There's just one opportunity I had with that man . . .

BEN: I must make a train, William. There are several properties I'm looking at in Alaska.

WILLY: Sure, sure! If I'd gone with him to Alaska that time, everything would've been totally different.

CHARLEY: Go on, you'd froze to death up there.

WILLY: What're you talking about?

BEN: Opportunity is tremendous in Alaska, William. Surprised you're not up there.

WILLY: Sure, tremendous.

CHARLEY: Heh?

WILLY: There was the only man I ever met who knew the answers.

CHARLEY: Who?

BEN: How are you all?

WILLY: [*taking a pot, smiling*] Fine, fine.

CHARLEY: Pretty sharp tonight.

BEN: Is Mother living with you?

WILLY: No, she died a long time ago.

CHARLEY: Who?

BEN: That's too bad. Fine specimen of a lady, Mother.

WILLY: [*to* CHARLEY] Heh?

BEN: I'd hoped to see the old girl.

CHARLEY: Who died?

BEN: Heard anything from Father, have you?

WILLY: [*unnerved*] What do you mean, who died?

CHARLEY: [*taking a pot*] What're you talkin' about?

BEN: [*looking at his watch*] William, it's half-past eight!

WILLY: [*as though to dispel his confusion he angrily stops* CHARLEY's *hand*] That's my build!

CHARLEY: I put the ace—

WILLY: If you don't know how to play the game I'm not gonna throw my money away on you!

CHARLEY: [*rising*] It was my ace, for God's sake!

WILLY: I'm through, I'm through!

BEN: When did Mother die?

WILLY: Long ago. Since the beginning you never knew how to play cards.

CHARLEY: [*picks up the cards and goes to the door*] All right! Next time I'll bring a deck with five aces.

WILLY: I don't play that kind of game!

CHARLEY: [*turning to him*] You ought to be ashamed of yourself!

WILLY: Yeah?

CHARLEY: Yeah! [*He goes out.*]

WILLY: [*slamming the door after him*] Ignoramus!

BEN: [*as* WILLY *comes toward him through the wall-line of the kitchen*] So you're William.

WILLY: [*shaking* BEN's *hand*] Ben! I've been waiting for you so long! What's the answer? How did you do it?

BEN: Oh, there's a story in that.

[LINDA *enters the forestage, as of old, carrying the wash basket.*]

LINDA: Is this Ben?

BEN: [*gallantly*] How do you do, my dear.

LINDA: Where've you been all these years? Willy's always wondered why you—

WILLY: [*pulling* BEN *away from her impatiently*] Where is Dad? Didn't you follow him? How did you get started?

BEN: Well, I don't know how much you remember.

WILLY: Well, I was just a baby, of course, only three or four years old—

BEN: Three years and eleven months.

WILLY: What a memory, Ben!

BEN: I have many enterprises, William, and I have never kept books.

WILLY: I remember I was sitting under the wagon in—was it Nebraska?

BEN: It was South Dakota, and I gave you a bunch of wild flowers.

WILLY: I remember you walking away down some open road.

BEN: [*laughing*] I was going to find Father in Alaska.

WILLY: Where is he?

BEN: At that age I had a very faulty view of geography, William. I discovered after a few days that I was heading due south, so instead of Alaska, I ended up in Africa.

LINDA: Africa!

WILLY: The Gold Coast!

BEN: Principally diamond mines.

LINDA: Diamond mines!

BEN: Yes, my dear. But I've only a few minutes—

WILLY: No! Boys! Boys! [YOUNG BIFF *and* HAPPY *appear.*] Listen to this. This is your Uncle Ben, a great man! Tell my boys, Ben!

BEN: Why, boys, when I was seventeen I walked into the jungle, and when I was twenty-one I walked out. [*he laughs*] And by God I was rich.

WILLY: [*to the boys*] You see what I been talking about? The greatest things can happen!

BEN: [*glancing at his watch*] I have an appointment in Ketchikan Tuesday week.

WILLY: No, Ben! Please tell about Dad. I want my boys to hear. I want them to know the kind of stock they spring from. All I remember is a man with a big beard, and I was in Mamma's lap, sitting around a fire, and some kind of high music.

BEN: His flute. He played the flute.

WILLY: Sure, the flute, that's right!

    [*New music is heard, a high, rollicking tune.*]

BEN: Father was a very great and a very wild-hearted man. We would start in Boston, and he'd toss the whole family into the wagon, and then he'd drive the team right across the country; through Ohio, and Indiana, Michigan, Illinois, and all the Western states. And we'd stop in the towns and sell the flutes that he'd made on the way. Great inventor, Father. With one gadget he made more in a week than a man like you could make in a lifetime.

WILLY: That's just the way I'm bringing them up, Ben—rugged, well liked, all-around.

BEN: Yeah? [*to* BIFF] Hit that, boy—hard as you can. [*he pounds his stomach*]
BIFF: Oh, no, sir!
BEN: [*taking boxing stance*] Come on, get to me! [*He laughs.*]
BIFF: Okay! [*He cocks his fists and starts in.*]
LINDA: [*to* WILLY] Why must he fight, dear?
BEN: [*sparring with* BIFF] Good boy! Good boy!
WILLY: How's that, Ben, heh?
HAPPY: Give him the left, Biff!
LINDA: Why are you fighting?
BEN: Good boy! [*Suddenly comes in, trips* BIFF, *and stands over him, the point of his umbrella poised over* BIFF's *eye.*]
LINDA: Look out, Biff!
BIFF: Gee!
BEN: [*patting* BIFF's *knee*] Never fight fair with a stranger, boy. You'll never get out of the jungle that way. [*taking* LINDA's *hand and bowing*] It was an honor and a pleasure to meet you, Linda.
LINDA: [*withdrawing her hand coldly, frightened*] Have a nice—trip.
BEN: [*to* WILLY] And good luck with your—what do you do?
WILLY: Selling.
BEN: Yes. Well . . . [*He raises his hand in farewell to all.*]
WILLY: No, Ben, I don't want you to think . . . [*He takes* BEN's *arm to show him.*] It's Brooklyn, I know, but we hunt too.
BEN: Really, now.
WILLY: Oh, sure, there's snakes and rabbits and—that's why I moved out here. Why, Biff can fell any one of these trees in no time! Boys! Go right over to where they're building the apartment house and get some sand. We're gonna rebuild the entire front stoop right now! Watch this, Ben!
BIFF: Yes, sir! On the double, Hap!
HAPPY: [*as he and* BIFF *run off*] I lost weight, Pop, you notice?
                    [CHARLEY *enters in knickers, even before the boys are gone.*]
CHARLEY: Listen, if they steal any more from that building the watchman'll put the cops on them!
LINDA: [*to* WILLY] Don't let Biff . . .
                    [BEN *laughs lustily.*]
WILLY: You shoulda seen the lumber they brought home last week. At least a dozen six-by-tens worth all kinds a money.
CHARLEY: Listen, if that watchman—
WILLY: I gave them hell, understand. But I got a couple of fearless characters there.
CHARLEY: Willy, the jails are full of fearless characters.
BEN: [*clapping* WILLY *on the back, with a laugh at* CHARLEY] And the stock exchange, friend!
WILLY: [*joining in* BEN's *laughter*] Where are the rest of your pants?
CHARLEY: My wife bought them.
WILLY: Now all you need is a golf club and you can go upstairs and go to sleep. [*to* BEN] Great athlete! Between him and his son Bernard they can't hammer a nail!

BERNARD: [*rushing in*] The watchman's chasing Biff!

WILLY: [*angrily*] Shut up! He's not stealing anything!

LINDA: [*alarmed, hurrying off left*] Where is he? Biff, dear! [*She exits.*]

WILLY: [*moving toward the left, away from* BEN] There's nothing wrong. What's the matter with you?

BEN: Nervy boy. Good!

WILLY: [*laughing*] Oh, nerves of iron, that Biff!

CHARLEY: Don't know what it is. My New England man comes back and he's bleedin', they murdered him up there.

WILLY: It's contacts, Charley, I got important contacts!

CHARLEY: [*sarcastically*] Glad to hear it, Willy. Come in later, we'll shoot a little casino. I'll take some of your Portland money. [*He laughs at* WILLY *and exits.*]

WILLY: [*turning to* BEN] Business is bad, it's murderous. But not for me, of course.

BEN: I'll stop by on my way back to Africa.

WILLY: [*longingly*] Can't you stay a few days? You're just what I need, Ben, because I—I have a fine position here, but I—well, Dad left when I was such a baby and I never had a chance to talk to him and I still feel—kind of temporary about myself.

BEN: I'll be late for my train.

[*They are at opposite ends of the stage.*]

WILLY: Ben, my boys—can't we talk? They'd go into the jaws of hell for me, see, but I—

BEN: William, you're being first-rate with your boys. Outstanding, manly chaps!

WILLY: [*hanging on to his words*] Oh, Ben, that's good to hear! Because sometimes I'm afraid that I'm not teaching them the right kind of— Ben, how should I teach them?

BEN: [*giving great weight to each word, and with a certain vicious audacity*] William, when I walked into the jungle, I was seventeen. When I walked out I was twenty-one. And, by God, I was rich! [*He goes off into darkness around the right corner of the house.*]

WILLY: . . . was rich! That's just the spirit I want to imbue them with! To walk into a jungle! I was right! I was right! I was right!

[BEN *is gone, but* WILLY *is still speaking to him as* LINDA, *in nightgown and robe, enters the kitchen, glances around for* WILLY, *then goes to the door of the house, looks out and sees him. Comes down to his left. He looks at her.*]

LINDA: Willy, dear? Willy?

WILLY: I was right!

LINDA: Did you have some cheese? [*He can't answer.*] It's very late, darling. Come to bed, heh?

WILLY: [*looking straight up*] Gotta break your neck to see a star in this yard.

LINDA: You coming in?

WILLY: Whatever happened to that diamond watch fob? Remember? When Ben came from Africa that time? Didn't he give me a watch fob with a diamond in it?

LINDA: You pawned it, dear. Twelve, thirteen years ago. For Biff's radio correspondence course.

WILLY: Gee, that was a beautiful thing. I'll take a walk.

LINDA: But you're in your slippers.

WILLY: [*starting to go around the house at the left*] I was right! I was! [*half to* LINDA, *as he goes, shaking his head*] What a man! There was a man worth talking to. I was right!

LINDA: [*calling after* WILLY] But in your slippers, Willy!

> [WILLY *is almost gone when* BIFF, *in his pajamas, comes down the stairs and enters the kitchen.*]

BIFF: What is he doing out there?

LINDA: Sh!

BIFF: God Almighty, Mom, how long has he been doing this?

LINDA: Don't, he'll hear you.

BIFF: What the hell is the matter with him?

LINDA: It'll pass by morning.

BIFF: Shouldn't we do anything?

LINDA: Oh, my dear, you should do a lot of things, but there's nothing to do, so go to sleep.

> [HAPPY *comes down the stairs and sits on the steps.*]

HAPPY: I never heard him so loud, Mom.

LINDA: Well, come around more often; you'll hear him. [*She sits down at the table and mends the lining of* WILLY's *jacket.*]

BIFF: Why didn't you ever write me about this, Mom?

LINDA: How would I write to you? For over three months you had no address.

BIFF: I was on the move. But you know I thought of you all the time. You know that, don't you, pal?

LINDA: I know, dear, I know. But he likes to have a letter. Just to know that there's still a possibility for better things.

BIFF: He's not like this all the time, is he?

LINDA: It's when you come home he's always the worst.

BIFF: When I come home?

LINDA: When you write you're coming, he's all smiles, and talks about the future, and—he's just wonderful. And then the closer you seem to come, the more shaky he gets, and then, by the time you get here, he's arguing, and he seems angry at you. I think it's just that maybe he can't bring himself to—to open up to you. Why are you so hateful to each other? Why is that?

BIFF: [*evasively*] I'm not hateful, Mom.

LINDA: But you no sooner come in the door than you're fighting!

BIFF: I don't know why. I mean to change. I'm tryin', Mom, you understand?

LINDA: Are you home to stay now?

BIFF: I don't know. I want to look around see what's doin'.

LINDA: Biff, you can't look around all your life, can you?

BIFF: I just can't take hold, Mom. I can't take hold of some kind of a life.

LINDA: Biff, a man is not a bird, to come and go with the springtime.

BIFF: Your hair . . . [*He touches her hair.*] Your hair got so gray.

LINDA: Oh, it's been gray since you were in high school. I just stopped dyeing it, that's all.

BIFF: Dye it again, will ya? I don't want my pal looking old. [*He smiles.*]

LINDA: You're such a boy! You think you can go away for a year and . . . You've got to get it into your head now that one day you'll knock on this door and there'll be strange people here—

BIFF: What are you talking about? You're not even sixty, Mom.

LINDA: But what about your father?

BIFF: [*lamely*] Well, I meant him too.

HAPPY: He admires Pop.

LINDA: Biff, dear, if you don't have any feeling for him, then you can't have any feeling for me.

BIFF: Sure I can, Mom.

LINDA: No. You can't just come to see me, because I love him. [*with a threat, but only a threat, of tears*] He's the dearest man in the world to me, and I won't have anyone making him feel unwanted and low and blue. You've got to make up your mind now, darling, there's no leeway any more. Either he's your father and you pay him that respect, or else you're not to come here. I know he's not easy to get along with—nobody knows that better than me—but . . .

WILLY: [*from the left, with a laugh*] Hey, hey, Biffo!

BIFF: [*starting to go out after* WILLY] What the hell is the matter with him? [HAPPY *stops him.*]

LINDA: Don't—don't go near him!

BIFF: Stop making excuses for him! He always, always wiped the floor with you. Never had an ounce of respect for you.

HAPPY: He's always had respect for—

BIFF: What the hell do you know about it?

HAPPY: [*surlily*] Just don't call him crazy!

BIFF: He's got no character— Charley wouldn't do this. Not in his own house —spewing out that vomit from his mind.

HAPPY: Charley never had to cope with what he's got to.

BIFF: People are worse off than Willy Loman. Believe me, I've seen them!

LINDA: Then make Charley your father, Biff. You can't do that, can you? I don't say he's a great man. Willy Loman never made a lot of money. His name was never in the paper. He's not the finest character that ever lived. But he's a human being, and a terrible thing is happening to him. So attention must be paid. He's not to be allowed to fall into his grave like an old dog. Attention, attention must be finally paid to such a person. You called him crazy—

BIFF: I didn't mean—

LINDA: No, a lot of people think he's lost his—balance. But you don't have to be very smart to know what his trouble is. The man is exhausted.

HAPPY: Sure!

LINDA: A small man can be just as exhausted as a great man. He works for a company thirty-six years this March, opens up unheard-of territories to their trademark, and now in his old age they take his salary away.

HAPPY: [*indignantly*] I didn't know that, Mom.

LINDA: You never asked, my dear! Now that you get your spending money someplace else you don't trouble your mind with him.

HAPPY: But I gave you money last—

LINDA: Christmas time, fifty dollars! To fix the hot water it cost ninety-seven fifty! For five weeks he's been on straight commission, like a beginner, an unknown!

BIFF: Those ungrateful bastards!

LINDA: Are they any worse than his sons? When he brought them business, when he was young, they were glad to see him. But now his old friends, the old buyers that loved him so and always found some order to hand him in a pinch—they're all dead, retired. He used to be able to make six, seven calls a day in Boston. Now he takes his valises out of the car and puts them back and takes them out again and he's exhausted. Instead of walking he talks now. He drives seven hundred miles, and when he gets there no one knows him any more, no one welcomes him. And what goes through a man's mind, driving seven hundred miles home without having earned a cent? Why shouldn't he talk to himself? Why? When he has to go to Charley and borrow fifty dollars a week and pretend to me that it's his pay? How long can that go on? How long? You see what I'm sitting here and waiting for? And you tell me he has no character? The man who never worked a day but for your benefit? When does he get the medal for that? Is this his reward—to turn around at the age of sixty-three and find his sons, who he loved better than his life, one a philandering bum—

HAPPY: Mom!

LINDA: That's all you are, my baby! [*to* BIFF] And you! What happened to the love you had for him? You were such pals! How you used to talk to him on the phone every night! How lonely he was till he could come home to you!

BIFF: All right, Mom. I'll live here in my room, and I'll get a job. I'll keep away from him, that's all.

LINDA: No, Biff. You can't stay here and fight all the time.

BIFF: He threw me out of this house, remember that.

LINDA: Why did he do that? I never knew why.

BIFF: Because I know he's a fake and he doesn't like anybody around who knows!

LINDA: Why a fake? In what way? What do you mean?

BIFF: Just don't lay it all at my feet. It's between me and him—that's all I have to say. I'll chip in from now on. He'll settle for half my pay check. He'll be all right. I'm going to bed. [*he starts for the stairs*]

LINDA: He won't be all right.

BIFF: [*turning on the stairs, furiously*] I hate this city and I'll stay here. Now what do you want?

LINDA: He's dying, Biff.

[HAPPY *turns quickly to her, shocked.*]

BIFF: [*after a pause*] Why is he dying?

LINDA: He's been trying to kill himself.

BIFF: [*with great horror*] How?

LINDA: I live from day to day.

BIFF: What're you talking about?

LINDA: Remember I wrote you that he smashed up the car again? In February?

BIFF: Well?

LINDA: The insurance inspector came. He said that they have evidence. That all these accidents in the last year—weren't—weren't—accidents.

HAPPY: How can they tell that? That's a lie.

LINDA: It seems there's a woman . . . [*she takes a breath as*]

⎧ BIFF: [*sharply but contained*] What woman?
⎨
⎩ LINDA: [*simultaneously*] . . . and this woman . . .

LINDA: What?

BIFF: Nothing. Go ahead.

LINDA: What did you say?

BIFF: Nothing. I just said what woman?

HAPPY: What about her?

LINDA: Well, it seems she was walking down the road and saw his car. She says that he wasn't driving fast at all, and that he didn't skid. She says he came to that little bridge, and then deliberately smashed into the railing, and it was only the shallowness of the water that saved him.

BIFF: Oh, no, he probably just fell asleep again.

LINDA: I don't think he fell asleep.

BIFF: Why not?

LINDA: Last month . . . [*with great difficulty*] Oh, boys, it's so hard to say a thing like this! He's just a big stupid man to you, but I tell you there's more good in him than in many other people. [*she chokes, wipes her eyes*] I was looking for a fuse. The lights blew out, and I went down the cellar. And behind the fuse box—it happened to fall out—was a length of rubber pipe—just short.

HAPPY: No kidding?

LINDA: There's a little attachment on the end of it. I knew right away. And sure enough, on the bottom of the water heater there's a new little nipple on the gas pipe.

HAPPY: [*angrily*] That—jerk.

BIFF: Did you have it taken off?

LINDA: I'm—I'm ashamed to. How can I mention it to him? Every day I go down and take away that little rubber pipe. But, when he comes home, I put it back where it was. How can I insult him that way? I don't know what to do. I live from day to day, boys. I tell you, I know every thought in his mind. It sounds so old-fashioned and silly, but I tell you he put his whole life into you and you've turned your backs on him. [*she is bent over in the chair, weeping, her face in her hands*] Biff, I swear to God! Biff, his life is in your hands!

HAPPY: [*to* BIFF] How do you like that damned fool!

BIFF: [*kissing her*] All right, pal, all right. It's all settled now. I've been remiss. I know that, Mom. But now I'll stay, and I swear to you, I'll apply myself. [*kneeling in front of her, in a fever of self-reproach*] It's just—you see, Mom, I don't fit in business. Not that I won't try. I'll try, and I'll make good.

HAPPY: Sure you will. The trouble with you in business was you never tried to please people.

BIFF: I know, I—

HAPPY: Like when you worked for Harrison's. Bob Harrison said you were tops, and then you go and do some damn fool thing like whistling whole songs in the elevator like a comedian.

BIFF: [*against* HAPPY] So what? I like to whistle sometimes.

HAPPY: You don't raise a guy to a responsible job who whistles in the elevator!

LINDA: Well, don't argue about it now.

HAPPY: Like when you'd go off and swim in the middle of the day instead of taking the line around.

BIFF: [*his resentment rising*] Well, don't you run off? You take off sometimes, don't you? On a nice summer day?

HAPPY: Yeah, but I cover myself!

LINDA: Boys!

HAPPY: If I'm going to take a fade the boss can call any number where I'm supposed to be and they'll swear to him that I just left. I'll tell you something that I hate to say, Biff, but in the business world some of them think you're crazy.

BIFF [*angered*] Screw the business world!

HAPPY: All right, screw it! Great, but cover yourself!

LINDA: Hap, Hap!

BIFF: I don't care what they think! They've laughed at Dad for years, and you know why? Because we don't belong in this nuthouse of a city! We should be mixing cement on some open plain, or—or carpenters. A carpenter is allowed to whistle!

　　　　[WILLY *walks in from the entrance of the house, at left.*]

WILLY: Even your grandfather was better than a carpenter. [*Pause. They watch him.*] You never grew up. Bernard does not whistle in the elevator, I assure you.

BIFF: [*as though to laugh* WILLY *out of it*] Yeah, but you do, Pop.

WILLY: I never in my life whistled in an elevator! And who in the business world thinks I'm crazy?

BIFF: I didn't mean it like that, Pop. Now don't make a whole thing out of it, will ya?

WILLY: Go back to the West! Be a carpenter, a cowboy, enjoy yourself!

LINDA: Willy, he was just saying—

WILLY: I heard what he said!

HAPPY: [*trying to quiet* WILLY] Hey, Pop, come on now . . .

WILLY: [*continuing over Happy's line*] They laugh at me, heh? Go to Filene's, go to the Hub, go to Slattery's, Boston. Call out the name Willy Loman and see what happens! Big shot!

BIFF: All right, Pop.

WILLY: Big!

BIFF: All right!

WILLY: Why do you always insult me?

BIFF: I didn't say a word. [*to* LINDA] Did I say a word?

LINDA: He didn't say anything, Willy.

WILLY: [*going to the doorway of the living-room*] All right, good night, good night.

LINDA: Willy, dear, he just decided . . .

WILLY: [*to* BIFF] If you get tired hanging around tomorrow, paint the ceiling I put up in the living-room.

BIFF: I'm leaving early tomorrow.

HAPPY: He's going to see Bill Oliver, Pop.

WILLY: [*interestedly*] Oliver? For what?

BIFF: [*with reserve, but trying, trying*] He always said he'd stake me. I'd like to go into business, so maybe I can take him up on it.

LINDA: Isn't that wonderful?

WILLY: Don't interrupt. What's wonderful about it? There's fifty men in the City of New York who'd stake him. [*to* BIFF] Sporting goods?

BIFF: I guess so. I know something about it and—

WILLY: He knows something about it! You know sporting goods better than Spalding, for God's sake! How much is he giving you?

BIFF: I don't know, I didn't even see him yet, but—

WILLY: Then what're you talkin' about?

BIFF: [*getting angry*] Well, all I said was I'm gonna see him, that's all!

WILLY: [*turning away*] Ah, you're counting your chickens again.

BIFF: [*starting left for the stairs*] Oh, Jesus, I'm going to sleep!

WILLY: [*calling after him*] Don't curse in this house!

BIFF: [*turning*] Since when did you get so clean?

HAPPY: [*trying to stop them*] Wait a . . .

WILLY: Don't use that language to me! I won't have it!

HAPPY: [*grabbing* BIFF, *shouts*] Wait a minute! I got an idea. I got a feasible idea. Come here, Biff, let's talk this over now, let's talk some sense here. When I was down in Florida last time, I thought of a great idea to sell sporting goods. It just came back to me. You and I, Biff—we have a line, the Loman Line. We train a couple of weeks, and put on a couple of exhibitions, see?

WILLY: That's an idea!

HAPPY: Wait! We form two basketball teams, see? Two waterpolo teams. We play each other. It's a million dollars' worth of publicity. Two brothers, see? The Loman Brothers. Displays in the Royal Palms—all the hotels. And banners over the ring and the basketball court: "Loman Brothers." Baby, we could sell sporting goods!

WILLY: That is a one-million-dollar idea!

LINDA: Marvelous!

BIFF: I'm in great shape as far as that's concerned.

HAPPY: And the beauty of it is, Biff, it wouldn't be like a business. We'd be out playin' ball again . . .

BIFF: [*enthused*] Yeah, that's . . .

WILLY: Million-dollar . . .

HAPPY: And you wouldn't get fed up with it, Biff. It'd be the family again. There'd be the old honor, and comradeship, and if you wanted to go off for a swim or somethin'—well, you'd do it! Without some smart cooky gettin' up ahead of you!

WILLY: Lick the world! You guys together could absolutely lick the civilized world.

BIFF: I'll see Oliver tomorrow. Hap, if we could work that out . . .

LINDA: Maybe things are beginning to—

WILLY: [*wildly enthused, to* LINDA] Stop interrupting! [*to* BIFF] But don't wear sport jacket and slacks when you see Oliver.

BIFF: No, I'll—

WILLY: A business suit, and talk as little as possible, and don't crack any jokes.

BIFF: He did like me. Always liked me.

LINDA: He loved you!

WILLY: [*to* LINDA] Will you stop! [*to* BIFF] Walk in very serious. You are not applying for a boy's job. Money is to pass. Be quiet, fine, and serious. Everybody likes a kidder, but nobody lends him money.

HAPPY: I'll try to get some myself, Biff. I'm sure I can.

WILLY: I see great things for you kids, I think your troubles are over. But remember, start big and you'll end big. Ask for fifteen. How much you gonna ask for?

BIFF: Gee, I don't know—

WILLY: And don't say "Gee." "Gee" is a boy's word. A man walking in for fifteen thousand dollars does not say "Gee!"

BIFF: Ten, I think, would be top though.

WILLY: Don't be so modest. You always started too low. Walk in with a big laugh. Don't look worried. Start off with a couple of your good stories to lighten things up. It's not what you say, it's how you say it—because personality always wins the day.

LINDA: Oliver always thought the highest of him—

WILLY: Will you let me talk?

BIFF: Don't yell at her, Pop, will ya?

WILLY: [*angrily*] I was talking, wasn't I?

BIFF: I don't like you yelling at her all the time, and I'm tellin' you, that's all.

WILLY: What're you, takin' over this house?

LINDA: Willy—

WILLY: [*turning on her*] Don't take his side all the time, goddammit!

BIFF: [*furiously*] Stop yelling at her!

WILLY: [*suddenly pulling on his cheek, beaten down, guilt ridden*] Give my best to Bill Oliver—he may remember me.

[*He exits through the living-room doorway.*]

LINDA: [*her voice subdued*] What'd you have to start that for? [BIFF *turns away.*] You see how sweet he was as soon as you talked hopefully? [*She goes over to* BIFF] Come up and say good night to him. Don't let him go to bed that way.

HAPPY: Come on, Biff, let's buck him up.

LINDA: Please, dear. Just say good night. It takes so little to make him happy. Come. [*She goes through the living-room doorway, calling upstairs from within the living-room:*] Your pajamas are hanging in the bathroom, Willy!

HAPPY: [*looking toward where* LINDA *went out*] What a woman! They broke the mold when they made her. You know that, Biff?

BIFF: He's off salary. My God, working on commission!

HAPPY: Well, let's face it: he's no hot-shot selling man. Except that sometimes, you have to admit, he's a sweet personality.

BIFF: [*deciding*] Lend me ten bucks, will ya? I want to buy some new ties.

HAPPY: I'll take you to a place I know. Beautiful stuff. Wear one of my striped shirts tomorrow.

BIFF: She got gray. Mom got awful old. Gee, I'm gonna go in to Oliver tomorrow and knock him for a—

HAPPY: Come on up. Tell that to Dad. Let's give him a whirl. Come on.

BIFF: [*steamed up*] You know, with ten thousand bucks, boy!

HAPPY: [*as they go into the living-room*] That's the talk, Biff, that's the first time I've heard the old confidence out of you! [*from within the living-room, fading off*] You're gonna live with me, kid, and any babe you want just say the word . . . [*The last lines are hardly heard. They are mounting the stairs to their parents' bedroom.*]

LINDA: [*entering her bedroom and addressing* WILLY, *who is in the bathroom. She is straightening the bed for him*] Can you do anything about the shower? It drips.

WILLY: [*from the bathroom*] All of a sudden everything falls to pieces! Goddam plumbing, oughta be sued, those people. I hardly finished putting it in and the thing . . . [*his words rumble off.*]

LINDA: I'm just wondering if Oliver will remember him. You think he might?

WILLY: [*coming out of the bathroom in his pajamas*] Remember him? What's the matter with you, you crazy? If he'd've stayed with Oliver he'd be on top by now! Wait'll Oliver gets a look at him. You don't know the average caliber any more. The average young man today—[*he is getting into bed*]—is got a caliber of zero. Greatest thing in the world for him was to bum around.

[BIFF *and* HAPPY *enter the bedroom. Slight pause.*]

WILLY: [*stops short, looking at* BIFF] Glad to hear it, boy.

HAPPY: He wanted to say good night to you, sport.

WILLY: [*to* BIFF] Yeah. Knock him dead, boy. What'd you want to tell me?

BIFF: Just take it easy, Pop. Good night. [*He turns to go.*]

WILLY: [*unable to resist*] And if anything falls off the desk while you're talking to him—like a package or something—don't you pick it up. They have office boys for that.

LINDA: I'll make a big breakfast—

WILLY: Will you let me finish? [*to* BIFF] Tell him you were in the business in the West. Not farm work.

BIFF: All right, Dad.

LINDA: I think everything—

WILLY: [*going right through her speech*] And don't undersell yourself. No less than fifteen thousand dollars.

BIFF: [*unable to bear him*] Okay. Good night, Mom. [*He starts moving.*]

WILLY: Because you got a greatness in you, Biff, remember that. You got all kinds a greatness . . . [*He lies back, exhausted.*]
[BIFF *walks out.*]

LINDA: [*calling after* BIFF] Sleep well, darling!

HAPPY: I'm gonna get married, Mom. I wanted to tell you.

LINDA: Go to sleep, dear.

HAPPY: [*going*] I just wanted to tell you.

WILLY: Keep up the good work. [HAPPY *exits.*] God . . . remember that Ebbets Field game? The championship of the city?

LINDA: Just rest. Should I sing to you?

WILLY: Yeah. Sing to me. [LINDA *hums a soft lullaby.*] When that team came out—he was the tallest, remember?

LINDA: Oh, yes. And in gold.
[BIFF *enters the darkened kitchen, takes a cigarette, and leaves the house. He comes downstage into a golden pool of light. He smokes, staring at the night.*]

WILLY: Like a young god. Hercules—something like that. And the sun, the sun all around him. Remember how he waved to me? Right up from the field, with the representatives of three colleges standing by? And the buyers I brought, and the cheers when he came out—Loman, Loman, Loman! God Almighty, he'll be great yet. A star like that, magnificent, can never really fade away!
[*The light on* WILLY *is fading. The gas heater begins to glow through the kitchen wall, near the stairs, a blue flame beneath red coils.*]

LINDA: [*timidly*] Willy dear, what has he got against you?

WILLY: I'm so tired. Don't talk any more.
[BIFF *slowly returns to the kitchen. He stops, stares toward the heater.*]

LINDA: Will you ask Howard to let you work in New York?

WILLY: First thing in the morning. Everything'll be all right.
[BIFF *reaches behind the heater and draws out a length of rubber tubing. He is horrified and turns his head toward Willy's room, still dimly lit, from which the strains of* LINDA'S *desperate but monotonous humming rise.*]

WILLY: [*staring through the window into the moonlight*] Gee, look at the moon moving between the buildings!
[BIFF *wraps the tubing around his hand and quickly goes up the stairs.*]

ACT II

[*Music is heard, gay and bright. The curtain rises as the music fades away.* WILLY, *in shirt sleeves, is sitting at the kitchen table, sipping coffee, his hat in his lap.* LINDA *is filling his cup when she can.*]

WILLY: Wonderful coffee. Meal in itself.

LINDA: Can I make you some eggs?

WILLY: No. Take a breath.

LINDA: You look so rested, dear.

WILLY: I slept like a dead one. First time in months. Imagine, sleeping till ten on a Tuesday morning. Boys left nice and early, heh?

LINDA: They were out of here by eight o'clock.

WILLY: Good work!

LINDA: It was so thrilling to see them leaving together. I can't get over the shaving lotion in this house!

WILLY: [*smiling*] Mmm—

LINDA: Biff was very changed this morning. His whole attitude seemed to be hopeful. He couldn't wait to get downtown to see Oliver.

WILLY: He's heading for a change. There's no question, there simply are certain men that take longer to get—solidified. How did he dress?

LINDA: His blue suit. He's so handsome in that suit. He could be a—anything in that suit!

[WILLY *gets up from the table.* LINDA *holds his jacket for him.*]

WILLY: There's no question, no question at all. Gee, on the way home tonight I'd like to buy some seeds.

LINDA: [*laughing*] That'd be wonderful. But not enough sun gets back there. Nothing'll grow any more.

WILLY: You wait, kid, before it's all over we're gonna get a little place out in the country, and I'll raise some vegetables, a couple of chickens . . .

LINDA: You'll do it yet, dear.

[WILLY *walks out of his jacket.* LINDA *follows him.*]

WILLY: And they'll get married, and come for a weekend. I'd built a little guest house. 'Cause I got so many fine tools, all I'd need would be a little lumber and some peace of mind.

LINDA: [*joyfully*] I sewed the lining . . .

WILLY: I could build two guest houses, so they'd both come. Did he decide how much he's going to ask Oliver for?

LINDA: [*getting him into the jacket*] He didn't mention it, but I imagine ten or fifteen thousand. You going to talk to Howard today?

WILLY: Yeah. I'll put it to him straight and simple. He'll just have to take me off the road.

LINDA: And Willy, don't forget to ask for a little advance, because we've got the insurance premium. It's the grace period now.

WILLY: That's a hundred . . . ?

LINDA: A hundred and eight, sixty-eight. Because we're a little short again.

WILLY: Why are we short?

LINDA: Well, you had the motor job on the car . . .

WILLY: That goddam Studebaker!

LINDA: And you got one more payment on the refrigerator . . .

WILLY: But it just broke again!

LINDA: Well, it's old, dear.

WILLY: I told you we should've bought a well-advertised machine. Charley bought a General Electric and it's twenty years old and it's still good, that son-of-a-bitch.

LINDA: But, Willy—

WILLY: Whoever heard of a Hastings refrigerator? Once in my life I would like to own something outright before it's broken! I'm always in a race with the junkyard! I just finished paying for the car and it's on its last legs. The refrigerator consumes belts like a goddam maniac. They time those things. They time them so when you finally paid for them, they're used up.

LINDA: [*buttoning up his jacket as he unbuttons it*] All told, about two hundred dollars would carry us, dear. But that includes the last payment on the mortgage. After this payment, Willy, the house belongs to us.

WILLY: It's twenty-five years!

LINDA: Biff was nine years old when we bought it.

WILLY: Well, that's a great thing. To weather a twenty-five year mortgage is—

LINDA: It's an accomplishment.

WILLY: All the cement, the lumber, the reconstruction I put in this house! There ain't a crack to be found in it any more.

LINDA: Well, it served its purpose.

WILLY: What purpose? Some stranger'll come along, move in, and that's that. If only Biff would take this house, and raise a family . . . [*he starts to go*] Good-by, I'm late.

LINDA: [*suddenly remembering*] Oh, I forgot! You're supposed to meet them for dinner.

WILLY: Me?

LINDA: At Frank's Chop House on Forty-eighth near Sixth Avenue.

WILLY: Is that so! How about you?

LINDA: No, just the three of you. They're gonna blow you to a big meal!

WILLY: Don't say! Who thought of that?

LINDA: Biff came to me this morning, Willy, and he said, "Tell Dad, we want to blow him to a big meal." Be there six o'clock. You and your two boys are going to have dinner.

WILLY: Gee whiz! That's really somethin'. I'm gonna knock Howard for a loop, kid. I'll get an advance, and I'll come home with a New York job. Goddammit, now I'm gonna do it!

LINDA: Oh, that's the spirit, Willy!

WILLY: I will never get behind a wheel the rest of my life!

LINDA: It's changing, Willy, I can feel it changing!

WILLY: Beyond a question. G'by, I'm late. [*He starts to go again.*]

LINDA: [*calling after him as she runs to the kitchen table for a handkerchief*] You got your glasses?

WILLY: [*feels for them, then comes back in*] Yeah, yeah, got my glasses.

LINDA: [*giving him the handkerchief*] And a handkerchief.

WILLY: Yeah, handkerchief.

LINDA: And your saccharine?

WILLY: Yeah, my saccharine.

LINDA: Be careful on the subway stairs.

[*She kisses him, and a silk stocking is seen hanging from her hand.* WILLY *notices it.*]

WILLY: Will you stop mending stockings? At least while I'm in the house. It gets me nervous. I can't tell you. Please.

[LINDA *hides the stocking in her hand as she follows* WILLY *across the forestage in front of the house.*]

LINDA: Remember, Frank's Chop House.

WILLY: [*passing the apron*] Maybe beets would grow out there.

LINDA: [*laughing*] But you tried so many times.

WILLY: Yeah. Well, don't work hard today. [*He disappears around the right corner of the house.*]

LINDA: Be careful!

[*As* WILLY *vanishes,* LINDA *waves to him. Suddenly the phone rings. She runs across the stage and into the kitchen and lifts it.*]

LINDA: Hello? Oh, Biff! I'm so glad you called, I just . . . Yes, sure, I just told him. Yes, he'll be there for dinner at six o'clock, I didn't forget. Listen, I was just dying to tell you. You know that little rubber pipe I told you about? That he connected to the gas heater? I finally decided to go down the cellar this morning and take it away and destroy it. But it's gone! Imagine? He took it away himself, it isn't there! [*She listens.*] When? Oh, then you took it. Oh—nothing, it's just that I'd hoped he'd taken it away himself. Oh, I'm not worried, darling, because this morning he left in such high spirits, it was like the old days! I'm not afraid any more. Did Mr. Oliver see you? . . . Well, you wait there then. And make a nice impression on him, darling. Just don't perspire too much before you see him. And have ˙ nice time with Dad. He may have big news too! . . . That's right, a New York job. And be sweet to him tonight, dear. Be loving to him. Because he's only a little boat looking for a harbor. [*she is trembling with sorrow and joy*] Oh, that's wonderful, Biff, you'll save his life. Thanks, darling. Just put your arm around him when he comes into the restaurant. Give him a smile. That's the boy . . . Good-by, dear. . . . You got your comb? . . . That's fine Good-by, Biff dear.

[*In the middle of her speech,* HOWARD WAGNER, *thirty-six, wheels on a small typewriter table on which is a wire-recording machine and proceeds to plug it in. This is on the left forestage. Light slowly fades on* LINDA *as it rises on* HOWARD. HOWARD *is intent on threading the machine and only glances over his shoulder as* WILLY *appears.*]

WILLY: Pst! Pst!

HOWARD: Hello, Willy, come in.

WILLY: Like to have a little talk with you, Howard.

HOWARD: Sorry to keep you waiting. I'll be with you in a minute.

WILLY: What's that, Howard?

HOWARD: Didn't you ever see one of these? Wire recorder.

WILLY: Oh. Can we talk a minute?

HOWARD: Records things. Just got delivery yesterday. Been driving me crazy, the most terrific machine I ever saw in my life. I was up all night with it.

WILLY: What do you do with it?

HOWARD: I bought it for dictation, but you can do anything with it. Listen to this. I had it home last night. Listen to what I picked up. The first one is my daughter. Get this. [*he flicks the switch and "Roll out the Barrel" is heard being whistled*] Listen to that kid whistle.

WILLY: That is lifelike, isn't it?

HOWARD: Seven years old. Get that tone.

WILLY: Ts, ts. Like to ask a little favor if you . . .

> [*The whistling breaks off, and the voice of* HOWARD'S DAUGHTER *is heard.*]

HIS DAUGHTER: "Now you, Daddy."

HOWARD: She's crazy for me! [*Again the same song is whistled.*] That's me! Ha! [*He winks.*]

WILLY: You're very good!

> [*The whistling breaks off again. The machine runs silent for a moment.*]

HOWARD: Sh! Get this now, this is my son.

HIS SON: "The capital of Alabama is Montgomery; the capital of Arizona is Phoenix; the capital of Arkansas is Little Rock; the capital of California is Sacramento . . ." [*and on, and on*]

HOWARD: [*holding up five fingers*] Five years old, Willy!

WILLY: He'll make an announcer some day!

HIS SON: [*continuing*] "The capital . . ."

HOWARD: Get that—alphabetical order! [*The machine breaks off suddenly.*] Wait a minute. The maid kicked the plug out.

WILLY: It certainly is a—

HOWARD: Sh, for God's sake!

HIS SON: "It's nine o'clock, Bulova watch time. So I have to go to sleep."

WILLY: That really is—

HOWARD: Wait a minute! The next is my wife.

> [*They wait.*]

HOWARD'S VOICE: "Go on, say something." [*pause*] "Well, you gonna talk?"

HIS WIFE: "I can't think of anything."

HOWARD'S VOICE: "Well, talk—it's turning."

HIS WIFE: [*shyly, beaten*] "Hello." [*silence*] "Oh, Howard, I can't talk into this . . ."

HOWARD: [*snapping the machine off*] That was my wife.

WILLY: That is a wonderful machine. Can we—

HOWARD: I tell you, Willy, I'm gonna take my camera, and my bandsaw, and all my hobbies, and out they go. This is the most fascinating relaxation I ever found.

WILLY: I think I'll get one myself.

HOWARD: Sure, they're only a hundred and a half. You can't do without it. Supposing you wanna hear Jack Benny, see? But you can't be at home at that hour. So you tell the maid to turn the radio on when Jack Benny comes on, and this automatically goes on with the radio . . .

WILLY: And when you come home you . . .

HOWARD: You can come home twelve o'clock, one o'clock, any time you like, and you get yourself a Coke and sit yourself down, throw the switch, and there's Jack Benny's program in the middle of the night!

WILLY: I'm definitely going to get one. Because lots of time I'm on the road, and I think to myself, what I must be missing on the radio!

HOWARD: Don't you have a radio in the car?

WILLY: Yeah, but who ever thinks of turning it on?

HOWARD: Say, aren't you supposed to be in Boston?

WILLY: That's what I want to talk to you about, Howard. You got a minute? [*He draws a chair in from the wing.*]

HOWARD: What happened? What're you doing here?

WILLY: Well . . .

HOWARD: You didn't crack up again, did you?

WILLY: Oh, no. No . . .

HOWARD: Geez, you had me worried there for a minute. What's the trouble?

WILLY: Well, tell you the truth, Howard. I've come to the conclusion that I'd rather not travel any more.

HOWARD: Not travel! Well, what'll you do?

WILLY: Remember, Christmas time, when you had the party here? You said you'd try to think of some spot for me here in town.

HOWARD: With us?

WILLY: Well, sure.

HOWARD: Oh, yeah, yeah. I remember. Well, I couldn't think of anything for you, Willy.

WILLY: I tell ya, Howard. The kids are all grown up, y'know. I don't need much any more. If I could take home—well, sixty-five dollars a week, I could swing it.

HOWARD: Yeah, but Willy, see I—

WILLY: I tell ya why, Howard. Speaking frankly and between the two of us, y'know—I'm just a little tired.

HOWARD: Oh, I could understand that, Willy. But you're a road man, Willy, and we do a road business. We've only got a half-dozen salesmen on the floor here.

WILLY: God knows, Howard, I never asked a favor of any man. But I was with the firm when your father used to carry you up here in his arms.

HOWARD: I know that, Willy, but—

WILLY: Your father came to me the day you were born and asked me what I thought of the name of Howard, may he rest in peace.

HOWARD: I appreciate that, Willy, but there just is no spot here for you. If I had a spot I'd slam you right in, but I just don't have a single solitary spot.

[*He looks for his lighter.* WILLY *has picked it up and gives it to him. Pause.*]

WILLY: [*with increasing anger*] Howard, all I need to set my table is fifty dollars a week.

HOWARD: But where am I going to put you, kid?

WILLY: Look, it isn't a question of whether I can sell merchandise, is it?

HOWARD: No, but it's a business, kid, and everybody's gotta pull his own weight.

WILLY: [*desperately*] Just let me tell you a story, Howard—

HOWARD: 'Cause you gotta admit, business is business.

WILLY: [*angrily*] Business is definitely business, but just listen for a minute. You don't understand this. When I was a boy—eighteen, nineteen—I was already on the road. And there was a question in my mind as to whether selling had a future for me. Because in those days I had a yearning to go to Alaska. See, there were three gold strikes in one month in Alaska, and I felt like going out. Just for the ride, you might say.

HOWARD: [*barely interested*] Don't say.

WILLY: Oh, yeah, my father lived many years in Alaska. He was an adventurous man. We've got quite a little streak of self-reliance in our family. I thought I'd go out with my older brother and try to locate him, and maybe settle in the North with the old man. And I was almost decided to go, when I met a salesman in the Parker House. His name was Dave Singleman. And he was eighty-four years old, and he'd drummed merchandise in thirty-one states. And old Dave, he'd go up to his room, y'understand, put on his green velvet slippers—I'll never forget—and pick up his phone and call the buyers, and without ever leaving his room, at the age of eighty-four, he made his living. And when I saw that, I realized that selling was the greatest career a man could want. 'Cause what could be more satisfying than to be able to go, at the age of eighty-four, into twenty or thirty different cities, and pick up a phone, and be remembered and loved and helped by so many different people? Do you know? when he died—and by the way he died the death of a salesman, in his green velvet slippers in the smoker of the New York, New Haven and Hartford, going into Boston—when he died, hundreds of salesmen and buyers were at his funeral. Things were sad on a lotta trains for months after that. [*He stands up.* HOWARD *has not looked at him.*] In those days there was personality in it, Howard. There was respect, and comradeship, and gratitude in it. Today, it's all cut and dried, and there's no chance for bringing friendship to bear—or personality. You see what I mean? They don't know me any more.

HOWARD: [*moving away, to the right*] That's just the thing, Willy.

WILLY: If I had forty dollars a week—that's all I'd need. Forty dollars, Howard.

HOWARD: Kid, I can't take blood from a stone, I—

WILLY: [*desperation is on him now*] Howard, the year Al Smith was nominated, your father came to me and—

HOWARD: [*starting to go off*] I've got to see some people, kid.

WILLY: [*stopping him*] I'm talking about your father! There were promises made across this desk! You mustn't tell me you've got people to see—I put thirty-four years into this firm, Howard, and now I can't pay my insurance! You can't eat the orange and throw the peel away—a man is not a piece of fruit! [*after a pause*] Now pay attention. Your father—in 1928 I had a big year. I averaged a hundred and seventy dollars a week in commissions.

HOWARD: [*impatiently*] Now, Willy, you never averaged—

WILLY: [*banging his hand on the desk*] I averaged a hundred and seventy dollars a week in the year of 1928! And your father came to me—or rather, I was in the office here—it was right over this desk—and he put his hand on my shoulder—

HOWARD: [*getting up*] You'll have to excuse me, Willy, I gotta see some people. Pull yourself together. [*going out*] I'll be back in a little while.

    [*On* HOWARD's *exit, the light on his chair grows very bright and strange.*]

WILLY: Pull myself together! What the hell did I say to him? My God, I was yelling at him! How could I! [WILLY *breaks off, staring at the light, which occupies the chair, animating it.*] Frank, Frank, don't you remember what you told me that time? How you put your hand on my shoulder, and Frank . . . [*He leans on the desk and as he speaks the dead man's name he accidentally switches on the recorder, and instantly*]

HOWARD'S SON: ". . . of New York is Albany. The capital of Ohio is Cincinnati, the capital of Rhode Island is . . ." [*The recitation continues.*]

WILLY: [*leaping way with fright, shouting*] Ha! Howard! Howard! Howard!

HOWARD: [*rushing in*] What happened?

WILLY: [*pointing at the machine, which continues nasally, childishly, with the capital cities*] Shut it off! Shut it off!

HOWARD: [*pulling the plug out*] Look, Willy . . .

WILLY: [*pressing his hands to his eyes*] I gotta get myself some coffee. I'll get some coffee . . .

    [WILLY *starts to walk out.* HOWARD *stops him.*]

HOWARD: [*rolling up the cord*] Willy, look . . .

WILLY: I'll go to Boston.

HOWARD: Willy, you can't go to Boston for us.

WILLY: Why can't I go?

HOWARD: I don't want you to represent us. I've been meaning to tell you for a long time now.

WILLY: Howard, are you firing me?

HOWARD: I think you need a good long rest, Willy.

WILLY: Howard—

HOWARD: And when you feel better, come back, and we'll see if we can work something out.

WILLY: But I gotta earn money, Howard. I'm in no position to—

HOWARD: Where are your sons? Why don't your sons give you a hand?

WILLY: They're working on a very big deal.

HOWARD: This is no time for false pride, Willy. You go to your sons and you tell them that you're tired. You've got two great boys, haven't you?

WILLY: Oh, no question, no question, but in the meantime . . .

HOWARD: Then that's that, heh?

WILLY: All right, I'll go to Boston tomorrow.

HOWARD: No, no.

WILLY: I can't throw myself on my sons. I'm not a cripple!

HOWARD: Look, kid, I'm busy this morning.

WILLY: [*grasping* HOWARD's *arm*] Howard, you've got to let me go to Boston!

HOWARD: [*hard, keeping himself under control*] I've got a line of people to see this morning. Sit down, take five minutes, and pull yourself together, and then go home, will ya? I need the office, Willy. [*He starts to go, turns, remembering the recorder, starts to push off the table holding the recorder.*] Oh, yeah. Whenever you can this week, stop by and drop off the samples. You'll feel better, Willy, and then come back and we'll talk. Pull yourself together, kid, there's people outside.

> [HOWARD *exits, pushing the table off left.* WILLY *stares into space, exhausted. Now the music is heard—*BEN's *music—first distantly, then closer. As* WILLY *speaks,* BEN *enters from the right. He carries valise and umbrella.*]

WILLY: Oh, Ben, how did you do it? What is the answer? Did you wind up the Alaska deal already?

BEN: Doesn't take much time if you know what you're doing. Just a short business trip. Boarding ship in an hour. Wanted to say good-by.

WILLY: Ben, I've got to talk to you.

BEN: [*glancing at his watch*] Haven't much time, William.

WILLY: [*crossing the apron to* BEN] Ben, nothing's working out. I don't know what to do.

BEN: Now, look here, William. I've bought timberland in Alaska and I need a man to look after things for me.

WILLY: God, timberland! Me and my boys in those grand outdoors!

BEN: You've a new continent at your doorstep, William. Get out of these cities, they're full of talk and time payments and courts of law. Screw on your fists and you can fight for a fortune up there.

WILLY: Yes, yes! Linda, Linda!

> [LINDA *enters as of old, with the wash.*]

LINDA: Oh, you're back?

BEN: I haven't much time.

WILLY: No, wait! Linda, he's got a proposition for me in Alaska.

LINDA: But you've got—[*to* BEN] He's got a beautiful job here.

WILLY: But in Alaska, kid, I could—

LINDA: You're doing well enough, Willy!

BEN: [*to* LINDA] Enough for what, my dear?

LINDA: [*frightened of* BEN *and angry at him*] Don't say those things to him! Enough to be happy right here, right now. [*to* WILLY, *while* BEN *laughs*] Why must everybody conquer the world? You're well liked, and the boys love you, and someday—[*to* BEN]—why old man Wagner told him just the other day that if he keeps it up he'll be a member of the firm, didn't he, Willy?

WILLY: Sure, sure. I am building something with this firm, Ben, and if a man is building something he must be on the right track, mustn't he?

BEN: What are you building? Lay your hand on it. Where is it?

WILLY: [*hesitantly*] That's true, Linda, there's nothing.

LINDA: Why? [*to* BEN] There's a man eighty-four years old—

WILLY: That's right, Ben, that's right. When I look at that man I say, what is there to worry about?

BEN: Bah!

WILLY: It's true, Ben. All he has to do is go into any city, pick up the phone, and he's making his living and you know why?

BEN: [*picking up his valise*] I've got to go.

WILLY: [*holding* BEN *back*] Look at this boy!

　　　[BIFF, *in his high school sweater, enters carrying suitcase.* HAPPY *carries* BIFF's *shoulder guards, gold helmet, and football pants.*]

WILLY: Without a penny to his name, three great universities are begging for him, and from there the sky's the limit, because it's not what you do, Ben. It's who you know and the smile on your face! It's contacts, Ben, contacts! The whole wealth of Alaska passes over the lunch table at the Commodore Hotel, and that's the wonder, the wonder of this country, that a man can end with diamonds here on the basis of being liked! [*he turns to* BIFF] And that's why when you get out on that field today it's important. Because thousands of people will be rooting for you and loving you. [*to* BEN, *who has again begun to leave*] And Ben! when he walks into a business office his name will sound out like a bell and all the doors will open to him! I've seen it, Ben, I've seen it a thousand times! You can't feel it with your hand like timber, but it's there!

BEN: Good-by, William.

WILLY: Ben, am I right? Don't you think I'm right? I value your advice.

BEN: There's a new continent at your doorstep, William. You could walk out rich. Rich! [*He is gone.*]

WILLY: We'll do it here, Ben! You hear me? We're gonna do it here!

　　　[YOUNG BERNARD *rushes. The gay music of the Boys is heard.*]

BERNARD: Oh, gee, I was afraid you left already!

WILLY: Why? What time is it?

BERNARD: It's half-past one!

WILLY: Well, come on, everybody! Ebbets Field next stop! Where's the pennants? [*He rushes through the wall-line of the kitchen and out into the living-room.*]

LINDA: [*to* BIFF] Did you pack fresh underwear?

BIFF: [*who has been limbering up*] I want to go!

BERNARD: Biff, I'm carrying your helmet, ain't I?

HAPPY: No, I'm carrying the helmet.

BERNARD: Oh, Biff, you promised me.

HAPPY: I'm carrying the helmet.

BERNARD: How am I going to get in the locker room?

LINDA: Let him carry the shoulder guards. [*She puts her coat and hat on in the kitchen.*]

BERNARD: Can I, Biff? 'Cause I told everybody I'm going to be in the locker room.

HAPPY: In Ebbets Field it's the clubhouse.

BERNARD: I meant the clubhouse. Biff!

HAPPY: Biff!

BIFF: [*grandly, after a slight pause*] Let him carry the shoulder guards.

HAPPY: [*as he gives* BERNARD *the shoulder guards*] Stay close to us now.

　　　[WILLY *rushes in with the pennants.*]

WILLY: [*handing them out*] Everybody wave when Biff comes out on the field. [HAPPY *and* BERNARD *run off.*] You set now, boy?
    [*The music has died away.*]

BIFF: Ready to go, Pop. Every muscle is ready.

WILLY: [*at the edge of the apron*] You realize what this means?

BIFF: That's right, Pop.

WILLY: [*feeling* BIFF's *muscles*] You're comin' home this afternoon captain of the All-Scholastic Championship Team of the City of New York.

BIFF: I got it, Pop. And remember, pal, when I take off my helmet, that touchdown is for you.

WILLY: Let's go! [*He is starting out, with his arm around* BIFF, *when* CHARLEY *enters, as of old, in knickers.*] I got no room for you, Charley.

CHARLEY: Room? For what?

WILLY: In the car.

CHARLEY: You goin' for a ride? I wanted to shoot some casino.

WILLY: [*furiously*] Casino! [*incredulously*] Don't you realize what today is?

LINDA: Oh, he knows, Willy. He's just kidding you.

WILLY: That's nothing to kid about!

CHARLEY: No, Linda, what's goin' on?

LINDA: He's playing in Ebbets Field.

CHARLEY: Baseball in this weather?

WILLY: Don't talk to him. Come on, come on! [*He is pushing them out.*]

CHARLEY: Wait a minute, didn't you hear the news?

WILLY: What?

CHARLEY: Don't you listen to the radio? Ebbets Field just blew up.

WILLY: You go to hell! [CHARLEY *laughs. Pushing them out.*] Come on, come on! We're late.

CHARLEY: [*as they go*] Knock a homer, Biff, knock a homer!

WILLY: [*the last to leave, turning to* CHARLEY] I don't think that was funny, Charley. This is the greatest day of his life.

CHARLEY: Willy, when are you going to grow up?

WILLY: Yeah, heh? When this game is over, Charley, you'll be laughing out the other side of your face. They'll be calling him another Red Grange. Twenty-five thousand a year.

CHARLEY: [*kidding*] Is that so?

WILLY: Yeah, that's so.

CHARLEY: Well, then, I'm sorry, Willy. But tell me something.

WILLY: What?

CHARLEY: Who is Red Grange?

WILLY: Put up your hands. Goddam you, put up your hands!
    [CHARLEY, *chuckling, shakes his head and walks away, around the left corner of the stage.* WILLY *follows him. The music rises to a mocking frenzy.*]

WILLY: Who the hell do you think you are, better than everybody else? You don't know everything, you big, ignorant, stupid. . . . Put up your hands!
    [*Light rises, on the right side of the forestage, on a small table in the reception room of* CHARLEY's *office Traffic sounds are heard.*

BERNARD, *now mature, sits whistling to himself. A pair of tennis rackets and an overnight bag are on the floor beside him.*]

WILLY: [*offstage*] What are you walking away for? Don't walk away! If you're going to say something say it to my face! I know you laugh at me behind my back. You'll laugh out of the other side of your goddam face after this game. Touchdown! Touchdown! Eighty thousand people! Touchdown Right between the goal posts.

[BERNARD *is a quiet, earnest, but self-assured young man.* WILLY's *voice is coming from right upstage now.* BERNARD *lowers his feet off the table and listens.* JENNY, *his father's secretary, enters.*]

JENNY: [*distressed*] Say, Bernard, will you go out in the hall?

BERNARD: What is that noise? Who is it?

JENNY: Mr. Loman. He just got off the elevator.

BERNARD: [*getting up*] Who's he arguing with?

JENNY: Nobody. There's nobody with him. I can't deal with him any more, and your father gets all upset everytime he comes. I've got a lot of typing to do, and your father's waiting to sign it. Will you see him?

WILLY: [*entering*] Touchdown! Touch—[*he sees* JENNY.] Jenny, Jenny, good to see you. How're ya? Workin'? Or still honest?

JENNY: Fine. How've you been feeling?

WILLY: Not much any more, Jenny. Ha, ha! [*He is surprised to see the rackets.*]

BERNARD: Hello, Uncle Willy.

WILLY: [*almost shocked*] Bernard! Well, look who's here! [*He comes quickly, guiltily, to* BERNARD *and warmly shakes his hand.*]

BERNARD: How are you? Good to see you.

WILLY: What are you doing here?

BERNARD: Oh, just stopped off to see Pop. Get off my feet till my train leaves. I'm going to Washington in a few minutes.

WILLY: Is he in?

BERNARD: Yes, he's in his office with the accountants. Sit down.

WILLY: [*sitting down*] What're you going to do in Washington?

BERNARD: Oh, just a case I've got there, Willy.

WILLY: That so? [*indicating the rackets*] You going to play tennis there?

BERNARD: I'm staying with a friend who's got a court.

WILLY: Don't say. His own tennis court. Must be fine people, I bet.

BERNARD: They are, very nice. Dad tells me Biff's in town.

WILLY: [*with a big smile*] Yeah, Biff's in. Working on a very big deal, Bernard.

BERNARD: What's Biff doing?

WILLY: Well, he's been doing very big things in the West. But he decided to establish himself here. Very big. We're having dinner. Did I hear your wife had a boy?

BERNARD: That's right. Our second.

WILLY: Two boys! What do you know!

BERNARD: What kind of a deal has Biff got?

WILLY: Well, Bill Oliver—very big sporting-goods man—he wants Biff very badly. Called him in from the West. Long distance, carte blanche, special deliveries. Your friends have their own private tennis court?

BERNARD: You still with the old firm, Willy?

WILLY: [*after a pause*] I'm—I'm overjoyed to see how you made the grade, Bernard, overjoyed. It's an encouraging thing to see a young man really— really— Looks very good for Biff—very—[*He breaks off, then:*] Bernard— [*He is so full of emotion, he breaks off again.*]

BERNARD: What is it, Willy?

WILLY: [*small and alone*] What—what's the secret?

BERNARD: What secret?

WILLY: How—how did you? Why didn't he ever catch on?

BERNARD: I wouldn't know that, Willy.

WILLY: [*confidentially, desperately*] You were his friend, his boyhood friend. There's something I don't understand about it. His life ended after that Ebbets Field game. From the age of seventeen nothing good ever happened to him.

BERNARD: He never trained himself for anything.

WILLY: But he did, he did. After high school he took so many correspondence courses. Radio mechanics; television; God knows what, and never made the slightest mark.

BERNARD: [*taking off his glasses*] Willy, do you want to talk candidly?

WILLY: [*rising, faces* BERNARD] I regard you as a very brilliant man, Bernard. I value your advice.

BERNARD: Oh, the hell with the advice, Willy. I couldn't advise you. There's just one thing I've always wanted to ask you. When he was supposed to graduate, and the math teacher flunked him—

WILLY: Oh, that son-of-a-bitch ruined his life.

BERNARD: Yeah, but, Willy, all he had to do was go to summer school and make up that subject.

WILLY: That's right, that's right.

BERNARD: Did you tell him not to go to summer school?

WILLY: Me? I begged him to go. I ordered him to go!

BERNARD: Then why wouldn't he go?

WILLY: Why? Why! Bernard, that question has been trailing me like a ghost for the last fifteen years. He flunked the subject, and laid down and died like a hammer hit him!

BERNARD: Take it easy, kid.

WILLY: Let me talk to you—I got nobody to talk to. Bernard, Bernard, was it my fault? Y'see? It keeps going around in my mind, maybe I did something to him. I got nothing to give him.

BERNARD: Don't take it so hard.

WILLY: Why did he lay down? What is the story there? You were his friend!

BERNARD: Willy, I remember, it was June, and our grades came out. And he'd flunked math.

WILLY: That son-of-a-bitch!

BERNARD: No, it wasn't right then. Biff just got very angry, I remember, and he was ready to enroll in summer school.

WILLY: [*surprised*] He was?

BERNARD: He wasn't beaten by it at all. But then, Willy, he disappeared from the block for almost a month. And I got the idea that he'd gone up to New England to see you. Did he have a talk with you then?

[WILLY *stares in silence.*]

BERNARD: Willy?

WILLY: [*with a strong edge of resentment in his voice*] Yeah, he came to Boston. What about it?

BERNARD: Well, just that when he came back—I'll never forget this, it always mystifies me. Because I'd thought so well of Biff, even though he'd always taken advantage of me. I loved him, Willy, y'know? And he came back after that month and took his sneakers—remember the sneakers with "University of Virginia" printed on them? He was so proud of those, wore them every day. And he took them down in the cellar, and burned them up in the furnace. We had a fist fight. It lasted at least half an hour. Just the two of us, punching each other down the cellar, and crying right through it. I've often thought of how strange it was that I knew he'd given up his life. What happened in Boston, Willy?

[WILLY *looks at him as at an intruder.*]

BERNARD: I just bring it up because you asked me.

WILLY: [*angrily*] Nothing. What do you mean, "What happened?" What's that got to do with anything?

BERNARD: Well don't get sore.

WILLY: What are you trying to do, blame it on me? If a boy lays down is that my fault?

BERNARD: Now, Willy, don't get—

WILLY: Well, don't—don't talk to me that way! What does that mean, "What happened?"

[CHARLEY *enters. He is in his vest, and he carries a bottle of bourbon.*]

CHARLEY: Hey, you're going to miss that train. [*He waves the bottle.*]

BERNARD: Yeah, I'm going. [*He takes the bottle.*] Thanks, Pop. [*He picks up his rackets and bag.*] Good-by, Willy, and don't worry about it. You know, "If at first you don't succeed . . ."

WILLY: Yes, I believe in that.

BERNARD: But sometimes, Willy, it's better for a man just to walk away.

WILLY: Walk away?

BERNARD: That's right.

WILLY: But if you can't walk away?

BERNARD: [*after a slight pause*] I guess that's when it's tough. [*Extending his hand*] Good-by, Willy.

WILLY: [*shaking* BERNARD's *hand*] Good-by, boy.

CHARLEY: [*an arm on* BERNARD's *shoulder*] How do you like this kid? Gonna argue a case in front of the Supreme Court.

BERNARD: [*protesting*] Pop!

WILLY: [*genuinely shocked, pained, and happy*] No! The Supreme Court!

BERNARD: I gotta run. 'By, Dad!

CHARLEY: Knock 'em dead, Bernard!

[BERNARD *goes off.*]

WILLY: [*as* CHARLEY *takes out his wallet*] The Supreme Court! And he didn't even mention it!

CHARLEY: [*counting out money on the desk*] He don't have to—he's gonna do it.

WILLY: And you never told him what to do, did you? You never took any interest in him.

CHARLEY: My salvation is that I never took any interest in anything. There's some money—fifty dollars. I got an accountant inside.

WILLY: Charley, look . . . [*with difficulty*] I got my insurance to pay. If you can manage it—I need a hundred and ten dollars.

[CHARLEY *doesn't reply for a moment; merely stops moving.*]

WILLY: I'd draw it from my bank but Linda would know, and I . . .

CHARLEY: Sit down, Willy.

WILLY: [*moving toward the chair*] I'm keeping an account of everything, remember. I'll pay every penny back. [*He sits.*]

CHARLEY: Now listen to me, Willy.

WILLY: I want you to know I appreciate . . .

CHARLEY: [*sitting down on the table*] Willy, what're you doin'? What the hell is goin' on in your head?

WILLY: Why? I'm simply . . .

CHARLEY: I offered you a job. You can make fifty dollars a week. And I won't send you on the road.

WILLY: I've got a job.

CHARLEY: Without pay? What kind of a job is a job without pay? [*He rises.*] Now, look, kid, enough is enough. I'm no genius but I know when I'm being insulted.

WILLY: Insulted!

CHARLEY: Why don't you want to work for me?

WILLY: What's the matter with you? I've got a job.

CHARLEY: Then what're you walkin' in here every week for?

WILLY: [*getting up*] Well, if you don't want me to walk in here—

CHARLEY: I am offering you a job.

WILLY: I don't want your goddam job!

CHARLEY: When the hell are you going to grow up?

WILLY: [*furiously*] You big ignoramus, if you say that to me again I'll rap you one! I don't care how big you are! [*He's ready to fight.*]

[*Pause.*]

CHARLEY: [*kindly, going to him*] How much do you need, Willy?

WILLY: Charley, I'm strapped. I'm strapped. I don't know what to do. I was just fired.

CHARLEY: Howard fired you?

WILLY: That snotnose. Imagine that? I named him. I named him Howard.

CHARLEY: Willy, when're you gonna realize that them things don't mean anything? You named him Howard, but you can't sell that. The only thing you got in this world is what you can sell. And the funny thing is that you're a salesman, and you don't know that.

WILLY: I've tried to think otherwise, I guess. I always felt that if a man was impressive, and well liked, that nothing—

CHARLEY: Why must everybody like you? Who liked J. P. Morgan? Was he impressive? In a Turkish bath he'd look like a butcher. But with his pockets on he was very well liked. Now listen, Willy, I know you don't like me, and nobody can say I'm in love with you, but I'll give you a job because—just for the hell of it, put it that way. Now what do you say?

WILLY: I—I just can't work for you, Charley.

CHARLEY: What're you, jealous of me?

WILLY: I can't work for you, that's all, don't ask me why.

CHARLEY: [*angered, takes out more bills*] You been jealous of me all your life, you damned fool! Here, pay your insurance. [*He puts the money in* WILLY'*s hand.*]

WILLY: I'm keeping strict accounts.

CHARLEY: I've got some work to do. Take care of yourself. And pay your insurance.

WILLY: [*moving to the right*] Funny, y'know? After all the highways, and the trains, and the appointments, and the years, you end up worth more dead than alive.

CHARLEY: Willy, nobody's worth nothin' dead. [*after a slight pause*] Did you hear what I said?

[WILLY *stands still, dreaming.*]

CHARLEY: Willy!

WILLY: Apologize to Bernard for me when you see him. I didn't mean to argue with him. He's a fine boy. They're all fine boys, and they'll end up big— all of them. Someday they'll all play tennis together. Wish me luck, Charley. He saw Bill Oliver today.

CHARLEY: Good luck.

WILLY: [*on the verge of tears*] Charley, you're the only friend I got. Isn't that a remarkable thing? [*He goes out.*]

CHARLEY: Jesus!

[CHARLEY *stares after him a moment and follows. All light blacks out. Suddenly raucous music is heard, and a red glow rises behind the screen at right.* STANLEY, *a young waiter, appears, carrying a table, followed by* HAPPY, *who is carrying two chairs.*]

STANLEY: [*putting the table down*] That's all right, Mr. Loman, I can handle it myself. [*he turns and takes the chairs from* HAPPY *and places them at the table*]

HAPPY: [*glancing around*] Oh, this is better.

STANLEY: Sure, in the front there you're in the middle of all kinds of noise. Whenever you got a party, Mr. Loman, you just tell me and I'll put you back here. Y'know, there's a lotta people they don't like it private, because when they go out they like to see a lotta action around them because they're sick and tired to stay in the house by theirself. But I know you, you ain't from Hackensack. You know what I mean?

HAPPY: [*sitting down*] So how's it coming, Stanley?

STANLEY: Ah, it's a dog's life. I only wish during the war they'd a took me in the Army. I coulda been dead by now.

HAPPY: My brother's back, Stanley.

STANLEY: Oh, he come back, heh? From the Far West.

HAPPY: Yeah, big cattle man, my brother, so treat him right. And my father's coming too.

STANLEY: Oh, your father too!

HAPPY: You got a couple of nice lobsters?

STANLEY: Hundred per cent, big.

HAPPY: I want them with claws.

STANLEY: Don't worry, I don't give you no mice. [HAPPY *laughs*.] How about some wine? It'll put a head on the meal.

HAPPY: No. You remember, Stanley, that recipe I brought you from overseas? With the champagne in it?

STANLEY: Oh, yeah, sure. I still got it tacked up yet in the kitchen. But that'll have to cost a buck apiece anyways.

HAPPY: That's all right.

STANLEY: What'd you, hit a number or somethin'?

HAPPY: No, it's a little celebration. My brother is—I think he pulled off a big deal today. I think we're going into business together.

STANLEY: Great! That's the best for you. Because a family business, you know what I mean?—that's the best.

HAPPY: That's what I think.

STANLEY: 'Cause what's the difference? Somebody steals? It's in the family. Know what I mean? [*sotto voce*] Like this bartender here. The boss is goin' crazy what kinda leak he's got in the cash register. You put it in but it don't come out.

HAPPY: [*raising his head*] Sh!

STANLEY: What?

HAPPY: You notice I wasn't lookin' right or left, was I?

STANLEY: No.

HAPPY: And my eyes are closed.

STANLEY: So what's the—?

HAPPY: Strudel's comin'.

STANLEY: [*catching on, looks around*] Ah, no, there's no—

      [*He breaks off as a furred, lavishly dressed* GIRL *enters and sits at the next table. Both follow her with their eyes.*]

STANLEY: Geez, how'd ya know?

HAPPY: I got radar or something. [*staring directly at her profile*] Oooooooo . . . Stanley.

STANLEY: I think that's for you, Mr. Loman.

HAPPY: Look at that mouth. Oh God. And the binoculars.

STANLEY: Geez, you got a life, Mr. Loman.

HAPPY: Wait on her.

STANLEY: [*going to the* GIRL's *table*] Would you like a menu, ma'am?

GIRL: I'm expecting someone, but I'd like a—

HAPPY: Why don't you bring her—excuse me, miss, do you mind? I sell champagne, and I'd like you to try my brand. Bring her a champagne, Stanley.

GIRL: That's awfully nice of you.

HAPPY: Don't mention it. It's all company money. [*He laughs.*]

GIRL: That's a charming product to be selling, isn't it?

HAPPY: Oh, gets to be like everything else. Selling is selling, y'know.

GIRL: I suppose.

HAPPY: You don't happen to sell, do you?

GIRL: No, I don't sell.

HAPPY: Would you object to a compliment from a stranger? You ought to be on a magazine cover.

GIRL: [*looking at him a little archly*] I have been.

[STANLEY *comes in with a glass of champagne.*]

HAPPY: What'd I say before, Stanley? You see? She's a cover girl.

STANLEY: Oh, I could see, I could see.

HAPPY: [*to the* GIRL] What magazine?

GIRL: Oh, a lot of them. [*she takes the drink*] Thank you.

HAPPY: You know what they say in France, don't you? "Champagne is the drink of the complexion"—Hya, Biff!

[BIFF *has entered and sits with* HAPPY.]

BIFF: Hello, kid. Sorry I'm late.

HAPPY: I just got here. Uh, Miss—?

GIRL: Forsythe.

HAPPY: Miss Forsythe, this is my brother.

BIFF: Is Dad here?

HAPPY: His name is Biff. You might've heard of him. Great football player.

GIRL: Really? What team?

HAPPY: Are you familiar with football?

GIRL: No, I'm afraid I'm not.

HAPPY: Biff is quarterback with the New York Giants.

GIRL: Well, that is nice, isn't it? [*She drinks.*]

HAPPY: Good health.

GIRL: I'm happy to meet you.

HAPPY: That's my name. Hap. It's really Harold, but at West Point they called me Happy.

GIRL: [*now really impressed*] Oh, I see. How do you do? [*She turns her profile.*]

BIFF: Isn't Dad coming?

HAPPY: You want her?

BIFF: Oh, I could never make that.

HAPPY: I remember the time that idea would never come into your head. Where's the old confidence, Biff?

BIFF: I just saw Oliver—

HAPPY: Wait a minute. I've got to see that old confidence again. Do you want her? She's on call.

BIFF: Oh, no. [*He turns to look at the* GIRL.]

HAPPY: I'm telling you. Watch this. [*turning to the* GIRL] Honey? [*she turns to him*] Are you busy?

GIRL: Well, I am . . . but I could make a phone call.

HAPPY: Do that, will you, honey? And see if you can get a friend. We'll be here for a while. Biff is one of the greatest football players in the country.

GIRL: [*standing up*] Well, I'm certainly happy to meet you.

HAPPY: Come back soon.

GIRL: I'll try.

HAPPY: Don't try, honey, try hard.

> [*The* GIRL *exits.* STANLEY *follows, shaking his head in bewildered admiration.*]

HAPPY: Isn't that a shame now? A beautiful girl like that? That's why I can't get married. There's not a good woman in a thousand. New York is loaded with them, kid!

BIFF: Hap, look—

HAPPY: I told you she was on call!

BIFF: [*strangely unnerved*] Cut it out, will ya? I want to say something to you.

HAPPY: Did you see Oliver?

BIFF: I saw him all right. Now look, I want to tell Dad a couple of things and I want you to help me.

HAPPY: What? Is he going to back you?

BIFF: Are you crazy? You're out of your goddam head, you know that ?

HAPPY: Why? What happened?

BIFF: [*breathlessly*] I did a terrible thing today, Hap. It's been the strangest day I ever went through. I'm all numb, I swear.

HAPPY: You mean he wouldn't see you?

BIFF: Well, I waited six hours for him, see? All day. Kept sending my name in. Even tried to date his secretary so she'd get me to him, but no soap.

HAPPY: Because you're not showin' the old confidence, Biff. He remembered you, didn't he?

BIFF: [*stopping* HAPPY *with a gesture*] Finally, about five o'clock, he comes out. Didn't remember who I was or anything. I felt like such an idiot, Hap.

HAPPY: Did you tell him my Florida idea?

BIFF: He walked away. I saw him for one minute. I got so mad I could've torn the walls down! How the hell did I ever get the idea I was a salesman there? I even believed myself that I'd been a salesman for him! And then he gave me one look and—I realized what a ridiculous lie my whole life has been! We've been talking in a dream for fifteen years. I was a shipping clerk.

HAPPY: What'd you do?

BIFF: [*with great tension and wonder*] Well, he left, see. And the secretary went out. I was all alone in the waiting-room. I don't now what came over me, Hap. The next thing I know I'm in his office—paneled walls, everything. I can't explain it. I—Hap, I took his fountain pen.

HAPPY: Geez, did he catch you?

BIFF: I ran out. I ran down all eleven flights. I ran and ran and ran.

HAPPY: That was an awful dumb—what'd you do that for?

BIFF: [*agonized*] I don't know, I just—wanted to take something, I don't know. You gotta help me, Hap, I'm gonna tell Pop.

HAPPY: You crazy? What for?

BIFF: Hap, he's got to understand that I'm not the man somebody lends that kind of money to. He thinks I've been spiting him all these years and it's eating him up.

HAPPY: That's just it. You tell him something nice.

BIFF: I can't.

HAPPY: Say you got a lunch date with Oliver tomorrow.

BIFF: So what do I do tomorrow?

HAPPY: You leave the house tomorrow and come back at night and say Oliver is thinking it over. And he thinks it over for a couple of weeks, and gradually it fades away and nobody's the worse.

BIFF: But it'll go on forever!

HAPPY: Dad is never so happy as when he's looking forward to something!
  [WILLY *enters.*]

HAPPY: Hello, scout!

WILLY: Gee, I haven't been here in years!
  [STANLEY *has followed* WILLY *in and sets a chair for him.* STANLEY *starts off but* HAPPY *stops him.*]

HAPPY: Stanley!
  [STANLEY *stands by, waiting for an order.*]

BIFF: [*going to* WILLY *with guilt, as to an invalid*] Sit down, Pop. You want a drink?

WILLY: Sure, I don't mind.

BIFF: Let's get a load on.

WILLY: You look worried.

BIFF: N-no. [*to* STANLEY] Scotch all around. Make it doubles.

STANLEY: Doubles, right. [*he goes*]

WILLY: You had a couple already, didn't you?

BIFF: Just a couple, yeah.

WILL: Well, what happened, boy? [*nodding affirmatively, with a smile*] Everything go all right?

BIFF: [*takes a breath, then reaches out and grasps* WILLY's *hand*] Pal . . . [*He is smiling bravely, and* WILLY *is smiling too.*] I had an experience today.

HAPPY: Terrific, Pop.

WILLY: That so? What happened?

BIFF: [*high, slightly alcoholic, above the earth*] I'm going to tell you everything from first to last. It's been a strange day. [*Silence. He looks around, composes himself as best he can, but his breath keeps breaking the rhythm of his voice.*] I had to wait quite a while for him, and—

WILLY: Oliver?

BIFF: Yeah, Oliver. All day, as a matter of cold fact. And a lot of—instances—facts, Pop, facts about my life came back to me. Who was it, Pop? Who ever said I was a salesman with Oliver?

WILLY: Well, you were.

BIFF: No, Dad, I was a shipping clerk.

WILLY: But you were practically—

BIFF: [*with determination*] Dad, I don't know who said it first, but I was never a salesman for Bill Oliver.

WILLY: What're you talking about?

BIFF: Let's hold on to the facts tonight, Pop. We're not going to get anywhere bullin' around. I was a shipping clerk.

WILLY: [*angrily*] All right, now listen to me—

BIFF: Why don't you let me finish?

WILLY: I'm not interested in stories about the past or any crap of that kind because the woods are burning, boys, you understand? There's a big blaze going on all around. I was fired today.

BIFF: [*shocked*] How could you be?

WILLY: I was fired, and I'm looking for a little good news to tell your mother, because the woman has waited and the woman has suffered. The gist of it is that I haven't got a story left in my head, Biff. So don't give me a lecture about facts and aspects. I am not interested. Now what've you got to say to me?

[STANLEY *enters with three drinks. They wait until he leaves.*]

WILLY: Did you see Oliver?

BIFF: Jesus, Dad!

WILLY: You mean you didn't go up there?

HAPPY: Sure he went up there.

BIFF: I did.—I saw him. How could they fire you?

WILLY: [*on the edge of his chair*] What kind of a welcome did he give you?

BIFF: He won't even let you work on commission?

WILLY: I'm out! [*driving*] So tell me, he gave you a warm welcome?

HAPPY: Sure, Pop, sure!

BIFF: [*driven*] Well, it was kind of—

WILLY: I was wondering if he'd remember you. [*to* HAPPY] Imagine, man doesn't see him for ten, twelve years and gives him that kind of a welcome!

HAPPY: Damn right!

BIFF: [*trying to return to the offensive*] Pop, look—

WILLY: You know why he remembered you, don't you? Because you impressed him in those days.

BIFF: Let's talk quietly and get this down to the facts, huh?

WILLY: [*as though Biff had been interrupting*] Well, what happened? It's great news, Biff. Did he take you into his office or'd you talk in the waiting-room?

BIFF: Well, he came in, see, and—

WILLY: [*with a big smile*] What'd he say? Betcha he threw his arm around you.

BIFF: Well, he kinda—

WILLY: He's a fine man. [*to* HAPPY] Very hard man to see, y'know.

HAPPY: [*agreeing*] Oh, I know.

WILLY: [*to* BIFF] Is that where you had the drinks?

BIFF: Yeah, he gave me a couple of—no, no!

HAPPY: [*cutting in*] He told him my Florida idea.

WILLY: Don't interrupt. [*to* BIFF] How'd he react to the Florida idea?

BIFF: Dad, will you give me a minute to explain?

WILLY: I've been waiting for you to explain since I sat down here! What happened? He took you into his office and what?

BIFF: Well—I talked. And—and he listened, see.

WILLY: Famous for the way he listens, y'know. What was his answer?

BIFF: His answer was—[*he breaks off, suddenly angry*] Dad, you're not letting me tell you what I want to tell you!

WILLY: [*accusing, angered*] You didn't see him, did you?

BIFF: I did see him!

WILLY: What'd you insult him or something? You insulted him, didn't you?

BIFF: Listen, will you let me out of it, will you just let me out of it!

HAPPY: What the hell!

WILLY: Tell me what happened!

BIFF: [*to* HAPPY] I can't talk to him!

[*A single trumpet note jars the ear. The light of green leaves stains the house, which holds the air of night and a dream.* YOUNG BERNARD *enters and knocks on the door of the house.*]

YOUNG BERNARD: [*frantically*] Mrs. Loman, Mrs. Loman!

HAPPY: Tell him what happened!

BIFF: [*to* HAPPY]Shut up and leave me alone!

WILLY: No, no! You had to go and flunk math!

BIFF: What math? What're you talking about?

YOUNG BERNARD: Mrs. Loman, Mrs. Loman!

[LINDA *appears in the house, as of old.*]

WILLY: [*wildly*] Math, math, math!

BIFF: Take it easy, Pop!

YOUNG BERNARD: Mrs. Loman!

WILLY: [*furiously*] If you hadn't flunked you'd've been set by now!

BIFF: Now, look, I'm gonna tell you what happened, and you're going to listen to me.

YOUNG BERNARD: Mrs. Loman!

BIFF: I waited six hours—

HAPPY: What the hell are you saying?

BIFF: I kept sending in my name but he wouldn't see me. So finally he . . .

[*He continues unheard as light fades low on the restaurant.*]

YOUNG BERNARD: Biff flunked math!

LINDA: No!

YOUNG BERNARD: Birnbaum flunked him! They won't graduate him!

LINDA: But they have to. He's gotta go to the university. Where is he? Biff! Biff!

YOUNG BERNARD: No, he left. He went to Grand Central.

LINDA: Grand—You mean he went to Boston!

YOUNG BERNARD: Is Uncle Willy in Boston?

LINDA: Oh, maybe Willy can talk to the teacher. Oh, the poor, poor boy!

[*Light on house area snaps out.*]

BIFF: [*at the table, now audible, holding up a gold fountain pen*] . . . so I'm washed up with Oliver, you understand? Are you listening to me?

WILLY: [*at a loss*] Yeah, sure. If you hadn't flunked—

BIFF: Flunked what? What're you talking about?

WILLY: Don't blame everything on me! I didn't flunk math—you did! What pen?

HAPPY: That was awful dumb, Biff, a pen like that is worth—

WILLY: [*seeing the pen for the first time*] You took Oliver's pen?

BIFF: [*weakening*] Dad, I just explained it to you.

WILLY: You stole Bill Oliver's fountain pen!

BIFF: I didn't exactly steal it! That's just what I've been explaining to you!

HAPPY: He had it in his hand and just then Oliver walked in, so he got nervous and stuck it in his pocket!

WILLY: My God, Biff!

BIFF: I never intended to do it, Dad!

OPERATOR'S VOICE: Standish Arms, good evening!

WILLY: [*shouting*] I'm not in my room!

BIFF: [*frightened*] Dad, what's the matter? [*He and* HAPPY *stand up.*]

OPERATOR: Ringing Mr. Loman for you!

WILLY: I'm not there, stop it!

BIFF: [*horrified, gets down on one knee before* WILLY] Dad, I'll make good, I'll make good. [WILLY *tries to get to his feet.* BIFF *holds him down.*] Sit down now.

WILLY: No, you're no good, you're no good for anything.

BIFF: I am, Dad, I'll find something else, you understand? Now don't worry about anything. [*He holds up* WILLY's *face*] Talk to me, Dad.

OPERATOR: Mr. Loman does not answer. Shall I page him?

WILLY: [*attempting to stand, as though to rush and silence the* OPERATOR] No, no, no!

HAPPY: He'll strike something, Pop.

WILLY: No, no . . .

BIFF: [*desperately, standing over* WILLY] Pop, listen! Listen to me! I'm telling you something good. Oliver talked to his partner about the Florida idea. You listening? He—he talked to his partner, and he came to me . . . I'm going to be all right, you hear? Dad, listen to me, he said it was just a question of the amount!

WILLY: Then you . . . got it?

HAPPY: He's gonna be terrific, Pop!

WILLY: [*trying to stand*] Then you got it, haven't you? You got it! You got it!

BIFF: [*agonized, holds* WILLY *down*] No, no. Look, Pop. I'm supposed to have lunch with them tomorrow. I'm just telling you this so you'll know that I can still make an impression, Pop. And I'll make good somewhere, but I can't go tomorrow, see?

WILLY: Why not? You simply—

BIFF: But the pen, Pop!

WILLY: You give it to him and tell him it was an oversight!

HAPPY: Sure, have lunch tomorrow!

BIFF: I can't say that—

WILLY: You were doing a crossword puzzle and accidentally used his pen!

BIFF: Listen, kid, I took those balls years ago, now I walk in with his fountain pen? That clinches it, don't you see? I can't face him like that! I'll try elsewhere.

PAGE'S VOICE: Paging Mr. Loman!

WILLY: Don't you want to be anything?

BIFF: Pop, how can I go back?

WILLY: You don't want to be anything, is that what's behind it?

BIFF: [*now angry at* WILLY *for not crediting his sympathy*] Don't take it that way! You think it was easy walking into that office after what I'd done to him? A team of horses couldn't have dragged me back to Bill Oliver!

WILLY: Then why'd you go?

BIFF: Why did I go? Why did I go! Look at you! Look at what's become of you!

[*Off left,* THE WOMAN *laughs.*]

WILLY: Biff, you're going to go to that lunch tomorrow, or—

BIFF: I can't go. I've got no appointment!

HAPPY: Biff, for . . . !

WILLY: Are you spiting me?

BIFF: Don't take it that way! Goddammit!

WILLY: [*strikes* BIFF *and falters away from the table*] You rotten little louse! Are you spiting me?

THE WOMAN: Someone's at the door, Willy!

BIFF: I'm no good, can't you see what I am?

HAPPY: [*separating them*] Hey, you're in a restaurant! Now cut it out, both of you! [*The girls enter.*] Hello, girls, sit down.

[THE WOMAN *laughs, off left.*]

MISS FORSYTHE: I guess we might as well. This is Letta.

THE WOMAN: Willy, are you going to wake up?

BIFF: [*ignoring* WILLY] How're ya, miss, sit down. What do you drink?

MISS FORSYTHE: Letta might not be able to stay long.

LETTA: I gotta get up very early tomorrow. I got jury duty. I'm so excited! Were you fellows ever on a jury?

BIFF: No, but I been in front of them! [*The girls laugh.*] This is my father.

LETTA: Isn't he cute? Sit down with us, Pop.

HAPPY: Sit him down, Biff!

BIFF: [*going to him*] Come on, slugger, drink us under the table. To hell with it! Come on, sit down, pal.

[*On* BIFF'S *last insistence,* WILLY *is about to sit.*]

THE WOMAN: [*now urgently*] Willy, are you going to answer the door!

[THE WOMAN'S *call pulls* WILLY *back. He starts right, befuddled.*]

BIFF: Hey, where are you going?

WILLY: Open the door.

BIFF: The door?

WILLY: The washroom . . . the door . . . where's the door?

BIFF: [*leading* WILLY *to the left*] Just go straight down.

[WILLY *moves left.*]

THE WOMAN: Willy, Willy, are you going to get up, get up, get up, get up?

[WILLY *exits left.*]

LETTA: I think it's sweet you bring your daddy along.

MISS FORSYTHE: Oh, he isn't really your father!

BIFF: [*at left, turning to her resentfully*] Miss Forsythe, you've just seen a prince walk by. A fine, troubled prince. A hard-working, unappreciated prince. A pal, you understand? A good companion. Always for his boys.

LETTA: That's so sweet.

HAPPY: Well, girls, what's the program? We're wasting time. Come on, Biff. Gather round. Where would you like to go?

BIFF: Why don't you do something for him?

HAPPY: Me!

BIFF: Don't you give a damn for him, Hap?

HAPPY: What're you talking about? I'm the one who—

BIFF: I sense it, you don't give a good goddam about him. [*He takes the rolled-up hose from his pocket and puts it on the table in front of* HAPPY] Look what I found in the cellar, for Christ's sake. How can you bear to let it go on?

HAPPY: Me? Who goes away? Who runs off and—

BIFF: Yeah, but he doesn't mean anything to you. You could help him—I can't! Don't you understand what I'm talking about? He's going to kill himself, don't you know that?

HAPPY: Don't I know it! Me!

BIFF: Hap, help him! Jesus . . . help him . . . Help me, help me, I can't bear to look at his face! [*Ready to weep, he hurries out, up right.*]

HAPPY: [*starting after him*] Where are you going?

MISS FORSYTHE: What's he so mad about?

HAPPY: Come on, girls, we'll catch up with him.

MISS FORSYTHE: [*as* HAPPY *pushes her out*] Say, I don't like that temper of his!

HAPPY: He's just a little overstrung, he'll be all right!

WILLY: [*off left, as* THE WOMAN *laughs*] Don't answer! Don't answer!

LETTA: Don't you want to tell your father—

HAPPY: No, that's not my father. He's just a guy. Come on, we'll catch Biff, and, honey, we're going to paint this town! Stanley, where's the check! Hey, Stanley!

[*They exit.* STANLEY *looks toward left.*]

STANLEY: [*calling to* HAPPY *indignantly*] Mr. Loman! Mr. Loman!

[STANLEY *picks up a chair and follows them off. Knocking is heard off left.* THE WOMAN *enters, laughing.* WILLY *follows her. She is in a black slip; he is buttoning his shirt. Raw, sensuous music accompanies their speech.*]

WILLY: Will you stop laughing? Will you stop?

THE WOMAN: Aren't you going to answer the door? He'll wake the whole hotel.

WILLY: I'm not expecting anybody.

THE WOMAN: Whyn't you have another drink, honey, and stop being so damn self-centered?

WILLY: I'm so lonely.

THE WOMAN: You know you ruined me, Willy? From now on, whenever you come to the office, I'll see that you go right through to the buyers. No waiting at my desk any more, Willy. You ruined me.

WILLY: That's nice of you to say that.

THE WOMAN: Gee, you are self-centered! Why so sad? You are the saddest, self-centeredest soul I ever did see-saw. [*She laughs.*] [*He kisses her.*] Come on inside, drummer boy. It's silly to be dressing in the middle of the night. [*as knocking is heard*] Aren't you going to answer the door?

WILLY: They're knocking on the wrong door.

THE WOMAN: But I felt the knocking. And he heard us talking in here. Maybe the hotel's on fire!

WILLY: [*his terror rising*] It's a mistake.

THE WOMAN: Then tell him to go away!

WILLY: There's nobody there.

THE WOMAN: It's getting on my nerves, Willy. There's somebody standing out there and it's getting on my nerves!

WILLY: [*pushing her away from him*] All right, stay in the bathroom here, and don't come out. I think there's a law in Massachusetts about it, so don't come out. It may be that new room clerk. He looked very mean. So don't come out. It's a mistake, there's no fire.

> [*The knocking is heard again. He takes a few steps away from her, and she vanishes into the wing. The light follows him, and now he is facing* YOUNG BIFF, *who carries a suitcase.* BIFF *steps toward him. The music is gone.*]

BIFF: Why didn't you answer?

WILLY: Biff! What are you doing in Boston?

BIFF: Why didn't you answer? I've been knocking for five minutes, I called you on the phone—

WILLY: I just heard you. I was in the bathroom and had the door shut. Did anything happen home?

BIFF: Dad—I let you down.

WILLY: What do you mean?

BIFF: Dad . . .

WILLY: Biffo, what's this about? [*putting his arm around* BIFF] Come on, let's go downstairs and get you a malted.

BIFF: Dad, I flunked math.

WILLY: Not for the term?

BIFF: The term. I haven't got enough credits to graduate.

WILLY: You mean to say Bernard wouldn't give you the answers?

BIFF: He did, he tried, but I only got a sixty-one.

WILLY: And they wouldn't give you four points?

BIFF: Birnbaum refused absolutely. I begged him, Pop, but he won't give me those points. You gotta talk to him before they close the school. Because if he saw the kind of man you are, and you just talked to him in your way, I'm sure he'd come through for me. The class came right before practice, see, and I didn't go enough. Would you talk to him? He'd like you, Pop. You know the way you could talk.

WILLY: You're on. We'll drive right back.

BIFF: Oh, Dad, good work! I'm sure he'll change it for you!

WILLY: Go downstairs and tell the clerk I'm checkin' out. Go right down.

BIFF: Yes, sir! See, the reason he hates me, Pop—one day he was late for class so I got up at the blackboard and imitated him. I crossed my eyes and talked with a lithp.

WILLY: [*laughing*] You did? The kids like it?

BIFF: They nearly died laughing!

WILLY: Yeah? What'd you do?

BIFF: The thquare root of thixthy twee is . . . [WILLY *bursts out laughing;* BIFF *joins him.*] And in the middle of it he walked in!

[WILLY *laughs and* THE WOMAN *joins in offstage.*]

WILLY: [*without hesitation*] Hurry downstairs and—

BIFF: Somebody in there?

WILLY: No, that was next door.

BIFF: Somebody got in your bathroom!

[THE WOMAN *laughs offstage.*]

WILLY: No, it's the next room, there's a party—

THE WOMAN: [*enters, laughing. She lisps this*] Can I come in? There's something in the bathtub, Willy, and it's moving!

[WILLY *looks at* BIFF, *who is staring open-mouthed and horrified at* THE WOMAN.]

WILLY: Ah—you better go back to your room. They must be finished painting by now. They're painting her room so I let her take a shower here. Go back, go back . . . [*He pushes her.*]

THE WOMAN: [*resisting*] But I've got to get dressed, Willy, I can't—

WILLY: Get out of here! Go back, go back . . . [*suddenly striving for the ordinary*] This is Miss Francis, Biff, she's a buyer. They're painting her room. Go back, Miss Francis, go back . . .

THE WOMAN: But my clothes, I can't go out naked in the hall!

WILLY: [*pushing her offstage*] Get outa here! Go back, go back!

[BIFF *slowly sits down on his suitcase as the argument continues offstage.*]

THE WOMAN: Where's my stockings? You promised me stockings, Willy!

WILLY: I have no stockings here!

THE WOMAN: You had two boxes of size nine sheers for me, and I want them!

WILLY: Here, for God's sake, will you get outa here!

THE WOMAN: [*enters holding a box of stockings*] I just hope there's nobody in the hall. That's all I hope. [*to* BIFF] Are you football or baseball?

BIFF: Football.

THE WOMAN: [*angry, humiliated*] That's me too. G'night. [*She snatches her clothes from* WILLY, *and walks out.*]

WILLY: [*after a pause*] Well, better get going. I want to get to the school first thing in the morning. Get my suits out of the closet. I'll get my valise. [BIFF *doesn't move.*] What's the matter? [BIFF *remains motionless, tears falling.*] She's a buyer. Buys for J. H. Simmons. She lives down the hall—they're painting. You don't imagine—[*He breaks off. After a pause:*] Now listen, pal, she's just a buyer. She sees merchandise in her room and they have to keep it looking just so . . . [*Pause. Assuming command:*] All right, get my suits. [BIFF *doesn't move.*] Now stop crying and do as I say. I gave you an order. Biff, I gave you an order! Is that what you do when I give you an order? How dare you cry! [*putting his arm around* BIFF] Now look, Biff, when you grow up you'll understand about these things. You mustn't —you mustn't overemphasize a thing like this. I'll see Birnbaum first thing in the morning.

BIFF: Never mind.

WILLY: [*getting down beside* BIFF] Never mind! He's going to give you those points. I'll see to it.

BIFF: He wouldn't listen to you.

WILLY: He certainly will listen to me. You need those points for the U. of Virginia.

BIFF: I'm not going there.

WILLY: Heh? If I can't get him to change that mark you'll make it up in summer school. You've got all summer to—

BIFF: [*his weeping breaking from him*] Dad . . .

WILLY: [*infected by it*] Oh, my boy . . .

BIFF: Dad . . .

WILLY: She's nothing to me, Biff. I was lonely, I was terribly lonely.

BIFF: You—you gave her Mama's stockings! [*His tears break through and he rises to go.*]

WILLY: [*grabbing for* BIFF] I gave you an order!

BIFF: Don't touch me, you—liar!

WILLY: Apologize for that!

BIFF: You fake! You phony little fake! You fake! [*Overcome, he turns quickly and weeping fully goes out with his suitcase.* WILLY *is left on the floor on his knees.*]

WILLY: I gave you an order! Biff, come back here or I'll beat you! Come back here! I'll whip you!

> [STANLEY *comes quickly in from the right and stands in front of* WILLY.]

WILLY: [*shouts at* STANLEY] I gave you an order . . .

STANLEY: Hey, let's pick it up, pick it up, Mr. Loman. [*He helps* WILLY *to his feet*] Your boys left with the chippies. They said they'll see you home.

> [A SECOND WAITER *watches some distance away.*]

WILLY: But we were supposed to have dinner together.

> [*Music is heard,* WILLY's *theme.*]

STANLEY: Can you make it?

WILLY: I'll—sure, I can make it. [*suddenly concerned about his clothes*] Do I —I look all right?

STANLEY: Sure, you look all right. [*He flicks a speck off* WILLY's *lapel.*]

WILLY: Here—here's a dollar.

STANLEY: Oh, your son paid me. It's all right.

WILLY: [*putting it in* STANLEY's *hand*] No, take it. You're a good boy.

STANLEY: Oh, no, you don't have to . . .

WILLY: Here—here's some more, I don't need it any more. [*after a slight pause*] Tell me—is there a seed store in the neighborhood?

STANLEY: Seeds? You mean like to plant?

> [*As* WILLY *turns,* STANLEY *slips the money back into his jacket pocket.*]

WILLY: Yes. Carrots, peas . . .

STANLEY: Well, there's hardware stores on Sixth Avenue, but it may be too late now.

WILLY: [*anxiously*] Oh, I'd better hurry. I've got to get some seeds. [*He starts off to the right.*] I've got to get some seeds, right away. Nothing's planted. I don't have a thing in the ground.

> [WILLY *hurries out as the light goes down.* STANLEY *moves over to the right after him, watches him off. The other waiter has been staring at* WILLY.]

STANLEY: [*to the* WAITER] Well, whatta you looking at?

> [*The* WAITER *picks up the chairs and moves off right.* STANLEY *takes the table and follows him. The light fades on this area. There is a long pause, the sound of the flute coming over. The light gradually rises on the kitchen, which is empty.* HAPPY *appears at the door of the house, followed by* BIFF. HAPPY *is carrying a large bunch of long-stemmed roses. He enters the kitchen, looks around for* LINDA. *Not seeing her, he turns to* BIFF, *who is just outside the house door, and makes a gesture with his hands, indicating "Not here, I guess." He looks into the living-room and freezes. Inside,* LINDA, *unseen, is seated,* WILLY's *coat on her lap. She rises ominously and quietly and moves toward* HAPPY, *who backs up into the kitchen, afraid.*]

HAPPY: Hey, what're you doing up? [LINDA *says nothing but moves toward him implacably*] Where's Pop? [*He keeps backing to the right, and now* LINDA *is in full view in the doorway to the living-room*] Is he sleeping?

LINDA: Where were you?

HAPPY: [*trying to laugh it off*] We met two girls, Mom, very fine types. Here, we brought you some flowers. [*offering them to her*] Put them in your room, Ma.

> [*She knocks them to the floor at* BIFF's *feet. He has now come inside and closed the door behind him. She stares at* BIFF, *silent.*]

HAPPY: Now what'd you do that for? Mom, I want you to have some flowers—

LINDA: [*cutting* HAPPY *off, violently to* BIFF] Don't you care whether he lives or dies?

HAPPY: [*going to the stairs*] Come upstairs, Biff.

BIFF: [*with a flare of disgust, to* HAPPY] Go away from me! [*to* LINDA] What do you mean, lives or dies? Nobody's dying around here, pal.

LINDA: Get out of my sight! Get out of here!

BIFF: I wanna see the boss.

LINDA: You're not going near him!

BIFF: Where is he? [*He moves into the living-room and* LINDA *follows.*]

LINDA: [*shouting after* BIFF] You invite him for dinner. He looks forward to it all day—[BIFF *appears in his parents' bedroom, looks around, and exits*]—and then you desert him there. There's no stranger you'd do that to!

HAPPY: Why? He had a swell time with us. Listen, when I—[LINDA *comes back into the kitchen*]—desert him I hope I don't outlive the day!

LINDA: Get out of here!

HAPPY: Now look, Mom . . .

LINDA: Did you have to go to women tonight? You and your lousy rotten whores!

> [BIFF *re-enters the kitchen.*]

HAPPY: Mom, all we did was follow Biff around trying to cheer him up! [*to* BIFF] Boy, what a night you gave me!

LINDA: Get out of here, both of you, and don't come back! I don't want you tormenting him any more. Go on now, get your things together! [*to* BIFF] You can sleep in his apartment. [*She starts to pick up the flowers and stops herself*] Pick up this stuff, I'm not your maid any more. Pick it up, you bum, you!

> [HAPPY *turns his back to her in refusal.* BIFF *slowly moves over and gets down on his knees, picking up the flowers.*]

LINDA: You're a pair of animals! Not one, not another living soul would have had the cruelty to walk out on that man in a restaurant!

BIFF: [*not looking at her*] Is that what he said?

LINDA: He didn't have to say anything. He was so humiliated he nearly limped when he came in.

HAPPY: But, Mom, he had a great time with us—

BIFF: [*cutting him off violently*] Shut up!

> [*Without another word,* HAPPY *goes upstairs.*]

LINDA: You! You didn't even go in to see if he was all right!

BIFF: [*still on the floor in front of* LINDA, *the flowers in his hand; with self-loathing*] No. Didn't. Didn't do a damned thing. How do you like that, heh? Left him babbling in a toilet.

LINDA: You louse. You . . .

BIFF: Now you hit it on the nose! [*He gets up, throws the flowers in the waste-basket*] The scum of the earth, and you're looking at him!

LINDA: Get out of here!

BIFF: I gotta talk to the boss, Mom. Where is he?

LINDA: You're not going near him. Get out of this house!

BIFF: [*with absolute assurance, determination*] No. We're gonna have an abrupt conversation, him and me.

LINDA: You're not talking to him!

> [*Hammering is heard from outside the house, off right.* BIFF *turns toward the noise.*]

LINDA: [*suddenly pleading*] Will you please leave him alone?

BIFF: What's he doing out there?

LINDA: He's planting the garden!

BIFF: [*quietly*] Now? Oh, my God!

> [BIFF *moves outside,* LINDA *following. The light dies down on them and comes up on the center of the apron as* WILLY *walks into it. He is carrying a flashlight, a hoe, and a handful of seed packets. He raps the top of the hoe sharply to fix it firmly, and then moves to the left, measuring off the distance with his foot. He holds the flashlight to look at the seed packets, reading off the instructions. He is in the blue of night.*]

WILLY: Carrots . . . quarter-inch apart. Rows . . . one-foot rows. [*he measures it off*] One foot. [*he puts down a package and measures off*] Beets. [*he puts down another package and measures again*] Lettuce. [*he reads the package, puts it down*] One foot—[*He breaks off as* BEN *appears at the right and moves slowly down to him.*] What a proposition, ts, ts. Terrific, terrific. 'Cause she's suffered, Ben, the woman has suffered. You understand me? A man can't go out the way he came in, Ben, a man has got to add up to something. You can't, you can't—[BEN *moves toward him as though to interrupt.*] You gotta consider, now. Don't answer so quick. Remember, it's a guaranteed twenty-thousand-dollar proposition. Now look, Ben, I want you to go through the ins and outs of this thing with me. I've got nobody to talk to, Ben, and the woman has suffered, you hear me?

BEN: [*standing still, considering*] What's the proposition?

WILLY: It's twenty thousand dollars on the barrelhead. Guaranteed, gilt-edged, you understand?

BEN: You don't want to make a fool of yourself. They might not honor the policy.

WILLY: How can they dare refuse? Didn't I work like a coolie to meet every premium on the nose? And now they don't pay off? Impossible!

BEN: It's called a cowardly thing, William.

WILLY: Why? Does it take more guts to stand here the rest of my life ringing up a zero?

BEN: [*yielding*] That's a point, William. [*He moves, thinking, turns.*] And twenty thousand—that *is* something one can feel with the hand, it is there.

WILLY: [*now assured, with rising power*] Oh, Ben, that's the whole beauty of it! I see it like a diamond, shining in the dark, hard and rough, that I can pick up and touch in my hand. Not like—like an appointment! This would not be another damned-fool appointment, Ben, and it changes all the aspects. Because he thinks I'm nothing, see, and so he spites me. But the funeral—[*straightening up*] Ben, that funeral will be massive! They'll come from Maine, Massachusetts, Vermont, New Hampshire! All the old-timers with the strange license plates—that boy will be thunder-struck, Ben, because he never realized—I am known! Rhode Island, New York, New Jersey—I am known, Ben, and he'll see it with his eyes once and for all. He'll see what I am, Ben! He's in for a shock, that boy!

BEN: [*coming down to the edge of the garden*] He'll call you a coward.

WILLY: [*suddenly fearful*] No, that would be terrible.

BEN: Yes. And a damned fool.

WILLY: No, no, he mustn't, I won't have that! [*He is broken and desperate.*]

BEN: He'll hate you, William.

    [*The gay music of the Boys is heard.*]

WILLY: Oh, Ben, how do we get back to all the great times? Used to be so full of light, and comradeship, the sleigh-riding in winter, and the ruddiness on his cheeks. And always some kind of good news coming up, always something nice coming up ahead. And never even let me carry the valises in the house, and simonizing, simonizing that little red car! Why, why can't I give him something and not have him hate me?

BEN: Let me think about it. [*He glances at his watch.*] I still have a little time. Remarkable proposition, but you've got to be sure you're not making a fool of yourself.

[BEN *drifts off upstage and goes out of sight.* BIFF *comes down from the left.*]

WILLY: [*suddenly conscious of* BIFF, *turns and looks up at him, then begins picking up the packages of seeds in confusion*] Where the hell is that seed? *Indignantly:* You can't see nothing out here! They boxed in the whole goddam neighborhood!

BIFF: There are people all around here. Don't you realize that?

WILLY: I'm busy. Don't bother me.

BIFF: [*taking the hoe from* WILLY] I'm saying good-by to you, Pop. [WILLY *looks at him, silent, unable to move.*] I'm not coming back any more.

WILLY: You're not going to see Oliver tomorrow?

BIFF: I've got no appointment, Dad.

WILLY: He put his arm around you, and you've got no appointment?

BIFF: Pop, get this now, will you? Everytime I've left it's been a fight that sent me out of here. Today I realized something about myself and I tried to explain it to you and I—I think I'm just not smart enough to make any sense out of it for you. To hell with whose fault it is or anything like that. [*he takes* WILLY's *arm*] Let's just wrap it up, heh? Come on in, we'll tell Mom. [*He gently tries to pull* WILLY *to left.*]

WILLY: [*frozen, immobile, with guilt in his voice*] No, I don't want to see her.

BIFF: Come on! [*He pulls again, and* WILLY *tries to pull away.*]

WILLY: [*highly nervous*] No, no, I don't want to see her.

BIFF: [*tries to look into* WILLY's *face, as if to find the answer there*] Why don't you want to see her?

WILLY: [*more harshly now*] Don't bother me, will you?

BIFF: What do you mean, you don't want to see her? You don't want them calling you yellow, do you? This isn't your fault; it's me, I'm a bum. Now come inside! [WILLY *strains to get away.*] Did you hear what I said to you?
      [WILLY *pulls away and quickly goes by himself into the house.* BIFF *follows.*]

LINDA: [*to* WILLY] Did you plant, dear?

BIFF: [*at the door, to* LINDA] All right, we had it out. I'm going and I'm not writing any more.

LINDA: [*going to* WILLY *in the kitchen*] I think that's the best way, dear. 'Cause there's no use drawing it out, you'll just never get along.
      [WILLY *doesn't respond.*]

BIFF: People ask where I am and what I'm doing, you don't know, and you don't care. That way it'll be off your mind and you can start brightening up again. All right? That clears it, doesn't it? [WILLY *is silent, and* BIFF *goes to him.*] You gonna wish me luck, scout? [*He extends his hand.*] What do you say?

LINDA: Shake his hand, Willy.

WILLY: [*turning to her, seething with hurt*] There's no necessity to mention the pen at all, y'know.

BIFF: [*gently*] I've got no appointment, Dad.

WILLY: [*erupting fiercely*] He put his arm around . . . ?

BIFF: Dad, you're never going to see what I am, so what's the use of arguing? If I strike oil I'll send you a check. Meantime forget I'm alive.

WILLY: [*to* LINDA] Spite, see?

BIFF: Shake hands, Dad.

WILLY: Not my hand.

BIFF: I was hoping not to go this way.

WILLY: Well, this is the way you're going. Good-by.

> [BIFF *looks at him a moment, then turns sharply and goes to the stairs.*]

WILLY: [*stops him with*] May you rot in hell if you leave this house!

BIFF: [*turning*] Exactly what is it that you want from me?

WILLY: I want you to know, on the train, in the mountains, in the valleys, wherever you go, that you cut down your life for spite!

BIFF: No, no.

WILLY: Spite, spite, is the word of your undoing! And when you're down and out, remember what did it. When you're rotting somewhere beside the railroad tracks, remember, and don't you dare blame it on me!

BIFF: I'm not blaming it on you!

WILLY: I won't take the rap for this, you hear?

> [HAPPY *comes down the stairs and stands on the bottom step, watching.*]

BIFF: That's just what I'm telling you!

WILLY: [*sinking into a chair at the table, with full accusation*] You're trying to put a knife in me—don't think I don't know what you're doing!

BIFF: All right, phony! Then let's lay it on the line. [*He whips the rubber tube out of his pocket and puts it on the table.*]

HAPPY: You crazy—

LINDA: Biff! [*She moves to grab the hose, but* BIFF *holds it down with his hand.*]

BIFF: Leave it there! Don't move it!

WILLY: [*not looking at it*] What is that?

BIFF: You know goddam well what that is.

WILLY: [*caged, wanting to escape*] I never saw that.

BIFF: You saw it. The mice didn't bring it into the cellar! What is this supposed to do, make a hero out of you? This supposed to make me sorry for you?

WILLY: Never heard of it.

BIFF: There'll be no pity for you, you hear it? No pity!

WILLY: [*to* LINDA] You hear the spite!

BIFF: No, you're going to hear the truth—what you are and what I am!

LINDA: Stop it!

WILLY: Spite!

HAPPY: [*coming down toward* BIFF] You cut it now!

BIFF: [*to* HAPPY] The man don't know who we are! The man is gonna know! [*to* WILLY] We never told the truth for ten minutes in this house!

HAPPY: We always told the truth!

BIFF: [*turning on him*] You big blow, are you the assistant buyer? You're one of the two assistants to the assistant, aren't you?

HAPPY: Well, I'm practically—

BIFF: You're practically full of it! We all are! And I'm through with it. [*to* WILLY] Now hear this, Willy, this is me.

WILLY: I know you!

BIFF: You know why I had no address for three months? I stole a suit in Kansas City and I was in jail. [*to* LINDA, *who is sobbing*] Stop crying. I'm through with it.

    [LINDA *turns away from them, her hands covering her face.*]

WILLY: I suppose that's my fault!

BIFF: I stole myself out of every good job since high school!

WILLY: And whose fault is that?

BIFF: And I never got anywhere because you blew me so full of hot air I could never stand taking orders from anybody! That's whose fault it is!

WILLY: I hear that!

LINDA: Don't, Biff!

BIFF: It's goddam time you heard that! I had to be boss big shot in two weeks, and I'm through with it!

WILLY: Then hang yourself! For spite, hang yourself!

BIFF: No! Nobody's hanging himself, Willy! I ran down eleven flights with a pen in my hand today. And suddenly I stopped, you hear me? And in the middle of that office building, do you hear this? I stopped in the middle of that building and I saw—the sky. I saw the things that I love in this world. The work and the food and time to sit and smoke. And I looked at the pen and said to myself, what the hell am I grabbing this for? Why am I trying to become what I don't want to be? What am I doing in an office, making a contemptuous, begging fool of myself, when all I want is out there, waiting for me the minute I say I know who I am! Why can't I say that, Willy?

    [*He tries to make* WILLY *face him, but* WILLY *pulls away and moves to the left.*]

WILLY: [*with hatred, threateningly*] The door of your life is wide open!

BIFF: Pop! I'm a dime a dozen, and so are you!

WILLY: [*turning on him now in an uncontrolled outburst*] I am not a dime a dozen! I am Willy Loman, and you are Biff Loman!

    [BIFF *starts for* WILLY, *but is blocked by* HAPPY. *In his fury,* BIFF *seems on the verge of attacking his father.*]

BIFF: I am not a leader of men, Willy, and neither are you. You were never anything but a hard-working drummer who landed in the ash can like all the rest of them! I'm one dollar an hour, Willy! I tried seven states and couldn't raise it. A buck an hour! Do you gather my meaning? I'm not bringing home any prizes any more, and you're going to stop waiting for me to bring them home!

WILLY: [*directly to* BIFF] You vengeful, spiteful mut!

    [BIFF *breaks from* HAPPY. WILLY, *in fright, starts up the stairs.* BIFF *grabs him.*]

BIFF: [*at the peak of his fury*] Pop, I'm nothing! I'm nothing, Pop. Can't you understand that? There's no spite in it any more. I'm just what I am, that's all.

[BIFF's *fury has spent itself, and he breaks down, sobbing, holding on to* WILLY, *who dumbly fumbles for* BIFF's *face.*]

WILLY: [*astonished*] What're you doing? What're you doing? [*to* LINDA] Why is he crying?

BIFF: [*crying, broken*] Will you let me go, for Christ's sake? Will you take that phony dream and burn it before something happens? [*struggling to contain himself, he pulls away and moves to the stairs*] I'll go in the morning. Put him—put him to bed. [*Exhausted,* BIFF *moves up the stairs to his room.*]

WILLY: [*after a long pause, astonished, elevated*] Isn't that—isn't that remarkable? Biff—he likes me!

LINDA: He loves you, Willy!

HAPPY: [*deeply moved*] Always did, Pop.

WILLY: Oh, Biff! [*staring wildly*] He cried! Cried to me. [*He is choking with his love, and now cries out his promise:*] That boy—that boy is going to be magnificent!

[BEN *appears in the light just outside the kitchen.*]

BEN: Yes, outstanding, with twenty thousand behind him.

LINDA: [*sensing the racing of his mind, fearfully, carefully*] Now come to bed, Willy. It's all settled now.

WILLY: [*finding it difficult not to rush out of the house*] Yes, we'll sleep. Come on. Go to sleep, Hap.

BEN: And it does take a great kind of a man to crack the jungle.

[*In accents of dread,* BEN's *idyllic music starts up.*]

HAPPY: [*his arm around* LINDA] I'm getting married, Pop, don't forget it. I'm changing everything. I'm gonna run that department before the year is up. You'll see, Mom. [*he kisses her*]

BEN: The jungle is dark but full of diamonds, Willy.

[WILLY *turns, moves, listening to* BEN.]

LINDA: Be good. You're both good boys, just act that way, that's all.

HAPPY: 'Night, Pop. [*He goes upstairs.*]

LINDA: [*to* WILLY] Come, dear.

BEN: [*with greater force*] One must go in to fetch a diamond out.

WILLY: [*to* LINDA, *as he moves slowly along the edge of the kitchen, toward the door*] I just want to get settled down, Linda. Let me sit alone for a little.

LINDA: [*almost uttering her fear*] I want you upstairs.

WILLY: [*taking her in his arms*] In a few minutes, Linda. I couldn't sleep right now. Go on, you look awful tired. [*He kisses her.*]

BEN: Not like an appointment at all. A diamond is rough and hard to the touch.

WILLY: Go on now. I'll be right up.

LINDA: I think this is the only way, Willy.

WILLY: Sure, it's the best thing.

BEN: Best thing!

WILLY: The only way. Everything is gonna be—go on, kid, get to bed. You look so tired.

LINDA: Come right up.

WILLY: Two minutes.

> [LINDA *goes into the living-room, then reappears in her bedroom.* WILLY *moves just outside the kitchen door.*]

WILLY: Loves me. [*wonderingly*] Always loved me. Isn't that a remarkable thing? Ben, he'll worship me for it!

BEN: [*with promise*] It's dark there, but full of diamonds.

WILLY: Can you imagine that magnificence with twenty thousand dollars in his pocket?

LINDA: [*calling from her room*] Willy! Come up!

WILLY: [*calling into the kitchen*] Yes! Yes. Coming! It's very smart, you realize that, don't you, sweetheart? Even Ben sees it. I gotta go, baby. 'By! 'By! [*going over to* BEN, *almost dancing*] Imagine? When the mail comes he'll be ahead of Bernard again!

BEN: A perfect proposition all around.

WILLY: Did you see how he cried to me? Oh, if I could kiss him, Ben!

BEN: Time, William, time!

WILLY: Oh, Ben, I always knew one way or another we were gonna make it, Biff and I!

BEN: [*looking at his watch*] The boat. We'll be late. [*He moves slowly off into the darkness.*]

WILLY: [*elegiacally, turning to the house*] Now when you kick off, boy, I want a seventy-yard boot, and get right down the field under the ball, and when you hit, hit low and hit hard, because it's important, boy. [*he swings around and faces the audience*] There's all kinds of important people in the stands, and the first thing you know . . . [*suddenly realizing he is alone*] Ben! Ben, where do I . . . ? [*he makes a sudden movement of search*] Ben, how do I . . . ?

LINDA: [*calling*] Willy, you coming up?

WILLY: [*uttering a gasp of fear, whirling about as if to quiet her*] Sh! [*He turns around as if to find his way; sounds, faces, voices, seem to be swarming in upon him and he flicks at them, crying*] Sh! Sh! [*Suddenly music, faint and high, stops him. It rises in intensity, almost to an unbearable scream. He goes up and down on his toes, and rushes off around the house.*] Shhh!

LINDA: Willy?

> [*There is no answer.* LINDA *waits.* BIFF *gets up off his bed. He is still in his clothes.* HAPPY *sits up.* BIFF *stands listening.*]

LINDA: [*with real fear*] Willy, answer me! Willy!

> [*There is the sound of a car starting and moving away at full speed.*]

LINDA: No!

BIFF: [*rushing down the stairs*] Pop!

> [*As the car speeds off, the music crashes down in a frenzy of sound, which becomes the soft pulsation of a single cello string.* BIFF *slowly returns to his bedroom. He and* HAPPY *gravely don their jackets.* LINDA *slowly walks out of her room. The music has developed into a dead march. The leaves of day are appearing over everything.*

CHARLEY *and* BERNARD, *somberly dressed, appear and knock on the kitchen door.* BIFF *and* HAPPY *slowly descend the stairs to the kitchen as* CHARLEY *and* BERNARD *enter. All stop a moment when* LINDA, *in clothes of mourning, bearing a little bunch of roses, comes through the draped doorway into the kitchen. She goes to* CHARLEY *and takes his arm. Now all move toward the audience, through the wall-line of the kitchen. At the limit of the apron,* LINDA *lays down the flowers, kneels, and sits back on her heels. All stare down at the grave.*]

REQUIEM

CHARLEY: It's getting dark, Linda.

[LINDA *doesn't react. She stares at the grave.*]

BIFF: How about it, Mom? Better get some rest, heh? They'll be closing the gate soon.

[LINDA *makes no move. Pause.*]

HAPPY: [*deeply angered*] He had no right to do that. There was no necessity for it. We would've helped him.

CHARLEY: [*grunting*] Hmmm.

BIFF: Come along, Mom.

LINDA: Why didn't anybody come?

CHARLEY: It was a very nice funeral.

LINDA: But where are all the people he knew? Maybe they blame him.

CHARLEY: Naa. It's a rough world, Linda. They wouldn't blame him.

LINDA: I can't understand it. At this time especially. First time in thirty-five years we were just about free and clear. He only needed a little salary. He was even finished with the dentist.

CHARLEY: No man only needs a little salary.

LINDA: I can't understand it.

BIFF: There were a lot of nice days. When he'd come home from a trip; or on Sundays, making the stoop; finishing the cellar; putting on the new porch; when he built the extra bathroom; and put up the garage. You know something, Charley, there's more of him in that front stoop than in all the sales he ever made.

CHARLEY: Yeah. He was a happy man with a batch of cement.

LINDA: He was so wonderful with his hands.

BIFF: He had all the wrong dreams. All, all, wrong.

HAPPY: [*almost ready to fight* BIFF] Don't say that!

BIFF: He never knew who he was.

CHARLEY: [*stopping* HAPPY's *movement and reply. To* BIFF:] Nobody dast blame this man. You don't understand. Willy was a salesman. And for a salesman, there is no rock bottom to the life. He don't put a bolt to a nut, he don't tell you the law or give you medicine. He's a man way out there in the blue, riding on a smile and a shoeshine. And when they start not smiling back—that's an earthquake. And then you get yourself a couple of spots on your hat, and you're finished. Nobody dast blame this man. A salesman is got to dream, boy. It comes with the territory.

BIFF: Charley, the man didn't know who he was.

HAPPY: [*infuriated*] Don't say that!

BIFF: Why don't you come with me, Happy?

HAPPY: I'm not licked that easily. I'm staying right in this city, and I'm gonna beat this racket! [*He looks at* BIFF, *his chin set.*] The Loman Brothers!

BIFF: I know who I am, kid.

HAPPY: All right, boy. I'm gonna show you and everybody else that Willy Loman did not die in vain. He had a good dream. It's the only dream you can have—to come out number-one man. He fought it out here, and this is where I'm gonna win it for him.

BIFF: [*with a hopeless glance at* HAPPY, *bends toward his mother*] Let's go, Mom.

LINDA: I'll be with you in a minute. Go on, Charley. [*he hesitates*] I want to, just for a minute. I never had a chance to say good-by.

[CHARLEY *moves away, followed by* HAPPY. BIFF *remains a slight distance up and left of* LINDA. *She sits there, summoning herself. The flute begins, not far away, playing behind her speech.*]

LINDA: Forgive me, dear. I can't cry. I don't know what it is, but I can't cry. I don't understand it. Why did you ever do that? Help me, Willy, I can't cry. It seems to me that you're just on another trip. I keep expecting you. Willy, dear, I can't cry. Why did you do it? I search and search and I search, and I can't understand it, Willy. I made the last payment on the house today. Today, dear. And there'll be nobody home. [*a sob rises in her throat*] We're free and clear. [*sobbing more fully, released*] We're free. [BIFF *comes slowly toward her.*] We're free . . . We're free . . .

[BIFF *lifts her to her feet and moves out up right with her in his arms.* LINDA *sobs quietly.* BERNARD *and* CHARLEY *come together and follow them, followed by* HAPPY. *Only the music of the flute is left on the darkening stage as over the house the hard towers of the apartment buildings rise into sharp focus, and*]

THE CURTAIN FALLS

EUGENE IONESCO

THE NEW TENANT

Translated by
Donald Watson

CHARACTERS

THE GENTLEMAN
THE CARETAKER
THE FIRST FURNITURE MOVER
THE SECOND FURNITURE MOVER

SCENE 1—*A bare room, without any furniture. In the centre of the back wall, an open window. Double doors on the right and on the left. Light-coloured walls. Like the set and the furniture that will be brought on the stage later, the style of acting must be completely realistic.*

> [*As the curtain rises, a considerable din is heard offstage: the sounds of voices, and hammers, snatches of song, children shouting, the noise of feet going up and coming down stairs, a barrel-organ, etc. For a moment, as the noise goes on, the stage is empty: then* THE CARETAKER *comes in from the right, crashing the door open and singing in a loud voice; she is holding a bunch of keys.*]

CARETAKER: [*as she enters singing*] La, la, la, tralalala, tralali, tralalalala-a-a! [*And rattling the keys.*] La, la, la, la! [*She interrupts her singing to go and lean out of the open window:*] Bill! Oh, Bill! Bill! Hullo there, George! Go and tell Bill 'e's got to see Mr Clarence! . . . George . . . [*Silence*] George . . . [*Silence*] Well! If 'e ain't missing too! [*She tries to lean still further out of the window, singing at the top of her voice:*] La, la, la, la, la, la, la!

> [*While the row continues and* THE CARETAKER *is still craning out of the window,* THE GENTLEMAN *comes silently in from the left: he is middle-aged, with a little black moustache, dressed in dark clothes; he is wearing a bowler hat, black jacket and striped trousers, his shoes are of patent leather; he is carrying gloves, and an overcoat over one arm, and he has a little attaché-case of black leather. He closes the door quietly behind him and walks silently up to* THE CARETAKER, *who does not notice him; he stops beside her and waits for an instant without moving while* THE CARETAKER *suddenly interrupts her singing as she becomes aware of the stranger's presence; but for some moments she does not change her position and turns round only when* THE GENTLEMAN *speaks.*]

GENTLEMAN: Excuse me, are you the caretaker?
CARETAKER: [*putting her hand to her heart, she cries out*] Oh! Oh! Oh! [*And*

504

then hiccups.] I beg pardon, Sir. I've got the hiccups. [THE GENTLEMAN *does not stir.*] 'Ave you only just come in?

GENTLEMAN: Just this moment.

CARETAKER: I was tryin' to see if Bill—or George perhaps—or someone else anyway, was in the yard . . . It's about going to see Mr Clarence. Well! . . . so you've arrived then?

GENTLEMAN: As you can see.

CARETAKER: I wasn't expectin' you, not for today I wasn't . . . I thought you was meant to come tomorrow . . . Pleased to see you, anyway. Did you 'ave a good journey? Not too tired, I 'ope? Give me quite a turn, you did! I suppose you got finished sooner than you expected! That must be it. It's just because it took me by surprise, like. [*She hiccups.*] It's the hiccups. Shock, you know. It's only what you might expect. Good thing the last lot—the people what was 'ere before you, you know—moved everything out in time. I'm not sure as 'ow I know what he used to do, mind. They said they'd send me some postcards. Worked for the government. Not a bit nervy, 'e wasn't. I suppose you wouldn't be? Would you? Don't know what department 'e worked for. I've forgot. 'E told me once. Me and them government departments! And my first 'usband was an office-boy. They was good folks. Used to tell me everything, they did. I get used to folks' little secrets, I do. Mum's the word for me! 'Er—the old lady, I mean—she didn't used to work. Never lifted a finger in 'er life. I used to look after the place for 'em, she used to 'ave someone in to run errands for 'er and when she didn't used to come, it was me again! [*She hiccups.*] What a fright you gave me! I wasn't expectin' you till tomorrow. Or the day after. Used to have a little dog, they did, they 'ated cats, but then cats isn't allowed in this establishment. 'Course it's all the same to me, it's the landlord what says so! Regular sort of folk they were—no children, of course—off they'd go to the country every Sunday to some cousins of theirs, 'olidays in Devonshire, that's where the old gentleman come from, that's where they've gone to live now, but they didn't used to like the cider they 'ave there—said it used to go to their heads, like a drop of port now and again, just a drop, of course—*old* they were, even when they were young—well, there it is we 'aven't all got the same ideas, 'ave we? Take me, for instance. I'm not like that. Still, they was nice folks. And what about you? In business, are you? Clerk? Got your own money, perhaps? Pension? Oh, but not yet, you're too young for that, though you never know, some of them give up early when they're tired, don't they? And when they've *got* a little money, 'course everybody can't, good luck to them that can, that's what I say. Got any family?

GENTLEMAN: [*laying his case and overcoat on the floor*] No, I'm afraid not.

CARETAKER: That's right, put your case down. Nice bit of leather—mustn't 'ave an Irishman's rest! You can put it where you like. Well I'm blowed! 'Iccups 'ave gone! Got over me fright! Why don't you take your 'at off and make yourself comfortable? [THE GENTLEMAN *adjusts his hat more firmly on his head.*] Oh, I shouldn't bother to take your 'at off, Sir. Of course, you're at 'ome now, aren't you? Last week it wasn't your 'ome yet—there's always change—it was *their* 'ome—well, can't be helped—you 'ave to get old—it's all a question of age—now this is *your* 'ome, I'm not the one to say it ain't—very nice 'ere it is, a good 'ouse—must be twenty years now—my, that's a good long stretch . . .

> [*Without saying a word,* THE GENTLEMAN *takes a few paces in the empty room, and looks around carefully, at the walls, the doors, the ceiling: now he has his hands behind his back.*]

Ooh! They left everything proper, Sir! Clean folks they was, really nice people. Mm? Well, of course they 'ad their faults like you and me—bit proud they was and not what you might call talkative, not talkative by a long chalk—never said anything much about anything to me, they didn't— only silly things—'im—the old 'un, I mean—well, 'e was what you might call all right—but 'er, not 'er—threw 'er cat out of the window, she did— 'it the landlord on the 'ead—what a thud!—still, didn't 'urt my flowers. And as for 'im, 'e didn't 'alf used to beat 'er, if you can believe it, Sir, in these days—oh, that was their business—didn't go poking my nose in— when I come up once, 'e was going for 'er with 'is fists, something awful —Screaming she was, 'You brute! You bleeding bastard!' [*She bursts out laughing: at this moment* THE GENTLEMAN *is having a closer look at the state of the walls, still without uttering a word; he inspects the doors and the locks, moves his hand over them, shakes his head, etc., while the* CARE- TAKER *watches every movement as she goes on talking; the din outside continues.*] Oh, I 'ad to laugh, Sir—but there, they're away now, mustn't tell tales—just as though they was dead, not *just* the same p'raps, specially as it's all the same really—very nice they was, can't say I 'ad anything to grumble about, except for New Year's Day . . . Oh, don't you go worrying yourself about the 'ouse, Sir, *that's* sound enough—this 'ouse wasn't born yesterday, don't make 'em like that nowadays . . . You'll be all right 'ere, that you will . . . the neighbours are good folk, it's all 'armony 'ere, always nice and quiet—I've never once 'ad to call the police in, 'cept for the third floor front—Hinspector 'e is, shouts out all the time, wants to arrest everybody, 'e does . . .

GENTLEMAN: [*pointing*] I beg your pardon, the window! [*In an even, expressionless tone of voice.*]

CARETAKER: Oh, but of course, Sir—I'm only too willing to do for you. I don't ask very much, Sir. Get on fine, you an' me will, you won't 'ave any insurance stamps to worry you . . .

GENTLEMAN: [*same gesture, same calm*] The window, please!

CARETAKER: Oh yes, Sir, I *am* sorry—I was forgettin'. [*As she closes the window, there is a little less noise to be heard.*] . . . You know 'ow it is, Sir, one word leads to the next and don't time fly? [THE GENTLEMAN *continues his inspection.*] I've closed the window for you, just as you wanted—closes nice and easy. [THE GENTLEMAN *inspects the window fasteners and the window itself.*] Of course it looks out on the yard, but it's nice and bright as you can see, that's because it's on the sixth floor . . .

GENTLEMAN: There was nothing available on the ground floor.

CARETAKER: Oh! Don't think I don't know what you mean—it's no joke, the sixth floor, not when there's no lift . . .

GENTLEMAN: [*rather to himself*] That's not the point. I'm not at all tired.

CARETAKER: Oh, I see. Then why, Sir? . . . I suppose you don't like the sun? 'Course, it's true it can 'urt your eyes! When you get to a certain age, you can get on quite well without it, burns your skin right off, it does . . .

GENTLEMAN: Not at all.

CARETAKER: Well, not *right* off, of course. You 'aven't anything to sleep on tonight, 'ave you? I can lend you a bed! [*For some minutes,* THE GENTLE-MAN, *still engrossed in his examination of the room, has been deciding where to put the furniture that will be arriving, pointing out to himself the various positions; he takes a tape-measure out of his pocket and starts measuring.*] I'll 'elp you to arrange the furniture, don't you worry about that, I'll give you some ideas—plenty of them about—won't be the first time, neither—since I'm going to look after you—you won't see it come today, your furniture, at any rate, they won't be bringing it as quick as that, just you see, I know all their little tricks, them tradespeople's all the same . . .

GENTLEMAN: Yes, indeed.

CARETAKER: *You* think they're going to bring all your things today, do you? No 'arm in *thinking*—suits me all right, I've got no bed to lend you, but mind it'd surprise *me*, 'cause I *know* 'em. My, but I've seen 'em before, this lot's not the first, they won't come, you mark my words, it's a Saturday—no, it ain't, it's a Wednesday—I've got a bed for you . . . since I'm going to do for you . . . [*She goes to open the window.*]

GENTLEMAN: If you don't mind!

CARETAKER: What's the matter? [*She turns again to open the window.*] I've got to call George to tell 'im to tell Bill to go and see Mr Clarence . . .

GENTLEMAN: Leave the window alone, please.

CARETAKER: It's all on account of Mr Clarence, what wants to know if Mr Eustace, who's a friend of Bill and George's too, since they're what you might call relations, not exactly, but in a kind of way . . .

GENTLEMAN: Please leave the window alone.

CARETAKER: All right, all right, I 'eard you, you don't want me to—wouldn't 'ave done no 'arm—you're in your rights of course, it's your window, not mine. I don't want no window—I get you, it's you gives the orders, it's just as *you* like, I won't touch it, you're the boss in your own place—don't pay much for it either—still, no business of mine—the window, that's yours, too, you can buy anything when you've got a spot of money, that's life for you—I don't say nothing, I keeps to myself, it's your affair—'ave to go down six flights of stairs now to look for Bill, poor old woman like me—Ah, well! Can't 'elp men 'aving their little ways, don't think about nothing they don't—but I'll do just what you like, you know, it's all right with me, that don't worry me, suits me fine that does, I'm going to look after you, be as though I was your servant, like, won't it, Sir?

GENTLEMAN: No, I'm afraid it won't.

CARETAKER: Beg pardon, Sir?

GENTLEMAN: I shan't be needing your services, I'm afraid.

CARETAKER: Well, I like that! After all the time you've been asking me to do
for you! Bit of bad luck I didn't 'ave no witness, took you at your word,
I did, got proper took in . . . Too kind'earted, that's me . . .

GENTLEMAN: I beg your pardon. Please don't get upset about it.

CARETAKER: Well, that's all right then.

[*A knock at the door, left.*]

GENTLEMAN: The furniture!

CARETAKER: I'll open the door. Don't you disturb yourself. I'm the one to open
the door. Must wait on you, you know. I'm your servant. [*She goes to open
the door, but* THE GENTLEMAN *steps in front of her and stops her.*]

GENTLEMAN: [*still very calmly*] Please don't do anything like that!

[*He walks to the door on the left and opens it, while* THE CARETAKER,
hands on hips, exclaims:]

CARETAKER: Well, that's a bit of all right! They make up to you, promise you
the 'ole world, and then they go back on their word!

[THE GENTLEMAN *opens the door and the* FIRST FURNITURE MOVER
comes in.]

FIRST FURNITURE MOVER: 'Day to you!

GENTLEMAN: Is the furniture here?

1ST FURNITURE MOVER: Can we bring it up?

GENTLEMAN: Yes, if you like.

1ST FURNITURE MOVER: Very well, Sir. [*He goes out.*]

CARETAKER: You won't never be able to arrange all that furniture by yourself,
Sir.

GENTLEMAN: That will be all right. I shall have the removal men to help me.

CARETAKER: Well, you 'ardly want *strangers* to do it, do you? I don't even know
that one, I've never seen 'im before, it's not safe! You ought to 'ave asked
my 'ubby. Ought never to have let 'im come in, don't do to trust no one—
you never know, you know, that's just 'ow things 'appen—foolish I call
it when there's my old man, my second you know, don't know what
'appened to the first—he's down below, got nothing to do, 'asn't got a
job—'e's 'efty enough you know, would 'elp 'im to earn a bit, why give
your money away to other people, it don't do no good, 'e could bring it
up all right, 'e's tubercular you know, still, got to earn 'is bit, 'asn't 'e?—
Them strikers is right, so was my first 'ubby, 'e'd 'ad enough of it, so
off 'e went and then everyone's surprised!—Oh well, I'm not a bad sort
really, you know, I'll look after you, wouldn't mind looking after you at
all . . .

GENTLEMAN: I'm afraid I really shan't be needing your services. I'm extremely
sorry. I shall be looking after myself, you see.

CARETAKER: [*losing her temper and shouting*] 'E says 'e's sorry, does 'e! Thinks
'e can do what he likes, does 'e!—Oooh! I don't like these sort of goings
on, you can't make no fool out of me! I wish the old couple 'adn't gone,
they weren't like that at all. As kind and obliging as you could wish for!
They're all alike, one's as bad as another! Make you waste all your time,
as though I 'adn't got nothing else to do! Tells me to come up, 'e does,
and then . . .

[*The noise increases offstage, especially the sound of hammers.* THE
GENTLEMAN *pulls a wry face;* THE CARETAKER *screams out into the
wings.*]

Don't make so much noise! I can't 'ear myself speak. [*To* THE GENTLE-
MAN:] It's all right, I'm not going to open your window, *I* don't want to
break nobody's window-panes—I'm respectable, I am, no one never 'ad
anything to say about that—So I've been wasting my time, 'ave I?—and
all that washing to do, better for me if I 'adn't listened to you!

[*The door on the left opens noisily and lets the* 1ST FURNITURE MOVER
appear, carrying two very small stools, while THE CARETAKER's *tirade
goes on.*]

1ST FURNITURE MOVER: [*to* GENTLEMAN] Here's the first lot, anyway!

CARETAKER: [*to the* 1ST FURNITURE MOVER, *who takes no notice*] Don't you
believe a word 'e says, my lad . . .

1ST FURNITURE MOVER: [*to* GENTLEMAN] Where shall I put them?

CARETAKER: [*as before*] . . . A pack of lies, you needn't think 'e'll pay you for
it, think they can buy everything with money!

GENTLEMAN: [*calmly to the* 1ST FURNITURE MOVER] Would you mind putting
one of them there? And one there! [*He points either side of the door on
the left.*]

CARETAKER: [*as before*] 'E'll make you sweat, 'e will.

1ST FURNITURE MOVER: [*as before*] Very good, Sir! [*He sets the stools down as
directed.*]

CARETAKER: [*as before*] . . . Work yourself to death, that's all life is for the
likes of us . . .

[*The* 1ST FURNITURE MOVER *goes out;* THE CARETAKER *turns towards*
THE GENTLEMAN.]

I don't know who you *are*, but I know who *I* am. I know your sort . . .
Mrs Fairchild, that's me.

GENTLEMAN: [*still calm, taking money from his pocket*] Please take this for
your trouble! [*Offering her money.*]

CARETAKER: Well, I never! Who do you take me for? . . . I'm no pauper,
wasn't my fault if I couldn't 'ave any kids, that's on account of my old
man, they'd be grown up now, they would—I don't want your money!
[*She takes the money and puts it in her apron-pocket.*] Very good of you,
I'm sure, Sir! . . . No! It's no good, you can make as much fuss as you
like, you won't catch me looking after you, not the likes of you, you
won't, your sort's not for me—'e don't need no one, 'e don't, wants to do
it all for 'isself, 'e does—fine thing that is, too, at your time o' life . . .
[*She rambles on, while* THE GENTLEMAN *walks calmly to the door on the
left, exchanges the position of the two stools and moves back to judge the
effect.*] . . . a bad lot, that's what 'e is, a bad lot in the 'ouse, don't need
nobody 'e don't, not even a blessed dog to keep 'im comp'ny—that's the
sort that prowls round the streets at night—what a time to live in! Never
wanted nobody like that, I didn't, fine state of affairs, we only 'ave
respectable folks in our 'ouse—[*Still louder.*]—that's the sort that frightens
folks on purpose when they're looking out of the window, might have
broken my neck and don't need nothing 'e don't. Only wanted to pass

the time o' day, don't do no one no harm, don't get much fun I don't, 'cept the pictures now and again and that's about all, don't even know what they want, they don't . . . [THE GENTLEMAN, *who has finally put the stools back where they were, moves off again to admire them.*] . . . don't know much about life, that sort don't, don't do nothing but kick up a fuss . . .

GENTLEMAN: [*inspecting the stools with a satisfied look, but he is too phlegmatic to show much emotion*] Yes, they're better that way!

    [*The* 1ST FURNITURE MOVER *comes in through the left-hand door, noisily, with a vase in his hand.*]

CARETAKER: [*going on in the same way*] Don't 'alf 'ave a fine opinion of themselves either, they do—nothing but a lot of thieves, louts and good-for-nothings . . .

GENTLEMAN: [*to* 1ST FURNITURE MOVER] Here, you may put it here. [*Points to the left-hand corner of the stage, at the back.*]

1ST FURNITURE MOVER: There? Very good, Sir! [*Goes to the spot indicated.*]

CARETAKER: Makes all sorts of shameful suggestions to you, they does—for money . . .

GENTLEMAN: [1ST FURNITURE MOVER, *who has not put the object down right in the corner*] No! In the corner, right in the corner, there . . .

CARETAKER: That sort of lark don't cut no ice with me, not with me, it don't!

1ST FURNITURE MOVER: Here?

GENTLEMAN: Yes, there, it's fine like that . . .

CARETAKER: Oh, no! Money don't buy everything, money don't pervert everyone . . . I won't 'ave it any'ow!

1ST FURNITURE MOVER: [*to* THE GENTLEMAN] But where are you going to put the rest?

GENTLEMAN: [*to the* 1ST FURNITURE MOVER] Oh, please don't trouble about that, I've thought it all out, you'll see, there'll be room . . .

    [*The* 1ST FURNITURE MOVER *goes off left.*]

CARETAKER: Not that it's not what I weren't expecting, your sort don't catch me napping, I know 'em, I do, all of them fine gentlemen prowling round the streets, I've got my eyes open, I 'ave, you don't catch me 'aving any, run after anything in a skirt they will, but they don't 'ave me on! I know what you're up to, I know your little game, wanted to make a proper tart out of me, didn't you? Me! Mother of five kids too! Fine cheek you 'ave, come making nasty suggestions to a mother, with five kids too—I'm not so daft as you think I am, I've got my 'ead screwed on all right, good thing for me I 'ave. Listen 'ere, Sir, there's a police hinspector lives right in this very 'ouse, I'll charge you, I will, I'll 'ave you arrested, and then there's my old man too to look after my hinterests . . . Oh, no! Don't need nobody, 'e don't, eh? We'll see about that!

GENTLEMAN: [*who does not look at all menacing, turns towards* THE CARETAKER; *he is extremely calm, does not raise his voice and keeps his dignity perfectly, but he gives a surprising impression of authority*] Please don't upset yourself! Take my advice and accept my apologies; otherwise you will only make yourself ill!

CARETAKER: [*somewhat intimidated*] How dare you talk to me like that! To me! Mother of five children! You won't 'ave me on like that, you won't! Now just you listen to me! You no sooner get 'ere and you 'ave me come upstairs, you takes me on, and then, without not so much as a by-your-leave, you turns me out again! When the old couple were 'ere, 'ere in this very room where you're standing now . . .

GENTLEMAN: [*without making a gesture—his hands folded behind his back*] May I suggest you go back to your work? The postman may have called.
[THE CARETAKER *stops talking as though she were suddenly really frightened;* THE GENTLEMAN, *motionless, stares at her; then he goes back to the vase to admire it; taking advantage of the fact that* THE GENTLEMAN'S *back is turned,* THE CARETAKER *makes a dash for the door on the right, muttering to herself.*]

CARETAKER: The vase is a bit of all right! [*Then, having reached the door, she cries in a louder voice:*] A mother of five kids! You won't 'ave me on a bit of string! I'll go and see the hinspector, I will! [*As she turns to go out she bumps into the* 2ND FURNITURE MOVER, *who is just coming in.*] Watch where you're going! [*Then she goes out, still shouting:*] You won't 'ave me on! You won't 'ave me on!
[*While* THE GENTLEMAN *turns to the newcomer.*]

2ND FURNITURE MOVER: Good-day, Sir. I've come about your furniture, Sir.

GENTLEMAN: Ah, yes! Good morning. Thank you. Your associate is here already. [*He points to the left, over his shoulder.*]

2ND FURNITURE MOVER: Good, I'll go and help him. [*He crosses the stage towards the door on the left; as he does so he catches sight of the two little stools and the little vase in the corner, which must be about eighteen inches high.*] I see he's already started bringing them up.

GENTLEMAN: Oh, yes! He's already started bringing them up.

2ND FURNITURE MOVER: Has he been here long?

GENTLEMAN: No, only a few minutes.

2ND FURNITURE MOVER: Is there much left?

GENTLEMAN: Quite a lot, yet. [*Noise off left.*] He's coming up now.

1ST FURNITURE MOVER: [*offstage*] Are you there, Fred? Come and give me a hand, will you?
[*The* 2ND FURNITURE MOVER *goes off left, disappears for a moment and then he can just be seen coming in again backwards and straining hard; meanwhile* THE GENTLEMAN *holds out his arm to indicate different places in the room, pointing to the floor, to the walls, etc., as though it were helping him to imagine the arrangement of the furniture, saying:*]

GENTLEMAN: One . . . two . . . three . . . four . . . one . . .
[*The* 2ND FURNITURE MOVER, *coming in backwards, is almost completely visible, though it is still not possible to see what he is carrying with so much difficulty; from the wings can be heard the voice of the—*]

1ST FURNITURE MOVER: [*straining*] That's it . . . go ahead now!

GENTLEMAN: [*as before*] One . . . two . . . three . . . four . . . one . . .

[*Both* FURNITURE MOVERS *are now visible, struggling to carry between them another empty vase, identical with the first, and obviously extremely light in weight; but their united effort should appear tremendous, so much so that they are in fact stumbling under their burden.*]

1ST FURNITURE MOVER: Come on now—once more! . . .

2ND FURNITURE MOVER: Keep a good grip on it, there! . . .

GENTLEMAN: [*as before*] One . . . two . . . three . . .

1ST FURNITURE MOVER: [*to* THE GENTLEMAN] Where's this one got to go?

GENTLEMAN: [*turning towards them*] Let's see . . . yes, put it there, please! [*He points to a spot to the left of the door on the left, near the footlights.*] That's it!

[*The two* FURNITURE MOVERS *have put the vase down; they straighten up, rubbing their arms and their backs, taking off their caps to wipe their forehead; meanwhile* THE CARETAKER's *voice can be heard from time to time raised in conversation and mixed up with other voices, but all the noise will subside gradually.*]

2ND FURNITURE MOVER: Well, I hope everything's not going to be like that!

GENTLEMAN: Are you tired, gentlemen?

1ST FURNITURE MOVER: Oh, it's nothing . . . we're used to it, you know . . . [*To his colleague:*] Mustn't waste time! Shall we go? [*They both go out through the door on the left, while—*]

GENTLEMAN: [*counting*] One . . . two . . . three . . . four . . . one . . . two . . . three . . . [*Then he moves about choosing the places to put things and sometimes using the tape-measure he is holding in his hand.*] There, that will be fine . . . and we can put that there . . . and that can go here . . . That's it . . .

[*The* 1ST FURNITURE MOVER *comes in from the left carrying another vase, this time by himself but still with difficulty.* THE GENTLEMAN *points towards the other side of the stage, to the righthand corner at the back. The* 1ST FURNITURE MOVER *goes and puts the object down, while* THE GENTLEMAN *goes on measuring:*] One . . . two . . . three . . . five . . . one . . . two . . . seven . . . Good . . . that's it . . . that'll be fine . . .

1ST FURNITURE MOVER: Is that where you want it, Sir?

[*The larger and heavier the articles that the* FURNITURE MOVERS *bring on, the easier they seem to carry them, until finally it looks like child's play.*]

GENTLEMAN: Yes, that will do nicely.

[*Then the* 1ST FURNITURE MOVER *goes off left while the* 2ND FURNITURE MOVER *comes in through the same door, carrying another vase exactly like the rest.*]

Will you put it there, please? [*He points to the right-hand corner, near the footlights.*]

2ND FURNITURE MOVER: Ah, yes! [*He puts it down and goes off left while the* 1ST FURNITURE MOVER *comes in through the same door carrying two more tiny stools, exactly like the first ones, and still with great effort.*]

1ST FURNITURE MOVER: And where are these to go, Sir?

GENTLEMAN: [*pointing either side of the door on the right*] There and there, of course; then they'll match the two on the other side.

1ST FURNITURE MOVER: Of course, I should have thought . . . [*The* 1ST FURNITURE MOVER *sets the objects down in their place.*] Phew! Is there still any room left? [*He stops for a moment, with nothing in his hands, in the middle of the room, then he goes off left.*]

GENTLEMAN: There'll be enough. There's sure to be enough. I have it all worked out. [*To the* 2ND FURNITURE MOVER, *who enters from the left, with a suitcase:*] Put it there please . . . [*He points to the right of the window at the back; as the* 2ND FURNITURE MOVER *moves towards the spot,* THE GENTLEMAN *stops him.*] I'm sorry. Not there. There . . . [THE GENTLEMAN *points to the left of the window; the* 2ND FURNITURE MOVER *sets the object down, saying:*]

2ND FURNITURE MOVER: Right, Sir. It would help if you could be a little more definite, Sir.

GENTLEMAN: Why, yes, of course.

2ND FURNITURE MOVER: And then we won't tire ourselves out unnecessarily.

GENTLEMAN: Of course, I understand.

1ST FURNITURE MOVER: [*coming in from the left with a pedestal table while the* 2ND FURNITURE MOVER *goes out left*] And this? Where shall I put this?

GENTLEMAN: Ah yes . . . let me see . . . it's not easy to find the right little place for that . . .

1ST FURNITURE MOVER: Here, perhaps, Sir! [*He carries the table to the left of the window.*]

GENTLEMAN: The ideal place! [*These tables are all in different shapes and colours.*] Ideal!

2ND FURNITURE MOVER: [*coming in left with another pedestal table*] And this?

GENTLEMAN: [*indicating a place to the left of the first table*] Here, if you don't mind.

2ND FURNITURE MOVER: [*puts it down*] But there won't be any room for your plates!

GENTLEMAN: Everything's been accounted for.

2ND FURNITURE MOVER: [*looking round the stage*] I don't quite see . . .

GENTLEMAN: Yes, I assure you.

2ND FURNITURE MOVER: Well, if you say so. [*He goes off left, while the* 1ST FURNITURE MOVER *arrives, with another table.*]

GENTLEMAN: [*to* 1ST FURNITURE MOVER] Beside the last one. [*Then while the* 1ST FURNITURE MOVER *places the table in position and goes out, and the* 2ND FURNITURE MOVER *comes in, still from the left, with another table,* THE GENTLEMAN *traces a circle on the floor in chalk; then, more carefully, a larger circle in the middle of the stage;* THE GENTLEMAN *stops and straightens up to show the* 2ND FURNITURE MOVER *where to put his latest pedestal table:*] There, along by the wall, next to the other! [*While the* 2ND FURNITURE MOVER *puts it down,* THE GENTLEMAN, *who has finished tracing his circle, straightens up again and says:*] That will be fine! [*While the* 2ND FURNITURE MOVER *goes off, still on the left, the* 1ST FURNITURE MOVER *arrives with another pedestal table:*] Next to the last one!

[*He points out the place, the* 1ST FURNITURE MOVER *puts it down*

and goes off left. THE GENTLEMAN, *alone for a moment, counts the pedestal tables.*]
Yes . . . that's it . . . now we shall have to . . . [*The* 2ND FURNITURE MOVER *comes in from the right with another pedestal table.*] All round the room . . . [*Then, from the left, the* 1ST FURNITURE MOVER.] All around . . .

> [*Both* FURNITURE MOVERS *go off, the* 1ST *on the left, to come on again from the right, the* 2ND *on the right, to come in again from the left, and they bring on more tables and other objects such as chairs, screens, table-lamps, piles of books, etc., which they set down, one after the other, all round the stage and along the walls, meeting and passing each other as they do so. The movement is carried out in such a way that there is always one* FURNITURE MOVER *on the stage throughout the scene that follows.*]

All around the room, all around . . . all around . . . [*Then, when the walls are all lined with the first row of furniture,* THE GENTLEMAN *says to the* 1ST FURNITURE MOVER, *who comes in, empty-handed, from the left:*] Now you can bring a step-ladder! [*The* 1ST FURNITURE MOVER *goes out the way he came in, the* 2ND FURNITURE MOVER *comes on from the right.*] A step-ladder! [*The* 2ND FURNITURE MOVER *goes out the way he came in.* THE GENTLEMAN *is looking round the walls and rubbing his hands together:*] There now! Now it's beginning to take shape. It'll be a very comfortable sort of place. It won't be at all bad.

> [*The two* FURNITURE MOVERS *come in from the left and right, each from the side opposite to the one they went out;* THE GENTLEMAN *indicates to the one coming from the left the wall on the right, and vice-versa; he says nothing.*]

1ST FURNITURE MOVER: Right ho!
2ND FURNITURE MOVER: Right ho!

> [*They cross and place their ladders against the walls indicated.*]

GENTLEMAN: Leave the ladders there. You can bring in the pictures now! [*They come down their ladders and go off right and left. As he moves towards the exit, the* 2ND FURNITURE MOVER *steps on one of the chalk circles, the one in the middle of the stage.*] Be careful there! Don't spoil my circle.
2ND FURNITURE MOVER: Oh, yes! We'll try not to.
GENTLEMAN: Be careful! [*The* 2ND FURNITURE MOVER *goes out while the* 1ST FURNITURE MOVER *enters from the opposite side with a large painting representing the head of a hideous old man.*] Be careful, be careful of my circles. [*This said in a calm and neutral tone.*]
1ST FURNITURE MOVER: I'll try. It's not easy when you're loaded . . .
GENTLEMAN: Now hang the picture up . . .
1ST FURNITURE MOVER: Yes, Sir. [*He climbs up the ladder and carefully hangs the picture. The* 2ND FURNITURE MOVER *enters from the side opposite the one from which the* 1ST FURNITURE MOVER *has just come in, also carrying a large painting representing another hideous old man.*]
GENTLEMAN: My ancestors. [*To the* 2ND FURNITURE MOVER:] Now go up the ladder and hang the picture.

2ND FURNITURE MOVER: [*going up the ladder against the opposite wall, holding the picture*] It's not easy, with all your circles. Especially when we come to the heavy objects. We can't watch out for everything. [*He busies himself hanging the picture.*]

GENTLEMAN: Oh yes, you can, if you really want to. [THE GENTLEMAN *picks up from amongst the various objects brought on the stage a book or a box or some other still smaller object and takes it to the centre of the stage where he sets it down after having inspected it by raising it above his head; meanwhile, the workmen are busy fixing the paintings carefully on the two walls;* THE GENTLEMAN *could also adjust the position of some of the furniture slightly or retrace his chalk circles again; all this without a word spoken. A slight sound of hammers and the other exterior noises can still be heard, but already transformed into music.* THE GENTLEMAN *contemplates the painting and the room in general with an air of satisfaction. The two workmen have finished, and so has* THE GENTLEMAN: *the work should have lasted some time, acted without words. The* FURNITURE MOVERS *come down from their ladders; they go and put the ladders where there is still a little space, as for example near the two doors; then they join* THE GENTLEMAN, *who studies first one of the pictures, then the other.*]

1ST FURNITURE MOVER: [*pointing to the two pictures, speaking to* THE GENTLEMAN] All right?

GENTLEMAN: [*to* FURNITURE MOVER] All right?

2ND FURNITURE MOVER: Looks all right to me.

GENTLEMAN: [*inspecting the pictures*] They're firmly fixed. [*Pause*] Bring in the heavy objects.

2ND FURNITURE MOVER: It's thirsty work! [*Mops his brow.*]

GENTLEMAN: We must have the sideboard then. [*Both* FURNITURE MOVERS *go towards the door on the right;* THE GENTLEMAN *turns towards the window.*] One . . . yes . . . one here . . .

> [*Before the two* FURNITURE MOVERS *can reach the door on the right, the two folding doors open of themselves and a sideboard slides onto the stage, propelled by an invisible force; the folding doors close again and the* FURNITURE MOVERS *seize the sideboard and glance towards* THE GENTLEMAN, *who with a gesture shows them where to put it.*]

BOTH FURNITURE MOVERS: [*who are now near the centre of the stage*] Where?

GENTLEMAN: [*his back to the audience, his hands extended towards the window*] But there, of course! . . .

1ST FURNITURE MOVER: You'll shut out all the light.

GENTLEMAN: There's electric light, isn't there?

> [*The* 1ST FURNITURE MOVER *pushes the sideboard against the window; it fails to block it up completely; it is not high enough. The* 2ND FURNITURE MOVER *goes to one of the doors and switches on the ceiling light; he takes hold of a picture representing a winter landscape, which has glided on to the stage by itself through the folding doors, and places it on top of the sideboard: this time the window is completely masked. The* 1ST FURNITURE MOVER *opens the side-*

> board, takes a bottle out, takes a swig from it, passes it to the 2ND
> FURNITURE MOVER, who does the same, and then offers it to THE
> GENTLEMAN.]

No, thank you. I never touch it.

> [Then both the FURNITURE MOVERS drink in turn out of the bottle,
> handing it backwards and forwards, and looking at the blocked-up
> window.]

Much better, like that.

> [The two FURNITURE MOVERS, too, still drinking from time to time,
> turn to face the window concealed by the sideboard and the canvas
> representing winter, so that, in this way, all three have their backs
> to the audience.]

1ST FURNITURE MOVER: [with approval] Ah ha!

2ND FURNITURE MOVER: [with approval] Ah ha!

GENTLEMAN: It's not quite right [Indicating the picture.] I don't like it . . .
Turn it round!

> [The two FURNITURE MOVERS turn the picture round while THE GEN-
> TLEMAN watches them; only the back of the picture is to be seen, with
> its dark frame and hanging cord; then the two FURNITURE MOVERS step
> away a little and again pick up the bottle and go on drinking; then
> they go and stand on either side of THE GENTLEMAN, still with their
> backs to the audience, and again gaze at the sideboard with the
> picture on top of it in silence for several moments.]

I like it better like that.

1ST FURNITURE MOVER: It's much nicer.

GENTLEMAN: Much nicer. More restrained.

2ND FURNITURE MOVER: Much nicer. More restrained.

GENTLEMAN: Ah, yes, it's very much nicer, more restrained.

1ST FURNITURE MOVER: Ah yes . . .

2ND FURNITURE MOVER: Ah yes . . .

GENTLEMAN: You can't see anything now.

1ST FURNITURE MOVER: Well, that's something.

> [Silence]

2ND FURNITURE MOVER: [after a moment, turning the bottle neck downwards]
There isn't any more.

1ST FURNITURE MOVER: The last drop.

2ND FURNITURE MOVER: [still holding the bottle in the same way, to THE GEN-
TLEMAN] There isn't any more.

GENTLEMAN: I don't think so either. [The 1ST FURNITURE MOVER takes the
bottle from the 2ND FURNITURE MOVER and puts it in the sideboard, which
he closes.] Won't have any more trouble from the neighbours now.

1ST FURNITURE MOVER: Better for everybody.

2ND FURNITURE MOVER: Everybody will be happy.

GENTLEMAN: Everyone will be happy. [A moment of silence.] To work. Let's
go on. My armchair.

1ST FURNITURE MOVER: Where can we put it?

2ND FURNITURE MOVER: Where can we put it?

GENTLEMAN: In the circle. [*He points to the circle in the middle.*] You won't be able to spoil my circle any more.

1ST FURNITURE MOVER: [*to* THE GENTLEMAN] You'll be able to see it better.

GENTLEMAN: [*to the* 1ST FURNITURE MOVER] Will you go and fetch it?

> [*The* 1ST FURNITURE MOVER *goes to the door on the right. To the* 2ND FURNITURE MOVER:] Now for the heavy furniture in pink wood. [*The* 1ST FURNITURE MOVER *arrives at the door on the right; the armchair glides on, pushed from behind; he takes hold of it. The* 2ND FURNITURE MOVER *goes to the door on the left; half a wardrobe appears; he seizes hold of it and pulls it towards the centre of the stage; all the movements have slowed down; from now on all the furniture comes on through the two doors alternately, propelled from behind; each item only half appears; the* FURNITURE MOVERS *pull it towards them, and when it has been pulled right into the room, something else slides on, half visible, and so on. The* 1ST FURNITURE MOVER, *then, has hold of the armchair, while the other man is pulling through the other doorway a huge wardrobe lying on its side; the* 1ST FURNITURE MOVER *sets the armchair down within the circle.*]

GENTLEMAN: [*looking at the pink wardrobe*] It's a beautiful pink, isn't it?

1ST FURNITURE MOVER: [*after placing the armchair within the circle*] Good armchair.

GENTLEMAN: [*feeling the upholstery*] Yes, it's very soft. Well-upholstered. [*To the* 1ST FURNITURE MOVER:] Please don't stop bringing the things in. [*The* 1ST FURNITURE MOVER *goes to the door on the right, where he finds a second pink wardrobe on its side; the* 2ND FURNITURE MOVER, *still dragging his wardrobe on, glances at* THE GENTLEMAN, *as though asking silently where to put it.*]

There!

> [*The wardrobes in question—there could be four in all—will be disposed, always according to* THE GENTLEMAN's *directions, along the three walls, parallel to the other rows of furniture; first one, then the other of the two* FURNITURE MOVERS *will dart a questioning look at* THE GENTLEMAN *each time they have succeeded in dragging the furniture clear of the folding doors and* THE GENTLEMAN *will point and say to them:*]

There! There! There! There!

> [*At each 'There!', the* FURNITURE MOVERS *nod their heads affirmatively and bring the furniture in; after the four wardrobes come smaller items—some more tables, settees too, wickerwork baskets, strange furniture never seen before, etc. It is all placed in front of the rest along the three walls, so that* THE GENTLEMAN *is confined in an ever-diminishing space in the centre of the stage; the action is like a ponderous kind of ballet and all the movements are made very slowly. While the* FURNITURE MOVERS *are still bringing on the furniture and questioning him silently, while the furniture is still sliding on to the stage, pushed on from behind,* THE GENTLEMAN *is in the center, with one hand on the back of the armchair and the other pointing:*]

There . . . There . . . There . . . There . . . There . . . There . . .
There . . . There . . . There . . . There . . . There . . . There . . .
There . . . There . . . There . . . There . . . [*It should be arranged so
that this action lasts a long time; in a slow and broken rhythm. Then,
at a certain moment, the* 1ST FURNITURE MOVER *brings on a radio set
from the right; when his questioning glance alights on* THE GENTLEMAN,
the latter says, in a voice scarcely louder than before:] Oh no! Oh dear
me no!

1ST FURNITURE MOVER: It doesn't work.

GENTLEMAN: Well, in that case . . . yes. Here. [*He indicates a spot near the
armchair; the* 1ST FURNITURE MOVER *deposits the article and moves off
towards the right for more, while the* 2ND FURNITURE MOVER *comes up
from the left, with the same look of interrogation, carrying a chamber-pot;
to the* 2ND FURNITURE MOVER:] Why yes, of course . . . here.

[*He points to the other side of the armchair; the* 2ND FURNITURE
MOVER *lays the chamber-pot down and then they both move off
their own side and come back again with other furniture so that the
space surrounding* THE GENTLEMAN *gets smaller and smaller; now
the action continues without words, in complete silence; little by little
the sounds from outside,* THE CARETAKER's *voice, etc., have died
away; the* FURNITURE MOVERS *pad about noiselessly; the furniture
appears on the stage quite silently; each time the* FURNITURE MOVERS
introduce a new item they still look questioningly at THE GENTLEMAN
*and the latter still indicates by gesture, without uttering a word,
where to put the various articles, which are slowly but surely closing
in on him. This dumb show, with its broken mechanical movements,
should also last a long time, even longer, perhaps, than the previous
scene of* THE GENTLEMAN's '*There . . . There . . . There . . . There*':
finally the 2ND FURNITURE MOVER *brings on an enormous wall-clock
from the left, while the other* FURNITURE MOVER *continues as before;
when* THE GENTLEMAN *sees the clock, he shows surprise and uncertainty, then finally makes a sign of refusal; while the* 2ND FURNITURE
MOVER *takes the clock away to bring up another piece of furniture
the* 1ST FURNITURE REMOVER *arrives with a second clock that resembles the first in every respect;* THE GENTLEMAN *dismisses him with a
gesture, then changes his mind.*]

GENTLEMAN: But wait . . . after all, why not? [*The clock is brought up to the
armchair, and* THE GENTLEMAN *points to a place near it; next the* 2ND
FURNITURE MOVER *comes back with a large and very high screen; as he
reaches the armchair the* 1ST FURNITURE MOVER *comes up from his side
also carrying a screen of the same height.*]

2ND FURNITURE MOVER: There'll be no room left!

GENTLEMAN: Oh, yes, there will. [*He sits down in his armchair within the
circle.*] Like this there will.

[*The* FURNITURE MOVERS *bring up a second and then a third screen
and enclose* THE GENTLEMAN *on three sides, within the circle. Only
the side facing the audience remains open.* THE GENTLEMAN *is sitting
in the armchair, with his hat on his head, his face turned towards*

the public; on each side, the two FURNITURE MOVERS, *their bodies hidden behind the screens, poke their heads round to have a look at* THE GENTLEMAN.]

1ST FURNITURE MOVER: All right? You comfortable now?

[THE GENTLEMAN *nods his head.*]

It's good to feel at home.

2ND FURNITURE MOVER: You must have got tired. I should have a little rest.

GENTLEMAN: Don't stop, will you? . . . Is there still much left?

[*Dumb show.* THE GENTLEMAN *is seated, motionless, hat on head, facing the audience; the two* FURNITURE MOVERS *make their way, each to one of the two entrances; the folding doors are wide open; the two openings are completely blocked and one can only see great wooden boards, green on the left, purple on the right, as high as the doors themselves, apparently the backs of tall, wide wardrobes; synchronizing their movements, each man looks at the door in front of him and scratches his head underneath his cap in a puzzled way; they shrug their shoulders and put their hands on their hips simultaneously; then, still moving together, they step back amongst the furniture, each man on his own side of the stage and gape at each other. Then:*]

1ST FURNITURE MOVER: What shall we do?

2ND FURNITURE MOVER: What shall we do?

GENTLEMAN: [*without moving*] Is there still much left? Isn't it finished yet?

[*The* 1ST FURNITURE MOVER, *without answering* THE GENTLEMAN, *makes a meaningful gesture directed at the* 2ND FURNITURE MOVER, *a gesture expressing bewilderment, which the* 2ND FURNITURE MOVER *repeats. Without moving, still very calm:*]

Have you brought up *all* the furniture?

[*Dumb show for a moment. Both* FURNITURE MOVERS, *still standing where they were, turn towards their respective doors, and then towards* THE GENTLEMAN, *who can no longer see them.*]

1ST FURNITURE MOVER: It's really rather awkward, Sir.

GENTLEMAN: What is?

2ND FURNITURE MOVER: The rest of the furniture's very big and the doors aren't.

1ST FURNITURE MOVER: Can't get it in.

GENTLEMAN: What is it that's left?

1ST FURNITURE MOVER: Wardrobes.

GENTLEMAN: The green and the purple ones?

2ND FURNITURE MOVER: Yes.

1ST FURNITURE MOVER: And that's not all. There's more to come.

2ND FURNITURE MOVER: The staircase is jammed from top to bottom. Nobody can get up or down.

GENTLEMAN: The yard is cram-full too. So is the street.

1ST FURNITURE MOVER: The traffic's come to a standstill in the town. Full of furniture.

2ND FURNITURE MOVER: [*to* THE GENTLEMAN] At least you've nothing to complain about, Sir. You've got somewhere to sit.

1ST FURNITURE MOVER: Perhaps the tube's still running.

2ND FURNITURE MOVER: No, it isn't.

GENTLEMAN: [*still as before*] No. All the underground lines are blocked.

2ND FURNITURE MOVER: [*to* THE GENTLEMAN] Some furniture! It's cluttering up the whole country.

GENTLEMAN: The Thames has stopped flowing, too. Dammed up. No more water.

1ST FURNITURE MOVER: What can we do then, if we can't get any more in?

GENTLEMAN: It can't be left outside, because of the weather.

[*The* FURNITURE MOVERS *are still speaking from their respective positions.*]

1ST FURNITURE MOVER: Might be able to get it in through the attic. But then . . . we'd have to break the ceiling in.

2ND FURNITURE MOVER: Not necessary. Modern house. Sliding ceiling. [*To* THE GENTLEMAN:] Did you know?

GENTLEMAN: No.

2ND FURNITURE MOVER: Well, there you are. It's easy. Just have to clap your hands. [*He makes the gesture.*] The ceiling opens.

GENTLEMAN: [*from his armchair*] No . . . I'm afraid of the rain on the furniture. It's new and easily spoilt.

2ND FURNITURE MOVER: No fear of that, Sir. I know how it works. The ceiling opens and closes, opens and closes, just as you want.

1ST FURNITURE MOVER: Come on then, perhaps we can . . .

GENTLEMAN: [*from his armchair*] Providing you close it again at once. No carelessness, mind.

1ST FURNITURE MOVER: We won't forget. *I'm* on the job. [*To the* 2ND FURNITURE MOVER:] Ready?

2ND FURNITURE MOVER: Yes.

1ST FURNITURE MOVER: [*to* THE GENTLEMAN] All right?

GENTLEMAN: Right.

1ST FURNITURE MOVER: [*to the* 2ND FURNITURE MOVER] Go ahead.

[*The* 2ND FURNITURE MOVER *claps his hands. From the ceiling huge planks descend at the front of the stage, completely hiding from view* THE GENTLEMAN *in his high-walled enclosure; a few could also come down on to the stage amongst the furniture; the new tenant is thus completely walled-in; clambering over the furniture the* 1ST FURNITURE MOVER, *after knocking three times without response on one of the screens at the side, makes his way, with a ladder, to the place where the planks have completed the enclosure; he holds in one hand a bunch of flowers that he tries to hide from the audience; silently he leans his ladder up against the end plank on the right; when he has reached the top, he looks down into the enclosure and calls out to* THE GENTLEMAN:]

That's it, Sir. Everything in. Are you nice and comfortable? Has the move gone off to your satisfaction?

GENTLEMAN'S VOICE: [*just as it has always been; slightly muffled, that's all*] Ceiling. Close ceiling, please.

1ST FURNITURE MOVER: [*from the top of the ladder to his mate*] He wants you to close the ceiling. You forgot.

2ND FURNITURE MOVER: [*in the same spot*] Oh, yes. [*He claps for the ceiling to close again.*] There you are.

GENTLEMAN'S VOICE: Thank you.

1ST FURNITURE MOVER: [*on the ladder*] Ah well, you've got a good sheltered spot there, you won't be cold . . . Are you all right?

GENTLEMAN'S VOICE: [*after a silence*] All right.

1ST FURNITURE MOVER: Hand me your hat, Sir, it might worry you.

[*After a short pause,* THE GENTLEMAN's *hat can be seen appearing from within the enclosure.*]

1ST FURNITURE MOVER: [*taking the hat and throwing the flowers down inside*] That's right. You'll be more comfortable like that. Here are some flowers for you. [*To the* 2ND FURNITURE MOVER:] Is that all?

2ND FURNITURE MOVER: That's all.

1ST FURNITURE MOVER: Good. [*To* THE GENTLEMAN:] We've brought every-thing, Sir, you're really at home now. [*He comes down off the ladder.*] We'll be off. [*He leans the ladder against the wall, or perhaps he can prop it up, gently, without making a noise, somewhere amongst the other objects that hem* THE GENTLEMAN *in. To the* 2ND FURNITURE MOVER:] Come on.

[*The two* FURNITURE MOVERS, *each still keeping to his own side, make their way, blindly and tentatively, to the back of the stage, towards invisible and problematical exits, Heaven knows where; for the window is stopped up and through the open folding doors you can still see the violently coloured wood that blocks the way.*]

1ST FURNITURE MOVER: [*at a certain moment, he stops,* THE GENTLEMAN's *hat in his hand, turns round and directs his words from one end of the stage towards the concealed* GENTLEMAN] Is there anything you want?

[*Silence*]

2ND FURNITURE MOVER: Is there anything you want?

GENTLEMAN'S VOICE: [*after a silence; not a movement on the stage*] Put out the light. [*Utter darkness.*] Thank you.

CURTAIN

DAVID RABE

STICKS AND BONES

CHARACTERS

OZZIE
HARRIET
DAVID
RICK
ZUNG (THE GIRL)
FATHER DONALD
SERGEANT MAJOR

TIME: *Autumn*
PLACE: *The family home*

ACT I

Place: the family home.

Darkness; silence. Slides appear on both sides of the stage: the first is a black-and-white medium close-up of a young man, mood and clothing of the early 1900s; he is lean, reasonably handsome, black hair parted in the center. Voices speak. They are slow and relaxed, with an improvisational quality.

1ST CHILD'S VOICE: Who zat?

MAN'S VOICE: Grandpa Jacob's father.

    [New slide: group photo, same era, eight or ten people, all ages.]

2ND CHILD'S VOICE: Look at 'em all!

1ST CHILD'S VOICE: How come they're all so serious?

    [New slide: small boy, black hair, black knickers.]

WOMAN'S VOICE: There's Grandpa Oswald as a little boy.

1ST CHILD'S VOICE: Grandpa?

    [New slide: different boy, same pose.]

WOMAN'S VOICE: And that's his brother Thomas. He died real young.

MAN'S VOICE: Scarlet fever.

    [New slide: young girl, seventeen or eighteen.]

    And that's his sister Christina.

WOMAN'S VOICE: No, that's Grandma.

MAN'S VOICE: No.

WOMAN'S VOICE: Sure.

    [New slide: Ozzie and Harriet, young, 1940s era.]

    There's the two of them.

MAN'S VOICE: Mmmmm, you're right, because that's Grandpa.

[*New slide: two boys, five and nine years old.*]

WOMAN'S VOICE: The taller one's David, right?

[*New slide: color close-up of David from the last moment of the play, a stricken look.*]

1ST CHILD'S VOICE: What's that one?

MAN'S VOICE: Somebody sick.

1ST CHILD'S VOICE: Boy . . . !

[*New slide: color photo of Ozzie, Harriet, and Father Donald. Father Donald, wearing a gym suit, his back to the camera, stands holding a basketball in one hand. Ozzie and Harriet face him, one on either side.*]

2ND CHILD'S VOICE: Oh, look at that one!

MAN'S VOICE: That's a funny one, isn't it.

WOMAN'S VOICE: That's one—I bet somebody took it—they didn't know it was going to be taken.

[*There is a bright flash and the stage is immediately illuminated. The set is an American home, very modern, with a quality of brightness, green walls, green rug. Stairs lead up to a bedroom—not lighted now —with a hallway leading off to the rest of the upstairs beyond. There is a naturalness, yet a sense of space and, oddly, a sense also that this room, these stairs belong in the gloss of an advertisement.*]

[*Downstage, a TV on wheels faces upstage, glowing, murmuring. Ozzie, Harriet, and Father Donald—a slightly rotund, serious man— are standing as they were in the slide last seen.*]

FATHER DONALD: A feel for it is the big thing. A feel for the ball. You know, I mean, bouncing it, dribbling it. You don't even look at it.

[*Phone rings.*]

OZZIE: I'll get it.

FATHER DONALD: You can do it, Harriet. Give it a try. [*He bounces the ball to Harriet.*]

OZZIE: Hello? . . .

FATHER DONALD: [*as Harriet catches the ball*]. That a girl.

HARRIET: Oh, Father . . .

OZZIE: [*hanging up*] Nobody there.

FATHER DONALD: That's what I'm telling you. You gotta help kids. Keeps 'em outa trouble. We help. Organized sports activities; it does 'em a world a good. You know that. And they need you.

OZZIE: I was a track and field man. Miler. Dash man—I told you.

[*Phone rings.*]

FATHER DONALD: But this is basketball season. [*He moves toward Harriet and then the door, as Ozzie goes to the phone, says "Hello," then listens intently.*] You listen to me, you get that husband of yours out there to help us. It'll do him good. Tell him he'd be a good little guard. A play maker.

HARRIET: Oh, Father Donald, bless me.

FATHER DONALD: Of course. [*He blesses her, holding the ball under his left arm.*] Bye-bye.

HARRIET: [*as Father Donald goes*] Good-bye, Father.

[*And she turns to look for a moment at* OZZIE *on the phone.*]
Why aren't you talking?

[*Silence: she is looking at him.*]
Ozzie, why aren't you talking?

OZZIE: [*slowly lowering the phone.*] They're gone. They hung up.

HARRIET: You didn't say a word. You said nothing.

OZZIE: I said my name.

HARRIET: What did they want?

OZZIE: I said hello.

HARRIET: Were they selling something—is that what they wanted?

OZZIE: No, no.

HARRIET: Well . . . who was it?

OZZIE: What?

HARRIET: What are we talking about?

OZZIE: The Government. It was . . . you know. . . .

HARRIET: Ozzie! [*In fear*] No!

OZZIE: [*some weariness in him*] No, he's all right, he's coming home!

HARRIET: Why didn't you let me speak? Who was it?

OZZIE: No, no.

HARRIET: It was David.

OZZIE: No, somebody else. Some clerk. I don't know who.

HARRIET: You're lying.

OZZIE: No. There was just all this static—it was hard to hear. But he was coming home was part of it, and they had his records and papers but I couldn't talk to him directly even though he was right there, standing right there.

HARRIET: I don't understand.

OZZIE: That's what they said. . . . And he was fine and everything. And he wanted them to say hello for him. He'd lost some weight. He would be sent by truck. I could hear truck engines in the background—revving. They wanted to know my name. I told them.

HARRIET: No more?

OZZIE: They were very professional. Very brusque . . .

HARRIET: No more . . . at all? . . .

[*The front door opens and* RICK *comes in. And the door slams. He is young, seventeen. His hair is long and neat, with sideburns. His clothing is elaborate—very, very up to date. He carries a guitar on his shoulder.*]

RICK: Hi, Mom. Hi, Dad.

HARRIET: Hi, Rick.

OZZIE: Hi, Rick.

HARRIET: Ohhh, Ricky, Ricky, your brother's on his way home. David's coming home!

OZZIE: We just got a call.

RICK: Ohhh, boy!

HARRIET: Isn't that wonderful? Isn't it? Your father talked to him. Oh, I bet you're starving. Sit, sit.

OZZIE: I talked to *somebody*, Rick.

HARRIET: There's fudge and ice cream in the fridge; would you like that?

RICK: Oh, yeah, and could I have some soda?

[*She is on her way to the kitchen, nodding.*]

Wow, some news. I'm awful hungry.

OZZIE: Never had a doubt. A boy like that—if he leaves, he comes back.

RICK: [*as he picks up a comic book*] How about me? What if I left?

OZZIE: Absolutely. Absolutely.

[*Silence. Rick reads the comic.*]

I built jeeps . . . tanks, trucks.

RICK: What?

OZZIE: In the other war, I mean. Number Two. I worked on vehicles. Vehicles were needed and I worked to build them. Sometimes I put on wheels, tightened 'em up. I never . . . served . . . is what I mean. [*Slight pause.*] They got all those people—soldiers, Rick—you see what I mean? They get 'em across the ocean, they don't have any jeeps or tanks or trucks, what are they gonna do, stand around? Wait for a bus on the beachhead? Call a cab?

RICK: No public transportation in a war.

OZZIE: That's right, that's right.

[*Harriet enters, carrying fudge and ice cream.*]

HARRIET: Oh, Ozzie, Ozzie, do you remember—I just remembered that time David locked himself in that old icebox. We didn't know where he was. We looked all over. We couldn't find him. And then there was this icebox in this clearing . . . out in the middle. I'll bet you don't even remember.

OZZIE: Of course I remember.

HARRIET: And he leaped to us. So frightened.

OZZIE: He couldn't even speak—he couldn't even speak—just these noises.

HARRIET: Or that time he fell from that tree.

OZZIE: My God, he was somethin'! If he wasn't fallin', he was gettin' hit.

HARRIET: And then there was that day we went out into the woods. It was just all wind and clouds. We sailed a kite!

OZZIE: I'd nearly forgotten! . . .

RICK: Where was I?

HARRIET: You were just a baby, Rick. We had a picnic.

RICK: I'm gonna get some more soda, okay?

[*Harriet touches him as he passes.*]

OZZIE: What a day that was. I felt great that day.

HARRIET: And then Hank came along. Hank Grenweller. He came from out of the woods calling that—

OZZIE: That's right.

HARRIET: He was happy.

OZZIE: We were all happy. Except he'd come to tell us he was going away, leaving. And then we had that race. Wasn't that the day?

HARRIET: I don't remember.

OZZIE: Hank and me! Hank Grenweller. A foot race. And I beat him. I did it; got him.

HARRIET: Noooo.

OZZIE: It was only inches, but—

HARRIET: Ozzie, he took it easy. He wasn't trying.

OZZIE: He had to do his very best. Always. Never less. That was one thing you knew—no matter what he did or said, it was meant and true. All those long talks. Do you ever miss him?

HARRIET: He was a fine strong man.

OZZIE: I don't know why he left.

HARRIET: Do you remember when he showed us this house?

OZZIE: I remember when he showed me you.

HARRIET: You know that's not true. If it was close—and it was—that race you ran—[*This is not loud: there is intimacy; they are near one another.*] I remember now—it was because he let it be—no other reason. We were all having fun. He didn't want to make you feel badly. He didn't want to ruin all the fun. You know that. You know you do.

RICK: [*calling from the kitchen*] You people want some fudge?

HARRIET: No, Rick.

OZZIE: I don't know he didn't try. I don't know that. [*He stares at Harriet.*]

HARRIET: I think I'll be going up to bed; take a little nap.

RICK: Sleepy, Mom?

HARRIET: A little. [*She is crossing toward Ozzie.*]

RICK: That's a good idea then.

HARRIET: Call me.

RICK: Okay.

HARRIET: Do you know, the day he left? It was a winter day. November, Ozzie. [*She moves toward the stairs.*]

OZZIE: I know.

HARRIET: I prayed; did you know that? Now he's home.

OZZIE: It was a winter day.

HARRIET: [*at the top of the stairs.*] I know.

RICK: [*toying with his guitar*] Night, Mom.
    [*She doesn't answer but disappears down the hall. He looks up and yells after her.*]
    Night, Mom!

HARRIET: [*from off*] Turn off the TV, somebody.
    [RICK *crosses to the TV. He turns it off and wheels it back under the stairs.* OZZIE *watches. Silence.*]

OZZIE: I knew she was praying. She moves her lips.
    [RICK *does not look up. He begins, softly, to strum and tune the guitar.*]
    And something else—yes, sir, boy, oh, boy, I tell you, huh? What a day, huh? [*Slight pause.*] They got seventeen hundred million men they gotta deal with, how they gonna do that without any trucks and tanks and jeeps? But I'm some kinda jerk because I wasn't out there blastin' away,

huh? I was useful. I put my time to use. I been in fights. Fat Kramer.
. . . How we used to fight!
[*Rick strums some notes on the guitar. Ozzie stares at him.*]
How come I'm restless? I . . . seen him do some awful, awful things, ole
Dave. He was a mean . . . foul-tempered little baby. I'm only glad I was
here when they sent him off to do his killing. That's right. [*Silence.*]
I feel like I swallowed ants, that's how restless I am. Outran a bowlin'
ball one time. These guys bet me I couldn't do it and I did, beat it to
the pins. Got a runnin' start, then the—
[*A faint, strange rapping sound has stopped him, spun him around.*]
Did you do that?

RICK: Somebody knockin'.

OZZIE: Knockin'?

RICK: The door, Dad.

OZZIE: Oh.

RICK: You want me to get it?

OZZIE: No, no. It's just so late. [*He moves for the door.*]

RICK: That's all right.

OZZIE: Sure.
[*He opens the door just a crack, as if to stick his head around. But
the door is thrust open and a man enters abruptly. He is black or of
Spanish descent, and is dressed in the uniform of a sergeant major
and wearing many campaign ribbons.*]

SGT. MAJOR: Excuse me. Listen to me. I'd like to speak to the father here.
I'd like to know who . . . is the father? Could . . . you tell me the address?

OZZIE: May I ask who it is who's asking?

SGT. MAJOR: I am. I'm asking. What's the address of this house?

OZZIE: But I mean, who is it that wants to know?

SGT. MAJOR: We called; we spoke. Is this seven-seventeen Dunbar?

OZZIE: Yes.

SGT. MAJOR: What's wrong with you?

OZZIE: Don't you worry about me.

SGT. MAJOR: I have your son.

OZZIE: What?

SGT. MAJOR: Your son.

OZZIE: No.

SGT. MAJOR: But he is. I have papers, pictures, prints. I know your blood and
his. This is the right address. Please. Excuse me. [*He pivots, reaches out
into the dark.*] I am very busy. I have your father, David.
[*He draws DAVID in—a tall, thin boy, blond and, in the shadows,
wearing sunglasses and a uniform of dress greens. In his right hand
is a long, white, red-tipped cane. He moves, probing the air, as the
sergeant major moves him past OZZIE toward the couch, where he
will sit the boy down like a parcel.*]

OZZIE: Dave? . . .

SGT. MAJOR: He's blind.

OZZIE: What?

SGT. MAJOR: Blind.

OZZIE: I don't . . . understand.

SGT. MAJOR: We're very sorry.

OZZIE: [*realizing*] Ohhhhh. Yes. Ohhhh. I see . . . sure. I mean, we didn't know. Nobody said it. I mean, sure, Dave, sure; it's all right—don't you worry. Rick's here, too, Dave—Rick, your brother, tell him hello.

RICK: Hi, Dave.

DAVID: [*worried*] You said . . . "father."

OZZIE: Well . . . there's two of us, Dave; two.

DAVID: Sergeant, you said "home." I don't think so.

OZZIE: Dave, sure.

DAVID: It doesn't feel right.

OZZIE: But it is, Dave—me and Rick—Dad and Rick. Harriet! [*Calling up the stairs*] Harriet!

DAVID: Let me touch their faces. . . . I can't see. [*Rising, his fear increasing*] Let me put my fingers on their faces.

OZZIE: [*hurt, startled*] What? Do what?

SGT. MAJOR: Will that be all right if he does that?

OZZIE: Sure. . . . Sure. . . . Fine.

SGT. MAJOR: [*helping* DAVID *to* OZZIE]. It will take him time.

OZZIE: That's normal and to be expected. I'm not surprised. Not at all. We figured on this. Sure, we did. Didn't we, Rick?

RICK: [*occupied with his camera, an Instamatic*]. I wanna take some pictures, okay? How are you, Dave?

DAVID: What room is this?

OZZIE: Middle room, Dave. TV room. TV's in—

HARRIET: [*on the stairs*] David; . . . Oh, David! . . . David . . .

[*And* OZZIE, *leaving* DAVID, *hurries toward the stairs and looks up at her as she falters, stops, stares.* RICK, *moving near, snaps a picture of her.*]

OZZIE: Harriet . . . don't be upset. . . . They say . . . Harriet, Harriet . . . he can't see! . . . Harriet . . . they say—he—can't . . . see. That man.

HARRIET: [*standing very still*] Can't see? What do you mean?

SGT. MAJOR: He's blind.

HARRIET: No. Who says? No, no.

OZZIE: Look at him. He looks so old. But it's nothing, Harriet, I'm sure.

SGT. MAJOR: I hope you people understand.

OZZIE: It's probably just how he's tired from his long trip.

HARRIET: [*moving toward him*] Oh, you're home now, David.

SGT. MAJOR: [*with a large sheet of paper waving in his hands*]. Who's gonna sign this for me, Mister? It's a shipping receipt. I got to have somebody's signature to show you got him. I got to have somebody's name on the paper.

OZZIE: Let me. All right?

SGT. MAJOR: Just here and here, you see? Your name or mark three times.

As they move toward a table and away from HARRIET, who is near DAVID.

OZZIE: Fine, listen, would you like some refreshments?

SGT. MAJOR: No.

OZZIE: I mean while I do this. Cake and coffee. Of course, you do.

SGT. MAJOR: No.

OZZIE: Sure.

SGT. MAJOR: No. I haven't time. I've got to get going. I've got trucks out there backed up for blocks. Other boys. I got to get on to Chicago, and some of them to Denver and Cleveland, Reno, New Orleans, Boston, Trenton, Watts, Atlanta. And when I get back they'll be layin' all over the grass; layin' there in pieces all over the grass, their backs been broken, their brains jellied, their insides turned into garbage. One-legged boys and no-legged boys. I'm due in Harlem; I got to get to the Bronx and Queens, Cincinnati, Saint Louis, Reading. I don't have time for coffee. I got deliveries to make all across this country.

DAVID: [*with Harriet, his hands on her face, a kind of realization*] Nooooooo. . . . Sergeant . . . nooo; there's something wrong; it all feels wrong. Where are you? Are you here? I don't know these people!

SGT. MAJOR: That's natural, Soldier; it's natural you feel that way.

DAVID: Nooooo.

HARRIET: [*attempting to guide him back to a chair*] David, just sit, be still.

DAVID: Don't you hear me?

OZZIE: Harriet, calm him.

DAVID: The air is wrong; the smells and sounds, the wind.

HARRIET: David, please, please. What is it? Be still. Please . . .

DAVID: GODDAMN YOU, SERGEANT, I AM LONELY HERE! I AM LONELY!

SGT. MAJOR: I got to go. [*And he pivots to leave.*]

DAVID: [*following the sound of the sergeant major's voice*] Sergeant!

SGT. MAJOR: [*whirling, bellowing*] You shut up. You piss-ass soldier, you shut the fuck up!

OZZIE: [*walking to the sergeant major, putting his hand on the man's shoulder*]. Listen, let me walk you to the door. All right? I'd like to take a look at that truck of yours. All right?

SGT. MAJOR: There's more than one.

OZZIE: Fine.

SGT. MAJOR: It's a convoy.

OZZIE: Good.

> [*They exit, slamming the door, and* RICK, *running close behind them, pops it open, leaps out. He calls from off.*]

RICK: Sure are lots a trucks, Mom!

HARRIET: [*as he re-enters.*] Are there?

RICK: Oh, yeah. Gonna rain some more too. [*And turning, he runs up the stairs.*] See you in the morning. Night, Dave.

HARRIET: It's so good to have you here again; so good to see you. You look . . . just . . .

> [*Ozzie has slipped back into the room behind her, he stands, looking.*]

fine. You look—

> [*She senses* OZZIE's *presence, turns, immediately, speaking.*]

He bewilders you, doesn't he?

[*And* OZZIE, *jauntily, heads for the stairs.*]
Where are you going?

[*He stops; he doesn't know. And she is happily sad now as she speaks —sad for poor* OZZIE *and* DAVID, *they are so whimsical, so childlike.*]
You thought you knew what was right, all those years, teaching him sports and fighting. Do you understand what I'm trying to say? A mother knows *things* . . . a father cannot ever know them. The measles, smallpox, cuts and bruises. Never have you come upon him in the night as he lay awake and staring . . . praying.

OZZIE: I saw him put a knife through the skin of a cat. I saw him cut the belly open.

DAVID: Noooo. . . .

HARRIET: [*moving toward him in response*] David, David. . . .

DAVID: Ricky!

[*There is a kind of accusation in this as if he were saying Ricky did the killing of the cat. He says it loudly and directly into her face.*]

HARRIET: He's gone to bed.

DAVID: I want to leave.

[*There is furniture around him; he is caged. He pokes with his cane.*]

HARRIET: What is it?

DAVID: Help me. [*He crashes.*]

OZZIE: Settle down! Relax.

DAVID: I want to leave! I want to leave! I want to leave. I . . .

[*And he smashes into the stairs, goes down, flails, pounding his cane.*]
want to leave.

OZZIE AND HARRIET: Dave! David! Davey!

DAVID: . . . to leave! Please.

[*He is on the floor, breathing. Long, long silence in which they look at him sadly, until* HARRIET *announces the problem's solution.*]

HARRIET: Ozzie, get him some medicine. Get him some Ezy Sleep.

OZZIE: Good idea.

HARRIET: It's in the medicine cabinet; a little blue bottle, little pink pills.
[*And when* OZZIE *is gone up the stairs, there is quiet. She stands over* DAVID.]
It'll give you the sleep you need, Dave—the sleep you remember. You're our child and you're home. Our good . . . beautiful boy.
[*And front door bursts open. There is a small girl in the doorway, an Asian girl. She wears the Vietnamese ao dai, black slacks and white tunic slit up the sides. Slowly, she enters, carrying before her a small straw hat.* HARRIET *is looking at the open door.*]

HARRIET: What an awful . . . wind. [*She shuts the door.*]
[*Blackout. Guitar music.*]

[*A match flickers as Harriet lights a candle in the night. And the girl silently moves from before the door across the floor to the stairs, where she sits, as* HARRIET *moves toward the stairs and* OZZIE, *asleep sitting up in a chair, stirs.*]

HARRIET: Oh! I didn't mean to wake you. I lit a candle so I wouldn't wake you.

[*He stares at her.*]

I'm sorry.

OZZIE: I wasn't sleeping.

HARRIET: I thought you were.

OZZIE: Couldn't. Tried. Couldn't. Thinking. Thoughts running very fast. Trying to remember the night David . . . was made. Do you understand me? I don't know why. But the feeling in me that I had to figure something out and if only I could remember that night . . . the mood . . . I would be able. You're . . . shaking your head.

HARRIET: I don't understand.

OZZIE: No.

HARRIET: Good night.

[*She turns and leaves* OZZIE *sitting there, gazing at the dark. Arriving at David's door, she raps softly and then opens the door.* DAVID *is lying unmoving on the bed. She speaks to him.*]

I heard you call.

DAVID: What?

HARRIET: I heard you call.

DAVID: I didn't.

HARRIET: Would you like a glass of warm milk?

DAVID: I was sleeping.

HARRIET: [*after a slight pause*] How about that milk? Would you like some milk?

DAVID: I didn't call. I was sleeping.

HARRIET: I'll bet you're glad you didn't bring her back. Their skins are yellow, aren't they?

DAVID: What?

HARRIET: You're troubled, warm milk would help. Do you pray at all any more? If I were to pray now, would you pray with me?

DAVID: What . . . do you want?

HARRIET: They eat the flesh of dogs.

DAVID: I know. I've seen them.

HARRIET: Pray with me; pray.

DAVID: What . . . do . . . you want?

HARRIET: Just to talk, that's all. Just to know that you're home and safe again. Nothing else; only that we're all together, a family. You must be exhausted. Don't worry; sleep. [*She is backing into the hallway. In a whisper*] Good night.

[*She blows out the candle and is gone, moving down the hall. Meanwhile the girl is stirring, rising, climbing from the living room up toward David's room, which she enters, moving through a wall, and* DAVID *sits up.*]

DAVID: Who's there?

[*As she drifts by, he waves the cane at the air.*]

Zung? [*He stands.*] Chào, Cô Zung.

[*He moves for the door, which he opens, and steps into the hall, leaving her behind him in the room.*]

Zung. Chào, Cô Zung.

[*And he moves off up the hallway. She follows*]

Zung! . . .

[*Blackout. Music.*]

Lights up. It is a bright afternoon, and ozzie *is under the stairs with a screwdriver in his hand, poking about at the TV set.*

ozzie: C'mon, c'mon. Ohhhh, c'mon, this one more game and ole State's Bowl-bound. C'mon, what is it? Ohhh, hey . . . ohhhhh. . . .

harriet: [*entering from the kitchen carrying a tray with a bowl of soup and a glass of juice*] Ozzie, take this up to David; make him eat it.

ozzie: Harriet, the TV is broke.

harriet: What?

ozzie: There's a picture but no sound. I don't—

[*Grabbing her by the arm, he pulls her toward a place before the set.*]

harriet: Stoppit, you're spilling the soup. [*She pulls free.*]

ozzie: It's Sunday. I want to watch it. I turned it on, picture came on just like normal. I got the volume up full blast.

[*Having set the tray down,* harriet *now shoves the TV set deeper under the stairs, deeper into the place where it is kept when not in use.*]

Hey! I want to watch it!

harriet: I want to talk about David.

ozzie: David's all right.

[*He turns, crosses toward the phone, picks up the phone book.*]

I'm gonna call the repairman.

harriet: [*following him*] Ozzie, he won't eat. He just lays there. I offer him food, he won't eat it. No, no. The TV repairman won't help, you silly. [*She takes the phone book from him.*] He doesn't matter. There's something wrong with David. He's been home days and days and still he speaks only when spoken to; there's no light in his eye, no smile; he's not happy to be here and not once has he touched me or held me, nor has he even shaken your hand.

[ozzie *flops down in a chair.*]

ozzie: Oh, I don't mind that. Why should I mind—

harriet: And now he's talking to himself! What about that? Do you mind that? He mutters in his sleep.

ozzie: [*exasperated*] Ohhhhh.

harriet: Yes. And it's not a regular kind of talking at all. It's very strange—very spooky.

ozzie: Spooky?

harriet: That's right.

ozzie: I never heard him.

harriet: You sleep too deeply. I took a candle and followed. I was in his room. He lay there, speaking.

OZZIE: Speaking what?

HARRIET: I don't know. I couldn't understand.

OZZIE: Was it words?

HARRIET: All kind of funny and fast.

OZZIE: Maybe prayer; praying.

HARRIET: No. No, it was secret. Oh, Ozzie, I know praying when I hear it and it wasn't praying he was doing. We meant our son to be so different —I don't understand—good and strong. And yet . . . perhaps he is. But there are moments when I see him . . . hiding . . . in that bed behind those awful glasses, and I see the chalkiness that's come into—

OZZIE: [*headed for the kitchen, looking for juice to drink*] Those glasses are simply to ease his discomfort.

HARRIET: I hate them.

OZZIE: They're tinted glass and plastic. Don't be so damn suspicious.

HARRIET: I'm not, I'm not. It's seeing I'm doing, not suspicion. Suspicion hasn't any reasons. It's you—now accusing me for no reason when I'm only worried.

OZZIE: [*returning from the kitchen, angered*] Where's my juice?

HARRIET: I want to talk.

OZZIE: The hell with David for a minute—I want some juice.

HARRIET: Shut up. You're selfish. You're so selfish.

OZZIE: [*walking to the tray and juice, attempting to threaten her*] I'll pour it on the floor. I'll break the glass.

  [*She turns to move to get the juice.*]

HARRIET: A few years ago you might have done that kind of thing.

OZZIE: I woke up this morning, I could see so clearly the lovely way you looked when you were young. Beside me this morning, you were having trouble breathing. You kept . . . trying . . . to breathe.

  [*She approaches him to hand him the juice.*]

  What do you give me when you give me this?

HARRIET: I always looked pretty much as I do now. I never looked so different at all.

  [DAVID *appears from off upstairs, dressed in a red robe, and descends toward them.*]

DAVID: [*sounding happy, yet moving with urgency*] Good morning.

OZZIE: Oh, David! Ohhh, good morning. Hello. How do you feel this fine bright morning; how do you feel?

DAVID: He was a big man, wasn't he?

OZZIE: What?

DAVID: Hank. You were talking about Hank Grenweller. I thought you were.

OZZIE: Oh, yes. Hank. Very big. Big. A good fine friend, ole Hank.

DAVID: You felt when he was with you he filled the room.

OZZIE: It was the way he talked that did that. He boomed. His voice just boomed.

DAVID: He was here once and you wanted me to sit on his lap, isn't that right? It was after dinner. He was in a chair in the corner.

HARRIET: That's right.

DAVID: His hand was gone—the bone showed in the skin.

OZZIE: My God, what a memory—did you hear that, Harriet? You were only four or five. He'd just had this terrible, awful auto accident. His hand was hurt, not gone.

DAVID: No. It was congenital and none of us knew.

OZZIE: What?

DAVID: That hand. The sickness in it.

OZZIE: Congenital?

DAVID: Yes.

OZZIE: What do you mean? What do you think you mean?

DAVID: I'd like some coffee.

> [*He is seated now, but not without tension.*]

OZZIE: Hank's parents were good fine people, David.

DAVID: I know.

OZZIE: Well, what are you saying then?

DAVID: I'd like that coffee.

HARRIET: Of course. And what else with it?

DAVID: Nothing.

HARRIET: Oh, no, no, you've got to eat. To get back your strength. You must. Pancakes? How do pancakes sound? Or wheat cakes? Or there's eggs? And juice? Orange or prune: or waffles. I bet it's eggs you want. Over, David? Over easy? Scrambled?

DAVID: I'm only thirsty.

HARRIET: Well, all right then, coffee is what you'll have and I'll just put some eggs on the side, you used to love them so; remember?

> [*And, picking up the tray, she is off toward the kitchen. There is a pause.*]

OZZIE: I mean, I hate to harp on a thing, but I just think you're way off base on Hank, Dave. I just think you're dead wrong.

DAVID: He told me.

OZZIE: Who?

DAVID: Hank.

OZZIE: You . . . talked to Hank?

DAVID: In California. The day before they shipped me overseas.

OZZIE: No, no. He went to Georgia when he left here. We have all his letters postmarked Georgia.

DAVID: [*with great urgency*] It was California, I'm telling you. I was in the barracks. The C.Q. came to tell me there was someone to see me. It was Hank asking did I remember him? He'd seen my name on a list and wondered if I was Ozzie's boy. He was dying, he said. The sickness was congenital. We had a long, long talk.

OZZIE: But his parents were good fine people, David.

DAVID: Don't you understand? We spoke. Why did you make me think him perfect? It was starting in his face the way it started in his hand.

OZZIE: Oh! I didn't realize—I didn't know. You weren't blind. You could see. I didn't realize, Dave.

DAVID: What?

OZZIE: Did he wanna know about me? Did he mention me?

DAVID: [*after thinking a moment*] He asked . . . how you were.

OZZIE: Well, I'm fine. Sure. You told him.

HARRIET: [*entering with a cup of coffee*] It must be so wonderful for you to be home. It must just be so wonderful. A little strange, maybe . . . just a little, but time will take care of all that. It always does. You get sick and you don't know how you're going to get better and then you do. You just do. You must have terrible, awful, ugly dreams, though.

    [*Slight pause.*]

OZZIE: She said you probably have terrible, awful, ugly dreams . . . though.

DAVID: What?

HARRIET: Don't you remember when we spoke last night?

DAVID: Who?

HARRIET: You called to me and then you claimed you hadn't.

DAVID: I didn't.

HARRIET: Ohhh, we had a lovely conversation, David. Of course you called. You called; we talked. We talked and laughed and it was very pleasant. Could I see behind your glasses?

DAVID: What? [*Moving away, crossing in flight from them*] Do . . . what?

HARRIET: See behind your glasses; see your eyes.

OZZIE: Me too, Dave; could we?

DAVID: My eyes . . . are ugly.

OZZIE: We don't mind.

HARRIET: We're your parents, David.

DAVID: I think it better if you don't.

OZZIE: And something else I've been meaning to ask you—why did you cry out against us that first night—to that stranger, I mean, that sergeant?

HARRIET: And you do dream. You do.

OZZIE: Sure. You needn't be ashamed.

HARRIET: We all do it. All of us.

OZZIE: We have things that haunt us.

HARRIET: And it would mean nothing at all—it would be of no consequence at all—if only you didn't speak.

DAVID: I don't understand.

OZZIE: She says she heard you, Dave.

HARRIET: I stood outside your door.

DAVID: No.

OZZIE: A terrible experience for her, Dave; you can see that.

HARRIET: Whatever it is, David, tell us.

OZZIE: What's wrong?

DAVID: No.

HARRIET: We'll work it out.

OZZIE: You can't know how you hurt us.

DAVID: I wasn't asleep.

OZZIE: Not until you have children of your own.

HARRIET: What?

    [*Silence.*]

    Not . . . asleep? . . .

DAVID: I was awake; lying awake and speaking.

OZZIE: Now wait a minute.

DAVID: Someone was with me—there in the dark—I don't know what's wrong with me.

HARRIET: It was me. I was with you. There's nothing wrong with you.

DAVID: No. In my room. I could feel it.

HARRIET: I was there.

[*And they have him cornered in another chair.*]

DAVID: No.

OZZIE: Harriet, wait!

HARRIET: What are you saying, "Wait"? I was there.

OZZIE: Oh, my God. Oh, Christ, of course. Oh, Dave, forgive us.

HARRIET: What?

OZZIE: Dave, I understand. It's buddies left behind.

DAVID: No.

OZZIE: But I do. Maybe your mother can't but I can. Men serving together in war, it's a powerful thing—and I don't mean to sound like I think I know it—all of it, I mean—I don't, I couldn't—but I respect you having had it—I almost envy you having had it, Dave. I mean . . . true comradeship.

DAVID: Dad . . .

OZZIE: I had just a taste—not that those trucks and factory were any battlefield, but there was a taste of it there—in the jokes we told and the way we saw each other first in the morning. We told dirty, filthy jokes, Dave. We shot pool, played cards, drank beer late every night, singing all these crazy songs.

DAVID: That's not right, Dad.

OZZIE: But all that's nothing, I'm sure, to what it must be in war. The things you must touch and see. Honor. You must touch honor. And then one of you is hurt, wounded . . . made blind . . .

DAVID: No. I had fear of all the kinds of dying that there are when I went from here. And then there was this girl with hands and hair like wings. [*The poetry is like a thing possessing him, a frenzy in which he does not know where he is.*] There were candles above the net of gauze under which we lay. Lizards. Cannon could be heard. A girl to weigh no more than dust.

HARRIET: A nurse, right . . . David?

OZZIE: No, no, one of them foreign correspondents, English maybe or French. [*Silence.*]

HARRIET: Oh, how lovely! A Wac or Red Cross girl? . . .

DAVID: No.

OZZIE: Redhead or blonde, Dave?

DAVID: No.

[*Harriet is shaken.*]

OZZIE: I mean, what you mean is you whored around a lot. Sure. You whored around. That's what you're saying. You banged some whores . . . had some intercourse. Sure, I mean, that's my point.

[DAVID, *turning away, seems about to rise.*]

Now Dave, take it easy. What I mean is, okay, sure, you shacked up with.
I mean, hit on. Hit on, Dave. Dicked. Look at me. I mean, you pronged it,
right? Right? Sure, attaboy. [*Patting* DAVID *on the shoulder*] I mean, it's
like going to the bathroom. All glands and secretions. Look, Dave, what
are you doing?

> [*A rage is building in* DAVID, *tension forcing him to stand, his cane
> pressing the floor.*]

We can talk this over. We can talk this over.

> [DAVID, *heading for the stairs, crashes into* OZZIE.]

Don't—goddamnit, don't walk away from me. [*He pushes* DAVID *backward.*] What the hell do you think you're doing? It's what you did. Who
the hell you think you are? You screwed it. A yellow whore. Some yellow
ass. You put in your prick and humped your ass. You screwed some
yellow fucking whore!

> [*He has chased* DAVID *backward,* HARRIET *joining in with him.*]

HARRIET: That's right, that's right. You were lonely and young and away from
home for the very first time in your life, no white girls around—

DAVID: They are the color of the earth, and what is white but winter and the
earth under it like a suicide?

> [HARRIET'*s voice is a high humming in her throat.*]

Why didn't you tell me what I was?

> [*And* HARRIET *vomits, her hands at her mouth, her back turning.
> There is a silence. They stand.* OZZIE *starts toward her, falters, starts,
> reaches, stops.*]

OZZIE: Why . . . don't . . . you ask her to cook something for you, David,
will you? Make her feel better . . . okay.

DAVID: I think . . . some eggs might be good, Mom.

OZZIE: [*wanting to help her*] Hear that, Harriet? David wants some eggs.

HARRIET: I'm *all right.*

OZZIE: Of course you are. [*Patting her tenderly, he offers his clean white
handkerchief.*] Here, here: wipe your mouth; you've got a little something
—on the corner, left side. That's it. Whattayou say, David?

HARRIET: What's your pleasure, David?

DAVID: Scrambled.

OZZIE: There you go. Your specialty, his pleasure.

> [OZZIE, *between them, claps his hands; off she goes for the kitchen.*
> OZZIE, *looking about the room like a man in deep water looking for
> something to keep him afloat, sees a pack of cigarettes.*]

How about a cigarette? [*Running to grab them, show them.*] Filter, see,
I switched. Just a little after you left, and I just find them a lot smoother,
actually. I wondered if you'd notice. [*And speaking now, his voice and
manner take on a confidence; he demonstrates; he is self-assured.*] The
filter's granulated. It's an off-product of corn husks. I light up—I feel like
I'm on a ship at sea. Isn't that one hell of a good tasting cigarette? Isn't
that one beautiful goddamn cigarette?

> [HARRIET *enters with two bowls. One has a grapefruit cut in half;
> the second has eggs and a spoon sticking out.*]

HARRIET: Here's a little grapefruit to tide you over till I get the eggs.

[*And now she stirs the eggs in preparation for scrambling them.*] Won't be long, I promise—but I was just wondering, wouldn't it be nice if we could all go to church tonight. All together and we could make a little visit in thanksgiving of your coming home.

[DAVID *is putting his cigarette out in his grapefruit. They see.*] I wouldn't ask that it be long—just—

[*He is rising now, dropping the grapefruit on the chair.*] I mean, we could go to whatever saint you wanted, it wouldn't . . . matter . . .

[*He has turned his back, is walking toward the stairs.*] Just in . . . just out . . .

[*He is climbing the stairs.*] David.

OZZIE: Tired . . . Dave?

[*They watch him plodding unfalteringly toward his room.*] Where you going . . . bathroom?

DAVID: No.

OZZIE: Oh.

[DAVID *disappears into his room and* HARRIET *whirls and heads for the telephone.* OZZIE, *startled, turns to look at her.*] Harriet, what's up?

HARRIET: I'm calling Father Donald.

OZZIE: Father Donald?

HARRIET: [*dialing*] We need help, I'm calling for help.

OZZIE: Now wait a minute. No; oh, no, we—

HARRIET: Do you still refuse to see it? He was involved with one of them. You know what the Bible says about those people. You heard him.

OZZIE: Just not Father Donald; please, please. That's all I ask—just—

[*She is obstinate, he sees. She turns her back waiting for someone to answer.*] Why must everything be personal vengeance?

[*The front door pops open and in comes bounding* RICK, *guitar upon his back.*]

RICK: [*happy*] Hi, Mom. Hi, Dad.

HARRIET: [*waiting, telephone in hand—overjoyed*] Hi, Rick!

RICK: [*happy*] Hi, Mom.

OZZIE: [*feeling fine*] Hi, Rick.

RICK: Hi, Dad.

OZZIE: How you doin', Rick? [*He is happy to see good ole regular Rick.*]

RICK: Fine, Dad. You?

OZZIE: Fine.

RICK: Good.

HARRIET: I'll get you some fudge in just a minute, Rick!

RICK: Okay. How's Dave doin', Dad?

[*He is fiddling with his camera.*]

OZZIE: Dave's doin' fine, Rick.

RICK: Boy, I'm glad to hear that. I'm really glad to hear that, because, boy, I'll sure be glad when everything's back to the regular way. Dave's too serious, Dad; don't you think so? That's what I think. Whattayou think, Dad?

[*He snaps a picture of* OZZIE, *who is posing, smiling, while* HARRIET *waves angrily at them.*]

HARRIET: SHHHHHHH! *Everybody!* [*And then, more pleasantly she returns to the phone.*] Yes, yes. Oh, Father, I didn't recognize your voice. No, I don't know who. Well, yes, it's about my son, Father, David. Yes. Well, I don't know if you know it or not, but he just got back from the war and he's troubled. Deeply. Yes.

[*As she listens silently for a moment,* RICK, *crouching, snaps a picture of her. She tries to wave him away.*]

Deeply.

[*He moves to another position, another angle, and snaps another picture.*]

Deeply, yes. Oh. So do you think you might be able to stop over some time soon to talk to him or not? Father, any time that would be convenient for you. Yes. Oh, that would be wonderful. Yes. Oh, thank you. And may God reward *you,* Father.

[*Hanging up the phone, she stands a moment, dreaming.*]

OZZIE: I say to myself, what does it mean that he is my son? How the hell is it that . . . he . . . is my son? I mean, they say something of you joined to something of me and became . . . him . . . but what kinda goddamn thing is that? One mystery replacing another? Mystery doesn't explain mystery!

RICK: [*scarcely looking up from his comic*] Mom, hey, c'mon, how about that fudge, will ya?

HARRIET: Ricky, oh, I'm sorry. I forgot.

OZZIE: They've got . . . diseases! . . .

HARRIET: [*having been stopped by his voice*] What? . . .

OZZIE: Dirty, filthy diseases. They got 'em. Those girls. Infections. From the blood of their parents into the very fluids of their bodies. Malaria, TB. An actual rot alive in them . . . gonorrhea, syphilis. There are some who have the plague. He touched them. It's disgusting. It's—

RICK: Mom, I'm starving, honest to God; and I'm thirsty too.

HARRIET: [*as she scurries off, clapping, for the kitchen*] Yes, of course. Oh, oh.

RICK: And bring a piece for Dad, too; Dad looks hungry.

OZZIE: No.

RICK: Sure, a big sweet chocolate piece of fudge.

OZZIE: No. Please. I don't feel well.

RICK: It'll do you good.

HARRIET: [*entering with fudge and milk in each hand*] Ricky, here, come here.

RICK: [*hurrying toward her*] What?

HARRIET: [*hands him fudge and milk*] Look good? [*And she moves toward* OZZIE.]

OZZIE: And something else—maybe it could just be that he's growing away from us, like we did ourselves, only we thought it would happen in some other way, some lesser way.

HARRIET: [*putting the fudge and milk into* OZZIE's *hands*] What are you talking about, "going away"? He's right upstairs.

OZZIE: I don't want that.

HARRIET: You said you did.

OZZIE: He said I did.

RICK: [*having gobbled the fudge and milk*] You want me to drive you, Mom?

HARRIET: Would you, Ricky, please?

RICK: [*running*] I'll go around and get the car.

HARRIET: [*scolding, as* OZZIE *has put the fudge and milk down on a coffee table*] It's all cut and poured, Ozzie; it'll just be a waste.

OZZIE: I don't care.

HARRIET: You're so childish.

> [*She marches off toward the front door, where she takes a light jacket from a hook, starts to slip it on.*]

OZZIE: Don't you know I could throw you down onto this floor and make another child live inside you . . . now! . . .

HARRIET: I . . . doubt that . . . Ozzie.

OZZIE: You want me to do it?

HARRIET: [*going out the door*] Ohhh, Ozzie, Ozzie.

OZZIE: Sure. Bye-bye. Bye-bye. [*After a pause.*] They think they know me and they know nothing. They don't know how I feel. . . . How I'd like to beat Ricky with my fists till his face is ugly! How I'd like to banish David to the streets. . . . How I'd like to cut her tongue from her mouth.

> [*David moves around upstairs.*]

I was myself.

> [*And now he is clearly speaking to the audience, making them see his value. They are his friends and buddies, and he talks directly to them.*]

I lived in a time beyond anything they can ever know—a time beyond and separate, and I was nobody's goddamn father and nobody's goddamn husband! I was myself! And I could run. I got a scrapbook of victories, a bag of medals and ribbons. In the town in which I lived my name was spoken in the factories and in the fields all around because I was the best there was. I'd beaten the finest anybody had to offer. Summer . . . I would sit out on this old wood porch on the front of our house and my strength was in me, quiet and mine. Round the corner would come some old Model T Ford and scampering up the walk this ancient, bone-stiff, buck-toothed farmer, raw as winter and cawing at me like a crow: they had one for me. Out at the edge of town. A runner from another county. My shoes are in a brown-paper bag at my feet. I snatch 'em up. I set out into the dusk, easy as breathing. There's an old white fence and we run for the sun. . . . For a hundred yards or a thousand yards or a thousand thousand. It doesn't matter. Whatever they want. We run the race they think their specialty and I beat them. They sweat and struggle; I simply glide on, one step beyond, no matter what their effort, and the sun bleeds before me. . . . We cross rivers and deserts; we clamber over mountains. I run the races the farmers arrange and win the bets they make. And then a few days after the race, money comes to me anonymously in the mail;

but it's not for the money that I run. In the fields and factories they speak my name when they sit down to their lunches. If there's a prize to be run for, it's me they send for. It's to be the-one-sent-for that I run.

[DAVID, *entering from his room, has listened to the latter part of this.*]

DAVID: And . . . then . . . you left.

OZZIE: [*whirling to look at him*] What?

DAVID: I said . . . "And . . . then you left." That town.

OZZIE: Left?

DAVID: Yes. Went away; traveled.

OZZIE: No. What do you mean?

DAVID: I mean, you're no longer there; you're here . . . now.

OZZIE: But I didn't really *leave* it. I mean, not *leave*. Not really.

DAVID: Of course you did. Where are you?

OZZIE: That's not the point, Dave. Where I am isn't the point at all.

DAVID: But it is. It's everything; all that other is gone. Where are you going?

OZZIE: Groceries. Gotta go get groceries. You want anything at the grocery store? [*He looks at his watch.*] It's late. I gotta get busy.

DAVID: [*as* OZZIE *exits*] That's all right, Dad. That's fine.

[*Blackout.*]

The lights rise to brightness, and RICK *enters from the kitchen, carrying his guitar, plinking a note or two as* HARRIET *emerges also from the kitchen, carrying a bowl of chips and a tray of drinks, and* OZZIE *appears upstairs, coming down the hall carrying an 8-mm movie projector already loaded with film.*

HARRIET: Tune her up now, Rick.

OZZIE: What's the movie about anyway?

HARRIET: It's probably scenery, don't you think?—trees and fields and those little ponds. Everything over there's so green and lovely. Enough chips, Ricky?

[*All during this, they scurry about with their many preparations.*]

RICK: We gonna have pretzels too? 'Cause if there's both pretzels and chips then there's enough chips.

OZZIE: [*at the projector*] David shoot it or somebody else? . . . Anybody know? I tried to peek—put a couple feet up to the light . . .

HARRIET: What did you see?

OZZIE: Nothing. Couldn't.

HARRIET: Well, I'll just bet there's one of those lovely little ponds in it some-where.

OZZIE: Harriet . . . you know when David was talking about that trouble in Hank's hand being congenital, what did you think? You think it's possible? I don't myself. I mean, we knew Hank well. I think it's just something David got mixed up about and nobody corrected him. What do you think? Is that what you think? Whatsamatter? Oh.

[*He stops, startled, as he sees she is waving at him. Looking up the stairs, which are behind him, he sees* DAVID *is there, preparing to descend.* DAVID *wears his robe and a bright-colored tie.*]

HARRIET: Hello!

OZZIE: Oh. Hey, oh, let me give you a hand. Yes. Yes. You look good. Good to see you.

[*And he is on the move to* DAVID *to help him down the stairs.*]

Yes, sir. I think, all things considered, I think we can figure we're over the hump now and it's all downhill and good from here on in. I mean, we've talked things over, Dave, what do you say? The air's been cleared, that's what I mean—the wounds acknowledged, the healing begun. It's the ones that aren't acknowledged—the ones that aren't talked over— they're the ones that do the deep damage. That's always what happens.

HARRIET: [*moving to* DAVID] I've baked a cake, David. Happy, happy being home.

[DAVID, *on his own, finds his way to a chair and sits.*]

OZZIE: And we've got pop and ice and chips, and Rick is going to sing some songs.

HARRIET: Maybe we can all sing along if we want.

RICK: Anything special you'd like to hear, Dave?

OZZIE: You just sing what you know, Rick; sing what you care for and you'll do it best.

[*And he and* HARRIET *settle down upon the couch to listen, all smiles.*]

RICK: How about "Baby, When I Find You"?

HARRIET: Ohhh, that's such a good one.

RICK: Dave, you just listen to me go! I'm gonna build! [*He plays an excited lead into the song.*] I'm gonna build, build, build.

[*And he sings.*]

Baby, when I find you,
never gonna stand behind you,
gonna, gonna lead
softly at the start,
gently by the heart,
Sweet . . . Love! . . .
Slipping softly to the sea
you and me both mine
wondrous as a green
growing forest vine. . . .
Baby, when I find you,
never gonna stand behind you,
gonna, gonna lead you
softly at the start,
gently by the heart,
Sweet . . . Love! . . .
Baby, when I find you.

OZZIE: [*as both he and* HARRIET *clap and laugh*] Ohhh, great, Rick, great. You burn me up with envy, honest to God.

HARRIET: It was just so wonderful. Oh, thank you so much.

RICK: I just love to do it so much, you know?

OZZIE: Has he got something goin' for him, Dave? Huh? Hey! You don't even have a drink. Take this one; take mine!

[*Now they hurry back and forth from* DAVID *to the table.*]

HARRIET: And here's some cake.

OZZIE: How 'bout some pretzels, Dave?

RICK: Tell me what you'd like to hear.

DAVID: I'd like to sing.

[*This stops them. They stare at* DAVID *for a beat of silence.*]

RICK: What?

OZZIE: What's that?

DAVID: I have something I'd like to sing.

RICK: Dave, you don't sing.

DAVID: [*reaching at the air*] I'd like to use the guitar, if I could.

HARRIET: What are you saying?

OZZIE: C'mon, you couldn't carry a tune in a bucket and you know it. Rick's the singer, Rick and your mom.

[*Not really listening, thinking that his father has gotten everything back to normal,* RICK *strums and strums the guitar, drifting nearer to* DAVID.]

C'mon, let's go, that all we're gonna hear?

DAVID: You're so selfish, Rick. Your hair is black; it glistens. You smile. You sing. People think you are the songs you sing. They never see you. Give me the guitar.

[*And he clamps his hand closed on the guitar, stopping the music.*]

RICK: Mom, what's wrong with Dave?

DAVID: Give me.

RICK: Listen, you eat your cake and drink your drink, and if you still wanna, I'll let you.

[DAVID *stands, straining to take the guitar.*]

DAVID: Now!

HARRIET: Ozzie, make David behave.

OZZIE: Don't you play too roughly. . . .

DAVID: Ricky! . . .

RICK: I don't think he's playing, Dad.

OZZIE: [*as* DAVID, *following* RICK, *bumps into a chair*]. You watch out what you're doing . . .

[DAVID *drops his glass on the floor, grabs the guitar.*]

You got cake all over your fingers, you'll get it all sticky, the strings all sticky—[*Struggling desperately to keep his guitar*] Just tell me what you want to hear, I'll do it for you!

HARRIET: What is it? What's wrong?

DAVID: GIVE ME! [*With great anger*] GIVE ME!

OZZIE: David! . . .

[*And* DAVID *wrenches the guitar from* RICK'S *hands, sends Rick sprawling, and loops the strap of the guitar over his shoulder, smiling, smiling.*]

HARRIET: Ohhhh, no, no, you're ruining everything. What's wrong with you?

OZZIE: I thought we were gonna have a nice party—

DAVID: I'm singing! We are!

OZZIE: No, no, I mean a *nice* party—one where everybody's happy!

DAVID: I'm happy. I'm singing. Don't you see them? Don't you see them?

OZZIE: Pardon, Dave?

HARRIET: What . . . are you saying?

DAVID: [*changing, turning*] I have some movies. I thought you . . . knew.

HARRIET: Well . . . we . . . do.

OZZIE: Movies?

DAVID: Yes, I took them.

RICK: I thought you wanted to sing.

OZZIE: I mean, they're what's planned, Dave. That's what's up. The projector's all wound and ready. I don't know what you had to get so angry for.

HARRIET: Let's get everything ready.

OZZIE: Sure, sure. No need for all that yelling.
      [*He moves to set up the projector.*]

DAVID: I'll narrate.

OZZIE: Fine, sure. What's it about anyway?

HARRIET: Are you in it?

OZZIE: Ricky, plug it in. C'mon, c'mon.

DAVID: It's a kind of story.

RICK: What about my guitar?

DAVID: No.

OZZIE: We oughta have some popcorn, though.

HARRIET: Oh, yes, what a dumb movie house, no popcorn, huh, Rick!
      [*Rick switches off the lights.*]

OZZIE: Let her rip, Dave.
      [*Dave turns on the projector;* OZZIE *is hurrying to a seat.*]
   Ready when you are, C.B.

HARRIET: Shhhhhhh!

OZZIE: [*a little child playing*] Let her rip, C.B. I want a new contract, C.B.
      [*The projector runs for a moment. (Note: In proscenium, a screen should be used if possible, or the film may be allowed to seem projected on the fourth wall; in three-quarter or round the screen may be necessary. If the screen is used, nothing must show upon it but a flickering of green.)*]

HARRIET: Ohhh, what's the matter? It didn't come out, there's nothing there.

DAVID: Of course there is.

HARRIET: Noooo. . . . . It's all funny.

DAVID: Look.

OZZIE: It's underexposed, Dave.

DAVID: [*moving nearer*] No. Look.

HARRIET: What?

DAVID: They hang in the trees. They hang by their wrists half-severed by the wire.

OZZIE: Pardon me, Dave?

HARRIET: I'm going to put on the lights.

DAVID: NOOOOOO! LOOK! They hang in the greenish haze afflicted by insects; a woman and a man, middle aged. They do not shout or cry.

He is too small. Look—he seems all bone, shame in his eyes; his wife even here come with him, skinny also as a broom and her hair is straight and black, hanging to mask her eyes.

[*The girl,* ZUNG, *drifts into the room.*]

OZZIE: I don't know what you're doing, David; there's nothing there.

DAVID: LOOK! [*And he points.*] They are all bone and pain, uncontoured and ugly but for the peculiar melon-swelling in her middle which is her pregnancy, which they do not see—look! these soldiers who have found her—as they do not see that she is not dead but only dying until saliva and blood bubble at her lips. Look. . . . Yet . . . she dies. Though a doctor is called in to remove the bullet-shot baby she would have preferred . . . to keep since she was dying and it was dead.

[*And* ZUNG *silently, drifting, departs.*]

In fact, as it turned out they would have all been better off left to hang as they had been strung on the wire—he with the back of his head blown off and she, the rifle jammed exactly and deeply up into her, with a bullet fired directly into the child living there. For they ended each buried in a separate place; the husband by chance alone was returned to their village, while the wife was dumped into an alien nearby plot of dirt, while the child, too small a piece of meat, was burned. Put into fire, as the shattered legs and arms cut off of men are burned. There's an oven. It is no ceremony. It is the disposal of garbage! . . .

[*Harriet gets to her feet, marches to the projector, pulls the plug, begins a little lecture.*]

HARRIET: It's so awful the things those yellow people do to one another. Yellow people hanging yellow people. Isn't that right? Ozzie, I told you— animals—Christ, burn them. David, don't let it hurt you. All the things you saw. People aren't themselves in war. I mean like that sticking that gun into that poor woman and then shooting that poor little baby, that's not human. That's inhuman. It's inhuman, barbaric and uncivilized and inhuman.

DAVID: I'm thirsty.

HARRIET: For what? Tell me. Water? Or would you like some milk? How about some milk?

DAVID: [*shaking his head*] No.

HARRIET: Or would you like some orange juice? All golden and little bits of ice.

OZZIE: Just all those words and that film with no picture and these poor people hanging somewhere—so you can bring them home like this house is a meat house—

HARRIET: Oh, Ozzie, no, it's not that—no—he's just young, a young boy . . . and he's been through terrible, terrible things and now he's home, with his family he loves, just trying to speak to those he loves—just—

DAVID: Yes! That's right. Yes. What I mean is, yes, of course, that's what I am—a young . . . blind man in a room . . . in a house in the dark, raising nothing in a gesture of no meaning toward two voices who are not speaking . . . of a certain . . . incredible . . . *connection!*

[*All stare.* RICK *leaps up, running for the stairs.*]

RICK: Listen, everybody, I hate to rush off like this, but I gotta. Night.

HARRIET: Good night, Rick.

OZZIE: [*simultaneously*] Good night.

    [DAVID *moves toward the stairs, looking upward.*]

DAVID: Because I talk of certain things . . . don't think I did them. Murderers don't even know that murder happens.

HARRIET: What are you saying? No, no. We're a family, that's all—we've had a little trouble—David, you've got to stop—please—no more yelling. Just be happy and home like all the others—why can't you?

DAVID: You mean take some old man to a ditch of water, shove his head under, talk of cars and money till his feeble pawing stops, and then head on home to go in and out of doors and drive cars and sing sometimes. I left her like you wanted . . . where people are thin and small all their lives. [*The beginning of realization*] Or did . . . you . . . think it was a . . . place . . . like this? Sinks and kitchens all the world over? Is that what you believe? Water from faucets, light from wires? Trucks, telephones, TV. Ricky sings and sings, but if I were to cut his throat, he would no longer and you would miss him—you would miss his singing. We are hoboes! [*And it is the first time in his life he has ever thought these things.*] We make signs in the dark. You know yours. I understand my own. We share . . . coffee!

    [*There is nearly joy in this discovery: a hint of new freedom that might be liberation. And somewhere in the thrill of it he has whirled, his cane has come near to* OZZIE, *frightening him, though* HARRIET *does not notice. Now* DAVID *turns, moving for the stairs, thinking.*]

    I'm going up to bed . . . now. . . . I'm very . . . tired.

OZZIE: Well . . . you have a good sleep, Son. . . .

DAVID: Yes, I think I'll sleep in.

OZZIE: You do as you please. . . .

DAVID: Good night.

HARRIET: Good night.

OZZIE: Good night.

HARRIET: Good night. [*Slight pause.*] You get a good rest. [*Silence.*] Try . . .

    [*Silence.* DAVID *has gone into his room.* OZZIE *and* HARRIET *stand.*]

    I'm . . . hungry . . . Ozzie. . . . Are you hungry?

OZZIE: Hungry? . . .

HARRIET: Yes.

OZZIE: No. Oh, no.

HARRIET: How do you feel? You look a little peaked. Do you feel all right?

OZZIE: I'm fine; I'm fine.

HARRIET: You look funny.

OZZIE: Really. No. How about yourself?

HARRIET: I'm never sick; you know that. Just a little sleepy.

OZZIE: Well . . . that's no wonder. It's been a long day.

HARRIET: Yes, it has.

OZZIE: No wonder.

HARRIET: Good night.

[*She is climbing the stairs toward bed.*]

OZZIE: Good night.

HARRIET: Don't stay up too late now.

OZZIE: Do you know when he pointed that cane at me, I couldn't breathe. I felt . . . for an instant I . . . might never breathe. . . .

HARRIET: Ohhh . . . I'm so sleepy. So . . . sooooo sleepy. Aren't you sleepy?

OZZIE: [*to make her answer*] Harriet! I couldn't breathe.

HARRIET: WHAT DO YOU WANT? TEACHING HIM SPORTS AND FIGHTING.

[*This moment—one of almost a primal rage—should be the very first shattering of her motherly self-sacrificing image.*]

WHAT . . . OZZIE . . . DO YOU WANT?

OZZIE: Well . . . I was . . . wondering, do we have any aspirin down here . . . or are they all upstairs?

HARRIET: I thought you said you felt well.

OZZIE: Well, I do, I do. It's just a tiny headache. Hardly worth mentioning.

HARRIET: There's aspirin in the desk.

OZZIE: [*crossing*] Fine. Big drawer?

HARRIET: Second drawer, right-hand side.

OZZIE: Get me a glass of water, would you, please?

HARRIET: Of course.

[*She gets a glass from a nearby table, a drink left over from the party, and hands it to him.*]

OZZIE. Thank you. It's not much of a headache, actually. Actually it's just a tiny headache.

[*He pops the tablets into his mouth and drinks to wash them down.*]

HARRIET: Aspirin makes your stomach bleed.

[*He tries to keep from swallowing the aspirin, but it is too late.*]

Did you know that? Nobody knows why. It's part of how it works. It just does it, makes you bleed. This extremely tiny series of hemorrhages in those delicate inner tissues.

[*He is staring at her: there is vengeance in what she is doing.*]

It's like those thin membranes begin, in a very minor way, to sweat blood and you bleed; inside yourself you bleed.

[*She crosses away.*]

OZZIE: That's not true. None of that. You made all that up. . . . Where are you going?

[*With a raincoat on, she is moving out the front door.*]

I mean . . . are you going out? Where . . . are you off to?

[*She is gone.*]

Goddamnit, there's something going on around here, don't you want to know what it is? [*Yelling at the shut door*] I want to know what it is. [*Turning, marching to the phone, dialing.*] I want to know what's going on around here. I want to; I do. Want to—got to. Police. That's right, goddamnit—I want one of you people to get on out to seven-seventeen Dunbar and do some checking, some checking at seven-seventeen—What? Ohhh— [*Hissing*] Christ! . . . [*And he is pulling a handkerchief from his pocket, and covering the mouthpiece.*] I mean, they got a kid living there who just got back from the war and something's going on and I want to know what it. . . . No, I don't wanna give my name—it's them, not me—Hey! Hey!

RICK: [*popping in at the hallway at the top of the stairs*] Hey, Dad! How you doin'?

> [OZZIE *slams down the phone.*]

OZZIE: Oh, Rick! Hi!

RICK: Hi! How you doin'?

> [*Guitar over his shoulder, he is heading down the stairs and toward the front door.*]

OZZIE: Fine. Just fine.

RICK: Good.

OZZIE: How you doin', Rick?

RICK: Well, I'll see you later.

OZZIE: [*running*] I WANT YOU TO TEACH ME GUITAR!

RICK: [*faltering*] What?

OZZIE: I want you to teach me . . . guitar! . . . To play it.

RICK: [*as* OZZIE *pulls the guitar from his hands*] Sure. Okay.

OZZIE: I want to learn to play it. They've always been a kind of mystery to me, pianos, guitars.

RICK: Mystery?

> [*And Ozzie is trying, awkwardly, desperately, to play.*]

OZZIE: I mean, what do you think? Do you ever have to think what your fingers should be doing? What I mean is do you ever have to say—I don't know what—"This finger goes there and this other one does—" I mean, "It's on *this* ridge; now I chord all the strings and then switch it all." See? And do you have to tell yourself, "Now switch it all—first finger this ridge—second finger, down—third—somewhere." I mean, does that kind of thing ever happen? I mean, *How do you play it?* I keep having this notion of wanting some . . . thing . . . some material thing, and I've built it. And then there's this feeling I'm of value, that I'm on my way—I mean, moving—and I'm going to come to something eventually, some kind of achievement. All these feelings of a child . . . in me. . . . They shoot through me and then they're gone and they're not anything . . . anymore. But it's . . . a . . . wall . . . and that I want . . . I think. I see myself doing it sometimes . . . all brick and stone . . . coils of steel. And then I finish . . . and the success of it is monumental and people come from far . . . to see . . . to look. They applaud. Ricky . . . teach me . . .

RICK: Ahhh . . . what, Dad?

OZZIE: Guitar, guitar.

RICK: Oh, sure. First you start with the basic C chord. You put the first finger on the second string—

OZZIE: But that's what I'm talking about. You don't do that. I know you don't.

RICK: [*not understanding*] Oh.

OZZIE: You just pick it up and play it. I don't have time for all that you're saying. That's what I've been telling you.

RICK: [*on his way for the door*] Well, maybe some other day then. Maybe Mom'll wanna learn, too.

[*All this dialogue is rapid, overlapping.*]

OZZIE: No, no.

RICK: Just me and you then.

OZZIE: Right. Me and you.

RICK: I'll see you later.

OZZIE: What?

RICK: Maybe tomorrow.

OZZIE: No.

RICK: Well, maybe the next day then.

[*And he is gone out the door.*]

OZZIE: NOW! Now!

[*And the door slams shut.*]

I grew too old too quick. I had no choice. It was just a town, I thought, and no one remained to test me. I didn't even know it was leaving I was doing. I thought I'd go away and come back. Not leave. [*And he looks up at* DAVID's *room.*] YOU SONOFABITCH [*running up to* DAVID's *room*], NOT LEAVE! [*He bursts into the room. Silence.*] Restless, Dave; restless. Got a lot on my mind. Some of us can't just lay around, you know. You said I left that town like I was wrong, but I was right. A man proved himself out there, tested himself. So I went and then I ended up in the goddamn Depression, what about that? I stood in goddamn lines of people begging bread and soup. You're not the only one who's had troubles. All of us, by God, David; think about that a little. [*Stepping out the door, slamming it*] Just give somebody besides yourself some goddamn thought for a change.

[*Pause. He talks to the audience again; they are his friends.*]

Lived in goddamn dirty fields, made tents of our coats. The whole length of this country again and again, soot in our fingers, riding the rails, a bum, a hobo, but young. I remember. And then one day . . . on one of those trains, Hank was there, the first time I ever saw him. Hank, the brakeman, and he sees me hunched down in that car and he orders me off. He stands distant, ordering that I jump! . . . I don't understand and then he stops speaking . . . and . . . when he speaks again, pain is in his eyes and voice—"You're a runner," he says. "Christ, I didn't know you were a runner." And he moves to embrace me and with both hands lifts me high above his head—holds me there trembling, then flings me far out and I fall, I roll. All in the air, then slam down breathless, raw from the cinders . . . bruised and dizzy at the outskirts of this town, and I'm here, gone from that other town. I'm here. We become friends, Hank and me, have good times even though things are rough. He likes to point young girls out on the street and tell me how good it feels to touch them. I start thinking of their bodies, having dreams of horses, breasts and crotches. I remember. And then one day the feeling is in me that I must see a

train go by and I'll get on it or I won't, something will happen, but half-
way down to where I was thrown off, I see how the grass in among the
ties is tall, the rails rusted. . . . Grass grows in abundance. No trains any
longer come that way; they all go some other way . . . and far behind
me Hank is calling, and I turn to see him coming, Harriet young and
lovely in his hand, weaving among the weeds. I feel the wonder of her body
moving toward me. She's the thing I think I'll enter to find my future.
"Hank," I yell, "you sonofabitch! Bring her here. C'mon. Bring her on."
Swollen with pride, screaming and yelling, I stand there, I stand: "I'm
ready. I'm ready . . . I'm ready."
[*He has come down the stairs. He stands, arms spread, yelling.*]
[*Blackout. Music.*]

Lights slowly up. OZZIE *sleeps on the couch.* RICK *sits in a chair, looking at his
guitar.* ZUNG *is in* DAVID's *room, sitting on the bed behind* DAVID, *who is
slouched in a chair.* HARRIET, *dressed in a blue robe, enters from the upstairs
hallway and comes down the stairs.*

HARRIET: Have you seen my crossword-puzzle book?
RICK: In the bathroom, Mom.
HARRIET: Bathroom? . . . Did I leave it there?
[*Turning, she heads back up the stairs.*]
RICK: Guess so, Mom.
DAVID: [*sitting abruptly up in his chair as if at a sudden, frightening sound*]
Who's there? There's someone there?
[RICK *looks up;* DAVID *is standing, poking the air with his cane.*]
Who's there?
[*He opens the door to his room and steps into the hallway.*]
RICK: Whatsamatter? It's just me and Dad, and Dad's sleeping.
DAVID: Sleeping? Is he?
RICK: On the davenport. . . . You want me to wake him?
DAVID: Nooo . . . nooo.
[*He moves swiftly to descend to the living room.*]
RICK: Hey . . . could I get some pictures, Dave? Would you mind?
DAVID: Of course not. No.
RICK: [*dashing off up the stairs, while* DAVID *gropes to find the couch*] Let me
just go get some film and some flashes, okay.
DAVID: [*standing behind the couch on which* OZZIE *sleeps and looking after*
RICK] Sure . . .
OZZIE: Pardon? Par . . . don?
DAVID: [*whispering into his father's ear*] I think you should know I've begun
to hate you. I feel the wound of you, yet I don't think you can tell me
any more, I . . . must tell you. If I had been an orphan with no one to
count on me, I would have stayed there. Now . . . she is everywhere
I look. I can see nothing to distract me.
[OZZIE *stirs.*]
You think us good, we steal all you have.

OZZIE: Good . . . ole Hank. . . .

DAVID: No, no, he has hated us always—always sick with rot.

OZZIE: Noooo . . . nooooooo. . . .·

DAVID: She would tell me you would not like her. She would touch her fingers to her eyes, and she knew how I must feel sometimes as you do.

OZZIE: Ohhh, noooo . . . sleeping. . . .

DAVID: You must hear me. It is only fraud that keep us sane, I swear it.

OZZIE: David, sleeping! . . . Oh, oh . . .

DAVID: It is not innocence I have lost. What is it I have lost?

OZZIE: Oh . . . oh . . .

[RICK *has appeared high in the hallway and hesitates there.*]

DAVID: Don't you know? Do you see her in your sleep?

RICK: [*hurrying down*] I meant to get some good shots at the party, but I never got a chance the way things turned out. You can stay right there.

DAVID: [*moving toward the chair on which* RICK'*s guitar rests*] I'll sit, all right? [RICK *rushes to save the guitar.*]

RICK: Sure. How you feelin' anyway, Dave? I mean, honest ta God, I'm hopin' you get better. Everybody is. I mean . . . [*He takes a picture.*] . . . you're not gonna go talkin' anymore crazy like about that guitar and all that, are you? You know what I mean. Not to Mom and Dad anyway. It scares 'em and then I get scared and I don't like it, okay? [*He moves on, taking more pictures.*]

DAVID: Sure. That guitar business wasn't serious anyway, Rick. None of that. It was all just a little joke I felt like playing, a kind of little game. I was only trying to show you how I hate you.

RICK: Huh? [*Stunned, he stares.*]

DAVID: To see you die is why I live, Rick.

RICK: Oh.

HARRIET: [*appearing from off upstairs, the crossword-puzzle book in her hands*] Goodness gracious, Ricky, it was just where you said it would be, though I'm sure I don't know how it got there because I didn't put it there. Hello, David.

OZZIE: OHHHHHHHHHHHHHHHHH! [*Screaming, he comes awake, falling off the couch.*] Oh, boy, what a dream! Oh. . . . [*Trying to get to his feet, but collapsing*] Ohhhhhhh! God, leg's alseep. Jesus! [*And he flops about, sits there rubbing his leg*] Ohhhh, everybody. Scared hell out of me, that dream. I hollered. Did you hear me? And my leg's asleep, too. [*He hits the leg, stomps the floor.* HARRIET *sits on the couch, working her crossword-puzzle book.* RICK, *slumped in a chair, reads a comic.* DAVID, *though, leans forward in his chair. He wants to know the effect of his whispering on his father.*] Did anybody hear me holler?

HARRIET: Not me.

RICK: What did you dream about, Dad?

OZZIE: I don't remember, but it was awful. [*Stomping the foot*] Ohhhh, wake up, wake up. Hank was in it, though. And Dave. They stood over me, whispering—I could feel how they hated me.

RICK: That really happened; he really did that, Dad.

OZZIE: Who did?

RICK: What you said.

OZZIE: No. No, I was sleeping. It scared me awful in my sleep. I'm still scared, honest ta God, it was so awful.

DAVID: It's that sleeping in funny positions, Dad. It's that sleeping in some place that's not a bed.

OZZIE: Pardon?

DAVID: Makes you dream funny. What did Hank look like?

HARRIET: Ozzie, how do you spell "Apollo"?

OZZIE: What?

RICK: Jesus, Dad, Schroeder got three home runs, you hear about that? Two in the second of the first and one in the third of the second. Goddamn, if he don't make MVP in the National, I'll eat my socks. You hear about that, Dad?

OZZIE: Yes, I did. Yes.

RICK: He's somethin'.

OZZIE: A pro.

HARRIET: Ozzie, can you think of a four letter word that starts with G and ends with B?

RICK: Glub.

HARRIET: Glub?

OZZIE: [*almost simultaneously*] Glub?

RICK: It's a cartoon word. Cartoon people say it when they're drowning. G-L-U-B.

OZZIE: [*on his feet now*] Ricky. Ricky, I was wondering . . . when I was sleeping, were my eyes open? Was I seeing?

RICK: I didn't notice, Dad.

HARRIET: *Glub* doesn't work, Rick.

RICK: Try *grub*. That's what sourdoughs call their food. It's G-R—

OZZIE: WAIT A MINUTE!

RICK: G-R—

OZZIE: ALL OF YOU WAIT A MINUTE! LISTEN! Listen. I mean, I look for explanations. I look inside myself. For an explanation. I mean, I look inside *my* self. As I would look into water . . . or the sky . . . the ocean. They're silver. Answers . . . silver and elusive . . . like fish. But if you can catch them in the sea . . . hook them as they flash by, snatch them . . . drag them down like birds from the sky . . . against all their struggle . . . when you're adrift . . . and starving . . . they . . . can help you live.

> [*He falters; he stands among them, straining to go further, searching some sign of comprehension in their faces.*]

RICK: Mom . . . Dad's hungry . . . I think. He wants some fish, I—

OZZIE: SHUT UP!

RICK: [*hurt deeply*] Dad?

OZZIE: PIECE OF SHIT! SHUT UP! SHUT UP!

HARRIET: Ozzie! . . .

OZZIE: [*roaring down at* DAVID] I don't want to hear about her. I'm not interested in her. You did what you did and I was no part of it. You understand me? I don't want to hear any more about her! Look at him. Sitting there. Listening. I'm tired of hearing you, Dave. You understand that? I'm tired of hearing you and your crybaby voice and your crybaby stories. And your crybaby slobbering and your . . . [*And his voice is possessed with astonished loathing.*] LOOK . . . AT . . . HIM! YOU MAKE ME WANT TO VOMIT! HARRIET! YOU— [*He whirls on* HARRIET.] YOU! Your internal organs—your internal female organs—they've got some kind of poison in them. They're backing up some kind of rot into the world. I think you ought to have them cut out of you. I MEAN, I JUST CAN'T STOP THINKING ABOUT IT. I JUST CAN'T STOP THINKING ABOUT IT. LITTLE BITTY CHINKY KIDS HE WANTED TO HAVE! LITTLE BITTY CHINKY YELLOW KIDS! DIDN'T YOU! FOR OUR GRANDCHILDREN! [*And he slaps* DAVID *with one hand.*] LITTLE BITTY YELLOW PUFFY—[*He breaks, groping for the word.*] . . . creatures! . . . FOR OUR GRANDCHILDREN! [*He slaps* DAVID *again, again.*] THAT'S ALL YOU CARED!

    [DAVID, *a howl in his throat, has stood up.*]

HARRIET: Ohhh, Ozzie, God forgive you the cruelty of your words. All children are God's children.

    [DAVID *is standing rigid. The front door blows open, and in a fierce and sudden light* ZUNG *steps forward to the edge of David's room, as he looks up at her.*]

DAVID: I didn't know you were here. I didn't know. I will buy you clothing. I have lived with them all my life. I will make them not hate you. I will buy you boots.

    [*And he is moving toward her, climbing the stairs.*]

They will see you. The seasons will amaze you. Texas is enormous. Ohio is sometimes green. There will be time. We will learn to speak. And it will be as it was in that moment when we looked in the dark and our eyes were tongues that could speak and the hurting . . . all of it . . . stopped, and there was total understanding in you of me and in me of you . . . and . . .

    [*Near her now, stepping into his room through the wall, he reaches in a tentative way toward her.*]

such delight in your eyes that I felt it;

    [*And she has begun to move away from him.*]

yet . . . I

    [*She is moving away and down the stairs.*]

discarded you. I discarded you. Forgive me. You moved to leave as if you were struggling not to move, not to leave. "She's the thing most possibly of value in my life," I said. "She is garbage and filth and I must get her back if I wish to live. Sickness. I must cherish her." Zung, there were old voices inside me I had trusted all my life as if they were my own. I didn't know I shouldn't hear them. So reasonable and calm they seemed a source of wisdom. "She's all of everything impossible made

possible, cast her down," they said. "Go home." And I did as they told;
and now I know that I am not awake but asleep, and in my sleep . . .
there is nothing. . . .

[ZUNG *is now standing before the open door, facing it, about to leave.*]
Nothing! . . . What do you want from me to make you stay? I'll do it.
I'll do what you want!

RICK: [*in the dark before his father, camera in hand*] Lookee here, Dad. Cheer
up! Cheer up!

DAVID: [*as* ZUNG *turns to look up at him*] Nooooooooo. . . .

[*And there is a flash as* RICK *takes the picture.*]
NOOOOOOOOOOOOOOO! STAAAAAAAY!

And the door slams shut, leaving ZUNG *still inside. A slide of* OZZIE *appears
on the screen, a close-up of his pained and puzzled face. Music, a falling of
notes. The lights are going to black. Perhaps "Intermission" is on the bottom
of the slide. The slide blinks out.*

ACT II

Blackness. Slide: color close-up of a man's ruddy, smiling, round face.

1ST CHILD'S VOICE: Who zat?

WOMAN'S VOICE: I don't know.

MAN'S VOICE: Looks like a neighbor.

WOMAN'S VOICE: How can you say it's a neighbor? You don't know.

[*New slide appears: scenery, in color.*]

2ND CHILD'S VOICE: Oh, that's a pretty one.

[*New slide: Father Donald in a boxing pose, color.*]

1ST CHILD'S VOICE: Oh, lookee that.

MAN'S VOICE: Father What's-his-name. You know.

[*Another slide: Father Donald, slightly different boxing pose.*]

WOMAN'S VOICE: There he is again.

2ND CHILD'S VOICE: Wow.

[*Lights up on the downstairs.* DAVID *is up in his room on his bed.
Downstairs,* HARRIET *sits on the couch,* FATHER DONALD *is on a
chair;* OZZIE *is in the chair beside him. We have the feeling they
have been there a long, long time.*]

FATHER DONALD: I deal with people and their uneasiness on a regular basis all
the time, you see. Everybody I talk to is nervous . . . one way or
another . . . so . . . I anticipate no real trouble in dealing with Dave. You
have no idea the things people do and then tell me once that confes-
sional door is shut. I'm looking forward actually, to speaking with him.
Religion has been sloughed off a lot lately, but I think there's a relevancy
much larger than the credit most give. We're growing—and our insights,
when we have them, are twofold. I for one have come recently to understand how very often what seems a spiritual problem is in fact a problem
of the mind rather than the spirit—not that the two can in fact be sepa-
rated, though, in theory, they very often are. So what we must do is

apply these theories to fact. At which point we would find that mind and spirit are one and I, a priest, am a psychiatrist, and psychiatrists are priests. I mean— I feel like I'm rambling. Am I rambling?

HARRIET: Oh, no, Father.

OZZIE: Nooo . . . noo.

HARRIET: Father, this is hard for me to say, but I . . . feel . . . his problem is he sinned against the sixth commandment with whores.

FATHER DONALD: That's very likely over there.

HARRIET: And then the threat of death each day made it so much worse.

FATHER DONALD: I got the impression from our earlier talk that he'd had a relationship of some duration.

HARRIET: A day or two, wouldn't you say, Ozzie?

OZZIE: [*distracted, oddly preoccupied with his chair*] A three-day pass I'd say . . . though I don't know, of course.

FATHER DONALD: They're doing a lot of psychiatric studies on that phenomenon right now, did you know that?

[*The front door pops open, and in bounds* RICK.]

HARRIET: Oh, Rick! . . .

RICK: Hi, Mom. Hi, Dad.

OZZIE: Hi, Rick.

FATHER DONALD: [*rising*] Rick, hello!

RICK: Oh, Father Donald . . . hi.

[*No time for Father Donald,* RICK *is speeding for the kitchen.*]

OZZIE: Look at him heading for the fudge.

FATHER DONALD: Well, he's a good big strong sturdy boy.

RICK: [*as he goes out*] Hungry and thirsty.

FATHER DONALD: And don't you ever feel bad about it, either!

[*He stands for an instant, a little uncertain what to do.*]

Dave's up in his room, I imagine, so maybe I'll just head on up and have my little chat. He is why I'm here, after all.

HARRIET: Fine.

OZZIE: [*standing, still distracted, he stares at the chair in which Father Donald was sitting*] First door top of the stairs.

FATHER DONALD: And could I use the bathroom, please, before I see ole Dave? Got to see a man about a horse.

HARRIET: Oh, Father, certainly: it's just down the hall. Fifth door.

OZZIE: [*stepping nearer to the chair*] What's wrong with that chair? . . .

HARRIET: It's the blue door, Father! . . .

OZZIE: I . . . don't like that chair. I think it's stupid . . . looking. . . .

[*As* RICK *enters from the kitchen, eating fudge.*]

Ricky, sit. Sit in that chair.

RICK: What? . . .

OZZIE: Go on, sit, sit.

[RICK *hurries to the chair, sits, eats.* OZZIE *is fixated on the chair.*]

HARRIET: Oh, Ricky, take your father's picture, he looks so silly.

OZZIE: I just don't think that chair is any good. I just don't think it's comfortable. Father Donald looked ill at ease all the while he was sitting there.

HARRIET: Well, he had to go to the bathroom, Ozzie, what do you expect?

OZZIE: [*to* RICKY] Get up. It's just not right.

> [RICK *gets up and* OZZIE *flops into the chair, sits, fidgets.* RICK *goes back out to the kitchen.*]

> Noooooo. It's just not a comfortable chair at all, I don't know why.

> [*He rises and moves toward the couch.*]

> I don't like it. How much did we pay?

HARRIET: What do you think you're doing?

OZZIE: And this couch isn't comfortable either.

HARRIET: It's a lovely couch.

OZZIE: [*tests it*] But it isn't comfortable. Noooo. And Im not really sure it's lovely, either. Did we pay two hundred dollars?

HARRIET: What? Oh, more.

OZZIE: How much?

HARRIET: I don't know, I told you.

OZZIE: You don't. I don't. It's gone anyway, isn't it?

HARRIET: Ozzie, what does it matter?

OZZIE: [*already on the move for the stairs*] I'm going upstairs. I'll be upstairs.

HARRIET: Wait a minute.

> [*As he keeps moving, up the stairs.*]

> I want to talk to you. *I think we ought to talk!*

> [*Emotion well beneath her voice stops him, turns him.*]

> I mean, it's nothing to worry about or anything, but you don't know about it and it's your house, you're involved—so it's just something I mention. You're the man of the house, you ought to know. The police were here . . . earlier today.

OZZIE: What? Oh, my God.

HARRIET: The police. Two of them. Two. A big and a small . . . they—

> [*He is dazed; he doesn't know whether to go up or down, listen or leave. He nods.*]

> It was just a little bit ago; not long at all.

OZZIE: Jesus Christ. [*He descends.*]

HARRIET: Oh, I know, I know. Just out of the blue like that—it's how I felt, too, I did, I did.

OZZIE: *What—police?*

HARRIET: It was when you were gone for groceries. I mean, they thought they were supposed to be here. We wanted it, they thought.

OZZIE: No, no.

HARRIET: Somebody called them to come here. They thought it had been us. They were supposed to look through David's luggage, they thought.

OZZIE: They . . . were . . . what?

HARRIET: That's when I mean. That's exactly what I—

OZZIE: *Look through his luggage? There's nothing wrong with his luggage!*

HARRIET: Isn't it incredible? Somebody called them—they didn't know who— no name was given and it sounded muffled through a handkerchief, they said. I said, "Well, it wasn't us." Told them, "Don't you worry; we're all all right here." It must have been a little joke by somebody.

OZZIE: What about Dave?

HARRIET: No, no.

OZZIE: Or Ricky? Did you ask Ricky?

HARRIET: Ricky?

OZZIE: RICKY! RICKY!

RICK: [*popping in from the kitchen, thinking he was called*] What's up, Dad?

OZZIE: I DON'T KNOW.

RICK: I thought you called.

> [*He pops back out into the kitchen.*]

OZZIE: [*to Harriet*] You ask him; you ask him. I think the whole thing's preposterous—absolutely—

HARRIET: [*as* RICK *re-emerges to look and listen*] Ricky, do you know anything about anybody calling the police to come here?

OZZIE: [*turning and moving for the stairs*] I'm going upstairs. I'll be upstairs.

RICK: The police?

> [*As* HARRIET *turns to look and half step after Ozzie.*]

Oh, no, Mom, not me. Okay if I use the car?

HARRIET: What?

FATHER DONALD: [*encountering* OZZIE *in the upstairs hallway*] Gonna take care of old Dave right now.

OZZIE: I'm going upstairs. I'll be upstairs.

> [*He exits. as* HARRIET *stands looking up at them.*]

RICK: Bye, Mom.

HARRIET: What? Oh. [*Looking back as* RICK *goes out the door*] BE CAREFUL!

FATHER DONALD: [*after a slight hesitation*] Ozzie said to tell you he was going upstairs.

HARRIET: What?

FATHER DONALD: Ozzie said to tell you he was going upstairs.

HARRIET: [*stares at him a moment*] Oh, Father, I'm so glad you're here.

> [*And she exits into the kitchen, leaving* FATHER DONALD. *He nods, knocks on David's door.*]

FATHER DONALD: Dave?

> [*He opens the door, eases into the semidark of the room.*]

Dave? It's me . . . Dave. . . .

> [*Finding a light, he flicks it on.*]

Ohh, Dave, golly, you look just fine. Here I expected to see you all worn out and there you are looking so good. It's me, Dave, Father Donald. Let me shake your hand.

> [DAVID's *rising hand comes up far off from* FATHER DONALD. *The priest, his own hand extended, has to move nearly around the bed before he can shake David's hand.*]

No, no, David. Here. Over here. Can't see me, can you? There you go. Yes, sir, let me tell you, I'm proud. A lot of people might tell you that, I know, but I mean it, and I'll stand behind it if there's anything I can do for you—anything at all.

DAVID: No. I'm all right.

FATHER DONALD: And that's the amazing part of it, Dave, you are. You truly are. It's plain as day. Golleee, I just don't know how to tell you how glad I am to see you in such high fine spirits. Would you like my blessing? [*He gets to his feet.*] Let me just give you my blessing and then we'll talk things over a little and—

> [DAVID *slashes with his cane and strikes the hand moving into the position to bless.*]

Ohhhhhhhhhhhhhh! [*Wincing, teeth gritted*] Oh, Dave; oh, watch out what you're doing!

DAVID: I know.

FATHER DONALD: No, no, I mean, you swung it in the air, you—hit me.

DAVID: Yes.

FATHER DONALD: No, no, you don't understand, you—

DAVID: I was trying to hit you, Father.

> [*Father Donald stares, taking this in.*]

FATHER DONALD: What?

DAVID: I didn't send for you.

FATHER DONALD: I know, I know, your poor mother—your poor mother—

DAVID: I don't want you here, Father; get out!

FATHER DONALD: David!

DAVID: Get out, I'm sick of you. You've been in one goddamn corner or another of this room all my life making signs at me, whispering, wanting to splash me with water or mark me with oil—some goddamn hocus-pocus. I feel reverence for the air and the air is empty, Father. Now get the fuck out of here.

FATHER DONALD: No, no, no, no, David. No, no. I can't give that to you. You'll have to get that from somewhere else.

DAVID: I don't want anything from you!

FATHER DONALD: I'm supposed to react now in some foolish way—I see—some foolish, foolish way that will discredit me—isn't that right? Oh, of course it is. It's an excuse to dismiss my voice that you're seeking, an excuse for the self-destruction your anger has made you think you want, and I'm supposed to give it. I'm supposed to find all this you're doing obscene and sacrilegious instead of seeing it as the gesture of true despair that it is. You're trying to make me disappear, but it's not going to happen. No, no. No such luck, David. I understand you, you see. Everything about you.

DAVID: Do you?

FATHER DONALD: The way you're troubled.

DAVID: I didn't know that, Father.

FATHER DONALD: You say that sarcastically—"Do you? I didn't know that." As if to imply you're so complicated I couldn't ever understand you when I already have. You see, I've been looking into a few things, David, giving some things some thought. [*Producing a magazine with a colorful cover*] I have in my hand a magazine—you can't see it, I know—but it's there. A psychiatric journal in which there is an article of some interest and it deals with soldiers and some of them carried on as you did and then there's some others who didn't. It's not all just a matter of hocus-pocus any longer.

DAVID: Carried . . . on . . . Father?

FATHER DONALD: That whore. That yellow whore. You understand. You knew I was bringing the truth when I came which is why you hit me.

DAVID: I thought you didn't even know the problem. You came in here all bubbly and jolly asking how did I feel.

FATHER DONALD: That was only a little ruse, David; a little maneuver to put you off your guard. I only did that to mislead you. That's right. Your mother gave me all the basics some weeks ago and I filled in the rest from what I know. You see, if it's a fight you want, it's what you'll get. Your soul is worth some time and sweat from me. You're valued by others, David, even if you don't value yourself. [*Waving the magazine in the air*] It's all here—right here—in these pages. It was demonstrated beyond any possible doubt that people—soldiers—who are compelled for some reason not even they themselves understand to establish personal sexual relationships with whores are inferior to those who don't; they're maladjusted, embittered, non-goal-oriented misfits. The sexual acceptance of another person, David, is intimate and extreme; this kind of acceptance of an alien race is in fact the rejection of one's own race—it is in fact the rejection of one's own self—it is sickness, David. Now I'm a religious man, a man of the spirit, but knowledge is knowledge and I must accept what is proven fact whether that fact come from science or philosophy or whatever. What kind of man are you that you think you can deny it? You're in despair, David, whether you think of it that way or not. It's only into a valley of ruin that you are trying to lock yourself. You can only die there, David. Accept me. Let God open your eyes; let Him. He will redeem you. Not I nor anyone, but only Him—yet if you reject me, you reject Him. My hand is His. His blessing.

[*The hand is rising as if the very words elevate it.*]

My blessing. Let me give you my blessing.

[*And* DAVID's *cane hits like a snake.* FATHER DONALD *cries out in surprise and pain. He recovers and begs.*]

Let me bless you. [*His hand is again rising in blessing.*] Please!

[DAVID, *striking again, stands. He hits again and again.*]

David! David! [*Terrified*] Stop it. Let me bless you.

[DAVID *hits* FATHER DONALD's *arm, hits his leg.*]

DAVID: I don't want you here!

FATHER DONALD: You don't know what you're saying.

[*But now the blow seems about to come straight down on his head. He yells and covers his head with his arms. The blow hits. He picks up a chair, holds it up for protection.*]

Stop it. Stop it. Goddamnit, stop hitting me. Stop it. You are in despair.

[*He slams the chair down.*]

A man who hits a priest is in despair!

[*Whistling, the cane slams into his arm.*]

Ohhhhh, this pain—this terrible pain in my arm—I offer it to earn you your salvation.

DAVID: Get out!

FATHER DONALD: Death! Do you understand that. Death. Death is your choice. You are in despair.

[*He turns to leave.*]

DAVID: And may God reward *you*, Father.

FATHER DONALD: [*turning back, as* DAVID *flops down on the bed*] Oh yes; yes of course, you're so confident now, young and strong. Look at you—full of spunk, smiling. But all that'll change. Your tune'll change in time. What about pain, Dave? Physical pain. What do you do when it comes? Now you send me away, but in a little while you'll call me back, run down by time, lying with death on your bed . . . in an empty house . . . gagging on your own spit you cannot swallow; you'll call me then, nothing left to you but fear and Christ's black judging eyes about to find and damn you; you'll call.

[*Slight pause.*]

DAVID: That's not impossible, Father.

FATHER DONALD: I don't even like you; do you know that? I DON'T EVEN LIKE YOU!

DAVID: Tell them I hit you when you go down.

FATHER DONALD: [*near the door, thinking about trying to bless from there*] No. No, they've pain enough already.

DAVID: Have they? You get the fuck out of here before I kill you.

[*As if he has read Father Donald's mind and knows what the man is thinking,* DAVID's *cane has risen like a spear; it aims at the priest's heart.*]

FATHER DONALD: [*moving not a muscle*] THOUGH I DO NOT MOVE MY HAND, I BLESS YOU! YOU ARE BLESSED!

[*And he exits hurriedly, heading straight down the hall toward the bathroom. Lights up downstairs: it seems a lovely afternoon as* RICK *and* HARRIET *enter from the kitchen, chatting.*]

HARRIET: So the thing I want to do—I just think it would be so nice if we could get Dave a date with some nice girl.

RICK: Oh, sure.

HARRIET: Do you think that would be a good idea?

[OZZIE, *descending from the attic, pauses to peek into David's room; he finds* DAVID *asleep, and, after a moment, continues on down.*]

RICK: Sure.

HARRIET: Do you know any girls you think might get along with David?

RICK: No, but I still think it's really a good idea and I'll keep it in mind for all the girls I meet and maybe I'll meet one. Here comes Dad. Hi, Dad. Bye, Mom.

HARRIET: Oh, Ozzie, did you see what they were doing?

OZZIE: Dave's sleeping, Harriet; Father Donald's gone.

HARRIET: What? He can't be gone.

OZZIE: I thought maybe he was down here. How about the kitchen?

HARRIET: No, no, I just came out of the kitchen. Where were you upstairs? Are you sure he wasn't in David's room?

OZZIE: I was in the attic.

HARRIET: Well, maybe he saw the light and came up to join you and you missed each other on the way up and down. Why don't you go check?

OZZIE: I turned off all the lights, Harriet. The attic's dark now.

HARRIET: Well, yell up anyway—

OZZIE: But the attic's dark now, Harriet.

HARRIET: Just in case.

OZZIE: What are you trying to say? Father Donald's up in the attic in the dark? I mean, if he was up there and I turned off the lights, he'd have said something—"Hey, I'm here," or something. It's stupid to think he wouldn't.

> [*And he sits down.*]

HARRIET: No more stupid to think that than to think he'd leave without telling us what happened with David.

OZZIE: All right, all right. [*Storming to the foot of the stairs.*] HEEEEEE-YYYYYYYYYYYYY! HEEEEEYYYYYYYYY! UP THEEEEEERRE! ANYBODY UP THERE?

> [*There is a brief silence. He turns toward* HARRIET.]

DAVID: [*on his bed in his room*] WHAT'S THAT, DAD?

OZZIE: [*falters, looks about*] What?

DAVID: WHAT'S UP, DAD?

OZZIE: OH, DAVE, NO, NOT YOU.

DAVID: WHY ARE YOU YELLING?

OZZIE: NO, NO, WE JUST THOUGHT FATHER DONALD WAS UP THERE IN THE ATTIC, DAVE. DON'T YOU WORRY ABOUT IT.

DAVID: I'M THE ONLY ONE UP HERE, DAD!

OZZIE: But . . . YOU'RE NOT IN THE ATTIC, SEE?

DAVID: I'M IN MY ROOM.

OZZIE: I KNOW YOU'RE IN YOUR ROOM.

DAVID: YOU WANT ME TO GO UP IN THE ATTIC?

OZZIE: NO! GODDAMNIT, JUST—

DAVID: I DON'T KNOW WHAT YOU WANT.

OZZIE: I WANT YOU TO SHUT UP, DAVE, THAT'S WHAT I WANT, JUST—

FATHER DONALD: [*appearing from off upstairs*] What's the matter? What's all the yelling?

HARRIET: Oh, Father!

OZZIE: Father, hello, hello.

HARRIET: How did it go? Did it go all right?

FATHER DONALD: [*coming down the steps, seeming as if nothing out of the ordinary has happened*] Fine, just fine.

HARRIET: Oh, you're perspiring so though—look at you.

FATHER DONALD: [*maneuvering from the door*] Well, I've got a lot on my mind. It happens. Nerves. I've other appointments. Many, many.

HARRIET: You mean you're leaving? What are you saying?

FATHER DONALD: I must.

HARRIET: But we've got to talk.

FATHER DONALD: Call me.

HARRIET: Father . . . bless me! . . .
FATHER DONALD: What? . . .
HARRIET: Bless me. . . .
FATHER DONALD: Of course.
    [*She bows her head, and the priest blesses her, murmuring the Latin.*]
HARRIET: Ohhh, Father, thank you so much. [*Touching his hand.*] Shall I
    walk you to your car?
FATHER DONALD: [*backing for the door*] Fine, fine. That's all right. Sure.
OZZIE: [*nodding*] DAVE, SAY GOOD-BYE TO FATHER DONALD, HE'S
    LEAVING NOW.
FATHER DONALD: GOOD-BYE, DAVE!
DAVID: GOOD-BYE, FATHER!

Blackout as HARRIET *and* FATHER DONALD *are going out the door. Music.*

    [OZZIE *is discovered in late night light, climbing the stairs to David's
    door, where, after hesitating an instant, he gently knocks.*]
OZZIE: Dave, I'd like to come in . . . if I could. [*Easing in.*] Awful dark;
    can I put on a light?
    [*Silence.*]
    I mean, we don't need one—not really. I just thought we might . . . I
    mean, first of all, I want to apologize for the way I hit you the other day.
    I don't know why I did it. I'm . . . gonna sit down here on the edge of
    the bed. Are you awake enough to understand? I am your father, you
    know, and I could command . . . if I wanted. I don't; but I could. I'm
    going to sit.
    [*Slight pause.*]
    I mean, it's so sad the way you just go on and on . . . and I'd like to
    have time for you, but you want so much; I have important things, too.
    I have plans; I'm older, you know; if I fail to fulfill them, who will do it:
    Not you, though you could. And Rick's too busy. Do you understand?
    There's no evidence in the world of me, no sign or trace, as if everything
    I've ever done were no more than smoke. My life has closed behind me
    like water. But I must not care about it. I must not. Though I have
    inside me a kind of grandeur I can't realize, many things and memories
    of a darker time when we were very different—harder—nearer to the air
    and we thought of nothing as a gift. But I can't make you see that. There's
    no way. It's what I am, but it's not what you are. Even if I had the
    guitar, I would only stand here telling my fingers what to do, but they
    would do nothing. You would not see. . . . I can't get beyond these
    hands. I jam in the fingers. I break on the bone. I am . . . lonely. I
    mean, oh, no, not exactly lonely, not really. That's a little strong,
    actually. . . .
    [*Silence.*]
    I mean . . . Dave . . . [*He pulls from his back pocket David's overseas
    cap.*] What's this?
DAVID: What?

OZZIE: This cap. What is it? I cut myself on it. I was rummaging in your stuff upstairs, your bags and stuff, and I grabbed it. It cut me.

DAVID: [*reaching for the cap*] Oh . . . yes.

OZZIE: There are razors sewn into it. Why is that?

DAVID: To cut people.

[*Slowly he puts the cap on his head.*]

OZZIE: Oh.

DAVID: Here . . . I'll show you. . . . [*Getting slowly to his feet.*] You're on the street, see. You walk . . . and see someone who's after you. . . . You wait. . . .

[*He tenses. His hand rises to the tip of the cap.*]

As they get near . . . slowly you remove the hat—they think you're going to toss it aside, see? You . . . *snap it! You snap it!*

[*Seizing the front edge of the cap between thumb and finger, he snaps it down. It whistles past* OZZIE, *who jumps.*]

It cuts them. They hold their face. However you want them, they're yours. You can stomp them, kick them. This is on the street. I'd like to do that to somebody, wouldn't you?

OZZIE: Huh?

DAVID: It'd be fun.

OZZIE: Oh, sure. I . . .

DAVID: Hank told you to buy this house, didn't he?

OZZIE: What?

DAVID: "Get that house," he said. "Get it."

OZZIE: It's a good house. Solid. Not one of those prefabs, those—

DAVID: It's a coffin. You made it big so you wouldn't know, but that's what it is, and not all the curtains and pictures and lamps in the world can change it. He threw you off a fast free train, Ozzie.

OZZIE: I don't believe you saw him.

DAVID: He told you gold, he gave you shit.

OZZIE: I don't believe you saw him. You're a liar, David.

[ZUNG *appears.*]

DAVID: Do you know, Dad, it seemed sometimes I would rise and slam with my fists into the walls of a city. Pointing at buildings, I turned them into fire. I took the fleeing people into my fingers and bent them to touch their heads to their heels, each screaming at the night of their brain turning black. And now sometimes I miss them, all those screaming people. I wish they were here with us, you and Mom and Rick and Zung and me.

[*Pause.*]

OZZIE: Mom and Rick and who and you, Dave?

DAVID: ZUNG.

[ZUNG *is moving nearer to them now.*]

OZZIE: Zung, Dave?

DAVID: She's here. They were all just hunks of meat that had no mind to know of me until I cared for her. It was simple. We lived in a house. She didn't want to come back here, Dad; she wanted me to stay there. And in all the time I knew her, she cost me six dollars that I had to sneak into her purse. Surprised? In time I'll show you some things. You'll see them. I will be your father.

[*He tosses the cap at* OZZIE.]

OZZIE: [*shaken, struggling to catch the cap*] Pardon, Dave?

DAVID: What's wrong? You sound like something's terribly wrong?

OZZIE: No. No, no. I'm fine. Your poor mother—she's why I'm here. Your poor mother, sick with grief. She's mine to care for, you know. It's me you're after, yet you torment her. No more. No more. That's what I came up here to tell you.

DAVID: [*getting to his feet*] Good.

OZZIE: You're phony, David—phony—trying to make up for the thousands you butchered, when if you were capable of love at all you would love us, your mother and me—not that we matter—instead of some poor little whore who isn't even here.

DAVID: [*exiting the room*] I know.

OZZIE: I want her happy.

DAVID: [*as* OZZIE *follows a little into the hall*] I know.

[*And* DAVID *is gone.* HARRIET *enters slowly from the kitchen, sees* OZZIE, *then the room's open door.*]

HARRIET: Did you have a nice talk?

OZZIE: [*heading toward her*] Harriet, what would you say if I said I wanted some checking done?

HARRIET: I don't know what you mean. In what way do you mean?

OZZIE: Take a look at that. But just be careful.

HARRIET: What is it?

OZZIE: His cap. There are razor blades sewn in it; all along the edge.

HARRIET: Ozzie . . . ohhh! Goodness.

OZZIE: That's what I mean. And I was reading just yesterday—some of them bring back guns and knives. Bombs. We've got somebody living in this house who's killed people, Harriet, and that's a fact we've got to face. I mean, I think we ought to do some checking. You know that test where they check teeth against old X-rays. I think—

HARRIET: Ohhh . . . my God! . . .

OZZIE: I know, I know, it scares me, too, but what are we talking about? We're talking about bombs and guns and knives, and sometimes I don't even think it's David up there. I feel funny . . . sometimes . . . I mean, and I want his fingerprints taken. I think we should have his blood type—

HARRIET: Oh, Ozzie, Ozzie, it was you.

OZZIE: Huh?

HARRIET: You did it. You got this out of his luggage, all his baggage upstairs. You broke in and searched and called the police.

OZZIE: No. What?

HARRIET: You told them to come here, and then you lied and said you didn't.

OZZIE: What?

HARRIET: You did, and then you lied and now you're lying again.

OZZIE: Oh, no. No.

HARRIET: What's wrong with you? What's happening to you?

OZZIE: But I didn't do that. I didn't.

> [DAVID *appears in the upstairs hallway, moving to return to his room.*]

I didn't. No, no. And even if I did, what would it mean but I changed my mind, that's all. Sure. [*Looking up at* DAVID *moving in the hall toward his room*] I called and then changed my mind and said I didn't when I did, and since when is there anything wrong in that? It would mean only that I have a little problem of ambivalence. I got a minor problem of ambiguity goin' for me here, is all, and you're exaggerating everything all out of proportion. You're distorting everything! All of you! [*And he whirls to leave.*] If I have to lie to live, I will! [*He runs.*]

HARRIET: Where are you going? Come back here, Ozzie. Where are you going?

OZZIE: Kitchen. Kitchen.

> [*He gallops away and out the front door. Blackout. Music.*]

Lights up. Bright afternoon. HARRIET *is alone, dusting.* RICK, *carrying books, enters from the kitchen and heads for the stairs to go to his room.*

HARRIET: One day, Ricky . . . there were these two kittens and a puppy all in our back yard fighting. The kittens were little fur balls, so angry, and the little puppy, yapping and yapping. I was just a girl, but I picked them up in my arms. I held them all in my arms and they got very, very quiet.

RICK: I'm going up to my bedroom and study my history and English and trigonometry, Mom.

HARRIET: Do you know, I've called Father Donald seven times now—seven times, and haven't got an answer. Isn't that funny? He's starting to act like Jesus. You never hear from him. Isn't that funny?

RICK: I'm going up to my bedroom and study my history and English and trigonometry, Mom, okay?

HARRIET: Fine, Ricky. Look in on David, would you?

RICK: Sure.

HARRIET: Good night.

RICK: [*calling as he passes David's door*] Hi, Dave.

DAVID: Hi, Rick.

RICK: DAVE'S OKAY, MOM.

> [*She is at the foot of the stairs.* RICK *goes from view. She turns back to her work, and the front door opens and* OZZIE *enters.*]

OZZIE: [*excited, upset*] Harriet! Can you guess what happened? You'll never guess what happened.

> [*She continues cleaning.*]

Harriet, wait. Stop.

HARRIET: Ozzie, I've got work to do.

OZZIE: But I want to tell you something.

HARRIET: All right, tell me; I can clean and listen; I can do both.

> [*As she moves away, he rushes toward her, stretching out the lapel of his jacket to show her a large stain on it. She must see.*]

OZZIE: Lookit; look at that. What do you think that is? That spot on my coat, do you see it? That yellow?

HARRIET: [*distressed, touching the spot*] Ohhh, Ozzie! . . .

OZZIE: And the red mark on my neck.

HARRIET: [*wincing*] Ohh, Ozzie, what happened? A bee sting! You got stung by a bee!

OZZIE: No, no; I was walking—thinking—trying to solve our problems. Somebody hit me with an egg. They threw it at me. I got hit with an egg.
[*She stares, incredulous.*]
That's right. I was just walking down the street and—bang—I was hit. I almost blacked out; I almost fell down.

HARRIET: Ozzie, my God, who would do such a thing?

OZZIE: I don't know. That's the whole point. I've racked my brain to understand and I can't. I was just walking along. That's all I was doing.

HARRIET: You mean you didn't even see them?

OZZIE: [*pacing, his excitement growing*] They were in a car. I saw the car. And I saw the hand, too. A hand. Somebody's hand. A very large hand. Incredibly large.

HARRIET: What kind of car?

OZZIE: I don't know. An old one—black—big high fenders.

HARRIET: A Buick.

OZZIE: I think so; yes. Cruising up and down, up and down.

HARRIET: Was it near here? Why don't you sit down? [*Trying to help him sit, to calm and comfort him*] Sit down. Relax.
[*He obeys, hardly aware of what he is doing, sort of squatting on the couch, his body rigid with tension, as the story obsesses him.*]

OZZIE: And I heard them, too. They were hollering.

HARRIET: What did they say?

OZZIE: I don't know. It was just all noise. I couldn't understand.

HARRIET: [*as if the realization doubles the horror*] It was more than one? My God!

OZZIE: I don't know. Two at least, at the very least. One to drive and one to throw. Maybe even three. A lookout sort of, peering up and down, and then he sees me. "There," he says; he points me out. I'm strolling along like a stupid ass, I don't even see them. The driver picks up speed.
[*And now he is rising from the couch, reliving the story, cocking his arm.*]
The thrower cocks his arm . . .

HARRIET: Ozzie, please, can't you relax? You look awful.

OZZIE: Nooo, I can't relax, goddamnit!
[*Off he goes, pacing again.*]

HARRIET: You look all flushed and sweating; please.

OZZIE: It just makes me so goddamn mad the more I think about it. It really does. GODDAMNIT! GODDAMNIT!

HARRIET: Oh, you poor thing.

OZZIE: Because it was calculated; it was calculated, Harriet, because that egg had been boiled to just the right point so it was hard enough to hurt but not so hard it wouldn't splatter. The filthy sonsabitches, but I'm gonna find 'em, I swear that to God, I'm gonna find 'em. I'm gonna kill 'em. I'm gonna cut out their hearts!
[RICK *appears at the top of the stairs.*]

RICK: Hey! What's all the racket? What's—

OZZIE: Ricky, come down here! . . . Goddamn 'em. . . .

HARRIET: Ricky, somebody hit your father with an egg!

RICK: Hit him? [*Descending hurriedly, worried*] Hit Dad?

OZZIE: They just threw it! Where's Dave? Dave here?

    [*He is suddenly looking around, moving for the stairs.*]

    I wanna tell Dave. DAVE!

HARRIET: Ozzie, give me your jacket!

    [*She follows him part way up the stairs, tugging at the jacket.*]

OZZIE: I wanna tell Dave!

    [*He and* HARRIET *struggle to get the jacket off.*]

HARRIET: I'll take the spot off.

OZZIE: I gotta tell ole Dave!

    [*And the jacket is in her arms. He races on up the stairs.*]

    DAVE? DAVE! HEY, DAVE?

    [*But David is not in his room. While* HARRIET *descends and goes to a wall counter with drawers,* OZZIE *hurries off down the hallway. From a drawer* HARRIET *takes a spray container and begins to clean the jacket.*]

RICK: [*wandering near to her*] Boy, that's something, huh. What you got there, Mom?

HARRIET: [*as* RICK *watches*] Meyer Spot Remover, do you know it? It gives just a sprinkling . . . like snow, which brushed away, leaves the fabric clean and fresh like spring.

    [OZZIE *and* DAVID *rush out from the hallway and down the stairs.* RICK *moves toward them to take a picture.*]

OZZIE: But it happened—and then there's this car tearin' off up the street. "Christ Jesus," I said, "I just been hit with an egg. Jesus Christ, that's impossible." And the way I felt—the way I feel—Harriet, let's have some beer; let's have some good beer for the boys and me.

    [*With a sigh, she moves to obey. As* OZZIE *continues, she brings beer, she brings peanuts.* OZZIE *now is pleased with his high energy, with his being the center of attention.*]

    It took me back to when I was a kid. Ole Fat Kramer. He lived on my street and we used to fight every day. For fun. Monday he'd win, and Tuesday, I'd beat him silly, my knees on his shoulders, blam, blam, blam. Later on, he grew up, became a merchant marine, sailed all over the world, and then he used to race sailboats up and down both coasts—he had one he lived on—anything that floated, he wanted to sail. And he wasn't fat either. We just called him that . . . and boy, oh boy, if he was around now—ohhhh, would we go get those punks threw that egg at me. We'd run 'em into the ground. We'd kill 'em like dogs . . . poor little stupid ugly dogs, we'd cut out their hearts.

RICK: [*suddenly coughing and coughing—having gulped down beer—and getting to his feet*] Excuse me, Dad; excuse me. Listen, I've got to get going. You don't mind, do you? Got places to go; you're just talking nonsense anyway. [*He moves for the front door.*]

HARRIET: Have a good time, Rick.

RICK: I'm too pretty not to, Mom! (*And he is gone.*)

OZZIE: Where is . . . he . . . going? Where does he always go? Why does he always go and have some place to go? Always! . . .

HARRIET: Just you never mind, Ozzie. He's young and you're not. I'm going to do the dishes, but you just go right ahead with your little story and I'll listen from the kitchen.

[*Gathering the beer and glasses, she goes.*]

OZZIE: [*following a little after her, not knowing quite what to do*] I . . . out-ran a bowling ball. . . . They bet I couldn't.

[*And he starts as if at a sound. He turns toward* DAVID.]

What are you . . . looking . . . at? What do you think you're seeing?

DAVID: I'm not looking.

OZZIE: I feel watched; looked at.

DAVID: No.

OZZIE: Observed.

DAVID: I'm blind.

OZZIE: Did you do it? Had you anything to do with it?

DAVID: What?

OZZIE: That egg.

DAVID: I can't see.

OZZIE: I think you did. I feel like you did it.

DAVID: I don't have a car. I can't drive. How could I?

HARRIET: [*hurrying in to clean up more of the party leftovers*] Ohh, it's so good to hear men's voices in the house again, my two favorite men in all the world—it's what I live for really. Would you like some coffee? Oh, of course you would. Let me put some on. Your humble servant at your command; I do your bidding, bid me be gone.

[*And she is gone without a pause, leaving* OZZIE *staring after her.*]

OZZIE: I could run again if I wanted. I'd . . . like . . . to want to. Christ, Fat Kramer is probably dead . . . now . . . not bouncing about in the ocean in some rattletrap, tin-can joke of a ship . . . but dust . . . locked in a box . . . held in old . . . cold hands. . . . And I just stand here, don't I? and let you talk any way you want. And Ricky gets up in the middle of some sentence I'm saying and walks right out and I let him. Because I fear him as I fear her . . . and you. Because I know the time is close when I will be of no use to any of you any longer . . . and I am so frightened that if I do not seem inoffensive . . . and pleasant . . . if I am not careful to never disturb any of you unnecessarily, you will all abandon me. I can no longer compel recognition. I can no longer impose myself, make myself seen.

HARRIET: [*entering now happily with a tray of coffee*] Here you go. One for each and tea for me. Cream for David . . . [*Setting a cup for* DAVID, *moving toward* OZZIE] and cream and sugar for—

OZZIE: Christ how you must have beguiled me!

HARRIET: Pardon?

OZZIE: Beguiled and deceived!

HARRIET: Pardon . . . Ozzie? . . .

OZZIE: And I don't even remember. I say "must" because I don't remember,

I was so innocent, so childish in my strength, never seeing that it was surrendering I was doing, innocently and easily giving to you the love that was to return in time as flesh to imprison, detain, disarm and begin . . . to kill.

HARRIET: [*examining him, scolding him*] Ozzie, how many beers have you had? You've had too many beers!

OZZIE: Get away!

    [*He whirls to point at* DAVID *who sits on the floor facing upstage.*]

Shut up! You've said enough! Detain and kill! Take and give nothing. It's what you meant, isn't it. You said it yesterday, a warning, nearly exactly this. This is your meaning!

DAVID: You're doing so well, Dad.

OZZIE: [*not understanding*] What?

DAVID: You're doing so well.

OZZIE: No.

DAVID: You are.

OZZIE: Nooo, I'm doing awful. I'm doing terrible.

DAVID: This is the way you start, Dad. We'll be runners. Dad and Dave!

OZZIE: What's he saying?

HARRIET: My God, you're shaking; you're shaking.

OZZIE: I don't know what he's talking about. What's he talking about? [*To* HARRIET] Just let me alone. Just please let me be. I don't really mean these things I'm saying. They're not really important. They'll go away and I don't mean them; they're just coming out of me; I'm just saying them, but I don't mean them. Oh, please, please, go away.

    [*And* DAVID, *behind them, pivots to go up the stairs. She whirls, drawn by his sudden movement.*]

HARRIET: [*dismayed*] David? . . .

DAVID: I'm going upstairs.

HARRIET: Oh, yes. Of course, of course.

DAVID: Just for a while.

HARRIET: Fine. Good. Of course.

DAVID: I'll see you all later.

    [*And he quietly enters his room, lies down.*]

OZZIE: [*coiled on the couch, constricted with pain*] I remember . . . there was a day . . . when I wanted to leave you, all of you, and I wanted desperately to leave, and Hank was there . . . with me. We'd been playing cards. "No," he told me. "No," I couldn't, he said. "Think of the children," he said. He meant something by that. He meant something and I understood it. But now . . . I don't. I no longer have it—that understanding. It's left me. What did he mean?

HARRIET: [*approaching, a little fearful*] You're trembling again. Look at you.

OZZIE: For a while . . . just a while, stay away. That's all I ask.

HARRIET: [*reaching to touch him*] What?

OZZIE: Stay the hell away from me!

HARRIET: Stay away? How far away? Ozzie, how far away? I'll move over . . . [*And she scurries, frightened.*] . . . here. Is this far enough away? Ozzie . . .

OZZIE: It's my hands, my feet. There's tiredness in me. I wake up each morning, it's in my fingers . . . sleep. . . .

HARRIET: Ohhh, it's such a hateful thing in you the way you have no love for people different than yourself . . . even when your son has come home to tell you of them. You have no right to carry on this way. He didn't bring her back—didn't marry her—we have those two things to thank God for. You've got to stop thinking only of yourself. We don't matter, only the children. When are you going to straighten out your thinking? Promise. You've got to straighten out your thinking.

OZZIE: I do. I know.

HARRIET: We don't matter; we're nothing. You're nothing, Ozzie. Only the children.

OZZIE: I know. I promise.

HARRIET: [*moving toward the stairs*] All right . . . just . . . rest . . . for a little; I'll be back. . . .

OZZIE: I promise, Harriet.

HARRIET: [*more to herself than to him*] I'll go see how he is.

OZZIE: [*coiled on the couch*] It's my hands; they hurt . . . I want to wrap them; my feet . . .

HARRIET: I'll tell him for you. I'll explain—how you didn't mean those terrible things you said. I'll explain.

OZZIE: It's going to be so cold; and I hurt . . . already. . . . So cold; my ankles! . . .

HARRIET: [*hesitating on the stairway*] Oh, Ozzie, Ozzie, we're all so worried, but I just think we must hope for the fine bright day coming when we'll be a family again, as long as we try for what is good, truly for one another, please.

[*And she goes upstairs. The front door pops open.*]

RICK: Hi, Mom. Hi, Dad.

OZZIE: Hi, Rick. Your mom's upstairs. You have a nice time? I bet you did.

RICK: Fine; sure. How about you?

OZZIE: Fine; sure.

RICK: Whata you doin', restin'?

OZZIE: Workin'. Measurin'. Not everybody can play the guitar, *you know*. I'm going to build a wall . . . I think—a wall. Pretty soon . . . or . . . six walls. Thinkin' through the blueprints, lookin' over the plans.

RICK: [*moving for the kitchen*] I'm gonna get some fudge, Dad; you want some?

OZZIE: No. Too busy.

RICK: I had the greatest piece a tail tonight, Dad; I really did. What a beautiful piece a ass.

OZZIE: Did you, Rick?

RICK: She was beee-uuuuu-ti-ful.

OZZIE: Who was it?

RICK: Nobody you'd know, Dad.

OZZIE: Oh. Where'd you do it—I mean, get it.

RICK: In her car.

OZZIE: You were careful, I hope.

RICK: [*laughing a little*] C'mon, Dad.

OZZIE: I mean, it wasn't any decent girl.

RICK: Hell, no. . . .

> [*He is still laughing, as* OZZIE *gets to his feet.*]

OZZIE: [*starting for the door*] Had a dream of the guitar last night, Rick. It was huge as a building—all flecked with ice. You swung it in the air and I exploded.

RICK: I did?

OZZIE: Yes. I was gone.

RICK: Fantastic.

OZZIE: [*exaggeratedly happy, almost singing*] Good night.

> *Ozzie is gone out the door.* [*Blackout. Music.*]

Late night. HARRIET *comes down the hall toward David's room. She is wearing a bathrobe and carries a towel, soap, a basin of water. Giving just the lightest tap on the door, she enters, smiling.*

HARRIET: A little bath . . . David? A little sponge bath, all right? You must be all hot and sticky always in that bed. And we can talk. Why don't you take your shirt off? We've an awful lot to talk about. Take your shirt off, David. Your poor father . . . he has no patience, no strength. Something has to be done. . . . A little sponge bath would be so nice. Have you talked to him lately? I think he thinks you're angry, for instance, with . . . us . . . for some reason . . . I don't know. [*Tugging at his shirt a little*] Take your shirt off, David. You'll feel cool. That's all we've ever wanted, your father and me—good sweet things for you and Rick—ease and lovely children, a car, a wife, a good job. Time to relax and go to church on Sundays . . . and on holidays all the children and grand-children come together, mingling. It would be so wonderful—everyone so happy—turkey. Twinkling lights! [*She is puzzled, a little worried.*] David, are you going to take your shirt off for me?

DAVID: They hit their children, did you know that? They hit them with sticks.

HARRIET: What?

DAVID: The yellow people. They punish the disobedience of their children with sticks. And then they sleep together, one family in a bed, limbs all entwined like puppies. They work. I've seen them . . . laugh. They go on picnics. They murder—out of petty jealousy. Young girls wet their cunts with spit when they are dry from wear and yet another GI stands in line. They spit on their hands and rub themselves, smiling, opening their arms.

HARRIET: That's not true.

DAVID: I saw—

HARRIET: [*smilingly scolding him*] None of what you say. No. No. All you did was something normal and regular, can't you see? And hundreds of boys have done it before you. Thousands and thousands. Even now. Now. Now. Why do you have to be so sick and morbid about something so ordinary?

DAVID: She wasn't always a whore. Not always. Not—

HARRIET: If she is now, she was then, only you didn't know. You didn't know.
[*She is reaching for him. He eludes her, stands above her, as she is left sitting on the bed, looking up.*]
Oh, David, David, I'm sure she was a lovely little girl, but I would be insane if I didn't want you to marry someone of your own with whom you could be happy, if I didn't want grandchildren who could be free and welcome in their world. I couldn't want anything else and still think I loved you. David, think of their faces, their poor funny little faces. . . .
[*And the cane is moving, slowly moving along the floor; it grazes her ankle.*]
DAVID: I know . . . I know. . . .
[*The cane moves now along her inner calf, rising under the hem of her robe, lifting. She tries to ignore it.*]
HARRIET: The human face was not meant to be that way. A nose is a thin-ness—you know that. And lips that are not thin are ugly, and it is we who disappear, David. They don't change, and we are gone. It is our triumph, our whiteness. We disappear. What are you doing?
[*The cane has driven her back along the bed; no longer can it be ignored. It has pressed against her.*]
They take us back and down if our children are theirs—it is not a mingling of blood, it is theft.
[*And she hits the cane away. In revulsion she stands, wanting only to flee.*]
Oh, you don't mean these awful things you do. Your room stinks—odors come from under the door. You don't clean yourself. David, David, you've lost someone you love and it's pain for you, don't you see? I know, I know. But we will be the same, lost from you—you from us—and what will that gain for anyone? What?
[*Now the cane begins to scrape along the floor. It begins to lift toward her, and, shuddering, she flees down the hall.* DAVID *opens the door, listens. Stepping into the hall, he carefully shuts the door before moving down the stairs. In the living room, he moves to plant himself before the front door.* HARRIET, *wearing a raincoat over her robe and a scarf on her head, comes down the stairs, when she turns toward the door and she sees* DAVID, *she stops, nods hello, and stands as he begins to advance upon her.*]
DAVID: Do you remember? It was a Sunday when we had all gone to church and there was a young man there with his yellow wife and child. You spoke to us . . . Dad and Rick and me, as if we were conspirators. "I feel so sorry for that poor man—the baby looks like *her*," you said, and your mouth twisted as if you had been forced to swallow someone's else's spit.
HARRIET: No, no. You want only to hurt us, don't you? Isn't that right? That's all you want. Only to give us unhappiness. You cheat her, David. That lovely, lovely little girl you spoke of. She merits more to be done in her memory than cruelty.

[*She has seated herself on the couch, clinging to some kind of normalcy, an odd and eerie calmness on both of them now.*]

DAVID: And I felt that I must go to her if I was to ever live, and I felt that to touch truly her secret stranger's tongue and mind would kill me. Now she will not forgive the way I was.

HARRIET: [*standing up*] No. No, no. No, you don't know how badly I feel. I've got a fever, the start of a cold or flu. Let me be. I can't hardly . . . [*And she is moving away from him, back toward the stairs*] move . . . or stand up. I just want to flop somewhere and not have to move. I'm so weak . . . don't hurt me anymore. Don't hurt me—no more—I've got fever; please, fever; don't hurt me. [*She is on the stairs.*]

DAVID: But I have so much to show you.

HARRIET: [*stops to stare helplessly down at him*] Who are you? I don't know who you are.

DAVID: David.

HARRIET: Noooooo.

DAVID: But I am.

HARRIET: No, no. Oh, no.

[*Moving now as in a trance, she walks up the stairs and down the hallway, all slowly, while* ZUNG *comes forward in David's room, and* DAVID, *in the living room, calls after his mother.*]

DAVID: But it's what you want, don't you see? You can see it. Her wrists are bound in coils of flowers. Flowers are strung in her hair. She hangs from the wind and men strike and kick her. They are blind so that they may not see her, yet they howl, wanting not to hurt her but only as I do, to touch and hold her . . . and they howl. I'm home. Little David. . . . Home.

[*And he is turning now to take possession of the house. As he speaks, he moves to take the space. A conquerer, he parades in the streets he has taken; among the chairs, around the lamp.*]

Little Davey . . . of all the toys and tops and sailor suits, the plastic cars and Tinkertoys. Drum-player, bed-wetter, home-run-hitter, I'm home . . . now . . . and I want to drink from the toilet, wash there.

[*As he climbs the stairs, he passes by* ZUNG, *who stands in his room looking out at him. He walks down the hall in the direction Harriet fled.*]

And you will join me. You . . . will . . . join me!

[*When he has gone,* ZUNG *sits to gaze down upon the living room, as the front door opens.* OZZIE, *dressed in a suit or perhaps even a tuxedo, enters from the outside. Under his arm he carries a packet of several hundred sheets of paper. He moves now with an absolute confidence, almost smugness, as he carefully sets down the papers and proceeds to arrange three items of furniture—perhaps two chairs and a footstool—in such a way that they face him. He is cocky. Now he addresses them.*]

OZZIE: [*to the large chair*] Harriet. . . . [*Nodding to the second chair.*] David. . . . [*Patting the footstool.*] Ricky.

[*He looks them over, the three empty chairs, and then speaks in the manner of a chairman of the board addressing the members of his board, explaining his position and plan of action for total solution. This is a kind of commercial on the value of Ozzie.*]

I'm glad we've gotten finally together here, because the thing I've decided to do—and you all, hopefully, will understand my reasoning—is to *combat* the weariness beginning in me. It's like stepping into a hole, the way I feel each morning when I awaken, I see the day and the sun and I'm looking upward into the sky with a sense of looking down. A sense of hovering over a great pit into which I am about to fall. The sky. Foolishness and deceit, you say, and I know you're right—a trick of feeling inside me being played against me, seeking to diminish me and increase itself until it is larger than me filling me and who will I be then? It. That feeling of being nothing. At first . . . at first . . . I thought the thing to do would be to learn the guitar. . . . But *that* I realized in just the nick of time was a folly that would have taken me into the very agony of frustration I was seeking to avoid. The skill to play like Ricky does is a great gift and only Ricky has it. He has no acids rotting his heart. He is all lies and music, his brain small and scaly, the brain of a snake forever innocent of the fact that it crawls. Lucky Ricky. But there are other things that people can do. And I've come at last to see the one that I must try if I am to become strong again in my opinion of myself. [*Holding up, with great confidence, one of the many packets of paper.*] What I have here is an inventory of everything I own. Everything. Every stick of furniture, pot and pan, every sock, T-shirt, pen or pencil. And opposite is its price. For instance—here—that davenport—five hundred an' twelve dollars an' ninety-eight cents. That chair—a hundred twenty ninety-nine. That table . . . [*He hurries to the table.*] . . . this table—thirty-two twenty-nine. Et cetera. Et cetera. Now the idea is that you each carry a number of these at all times.

[*He is distributing more papers to the chairs, his control, however, diminishing, so that the papers are thrown about.*]

Two or three copies at all times, and you are to pass them out at the slightest provocation. Let people know who I am, what I've done. Someone says to you, "Who are you?" You say, "I'm Ozzie's son." "I'm Ozzie's wife." Who?" they'll say. "Take a look at that!" you tell 'em. Spit it out, give 'em a copy, turn on your heel and walk right out. That's the way I want it; from all of you from here on out, that's the WAY I WANT IT!

[*And the room goes suddenly into eerie light.* ZUNG, *high behind him in David's room, is hit with a sudden light that makes* OZZIE *go rigid, as if some current from her has entered into him, and he turns slowly to look up at her.*]

Let him alone. Let David alone.

[HARRIET *is in the hallway.*]

HARRIET: Is there any aspirin down there? I don't feel well . . . Ozzie. I don't feel well at all. David poked me with his cane and I don't like . . . what's . . . going on.

[OZZIE *is only staring at* ZUNG.]

I don't want what's happening to happen.

[*She has halted on the stairway.*]

It must be some awful flu, I'm so weak, or some awful cold. There's an odor . . .

OZZIE: I'll go to the drugstore. My eyes hurt; funny . . .

HARRIET: Oh, Ozzie . . . oh my God. It was awful. I can't help it. He's crazy—he—

OZZIE: I don't want to hear about him. I don't want to hear. Oh, no, oh no. I can't. No more, no more. Let him do what he wants. No more of him, no more. Just you—you're all that I can see. All that I care for or want.

[*He has moved to her as she moved down, and they embrace.*]

HARRIET: David's crazy! . . .

OZZIE: You're everything.

HARRIET: Please . . .

OZZIE: Listen; we must hide; please.

HARRIET: [*moving to kneel and he, while helping her, kneels also*] Pray with me.

OZZIE: We won't move. We'll hide by not moving.

HARRIET: We must beg God to not turn against him; convince him. Ozzie, pray. . . .

OZZIE: Yes! . . .

HARRIET: Now! . . .

[*They pray: kneeling, murmuring, and it goes on and on. The front door opens.*]

RICK: Hi, Mom. Hi, Dad.

[*They contine. He stops.*]

Hi . . . Mom. Hi, Dad. . . . [*very puzzled*] Hi . . . Mom. . . . Hi Dad. . . .

[*He thinks and thinks.*]

DAVID!

[*He screams at David. He goes running up to look in David's room, but the room is empty.* DAVID, *in ragged combat fatigues, appears on the top of the stairs.* RICK, *frightened, backs away.*]

Dave . . . what have you got to say for yourself? What can you? Honest ta God, I've had it. I really have. I can't help it, even if you are sick, and I hate to complain, but you're getting them so mixed up they're not themselves anymore. Just a minute ago—one minute—they were on their knees, do you know that? Just a minute ago—right here on the living-room floor. Now what's the point of that? They're my mom and dad, too.

DAVID: He doesn't know, does he, Dad? Did you hear him?

RICK: [*as* OZZIE *and* HARRIET *are getting from their knees and struggling to sit on the couch*] Let Dad alone.

DAVID: [*on the landing, looking down on them*] He doesn't know how when you finally see yourself, there's nothing really there to see . . . isn't that right? Mom?

RICK: Dave, honest to God, I'm warning you, let them alone.

[DAVID *descends with* ZUNG *behind him. Calmly he speaks, growing slowly happy.*]

DAVID: Do you know how north of here, on farms, gentle loving dogs are raised, while in the forests, other dogs run wild? And upon occasion, one of those that's wild is captured and put in among the others that are tame, bringing with it the memory of when they had all been wild—the dark and terror—that had made them wolves. Don't you hear them?

[*And there is a rumbling.*]

RICK: What? Hear what?

[*It is windlike, the rumbling of many trucks.*]

DAVID: Don't you hear the trucks? They're all over town, lined up from the center of town into the country. Don't you hear? They've stopped bringing back the blind. They're bringing back the dead now. The convoy's broken up. There's no control . . . they're walking from house to house, through the shrubbery, under the trees, carrying one of the dead in a bright blue rubber bag for which they have no papers, no name or number. No one knows whose it is. They're at the Jensens' now. Now Al Jensen's at the door, all his kids behind him trying to peek. Al looks for a long, long time into the open bag before he shakes his head. They zipper shut the bag and turn away. They've been to the Mayers', the Kellys', the Irwins' and Kresses'. They'll be here soon.

OZZIE: Nooo.

DAVID: And Dad's going to let them in. We're going to let them in.

HARRIET: What's he saying?

DAVID: He's going to knock.

OZZIE: I DON'T KNOW.

DAVID: Yes. Yes.

[*A knocking sound. Is it* DAVID *knocking with his fist against the door or table?*]

OZZIE: Nooooo.

RICK: Mom, he's driving Dad crazy.

[*Knocking loud: it seems to be at the front door.*]

OZZIE: David, will I die?

[*He moves toward the door.*]

HARRIET: Who do you suppose it could be so late?

RICK: [*intercepting* OZZIE, *blocking the way to the door*] I don't think you should just go opening the door to anybody this time of the night, there's no telling who it might be.

DAVID: We know who it is.

OZZIE: Oh, David, why can't you wait? Why can't you rest?

[*But* DAVID *is the father now, and he will explain. He loves them all.*]

DAVID: Look at her. See her, Dad. Tell her to go to the door. Tell her yes, it's your house, you want her to open the door and let them in. Tell her yes, the one with no name is ours. We'll put it in that chair. We can bring them all here. I want them all here, all the trucks and bodies. There's room. [*Handing* RICK *the guitar*] Ricky can sing. We'll stack them along the walls . . .

OZZIE: Nooo . . .

DAVID: Pile them over the floor . . .

OZZIE: No, no . . .

DAVID: They will become the floor and they will become the walls, the chairs. We'll sit in them; sleep. We will call them "home." We will give them as gifts—call them "ring" and "pot" and "cup." No, no; it's not a thing to fear. . . . We will notice them no more than all the others.

[*He is gentle, happy, consoling to them.*]

OZZIE: What others? There are no others. Oh . . . please die. Oh, wait. . . .

[*And he scurries to the TV where it sits beneath the stairs.*]

I'll get it fixed. I'll fix it. Who needs to hear it? We'll watch it. [*Wildly turning TV channels.*] I flick my rotten life. Oh, there's a good one. Look at that one. Ohhh, isn't that a good one? That's the best one. That's the best one.

DAVID: They will call it madness. We will call it seeing.

[*Calmly he lifts* OZZIE.]

OZZIE: I don't want to disappear.

DAVID: Let her take you to the door. We will be runners. You will have eyes.

OZZIE: I will be blind. I will disappear.

[*Knocking is heard again. Again.*]

DAVID: You stand and she stands. "Let her go," you say; "she is garbage and filth and you must get her back if you wish to live. She is sickness, I must cherish her." Old voices you have trusted all your life as if they were your own, speaking always friendly. "She's all of everything impossible made possible!"

OZZIE: Ricky . . . nooo! . . .

DAVID: Don't call to Ricky. You love her. You will embrace her, see her and—

OZZIE: He has no right to do this to me.

DAVID: Don't call to Ricky!

OZZIE: [*suddenly raging, rushing at* DAVID, *pushing him*] You have no right to do this.

RICK: Noooooo!

[*Savagely he smashes his guitar down upon* DAVID, *who crumples.*] Let Dad alone. Let him alone. He's sick of you. What the hell's the matter with you? He doesn't wanna talk anymore about all the stupid stuff you talk. He wants to talk about cake and cookies and cars and coffee. He's sick a you and he wants you to shut up. We hate you, goddamn you.

[*Silence:* DAVID *lies still.*]

ZUNG: Chào ông!

[OZZIE *pivots, looks at her.*]

Chào ông! Hôm nay ông manh không?

OZZIE: Oh, what is it that you want? I'm tired. I mean it. Forgive me. I'm sick of the sight of you, squatting all the time. In filth like animals, talking gibberish, your breath sick with rot. . . . And yet you look at me with those sad pleading eyes as if there is some real thing that can come between us when you're not even here. You are deceit.

[*His hands, rising, have driven to her throat. The fingers close.*]

I'm not David. I'm not silly and soft . . . little David. The sight of you sickens me. YOU HEAR ME, DAVID? Believe me. I am speaking my honest true feelings. I spit on you, the both of you; I piss on you and your eyes and pain. Flesh is lies. You are garbage and filth. You are darkness. I cast you down. Deceit. Animal. Dirty animal.

[*And he is over her. They are sprawled on the ground. Silence as no one moves. She lies like a rag beneath him.*]

RICK: I saw this really funny movie last night. This really . . . funny, funny movie about this young couple and they were going to get a divorce but they didn't. It was really funny.

[OZZIE *is hiding the girl. In a proscenium production, he can drag her behind the couch; in three-quarter, he covers her with a blanket brought to him by* HARRIET *which matches the rug.*]

HARRIET: What's that? What's that?

RICK: This movie I saw.

HARRIET: Anybody want to go for groceries? We need Kleenex, sugar, milk.

RICK: What a really funny movie.

OZZIE: I'll go; I'll go.

HARRIET: Good. Good.

OZZIE: I think I saw it on TV.

[*They are cleaning up the house now, putting the chairs back in order, dumping all of Ozzie's leaflets in the waste can.*]

HARRIET: Did you enjoy it, Rick?

RICK: Oh, yeh. I loved it.

OZZIE: I laughed so much I almost got sick. It was really good. I laughed.

RICK: I bet it was; I bet you did.

OZZIE: Oh, I did.

[*Even* DAVID *helps with the cleaning: he gets himself off the floor and seated in a chair.*]

HARRIET: How are you feeling, Ricky?

RICK: Fine.

HARRIET: Good.

RICK: How do you feel?

HARRIET: Oh, I'm all right. I feel fine.

OZZIE: Me, too. I feel fine, too. What day is it anyway? Monday?

HARRIET: Wednesday.

RICK: Tuesday, Mom.

[*Now all three are seated on the couch.*]

OZZIE: I thought it was Monday.

RICK: Oh, no.

HARRIET: No, no. You're home now, David. . . .

RICK: [*moving to* DAVID, *who sits alone in a chair*] Hey, Dave, listen, will you. I mean I know it's not my place to speak out and give advice and everything because I'm the youngest, but I just gotta say my honest true feelings and I'd kill myself if I were you, Dave. You're in too much misery. I'd cut my wrists. Honestly speaking, brother to brother, you should have done it long ago.

[DAVID *is looking about.*]

You looking for her, Dave? You looking for her? She's not here.

DAVID: What?

RICK: Nooo. She's never been here. You just thought so. You decided not to bring her, Dave, remember? You decided, all things considered that you preferred to come back without her. Too much risk and inconvenience . . . you decided. Isn't that right? Sure. You know it is. You've always known.

[*Silence.* HARRIET *moves to look out the front door.*]

Do you want to use my razor, Dave? [*Pulling a straight razor from his pocket*] I have one right here and you can use it if you want.

[DAVID *seems to be looking at the razor.*]

Just take it if you want it, Dave.

HARRIET: Go ahead, David. The front yard's empty. You don't have to be afraid. The streets, too . . . still and empty.

RICK: It doesn't hurt like you think it will. Go ahead; just take it, Dave.

OZZIE: You might as well.

RICK: That's right.

OZZIE: You'll feel better.

RICK: I'll help you now, Dave, okay?

HARRIET: I'll go get some pans and towels.

RICK: [*moving about* DAVID, *patting him, buddying him*] Oh, you're so confused, you don't know what to do. It's just a good thing I got this razor, Boy, that's all I gotta say. You're so confused. You see, Dave, where you're wrong is your point of view, it's silly. It's just really comical because you think people are valuable or something and, given a chance like you were to mess with 'em, to take a young girl like that and turn her into a whore, you shouldn't, when of course you should or at least might . . . on whim . . . you see? I mean, you're all backwards, Dave— you're upside down. You don't know how to go easy and play—I bet you didn't have any fun the whole time you were over there—no fun at all— and it was there. I got this buddy Gerry, he was there, and he used to throw bags of cement at 'em from off the back a his truck. They'd go whizzin' through those villages, throwin' off these bags a cement. You could kill people, he says, you hit 'em right. Especially the kids. There was this once they knocked this ole man off his bicycle—fifty pounds a dry cement—and then the back a the truck got his legs. It was hysterical —can't you just see that, Dave? Him layin' there howlin', all the guys in the truck bowin' and wavin' and tippin' their hats. What a goddamn funny story, huh?

[HARRIET *has brought silver pans and towels with roosters on them. The towels cover the arms of the chair and* DAVID's *lap. The pans will catch the blood. All has been neatly placed.* DAVID, *with* RICKY's *help, cuts one wrist, then the other, as they talk.*]

DAVID: I wanted . . . to kill you . . . all of you.

RICK: I know, I know; but you're hurt; too weak.

DAVID: I wanted for you to need what I had and I wouldn't give it.

HARRIET: That's not possible.

OZZIE: Nooooo.

DAVID: I wanted to get you. Like poor bug-eyed fish flung up from the brief water to the lasting dirt, I would gut you.

HARRIET: David, no, no, you didn't want that.

OZZIE: No, no.

RICK: I don't even know why you'd think you did.

OZZIE: We kill you is what happens.

RICK: That's right.

OZZIE: And then, of course, we die, too. . . . Later on, I mean. And nothing stops it. Not words . . . or walls . . . or even guitars.

RICK: Sure.

OZZIE: That's what happens.

HARRIET: It isn't too bad, is it?

RICK: How bad is it?

OZZIE: He's getting weaker.

HARRIET: And in a little, it'll all be over. You'll feel so grand. No more funny talk.

RICK: You can shower; put on clean clothes. I've got deodorant you can borrow. After Roses, Dave. The scent of a thousand roses.

[*He is preparing to take a picture—crouching, aiming.*]

HARRIET: Take off your glasses, David.

OZZIE: Do as you're told.

RICK: [*as* DAVID's *hands are rising toward the glasses to remove them*]. I bet when you were away there was only plain water to wash in, huh? You prob'ly hadda wash in the rain.

[*He takes the picture; there is a flash. A slide appears on the screen: a close-up of* DAVID, *nothing visible but his face. It is the slide that, appearing at the start of the play, was referred to as "somebody sick." Now it hovers, stricken, sightless, revealed.*]

Mom, I like David like this.

HARRIET: He's happier.

OZZIE: We're all happier.

RICK: Too bad he's gonna die.

OZZIE: No, no, he's not gonna die, Rick. He's only gonna nearly die. Only nearly.

RICK: Ohhhhhhhhhhh.

HARRIET: Mmmmmmmmmmmmm.

[*And* RICK, *sitting, begins to play his guitar for* DAVID. *The music is alive and fast. It has a rhythm, a drive of happiness that is contagious. The lights slowly fade.*]